The Growth of the Seed

Notes on the Book of Genesis

Nathan Ward

DE WARD
PUBLISHING COMPANY

The Growth of the Seed: Notes on the Book of Genesis
© 2007 by DeWard Publishing Company, Ltd.
P.O. Box 6259, Chillicothe, Ohio 45601
www.deward.com

Cover art by Brooke Rombach. Used with permission.

Reasonable care has been taken to trace original sources for any excerpts and quotations appearing in this book and to document such information in the footnotes. For material not in the public domain, fair-use standards and practices were followed. Should any attribution be found to be incorrect or incomplete, the publisher welcomes written documentation supporting correction for subsequent printings.

Printed in the United States of America.

ISBN: 978-0-9798893-0-1

The words of the wise are like goads, and like nails firmly fixed are the collected sayings; they are given by one Shepherd. My son, beware of anything beyond these. Of making many books there is no end, and much study is weariness of the flesh.

—Ecclesiastes 12.11–12

Table of Contents

Acknowledgments..5

Preface 6

Abbreviations..10

Introduction 13

Major Divisions

    Creation..23

    Man in the Garden 45

    Enmity Between the Seeds 59

    The Flood 93

    From the Flood to Abraham............................123

    Abraham 131

    Isaac and Jacob 267

    Judah and Joseph..367

Special Studies

    Additional Notes on the Creation Account...................37

    God's Designation..52

    Genealogies...88

    The Sons of God and the Nephilim 100

    The Separation of Abram and Lot........................152

    The Priesthood of Melchizedek..........................162

The Duration of the Egyptian Bondage 173

The Angel of the Lord. 185

The Role of Egypt in the Life of Abraham 243

Wrestling with God 332

Was Dinah Raped? 347

Rachel and Leah 356

Sheol 381

The Sons of Jacob 464

Bibliography 503

Author Index. 515

General Index 517

Scripture Index 524

Acknowledgments

There are many to whom I must offer thanks and whose help I must acknowledge:

The congregations who gave me the responsibility to teach, thereby teaching me to love the book of Genesis;

Those who have encouraged me along the way;

Wes, whose teaching of Genesis as I was writing this prodded me onward;

Jeff, to whom I owe any skill in typesetting I have, and who deserves no blame for any bad habits I haven't yet broken;

Brent, for his skill and assistance in editing this manuscript;

The late Phil Roberts, who was always open to a question and always willing to offer his time and energy to give a thoughtful—and helpful—answer;

My parents who first taught me the Bible, who helped me think through many of the things you will find here, and who offered their proofreading services.

And mostly my wife Brooke:

Whose professional expertise has allowed for an index in this work;

Who put up with a dining room table covered with books and photocopies for more than a year when I first taught this;

Who reminded me by her good stewardship—and never once in word—that I was responsible to finish this after spending *our* money on *my* resources;

Who stood behind me when it seemed that few else did, offering her unconditional love and support in an awkward and uncomfortable situation.

If the following manuscript fails to live up to my hopes, it is certainly not for lack of support. If it is of any lasting value, it is surely due to what all of you have done for me.

Preface

A few years ago, I was asked by the brethren at the Belmont Heights congregation to teach the adult class on the book of Genesis. I was familiar with the book from growing up in the church. But for the most part, that familiarity was superficial. Like many Christians, I was unaware of the potential depth of study the book of Genesis offers.

At the time, I was shy of 25 and had only taught one adult class before: 1 Peter. And while I did a fair job on that class, it was hardly an in-depth study. This time, I wanted to dig deeper and to challenge both myself and my students to grow as much as possible.

I read through the entire text of Genesis five or six times. I wrote questions to help myself better understand the path of the text—questions that later became a study guide for the class. After I reached my own conclusions on the book, I spent hours at the Florida College library searching through a religious periodicals database, trying to find everything available on the book of Genesis (the bibliography will show you that I barely managed to scratch the surface of the materials out there). I read every *International Standard Bible Encyclopedia* article that had anything to do with Genesis. I sought various commentaries and books on Genesis. When all was said and done, I felt that I had put together a good class based on very thorough research.

A couple of years later, at a different congregation, I was asked to teach again. With this fresh in mind, I suggested Genesis. It was agreed upon. I took out the old notes to dust them off and add onto them. Since the completion of my first class, I'd found a few new commentaries and articles, and felt ready to take the class to another level. It was this second opportunity to teach when I decided to take the expanded study and transcribe the outline into a manuscript.

You'd never mistake me for a scholar. Sure, I know the Bible and can think for myself, but I'm no scholar. My one year of college Hebrew hardly qualifies me to make any definitive decisions on what a word means or doesn't mean; my lack of knowledge concerning ancient custom and archaeology hardly gives me room to inform you what so-and-so did (or didn't do) based on some obscure piece of data dug up at a tell in the near east; my *lack* of knowledge about some parts of the Bible—

the prophets, for example—could easily destroy what little credibility I might otherwise garner.

And so, I have replaced my lack of scholarship with the scholarship of others. I have assembled the comments of the some of the best conservative Old Testament scholars concerning Genesis. And I've purposefully gathered a quantity of material from varying viewpoints, so it would be virtually impossible for me to be led down the path of another thinker without weighing three or four other viewpoints—not to mention my own conclusions—first. I tell you this because you will find herein a large assembly of quotes. Primarily, you'll find a blend of seven conservative commentators: Bruce Waltke, Victor Hamilton, Gordon Wenham, Kenneth Mathews, Derek Kidner, H.C. Leupold, and C.F. Keil. In addition, I've found Robert Alter's translation and comments on Genesis helpful and have included his thoughts throughout. Finally, where they provided helpful information, I've offered quotes from various journal authors, encyclopedia articles, and other useful books including theologies and introductions.

But don't get me wrong, you *will* find my thoughts as well—that is, indeed, the backbone on which everything else is built. Because so many people have written from so many perspectives, I had to reach my own conclusions and compare the scholars' viewpoints with my own study in order to make decisions about what I would include and what I would leave out. And in a few places, I agreed with none of the major thinkers and only wrote my own interpretation. But, for the most part, after studying and deciding, I could find someone who had said it better than I could. And so I let those who are already considered scholars speak for themselves.[1]

Because I have quoted so frequently, I've forgone the normal style guides' rules of indenting long quotes. Also, because of the frequency with which I quote these eight authors listed above and the verse-by-verse nature of their volumes, I have omitted the page number when citing them. If you wish to see the context surrounding the quote, turn to the pages discussing the verse in question. Citations from other sources will include bibliographic information in a footnote. Finally, where needed, some minor

---

[1]My intention, of course, is not to quote so heavily that I replace those works. Even with the number of quotes from each of the eight above-listed commentators, I have barely scratched the surface of their works. Please do not suspect that after reading this you understand what each of those commentators believes about the book of Genesis. To understand that, you will need to read their entire works.

changes in the quotations were made for the sake of stylistic consistency without any notation.[2]

My thoughts are expressed throughout in the first person plural. I don't really know why, but *we* just seemed right as I was typing. Please forgive the grasping aspirations at scholarship that such usage might imply.

Finally, I need to acknowledge a couple of areas where this manuscript falls short. First, there is the general lack of comment on the debate that rages on between conservative and liberal theologians. I have familiarized myself with some of the writings of the key liberal theologians and most of their positions regarding various matters in Genesis. From time to time, I mention something one or more of them teaches, referring to them as *critical scholars*. In the end, however, I decided not to muddy the waters of my study with a debate in which I could make little headway and ultimately detract from the real point Genesis makes to those of faith. And so I've left those matters to those who are better suited to confront them.[3] Second, there is virtually no discussion herein concerning textual critical matters. Although such a study would be beneficial, it is outside the scope of this study, and certainly beyond my limited expertise. Finally, this fails to discuss the genealogical chapters in much detail. This is something of a bitter irony, as I spend some time discussing the importance of genealogical study and why genealogies should not simply be overlooked—yet, in the end, I decided to comment only briefly on those chapters.

The rest of this manuscript is the result of the study I've described above. I hope that you will find the study of Genesis as enriching as I have.

— Nathan Ward

---

[2]These modifications, of course, do not change the meaning of any of the quotations and are limited to things such as the format of references (*e.g.*, *Gen 3.15* rather than *Gen. 3:15*), the spelling of names (*e.g.*, *Abimelech* rather than *Abimelek*—Wenham consistently spells *ch*-ending names with a *k*), the change of names (*e.g.*, *Abram* rather than *Abraham*—Waltke uses *Abraham* throughout in his work), changing the case of pronouns referring to deity (*He* rather than *he*, though not when quoting the ESV), and transliteration of Hebrew letters (*e.g.*, אדם to *adam*).

[3]This may also help explain the glaring lack of information from one of the most monumental commentaries on Genesis—that of Westerman.

Abbreviations

Alter	*Genesis: Translation and Commentary*, Robert Alter
ASV	American Standard Version
AUSS	*Andrews University Seminary Studies*
BA	*Biblical Archaeologist*
BDB	F. Brown, S.R. Driver, and C.A. Briggs, *Hebrew and English Lexicon of the Old Testament*
BR	*Bible Review*
BSac	*Bibliotheca Sacra*
CBQ	*Catholic Bible Quarterly*
ESV	English Standard Version
EvQ	*Evangelical Quarterly*
GTJ	*Grace Theological Journal*
Hamilton	*The Book of Genesis*, 2 vol. Victor Hamilton. New International Commentary on the Old Testament
HALOT	*The Hebrew and Aramaic Lexicon of the Old Testament*, L. Koehler and W. Baumgartner.
Hard Sayings	*Hard Sayings of the Bible*, Walter C. Kaiser Jr., *et al.*
Interpretation	*Interpreatation: A Journal of Bible and Theology*
ISBE	*International Standard Bible Encyclopedia*, rev., ed. G.W. Bromiley
JBL	*Journal of Biblical Literature*
JETS	*Journal of the Evangelical Theological Society*
JSOT	*Journal for the Study of the Old Testament*
Keil	*Pentateuch.* C.F. Keil, Keil & Delitzsch Commentary on the Old Testament
Kidner	*Genesis: An Introduction and Commentary*, Derek Kidner, Tyndale Old Testament Commentaries

KJV	King James Version
Leupold	*Genesis*. 2 vol. Leupold on the Old Testament
LXX	Septuagint
Mathews	*Genesis*, 2 vol. The New American Commentary
MT	Masoretic Text
NAC	The New American Commentary
NASB	New American Standard Bible
NICOT	New International Commentary on the Old Testament
NIDOTTE	New International Dictionary of Old Testament Theology and Exegesis
NIV	New International Version
NKJV	New King James Version
RSV	Revised Standard Version
TWOT	*Theological Wordbook of the Old Testament*, ed. R.L. Harris, G.L. Archer, B.K. Waltke
Waltke	*Genesis: A Commentary*, Bruce K. Waltke with Cathi J. Fredricks
Wenham	*Genesis*, 2 vol. Gordon J. Wenham. Word Biblical Commentary
WBC	Word Biblical Commentary
WTJ	*Westminster Theological Journal*

A Brief Introduction

The value of Old Testament study should need no defense. It isn't something to be taken lightly. In Matthew 5.17–18, Jesus says that He came to fulfill the law, and thus ties Himself inextricably to the God of the Old Testament as well as the plan and prophecies of the Old Testament. If we are ever to *really* understand Jesus, we must *really* understand the Old Testament (*cf.* Luke 24.27; Acts 8.30–35). In statements like these, Jesus affirms His confidence in every word of the Old Testament writings (*cf.* Luke 24.44).

The Old Testament was the only Bible early Christians had. Jesus taught with it as did His apostles. Paul tells us that it is a tutor to bring us to Christ (Gal 3.22–25). Even though we have the more complete revelation from God now, certainly we can continue to use these writings to accomplish their original purpose—even as Jesus and His apostles did.

A Book of Beginnings.[1] The name Genesis is derived from the Greek word meaning *beginning*. This name was given in the LXX, retained in the Latin Vulgate, and has been transliterated into English Bibles as well. Certainly this name is appropriate based on the first chapter of the book—the beginning of the universe and life—but the beginnings in Genesis go beyond that.

---

[1]This introduction is not intended to be a comprehensive one. For further introductory material to Genesis, see the chapters in various Old Testament Introductions, such as R.K. Harrison's volume. Another valuable read, though not aimed at a scholarly audience, is Tremper Longman's *How to Read Genesis*. One can also find useful introductory information in the commentaries by Bruce Waltke, Victor Hamilton, and Kenneth Mathews.

Revelation from God. The book of Genesis contains the beginning of revelation from God, because, quite simply, it is the first place where God reveals to man what He would have man do. Though the laws given are not as complete as those given on Sinai—and certainly not as complete as we find in Jesus—God begins to reveal His will to man in the book of Genesis.

In addition, God begins to reveal Himself to man by His self-revelation in creation. As an author or painter is known by his work, so God is known by His creation: *He did not leave Himself without witness... for since the creation of the world His invisible attributes are clearly seen, being understood by the things that are made... the heavens declare the glory of God; and the firmament shows His handiwork* (Acts 14.17; Rom 1.20; Psa 19.1, NKJV). The Bible does not begin by explaining God, but presents Him as the explanation of everything else; the Presupposition; the Ultimate Cause. Many Christians through the centuries have come under severe attack because of their desire to reconcile natural observation with scriptural declaration. It must be understood, however, that to study the sciences *is* to study God. God has revealed His nature in His creation. "To try to correlate the data of Scripture and nature is not to dishonour biblical authority, but to honour God as Creator and to grapple with our proper task of interpreting His ways of speaking" (Kidner).

Finally, Genesis is the beginning of revelation from God simply due to the nature of the first two chapters. The creation account, by necessity, is pure revelation since no one was around to witness it. If we believe in the inspiration of the word, we can be certain that the first two chapters have come directly from God and contain precisely what He wanted to reveal about His methods of creation.

Mankind and Sin. God placed man in His newly created world. Man was the last of God's creations, the crown and climax of His work. All else was created in preparation for him. Man was similar to the other creations of God, but he was also different. He was similar to the other creation because of his physical nature. He was not created *ex nihilo* (from nothing) as the heavens and earth, but was formed from the dust of the ground. His name Adam is closely related to the Hebrew word for ground: *adamah.*

But man was also different. He was different because of his spiritual nature. Created in the image of God and granted a soul and free moral choice, man—though similar to creation—transcends it. He was given responsibilities by God and had a personal relationship with God. More-over, he had moral obligations to God. After creating man upright and placing him in a perfect environment, God gave man the ability to choose. He chose poorly and sin entered the world.

The problem of sin is typically described as the loss of man's relationship with God. Though accurate, this is a thoroughly anthropocentric descrip-tion. The theocentric description—no more accurate, but perhaps more apt—is that sin dethrones God. In man's decision to disregard the com-mands of God, he is declaring openly that he knows better than God—that he does not need God. In effect, man makes himself out to be God when he sins. The plan of salvation, then, also has a theocentric counter-part. The success of God's plan isn't merely the restoration of the rela-tionship between man and God; rather, it is the restoration of God to his rightful place as lord of all. Thus, when Paul looks back and describes this plan, he repeatedly says that it is *to the praise of his glory* (Eph 1.3–14).

The Plan of Salvation. God had a plan for when man faltered. The com-ing to pass of that plan becomes the theme of the Bible. The book of Gen-esis contains the beginning of that plan: the first promise of a redeemer; the first covenant made between man and God; the first foreshadowing of Jesus by men's lives.

Genesis 49 gives us an important clue to understanding the rest of the book of Genesis, and how the events recorded are related to the central theme of the Bible. There we read of the blessing of Judah and the pass-ing over of Reuben, Simeon and Levi for the blessing. In these few verses, we learn why so much of chapters 34–49 were recorded: they were direct-ly related to which son of Jacob was blessed. In fact, everything in chap-ters 34–49 is related either to Judah's blessing or the survival and growth of the nation of Israel.

This understanding can then be expanded to the remainder of Genesis. The things that are recorded in Genesis are related to God's covenant with man—most often, to the continuance of the Messianic line.

A comparison of several of the characters in Genesis reveals something very telling. Consider Seth, Isaac, Jacob and Judah. These four men have two things in common. First, they each carried the Messianic line. Sec-ond, each was a younger brother. This is perhaps the most often over-looked aspect of the book of Genesis: every account is a story being told of two or more individuals where the oldest does not receive the blessing, while the faithful, younger sibling does. Perhaps the reason we have the accounts of these individuals instead of those who are passed over in genealogical lists is due to this fact. When the oldest receives the blessing, there is no need for an explanation. But when the blessing comes through a younger son, further clarification is required.

Upon further examination, you find this to be true of the other characters in Genesis as well. Shem is not the oldest son of Noah. Noah began to bear sons at 500 years of age (5.32) and was 600 at the flood (7.6). If Shem was Noah's oldest son, he would have been 100 at the flood; however, Shem was 100 two years after the flood (11.10). Shem could not have been the oldest son. And Abram is not the oldest of Terah. Terah began to bear sons at 70 years of age (11.26). Terah died at 205 in the land of Haran (11.32). At that point, Abram and Lot left Haran (Acts 7.4). Abram was 75 (12.4). If Abram was 75 (at the most) when Terah was 205, then Terah was *at least* 130 when he had Abram—sixty years after he had his firstborn. In both of these instances, the son listed first isn't so listed because of his age, but because of his prominence.[2]

In fact, the only two men who carry the line of Christ in Genesis who are *not* the younger son are Adam and Noah—two men whose story and purpose are different than anyone else in the book.

Now, consider the brothers who are rejected. Cain, Ishmael, Esau, Reuben/Simeon/Levi. The reason they do not carry the Messianic line is at once evident: they were all unfaithful. The faithful ones carry the line of the promise. (Though Abel was the faithful son, his 'replacement' was also faithful, 4.26.)[3] Ishmael is older than Isaac. Esau is older than Jacob. Judah is the fourth in line of Jacob's sons. Ishmael was the product of faithlessness; Esau was faithless; Reuben, Simeon and Levi were each wicked in his own way.

This principle may also explain why so much is told of Rachel and Leah

---

[2] *Cf. Hard Sayings* 49–50. Most commentators jump through hoops to explain how these passages *don't* indicate that Shem and Abram were younger siblings, while they continue on to comment about how so often primogeniture is ignored in Genesis. To us, it seems more sensible to read these two accounts at face value and see them as continuing the theme that the younger sibling carries on the Messianic line in every Genesis narrative.

[3] Ham doesn't fit into this pattern (9.24). However, though he wasn't older than Shem, he certainly fits the pattern of one who is rejected for wickedness. Lot, also, though he is not a son, is a possible heir rejected for his poor choice. See Excursus E.

in Genesis. Both wives had a son who stood out among the brothers as faithful to God. Among the mothers, however, only Leah was faithful. She knew Yahweh (29.32–35). Rachel showed no indication of such knowledge—rather she stole, lied, and placed her faith in idols (31.19, 35). Thus, the line of Christ comes through Judah rather than Joseph.[4]

In each of these instances, the younger is not chosen haphazardly. In every case, it is due to the faithfulness of the younger.[5] The Messiah was not to come from the faithless and profane. Instead, He was to come through those who saw God's covenant as something important and worthy of giving their lives to. And so the book of Genesis records these specific events to explain who Jesus came from and why He came from those people. The story of Genesis, then, is the tracing of God's blessing to the faithful. To that end, the comments on each chapter are concluded with a note on *The Growth of the Seed*, a summary of the development of the progress of the Messianic line or some other aspect of man's covenant relationship with God.[6]

The Reliability of God's Word. There is a contrast throughout the book of Genesis between the word of man and the word of God. Throughout the book, everyone's word is untrustworthy. Beginning with the serpent and continuing through Adam, Cain, Abraham and Sarah, Isaac, Rebekah and Jacob, Laban, Rachel, Simeon and Levi, the ten sons of Jacob, Judah, Potiphar's wife, and Joseph, it seems as if everyone is lying all the time—everyone except God. Even when the most righteous people in the world cannot be counted on to tell the truth, the words of God are truth. Even when they may look like they cannot be true (17.15–17), even when it seems as though they have been forgotten (7.24–8.1), even when they are said to be untrue (3.4–5), it is only in the word of God that man can place his ultimate trust.

---

[4]See Excursus L.

[5]This, of course, may seem to break down somewhat at the *in utero* declaration that Jacob would be blessed over Esau. But the prophecy refers to the nations, not the individuals. And even if an individualistic interpretation is wrongly forced on the prophecy, Jacob and Esau live out the pattern that is displayed throughout Genesis: Jacob is faithful; Esau is not.

[6]The first chapter does not include this as its purpose is simply to describe the creation of the setting and people of the covenant.

Authorship

Moses. Among conservative scholars, it is pretty well agreed that Moses wrote Genesis. Since he was *learned in all the wisdom of the Egyptians and was mighty in words and in deeds* (Acts 7.22), he was certainly well prepared to author Genesis. He also received direct command from God to record the history of the Israelites on several occasions (*e.g.,* Exod 17.14; Num 33.2).

In New Testament times, he was believed to be the author of all the Pentateuch, a point which Jesus does not refute. Rather, He uses the standard *Law of Moses* as a description of all five books when speaking of them (Luke 24.44), certainly seeming to imply Mosaic authorship. Luke also accepted the Mosaic authorship of Genesis (24.27).

That is not to say that Mosaic authorship is without problem. Certainly there are things in the Pentateuch that Moses could not have known on his own—the creation story and the account of his death first come to mind. Moses calling himself the most humble man on the earth proves a stumbling block for others. And there are those pesky anachronisms—references to places and peoples that didn't yet exist (the city of Dan, 14.14; the Chaldeans, 11.28). Providing something of a solution, Harrison writes: "In attributing Mosaic authorship to the Pentateuch as a whole, conservative scholars have pointed out that the Torah in its entirety must not necessarily be assumed to have been the work of his own hands...but in general the ascription of Mosaicity to the Pentateuch implies its historicity and its formulation by Moses under divine inspiration, with the supposition that later editors may have revised the contents somewhat in accord with the traditions of the ancient Near Eastern scribes."[7]

Documentary Theory. Critical scholarship has taken a different approach to the composition of Genesis. In 1753, Astruc suggested that Genesis came from two source documents based on the name of God used (Yahweh or Elohim, source documents J and E). In 1792 and 1800 Geddes assigned the Pentateuch to the time of Solomon and attributed its compilation to a redactor. Later, a third, post-exilic priestly source (P) was added to the theory, making the composition of Genesis only a few hundred years before the coming of Christ.

The critical theory of the composition of Genesis can be summed up as follows: "A redactor in the postexilic period pieced together four formerly

---

[7]R.K. Harrison, *Introduction to the Old Testament,* 542.

continuous documents to compose the present work: J (Yahwist, 950 BC), E (Elohist, 850 BC), D (Deuteronomist, 620 BC), P (Priestly Code, 500 BC)" (Waltke). The source documents were traced by differences in vocabulary and style of writing.

"P shows decided preference for the divine names Elohim and El Shaddai. He was forever concerned with such other statistics as the total life span of the given individual, the age of a father at the birth of his oldest son... the names of other members of the family, and the like. J, on the other hand, used Yahweh exclusively. He was not given to stereotypes in either vocabulary or style; he was the literary genius behind the Book of Genesis. His writings are warmer and more intimate than P's, making freer use of anthropomorphisms. He probably belongs to the tenth century, which is about one hundred years earlier than scholars of the nineteenth century dated him. In general, E lacks the directness of J where man's relations with God are concerned. ...The center of E's world has not shifted all the way to heaven, as it has with P; neither is it earthbound, on the other hand, as in the case of J. E has a tendency, furthermore, to justify and explain rather than let actions speak for themselves. ...Basically, however, E is interested in events, whereas J is concerned with people. There are also other minor sources in the Book of Genesis; certain sections which do not fit into the above categories, so there must have been a redactor or redactors—R." [8]

While this idea is widely published and defended, we are not convinced by it. To conclude that difference in vocabulary from place to place throughout a body of literature indicates different authors is an invalid argument—at the very least, it is an argument that can be shown to be faulty in the world of extra-biblical literature. The use of multiple names for a god in a single text is common in other ancient Near Eastern documents. Or to use a popular example, no one disputes that J.R.R. Tolkien wrote all of *The Lord of the Rings,* even though Isildur's heir is called—in various places—Aragorn, Strider, Dunadan, and Elessar. Each of those names is used in different places to emphasize different aspects of his character, or because the character is in a specific place. Perhaps the author of Genesis had a similar motive. The consistency in which Yahweh, Elohim and El Shaddai are used does not necessarily point to different authors. It

---

[8]John J. Davis, *Paradise to Prison*, 22. Davis goes on to say that many critical commentators no longer see evidence for a source document D. See other OT Introductions for various viewpoints.

does, however, most likely point to a consistent theological emphasis being made by the author.[9]

Likewise, differing styles hardly proves different authors. A single man can write from a variety of different perspectives, a point which C.S. Lewis proves very well in his writing. How great is the disparity between *Mere Christianity, A Great Divorce, The Screwtape Letters,* and his Narnia chronicles! Each of these is unique from the others and no one doubts that a single author penned all of them. In the Bible, Paul shows this to be true: his letters to the Romans, Timothy and Philemon are quite different.

Moreover, certain parts of the text of Genesis have defied any attempt to separate them into such source documents, particularly some sections in which there was thought to be a mixture of J and E documents.[10] Overall, the book has far too much unity of thought and composition to be so divided. Other supposed evidence to this end—*e.g.,* repeated wife-sister stories—are not convincing.

If the documentary theory be upheld, it rests on a man who would singly stand as the worst editor who has ever lived.

Furthermore, archaeological discoveries have only hurt the theory and given credence to a more ancient date. "Of the many religious documents recovered from various sites in the Near East, not one of them can be shown to have been compiled in the manner described by nineteenth-century literary critics and their successors for the book of Genesis."[11]

Toledot Structure. Archaeology has, however, pointed us in a different direction. Ancient Near Eastern families kept their histories on clay tablets—a vast number of which have been found in digs in the Mesopotamian region. These tablets contain genealogies accompanied by significant historical notes on the back.[12] It has been suggested by several conservative scholars that the transmission of the history in Genesis may have been passed along by means of family history tablets.

The phrase *these are the **toledot** of* occurs eleven times in the book of Genesis. This phrase may refer to the previously recorded history, because "the preponderance of information given in relation to the person mentioned

---

[9]See Excursus B.

[10]R.K. Harrison, "Genesis," *ISBE,* 433.

[11]*Ibid.,* 434.

[12]Dale S. DeWitt, "Generations of Genesis," *EvQ.* 48 (1976): 200.

[13]R.K. Harrison, "Genesis," *ISBE,* 436.

in the phrase comes before, not after, the expression 'these are the generations of.'"[13] Following the notation about Adam in 5.1, for example, nothing else is said concerning him except a statement of his age at death. Likewise, after the mention of Jacob in 37.2, the only other references to him are incidental, with Joseph and Judah being the principal persons under consideration. This statement may then serve as a concluding remark to the previous history. Longman suggests, however, that it serves as an introductory remark to the history of that person's descendants. "The person named is not necessarily the main character but only the beginning point of the section of the book that also closes with the person's death."[14] Although either option is tenable, we are more inclined to follow the latter.

The eleven *these are the generations of* phrases could represent eleven distinct family history tablets. "The person mentioned in connection with [this phrase] could have been either the writer of the tablet, the owner, or both. ...It would have been a comparatively easy matter for a talented person such as Moses to compile the canonical book by arranging the tablets in a rough chronological order... and transcribing the entire corpus on a leather or papyrus roll."[15] All of this gives practical explanation to the recurring phrase *these are the generations of* in Genesis. Furthermore, it explains how Moses could have been so far removed from these events, yet know specifically what happened.

This theory takes nothing away from Jesus' reference to Genesis as a book of Moses, as he did the compiling and editing. Nor does it impugn the inspiration of God, as other books of the Bible were composed by means of research (most notably Luke's writings, *cf.* Luke 1.1–4). Should this approach be followed, the inspiration of Genesis is in the preservation of these materials for Moses and God working in Moses as he compiled the book. "The inspiration [is] in the choice of the material used. It would be parallel to Hezekiah's men copying out the proverbs of Solomon (Prov 25.1)."[16]

Is this a definite answer as to how Genesis came to be? We simply cannot know for certain.[17] It is, however, a plausible suggestion based on archaeology and the text without contradicting any other biblical teachings.

---

[14]Tremper Longman III, *How to Read Genesis,* 47.

[15]R.K. Harrison, "Genesis," *ISBE,* 436–437.

[16]Francis A. Schaeffer, *Genesis in Space and Time,* 128.

[17]Kidner remains unconvinced, 23–25.

Structure and Pattern in Genesis
The Primeval History: Alternating Structure[1]

A Creation story: first beginning; divine blessing (1.1–2.3)

    B Sin of Adam: nakedness; seeing/covering nakedness; curse (2.4–3.24)

        C No descendants of murdered younger, righteous son Abel (4.1–16)

            D Descendants of sinful son Cain (4.17–26)

                E Descendants of chosen son Seth: ten generations from Adam to Noah (5.1–32)

                    F Downfall: unlawful union (6.1–4)

                        G Brief introduction to Noah (6.5–8)

A' Flood story: reversal of creation; new beginning; divine blessing (6.9–9.19)

    B' Sin of Noah: nakedness, seeing/covering nakedness; curse (9.20–29)

        C' Descendants of younger, righteous son Japheth (10.1–5)

            D' Descendants of sinful son Ham (10.6–20)

                E' Descendants of chosen son Shem: ten generations from Noah to Terah (10.21–32)

                    F' Downfall: rebellious union (Tower of Babel) (11.1–9)

                        G' Brief Introduction of Abraham, through whom God will bless humanity (11.27–32)

---

[1] This structure is taken from Waltke. Three more will follow: preceding the Abraham narrative, the Jacob narrative, and the Joseph narrative. All three are adapted summaries of Gary Rendsburg's analysis of the main cycles of Genesis, modified in large measure from David Dorsey's *The Literary Structure of the Old Testament*. See Waltke, 19–21.

Creation

Why should we believe the Bible's account of creation?[1] Surely, Genesis 1 can be explained away as a creation of man—like all the other ancient myths about various gods and their creative works.

Comparison with ancient mythology, however, reveals something very different about the way Genesis is written. We follow Delitzsch in pointing to the manner in which it was written: sober, definite, clear, and concrete. And though it is full of potential for speculation and poetic beauty, the Genesis account of creation is free from human invention and philosophizing (Keil). "When it speaks of the origin of the heaven and earth, it presents no saga or myth or poetical fantasy but even then, according to its clear intention, presents history, which deserves faith and trust."[2]

Keil also points to the creation of man—the lord over the earth—as a differentiating mark from a man-made creation account. Surely man would have been created first if man had invented the creation account. Also, man probably would have been created distinctly and alone (*i.e.*, not on the same day as cattle, reptiles and other beasts of the field).

Furthermore, God's creation of the universe is taught consistently through the whole Bible. "In Exodus 20.11 the activity of God is present-

---

[1]As the introductory material was largely cursory, so also will be the comments on the first several chapters. The nature of these chapters is that they must be taken as literal by faith or explained away as something else. Much that can be, and often is, said of these chapters is largely speculative and counter-productive. The simpler parts of the text will be allowed to stand for themselves, while we will discuss some of the more difficult matters.

[2]Banvinck qtd. in Edward J. Young, *Studies in Genesis One*, 43.

ed to man as a pattern, and this fact presupposes that there was a reality in the activity of God which man is to follow."[3] Christ and His disciples accepted and taught this as truth. "The New Testament looks upon certain events of the creative week as genuinely historical. The creation itself (Heb 11.3)...the emerging of the earth (2 Pet 3.5). ...God's first fiat (2 Cor 4.6). ...Hebrews 6.7 seems to reflect upon the bringing forth of herbs on the third day, and Acts 17.24 to the work of filling the earth with its inhabitants. Likewise 1 Corinthians 11.7 asserts that man is in the image of God, and His creation is specifically mentioned in Matthew 19.4."[4] If we believe in Jesus, we must also believe as He did. Can we really believe that a God who can raise Jesus from the dead somehow cannot accurately record for us how He created the universe?

A Summary of Creation
Day One: light; day and night
Day Two: waters, sky, atmosphere
Day Three: land, oceans; vegetation
Day Four: sun, stars, moon for signs and time
Day Five: sea creatures and birds
Day Six: land animals and humankind
Day Seven: God rested

In addition to the linear structure (*i.e.*, seven consecutive days), the days of creation can be seen in a parallel structure:

A light
   B sea and sky
      C dry land
A' luminaries
   B' fish and birds
      C' land animals and humans
         D' Sabbath

"In both the linear and parallel structures, the Sabbath day stands in the position of emphasis: it culminates the linear arrangement; and it stands as unique and unmatched (and thus highlighted) in the parallel scheme."[5]

---

[3]Aalders qtd. in *ibid.*, 47.

[4]*Ibid.*, 51.

[5]David A. Dorsey, *The Literary Structure of the Old Testament*, 49. For a further explanation of the parallel structure, see *The Relationship of the Days* in Excursus A.

1 *1, In the beginning, God created the heavens and the earth.* Does this statement refer to a pre-first day, initial creative act of God, which left a void and formless earth, or is it merely a summary statement that stands for the specifics described in the rest of the chapter? Each position has been staunchly defended by different competent scholars.[6]

According to Waltke, "Although some have argued that 1.1 functions as merely the first event of creation, rather than a summary of the whole account, the grammar makes that interpretation improbable. ...'Beginning' refers to the entire created event, the six days of creation, not something before the six days." And Blocher: "'The heavens and the earth' is a formula which always designates the totality of the universe in its order and beauty. To apply the phrase to a confused mass is to make it mean its opposite." Further, "If we add that creation was achieved by the word (Psa 33.6) and that the first word is not heard until verse 3, we shall firmly exclude the possibility that verse 2 speaks of what was created according to verse 1."[7] Waltke concludes: "Logic will not allow us to entertain the contradictory notions: God created the organized heaven and earth [verse 1]; the earth was unorganized [verse 2]."[8]

The issue raised by some at this point is that such an interpretation does not explain where the earth comes from. Indeed, to accept verse 1 as a summary statement leaves God working with a planet that was in existence when He first speaks in verse 3. The solution to this lies in the fact that Genesis 1 is not meant to be an exhaustive account of all of creation. For example, Genesis says nothing of the creation of spiritual beings, yet Paul makes it clear that the spiritual realities are a part of God's creation (Col 1.16); nor is the method by which the land animals are made discussed. Their 'to dust they return' nature would seem to indicate that they were not created *ex nihilo.* So, did they pop out of the ground or were they formed and breathed into the same way that God formed and breathed into man? Genesis 1 does not seek to answer this question. Its purpose is not to document every particular act of God during His creative week.[9]

---

[6]For a well-reasoned defense of this verse describing an initial creative act, see Mark F. Rooker, "Genesis 1.1–3: Creation or Re-Creation?" in *Vital Old Testament Issues,* 11–27.

[7]Henri Blocher, *In the Beginning,* 64–65.

[8]Qtd. in Rooker, 13.

[9]Incidentally, this remains the strongest argument against verse 1 being a summary statement—not because it leaves a blank where we would like information, but because it removes a significant

1.2, The earth was without form and void. Those who would understand verse 1 as an initial creative act would continue that this verse shows the unformed and unfinished creation. This interpretation may be attractive as it would allow for scientists' billions of years to pass after the creation, but before time, *per se*, begins on Day One. But if it does not mean this, as we have followed, to what, then, does the earth being *without form and void* refer? Waltke suggests: "This phrase is an antonym to 'heavens and the earth,' signifying something uncreated or disordered (Jer 4.23–27)." It would seem best to understand the first half of verse 2 describing the state of the earth prior to verse 1—uncreated—"as it would be a contradiction to represent the creation as formed cosmos and the earth as unformed" (Waltke).

The Spirit of God was hovering over the face of the waters. As with nearly everything in the first chapter of Genesis, this phrase has been one of debate. As the word for *Spirit* can also be translated *wind* or *breath*, some have suggested (to great vilification) that this verse does not actually indicate that God's Spirit was hovering over the waters. Although *wind* certainly seems to be the appropriate understanding of the Hebrew word in God's *re-creation* (*cf.* 8.1), it does not seem to fit the context of this passage.

By contrast, many modern exegetes often read Trinitarian doctrine back into this passage, understanding the Spirit of God who hovered to be the Third Person of the Godhead. While this may be the case, God's *spirit* was more likely understood by the original audience—those who saw pillars of fire and smoke, and read about God's appearing to the patriarchs as a man—as simply a distinction from God's *physical* appearing. This passage, then, should not be pressed, with 1.26, into Trinitarian foreshadowing.

1.3, And God said. Cf. Psalm 33.6; Hebrews 11.3. "God's creative word does not refer to the utterance of a magic word, but to the expression of an effortless, omnipotent, unchallengeable word of a God who transcends the world."[10]

---

difference between this and the pagan creation accounts. In those, the pagan deities all work with preexisting matter. Should verse 1 be understood as the creation of all matter, it highlights the depth of the difference between the various accounts. See Excursus A.

[10]Gerhard F. Hasel, "The Significance of the Cosmology in Genesis 1 in Relation to Ancient Near Eastern Parallels," *AUSS* 10 No. 2. (1972): 11.

"Let there be light." God alone is the giver and source of light (*cf.* John 1.5–9; 12.35–36). "Since the sun is only later introduced as the immediate cause of light, the chronology of the text emphasizes that God is the *ultimate* source of light. The dischronologization probably functions as a polemic against pagan religions, which worship the creation or creatures, not the Creator upon whom the creation depends" (Waltke).

1.5, There was evening and there was morning. Those who argue for literal days often point to this phrase as the key to that understanding. But one must ask how *evening and morning* equals 24 hours. The author just spoke of the light being day and the darkness night. Surely, we understand that 24 hours is made up of day and night, not evening and morning.

A common suggestion is represented by Wenham: "Probably the mention of evening before morning reflects the Jewish concept that the day begins at dusk, not at dawn. ...On this view, the first day began in darkness (v 2) and ended, after the creation of light, with nightfall, the start of the second day." While this may be a plausible explanation, it seems convoluted for the first day to begin at any time other than the creation of light; would the first day not have begun when God first spoke? Hamilton reassures us: "The fact that *evening* is placed before *morning* throughout this chapter is not a foolproof indication that the OT reckons a day from sunset to sunset."

By contrast, Kidner suggests it be translated "evening came and morning came." And Waltke: "The idea, as expressed by the Hebrew is that the first day ends when the darkness of the evening is dispelled by the morning light." Thus, the first day began when God said *"Let there be light."* *Evening* brought to end the first day (*i.e.,* period of daylight). *Morning* brought to end the first 24 hour period, "For 'evening' marks the conclusion of the day, and 'morning' marks the conclusion of the night" (Leupold).

It has been argued that because the sun wasn't around until the fourth day, and because days are measured by a sunrise and sunset, we cannot know precisely how long the first three days were. While it is true that the sun was not created until the fourth day, the measure of the days did not change after that point. Before day four, the days were measured by the passing of light to darkness and the return of light. And nothing changed after the sun and moon were placed in the sky.

All of these questions, of course, are subtle attempts to press a theory that each day could have been millions of years, allowing for the reconciliation of the Bible with science. This theory, however, has bigger problems to overcome than the description of the days in Genesis. The primary problem with the day-age theory (*i.e.,* each day was thousands or millions of years) is that it takes a passage that uses a *figure of speech* and tries to bind that figure *literally* on another part of the Bible (*i.e.,* 2 Pet 3.8 onto Gen 1). As Wenham asserts, "There can be little doubt that here 'day' has its basic sense of a 24-hour period."

On the other hand, those who say that *day* never means anything other than 24-hours don't have an exegetical leg to stand on. This is clearly refuted three times in the first two chapters of Genesis. In 1.5, *God called the light Day, and the darkness he called Night.* Here, day clearly refers to daylight—the time between sunrise and sunset. In 2.4, we find *the day the* L ORD *made the earth and the heavens*—a use of *day* to refer to a week-long period. In 2.17, God warns Adam, *"The day you eat of it, you will surely die."* Physical death certainly didn't happen on that day, and while spiritual separation from God occurred on some level, spiritual death in its ultimate sense (*i.e.,* hell) did not occur that day either. And even if this verse is forced into meaning Adam's immediate spiritual separation from God by sin, it still wouldn't equal 24-hours: the separation was instant, not gradually developing while the earth made a full rotation.

The first day. Unfortunately, the ESV obscures what is immediately striking in the Hebrew text of the days' enumeration. The first day is the only one to use a cardinal number, while the remaining use ordinals. Thus, the description of the first day should either be rendered *one day* or *Day One,* depending on whether its significance is to mark how long the period of time is (one day) or where this period of time fell (Day One). In that the remaining numbers seek to identify the day by number (second, third, *etc.)*—and that the duration of the days is a purely modern question—we would choose to translate the first day as *day one.*

The ESV also fails to make another significant grammatical distinction. Each day except the sixth and seventh are indefinite. The author's reason is somewhat unclear and interpretations of its implications vary. It is, however, better rendered: *Day One... a second day... a third day... a fourth day... a fifth day... the sixth... the seventh day.*[11]

1.6, "An expanse." To what exactly does the *expanse* refer? Verse 17, where

---

[11]See Excursus A.

the heavenly bodies are put into the expanse, might indicate that the expanse refers to 'outer space.' A few verses later, however, we read that the birds fly through the expanse (v 20). It is probably best not to get too scientific in trying to pin down what the author had in mind. Wenham says, "The firmament occupies the space between earth's surface and the clouds. ...Quite how the OT conceives the nature of the firmament is less clear." Perhaps it's best to describe it as 'what you see when you look up.'[12]

1.7, The waters that were above the expanse. This may simply refer to the clouds. "The expanse separates the source of rain from the waters on the earth" (Waltke). Leupold writes, "Apparently, before this firmament existed, the earth waters on the surface of the earth and the cloud waters as we now have them were contiguous without an intervening clear air space. ...Now the physical laws that cause clouds and keep them suspended go into operation. These clouds constitute the upper waters."

Ancients believed that there was a dome around the earth with water on the outside, having openings through which rain would pass. Many Bible believers have modified this into a canopy theory—that this layer of water above the sky existed until the flood. Then, the *windows of the heavens were opened* (7.11), drained all this supernal water onto the earth, and subsequently, the entire atmosphere was changed. Unfortunately for this viewpoint, *windows of heavens* is used figuratively in the Bible, just as we use the similar expression 'the sky opened up.' One scholar wrote of the Canopy Theory: "It is no theory. It has no support either biblically or physically. If someone wants to use Scripture to support a canopy 'theory,' they had better be prepared to accept the Hebrews' and other ancients' concept of the sky as an upside-down metal bowl with the stars painted on it. That's the only canopy concept in Genesis."

1.11, "Let the earth sprout vegetation." "This emergence is no less 'creation' than was the first act. ...God has bound together all creatures in a common dependence on their native elements, while giving each the distinctive character of its kind. Each has an origin which is from one angle natural and from another supernatural; and the natural process is made self-perpetuating and, under God, autonomous. One implication of this

---

[12]Much could be said about how the ancients perceived the created world and, even, how the Bible's description often matches ancient concepts. For our purposes, however, this description will suffice.

is that it is part of godliness to respect the limitations within which we live as natural creatures, as from Him. Another is that fertility, so often deified in the ancient world, is a *created* capacity, from the hand of the one God" (Kidner).

1.14, "Let them be for signs and for seasons." Waltke notes: "The lights mark out a comprehensive divine order for Israel's sacred seasons, not the zodiac or astrology." And Kidner: "They will speak for God, not for fate (Jer 10.2; *cf.* Matt 2.9; Luke 21.25, 28), for they *rule* (vv 16, 18) only as lightbearers, not as powers. In these few simple sentences the lie is given to a superstition as old as Babylon and as modern as a newspaper-horoscope."

1.20, "Let the waters swarm." See comment on verse 11.

1.21, The great sea creatures. The word used would have been ominous, because in pagan literature, it "stood for the powers of chaos confronting Baal in the beginning" (Kidner). But as Fox notes: "The rebellious primeval monster of Psalm 74.13 (and common in ancient Near Eastern myth) is here depicted as merely another one of God's many creations,"[13] one that, as Waltke goes on to say, depends upon and ultimately serves God.[14]

1.24, "Let the earth bring forth living creatures." See comment on verse 11.
   Livestock and creeping things and beasts of the earth. "The *creeping thing,* which suggests to us only the reptiles, is not a scientific classification but a description of the smooth or crawling motion of various kinds of creature. The Hebrew verb has already appeared in verse 21 ('moves'), evidently to denote the gliding of fish, as in Psalm 104.25. Probably the three kinds of animal in verse 24 are, broadly, what we should call domesticated animals, small creatures and game" (Kidner). And Roop: "Certainly this represents some element of classification, but these expressions are also poetic. They call to mind pictures of animals not just abstract categories. ...Domesticated animals, wild animals, and creeping/crawling creatures represent ordering by an artist as much as by a systematician."[15]

1.26, "Let us make man." To whom does God speak in this passage? Per-

---

[13]Everett Fox, *Genesis and Exodus: A New Rendition with Commentary and Notes,* 13.

[14] "Psalm 104.26 reduces the Leviathan to a duck in God's bathtub" (Waltke).

[15]Eugene F. Roop, *Genesis,* 30.

haps the most long-standing interpretation of this passage is that God speaks to the other members of the deity. Kidner refers to this as the "plural of fullness, which is found in the regular word for God [a plural] used with a singular verb."[16]

The plurality of deity in creation is certainly supported in the New Testament writings of John and Paul which speak to the creative act of the *Logos*. But if this is nothing more than an expansion of the regular sense of *elohim*, why does it first appear with a plural verb (v 26) only to be replaced with a singular verb in the creative act (v 27)?

If it is not the regular sense of *elohim*, and it is God speaking to the rest of deity regarding what *They* were going to do (plural verb, v 26), why is it that *He* is the one who did it (singular verb, v 27)? Further, there is no evidence that the Hebrews and Israelites had any concept of 'godhead.' This view would have us believe that no one was able to properly understand this passage until the fuller revelation of the New Testament. While it is helpful to read through the lens of the New Testament, such a closed explanation does nothing to tell us what this passage meant to its original audience.

Many other suggestions have been raised. Some (such as Driver and Keil) have suggested that this is the Plural of Majesty (*cf.* the English royal 'we'). This theory, however, was rejected as it was realized that the plural of majesty is not used with verbs in Hebrew.

Another view, held by some past Jewish scholars, is that God is addressing the earthly elements, speaking to His creation. Thus, *in our image* would refer to man's likeness to both God and the earth ('You provide the dirt and I'll provide the breath'). For God to invite His creation to be a partner is strange indeed, and falls by the wayside when verse 27 announces that God alone (singular verb) created man.

A more plausible solution is that this is a plural of self-deliberation (*e.g.,* Westerman), comparable to the English 'Let's see.' There is one clear example of this usage elsewhere in the Bible where David speaks of himself in the plural (2 Sam 24.14). That this is the only other parallel, however, makes this option a less attractive, though not an impossible one. The greatest detriment to this line of thought is that it provides little interpretive help in 3.22 where God again speaks in the first person plural.

Many critical scholars see this as polytheism. In an effort to make the

---

[16]Hamilton and Hasel also follow this view.

Bible just another book of myths, in line with the rest of ancient mythology, they see this plurality a leftover of the supposed past polytheism from which Israelite religion came. However, "Genesis 1 is distinctly antimythological in its thrust, explicitly rejecting ancient Near Eastern views of creation" (Wenham).

Finally, many have come to see this passage as God speaking to the angelic host (Waltke, Wenham, *etc.*). There is precedent for this interpretation, as many other Old Testament passages speak of a heavenly council that God addresses (*e.g.,* 1 Kgs 22.19–22; Jer 23.18, 22; Isa 6.1–8; Job 1.6–7; *etc.*). Wenham suggests, "[This] should therefore be regarded as a divine announcement to the heavenly court, drawing the angelic host's attention to the master stroke of creation, man. As Job 38.4, 7 puts it: 'When I laid the foundation of the earth…all the sons of God shouted for joy.'" Waltke adds, "It is not surprising that God would address the heavenly court since angels play a prominent role in Scripture… and there is much commerce in Genesis between the angelic realm and human beings."

The primary objections to this suggestion are that it makes angels a part of creating man and it removes Jesus from the creation.

In response to angels playing a role in the creation of man, this suggestion clearly does no such thing. Indeed, the singular use of the verb in verse 27 emphasizes that it is God alone who creates. Nor does this remove Jesus from creation. Such an assertion comes from flawed logic: Jesus was not a part of creation in the minds of the original audience of this book. For the plural to refer to Jesus—when the people had no concept of such a being— would mean that this passage was nothing more than an enigma for several millennia. Not until John and Paul wrote was it clear of whom this passage spoke. But to an audience who *regularly* read about God speaking to a heavenly council, this passage would be easily understandable.

How then do we correlate the Old and New Testaments in this matter? Such is done by closely examining what each says of the creation. Here and throughout the Old Testament, it is made manifest that the agent of God's creation was His word. He spoke the universe into existence. The New Testament teaches that the agent of God's creation is the *Logos*—the word of God—but goes on to identify this word as the one who would become Jesus.

A proper reading of Genesis 1 inserts the *Logos* into God's speaking. Instead of trying to match the New Testament's Agent of Creation *(Logos)* with the Old Testament's Creator *(Us)*, a proper reading matches the New Testament's Agent of Creation *(Logos)* with the Old Testament's Agent of Creation (God's Word). Thus, instead of understanding God's speaking as His vocal utterance into the vast nothingness, the New Testament teaches that His speaking was the sending forth of the *Logos* to fulfill His creative will. This interpretation allows the Agent to match the Agent in fully revealing God's message.

The primary problem with this understanding is that it stretches the range of our vocabulary, so that words don't quite mean what they mean: *i.e.,* His speaking was a Being. But then, should we expect less when we are trying to understand God—a goal that has been sought after for millennia, yet never fully grasped? Or, as it has been well said elsewhere: "Try as we might, we will never understand this divine depth."[17]

While a Christian cannot help but see Jesus in creation, an Israelite would not have seen the same thing. And while it is right and good to recognize Jesus' work in creation, we must remember to see the book of Genesis first with its original intent.

"In our image." To speak of the image of God is to speak of something that is spiritual, eternal, free willed, capable of love and relationships, self-aware, a moral being, and that has dominion. Yet it also should remind us of our origin: "An image *is only an image.* It exists only by derivation. It is not the original, nor is it anything without the original. Mankind's being an image stresses the radical nature of his dependence."[18] Longman adds, "The Hebrew word for image *(tselem)* is also used for the construction of royal images. That is, while the king could not be physically present throughout his entire realm, he would set up images of himself throughout the kingdom to remind the people of his authority. In this sense, the image of God may be taken to mean that human beings are God's representations in the creation."[19]

It is also important to note that *mankind* was created in God's image, not males. Females equally share in God's image. God is often described with female imagery—in terms of motherhood as well as fatherhood. All that is good about the feminine nature and motherhood is as much a part

---

[17]*Hard Sayings*, 492.

[18]Henri Blocher, *In the Beginning*, 82.

[19]Tremper Longman III, *How to Read Genesis*, 105.

of God's character as the best of masculinity and fatherhood. And this, we believe speaks even higher things of the institution of marriage: when the two come together, they provide what the other is lacking; when the two become one, they become a little bit more like God.

Further, subordination does not equal having less of His image. It is wrong to conclude that "for the woman to be subordinate would make her inferior in value, ability, or as a human being. The man's headship over the woman is solely a position of rank. The man owes this authoritative position to God's appointment, not to personal achievement or any kind of superiority." Again, "Woman is an equal participant with man in respect to the image of God."[20]

"After our likeness." How *likeness* relates exactly to *image* is something of an uncertainty.[21] While we would agree with Kidner that their purpose is not to distinguish aspects of man's character, "whereby the 'image' is man's indelible constitution as a rational and morally responsible being, and the 'likeness' is that spiritual accord with the will of God which was lost at the fall," we would hesitate to say that they "reinforce one another." Hamilton seems to be on the right track in saying, "The physical nuance of the concrete term 'image' is toned down by the more abstract term 'likeness.'" And Waltke hits even closer to home: "The important addition of 'likeness' underscores that humanity is only a facsimile of God and hence distinct from him... the word *likeness* serves to clearly distinguish God from humans in the biblical worldview."

The use of the word *likeness* seems to indicate that while we are formed in God's image, we are only a simile of God. Much is gained by looking at the nature of a simile: a comparison of two things that—while they have a common feature—are intrinsically different. While we were created in the image of God, we must remember that we are far from being Him.

1.31, It was very good. God looked at everything created and judged it good. "His conclusion: Every step and every sphere of creation, and the whole thing put together—man himself and his total environment, the heavens and the earth—conforms to myself."[22]

---

[20]Michael F Stitzinger, "Genesis 1–3 and the Male/Female Role Relationship," *GTJ* 2 No. 1 (1981): 27–30.

[21]See Wenham for a fuller discussion of the debate.

[22]Francis A Schaeffer, *Genesis in Space and Time*, 55.

2.3, God rested. "Literally 'ceased.' ...It is the rest of achievement, not inactivity, for He nurtures what He creates; we may compare the symbolism of Jesus 'seated' after His finished redemption (Heb 8.1; 10.12), to dispense benefits" (Kidner). And Leupold: "Since the primary meaning of *shabbath* is 'to cease' or 'to desist,' we are freed from all misconceptions which may attach to God's inactivity. ...If God desisted from labor on this day, then no more work was done on it, then nothing had to be completed, then no unseemly thought about God's being weary needs to be rejected." The meaning suggested by these two commentators is supported by BDB (cease, desist, rest—that *rest* is the third meaning) and *TWOT*: "the basic thrust of the verb is... to desist, to come to an end."[23]

Pagan creation accounts end with the gods building temples as a sign of their victory over the wild forces of chaos. God's 'celebration,' however, is one that is man-focused (*cf.* Mark 2.23–28). Even so, Genesis 1 is probably not the institution of the Sabbath law as such. Certainly there is no indication that anyone before Sinai observed the Sabbath. This is, however, the basis of the Sabbath law (*cf.* Exod 20.9–11). More important is the lesson it teaches: "It relativizes the works of mankind, the contents of the six working days. It protects mankind from total absorption by the task of subduing the earth, it anticipates the distortion which makes work the sum and purpose of human life, and it informs mankind that he will not fulfill his humanity in his relation to the world which he is transforming but only when he raises his eyes above, in the blessed, holy hour of communion with the Creator."[24]

Waltke observes that the Sabbath reminds Israel again and again that God completes His work. As He consummates His work in creation, He will bring to perfection His work in history through His elect people. He who calls Israel to bring salvation will not fail. It also confesses regularly that their God is Lord of all. He made the Sabbath holy to celebrate His rest *from all the work of creating that he had done*. Thus, to observe the Sabbath is to confess Yahweh as Lord. Further, it accepts the blessing that God gave to man for rest. The rabbis made the Sabbath a burden, but Jesus, in teaching that the Sabbath is meant for people, releases them from this burden.

---

[23]Victor P. Hamilton, "Shabat." *TWOT,* 902.

[24]Henri Blocher, *In the Beginning,* 57.

Sabbath observance is also a sign that the creator has set Israel apart for a special covenant relationship with Him. In addition, it is a reminder that they were slaves in Egypt and that God has redeemed them from slavery into rest (Deut 5.12–15; Christ is our Sabbath—Col 2.16–17). Finally, it gives concrete expression to the hope of heaven. The Sabbath rest assures saints that, just as God entered His rest after working for six days, so also they live in the hope that when they cease from their labors after their fleeting days, they too shall enter an eternal rest.

Excursus A:
Additional Notes on the Creation Account

Two more things need to be said regarding the Creation account: first, there are several points to be made about the days of creation that were not addressed above—with what limited answers we can give; second, the issue of the creation narrative's purpose should be addressed.

The Days of Creation

The Relationship Between the Days. The first three days consist of a separation: darkness from light (day 1); waters from waters (day 2); waters from land (day 3).

Further, "The first three days describe the creation of realms or habitations. The second three narrate the inhabitants of these realms, so the realms created on day one (light, darkness) are filled on day four (sun, moon, stars), those of day two (sky, water) are filled on day five (birds, fish) and day three (land) is filled on day six (land animals, humans)."[1]

Also, as the creation week moves along, the creative activity increases. "The number of creative acts also increases within each triad: from a single creative act (days 1 and 4) to one creative act with two aspects (days 2 and 5) to two separate creative acts (days 3 and 6)" (Waltke).

The Nature of the Days. A common argument, in seeking to reconcile the Bible and science, is that the days are not 24 hour days.[2] Such a position seems to follow the teaching of Whitcomb: "Whenever there is apparent conflict between the conclusions of the scientist and the conclusions of the theologian, especially with regard to such problems as the origin of the universe, solar system, earth, animal life, and man; the effects of the Edenic curse; and the magnitude and effects of the Noahic Deluge, the theologian must rethink his interpretation of the Scriptures at these points in such a way as to bring it into harmony with the general consensus of scientific opinion on these matters, since the Bible is not a textbook on science, and these problems overlap the territory in which science alone must give us the detailed and authoritative answers."[3]

Young responds: "What strikes one immediately upon reading such a statement is the low estimate of the Bible which it entails. Whenever 'science' and the Bible are in conflict, it is always the Bible that, in one manner or anoth-

---

[1]Tremper Longman III, *How to Read Genesis*, 104–105. Young, however, argues that the parallelism is not exact. See *Studies in Genesis One*, 68–71.

[2]For our position on the length of the days, see comment on 1.5; for our position on the Bible and science, see below.

[3]Qtd. in Edward J. Young, *Studies in Genesis One*, 52.

er, must give way. We are not told that 'science' should correct its answers in the light of Scripture. Always it is the other way round. Yet this is surprising, for the answers which scientists have provided have frequently changed with the passing of time. The 'authoritative' answers of pre-Copernican scientists are no longer acceptable; nor, for that matter, are many of the views of twenty-five years ago."[4] While we agree with the sentiment of Young in his estimation of Scripture, we do not agree with the low estimation of science based solely on the changing interpretation of scientists. Such logic would also lead to saying that the Bible itself must be questionable since theologians have changed their interpretations of various passages so many times.

As believers in God's creation, we believe that science is also His creation. Indeed, Paul assures us that the creation reveals His divine nature (Rom 1.19–20). And while scientists may repeatedly change their interpretation of science, it does not mean that science itself is untrue. There is, however, truth in Young's appeal that we not place so much credence in the scientists' word that we run to rearrange our theology based on it. If we do such, we may find ourselves changing our theology every five years.

Consecutive Days? Proponents of the non-consecutive approach to the days of Genesis have often looked to the clear structure as evidence that the order of the days have been rearranged. However, "A schematic disposition of the material in Genesis 1 does not prove, nor does it even suggest, that the days are to be taken in a non-chronological sense. There appears to be a certain schematization, for example, in the genealogies of Matthew 1, but it does not follow that the names of the genealogies are to be understood in a non-chronological sense."[5]

Sterchi makes a more compelling argument for a non-chronological sequence based on the grammatical construction of the text. He argues, "The text itself does not actually require that it be read as a chronological sequence."[6] His argument stems from the numbering of the days in the Hebrew text. Day One is the only day spoken of with a cardinal number, the remainder use ordinal numbers. The second–fifth days are all indefinite—"a second day, a third day, *etc.*" The last two days are definite.[7] At best, however, Sterchi's argument is: "The text is not implying a chronological sequence

---

[4]*Ibid.*, 53.

[5]*Ibid.*, 66.

[6]David A. Sterchi, "Does Genesis 1 Provide a Chronological Sequence?" *JETS* 39 (1996): 535.

[7]Sterchi argues that the definite article on the last two days serve "to emphasize [their] uniqueness." *Ibid.*, 533.

of seven days. Instead it is simply presenting a list of seven days. It is not that the list is definitely not chronological. It may be chronological, but the syntax of the list does not require that we read it as such."[8] While a non-chronological reading may be a grammatical possibility, it does not necessarily make it a better reading.

That days two through five are indefinite also *grammatically* allows for periods of time to pass between the days. Again, though the grammar allows this, such a view is not necessary from the grammar.

Literal or Figurative? The problem with debates over whether something in the Bible is figurative or literal is that it diminishes a great biblical truth: everything in the Bible is, to some degree, figurative. That doesn't mean that it isn't real or that it didn't literally happen in the way it was described; rather, it means that there is a greater spiritual truth to it than a superficial glance will show: it is a *figure* of something more. The days of creation are an excellent illustration of this point.

God could have created the earth and universe any way He wanted to. The Bible reports that it was six days, but He could have created in six seconds, six years, six centuries or six millennia. Or He could have done it instantaneously. But He created in six days. Why? It would seem that His choice is supposed to teach us something—it is a figure of something greater. Even if they are literal days, they are still, in a sense, figurative.

So why did God create in six days? *His creation in six days is to set off and emphasize by contrast the seventh day, the Sabbath, and to highlight its purpose.*[9] That this is the purpose of the six days of creation is made evident by the reference to it in explaining the Sabbath laws (Exod 20.8–11).[10] This becomes even more evident as the theme of rest is further developed in the Old Testament.

---

[8]*Ibid.*, 533.

[9]See comment on 2.3.

[10]Although we would not press it as far as he does, this is essentially what Blocher is getting at in his 'literary' approach to the days of creation. "The literary interpretation takes the form of the week attributed to the work of creation to be an artistic arrangement, a modest example of anthropomorphism that is not to be taken literally. ...He wishes to bring out certain themes and provide a theology of the sabbath" *(In the Beginning,* 50). And, "Once we grasp that God creates in time and not in a single instant, we can understand that God is involved when He creates, that He *enters* into His work; and similarly we can understand from the finishing of that creation and from its completed time-span that God is *not absorbed into* what He creates. He remains sovereignly free, holding His creation before him and delighting in it with the joy of the seventh day. ...The theological treasures of the framework of the Genesis days come most clearly to light by means of the 'literary' interpretation. The writer has given us a masterly elaboration of a fitting, restrained anthropomorphic vision, in order to convey a whole complex of deeply meditated ideas" *(ibid.,* 59).

Not only are Sabbath days to be observed, but Sabbath years. Then, when the people are carried away into captivity, one of the main reasons is because of their forsaking of these Sabbaths—their captivity is to give the land the rest it deserves. This rest found its origin in the creation week.

All of this comes to a head in the New Testament when we learn that all of those literal Sabbath days and years are figurative of something even greater: the fuller rest that awaits God's people in heaven (*cf.* Heb 4.1–11). The creation week was a figure for the Old Testament Sabbaths which were a figure for the final Sabbath rest.

In all of this we see a fundamental truth: God's relationship with mankind is based, in a large degree, on rest—whether Sabbath laws in the Old Testament or looking forward to the heavenly rest that awaits now.

So, when we spend all of our time arguing about how long the days were, we miss the real point of why God chose to create in six days rather than instantaneously. God created in six days to emphasize a key element in our relationship with Him. And if we miss that—the real point—because of our arguing about the length of the days, it doesn't matter whether or not we're right: we've missed the message of God's word.

Genesis 1 and the *Enuma Elish* [11]

Modern exegetes of Genesis invariably seek to understand the first chapter in relation to modern science: 'How can it say seven days, and the genealogies only add up to a few thousand years, when we *know* that the world is billions of years old?' they ask. And so, countless pages are spent seeking to reconcile these supposed contradictions. But the reality of the issue is that such matters were outside the scope of Moses' intent. Longman makes this point well: "It is certain that the biblical account of creation was not written to counter Charles Darwin or Stephen Hawking, but it was written in the light of rival descriptions of creation." [12]

This is not to say that science has no place in the life of a believer. To completely ignore science would be to neglect a portion of the evidence for God. Not only does the creation tell us that He exists (Psa 19.1–6), but it teaches us about His nature (Rom 1.19–20). And so we agree with Kidner: "To try to corre-

---

[11]This portion of Excursus A was only added after much thought. It is, after all, outside the purview of this manuscript; there is no corresponding Excursus about *The Gilgamesh Epic.* Ultimately, it was included to be a pointed contrast to those scholars and theologians who insist on reading Genesis 1 as a response to modern scientific assertions. It was not *The Origin of Species* or *A Brief History of Time* that Moses sought to correct, but the *Enuma Elish* and other such creation accounts.

[12]Tremper Longman III, *How to Read Genesis,* 72.

late the data of Scripture and nature is not to dishonor biblical authority, but to honor God as Creator and to grapple with our proper task of interpreting His ways of speaking." Indeed, the cosmos seems to be designed for discovery and mankind has been placed in a one-in-a-million venue, perched in a spot in the universe amazingly situated for exploration: "The extraordinary conditions that create a hospitable environment on Earth also happen to make our planet strangely well-suited for viewing, analyzing, and understanding the universe." [13] It would seem that God wants us to study the sciences of His creation and to learn more about Him through those things. The rejection of all things scientific, it would seem, is a rejection of God Himself and the Scripture which testifies to His self-revelation in creation.

The problem is that we are looking for answers to questions in the Genesis account that it never intended to give. We read Genesis asking *how* and *when*, but those are not the questions it was written to answer. There is no timestamp on the creation account, and little information is given as to how God created.[14] Instead, the creation account was recorded to answer *who* and *why*. This becomes even clearer when compared with the false creation accounts of the Israelites' pagan neighbors.

The *Enuma Elish,* in summary, explains the origins of the gods to whom the inert waters Apsu and Tiamat gave birth. The lesser gods, threatened by Apsu, kill him, prompting the revenge of Tiamat. Marduk rose to power by combating and slaying Tiamat. Then, Marduk created the cosmos as we know it from the carcass of Tiamat, dividing it into two parts which became the earth and sky.[15] "The reward for his task is his elevation as king of the gods and ultimately the building of Babylon by the deities and of its temple for his permanent royal citadel and center of administration. …Mesopotamia's creation epic was shaped to justify the political ascendancy of Babylon and its chief deity Marduk by setting their origins and character of their ruler in the mythic, eternal present" (Mathews).

For years, critical scholars have sought to read Genesis in the light of the *Enuma Elish,* but only to explain the Genesis account as having been literarily dependent on it. After all, the *Enuma Elish* does predate the book of Gen-

---

[13]Lee Strobel, *The Case for a Creator,* 188.

[14]We know that God created by His word and that He used dirt to form man and a rib to form woman. Beyond that, we know little: how God separated the various elements; how He created the animals (with dirt or *ex nihilo);* how He created the plants; how and when He created the spiritual beings (*cf.* Col 1:16); *etc.*

[15]See D. Winton Thomas, *Documents from Old Testament Times,* 3–16 for the full text of the *Enuma Elish* or Tremper Longman III, *How to Read Genesis,* 74–75 for a more detailed summary.

esis and there are similarities between the two creation accounts. The similarities that these critical scholars point to include such things as the creation of light, firmament, dry land and luminaries as well as a divine rest on the seventh day (Speiser qtd. in Wenham). Further similarities include a period of chaos followed by order with the primordial chaos being pictured as a watery mass. The cosmos is created from the sea and man is made from clay mixed with another substance.

While these similarities may seem substantial on a superficial level, when they are looked at more closely, it is evident that the theory of Genesis being drawn from the *Enuma Elish* is difficult to sustain. Harrison argues: "A more careful study of similarities and differences, however, has made it evident that resemblances between the Babylonian and Israelite cosmogonies are not as close as had been imagined previously."[16]

A clear difference between the two accounts is that the *Enuma Elish* features conflict at the center of creation. But, "According to Genesis, conflict is introduced into the world not by the gods but by human rebellion (Gen 3)."[17] Further, the purpose of the two creation accounts cannot be harmonized: "The overall purpose of the *Enuma Elish* and many of its details were quite different from those of Genesis 1. *Enuma Elish* is concerned with glorifying Marduk and justifying his supremacy in the Babylonian pantheon. The creative acts of this god constitute very minor illustrations of his power: His victory of Tiamat is central to *Enuma Elish,* whereas in Genesis, of course, God's work of creation is the central theme of [Genesis] 1" (Wenham).

And what of man being created from clay and another substance? In the *Enuma Elish,* man is created from clay and the blood of a slain demon—this couldn't be farther from the biblical account of the dust of the ground and the breath of God. Further, "In Mesopotamian mythology the creation of man is almost incidental, presented as a kind of afterthought."[18] By contrast, Genesis presents the creation of man as the crowning of creation—the sole purpose for which everything else was made.

Finally, there is a difference too glaring to ignore: "The main contrast has to do with the identity and nature of the Creator. The biblical account presents one God, who alone is God, who created the world. This one God created unopposed."[19] And Waltke: "The essential difference between the Mosaic faith

---

[16]R.K. Harrison, *Introduction to the Old Testament.* 555.

[17]Tremper Longman III, *How to Read Genesis,* 79.

[18]Gerhard F. Hasel, "The Significance of the Cosmology in Genesis 1 in Relation to Ancient Near Eastern Parallels," *AUSS* 10 No. 2 (1972): 16.

[19]Tremper Longman III, *How to Read Genesis,* 79.

and the pagan faith differed precisely in their conceptualization of the relationship of God to the creation."[20] [21]

What's more: try as they might, the critical scholars are left at a loss when searching the Genesis creation account for the mythological elements that would nicely tie up their theory: "Wellhausen himself could discover no mythological ingredients in Genesis 1 save for chaos."[22] Further, "Many of the supposed parallels between *Enuma Elish* and Genesis are commonplace in many Near Eastern cosmologies—e.g., the watery origin of the world and the separation of land—while the creation of man and the rest of the gods is mentioned in other early Babylonian sources" (Wenham).

It seems evident from all this that the similarities aren't because Moses borrowed from the pagan creation accounts when he was making up Yahweh's creation account, but the opposite. The pagan nations had some knowledge of how creation came about, and, through their years of apostasy, accuracy was replaced with the perversion of paganism. The Genesis account, then, was intended as a correction of the pagan creation accounts. Hasel concludes: "[The Genesis cosmology] represents not only a complete break with the ancient Near Eastern mythological cosmologies but represents a parting of the spiritual ways which meant an undermining of the prevailing mythological cosmologies."[23] And Longman: "The purpose of the creation texts, when read in the light of alternative contemporary accounts, was to assert the truth about who was responsible."[24]

---

[20]Qtd. in Rooker, "Genesis 1.1–3: Creation or Re-Creation?" *Vital Old Testament Issues*. Grand Rapids: Kregel Resources, 1996.

[21]For a more detailed study of the similarities and differences between Genesis 1 and other ancient cosmologies, see Gerhard F. Hasel's "The Significance of the Cosmology in Genesis 1 in Relation to Ancient Near Eastern Parallels," *AUSS* 10 No. 2 (1972): 1–20.

[22]R.K. Harrison, *Introduction to the Old Testament*, 555.

[23]Gerhard F. Hasel, "The Significance of the Cosmology in Genesis 1 in Relation to Ancient Near Eastern Parallels," *AUSS* 10 No. 2 (1972): 20.

[24]Tremper Longman III, *How to Read Genesis*, 79.

Man in the Garden

The second chapter of Genesis is the cause of some consternation to many scholars. It is often read as a different creation account than chapter one. Due to this, we will first address the apparent contradiction between chapters 1 and 2 before commenting on the text.

When did the events of chapter 2 happen? The easy answer to this question is that it occurred on day six: the creation of man. It is, however, important to note verse 5, which tells us that at this point no plant was yet on the ground. On the surface, it would appear that if we take the position that creation was immediate (*i.e.*, God said 'Let there be plants' and they were full grown), this cannot be day six. Further, verses 8–9 seem to indicate that the Garden of Eden was planted *after* the creation of man.

Is there a contradiction? While there may seem to be one on the surface, the contradiction dissipates quickly when one looks to the purpose of the author in writing. Chapter 1 tells of creation from a cosmic viewpoint, while chapter 2 writes from the viewpoint of man. The former is intended to show the structure and design of God's handiwork, and so it has an emphasis on the chronological sequence of creation. The latter is not so bent. Its purpose is to show the creation of man and his relationship with the rest of creation.

It is important to note why no plants were yet on the ground. Two reasons are given. First, God had not sent rain. Second, there was no man present to till the ground. The plants' creation was contingent on man's creation. And so man is created in relationship with the *flora*. And notice what follows man's creation. The animals pass by him one at a time while he names them. And so man is created in relationship with the *fauna*.

The reference of chapter 2 to the rest of creative week is only a summary of what else went on, not a step by step progression. By showing the earth as barren prior to the existence of man, it shows the relationship between man and agriculture: that mankind is just as necessary for plant life as rain from God. That man's relationship with the animals immediately follows this supports this reading of the text. To see a contradiction, one must set aside the writer's intention in each chapter. Since his purpose is not the same in both places, these chapters will represent the same facts differently. The arrangement of chapters 1 and 2 "gives us first a harmonious cosmic overview of creation and then a plunge into the technological nitty-gritty and moral ambiguities of human origins" (Alter).

2 **4, *These are the generations.*** This phrase in Genesis always marks the beginning of a new unit of thought, though usually by clarifying whose descendants will be the object of focus. In this case, it is something of an accommodative use. "The account pertains to what the cosmos has generated, not the generation of the cosmos" (Waltke).

2.5, *For the L*ORD *God had not caused it to rain on the land.* This passage is often pointed to in teaching that it never rained before the flood. The logic proceeds as follows: this passage says that it had not rained; rain is not mentioned again until the flood; in reverence to the silence of the Scripture, we must conclude that it did not rain until the flood.

This passage, however, is not atmospheric in its intent. Its purpose is to emphasize relationship. Just as man was necessary for plants, so also rain was necessary for plants. The teaching of this passage is not that it did not rain before the *flood*, but that it did not rain before the *plants*. Its clear implication, then, is that there *was* rain after the creation of the plants.

For those who still cling to the silence of the Scripture in support of their argument, we would offer the following: there is *no support in Scripture* (*i.e.,* the Scripture is silent) for an atmospheric change following the flood. Nowhere does it say that after the flood, rain became a regular occurrence. Further, after the flood, rain is not mentioned again until the plague of the hail (Exod 9.33–34). By the reasoning that leads to the conclusion that it never rained before the flood, one must also reason that it did not rain again after the flood until Moses' time. Much simpler is the understanding that God created things as they are now and have always been.

2.7, The LORD God formed the man of the dust from the ground. The translation loses the force of the wordplay inherent in this verse. The Hebrew tells us that God formed the *adam* from the *adamah*.

And breathed into his nostrils the breath of life. The creation of man is described in some detail, but nothing that we would consider medical. Man is created from a combination of the dust of the earth and the breath of God. "Hence, the nature of man consists of a material substance and an immaterial principle of life" (Keil). Interestingly, the Hebrew uses a different word for *breath* than the usual one.

2.9, The tree of life was in the midst of the garden, and the tree of the knowledge of good and evil. In the garden, two trees of significance were planted: the tree of life and the tree of the knowledge of good and evil. The former was to give man eternal life on the earth (*cf.* 3.22), while the latter was planted with the command that the man was not to eat from it. "If with the book of Proverbs we should say of Wisdom, 'She is a tree of life,' then the tree of the knowledge of good and evil is nothing other than the tree of folly."[1]

2.10–14, A river flowed out of Eden to water the garden, and there it divided and became four rivers. While something of the Garden's location is known to us, it is largely an enigma. Its location is indicated by references to geography, which would have been better understood by the original audience. It was planted *in the east.* The point of reference was almost certainly Palestine.

The names of these four rivers are given: *the Pishon... that flowed around the whole land of Havilah, where there is gold... bdellium and onyx stone... the Gihon... which flowed around the whole land of Cush... the Tigris... and the Euphrates.*

Of these four rivers, only the Tigris and the Euphrates are universally agreed upon. Most scholars agree that the land of Havilah is Arabia. James Sauer has identified an underground riverbed along the Wadi al Batin as the Pishon,[2] which runs through Saudi Arabia and Kuwait, but

---

[1] Henri Blocher, *In the Beginning,* 133.

this is not accepted by all scholars. Kidner would place these unknown rivers further east: "Since [the Tigris and Euphrates] are listed as if reading from east to west, the unknown *Pishon* and *Gihon* seem implied to lie still further east." Hamilton identifies the Pishon and Gihon as "considerably smaller rivers than the Tigris and Euphrates" based on the *on* ending, which might be an indicator of a diminutive. He suggests that the Pishon "may be the Karun in Elam or less likely the Kerkha, both of which once flowed through separate mouths into the head of the Persian Gulf."

The mention of Cush makes locating the Gihon somewhat problematic. Usually when mentioned in the Bible, Cush refers to Ethiopia or Nubia, which is nowhere near any of the other rivers. In this instance, following Genesis 10.8, Cush probably refers to the Kassite territory east of the Tigris (as argued by Kidner, Hamilton and Hill). Hill identifies the Gihon with the Karun.[3] Hamilton, by contrast, notes that the Samaritan Pentateuch renders *Gihon* as *'Asqop*, which is the Kerkha river east of the Tigris. "If the identification of Gihon with Kerkha is correct, then the rivers of paradise are being listed in an east to west direction: Gihon, Tigris, Euphrates. Thus we would expect the Pishon to be further to the east, and the Karun in Elam fits this locale nicely" (Hamilton).

The identity of the one river which breaks into these four is unknown. It is not to be identified with the Persian Gulf, as these rivers flow to the gulf, not from it. Thus, while we cannot pinpoint the location of Eden, "On the basis of currently available information it would appear that the one that locates Eden near the head of the Persian Gulf combines the greatest number of probabilities of every kind."[4]

2.15, The LORD God took the man and put him in the garden of Eden. Eden was planted to be the home of God's creation—the place where man would work and God would commune with him in a perfect relationship. "'Eden' is often used in the plural for 'delight.' ...This must be the determinative connotation in Genesis 2. God had prepared for the man a place of pleasure, the very environment of happiness. The overtones that we associate with the word 'paradise' are in harmony with the purpose of the text."[5]

---

[2]Carol A. Hill, "The Garden of Eden: A Modern Landscape," *Perspectives on Science and Christian Faith*, 52 No. 1 (2000): 32.

[3]*Ibid.*, 38.

[4]R.K. Harrison, "Eden," *ISBE*, 17.

2.16–17, "You may surely eat… you shall not eat." After placing man in the garden, God issues a command to man concerning the tree of the knowledge of good and evil. This is the only place where the command is given, implying God left man with the responsibility to pass the command along to Eve after her creation. Man was also placed in the garden to work in it: work is not a result of the curse; God never intended man to be lazy.

2.18, "It is not good for man to be alone; I will make him a helper fit for him." Looking forward, it is clear that the woman was to be the created helper for man. That she is to be his *helper* does not necessitate subordination— "In the Old Testament, in fifteen cases out of twenty-one, it is God who is the help of man!"[6]—although it will become clear later that the man's position was always one of authority.[7]

Does this teach that God does not want a man to be single? In a broad sense, it would seem that this declaration is God's way of expressing His intention of marriage for mankind. But does that mean that every individual must be married for God to be happy? Paul might argue with such an interpretation (*cf.* 1 Cor 7.7–8).

Another point that some have argued from this verse finds expression in a statement such as this: 'This passage shows women can be single and content while men need a woman to be happy—such a statement was never said of the woman.' While such a statement may be welcomed in the women's liberation camp, it lacks the support of linguistic evidence, logic and empirical data.

The Hebrew is the generic for humankind—the same word used a few verses earlier when it was said *God created man in His own image* (1.27). Clearly, no one would argue that only the male was made in God's image while the female was not, because such a statement is not made of her. And while it is clear from the context that the male is the human in question (as the woman had not been created), arguing this position is equivalent with saying if God had created the woman first, he could have just stopped right then—she has no problem with being alone. Further, this statement utterly lacks sense if, in an effort to provide a companion for the man, God created a woman who had no need for companionship. It would

---

[5]Henri Blocher, *In the Beginning*, 113.

[6]*Ibid.*, 104.

[7]See comment on 3.16.

not be much help for the man who has that need if the woman God created for him had no mutual interest or need for companionship.

Finally, while some might contend that women are perfectly happy being alone, there have been no studies (to our knowledge) that support such an assertion, and common dealings with single men and women show that both fare equally when dealing with solitude.

Thus, *It is not good for man to be alone* is a general statement describing the condition of mankind. Because of God's knowledge of this, He created the woman for the man and instituted a system of companionship that is mutually necessary. And as it is a general statement it probably should not be applied to every human being in every situation. Paul's decree in 1 Corinthians 7 would seem to eliminate the ability for such a broad use of this Genesis passage.

2.19, The Lord God... brought [the animals] to man to see what he would call them. That this immediately follows God's statement that man needed a helper, and is followed by God creating woman seems to indicate that there is more to this parade of animals than just man's naming them. The context of this passage, as well as our understanding of this chapter to be about relationships, demands that this is not the only purpose of this parade of animals. The pretext to this parade is that *it is not good for man to be alone* and the concluding remark is: *but for Adam there was not found a helper fit for him. ...So God created woman.* Naming the animals was only a byproduct of this event's true purpose: to show man what God already knew—he lacked something. In so doing, we see that the relationship between man and the animals to be *dominion* (shown by the naming of them) and *distinction* (not a helper fit for him).

And whatever man called every living creature, that was its name. "In naming the animals Adam showed how utterly separate and completely different he was from them. ...This task of naming the animals demanded an exercise of intelligence upon his part such as the animals themselves did not possess."[8]

2.21–22, The Lord God caused a deep sleep to fall upon the man, and while he slept took one of his ribs. And so God creates woman. Notice that He did not create her with dust but from a rib. To follow Matthew Henry:

---

[8]Edward J. Young, *Genesis 3*, 17–18.

"...not made out of his head to top him, not out of his feet to be trampled on by him, but out of his side to be equal with him, under his arm to be protected, and near his heart to be beloved" (qtd. in Waltke).[9]

Notice also the reason she is created from a rib rather than dust: *"Therefore a man shall leave his father and his mother and hold fast to his wife, and they shall become one flesh."* Because they came from one flesh, they shall be joined together as one flesh. Because they came from one flesh, he is to leave his parents and hold fast to his wife. Because they were separated, they must come back together.

And the rib... he made into a woman. The Hebrew translated *made* is more literally *built,* an interesting word choice for the creation of the woman. "It complements the potter's term, *fashion,* used for the creation of the first human, and is more appropriate because the Lord is now working with hard material, not soft clay" (Alter).

2.24, They shall become one flesh. While this may speak on some level of the sexual relationship between a husband and wife, such is not the extent of the unity that is to be found in marriage. Certainly there is a kind of spiritual/mental union, a union of purpose, which patterns itself after the image of God—distinct personalities that are inseparably united. Leupold describes this aspect as something that "involves the complete identification of one personality with the other in a community of interest and pursuits."

One particular downfall of the sexual interpretation of this verse is that it fails to explain the permanence of the two being one flesh. A better explanation that details the permanence of this state of being without underemphasizing the fleshly aspect is given by Wenham: "It affirms that just as blood relations are one's flesh and bone, so marriage creates a similar kinship relation between man and wife. They become related to each other as brother and sister are." This has even been accepted as our custom. My wife, for example, is to my parents a daughter; to my brother, a sister.

Growth of the Seed: Man and woman are created and given the covenant of marriage.

---

[9]Some of the early church fathers, and more recently Karl Barth, have suggested that this contains a figure of the passion of Christ, whose side was wounded in order that His bride, the church, might be generated. While intriguing, such an interpretation is merely exaggerated allegorization. See Blocher, *In the Beginning,* 102.

Excursus B: God's Designation

It takes no more than two chapters of the Old Testament before we are faced with a perplexing question: is God known as Yahweh or Elohim? And the question becomes even more complex as the chapters of Genesis unfold. Soon, other names are added—El Shaddai, El Elyon, *et al*. Critical scholars understand this to be evidence of multiple source documents, a theory which we rejected at the outset.[1] What, then, is a valid explanation for the change in God's name throughout the book of Genesis?

Was His Name Used Before Exodus 6.3?

"I appeared to Abraham, to Isaac, and to Jacob, as God Almighty, but by my name the LORD I did not make myself known to them" (Exod 6.3).

What exactly are the implications of this verse on Genesis' use of the personal name of God (*i.e.*, Yahweh)? Bromiley suggests two options: it was used during the patriarchal period, but dropped out of use during the Egyptian bondage; that it was never used before this point: "It was given for the first time with the new step of the divine deliverance from Egypt, and was then quite correctly read back into the earlier stories in order to bring out the continuity of God's saving action through Israel."[2]

Bromiley's first option seems weak. It would be quite an accomplishment of linguistic gymnastics to make *"I did not make myself known to them"* mean *'They forgot my name.'* His second option is much more plausible and was held as the standard view for many years. Wenham stands against the trend of modern scholarship in continuing to hold this view.[3] In its favor, it is the simplest and most straightforward reading of the text: it means what it says and says what it means. It allows the theological implications of the use of the various names to rest solely in the inspired pen of Moses to whom God first revealed His name.

But this option is not without its problems. Meek says that Moses' mother's name, Jochebed, "is unquestionably a Yahweh name, and this would imply that the family of Moses at least were worshippers of Yahweh."[4] If this is true, it would seem unquestionable that Yahweh was known prior to Exodus 6.3. But even this raises further questions. "It is a striking fact that not a single personal name with Yahweh as an element appears with the Hebrews until Jochebed."[5]

---

[1]See INTRODUCTION.

[2]G.W. Bromiley, "God," *ISBE*, 497.

[3]See his commentary for a further explanation of this view.

[4]Theophile J. Meek, *Hebrew Origins*, 97.

In ancient cultures, personal names regularly reflected the religious beliefs of the people. The total lack of other Yahweh names must cause one to wonder if Meek's assertion of the etymology of Jochebed's name is correct. Indeed, this may be the best argument in favor of the second view.

A third option, taken by most modern scholars, and that we will develop here, is that God's revealing of His name is not intended to be understood as a question of whether or not the Hebrews knew the name Yahweh, but that God would further display His character to them, so that they would understand what Yahweh meant.

Gianotti follows Motyer in translating *name* as *in the character of* in our passage. "It was the character expressed by the name that was withheld from the patriarchs and not the name itself... to know by a name means to have come into intimate and personal acquaintance with a person."[6] And Kaiser: "This phrase meant that while Abraham, Isaac and Jacob heard and used the name Yahweh, it was only in Moses' day that the realization of the character, nature and essence of what that name meant became clear."[7] And Mathews: "When we consider that *Yahweh* occurs 162 times in Genesis, often in direct discourse (34x), the modification required by the editor exhibits a remarkable license in altering the *theological* content of his sources. [It is better] to consider Exodus 6.2–3 on an exegetical basis that is not atomistic. ...Contextually, the issue is not the name of the deity *per se* (*e.g.,* Exod 7.5) but rather the nature of God. Revelation of the 'name' to Moses concerned the content and meaning of *Yahweh* that was not fully understood by the patriarchs."

This position seems to be strengthened by what *name* represents in other passages and the Hebrew used in Moses' question. Payne argues, "In the Orient a name is more than an identification. A man's name is not only descriptive of its bearer, it may stand as the equivalent to his very nature and individuality. Thus to change a man's name indicates power over his person. ...[God's] 'name' comes to punish (Isa 30.27), or it may equal the glory cloud in the Tabernacle or the Temple (Deut 12.11; 1 Kgs 8.29; Jer 3.17; 7.12). ...God's 'name' may even refer to specific attributes, as His might (Psa 54.1; 76.1) or His mercy (Psa 20.1–2). ...The names of God as they are revealed in Scripture serve to depict His Person and His attributes (Psa 23.3). ...They are descriptive of His activity in establishing the testament (Psa 111.9)."[8]

---

[5]*Ibid.,* 97.

[6]Motyer qtd. in Charles R. Gianotti, "The Meaning of the Divine Name YHWH," *Vital Old Testament Issues*, 28.

[7]*Hard Sayings*, 88.

[8]J. Barton Payne, *The Theology of the Older Testamnet*, 144.

Regarding the Hebrew in the question, Moses asked using *mah*, rather than *mi*. Gionatti writes: "The Hebrew term introducing the question indicates a concern for quality. ...In biblical Hebrew it is never used in asking a person's name; for this *[mi]* is used."[9] And Kaiser: "The latter *[mi]* only asked for the title or designation of a person while *mah*, especially when connected with the word 'name,' sought out the qualities, character, powers, and abilities resident in that name."[10]

Thus, it would seem to be at least conceivable that the name Yahweh was known to the patriarchs and that this statement to Moses and the Israelites was intended to mark a further development of their understanding of Him as Yahweh.

Elohim and the El Variants

Before progressing to this further meaning of the name Yahweh, let us stop for a moment to briefly examine the other names and descriptions used for God.

The most common Hebrew word used for deity is *elohim*, which is translated *God*, and simply means *deity*. It is, however, used in the Bible to speak of those who are not God. It is used of other gods and their idols (*e.g.*, Gen 31.30) and even men (*e.g.*, Exod 4.16; 7.1). "This does not mean, however, that God is brought under a general category, for the whole point of OT revelation is that Yahweh is *elohim* in the strict sense. That is, *elohim* is finally defined in terms of Yahweh, and all others who bear the name are then brought into relation to Him."[11]

Elohim, interestingly, is a plural word. Many have seen in this an early hint at what would later become the so-called Trinitarian doctrine of the New Testament. While there may be some merit to that position, we would agree with Payne: "The grammatical form of *Elohim* is that of an abstract plural of greatness or majesty, and not a true numeric plural. Unless referring to the gods of the pagans, *Elohim* is construed with other words in the singular. It signifies God as the one who bears the fullness of divine life."[12]

El is also compounded with other words to describe God, the most common form being *El Shaddai*, translated God Almighty. "*El Shaddai* became the characteristic divine name for patriarchal religion (Exod 6.3) with its sense of the 'overpowering' God (as Ruth 1.20–21)."[13] Of these compound descriptions of

---

[9]Charles R. Gianotti, "The Meaning of the Divine Name YHWH," *Vital Old Testament Issues*, 29.

[10]Walter C. Kaiser Jr., *Toward and Old Testament Theology*, 107.

[11]G.W. Bromiley, "God," *ISBE*, 497.

[12]J. Barton Payne, *The Theology of the Older Testament*, 145.

God, Bromiley writes, "These descriptive names are of great importance. They again make it clear that there is no such thing as God as an abstract concept; God is all these things in particular even though a generic name may often be used. Again, they specifically show that God stands in a personal relationship to mankind. Furthermore, they all indicate that God has the initiative in this relationship. Finally, they are not just poetic attributes; they are all based on actual dealings of God with His people. It is not that mankind has an idea of God and then selects and heaps up suitable epithets. Nor is it that mankind has certain experience of what he takes to be the divine and then puts these experiences into words. He is this God, whether we experience Him as such or not. He acts and manifests Himself thus. Beside Him there is none else."[14]

Yahweh
The meaning of Yahweh has been a subject of great debate for many years. Rather than dive into etymological suppositions, we would stand with Payne on this point: "As to the meaning of Yahweh, etymological speculation is rather fruitless. It is the biblical definition found in Exodus 3.14 and in the surrounding context that must be determinative. These verses indicate that the root of 'Yahweh' is the verb 'to be,' used in its simple, rather than its causative, stem: God spoke in the first person and said unto Moses, 'I am that I am' (Exod 3.14; *cf.* Hos 1.9). Then, when someone would speak about God in the third person, the form became, 'He is,' or, in Hebrew, in the archaic spelling, 'Yahweh.'"[15] With this, Gianotti agrees: "[The context] does suggest that the meaning of [to be] is meant to inform the meaning of the name YHWH."[16]

But even though this is agreed upon, we are still not clear to the meaning. The standard approach to God's statement—*I am who I am*—is that it explains the eternal self-existence of God. Although this is the simplest reading of the text, it is not the only plausible explanation. Payne argues: "The theology of the older testament is preeminently one of redemptive activity, and speculative thought on matters such as God's eternal self-existence is foreign to its nature."[17] And Bromiley: "The meaning given in Exodus 3.13–15 can hardly bear the metaphysical sense that has sometimes been read into it, namely that of self-existence... but seems to imply rather the abiding faithfulness of God. ...

---

[13]*Ibid.*, 146.

[14]G.W. Bromiley, "God," *ISBE*, 497.

[15]J. Barton Payne, *The Theology of the Older Testament*, 147–148.

[16]Charles R. Gianotti, "The Meaning of the Divine Name YHWH," *Vital Old Testament Issues*, 29.

[17]J. Barton Payne, *The Theology of the Older Testament*, 148.

Its distinctive significance for Israel is undoubtedly given with the Theophany at the burning bush."[18] Payne concludes: "The best translation of Exodus 3.14 seems, therefore, to be this: 'I am present is what I am.' This description is, in fact, the fundamental inheritance promise of the testament, 'I will be their God, and they shall be my people.' 'Yahweh' ('faithful presence') is God's testamental nature or name."[19]

This suggestion seems to bear out when looking closer at God's conversation with Moses. "The phrase [I am YHWH] occurs three times in [Exodus 6.6–8]. In the first occurrence God identified His name in respect to what follows. The second occurrence constituted what the people would recognize about God who would deliver them—that He is YHWH, the One who would meet their needs just as His name implies. The final occurrence again emphasized His name in relation to His work. Clearly the saving acts on behalf of His people will reveal YHWH's name."[20] And Bromiley: "God is named; this in itself is of the utmost significance. God is not an abstraction; He is the living God. But this Yahweh, who is God, is *elohim*, the God of creation, the Lord of the cosmos. He is not just a tribal deity like the deities of the nations. Yet He is in fact the God of Israel. He is the God who works in history, the God who has chosen this people as both the first object and the agent of His revealing and reconciling action. As the God of this people He is the covenant God, the God of relationship, the God who establishes a relationship of faithfulness and obedience, the God of a mutual relationship of love."[21] Kaiser adds, "'I am the God who will be there' (Exod 3.14) was not so much an ontological designation or a static notion of being (*e.g.,* 'I am that I am'); it was rather a promise of a dynamic, active *presence*. As God had revealed Himself in His supernatural control over nature for the patriarchs [*i.e.,* the character of *El Shaddai*], now Moses and Yahweh's son, Israel, would know His presence in a day-by-day experience as it was never known before [*i.e.,* the character of Yahweh]."[22]

Regardless of the precise meaning of God's statement, it has been well established that *Yahweh* is God's covenant name. Gianotti offers three illustrations of this point: the repeated introductions to the commandments at Sinai (*i.e.,* I am Yahweh, Exod 20.1; Lev 18.2, 4, 21, 30); the connection of the name Yahweh with the rewards and retributions of the law (Lev 26.3–13); the connection

---

[18]G.W. Bromiley, "God," *ISBE*, 497.

[19]J. Barton Payne, *The Theology of the Older Testament*, 148.

[20]Charles R. Gianotti, "The Meaning of the Divine Name YHWH," *Vital Old Testament Issues*, 29.

[21]G.W. Bromiley, "God," *ISBE*, 497.

[22]Walter C. Kaiser Jr., *Toward an Old Testament Theology*, 107.

of the name Yahweh with explicit references to the covenant with the patriarchs.[23] "This is the name God bears when He comes and visits His people and makes a covenant with them; this is His covenant name, His name for His 'marriage' with Israel."[24] Gianotti summarizes: "The name YHWH points to God's relationship to Israel in both His saving acts and His retributive acts, manifesting His phenomenological effectiveness in Israel's history. What God says, He will do. His name promises that. And He will act on behalf of His people."[25]

Yahweh vs. Elohim

We are, then, to understand the use of the various names of God in Genesis to be theologically pregnant. "Yahweh is used wherever the Bible stresses God's personal relationship with His people and the ethical aspect of His nature. Elohim, on the other hand, refers to God as the Creator of the whole universe of people and things, and especially of the material world: He was the ruler of nature, the source of all life."[26] And Payne: "[Yahweh] carries the connotation of God's nearness, of His concern for man, and of His redemptive, testamentary revelation. So Moses selected Elohim as the appropriate term for Genesis 1–2.3, God transcendent in creation; but Yahweh for Genesis 2.4–25, God immanent in Eden's revelations. Similar shifts in names, corresponding to God's shift in activity from general sovereignty to personal redemption, appear in the Genesis passages that follow."[27][28]

This distinction is one that is most easily seen in Psalm 19. The first half of the Psalm describes God's work in and His relationship to His creation. And the first half of the psalm uses Elohim. At the halfway point, however, the psalmist switches to Yahweh, just as the topic switches to God's law and the relationship He has with those who know Him. "Elohim conveys the more philosophically oriented concept that connects deity with the existence of the world and humanity. But for those who seek the more direct, personal and ethically oriented view of God, the term Yahweh was more appropriate."[29]

---

[23]Charles R. Gianotti, "The Meaning of the Divine Name YHWH," *Vital Old Testament Issues*, 34, 37.

[24]Blocher, Henri. *In the Beginning*, 111.

[25]Charles R. Gianotti, "The Meaning of the Divine Name YHWH," *Vital Old Testament Issues*, 38.

[26]*Hard Sayings*, 87–88.

[27]J. Barton Payne, *The Theology of the Older Testament*, 148.

[28]Some have argued against this position, citing Psalm 14 and 53, which are almost identical apart from the choice of Yahweh or Elohim. Although this may indicate that the two names can be used synonymously, it may also indicate that the teaching of the psalm is true, whether you look at God in terms of His personal relationship with man or His role as creator.

[29]*Hard Sayings*, 88.

Enmity Between the Seeds

Chapters 3–5

Though God created a perfect dwelling place for man, it did not take long before sin entered. And with it, enmity between the seed of woman and the seed of the serpent. Chapters 3–5 document the fall of man, the progression of sin, and the division of the seeds.

3 *1, Now the serpent was more crafty than any other beast of the field that the LORD God had made.* Beyond this, Genesis tells us nothing of the serpent. Many contend that this passage teaches that the serpent was a beast of the field, as the ESV implies—*any other beast;* however, there is nothing in the grammar of this passage that implies such an inclusive rendering. More literally, he was *more crafty than any beast of the field.* That he was a beast of the field may be ascertained through context, but it cannot be demanded based on grammar.[1]

Thus, it has been argued by some that the language is accommodative and symbolic. In the culture of the original audience, the image of a serpent would immediately be understood as an enemy of God. "Since ancient creation myths gave serpentine form to the being who opposed the order of creation, it was fitting that the tempter in the garden be depicted in this way."[2] That this is at least plausible should be evident by a com-

---

[1] The argument that his being *more crafty than any beast of the field* makes him one of the beasts of the field runs into a problem when we admit that we, also, are more crafty than any beast of the field.

[2] Martin Pickup, "The Seed of Woman," *The Gospel in the Old Testament: Florida College Annual Lectures*, 60.

parison to passages such as Psalm 74, where God is seen as going to war against the multi-headed mythological sea monster, Leviathan (vv 12–14) or Psalm 89.8–10, where God defeats another mythological creature, Rahab.[3] Such an interpretation is not meant to argue that Satan was not there tempting Eve, but that he was described in a way that would have immediately tipped the original audience off to his intentions.[4]

Of course, the flip side of this argument must also be considered. Rather than understanding the Bible as borrowing from pagan mythology to offer a clue to the original audience, it can be held that Satan did, in fact, appear in the garden as a literal serpent and that the pagan accounts borrowed from that truth. Then, as the oral tradition was passed down, it was perverted in pagan cultures into serpents that fought against gods. In this account, then, Moses sought to correct the false accounts with the truth of what happened. But whatever the case, it is hard to argue that, in the cultural context, the original audience would not have read more into *the serpent* than a modern audience does.

It is interesting to note that the serpent is not clearly identified until the last book in the Bible (*cf.* Rev 12). This clearly ties the whole Bible together. Not to trivialize the Bible, but it also seems like a *whodunit* mystery. Imagine reading the Bible for the first time, without the full knowledge of what happens in it. You read originally of an enemy of God who is a serpent. Throughout the Bible, you find hints as to who this serpent is—his identity becomes clear in some places, though at times you will find other people who could, just maybe, be the enemy. But there, in the end of the Bible, the serpent is finally identified. And so we find another illustration of the unity and literary brilliance of the Bible.

He said to the woman. The serpent talks! And perhaps the most surprising thing about the serpent talking is that Eve didn't seem to think it strange—

---

[3]Similar mythological language can also be found in Job 26.12–13; Isaiah 27.1; 51.9–10; *cf.* Job 7.12.

[4]Blocher does a good job of explaining the symbolic approach: "By linking the dragon with 'the ancient serpent,' Revelation gives any confirmation that may be needed that it is showing how to interpret symbolic language. ...[The dragon] represents the power of paganism rising up against the Lord and against His people. No-one imagines that the devil took possession of the body of a sea monster in order to deceive the nations! Revelation interprets the snake of Genesis 3 and the dragon from other passages in exactly the same way; thus it respects the laws of language which require a clear choice of the figurative meaning if it is necessary to depart from the literal. Learning from the approach of Revelation, we shall understand the information about the snake as a whole as extended symbolism; since the snake is the devil, we must transpose all that is said about the snake in terms that are suitable for the devil." *In The Beginning*, 152.

she just conversed with it as if that were normal. Then again, Balaam did the same thing when his donkey spoke to him (*cf.* Num 22.22–35).

Some have taken this to mean that, prior to the fall, animals could speak. That seems to be a stretch. More likely, this happened soon after Eve was created. Satan *never* waits long to attack. Further, they were told *before* they were expelled from the garden to be fruitful and multiply, but that didn't happen until after they left. Thus, they couldn't have been in the garden for too long before this happened. Perhaps Eve, in her innocence, didn't know whether or not animals could talk.

The act itself shows the pride of the serpent (*cf.* 1 Tim 3.6). "It raises itself above the beasts of the field which the Lord God had made and it elevates itself to an equality with man."[5]

"Did God actually say?" Satan starts off friendly: this almost seems like casual small talk. But he also starts off by trying to make God the bad guy: 'Did God really say you couldn't eat *anything* in here?' He exaggerates the point in an effort to emphasize the prohibition, rather than all the things that they were allowed to eat. "The tempter makes a massive affirmation, adopting a tone of surprise and indignation or else of feigned compassion, because he wishes to make the fact seem *outrageous*. …He presents the ban as a monstrous deprivation. It is not so much God's word on which he casts doubt as His *goodness*. Of the God who is generosity itself he sketches a portrait of miserliness. He projects the false perspective of a rivalry between God and man; he suggests that man will be the less free as God will be the more sovereign, and vice versa."[6]

3.3, "But God said, 'You shall not eat of the fruit of the tree.'" It is important first to note that the woman knows about the command. It is most likely that God left Adam with the responsibility to pass the word along to her. Apparently, he did.

"'Neither shall you touch it.'" But notice that her command does not match God's command (*cf.* 2.16–17). God never mentions *touching* the tree. It seems that Phariseeism was alive and well even in the first couple.[7] Whichever of them decided that they should not even touch the tree came up with a good idea—'This is so dangerous that I'm not even going

---

[5]Edward J. Young, *Genesis 3*, 19.

[6]Henri Blocher, *In the Beginning*, 139.

to touch it!' they thought. But to bind their good idea as God's law—'And if you touch it, you're sinning'—is the exact thing Jesus frequently chided the Pharisees for: *"teaching as doctrines the commandments of men"* (Mark 7.7). In any event, she knew that she was not supposed to eat of the fruit.[8]

3.4, "You will not die." Satan mixes truth with deceit. There *is* some truth in this: they did not die immediately, either physically or spiritually (though they were separated from God by sin, a complete spiritual death—hell— does not befall them). But this truth is mixed with deceit: they began to die physically, and it was this transgression that allowed spiritual death to become a possibility for the human race.

This does not contradict God's command that *in the day* they eat of it, they will die. As we noted before, *day* does not always refer to a specific 24-hour period of time. Further, Blocher points to a parallel passage in 1 Kings 2.36–46 which "proves the meaning of the Hebrew expression: 'on that day you will fall under the power of a death sentence.'"[9] And Kaiser: "Neither the 1 Kings nor the Genesis text implies *immediacy of action* on that same day; instead they point to the *certainty of the predicted consequence* that would be set in motion by the act initiated on that day."[10]

3.5, "You will become like God." Clearly there is truth in this. God later admits that *"man has become like one of us, knowing good and evil"* (v 22). But even this obvious truth is mixed with deceit. They were *already* like God— He made them in His image. In fact, by doing this, they became *less* like God. No longer were they sinless and holy, instead they had separated themselves from His pure nature.

3.6, When the woman saw. The serpent convinces her to look at the situation from her perspective. "She believed herself capable of evaluating

---

[7]Young argues that the word used for *touch* may involve more than just handling, but (comparing its use in 20.6 and 26.11), "touching in the sense of consuming or making the fruit one's own." If this is the meaning in this instance, his assessment should be accepted: "She was not referring to handling the fruit as such, but in all probability to that touching which would result in taking possession of the fruit and so consuming it." *Genesis 3*, 30–31.

[8]Young notes, "The old tradition that the fruit was an apple rests upon a confusion of the Latin word *malum* (apple) with the Latin word *malus* (evil). In the genitive case the two words would have had the same form, namely, *mali*." *Genesis 3*, 45.

[9]Henri Blocher, *In the Beginning*, 184.

[10]*Hard Sayings*, 92.

all the facts of reality, including the fact of God and His commands and passing upon them an impartial judgment."[11] And Schaeffer: "The flow is from the internal to the external; the sin began in the thought-world and flowed outward. The sin was, therefore, committed in that moment she believed Satan instead of God."[12]

Then, the woman shared her sin with someone else.

Her husband, who was with her. Paul makes it clear that the woman's sin was the man's responsibility when he attributes the curse to Adam. This verse might may implicate him as well. Mathews writes, "Although 'with her' does not in itself demand that he is present since the serpent speaks 'to the woman,' nevertheless, the action of the verse implies that Adam is a witness to the dialogue. 'You' at each place in 3.1–5 is plural and thus suggests his presence." If he were present from the arrival of the serpent, his failure as a leader is doubled: not only did his relation of God's word to Eve go unheeded, but he stood by and allowed it to happen.

Paul clues us in to the difference between his sin and hers in 1 Timothy 2.14. According to Paul, the woman was deceived and fell into sin, but the man was not. Apparently, his sin was blatant rebellion. Yet many have blamed the predicament that we are in on the woman. At least she can say that she was tricked. Adam knew what he was doing when he sinned. Paul twice points to Adam—not Eve—as the cause of the mess we're in (Rom 5.12–21; 1 Cor 15.22). The point is not that Eve is excused in the matter; certainly she isn't. The point, rather, is that the men who cast the blame on her need to reevaluate the Bible's teaching as to whose fault it is.

And he ate. "The sinners of Genesis 3, like so many after them, imagined themselves greater in the arrogance of their gesture. Were they not making a superhuman challenge against heaven? Rebellion seeks to masquerade as heroism. But it is a laughable disguise, for at the very moment that the sinner is intoxicated with the sense of his own power, he is being manipulated by *another* mind. In actual fact, sin is defeat."[13]

3.7, *They knew that they were naked. And they sewed fig leaves together and made themselves loincloths.* With the loss of innocence came the realization of nakedness. "It is impossible for them not to discover at once the gulf be-

---

[11]Edward J. Young, *Genesis 3*, 39.

[12]Francis A. Schaeffer, *Genesis in Space and Time*, 85.

[13]Henri Blocher, *In the Beginning*, 142.

tween their intent [to be like God] and their resources. How vulnerable are they in their finitude, how tender and defenseless is their flesh."[14] But notice that their desire to hide themselves was not because of their physical nakedness. Even after they were covered, they were afraid to be seen (v 11).

Further, *this* passage does not teach that nakedness is a shameful thing. No one would see them but each other. Unless we are willing to teach that it is shameful for a husband and wife to be naked before each other, we must not use this passage to teach modesty. As Young notes: "Man's attempt to clothe himself is not necessarily praiseworthy; it is even rejected by God. …Man cannot be regarded as clothed until he is properly clothed with the clothing provided by God Himself."[15]

Instead, the problem is spiritual nakedness—what was previously a completely pure soul was suddenly separated from God. They were trying to hide from God, not from each other (Wenham). That they hid themselves from God points to their shame being due to their separation from Him. Their consciences were guilty because of what they did. Coinciding with this was the realization, for the first time, that they were naked. And so they tried to compensate for their spiritual emptiness by covering their physical nakedness, which they first saw in this loss of innocence (Keil). The shame was not that the husband and wife were naked before each other, but that they were guilty before God.

But their conscience did not lead them in the right direction. *They made themselves loincloths.* "Rather than driving them back to God, their guilt leads them into a self-atoning, self-protecting procedure" (Hamilton). And that's not the worst of it: "God's excellent gifts are used as a screen or as a shield against Him! And thus there emerges not only man's powerlessness but also his ingratitude."[16]

3.8–9, *The sound of the Lord God walking in the garden.* Apparently, when man was in the garden, God came down and conversed with him in some kind of visible shape. This does not mean, of course, that Adam and Eve saw God. (Or could sinless man commune with God in all His glory?) Rather, they saw the form that God used to present Himself to them.

"Where are you?" Certainly, God was not ignorant of where they were.

---

[14]*Ibid.,* 173.

[15]Edward J. Young, *Genesis 3,* 144–145. See comment on verse 21.

[16]Henri Blocher, *In the Beginning,* 177.

Rather, God used this as an opportunity to prompt a confession. Rather than coming down in raging judgment, He came with open arms, ready to accept the penitent sinner. But Adam does not confess.

3.10–11, *"Because I was naked... I hid myself."* He said, *"Who told you that you were naked?"* God gives Adam a second opportunity to confess, even going so far as to prompt the confession: *"Have you eaten of the tree of which I commanded you not to eat?"*

And the blame game begins. Rather than admitting sin, Adam points elsewhere: to the woman (and to God). The woman, in turn, points to the serpent. It's almost comical: God points to the man, who points to the woman, who points to the serpent. But sadly, it is a game that man has never gotten over. Just like they did, the sinner today "first of all endeavors to throw the blame upon others as tempters, and then upon circumstances which God ordained" (Keil), rather than simply confessing the sin that he or she has committed.

3.14, *The Lord God said.* It is more appropriate to refer to this section as *judgments* than *curses*. While Satan and the ground (for man's sake) are cursed, the section, as a whole, is a decree of judgment rather than curse.

The Serpent. "God asks the serpent no questions, for the serpent has no right to speak before God."[17] The serpent is to be cursed *above all livestock*. The word translated thus is the Hebrew *min*, which has a basic meaning of *from* or *out of*. That the serpent is cursed *from* the other animals leaves some question as to whether this should be rendered to mean a higher level of curse (Wenham) or a distinct kind of curse (Keil). Both interpretations may have merit and we cannot say whether favoring one over the other is a necessity.

"On your belly you shall go." Perhaps this indicates a change in structure or mode of locomotion than the serpent previously used. But "if before the fall the serpent possessed some other mode of locomotion, we do not know that fact, and there is really nothing in the Scripture to indicate it."[18] We believe it preferable to see in this statement a change in significance of what already existed. That this is what is done throughout these judgments (*i.e.*, change in significance) becomes evident as the judgments continue.

---

[17]Edward J. Young, *Genesis 3*, 94.

[18]*Ibid.*, 98.

Further, *you will eat dust* is clearly not to be taken literally; rather, a figure of speech, it shows how low the serpent will be considered. "If one is prepared to see in the decree *On your belly you shall crawl* a change in the snake's mode of locomotion, then to be consistent one must also see in the decree *dust shall you eat* a change in the snake's diet" (Hamilton). And Pickup: "[This is] a poetic way of predicting the humiliation and degradation of the serpent by using language that reflected a snake's means of locomotion. Since snakes crawl in the dust, this prompted the use of that image to indicate the serpent's subjugation"[19]—"just as in 9.13 a new significance, not new existence, will be decreed for the rainbow" (Kidner). Likewise, the snake probably already crawled, but now his crawling would stand as his badge of degradation.

3.15, "I will put enmity between." Several people are mentioned in verse 15: *you, woman, your offspring, her offspring, he [i.e., her offspring], you*. It is best to understand these as three couplets.

"You… woman." In the first couplet, *you* could refer to either the serpent (as a creature of the field) or Satan. Since *you* is clearly Satan in the later instance, it is best to interpret it as Satan here. *The Woman* clearly refers to Eve (who, at this point, was not yet named Eve).

"Your offspring and her offspring." Though often interpreted as the apparent animosity between serpents and mankind, there is probably a more spiritual meaning intended. "The seed of the serpent refers to natural humanity whom he has led into rebellion against God. Humanity is now divided into two communities: the elect, who love God, and the reprobate, who love self (John 8.41–42, 44; 1 John 3.8). Each of the characters of Genesis will be either the seed of the woman that reproduces her spiritual propensity or of the seed of the Serpent that reproduces his unbelief" (Waltke). This understanding of *your offspring/her offspring* clearly follows the outline of Genesis with which we began—the separation of the righteous from the wicked. Further, "There would be something supremely trivial about this solemn utterance if it did no more in the expression, the serpent's 'seed,' than to think of generations of serpents as yet unhatched. There must be meant the children of the evil one who are of their father the devil and will do the lusts of their father (John 8.44). …So the second part of the verse points to an en-

---

[19]Martin Pickup, "The Seed of Woman," *The Gospel in the Old Testament: Florida College Annual Lectures*, 51–52.

mity…involving on the one side the posterity or children of the evil one and on the other side the posterity or children of the woman, those who share her definite opposition to the evil one" (Leupold).

"He." This clearly refers to a specific seed whose battle will be with *you*, Satan. This passage becomes clearly Messianic in its nature when it is considered against the backdrop of the rest of the Old Testament. In Micah 7.17, when the Messiah defeats His enemies, the defeated nations will *lick the dust like a serpent.* In Isaiah 65.25 we find another Messianic victory and again, *dust shall be the serpent's food.* Psalm 91.11–13, the passage that Satan quotes to Jesus, finishes with *the serpent you will trample underfoot.* That Jesus was *born of a woman* (Gal 4.4) brings this passage to mind as well, though the most convincing New Testament cross-reference is in Revelation 12: the Messiah comes to earth and Satan is defeated and cast out of heaven.

It is important to note that though Satan is judged here, the judgment is not executed for several thousand more years. This should be clear from the prophecy that the Messiah will be the one to crush the serpent's head—to execute judgment. The remainder of the Old Testament also makes this clear. Consider, for instance, that throughout the Old Testament, Satan has full access to the throne room of God. In 1 Kings 22.19–23, Satan, identified as *the lying spirit,* volunteers to go forth from the heavenly court and deceive Ahab. In Job 1 and 2, Satan appears when the sons of God present themselves at the heavenly court. In Zechariah 3.2, Satan appears before the heavenly throne as an accuser of Israel. Even in Eden—paradise on earth—a fallen Satan had full access to enter, tempt man, and remain there before God.

The New Testament also acknowledges that Satan was the spiritual sovereign of the world at the time of Christ's coming. Jesus refers to Satan as *the prince of this world* in John 12.31, a claim that becomes evidently more-than-spiritual in nature when Satan offers Jesus rule over all the kingdoms of the world, and Jesus does not refute his ability to offer such (*cf.* Matt 4.9). In Revelation 13 and 17, the Roman Empire, the dominant kingdom of the world, is depicted as the kingdom of Satan himself.

The execution of the judgment pronounced in Genesis 3 is found in the death and resurrection of Jesus. In John 12.31, before His crucifixion and resurrection, Jesus declares that *now* is the time to cast Satan out. This is played out even further in Revelation 12.1–13. There, Satan is unable to prevent Christ's birth or resurrection on the earth which he claims to be ruling from heaven. The heavenly counterpart to this is that Satan is defeated by Michael and finally cast out of heaven and down to earth. And the heavenly war was won with *the blood of the Lamb* (v 11). But even the execution of this judgment isn't final. Revelation 20.7–10 let us know that his judgment will coincide with the rest of the created world—spiritual and physical. And he will be cast into hell the same time everyone else who goes there is sent.[20]

3.16, The woman. Though God begins with judging the evil, the judgment on mankind is withheld until the prospect of victory is presented. "The combination in Yahweh of justice and love—condemnation of sin, yet salvation for the sinner—tends to assume a fixed pattern in the OT. Justice is executed first, yet never completely or to the limit; love intervenes, to forgive and restore. It is this sequence that Isaiah expresses with his doctrine of the Remnant, Jeremiah with the New Covenant, Ezekiel with the hope held out to individuals. ...He is shown as having the qualities of an ideal judge. He is merciful by preference, not hasty to condemn; He will investigate and know for certain. But if it is indeed so, then He will act, and drastically."[21]

"Multiply your pain in childbearing." She who sought sweet delights in eating the forbidden fruit finds not delights but pain—not joy, but sorrow. God had planned that women would conceive and give birth. Henceforth, however, she would bear them in sorrow and pain. Here, God clearly takes something that already existed and used it in the judgment.

"Your desire shall be for your husband, and he shall rule over you." She who sought freedom in becoming like God will instead find the rule of her husband difficult. This *desire* is not to be explained, as Leupold, Keil and others do, as a sexual desire. This interpretation seeks to combine the two parts of the woman's judgment, described by Mathews as follows: "Despite her painful experience in childbirth, she will still have (sexual) desires for her husband. The promissory blessing of procreation will persist despite any possible reluctance on her part due to the attendant pain of delivery."

The primary downfall in this interpretation is that it makes something

---

[20]Much of the previous three paragraphs is adapted from Dr. Phil Roberts' unpublished article "The Role of Satan in the Bible."

[21]R.A.F. MacKenzie, "The Divine Soliloquies in Genesis," *CBQ* 17 (1955): 164–165.

that is a blessing from God (the sexual relationship found in marriage) a part of the judgment. And how badly would all the men who spend so much time trying to make women desire them by working out and exercise (or, those who better understand women, by doing the dishes and talking with them) feel if they found out that women are *cursed* to desire us! A further consideration is how this interpretation divorces the two halves of this bicolon, unless *he shall rule over you* is to be understood as some sort of sexual domination. To interpret the desire of woman to be sexual desire simply does not fit what the Bible teaches about marriage.

Longman points out, "The Hebrew word used here… is only used two other places (Gen 4.7; Song 7.10). The first of these is most telling because it is in the same context."[22] And understanding this passage becomes much easier when it is compared with 4.7, where God says to Cain, *"[Sin's] desire is for you, but you must control it."* Mathews says, "If we are to take the lexical and structural similarities as intentional, we must read these verses in concert." Then, understanding one passage illuminates us to understanding the other.

In 4.7, sin, pictured as a wild beast, is crouching and ready to pounce on and control its victim—sin desires to rule over Cain. Cain is told that he must instead rule over sin. Now when we take this back to 3.16, it clarifies our verse: *"Your desire shall be for your husband, [but] he shall rule over you."* The Hebrew conjunction, which can mean either *and* or *but* is better translated as the latter here. "This recommends that 3.16b also describes a struggle for mastery between the sexes. The 'desire' of the woman is her attempt to control her husband, but she will fail because God ordained that the man exercise his leadership function" (Mathews).

"In Genesis 4.7 sin's desire is to enslave Cain—to possess or control him, but the Lord commands, urges Cain to overpower sin, to master it. … As the Lord tells Cain what he should do, *i.e.*, master or rule sin, the Lord also states what the husband should do, rule over his wife."[23] And Hamilton: "The desire of the woman for her husband is akin to the desire of sin that lies poised ready to leap at Cain. It means a desire to break the relationship of equality and turn it into a relationship of servitude and domination." And, Waltke, from a standpoint more rooted in the poetic struc-

---

[22]Tremper Longman III, *How to Read Genesis*, 113.

[23]Susan T. Foh, "What is the Woman's Desire?" *WTJ* 37 (1975): 380–382.

ture: "The chiastic structure of the phrase pairs the terms 'desire' and 'rule over,' suggesting that her desire will be to dominate. This interpretation of an ambiguous passage is validated by the same pairing in the unambiguous context of 4.7."

And to the feminist who would refuse to follow the creation order, Ward offers the following: "Do you see what that does for the woman in subjection? It makes *her* the strong woman who exercises self-control, and the feminist the weak one who gives in to her desires."[24]

As with everything else in the judgments, this takes something that already existed and changes its significance as the means of judgment. Woman was already to be subordinate to man. Man was created before the woman (1 Tim 2.13). Further, "In that the woman was made from man to be his helper and is twice named by man indicates his authority over her" (Wenham). Man was also the one with whom God spoke and to whom God gave responsibilities. "He was commanded to 'cultivate' and 'keep' the garden. He was also restricted from eating of the tree of the knowledge of good and evil."[25] And Mathews: "[In 3.16], the directive for 'rule' is not given to the man, for that has already been given and is assumed (2.15, 18)." Finally, God gives man the command to leave and cleave. "It is important to notice that God addresses *the man* and not the woman to accomplish this activity. He is placing the responsibility primarily upon Adam (and his male descendants) as he has done thus far with other commands. ...This appears to be a sign of leadership on Adam's part."[26]

So, while 1 Timothy 2.13–14 may show that the woman being deceived is a part of why women are *to learn* in submission, it is clear from Genesis that women were already to be in submission. After sin, however, submission won't come easily.

3.17, To Adam. Just as the judgment on the woman *(ishshah)* showed the change in her relationship to her husband *(ish)*, the judgment on the man *(adam)* is concerned with his relationship to the earth *(adamah)*.[27]

---

[24]Dene Ward, *Born of a Woman: Teacher's Manual*, 11.

[25]Michael F. Stitzinger, "Genesis 1–3 and the Male/Female Role Relationship," *GTJ* 2 No. 1 (1981): 30.

[26]*Ibid.*, 33.

[27]Henri Blocher, *In the Beginning*, 182.

"Because you have listened to the voice of your wife." The reason for this judgment is given first: because he chose the woman over God. "In hearkening to the voice of his wife Adam had forfeited his position as the crown of creation and the head of the wife, and had placed himself in the subordinate position which belonged to the woman. ...Furthermore, he had listened to her when she was deceived by the serpent. Hence, Adam has abandoned his place of superiority over the creatures."[28]

"Cursed is the ground because of you." Again, neither Adam nor Eve is ever cursed. The ground, however, is cursed for man's sake. "And as the earth rebels against its lord, man is reminded of his rebellion against *his* Lord."[29]

"In pain you shall eat." The play on words is clear in this judgment. 'Because you ate, this is how you will eat: in pain, through thorns and thistles, and by the sweat of your face.' Again, the judgment uses what already existed and changes its significance. Man was already commissioned to work (2.15). Now, the work would be difficult.[30] "That the woman is cursed in relationships and the man in work certainly doesn't mean that women shouldn't work or men don't care about relationships, but it may indicate where the genders have tended to place their respective deepest significance."[31]

3.19, "To dust you shall return." Death. Just as God promised. But here, the focus isn't so much on the death, but the futility of life. 'Because of what you've done, the ground is cursed. Thus, you will have to labor hard all the days of your life to produce what you want from the ground until you go back to it yourself.' Adam was promised that he would work his life away, toiling to produce the things necessary to live; the end result: he will die. The writer of Ecclesiastes may have had this passage in mind when he said, *All is vanity and a striving after wind* (1.14)—and that the only thing worthwhile is serving and obeying God (12.13). Death is the *only* brand

---

[28]Edward J. Young, *Genesis 3*, 130.

[29]Jim McGuiggan, *Genesis and Us*, 17.

[30]Blocher argues that the change may be related more to the man than to the ground: "The Psalms which sing of God's creation as we now see it and the texts in the book of Job which celebrate its awesome beauty stand as a warning against the temptation to exaggerate the difference for nature in itself. Genesis 3.17f considers the earth in so far as it responds to man within that relationship. It is permissible to think that the disruption affects that relationship before anything else, beginning with the weakening and disorder of man himself." *In the Beginning*, 183.

[31]Tremper Longman III, *How to Read Genesis*, 114.

new thing given in these judgments (and even it was promised): "The crazy little god with his absurd pretensions is not God and never shall be. All he can do is die."[32]

3.20, The man called his wife's name Eve. His belief in God's promise manifested itself in the naming of his wife. "Man is dust, yet he calls his wife the mother of all living."[33] And Waltke: "To the woman's generic designation, Adam adds a personal name that defines her destiny. …Adam's naming of Eve is the beginning of hope. Adam shows his restoration to God by believing the promise that the faithful woman will bear offspring that will defeat Satan."

3.21, The Lord God made for Adam and for his wife garments. God provided for them new clothes. What verse 7 does not teach in regard to modesty,[34] this passage does. In verse 7, it was man's judgment that he needed clothes (man's judgment also led him to eating the fruit!); here God clothes them before sending them out into the world. Here, we learn that it is no longer God's plan for mankind to be naked. Giving this clothing to the couple is a combination of God's grace and a reminder of sin. It is an act of grace, as "They are not sent beyond the garden totally vulnerable" (Hamilton). But as Wenham notes, "Prior to their disobedience, they, and apparently God, had been quite unconcerned about their nakedness. In this context God's provision of clothes appears… as a reminder of their sinfulness." Their clothes would stand as a memorial of what they had lost and, more importantly, what they did to incur that loss.

Of skins. It would seem that this would mark the first death. As animals died in man's stead throughout the Old Testament, so also they did in the instance of the first sin. "Man could not stand before God in his own covering. Rather, he needed a covering from God—a covering of a specific nature—a covering that required sacrifice and death, a covering not provided by man but by God."[35] And Young: "God alone must decide what clothing is suitable for man, and it may be, that in order to make the con-

[32]Henri Blocher, *In the Beginning,* 190.

[33]Edward J. Young, *Genesis 3,* 140.

[34]See comment on verse 7.

[35]Francis A. Schaeffer, *Genesis in Space and Time,* 105.

trast stronger, inasmuch as man had chosen the leaves of the fig tree, God chose the skins of animals." [36]

3.22, "Like one of us." Following our interpretation of 1.26, this refers to the heavenly court. Man has become like other heavenly beings concerning the knowledge of good and evil.

As to becoming *like God* (v 5, see above), MacKenzie offers the following: "By deciding to treat as good something that Yahweh treated as evil (his eating from the tree), the man has acted like a god; he has aped God, and in this one respect he *has* made himself 'like Elohim.' But this has not made him like God in any other way, still less made him like a god. By this attempted usurpation, this god-like action, he has corrupted his nature as man." [37]

"Lest he… live forever." In his fallen state, man must not participate in immortality. Exposure to physical death is the only way to be saved from spiritual death. To live forever on the cursed earth would have been a far greater punishment than separation from the tree of life. Only by dying can we partake in Christ's power over death. "The expulsion from paradise, therefore, was a punishment inflicted for man's good, intended, while exposing him to temporal death, to preserve him from eternal death." [38]

3.24, The cherubim and a flaming sword that turned every way. These were placed to prevent reentry into the garden. Entrance into paradise is not something man can accomplish on his own. The way is blocked. Man cannot save himself. Only through God's plan can man ever reenter the paradise he lost.

Exactly what cherubim are is unknown. Traditionally, they have been understood to be a special class of angel, but Blocher convincingly argues that this is not necessarily the case. There is no Scripture that identifies them with angels or even links them together. Their faces are those of earthly creatures: mankind, the lion, the ox, and the eagle (Ezek 1.5ff; 10.15; Rev 4.6ff). Finally, he cites Fairbairn as pointing out that, in the Revelation, they join with the choir of men and not with the choir of angels (Rev 5.8, 11). He concludes: "The simplest solution is to… see in them

---

[36] Edward J. Young, *Genesis 3*, 148. *Cf.* Galatians 3.27.

[37] R.A.F. MacKenzie, "The Divine Soliloquies in Genesis," *CBQ* 17 (1955): 162–163.

[38] Edward J. Young, *Genesis 3*, 159.

the symbol of divine power, as it is manifested in the universe, or, more precisely still, a concentrated form of the universe itself, summed up in its more glorious figures, but in so far as it remains at the disposal of the Lord and acts as the instrument of His power."[39]

Finally, regarding what happened to the garden after man's expulsion, Leupold answers well: "All speculations as to how long the Garden of Eden continued upon earth after the Fall are bound to be quite hopeless. Certainly, for at least a time after the expulsion the garden was still upon the earth, and both the cherubim and the vibrant flame of fire continued in their God-appointed place. But to venture to say that the garden as such remained until it was destroyed by the Flood is an assertion that can be as little proved as the other claim that it was removed or [as Keil says] 'vanished from the earth with the expulsion of men from the Garden of Eden.'"

Growth of the Seed: Following the Fall, the Seed is promised.

Theological Reflection: Falling Prey to Sin

Satan *will* use truth to accomplish evil. He will intermingle truth and lies in order to confuse our judgment. We must be wary, even when we know the truth of the matter, that Satan is not using that truth against us. With the truth, Satan deceived Eve.

And Satan attacks at every level. A brief comparison between this passage and John's description of worldliness (1 John 2.15–16) makes this evident. She saw that it was good for food (lust of the flesh), that it was a delight to the eyes (lust of the eyes) and that it was desirable to make one wise (pride of life).

From this first sin, we learn that sin, at its most fundamental level is a combination of three things: a doubt in God's commands or promises, a concern with oneself, and trusting in what one feels. This is exactly what Eve did—and exactly what we do when we fall prey to sin. If Satan can get a person to do these three things, sin is inevitable.

Perhaps the most dangerous thing we can ever do is look at temptation through our eyes; rather, we must look at everything—especially temptation—through the lens of God's word. In our eyes, it will *always* look good. Through the lens of the Bible, it will always look bad.

---

[39]Henri Blocher, *In the Beginning*, 188–189.

Crushing the Serpent. There is a part in crushing the serpent that goes beyond Jesus' death and resurrection. There is a part that Christians play in the crushing of Satan. Romans 16.18–20 speaks to this, perhaps most clearly when Paul says, *The God of peace will crush Satan under your feet shortly.* We strike a blow against the serpent when we diligently keep God's law and live like Christ.

Further, the kingdom is to be on the attack. When Jesus promised that the gates of Hades would not prevail against the kingdom, He was not speaking of the kingdom being safe against Hades' attack. In His audience's mind, gates were primarily defensive. That the gates of Jerusalem didn't prevail against Rome didn't mean that Rome was safe from the attacks of Jerusalem. Likewise, the gates of Hades not prevailing against the kingdom put Christians on the offensive, not the defensive: God crushing Satan under *our feet;* the church tearing down the gates of Hades.

4 *1, Adam knew Eve his wife.* Without entering the world of Hebrew euphemisms, it is at once obvious that this is not a 'Hi, how are you' kind of knowledge, because of its result: *she conceived.*[1]

4.3, Brought to the LORD an offering. This is probably not the first-ever sacrifice. The casual way it is presented would indicate that this is something that had been done before. Surely Adam and Eve would have offered sacrifices sometime between their exile from the garden and their sons being old enough to each have a profession and make his own offering.

Each brought of his profession. Cain, a farmer, brought fruit of the ground. Abel, a shepherd, brought sheep of his flock.

4.4–5, And the LORD had regard for Abel and his offering, but for Cain and his offering he had no regard. Because God made a distinction between the two, we must ask what the difference was. The first difference that is noticed is that one is a vegetable sacrifice and the other an animal. This could be the difference; some offerings required blood to be pleasing to God (remit sins). But notice also that Abel brought *the firstborn of his flock and their fat portions* while Cain brought *some fruit* (NKJV). This seems to indicate that Abel brought his best, while Cain just brought something. This could be the difference; God doesn't take second-best.

As to determining where the fault was, we must remember that all the relevant information is not revealed. If the fault was the type of sacrifice, it means that God told them exactly what He wanted and Cain failed to obey. If it was a 'thanksgiving offering,' they each brought what they produced. Cain's was rejected because he failed to give from his heart.

Most commentators take the position that the difference was in the quality of the offering, not the type. Waltke summarizes this position well: "Abel's sacrifice represents acceptable, heartfelt worship; Cain's represents unacceptable tokenism."[2] While we may lean toward this interpretation above the other on the basis of what the passage *doesn't* say about

---

[1]As an aside, God expects us to *know* Him. Thus, our knowledge of God cannot be superficial; rather, it must be a deep and intimate knowledge. This should seem logical, since the relationship of God with His people is constantly compared to a marriage; sin (especially idolatry) is always compared with adultery. It should be no surprise that the word God uses to further elucidate that relationship—to *know* Him—is the same word used to describe the sexual relationship between a husband and wife.

[2]R.K. Harrison, "Cain," *ISBE*, 369.

Cain's sacrifice, we also take careful note of Lewis' warning: "If we wish to make much of silence, we might observe that only in connection with Cain's offering is it said to be brought 'to the Lord.' Though certainly to be understood, such is not specifically stated for Abel's offering."[3] In any event, it seems clear from God's rebuke of Cain in verse 7 that Cain knew what was *well*, and, for whatever reason, refused to do it.

Ultimately, we are not told why God accepted Abel's sacrifice and rejected Cain's, except by what the author of Hebrews tells us: Abel's offering was *by faith*. Anything beyond that finds itself in the realm of speculation. But, because it was faithless, Cain's worship would have been rejected no matter which way it failed. The silence in this matter may be intended to inform us that either failing was enough to make it unacceptable. From the beginning, God has wanted worship that is correct in both form and motive.

4.5, Cain was very angry. This should have served as a warning sign to Cain: if *God* is not pleased and *we* get angry, something is wrong with our thinking.

His face fell. Leupold suggests *his glance fell* is what is meant by this statement. "For anger that does not break out into violence seeks to hide itself by not looking freely into the eye of the one at whom it is directed. …So there was an inward passion and the visible outward indication of its presence." Further, he "sought to hide his internal thoughts from the omniscient God who knows his anger" (Waltke).

God responds with a series of questions. The first question—*"Why are you angry, and why has your face fallen?"*—is probably intended to make Cain think about the cause of his anger. Indeed, it should have made him realize that anger was not his right, but God's. The latter question—*"If you do well, will you not be accepted?"*—is to serve as a warning. Not doing well will lead to sin. Sin desires to rule over man, but man must, instead, rule over it.

4.7, "If you do well, will you not be accepted? …[Sin's] desire is for you, but you must rule over it." "God… knowing how crucial this moment is for the sinning man, tries to rally him for the fight of his young life."[4] But Cain would rather fight against God than with Him.

---

[3]Jack Lewis, "The Offering of Abel (Gen 4.4): A History of Interpretation," *JETS* 37 (1994): 496.

[4]Jim McGuiggan, *Genesis and Us,* 51.

4.8, His brother. This phrase shows up twice in this verse—four times in six verses—emphasizing their relationship, which in turn emphasizes the horror of the crime. By the second generation of life on the earth, sin has already grown to murder. It doesn't take long for sin to display its potential. The warning to us is clear: if we are participating in 'little sins' because 'it's really not that bad,' we're deceiving ourselves and setting ourselves up for a big fall.

And already we see developing the enmity between the seed of the woman (Abel) and the seed of the serpent (Cain).[5]

4.9, "Where is Abel your brother?" God again begins with a question. As with Adam and Eve, His question is designed to elicit a confession, to remind Cain that He already knows. But notice how different Cain's response is from Adam and Eve's. Their response was filled with fear and guilt. Cain's is brash and impudent. They cast the blame on another, while admitting the sin. Cain claims no knowledge of Abel's whereabouts. How much sin has grown in so short a time!

"Am I my brother's keeper?" Cain asks this rhetorical question in such a way that it obviously expects a negative answer. But is Cain's denial of being his brother's keeper an additional aspect of his sin, or is he correct in his assessment that we are not to be such?

We must begin by determining what it means to be a *keeper.* Related to God's question, it would seem to mean knowing the whereabouts of your brother all the time. Clearly, we all fail at that. One's own spouse does not know his exact whereabouts at every moment of every day. How much less our fellow man! But few believe that God expects such.

"The Hebrew word 'keeper' is a participle form of a verb which occurs frequently (more than 450 times) in the Old Testament. In all these occurrences there is not a single instance where a man's keeping another man is an expressed covenant norm or even a recognized social obligation. ...It is rare to find one man keeping another, and it is always a special circumstance. Such a keeper may be a servant or subordinate serving as a bodyguard. But a man may also keep a man by detaining or restraining him, holding him in custody."[6] Thus, Riemann suggests translating it *custodian,*

---

[5]See comment on verse 11.

[6]Paul Riemann, "Am I My Brother's Keeper?" *Interpretation* 24 (1970): 483–484.

guard, warden, or the like. Hamilton seems to be in agreement with this analysis: "To *keep* means not only to preserve and sustain but to control, regulate, exercise authority over. For this reason, today we say that zoos and prisons have keepers."

Riemann continues: "Man is enjoined to continually remember those in need, to provide for the poor, to guard the rights of the weak—indeed, to love his neighbor as himself. But not to *keep him.* …It is only God Himself, as lord and suzerain over the whole world, who is the keeper of men (Psa 12.7; 25.20; 121.4–8). …For keeping is more than protecting and assisting; it necessarily involves rule and control." [7] Perhaps this is why Jesus never prays for the disciples to keep one another—He only prays for God to keep them, and for them to be united (*cf.* John 17).

Thus, Cain's denial implicit in this question wasn't whether or not he had responsibilities to his brother; rather, his point was that his job wasn't to follow Abel around all day and know his precise location. (Of course, he already showed the denial of those other responsibilities when he murdered Abel.) How could Cain know, off the top of his head, where Abel was? If he had that kind of knowledge, he would have to be his brother's keeper—his custodian. But he is not.[8]

And consider how this changes what Cain is saying: he's not shirking a God-given responsibility in the face of God; rather, he's using a legitimate argument to try to hide what he has done. Instead of seeing Cain as foolish in this declaration, we see him as calm and calculating, devious and scheming, trying to deceive God by way of the truth. Cain remains guilty, but it's not because he denies being his brother's keeper. He's guilty because he is a murderer.

And, ultimately, this response is a lie. Clearly, his point was that he did not know Abel's whereabouts. Just as clearly, he did know where Abel was.

4.10, "What have you done?" God does not address the issue of whether or not Cain was to be Abel's keeper. Rather than addressing the lie, He proceeds to Cain's sin. According to Leupold, "The 'what' naturally im-

---

[7]*Ibid.,* 488–489.

[8]And we further agree with Riemann in this statement: "It is the last thing we really need to be encouraged to do since we are so naturally inclined to do it anyway. Either we ignore our fellow in need, or we appoint ourselves his keeper" (489).

plies: 'What horrible thing?'" to the end that "the divine word attempts to waken in the man a realization of the enormity of his misdeed." Having asked a question to promote a confession, He asks this one by way of accusation, "A question we punctuate with an exclamation point rather than a question mark, for God is making an accusation, not seeking information" (Hamilton).

"Your brother's blood is crying to me from the ground." Leupold notes: "That a voice should be attributed to blood should not be strange inasmuch as the soul is regarded as lodged in the blood of man (Lev 17.11), and the death of God's saints is precious in his sight (Psa 116.15). That God... avenges all instances of unjust shedding of blood, appears from Job 16.18; Genesis 9.5; Ezekiel 3.18; 24.7–8; 33.6; and Psalm 9.12." And Wenham: "Consequently, unatoned-for murders pollute the holy land, making it unfit for the divine presence." This, however, "should still be read... as a metaphor" (Kidner). Blood does not literally cry out from the ground. But even as a metaphor, it is clear that, as Keil says, "Murder is one of the sins that cries to heaven."

4.11–12, "You are cursed from the ground." Cain finds himself distinguished as the first person to have a curse placed directly on him. Among other things, this clearly marks Cain as the seed of the serpent, a point made explicitly clear in 1 John 3.12. The curse includes being driven away from the cultivated portion of the land and being compelled to live the life of a nomad. The first part of the curse makes perfect sense, as he was a farmer. "Because the earth has been compelled to drink innocent blood, it rebels against the murderer, and when he tills, it withdraws its strength, so that the soil yields no produce" (Keil). *Cursed are you so there is no ground for you* is Leupold's paraphrase—God is taking away his livelihood.

"You shall be a fugitive and a wanderer on the earth." The second part of the curse explains how the first part will happen: "Far from being sedentary and having the time to harvest crops, Cain will be a *wandering fugitive.* ...It is to lose all sense of belonging and identification with a community. It is to become rootless and detached" (Hamilton).

4.13, "My punishment is greater than I can bear." Cain's response marks a clear change in tune. His impudence and irreverence gives way to despair. But even in this, he has not reached penitence; rather, he questions God's judgment. Even in his despair, a hint of insolence remains. Irony abounds as he is afraid that he will be killed. He is not hesitant to kill his brother, but a coward in the face of his own demise.

4.15, "If anyone kills Cain, vengeance shall be taken on him sevenfold." God protects Cain. *Why?* "God reserved for Himself the right to determine which life should be terminated and which not" (Leupold)—"to take punishment into His own hands, and protect human life from the passion and willfulness of human vengeance" (Keil). Further, "The tares were to grow with the wheat, and sin develop itself to its utmost extent" (Keil), that sin may "run a free course and... develop to the full the potentialities that lie in it, so that the nature of evil as evil may be fully revealed in the historical development of mankind" (Leupold).

Or perhaps it is more simple than all that. Perhaps even in the first cursing of a human, there is the ever-present grace of God. "God's concern for the innocent (v 10) is only matched by his care for the sinner" (Kidner).

4.16, Then Cain went away from the presence of the LORD. This last phrase summarizes the worst curse that could be placed on man. The only curse worse than death is separation from God—Cain found himself in a literal hell on earth.

And settled in the land of Nod. That he *settled in Nod* does not contradict God's decree that Cain would be a nomad. *Nod* means *wandering*. We do not know that there was ever a literal *land of Nod* that he went to; rather, it seems better to understand that to *settle in Nod* means to enter a state of perpetual wandering.

4.17, Cain knew his wife. She must have been a sister, though it is conceivable that she was a niece. "This verse simply assumes that the marriage had already taken place. Cain's wife is not named, but must be one of the 'other daughters' of Adam mentioned in 5.4" (Hamilton). Just because Seth was not born until after Abel's death does not mean that the other daughters weren't, as Leupold suggests. Names of children in genealogies are not listed by birth order, but by prominence. Further, "The text assumes it as self-evident that she accompanied him into exile" (Keil). If this is not the case, she went looking for him later or they met by happenstance. It is most likely that they were married before Cain left. We have a hard time understanding why she would accompany him otherwise.

As to the matter of incest: "Marriage to a sister at this early stage of the development of the human race [cannot] be considered wrong or unnatural. If according to divine purpose the human race is to develop from one pair, then the marriage of brothers and sisters as well as of other close relatives will for a time be a necessity" (Leupold). Ultimately, the point is not to debate the identity of Cain's wife, but to emphasize that the line of Cain continues.

He built a city. This was probably an attempt to fly in the face of the curse and settle down somewhere. Some scholars (*e.g.,* Wenham, Leupold) have noted that the Hebrew is more properly translated, *he was building a city.* "The city may have been finished, but not by Cain. Others may have lived there, not he. Nothing points to an amelioration of the original divine sentence" (Leupold). The city was named after his son. "Instead of honoring God, the unbeliever honors humanity. This perverse reversal will give rise to a self-idolizing, Machiavellian state" (Waltke).

Phil Roberts noted that in the beginning, God planted a garden; He did not build a city. And, in the end, man will return to a garden. The first city was built by man, not by God. And since, cities have become synonymous with wickedness: Sodom and Gomorrah, Tyre and Sidon, Nineveh, Babylon, Rome; Las Vegas, San Francisco, New Orleans, Amsterdam, Rio.... Interestingly, even in the greatest of men's work, the builders still long for a garden in the midst of their city, whether the fabled Hanging Gardens of Babylon or New York's Central Park. Mankind longs for the garden paradise he lost, but he doesn't know the way back.[9] But to those who believe—to the seed of the woman—He has shown the way. It begins by rejecting the wisdom of man, the seed of the serpent. And it ends—though *ends* isn't really the right word—in the second garden.

4.19, Lamech. The seventh from Adam through Cain (*cf.* 5.22–24; Jude14). Here is a man who epitomized evil: the first bigamist (v 19); a murderer (v 23); and one who took God's authority upon himself (v 24).

4.23, "I have killed a man for wounding me." Lamech boasts to his wives of his strength and crime. "In the context of this genealogy, the poem introduces a world of uncontrolled violence. This stands in an ambiguous relationship to the spread of culture portrayed in the sons of Lamech (vv 19–

---

[9]Phil Roberts, "The City of God," *The Gospel in the Old Testament: Florida College Annual Lectures,* 233–254.

22). The text does not tie violence and culture together in such a way as to make one dependent on the other. At the same time we know well that the same energy in the human community that builds up can also be used to destroy. Living in a distorted world means we see both. By placing side by side a genealogy of the rise of human culture with a violent poem of male boasting, the reader experiences both the drama and danger of life."[10]

4.24, "If Cain's revenge is sevenfold, then Lamech's is seventy-sevenfold." Waltke says, "This formulaic number represents unlimited violence. ... Cain's identity, which was *marred* by violence, engenders his progeny's identity, which is *marked* by violence (*cf.* 6.1–6)."

4.25–26, Called his name Seth. Seth was born to take the place of Abel (v 25). And Seth proved to be a replacement in a spiritual sense as well, for it was in the line of Seth that *people began to call upon the name of the* LORD—to worship God. This is the quality that tells us *why* Seth was chosen: he was righteous, like his brother Abel. "While the family of Cainites... were laying the foundation for the kingdom of this world; the family of the Sethites began... to found and to erect the kingdom of God" (Keil). Worship of Yahweh did not begin with Moses or even Abraham, but with Seth.

Does this passage have negative implications on Adam and Eve? If calling on the name of the Lord began with Seth, are we to assume that Adam and Eve never returned to God after the fall? We know little about Adam and Eve's spiritual life after the fall, but what we do know is telling. Adam displayed faith when he named Eve (3.20). Eve displayed faith when she named Seth (4.26). That Abel and Seth were righteous would indicate they were taught. Further, *began* cannot be an absolute use here; Abel worshiped God. Leupold suggests that this is public worship. Ultimately, the point is not whether or not Adam and Eve were faithful or apostate after chapter three, but that, because of Seth, the brightness of the Messianic hope continued to shine; men worshipped the almighty God.

It is significant to note how far things have gone by the time Moses records this book. Here, the whole world knew who Yahweh was—and the righteous worshipped Him as the creator of all. But when Moses first meets Yahweh in the bush, he has to ask for God's name. He takes the

---

[10]Eugene Roop, *Genesis*, 55.

name of Yahweh to Pharaoh who has never heard of this God—Yahweh—before. After the Exodus, the people of Israel—knowing so little about Him, and so colored by the polytheistic world around them—promptly build an idol and say that it is Yahweh. We said in the introduction that the theocentric result of sin is that it dethrones God. The time of Moses saw this dethronement to its fullest: even His people no longer knew who He was.[11]

Growth of the Seed: Cain is rejected from the Messianic line due to his faithlessness and murder. The Seed will come through the faithful Seth (v 26), replacement of the faithful Abel.

---

[11]On why God's statement in Exodus 6 does not necessarily mean that no one before Moses had heard God's name, see Excursus B.

5 Having just documented the proliferation of the seed of the serpent, the Genesis author now turns his attention to the expansion of the seed of woman, highlighted by the walk of Enoch.

5.3, After his image. This may refer to something as simple as his son being a human baby rather than, say, a baby elephant. And that Adam was created in God's image, his fathering a son in his image would transfer God's image into his child. Mathews suggests that this reference "shows the perpetuation of the divine image and blessing, which had its beginnings in the creation of mankind" and Waltke furthers this in saying, "The verbal linkage with 1.26–28 presents human procreation as the continuation of God's creative act."

Even at this, we see wisdom in the words of Keil that this image and likeness was "not in the purity in which it came direct from God, but in the form given to it by his own self-determination, modified and corrupted by sin." The emphasis is that Adam's child was born in *his* image, which may be juxtaposed with Adam being created in God's image. Perhaps the image of God was somehow modified by the presence of sin on earth and separation from the tree of life. Perhaps the image of God in man is somehow less complete than that with which Adam and Eve were endowed, or that man will have after the final resurrection. But, as Kidner suggests, we should not press this contrast too far. While we suggest those possibilities, such a change in the image of God is not specifically stated. Nor would we infer from this verse the presence of an inherited, corrupt sinful nature. The point of this statement, to which everyone agrees, is that God's image continued from Adam to the rest of humankind.

5.5, 8, 11, 14, 17, 20, 27, 31, And he died. Even Methuselah, the oldest recorded man (v 27), succumbed to death. That this phrase shows up eight times in one chapter is not by happenstance. It is at once clear that the theme of this genealogy is the end of life. While it shows the fulfillment of God's command to *"Be fruitful and multiply,"* it also documents the fulfillment of God's promise that *"You will surely die."*

And so, it would seem, the point of this chapter is twofold: Man filled the earth as he was commanded; man died as was promised (*death reigned from Adam to Moses,* Rom 5.14).

5.21–24, Enoch. What is the point of the repeated *and he died?* If Adam's life consisted of 930 years, what do you suppose he did after that period of time was up? Keep living? To say, *All the days of Seth were 912 years; and he died* is redundant. Of course he died after the days of his life were up! What else could he have done? "If a person's entire life consists of *X* number of years, it is assumed (logically) that he died."[1] The purpose it would seem is to highlight, by contrast, the account of Enoch. He did not die. God took him. "In a plot where a funeral bell continually tolls out its mournful drone there is a disjunctive ray of hope."[2] The contrast cannot be missed. Enoch escaping death leaps from the page.

It is significant to point out that Enoch did not break the pattern of death until he broke the pattern of life. As Hebrew genealogies tend to be, this one is very structured and built on a pattern: *And he lived, and he begat, and he lived, and he died; And he lived, and he begat, and he lived, and he died; And he lived, and he begat, and he lived, and he died....* Until you get to Enoch: *And he lived, and he begat, and he walked with God.*

Enoch didn't just live. He walked with God. It wasn't just his death—or lack thereof—which is outside the pattern of this chapter. His life broke the pattern. "This suggests that walking with God is a step above mere living... it's an exception to the normal pattern of life."[3]

Aside from Enoch, only Noah is said to have walked with God. Others walked *before God* (17.1) and *after God* (Deut 13.4), but these refer to a righteous life "under the law according to the directions of the divine commands" (Keil). "A bit more intimacy seems to be suggested by 'walking with' over against 'walking before.' 'Walking with' captures an emphasis on communion and fellowship" (Hamilton).

We are not told precisely what is meant by *walking with God*. Certainly, the duration of Enoch's walk (300 years) tells us that it involves the idea of a continuous or habitual manner of life.

Walking with God is a summary of Enoch's life. From the New Testament's testimony about Enoch and Noah, we learn something of the nature of walking with God. Jude speaks of Enoch prophesying of the coming of the Lord. Peter calls Noah a preacher of righteousness. Clear-

---

[1]T.J. Cole, "Enoch, A Man Who Walked with God," *BSac* 148 (1991): 290.

[2]*Ibid.*, 289.

[3]*Ibid.*, 291.

ly, walking with God includes testifying for Him. It is not a silent walk in the midst of a world of sin. It's an open and communicative walk.

And, needless to say, walking with God is a walk of faith (Heb 11.5).

But ultimately, walking with God was the reason Enoch did not die. "It is his 'walk with God' that explains why Enoch did not die" (Mathews). Here, in the genealogy of death, there is a glimpse of life. "In writing of Enoch's life, Moses' aim was to communicate hope. Death is not the final answer; for Enoch God overruled death."[4] "Enoch's life affirms that those who 'walk with God' in this fallen world will experience life, not death, as the last word" (Waltke).

"There is rescue from death. There is rescue from the effects of the curse. There is hope. There is a road back into the garden... there is access to the tree of life. One can indeed live forever. It is possible after all once again to fellowship with and worship the Lord God in the garden. How? By walking with God; thus the lesson of Enoch... is this: Life comes through walking with God."[5]

5.32, After Noah was 500 years old, Noah fathered Shem, Ham, and Japheth. As motioned in the introduction, Shem is listed first because of his place of prominence, not because he is the oldest son of Noah. Noah began to bear sons at 500 years of age (5.32) and was 600 at the flood (7.6). If Shem was Noah's oldest son, he would have been 100 at the flood; however, Shem was 100 two years after the flood (11.10). Thus, Noah was 503 when Shem was born—three years after the birth of his firstborn.[6]

Growth of the Seed: The Messianic line continues through Seth.

---

[4]*Ibid.*, 293.

[5]*Ibid.*, 293.

[6]The third year is the one they spent on the ark, which is implied by Noah being 600 at the beginning of the flood and Shem's age given in relation to being after the flood.

Excursus C: Genealogies

Most Bible readers will skip over chapter 5. Genealogies are often boring. They suffer in comparison to the narratives that surround them; however, they must serve some purpose or they would not find a place in the Bible.

Yes, they are boring. But then, they aren't supposed to be exciting. They are simply "a fitting expression of the continuity of fundamental elements of human life—birth, death, the continuation of the family line."[1] And they are a quick, compact way of expressing this. Remember, the purpose of the narratives in Genesis *isn't* to entertain us, but to tell us why Jesus came from the people He came from. If there is not a story to tell, Moses just records the genealogies and moves to the next important event that needs explanation.

Further, God had told man to be fruitful and multiply, to fill the earth. "These genealogies document the fruitfulness of humanity and thus become the expression of the fulfillment of God's mandate. ...Thanks to the genealogies, virtually every character in Genesis can be related to every other by specific degrees of kinship."[2]

What Genealogies Don't Do

There are some things that genealogies cannot do. For instance, they cannot determine the exact age of the earth. According to Kaiser, some have used genealogies to calculate the age of the earth, one arguing that "the human race was created on October 24, 4004 BC at 9:30 AM 45th Meridian Time."[3] Although biblical writers provide some numerical summaries for the purpose of delineating a timeline (*e.g.*, Exod 12.40; 1 Kgs 6.1; Jdg 11.26, *et al.*), "biblical writers never used [genealogical] numbers for this purpose."[4]

Skipping Generations. Of course, scientists will argue that there are historical and geological problems with the earth only being 6,000 years old. But more important for us, biblical genealogies often skip generations to abridge the lists and condense the information. In a comparison between Ezra 7.3–4 and 1 Chronicles 6.6–14, for example, Ezra skips six generations between Meraioth and Azariah. Comparing Matthew 1.8 with 1 Chronicles 3.11–12 reveals that Matthew skips three generations between Jehoram and Uzziah. The Bible *never* says that generations are not skipped in the genealogies; the Bible itself points to the fact that they are skipped.

---

[1] R.B. Robinson, "Literary Functions of the Genealogies of Genesis," *CBQ* 48 (1986): 598.

[2] *Ibid.*, 600–601.

[3] *Hard Sayings*, 103.

[4] *Ibid.*, 48.

Structure in Genealogies. In addition to the examples given, the clear structure of certain genealogies implies that they were arranged in such a way to aid in memorization. Matthew's genealogy of Christ is divided into three sets of 14 names: Abraham to David; David to captivity; captivity to Christ. Some generations were skipped—and David was repeated—for the purpose of creating this arrangement.

We find a similar arrangement in Genesis. There are two sets of ten between Adam and Abraham (chs 5 and 11). Each list of ten ends with a father who has three sons (Noah, Terah). And the symmetry does not end there. A comparison between chapters 4 and 5 shows the significance of the seventh from Adam, seven being the number symbolic of perfection or completeness. In the line of Seth, the seventh from Adam is Enoch, who is the epitome of righteousness. In Cain's line, the seventh is Lamech, "who made his sword his god" (Keil) and epitomized wickedness. It certainly seems that these genealogies were intentionally designed this way. Young explains this structure: "The genealogy of chapter 5 is not intended to furnish a chronology. Rather, Moses selected ten representative names in order to show the unrestrained, universal reign of death over man."[5]

Other Obstacles. There are a couple of other issues that come up in considering this subject. And while these are not conclusive to genealogies skipping generations, they may add support to the case that has already been well built.

Age Problems. If no generations are skipped, Adam and Noah's father are contemporaries; Abraham misses Noah by just two years; Nahor, Abraham's grandfather, dies before Noah (Abraham's great, great, great, great, great, great grandfather). Of course, none of these are impossible, but given the lack of other textual evidence that any of these people overlapped, they seem unlikely.

Population Problems. A more convincing problem arises in Numbers 3.19–38. There, we are told that the four sons of Kohath (Moses' grandfather, if no generations are skipped) gave rise to the families of the Amramites, Isharites, Hebronites, and Uzzielites, of which the males alone numbered 8,600 one year after the Exodus. Kaiser and Geisler both point out that, if no generations are skipped, this means Kohath had 8,600 *male* descendants in two generations—2,750 of whom were between the ages of 30 and 50.[6] *Nobody* is *that* fertile!

So why skip? If we are correct in presenting the genealogies as skipping generations, we must ask why they do so. This brings us back to the point of genealogies: to preserve an accurate lineage in a compact way. Their goal is

---

[5]Edward J. Young, *An Introduction to the Old Testament,* 57.

[6]See Norman L. Geisler, *Baker Encyclopedia of Christian Apologetics,* 267–270; *Hard Sayings,* 48–50.

to relay the continuation of a family line in the most condensed way possible. Further, these genealogies were memorized. Forming the genealogies with a certain symmetrical structure would aid in memorization while accurately preserving the family line.

It is essential, at this point, to emphasize that *beget,* while it can refer to direct lineage, can also mean something along the lines of *became the ancestor of.*[7] For example, Matthew's declaration that *Jehoram begat Uzziah* clearly does not mean direct parentage, since 1 Chronicles 3.11–12 fills in three missing generations.[8]

The Ages of the Antediluvians

'There's no way people really lived that long.'

Some scholars have suggested that the ages of the antediluvians were symbolic, drawing evidence from numbers such as 365, 777 and others. But, as Wenham notes, "If they are symbolic, it is not clear what they symbolize." If some symbolism is meant, it is completely lost to the modern reader.

Another suggestion is that the long ages account for skipped generations: the hundreds of years include the life spans of those who are not listed between the two listed descendants. This, however, is not a natural reading and, as Wenham again points out, "Lamech comments on Noah's birth, and Ham, Shem and Japheth were contemporaries of their father. It therefore requires special pleading to postulate long gaps elsewhere in the genealogy" (Wenham).

Others have argued that the years are to be understood as months. While this makes their ages more reasonable (*e.g.,* Adam lives to 77 or 93, depending on whether a 10 or 12 month calendar is used), "This theory runs into trouble when Nahor becomes the father of Terah at 29 years of age in Genesis 11.24. This would mean that he actually had a child when he was [less than three] years old"; further, "There are no known biblical examples of the word *year* meaning anything less than the solar year we are accustomed to in general speech."[9]

There is no reason to read these ages as anything other than what they are; all attempts to do otherwise have come up short. So, how did they live so long? While there may have been an atmospheric change afer the flood (*cf.* 2 Pet 3.5–7), it is not specific enough to postulate a theory that would explain

---

[7]See *Hard Sayings*, 102; Norman L. Geisler, *Baker Encyclopedia of Christian Apologetics*, 270; Waltke.

[8]A Caveat: While genealogies being open in nature allows for time passing between generations, this does not mean that there is a genealogical gap between every name or that one can randomly insert thousands of years between every name in the Genesis genealogies. Such would seem to defy a reasonable understanding of condensing the information.

[9]*Hard Sayings*, 103.

longer life. Ultimately, we must conclude that this is one of the questions to which God gave no answers.

Miscellaneous

A couple of last notes on genealogies are in order.

Most genealogies have a theme or purpose beyond listing names. We must not, however, ascribe a general theme to all genealogies. The folly of such will at once be evident if you think of applying the same theme to Genesis 5 and Matthew 1.

While we admit that genealogies are not the most exciting reading, they do offer facts that you can learn no where else. For example, it is in a genealogy that you learn Joab was David's nephew (perhaps that's why David put up with so much from him). It's in a list of names that you learn Uriah the Hittite was among David's most trusted men—an elite group of 37 (making the adultery and subsequent murder all-the-more treacherous). While the study of these ancient lists may be tedious and dry, taking the time and learning the techniques to study them is extremely valuable to increasing one's understanding of the Bible.

The Flood

Chapters 6–9

Within the broader literary structure (see page 22), the flood narrative shows a symmetrical pattern.[1]

A Genealogical note (6.9–10)

   B God sees that the earth is ruined (6.11–12)

      C God's instructions to Noah in light of His coming destruction of life on earth (6.13–22)

         D They enter the ark at God's command (7.1–9)

            E Flood begins; ark is closed (7.10–16)

               F Waters rise (7.17–20)

                  G Climax: All life on land dies; only Noah and those with him are spared (7.21–24)

               F' Waters recede (8.1–5)

            E' Flood ends; ark's window is opened (8.6–14)

         D' They exit the ark at God's command (8.15–22)

      C' God's instructions to Noah in light of His renewal of life on earth (9.1–7)

   B' God promises never again to ruin the earth (9.8–17)

A' Genealogical note (9.18–19)

"The story's symmetric structure emphasizes the highlighted center, which

---

[1]The following is taken from David A. Dorsey, *The Literary Structure of the Old Testament*, 52. His structural outline is more detailed than the following.

recounts the annihilation of all life on earth. This suggests that the central point of the story—its bottom line—is God's reversal of His creation."[2] [3]

6 Buried in the verses of the previous genealogy, we find Enoch—one of the highest points of human history. As is typical with mankind, it is not long before the pendulum makes a full swing and we reach one of the lowest points of human history. It is this swing of the pendulum which is recorded in Genesis 6.[4]

6.2, The sons of God saw that the daughters of man were attractive. See Excursus D.

6.3, My spirit shall not abide in man forever... his days shall be 120 years. A difficult passage, translated *abide in, contend with,* and even *judge among* (Leupold), though most often the first two. The etymology of this word is uncertain, making it all-the-more difficult to pin down a meaning.

If the correct translation is *abide in,* as most translations and commentators accept, it is hard to see this passage referring to something other than the shortening of the life of man.[5] But, based on the remainder of Genesis, that understanding is not the most obvious one. If this does refer to the shortening of the life of man, God takes a while to get to it. Following this declaration, Abraham, Sarah, Isaac, and Jacob all live well beyond 120. The first recorded age to fall short of 120 is Joseph who lived only to 110.[6] And while most modern ancients succumb before 120, Jeanne Calment of France made it to 122 before dying in 1997—did one manage to slip by or was God merely estimating? Further, if this is to be the life span, why do so few people live to that age? There is little explanation to be found both for the longevity of life found

---

[2]*Ibid.,* 52.

[3]See comment on 7.11.

[4]The purpose of our comments is not to compare and contrast the biblical flood with other ancient flood stories. For more information on those, Hammerly-Dupuy offers a good summary of various accounts ("Some Observations on the Assyro-Babylonian and Sumerian Flood Stories," *AUSS* 6 [1968]: 1–18). Wenham spends several pages of his commentary on this subject, as does Longman in *How to Read Genesis.*

[5]Waltke prefers *contend with,* a translation based on the LXX of 6.3. "Although the Greek translator only guessed at the meaning 'contend,' the most recent authoritative lexicon prefers this meaning."

[6]It may be that Aaron and Miriam lived beyond 120 as well, given that Moses lived to 120, and his older siblings died only shortly before him.

in humans after the flood and the subsequent drop to a number well below 120 (*cf.* Psa 90.10).

We follow Hamilton in feeling that, "[This declaration] seems to presage some event that is about to occur," though this is not without problem. If the 120 years is a period of grace prior to the flood, it is difficult to incorporate God's statement that His spirit will not abide in man beyond that point: clearly, it has and continues to.[7]

While both interpretations have difficulties, it is conceivable for *abide in* to be correct and still understand this to be a period of time before the flood. This is possible if Noah is understood as a second Adam and the flood as a second creation.[8] God's spirit stopped abiding in mankind after the 120 years were up. Then, God recreated. And, in the new creation, God has sought to dwell in man as He did with the first creation.

The notion of Noah as a second Adam—of the flood as a second creation—falls under attack in that such is never said of Noah. Parallels between their lives may or may not be of significance. The language of 7.11, however, argues that God is, in fact, destroying His creation to start again. Further, the language of chapter 8 clearly suggests a recreation (see *Seven Progressive Phases of Creation and Re-Creation* following chapter 8).

In the final analysis, both interpretations are problematic, and it remains difficult to pin down a meaning on this difficult phrase.

6.4, The Nephilim. See Excursus D.

6.5, The wickedness of man. This, not the Nephilim, is the progeny of the intermarriages (see Excursus D). The polluted seed of woman is overrun by the seed of the serpent. Wickedness prevails on the earth. The author uses extreme redundancy to emphasize the degree to which man had become wicked. He doesn't just tell us that man was bad, but that *every intention of the thoughts of his heart was only evil continually.* "A more emphatic statement of the wickedness of the human heart is hardly conceivable" (Vriezen qtd. in Kidner).

---

[7]Rendering this *contend with* does not alleviate the problem, for God's spirit still contended with man after those 120 years.

[8]Noah, with Adam, holds the distinction of being the only person in Genesis to carry the line of Christ and not be a younger son (see Introduction). Like Adam, Noah is the one man through whom all generations came. Noah, at once, saw all the animals of creation, as Adam did. See comment on 7.11 and the *Seven Progressive Phases of Creation and Re-Creation* following chapter 8.

In the earth. "The recurring phrase '[in] the earth' (vv 5–7) anticipates the necessary purging of the now-polluted land" (Mathews).

6.6, *The LORD was sorry that he had made man.* The Hebrew root for the word *sorry* may help explain God 'changing his mind.' Kaiser notes: "In its origins the root may well have reflected the idea of breathing or sighing deeply. It suggests a physical display of one's feelings—sorrow, compassion or comfort. …This denotes not change in His purpose or character. It only demonstrates that God has emotions and passions and that He can and does respond to us for good or ill when we deserve it."[9]

6.8, *But Noah found favor.* Noah is described as righteous and blameless, one who walked with God.[10] *Blameless,* as it is commonly used in the Bible, does not refer to sinless perfection. According to Kaiser, "The Hebrew root of the word *perfect* [blameless] involves the idea of completeness."[11] We may further see that Noah was not sinless in the verse we are presently considering: he found favor—or *grace,* as it is often translated—in the eyes of the Lord. While the Hebrew word does not connote the full New Testament concept of grace, it should be clear that those who are under the scope of God's grace are not sinless. God's grace, combined with Noah's obedient faith, resulted in salvation.

6.11, *Now the earth was corrupt in God's sight.* This is contrasted with Noah, who was *blameless* (v 9). This wickedness is repeated from the previous description (the Nephilim, v 4; the pervading evil, v 5). God's previous decision to destroy man is relayed to Noah, who will escape this destruction.

6.14, *"Make yourself an ark."* The ark was to be composed of *gopher wood,* a word that is used of an unknown species of tree. "The NIV opts for 'cypress' because of the similar consonants with the Hebrew (c/g-p-r) and because the ancients used it in their shipbuilding due to its resistance to rot" (Waltke).

---

[9]*Hard Sayings,* 109.

[10]*Walked with God* is only used to describe the lives of Enoch and Noah. While only Enoch was translated, both of these men, in a sense, escaped death. And so our conclusion from chapter five remains: life comes through walking with God.

[11]*Hard Sayings,* 111.

"Make rooms." Variously translated: Compartments, cells, nests. This was most likely to suit the needs of the various animals. While Gary Larson's sense of humor is appreciated, it is this feature of the ark that would have kept the lions from killing the unicorns. Finally, Noah was to *cover it inside and out with pitch*, to water-proof the ark.

The dimensions of the ark were to be roughly 450 feet long, 75 feet wide and 45 feet tall and it was probably more of a box than a ship, "as it was not meant for sailing, but merely to float upon the water" (Keil). And Waltke: "Accordingly, Heidel proposes that the ark 'was a flat-bottomed, rectangular construction, square on both ends and straight up on the sides. Such a craft is represented on bronze coins from the Phrygian city of Apameia.'"[12] Further, a chest-design would maximize the space available for its cargo, "enough space (an approximate total deck area of 95,700 sq. ft.) to accommodate all the animals" (Hamilton).

6.16, *"Make a roof for the ark."* This word, sometimes translated window, only shows up here in the Old Testament. Clearly, there is a window in the ark (8.6), but the standard word for window is used there. Understanding this as *roof*, however, runs into the same problem, as this is not the normal word that would be used for roof.

Another problem is understanding how this roof, or window, is to be finished *to a cubit above*, another obscure phrase. Hamilton understands it to refer "to the elevation of the crease of the roof above the level of the walls' tops." Mathews says that it refers to the roof being "constructed so as to overhang the sides of the vessel by one cubit (eighteen inches) or so that there is a gap of one cubit between the walls and the roof." Leupold understands it as a one-cubit window ("an opening of a cubit") that is to be made "toward the top" of the ark. Keil dismisses that this could be a window that was only a cubit square, and rather understands it to be "a hole or opening for light and air... within a cubit of the edge of the roof."

6.17–18, *"I will bring a flood."* Here, Noah receives the answer to the 'why' question that may have been in his thoughts. God explains that in this flood, all life will end. While this verse is not enough to declare a geographically universal flood (that will come later), it certainly emphasizes the universality of the destructive scope of the flood. All mortal life will end.

---

[12] Bruce K. Waltke, "Ark of Noah," *ISBE,* 291.

"But I will establish my covenant with you." Here, we first find this significant theological term—*covenant*—and, further, we learn why the ark worked.[13] "The formal expression of the 'covenant' and the giving of its 'sign' (rainbow) are 'established' in 9.8–17 following the deluge, but its early mention here explains why Noah and his family will survive" (Mathews).

The ark was to hold Noah and his wife, his three sons and their wives, two of every animal (more specific instructions will be given in chapter 7 regarding clean animals), and every sort of food. "The language of verses 19–21 reflects the creation account of chapter 1, indicating the continuity in the created order before and after the flood: 'male and female' (1.27), 'bird,' 'beast,' 'crawling creature' (1.25), 'kind' (1.11, *etc.*), and 'food' (1.30). God is saving that which was declared 'very good' at creation (1.31)" (Mathews).

6.20, "Two of every sort shall come in to you." Undoubtedly, Noah was wondering how he would accomplish the monumental task of gathering the animals while simultaneously building a 95,000 square foot ark. God sets his mind at easy by letting Noah know that the animals would do that part of the work—they would come to him to preserve their lives. Most likely, the animals hibernated while on the ark.[14]

6.22, Noah... did all that God commanded him. Noah obeyed every detail of God's word.

Growth of the Seed: God establishes a covenant with Noah (v 18); the Messianic line will continue despite the destruction of creation.

Theological Reflection: Escaping Destruction
As mentioned above, Noah was not saved because he was sinless, but because he *found grace in the eyes of the Lord* (Gen 6.8, NKJV).

It is not the sinless who need to find grace in the eyes of God, but the sinner. Noah did not live in sinless perfection, but he walked by faith, striving to do what God would have him do. Noah escaped destruction not because he never sinned, but because he sought after the Lord. And the grace of God took care of the rest. Further, Noah was saved because of

---

[13]See THEOLOGICAL REFLECTION, below.

[14]Whitcomb and Morris, *The Genesis Flood*, 70–75.

the relationship God sought to establish with him. God tells Noah, *"I will establish my covenant with you"* (v 18) after He had told him how to build the ark and about the flood that was coming.

Have you ever wondered what would have happened if Joe Nextdoor had decided to build an ark, too? 'Hey, Noah's building one,' Joe says to himself. 'I don't really believe in that God he's talking about or the flood that he says is coming, but let me build one just in case.' So, Joe follows the exact specifications given to Noah by God and builds his own ark—exactly like Noah's in every detail. Then, lo and behold, Noah was right. The flood comes. Joe gathers up his family and they all pile on to his ark. What happens to Joe then?

Joe's ark would sink. Joe would drown.

The fact that Noah's ark was structurally sound was only part of the reason it floated and life continued on the earth. The primary reason it worked is because God had established His covenant with Noah. If Joe Nextdoor tried to build his own ark, it would have sunk, no matter how structurally sound it was, nor whether or not he followed God's specific instructions—Joe was not in a covenant relationship with God.

If one is not in a covenant relationship with God, it doesn't matter how many 'right things' he does or how specifically he follows God's instructions. If one is not in that relationship with Him, those things will not avail. And being in a covenant relationship does not come from a one-time action like baptism, although that is a part of the process. Notice how many times God renewed the covenant with Abraham. The very concept of a covenant relationship is that of an *ongoing* relationship.

Finally, Noah accepted the relationship that God offered. *And Noah did according to all that God commanded him; so he did* (v 22).

If Noah had failed to obey the commands of God, the covenant-relationship would not have helped him; there would not have been one. If Noah had not built the ark, he could not have counted on God's grace to save him from the flood—God's grace had already acted, and he failed to do what was required of him. Had he not built the ark, Noah and his family would have drowned with the rest of the world.

So in the account of Noah, we find the three things most necessary to be saved from destruction: the grace of God, obedience to God's commands and being in a covenant relationship with Him. All three of these are essential and the omission of any will lead to certain destruction.

Excursus D: The Sons of God and the Nephilim

"This problematic expression [sons of God] has been defined as Sethites, angels, or a dynasty of tyrants who succeed Lamech. All three interpretations can be defended from the Hebrew grammar" (Waltke). "The three positions may be labeled 'the cosmologically mixed races view,' ... 'the religiously mixed races view,' ... and 'the sociologically mixed races view.' "[1] We will explore each of these options, in the order offered by Waltke, followed by a brief survey of the views and then discussion of the Nephilim. We will summarize the strengths and weaknesses of the positions mainly through quoting the scholars who support and oppose each of them before we offer concluding remarks.

The precise nature of the sin involved may vary, depending ultimately on the interpretation taken; however, Mathews describes well the basis of knowledge that there was sin committed: "The actions of the 'sons of God' are described in a language reminiscent of Eve's sin (3.6): she 'saw' that the fruit was 'good' and 'took.' While no sin or condemnation is specified in the text, the allusion to the garden rebellion suggests that the marriages are in some way tainted."

1. The traditional Christian interpretation—tracing its roots to such names as Augustine, Luther and Calvin; among commentators: Keil, Leupold and Mathews—is that this passage describes the intermarriage of the righteous and the wicked, namely the Sethites and the Cainites.

In its favor, the interpretation fits nicely with the immediate context. "[Chapters] 4 and 5 contrast the two lines of descent from Adam—the Cainites and Sethites. Genesis 6.1–8 relates how the two lines intermarry, resulting in a community of unprecedented wickedness. The flood account... is actually embedded within the Sethite genealogy, which is not completed until the notice of Noah's death (9.29). This provides the appropriate interpretive key for understanding 6.1–8" (Mathews).

"We have had no mention made of angels thus far in Genesis. We have met with other sons of the true God, in fact, the whole preceding chapter, even 4.25–5.32, has been concerned with them. Who will, then, be referred to here? Answer, the Sethites, without a doubt" (Leupold). While we would disagree with Leupold on no mention of angels,[2] they only appear before by implication. If this were to refer to angels, it would be the first explicit reference to them.

Further, this interpretation fits the context of the Genesis story that we have previously discussed: the growing enmity between the seed of woman

---

[1] *Hard Sayings*, 106.

[2] See comment on 1.26.

and the seed of the serpent. In addition, "The warning against marrying unbelievers is one theme of the Pentateuch. ...In this context, Genesis 6.1–4 furthers the practical aim of preventing indiscriminate marriage without regard
to spiritual status."[3]

Although Mathews argues that the *sons of God* are the Sethites, he stops
short of saying the *daughters of man* must be exclusively the Cainites: "'Daughters of men,' then, in verse 2 again refers to women regardless of parentage,
but among these 'daughters' are the offspring of Cain. 'Any of them they chose'
accentuates the Sethites' crime of inclusiveness. ...[This phrase] does not necessarily mean polygamy. Diversity may be intended here; the 'sons of God' selected wives from any family, including Cainite women. If so, the godly lineage
exercised a freedom that goes afoul when they embrace unrighteousness."

The primary argument against this interpretation is expressed well by Waltke
and Kaiser. "[This view] uses the term *men* in verses 1 and 2 in two different
senses: in verse 1 'men' is used to indicate humanity generically, while in verse
2 it is understood to refer to the Cainite line specifically. Suggesting such an
abrupt change in meaning without any indication in the text is unwarranted.
But even more alarming is the problem of the offspring. Why would religiously
mixed marriages produce [giants]?"[4] And Waltke: "[In 6.1] *adam* is generic for
humanity and *banot* refers to all their female offspring. It is arbitrary (*i.e.*, the
burden of proof rests upon the exegete to prove a change of meaning) in the
next verse to limit *adam* to the Sethites and *banot* to the Cainites."

However, "The OT does not lack instances of a shift from a generic to a specific use of a word in one context. Thus, *adam* as 'mankind' in verse 1 and as
'Cainites' in verse 2 is not impossible" (Hamilton). And, from a slightly different perspective: "It by no means follows, that because in verse 1 *adam* denotes man as a genus, *i.e.*, the whole human race, it must do the same in verse
2, where the expression 'daughters of men' is determined by the antithesis
'sons of God'" (Keil).

The problem suggested by Kaiser—*i.e.*, religiously mixed marriages producing giants—will be further discussed below under *Identifying the Nephilim*.

2. The oldest interpretation, tracing its roots back to the apocryphal book of
1 Enoch and finding support today by Kidner, Wenham, and VanGemeren is
that the sons of God are angels who left their proper abode and married human women.

------

[3]Leroy Birney, "An Exegetical Study of Genesis 6.1–4," *JETS* 13 (1970): 46.

[4]*Hard Sayings*, 107.

The primary argument in favor of this interpretation is that *sons of God* typically refers to angels (Job 1; 38.7, *etc.*), while other interpretations make this passage say something it isn't saying: "The alternative interpretations presuppose that what Genesis 6 really meant was that 'the sons of some men' married 'the daughters of other men.' The present phrase 'sons of God' is, to say the least, an obscure way of expressing such an idea" (Wenham).

This usage would also be familiar to the original audience. "In Ugaritic literature 'sons of God' refers to members of the divine pantheon, and it is likely that Genesis is using the phrase in a similar sense" (Wenham). And Mathews: "There is evidence of an ancient memory among pagan peoples that celestial beings cohabited with humans. ...Thus, in this view, the Hebrew account corrects the false notion that there was in antiquity a superhuman race of semidivine beings and shows that the culprits were not gods but degenerate angels whose offspring were merely sinful 'men [flesh] of renown,' subject to the same destruction of God's moral outrage as any mortal human."

The New Testament may have some bearing on interpreting this passage: "Possible New Testament support for 'angels' may be seen in 1 Peter 3.19–20; also in 2 Peter 3.4–6, where the fallen angels, the Flood, and the doom of Sodom form a series that could be based on Genesis, and in Jude 6, where the angels' offence is that they 'left their proper habitation'" (Kidner). And, as Longman argues: "In response to those who say that Jesus taught that angels were asexual, it may be said that a closer look at the passage only says that they do not marry."[5]

VanGemeren argues this view, in part, because of what *isn't* said: "The exact offence of the marriage is not stated. In the reconstruction of the human marriage, the wrong is assumed to lie in the intermarriage of the godly Sethites with the daughters of Cain. The mere statement of the relationship of angels with daughters of men needs no further explanation as to the wrong involved. It clearly contradicts the marriage ordinance (Gen 2.24)."[6]

But all is not clear by taking this interpretation. To begin, the term *sons of God,* while it may typically refer to angels, does not always do so and often refers to righteous men (*e.g.,* Psa 73.15; 80.17; Deut 32.5; Isa 43.6; Hos 1.10; *etc.*). There's also the problem of bodiless and sexless spirits cohabiting with humans. Add to that the point, which Longman concedes, that angels do not marry (Mark 12.25), which these sons of God are clearly doing. Mathews notes: "The NIV rightly renders *laqah* ('took') as 'married' since the term is the common Hebrew expression for wedlock."

---

[5]Tremper Longman III, *How to Read Genesis*, 117.

[6]Willem A. VanGemeren, "The Sons of God in Genesis 6.1–4" *WTJ* 43 (1981): 347.

"Also, it is difficult to reckon this view with procreation as a power bestowed by God upon the terrestrial order of animals and humanity (1.22, 28). There is no biblical evidence elsewhere that procreation is a trait of the heavenly hosts, although admittedly angels take on other human properties. Yet even here there is a significant difference between holy angels who acquire the ability to eat and rebellious angels who acquire sexual properties. By what line of reason does one propose that the fallen condition of angels somehow results in the exercise of corporeal procreation?" (Mathews).

"Even more serious is the problem of why judgment should fall on the humans and on the earth if the angels of heaven were the cause of the trouble."[7] Further, "This interpretation... does not fit the context of the flood, since the flood judgment is against humanity (Gen 6.3–5) and not the heavenly realm. God specifically labels the offenders in 6.3 as 'flesh' (*basar* 'mortal' in NIV)" (Waltke). And Birney: "Since this passage gives the background for the near extermination of the human race by the Flood, and since the 'sons of god' were the chief initiators of the wrong, they must have been a part of the human race."[8] "From beginning to end 6.1–8 concerns humanity and its outcome, not angels and their punishment" (Mathews).

We certainly agree with Kaiser and Waltke—indeed, we feel that this is the primary argument against this viewpoint—but it cannot be said, as some have argued, that the angels are not judged at all for their crime (if this refers to them). "The argument that the 'sons of God' are not judged assumes that all that happened is revealed or at least that all that is revealed is completely revealed. ...The lot of the angelic beings was not in the direct interest of the author of Genesis 6.1–4."[9]

How much bearing Jude's account of angels not keeping their proper domain has to do with this passage is also something of a question. "To argue from the phrase 'in a similar way' in Jude 7 that the sin of Sodom and Gomorrah is the same as the sin of Genesis 6.1–4 claims too much, for the sin of sodomy is not the same thing as marrying a wife from another part of the universe!"[10]

3. A third position, advanced by Kline,[11] and supported by Kaiser and Birney, interprets the sons of God as tyrants, a continuation of the cursed line of Cain,

[7]*Hard Sayings*, 107.

[8]Leroy Birney, "An Exegetical Study of Genesis 6.1–4," *JETS* 13 (1970): 45.

[9]Willem A. VanGemeren, "The Sons of God in Genesis 6.1–4" *WTJ* 43 (1981): 347.

[10]*Hard Sayings*, 107.

[11]See Meredith G. Kline, "Divine Kingship and Genesis 6.1–4," *WTJ* 24 (1961): 187–204.

who rather than administering justice claimed deity for themselves and perverted their mandate to rule the earth under God. Hamilton describes this view: "The sons of God are dynastic rulers, an early royal aristocracy. The daughters of men, whom they took as wives, constituted the royal harems of these despots. The sin, then, is polygamy, along the lines of Lamech, who also 'took wives.' ... The major advantages of this view are that it removes Genesis 6.1–4 from any mythological or nonhistorical understanding; it allows the unit to serve as an appropriate introduction to the flood story; and it attempts to be faithful to the immediately preceding context about Cainites and Sethites" (Hamilton). Further, it "finds historical support in an ancient Jewish interpretation that the 'sons of God' were nobles, aristocrats, and princes who married girls outside their social status and took great numbers of them into their harems. ...This interpretation best explains 'any of them they chose' (6.2). ...It also fits the immediate context of the Flood, the theme of Genesis, and connects the reference to the Nephilim and heroes in 6.4 to 6.1–3" (Waltke).

It also fits the vocabulary used: "'Sons of God' is an early, but typical, reference to the titularies for kings, nobles and aristocrats in the ancient Near Eastern setting. These power-hungry despots not only lusted after power but also were powerfully driven to become 'men of a name' (or 'men of renown'—Gen 6.4). In their thirst for recognition and reputation, they despotically usurped control of the states they governed as if they were accountable to no one but themselves. Thus they perverted the whole concept of the state and the provision that God had made from some immediate amelioration of earth's injustices and inequities (Gen 6.5–6; see also Gen 10.8–12). They also became polygamous, taking and marrying 'any of [the women] they chose' (Gen 6.2)."[12]

While Kaiser and Waltke presume polygamy and coercion to be the sin in question, Mathews suggests that such is not necessary. "The idea of polygamy derived from the phrase 'any of them they chose' is only inferential at best. Also there is no sense that coercion is taking place," since the Hebrew uses the regular word for marriage.

Although this interpretation may appear, at first, to be a stretch, "There is ample evidence for taking *elohim* as human 'judges' in the Old Testament. Psalm 82.1, 6–7 speaks of human rulers as *elohim* (82.6a), and, more importantly, the parallel member (82.6b) refers to them as 'the sons of the Most High' (*bene elyon*), a description analogous to *bene haelohim* in Genesis 6.2. The psalmist, as in Genesis 6.3, stresses the mortality of the judges despite their lofty assignment," and, "Hebrew tradition as well understood that divine rule was carried

---

[12] *Hard Sayings*, 108.

out by appointed (human) magistrates. Related to this is the biblical motif of 'sonship' in Davidic theology" (Mathews).

"[This interpretation] is tenable because [the Cainite tyrants represented by Lamech are] already indicated in chapter 4, the term is consistent with biblical usage and the usage of the entire ancient Middle East, and it fits the context by carrying forward and culminating the theme of human corruption as the basis for the flood."[13]

Of course, this interpretation is not without problem. "The major weakness is that while both within the OT and in other ancient Near Eastern texts individual kings were called God's son, there is no evidence that groups of kings were so styled" (Hamilton). Mathews also acknowledges this, while questioning how this approach satisfies the demands of context: "It fails to square with the contextual requirements since the larger passage does not speak of kingship. Though individual kings were referred to as 'son of God,' no evidence can be marshaled for groups of kings in the ancient Near East bearing the names 'sons of God.'" Waltke also questions this translation: "The meaning 'divine rulers' is somewhat questionable, whereas 'angels' is well established" (Waltke).

4. Waltke and Geisler have instead suggested a hybrid of two views, spiritual beings possessing humans. "Angels... who possessed real human beings, moving them to interbreed with the 'daughters of men,' thus producing a superior breed whose offspring were the 'giants' and 'men of renown.'"[14] "The best solution is to combine the 'angelic' interpretation with the 'divine king' view. The tyrants were demon possessed" (Waltke).

Birney argues against this view: "[The] suggestion that it was angels working through demoniacs does not alleviate the difficulty, for then 'sons of god' is used of demoniacs, which has no parallel in Scripture."[15] This view also fails to escape the primary problem with the angelic view, namely flesh being punished for the sins of spirit.

Other Views
The following viewpoints have also been suggested, but lack sufficient textual evidence to merit discussion.

Beginning with the assumption that this passage is about male gods coupling with mortal women, critical scholars dismiss this passage as myth de-

---

[13]Leroy Birney, "An Exegetical Study of Genesis 6.1–4," *JETS* 13 (1970): 48.

[14]Geisler and Howe, *When Critics Ask,* 40–41.

[15]Leroy Birney, "An Exegetical Study of Genesis 6.1–4," *JETS* 13 (1970): 45.

rived from the Hittite traditions of Asia Minor (see Speiser, Driver, *et al.*). If this work were more focused on the conservative/critical debate among religious academia, this view would warrant further discussion.

Harrison, in arguing against the critical approach offers a surprising suggestion: "To relegate [this passage] to myth...is to preclude immediately the possibility of any rational interpretation of the text, and to miss entirely the invaluable anthropological insights into the interrelation of *homo sapiens* and pre-Adamic species which the passage contains, and which are amenable to those scholars who are equipped to pursue them."[16]

"L. Eslinger (*JSOT* 13 [1979] 65–73) has reversed the identifications, claiming that the Cainites are the 'sons of God' and that the Sethites are the daughters of men, for in 4.19–24 it is Cain's descendant Lamech who is the polygamist and it is the Sethites of chapter 5 who have sons and *daughters*. Furthermore, he notes that the description of the sin of the sons of God, 'they saw...good...took,' echoes Eve's archetypal sin, so that they must be regarded as the sinful line, *i.e.*, the Cainites. Though Eslinger has observed interesting echoes of the fall in Genesis 6.2, he offers no explanation of why the wicked Cainites should be called 'sons of God'" (Wenham).

Summary Remarks

"Suffice it to say, it is impossible to be dogmatic about the identification of the 'sons of God' here. The best one can do is to consider the options. While it may not be comforting to the reader, perhaps it is best to say that the evidence is ambiguous and therefore defies clear-cut identifications and solutions" (Hamilton). And Mathews: "No view escapes criticism. The mysterious identity of the 'sons of God' continues to humble the expositor."

"More important than the detail of this episode is its indication that man is beyond self-help, whether the Sethites have betrayed their calling, or demonic posers have gained a stranglehold" (Kidner). "These disparate views hold an essential tenet in common: the narrative tells how human conduct transgressed divinely established boundaries. Precisely how this occurred is the problem the expositor faces" (Mathews).

Identifying the Nephilim

A key element to understanding the marriage of the sons of God and daughters of men is the identity of the Nephilim. Who—or, perhaps more precisely, *what*—were they? Were they, as Geisler suggests, descendants of the intermarriage of the sons of God and daughters of men? What clues does the meaning of the word afford?

---

[16]R.K. Harrison, *Introduction to the Old Testament*, 557.

Were they giants?

"The Hebrew root (*napal*) means 'to fall' and may suggest their fate (see Ezek 32.20–28). God will not allow any tyrant to oppress and terrorize the land forever" (Waltke). And Mathews: "The Nephilim are considered 'the Fallen Ones.' If so, does this refer to their expulsion from heaven, their death as 'fallen' in battle, or to their moral degeneracy?" Leupold does not follow this approach; instead, he suggests a change in the nature of the fall: "One meaning of this verb is to 'Fall upon, attack' (BDB)... this verb could readily yield this noun in the sense of 'attackers,' 'robbers,' 'bandits'" (Leupold). Most, however, render this to mean that they were the fallen ones, not the ones falling on others.

The translation 'giants' originates in the LXX, *gigantes*. Wenham suggests that this use supports an angelic interpretation, "for in Greek mythology the *gigantes* were the product of the union of earth and heaven." However, "We can attribute [the LXX translation of *gigantes*] most likely to the influence of the later account recorded in Numbers 13.33... Numbers 13.33, however, cannot be used confidently to interpret the meaning of 'Nephilim' in 6.4 because of the passage's own problems. From Numbers 13 we learn that the Anakites are said to be descendants of the Nephilim. If the Nephilim of Numbers 13.33 and Genesis 6.4 are taken as the same group, the verse indicates that the Nephilim and their descendants survived the flood. ...Defining the term on the basis of Numbers 13 may be misleading since the spies were certainly exaggerating ('grasshoppers') the opposition they encountered in Canaan" (Mathews). Also, "It does not follow from Numbers 13.33, even if there the 'attackers' should also happen to have been giants. For 'sons of Anak' means 'sons of the long-necked one,' and this *may* refer to gigantic stature. The unfortunate thing about this mistranslation is that it directs attention away from the moral issue (wicked bandits) and to a physical one (tall stature)" (Leupold). Linking *nephilim* ("to fall") with *gibborim* ("a mighty man of valor, strength, wealth or power.")—both terms in 6.4; *nephilim* in Numbers 13; *gibborim* in Gen 10.8: Nimrod, a *gibbor* who was clearly a king—Kaiser suggests, "The meaning of *nephilim/gibborim* is not 'giants,' but something more like 'princes,' 'aristocrats' or 'great men.'"[17]

Leupold summarizes: "Apparently, [they were] a type of men who were the climax of all such who inspired fear, as the only other passage where the term is used indicates, Numbers 13.33. For there the spies first call all Canaanites 'men of stature,' and then they mention that even 'Nephilim,' sons of Anak, were there. Consequently, we are driven to seek some meaning for the word which makes them awe-inspiring."

---

[17]*Hard Sayings*, 108.

By contrast, some have suggested that the mighty men are not to be identified with the Nephilim: "'The same were mighty men' might point back to the Nephilim; but it is a more natural supposition that it refers to the children born to the sons of God. 'These,' *i.e.,* the sons sprung from those marriages, 'are the heroes, the renowned heroes of old.'" (Keil). And Hamilton: "The translation we have offered understands the Nephilim to be distinct from the mighty men, who alone are the offspring of the union between the sons of God and the daughters of men."

Where did they come from?

"The primary question is whether the Nephilim are the offspring of the marriages or merely their contemporaries. …The primary exegetical challenge is understanding the logical relationship between verse 4 and the preceding verses, since there is no grammatical connection" (Mathews). "Had verse 4 preceded verse 3, the likelihood would have increased that we are to understand the Nephilim as the bastard offspring of this union. But the present order of the verses argues to the contrary" (Hamilton).

Further, "It is worth noting that the giants are not said to have sprung solely from this origin: if some arose in this way *(also after that)*, others existed already *(in those days)*" (Kidner). And Mathews: "The Nephilim are not specifically said to be the offspring of the marital unions. Rather, for the author, establishing the time of the Nephilim's era is prominent: they lived in 'those days'… and they existed 'when' the intermarriages took place and 'also afterward.' This establishes the period of the Nephilim as being before and after the marriages." Keil argues: "To an unprejudiced mind, the words, as they stand, represent the Nephilim, who were on the earth in those days, as existing before the sons of God began to marry the daughters of men, and clearly distinguish them from the fruits of those marriages." Thus, "no particular sin seems to have been attached to their parentage. What was condemned was the violence and corruption that characterized contemporary society (Gen 6.11f)."[18]

"Now if, according to the simple meaning of the passage, the *Nephilim* were in existence at the very time when the sons of God came in to the daughters of men, the appearance of the *Nephilim* cannot afford the slightest evidence that the 'sons of God' were angels, by whom a family of monsters were begotten" (Keil). "Verse 4 is best seen as an identification of those who were especially prominent in the wickedness leading to the corruption and hence the judgment of the earth… not the products of the polygamous marriages, but to their perpetrators."[19] "The presence of the Nephilim, then,

---

[18]H. Van Broekhoven Jr., "Nephilim," *ISBE*, 519.

was another evidence presented by the author to depict the wickedness that marked antediluvian society" (Mathews).

Final Thoughts

While we agree, in principle, with Hamilton that this passage is most likely beyond a dogmatic interpretation, further things may be said here.

The second approach (angels) lacks cohesiveness with the rest of Genesis 6. Appeals to the Nephilim as giants and, thus, proof of the angelic interpretation fails on several levels. Most destructive is that the Nephilim appear before the intermarriage of these two groups. Further, to argue from Numbers 13 that *these* Nephilim must be giants goes beyond the purview of Numbers 13. Finally, to suppose that an intermarriage of angels and humans—should it be conceived possible—would produce giant offspring is merely speculation.

Of the two remaining views, both of which seem to be grammatically and contextually plausible, we are more inclined to follow the traditional approach, not because it is thus, but because it most closely aligns with the context of the previous two chapters—even the entire book of Genesis.

Genesis is a book of separations, beginning with separations on the first three days of creation, followed by the command that man remain separate from the tree of the knowledge of good and evil. After the fall, man, being separated from God, was separated from the tree of life and cast from the garden. In that episode, Eve is told that enmity would exist between her seed and the serpent's seed. The enmity between the righteous and the wicked begins immediately with the murder of Abel, and the exile—the separation—of the wicked and faithless from the line of the Messiah, even to the point of a separate genealogy for the rebellious seed of the serpent. Rather than retaining that sanctification, the seed of the woman married into the line of the serpent's seed. The righteous line was polluted by evil, and wickedness ruled the earth, save Noah and his family.

---

[19]Leroy Birney, "An Exegetical Study of Genesis 6.1–4," *JETS* 13 (1970): 51–52.

7 2–4, *"Seven pairs of all clean animals… to keep their offspring alive on the face of the earth."* Noah is now given further instructions of what to take onto the ark. This is not a contradiction of the previous instruction to take two of every kind, but "in typical Semitic style, the summary injunction to take pairs of animals into the ark is now developed by the more specific injunction to take seven pairs of clean animals" (Waltke).

There is some contention as to whether this means 14 animals or three pairs plus one. Leupold, Keil, and Whitcomb and Morris all lean toward the latter: "The Hebrew expression 'take seven seven' means 'seven each.' …It would be a most clumsy method of trying to say 'fourteen'" (Leupold). In this view, the seventh would be the sacrificial animal of 8.20. However, Waltke argues, "The next phrase 'male and its female' calls [this] interpretation into question." This, however, would argue that the following phrase, *two of every kind of unclean animal, a male and its mate* (NIV) would require four of each. Most translations circumvent this problem by either using *seven* and *two* or *seven pairs* and *one pair*.

In either event, the purpose of the extra clean animals is at once evident: *to keep their offspring alive on the face of all the earth* (v 4). Following the flood, God would sanction the eating of animals (9.2–3). For this, and the sacrificial practices of God's people, there needed to be a larger population of clean animals than unclean.

This passage also serves as the one-week warning of the impending flood.

7.5, *And Noah did all that the LORD had commanded him.* Noah's obedience, as it was in 6.22, is highlighted in that he obeyed every detail of God's command. The details of his obedience are spelled out more clearly in verses 6–10.

7.11, *The fountains of the great deep burst forth, and the windows of the heavens were opened.* This is a poetic description "suggesting water gushing forth uncontrollably from wells and springs which draw from a great subterranean ocean ('the great deep') and an unrestrained downpour from the sky" (Wenham). "The expressions are deliberately evocative of chapter 1: the waters above and below the firmament are, in token, merged again, as if to reverse the very work of creation and bring back the featureless waste of waters" (Kidner). "The flood un-creates, and returns the earth to a pre-creation period when there was only 'waters'" (Hamilton). "The surge of waters from the great deep below and from the heavens above is, of course, a striking reversal of the second day of creation, when a vault was erected to divide the waters above from the waters below" (Alter).

Some have sought to justify a canopy theory from this verse. Prior to the flood, they argue, *the waters that were above the expanse* remained outside the atmosphere; here, the *windows of heaven were opened* and that water fell to the earth. This theory encounters a substantial obstacle when the *waters above the heavens* are called to praise God long after the flood (Psa 148.4). Appeals have been made to 2 Peter 3.5—*the heavens of old*—to support a postdiluvian change of atmosphere. While Peter does support a remaking of the earth, his writing is not intended to be a scientific treatise on pre- and postdiluvian atmospheric conditions. Further, a careful reading shows that Peter's point was not to talk about the nature of the heavens in ancient days, but that the heavens were ancient. Ultimately, we conclude that *the windows of heaven were opened* is simply a figure of speech to indicate a torrential downpour of rain.

7.13, And Noah's wife and the three wives of his sons with them. Kidner notes: "In spite of the early example of Lamech (4.19) and the general moral decline, Noah and his sons were monogamous: the family numbered eight in all (1 Pet 3.20). Among the godly the first mention of polygamy is in the story of Abraham."

7.16, And the Lord shut him in. That God shut him in the ark does not necessarily indicate that He physically closed the door, though such is certainly possible. The significance, rather, is that it was God's seal which kept them safe from the floodwaters. It is this action that "initiates His protective care over the vessel… [signaling] the divine protection that kept out the raging seas" (Mathews). It was not the structural integrity of the ark which kept them safe through the flood, it was that God shut them in.

7.19, And the waters prevailed so mightily on the earth that all the high mountains under the whole heaven were covered. This is where all theories of a localized flood must fall by the wayside. Though Kidner would argue otherwise, we follow Mathews: "There can be no dispute that the narrative depicts the flood in the language of a universal deluge." If water seeks its own level, and the tops of the highest mountains were covered, it becomes at once clear that Moses' wrote of a flood that covered the whole earth. Kaiser summarizes well: "The flood was extensive enough to wipe all living humans on earth except the eight persons who were on board the ark. ...That is the main point of the biblical narrative and the one nonnegotiable argument in the whole discussion."[1] [2]

7.20, Fifteen cubits. This is probably an approximation of how deeply covered the mountains were. The draught of a vessel this size would be half its height (*i.e.*, 30 cubits; 6.15). Thus, "The mountains are submerged to depth... sufficient to keep the ark from grounding" (Waltke). Psalm 104.8 seems to speak of God raising new mountains after the flood, which may indicate that the peaks before the flood were not as high as those which are on the earth now.[3] We are, however, wary of ascribing scientific detail to a poetic passage.

7.21, All flesh died. This is the ultimate result of the flood: the ending of all life that was not on the ark. The flood was an absolute, complete judgment on the people. Later, the flood is seen as a type of the final judgment (Matt 24.37; 2 Pet 3.5–7).

7.17, 24 The flood continued forty days on the earth... the waters prevailed on the earth 150 days. The former refers to the length of the primary deluge of rain,[4] the latter to the waters being at their peak. From this point forward— *i.e., God remembered Noah*, (8.1)—the waters begin to recede (*cf.* 8.3).

Growth of the Seed: Noah obeys God and is saved from destruction; the Messianic line continues.

---

[1]*Hard Sayings*, 112.

[2]Of all the opposing theories, perhaps the most interesting (yet not particularly convincing) is that the flood was a local event which occurred in the Mediterranean basin when it was a desiccated desert, see Glenn Morton, "The Mediterranean Flood, *Perspectives on Science and Christian Faith*, 49 (1997): 238–250.

[3]See Bert Thompson, *The Global Flood of Noah*, 42.

[4]Apparently, the rain continued in some form, *cf.* 8.3.

8 1, *But God remembered Noah.* Certainly this does not mean that God had previously forgotten about him. "When the Old Testament says that *God remembered,* it combines the ideas of faithful love (*cf.* Jer 2.2; 31.20) and timely intervention: God's remembering always implies His movement towards the object of His memory" (Kidner). It is "covenant language, designating covenant fidelity" (Mathews) (*cf.* 9.14–15). The Hebrew term "signifies to act upon a previous commitment to a covenant partner" (Waltke).[1] The point is that "when all appears helpless, God intervenes to prevent tragedy" (Hamilton).

The result of God's remembrance of Noah is threefold: God caused a wind to blow on the earth; the fountains of the deep were stopped; the windows of heaven were closed and the rain from heaven restrained. "The ending of the Flood precisely echoes the terms in which its beginning was represented, in the same order" (Alter).

8.4, *The mountains of Ararat.* This refers to the mountain range in what is now eastern Turkey, not a particular mountain. "The reference is too imprecise to specify the mountains, suggesting that the narrator himself is uncertain" (Waltke).

8.7–8, *Raven… dove.* The raven went to and fro until the waters dried up; the dove found no place to rest her foot, and returned to Noah. The answer to the begged question—*i.e.,* what place the raven found to rest her foot— is answered upon the realization that the raven is a carrion eater. Further, it is a stronger bird which can fly for longer periods of time (Waltke). Thus, the raven is useless in telling Noah anything about the receding waters. "The foremost significance of the raven is its symbolic value as an 'unclean' bird, unfit for consumption" (Mathews).

The dove was sent with a commission: *to see if the waters had subsided from the face of the ground.* But she finds no place to land and continues to return until the water has receded. After a week, the dove is sent again and it returns with the first testimony to life: a freshly plucked olive leaf (v 11). The earth was once again producing life, but it was not yet dry enough on the earth for the dove to stay (v 12). After another week, the dove was sent again and it did not return.

---

[1]Waltke references the following passages on this point: 9.14–15; 19.29; 30.22; Exod 2.24; 6.5; 32.13; 1 Sam 1.19; Judg 16.28; Job 14.13; Psa 8.4; 9.12; 74.1–3; 98.3; 105.8; 106.45; 111.5; Jer 15.15.

8.9, He put out his hand and took her and brought her into the ark with him. Waltke notes: "The narrative speed, which has been racing through weeks in one verse, slows dramatically to focus on this one brief event. This series of verbs provides a cameo of Noah. He has the heart of a conservationist (see Prov 12.10), modeling God's concern to preserve the creation. Skinner says, 'The description of the return and admission of the dove is unsurpassed... for tenderness and beauty.'"

8.11, A freshly plucked olive leaf. There is life on the earth; plants are growing again.

8.13–14, The ground was dry... the earth had dried out. The translations obscure that the Hebrew words for *dry* and *dried* are not the same word. The implication may be that though there was no longer standing water, the earth was not yet dry. Alter points to two instances where these verbs are used in temporal sequence (Isa 19.5; Job 14.11; *i.e.*, as opposed to poetic parallelism, where they are also found together), commenting, "First a water source dries up *(harev)*, then it is in a state of complete dryness *(yavesh)*." And Waltke: "Even after Noah sees that the earth has dried out... he waits patiently almost another two months until it is completely dry... waiting for the divine word that it is safe to disembark."

8.17, "Bring out with you every living thing... and be fruitful and multiply." To be simple, Noah is told to unload and refill. These final verses closely parallel 7.1–4, with the flood being book-ended by divine commands to Noah. His obedience to God is to the point of waiting for God's instruction to both enter and exit the ark. They also leave with the commission to refill the earth. "The commands given originally just to the fish and the birds (1.20, 22) are here extended to all the land animals, one of many hints in this story that the post-flood era represents the start of a new creation" (Wenham).

8.20, Built an altar to the LORD... burnt offerings. The offering that Noah made had at least two purposes. First, it served as an offering of thanksgiving that God had kept Noah safe—that He had closed the doors of the ark—through the flood. Second, and perhaps an indirect purpose, it served as a propitiation offering to God. This can be clearly seen as a result of the offering: *When the LORD smelled the pleasing aroma, the LORD said... "I will never again curse the ground."*

8.21, The Lord said in his heart. This phrase simply means that He said it to Himself (as opposed to saying it to Noah). As Alter notes, this specific terminology "pointedly echoes 6.6... [and] 6.5. The Flood story is thus enclosed by mutually mirroring reports of God's musing on human nature." God resolves to never again curse His creation on account of man or strike down all life; rather the normal cycle of events will continue as long as the earth exists.

Growth of the Seed: God establishes a covenant with creation (vv 21–22).

Seven Progressive Phases of Creation and Re-Creation

Seven progressive phases of renewing creation parallel the progression of creation during the first week.[2]

Phase 1: Precreation. Just as God's Spirit hovered over the abyss (1.2), God sends a wind over the engulfing waters to renew the earth.
  1.2, "earth," "deep," "Spirit" (*ruah*), "waters"
  8.1b–2, "wind" (*ruah*), "earth," "waters," "deep"

Phase 2: Second Day. Just as God initially divided the waters (1.6–7), God regathers the waters, reestablishing the boundaries between sky and earth.
  1.6–8, "waters," "sky"
  8.2b, "sky"

Phase 3: Third Day. Just as God separated the dry, arable ground from the water to sustain vegetation, so again, the dry ground emerges in successful stages.
  1.9, "water," "dry ground," "appear"
  8.3–5, "water," "tops of the mountains," "appear"

Phase 4: Fifth Day. The sky once again houses the winged creatures, as God first proclaimed it so to be.
  1.20–23, "birds," "above [*'al*] the ground"
  8.6–12, "raven," "dove," "from [*me'al*]... the ground"

---

[2] This entire section is taken from Waltke.

Phase 5: Sixth Day. The living creatures of sky and land are called out from the ark, as in their first creative calling from the voice of God.

1.24–25, "creatures," "livestock," "creatures that move along the ground," "wild animals"

8.17–19, "creature," "birds," "animals," "creatures that move along the ground"

Phase 6. The reappearance of the nuclear family, all of whom bear God's image, as the heads and sole representatives of the human race functions as a reprise of the creation of *adam*, male and female in God's image.

1.26–28, "man," "image of God," "male and female"

8.16, 18, Noah and his wife

9.6, "man," "image of God"

Phase 7. The heavenly King graciously grants His blessing on humanity, feeds them with the fruit of the restored earth, and, renewing the cultural mandate, restores them as lords over the creation.

1.28, "blessed," "be fruitful," "increase in number," "fill the earth," "rule…every living creature"

9.1–2 (see also 8.17), "blessed," "be fruitful," "increase in number," "fill the earth," "fear…of you…upon every creature"

9 *1, And God blessed Noah and his sons.* Following God's declaration to Himself of His future plans, He blesses Noah in the same way that He originally blessed the first couple: be fruitful and fill the earth. Included in this blessing was that God would put the fear of man in animals. "This appears remarkably different from the relationship that the first man and woman enjoyed in the garden with their animal residents (2.19–20)" (Mathews). Also, all animals would now be given to man for food. Certainly this does not necessarily imply that no animals were eaten prior to the flood—but if such was done, it was done without God's approval.

No distinction is made at this point between eating the clean and unclean—here *every moving thing* was given to them for food. Presumably, animals that die on their own are forbidden. The distinction between clean and unclean understood by the patriarchs must have been for the purposes of sacrifice only, and only in the time of Moses were the dietary restrictions added.

9.4, "But you shall not eat flesh with… its blood." Leviticus 17.11 also informs that the life is in the blood. Even a beast's life is a thing created by God. "Animal life, though given to humanity for sustenance, remained valuable in the eyes of God as a living creature and therefore merited proper care, not wanton abuse" (Mathews). The blood in which this life resides should be respectfully treated, not devoured. Further, the blood would play a special part in Mosaic sacrifices. It is probable that this command was a preparation for that sacrificial use of the blood.

9.5, "For your lifeblood I will require a reckoning." All life will be accounted for by God—both beast and man. The repetition of this phrase emphasizes the significance God places on this accounting. And this accounting signifies an exact compensation.

"By man his blood shall be shed." God allows man to be the avenger of blood. This is a foundational principle which runs even into the New Testament (*cf.* Rom 13.1–5). "If God… would no more bring an exterminating judgment upon the earthly creation, it was necessary that by commands and authorities He should erect a barrier against the supremacy of evil, and thus lay the foundation for a well-ordered civil development of humanity" (Keil). And Waltke: "Animal blood may be shed for food, but human blood may not be shed at all, except to compensate for homicide."

"[But] you, be fruitful and multiply." This is not merely a repetition of

the command, but a contrast between God's judgment of murder (vv 5–6) and God's desire for man.

9.9, 11, "I establish my covenant with you." God reveals to man His decision made in 8.21–22, and establishes a covenant stating thus. The covenant was with all mankind—both Noah and his offspring—and for every beast of the earth. "Any idea that a covenant is basically a bargain is forestalled by such an opening to the series. At the same time, the absence of any obligations laid on the recipients makes this an extreme example" (Kidner). And McGuiggan: "The covenant is simply the instrument through which the two 'persons' enter into fellowship. God doesn't want Noah and his descendants to be related to a covenant, He wants them in fellowship with *Him*."[1]

9.13, "I have set my bow in the cloud." The rainbow would serve as a sign of this covenant, to remind God of His covenant with man.[2] "Furthermore, the rainbow may contain an implicit curse that God takes on Himself. The Hebrew word for rainbow used is the same as the word for bow, a weapon. Taken in this sense, God hangs His bow up and its upward direction, pointing at God, may signify that God is saying that He will keep the covenant on the pain of death. Of course, God can't die, and that is precisely the point. He can't break the covenant either."[3]

"From these words certain eminent theologians have been induced to deny that there was any rainbow before the deluge: which is frivolous. For the words of Moses do not signify, that a bow was then formed, which did not previously exist; but that a mark was engraven upon it, which should give a sign of the divine favor towards man" (Calvin qtd. in Wenham). Calvin's suggestion to a prior existence of the rainbow fits with our take on the flood—this event did not change anything meteorologically (no prior rain to the flood) or atmospherically (no 'canopy' existed prior to the flood). Unless God changed the laws of physics and light at this point, it is safe to assume that the rainbow was already in existence, but this added a new significance to it, another pattern we have already seen (*cf.* 3.14–19).

---

[1] Jim McGuiggan, *Genesis and Us,* 80.

[2] On God remembering, see comment on 8.1.

[3] Tremper Longman III, *How to Read Genesis,* 119.

9.15, "I will remember." See comment on 8.1.

9.16, "I will see it." Waltke comments: "This stands in contrast to the evil God 'saw' in 6.12. The transcendent God, who humbles Himself to involve Himself with people, deliberately chooses to reflect on this colorful vision rather than humanity's evil."

9.19, These three were the sons of Noah, and from these people of the whole earth were dispersed. The ESV footnote more clearly renders the sense of the verse: *from these the whole earth was populated.* God blesses them and makes them fruitful as He uses them to repopulate the planet.

9.21–22, He drank of the wine and became drunk. ...And Ham, the father of Canaan, saw the nakedness of his father and told his two brothers outside. This is far from the only place in Scripture where we see an otherwise great man of faith exercising terribly poor judgment. Such instances should give us hope when we fall from the mountaintops of faith into the folly of sin.

Noah's sin was drunkenness. But his sin was quickly eclipsed by that of his son. Precisely what Ham did is of some debate. Kidner suggests that Ham's transgression was merely an act of disrespect toward his father—a transgression of what would later become the fifth commandment. Keil also: "Not content with finding pleasure himself in his father's shame, he just proclaimed his disgraceful pleasure to his brethren, and thus exhibited his shameless sensuality." Leupold adds a little more to this line of thought by saying that the expression used "is not a mere harmless and accidental 'and he saw,' but 'he looked at' (BDB) or 'he gazed with satisfaction.' ...Similarly, *wayyaggedh* is not a mere 'and he told,' though we know of no other way of translating it. The circumstances suggest that it means: 'and he told with delight.'"

How does such an explanation handle the declaration that *Noah... knew what his youngest son had done to him?* Translations vary, and many understand this not to be an immediate knowledge of what he had done, but something that he became aware of (perhaps Shem and Japheth told Noah later). Or perhaps Noah was aware enough to know his condition when he went to sleep—unclothed and uncovered—and waking up covered was enough. In any event, Hamilton writes: "It is unwarranted to press the verb *had done...* to mean some physical act or abuse."

The problem with any other interpretation is that it requires too much reading between the lines—or, in reality, adding to them. Suggestions have ranged from various sorts of homosexual acts to castration, though none are clearly supported by the text. Further, while *saw the nakedness* can be used as a euphemism for some sort of sexual act, Mathews notes that the expressions *to see nakedness* and *to uncover nakedness* are used of heterosexual actions. This cannot be interpreted on the basis of Reuben's *going up onto his father's bed* (35.22; 49.4), as the transgression involved Noah, not his wife.

9.25, "Cursed be Canaan." One must immediately ask why the brunt of Noah's curse fell upon Ham's son when Ham was the offender. Kaiser suggests: "Noah could not have cursed his son, for he and his brothers, along with Noah, had been the objects of a blessing in Genesis 9.1. Neither Noah nor anyone else could reverse [God's] blessing with a curse. Balaam the son of Beor learned this the hard way in Numbers 22–24."[4] Waltke adds, "As the youngest son wrongs his father, so the curse will fall on his youngest son, who presumably inherits his moral decadence. ... Noah's righteousness is reproduced in Shem and Japheth, his immorality in Ham. The hubris of Ham against his father will be worked out in his descendants, and the modesty of Shem and Japheth in theirs." Finally, Kidner sees in this curse an emphasis on the family relationship: "For his breach of the family, his own family would falter."

Although we would not argue that a sin is genetically passed along, sexual deviation was the norm among the Canaanites: "The Canaanites were notoriously deviant in their sexual behavior. Almost everywhere the archaeologist's spade has dug in that part of the world there have been fertility symbols accompanying texts explicit enough to make many a modern pornographic dealer seem a mere beginner in the trade of deviant sexuality. Sodom left its name for the vice these people practiced. Even the Romans, so depraved in their own practices, were shocked by the behavior of the Phoenicians at the colony of Carthage (the last vestige of the Canaanite race)."[5]

While these suggestions are helpful, it is clear that we do not know pre-

---

[4]*Hard Sayings*, 117.

[5]*Ibid.*, 117–118.

cisely why Canaan was cursed rather than Ham. The significance of the curse is the end result: *and let Canaan be his servant*—the native people of the Promised Land would serve the people of God. The seed of Woman would, for a little while, have an upper hand on the seed of the serpent.

Because Ham's descendants populated Africa, many have sought justification for the African slave trade from this passage. However, as Leupold points out, *"Ham* is not cursed, no matter how freely proslavery men may have employed this text." And Kaiser: "We're not talking about Africans or blacks, but the Canaanite peoples who inhabited ancient Palestine."[6] "Since it confines the curse to this one branch within the Hamites, those who reckon the Hamitic peoples in general to be doomed to inferiority have therefore misread the Old Testament as well as the New. It is likely, too, that the subjugation of the Canaanites to Israel fulfilled the oracle sufficiently" (Kidner).

Growth of the Seed: God gives the first 'sign of the covenant' (v 12); Ham is (possibly) rejected from the Messianic line due to his wickedness (vv 20–27).

---

[6]*Ibid.,* 117.

From the Flood to Abraham

The period of time between the flood and the establishment of the Abrahamic covenant passes in relative silence. Only one event of note occurs in this time, with most of the narrative describing how Noah's descendants filled the earth.[1]

10 Interestingly, sevens dominate the table of nations. Dorsey notes that the list traces through the descendants of Noah's seven grandsons; Japheth's genealogy lists seven sons and seven grandsons; Ham's genealogy lists seven descendants of Cush, seven cities controlled by Nimrod, and Egypt's seven son's; the entire list includes seventy nations that descended from Noah's three sons.[2] Unfortunately, no one is quite sure what to make of this particular phenomenon, though it may simply be a device to aid in memorization. A more symbolic interpretation would be that it was Moses' way of saying that, by God's blessing, Noah's sons perfectly filled the earth.

10.1, 32, These are the generations of the sons of Noah, Shem, Ham, and Japheth. ... These are the clans of Noah, according to their genealogies, in their nations, and from these nations spread abroad on the earth after the flood. In this table of nations, we learn how Noah's sons spread across the earth.

---

[1] Our comments here will be brief, and statements about the geography of the descendants of Noah's sons are largely generalizations. For a further description of how these people populated the earth, see Waltke. Also, *Baker's Bible Atlas* devotes a chapter to this matter, including a map that more specifically shows how the area surrounding Palestine and the Fertile Crescent were populated.

[2] David A. Dorsey, *The Literary Structure of the Old Testament*, 53.

10.2, The Sons of Japheth: Gomer, Magog, Madai, Javan, Tubal, Meshech, and Tiras. Some of the more well known descendants of Japheth include the Medes (through *Madai)* and the Greeks (*Javan* is the Hebrew name for the Ionians). In general, the sons of Japheth moved westward and populated Asia Minor and what became Europe.

10.6, The Sons of Ham: Cush, Egypt, Put, and Canaan. Cush became synonymous with Ethiopia and Nubia. Egypt is well known to all; from Egypt, the Philistines arose. From Canaan came a list of nations which is often repeated in Numbers and Joshua: Jebusites, Amorites, Hivites, *etc.* Also, from Canaan came Sidon. All of these names become familiar foes of the people of God.

The offspring of Ham followed the offspring of Cain in city-building. Nimrod was behind the building of Babel (Babylon) and Nineveh—the capitals of the two nations which would eventually take the people of Israel captive. Although it only appears as subtext, we can see the continuing war between the seed of woman and the seed of the serpent brewing.

10.22, The sons of Shem: Elam, Asshur, Arpachshad, Lud, and Aram. While the sons of Japheth moved westward and the Hamites moved southward, the Semites spread throughout the Mesopotamian region. In addition to those names listed, other familiar neighbors of the Israelites came from the Semitic line. Through Lot came the Moabites and the Ammonites (19.36). From Ishmael, the Arabs (25.12–18). From Keturah, the Midianites (25.1–4). And from Isaac, the Edomites (36.9) and the Israelites. It is, of course, this last group which makes the Semitic line of special interest to our author. Of the three groups, it is only the Semitic line which receives a full genealogical treatment (11.10–26).

10.25, The name of one was Peleg, for in his days the earth was divided. Clearly this is a reference to the Babel incident. From the ages and years given in chapter 11, we learn that this happened roughly 100 years after the flood.[3] Peleg also stands out because it was through him that the Messianic line continued (*cf.* 11.18).

Growth of the Seed: The earth is refilled; the Messianic line continues through Shem.

---

[3]This must remain an approximation as geneaologies often skip generations. See EXCURSUS C.

11 **2, *The land of Shinar.*** A comparison with Isaiah 11.11 and Zechariah 5.11 places this in the land where the city of Babylon (Babel) would grow up.[1] There is no certain answer to the question of when this happened, since the numbers in genealogies aren't recorded for the purpose of calculating dates;[2] however, if we understand Peleg's name to indicate the time he lived, we can be fairly sure that this event was at least 100 years after the flood.

11.4, "*Let us make a name for ourselves.*" Their stated purpose was not what we have so often heard—to get to heaven—but renown and unity. This movement was based on striving for pride and seeking to show the earth their greatness. Note also that their pride was not just in building the tower, but also in building the city[3] "*lest we be dispersed over the face of the whole earth.*" "Unity in thought, word, and action may be a worthy goal. But what is the focus of that unity? ...The people did not consult God about building the city. They did not seek God first."[4] Because they left the Lord out of their plans, the Lord thwarted their work. From this point on, Babylon becomes the symbol of the pride and arrogance of man arrayed against God.[5] Plans that are not God-focused—to modern readers: *freedom* that is not God-focused—will invariably lead to rebellion of the worst kind.

If the flood is the new creation, then Babel is the new tree of knowledge, as this passage "mirrors the attempt of humanity in the garden to achieve power independently of God. The attempt of the Babelites to transgress human limits is reminiscent of Eve's ambition (3.5–6). ...Broadly speaking, the setting is the same since the garden's Tigris and Euphrates Rivers (2.14) are in the same region as the 'plain of Shinar.' ...Genesis 1–11 then has come full circle from 'Eden' to 'Babel,' both remembered for the expulsion of their residents" (Mathews).

The great irony is one found throughout Scripture. People do some-

---

[1] *Babylon* is the form the name took in the Greek language where it transliterates the plural *babilani*, and is used in the Greek New Testament and most English translations of the Old. But the Hebrew term is always *babel*, Phil Roberts, "City of God," *The Gospel in the Old Testament: Florida College Annual Lectures*, 252.

[2] See Excursus C.

[3] Phil Roberts, "City of God," *The Gospel in the Old Testament: Florida College Annual Lectures*, 233.

[4] Paula Parker, "Between Text and Sermon: Genesis 11.1–9," *Interpretation* 54 (2000): 58.

[5] Phil Roberts, "City of God," *The Gospel in the Old Testament: Florida College Annual Lectures*, 234.

thing against or without God to avoid something else that ultimately comes to fruition because of what they did to avoid it.[6] The people desired to do something great so they would not be separated. Yet, it was this plan which led to their separation. "Building walled cities and towers to heaven does not create unity. Unity is connection to God and to each other through the Holy Spirit in the language of prayer and proclamation. ...God has never permitted humankind to realize a lasting social order from which God is excluded, nor will God ever do so. Unity cannot be captured and contained."[7]

11.6, "And nothing... will be impossible for them." This does not indicate that they could do *anything* and even God would not be able to stop them; rather, as God had just said, *"This is only the beginning of what they will do."* Because of their unity, there will be no roadblocks to what they desire—they can do anything they put their mind to. The only other place this verb *(to be impossible)* is used is in Job 42.2 and speaks of God. Only God may plan without limit. And man is not to emulate his creator in this way (Wenham). Waltke understands this statement to clarify that man's sin in building the tower is the refusal to live within God-given boundaries. "There is no sin as deadly as successful sin! What a blessing it is that God will not always let us succeed in our wickedness."[8]

And so God confused their languages and dispersed them all over the face of the earth. God had told them to fill the earth; here, He provides the motivation to do so. This may be analogous to the early church remaining in Jerusalem until persecution drove them to carry out Jesus' commission (Acts 8.1, 4).

The confusion of the languages is eventually reversed. Its reversal is seen in part on the day of Pentecost when, filled with the Holy Spirit, the apostles preach to all the languages in their various tongues (Acts 2.5–7). Ultimately, it will find its reversal in heaven.

11.7, "Let us." See comment on 1.26.

---

[6]For example, the Jews sought to kill Jesus so the Romans would not invade and destroy the city (John 11.48). Yet, if there was one event that sealed their fate and guaranteed their destruction, it was the rejection of God's Messiah.

[7]Paula Parker, "Between Text and Sermon: Genesis 11.1–9," *Interpretation* 54 (2000): 58–59.

[8]Jim McGuiggan, *Genesis and Us*, 92.

11.8, *The* LORD *dispersed them from there over the face of all the earth.* Waltke notes: "In spite of their rebellion, the Sovereign fulfills His design that people fill the earth" (*cf.* 9.19).

11.9, *Therefore its name was called Babel, because there the* LORD *confused the language of all the earth.* It is interesting that the Hebrew word for confusion is not *babel*, but *balal*. Babel means *gate of God*. It is this definition, coupled with their desire to build a tower whose *top is in the heavens*—with *heavens* misunderstood to mean God's dwelling place—that we get the teaching that their desire was to build a tower to God. "But God did not see either their tower or their city as a gateway to Himself."[9]

But if Babel does not mean confusion or anything like it, how does the author expect that we understand his description? "It seems probable... that the narrator of Genesis 11.9 is indulging in a play on words, a verbal irony, or else relating a folk etymology, rather than attempting a serious etymology of the name"[10]—a derisive play on the name, Roberts suggests.[11] Interestingly, the modern word "babble" (or a word like it) appears in a wide spectrum of languages from Greek, Latin and Sanskrit to Norwegian (Alter).

Notice also the monotheism taught. "It is not the local deities but Yahweh who controls the vicissitudes of Mesopotamian history."[12]

Structure of the Tower

It is often suggested that this tower was a *ziggurat:* a tower of successively smaller platforms so that the whole resembles a stepped pyramid. A ziggurat was also a temple tower, an artificial mountain with a temple to some deity at the top.[13] If this is the case, "The construction would have been displeasing to God, either because some sort of polytheism was in-

---

[9]Phil Roberts, "City of God," *The Gospel in the Old Testament: Florida College Annual Lectures,* 234–235.

[10]J. Barton Payne, "Tower of Babel," *ISBE,* 382.

[11]Phil Roberts, "City of God," *The Gospel in the Old Testament: Florida College Annual Lectures,* 253.

[12]J. Barton Payne, "Tower of Babel," *ISBE,* 382.

[13]A more detailed description of the *ziggurat* is offered by Harrison: "The *ziggurat* consisted of a low hill or mound, formed artificially by the accumulation of clay and debris, on which stood a religious shrine. The term *ziggurat* actually describes the tiered or staged towers that comprised the temples built on these mounds, but is often used in a wider sense to include the mound also. This type of construction reflected the desire of the builders to safeguard the temples of their patron deities from inundation when sudden floods threatened the community." *Old Testament Times,* 38.

volved, or because man actually believed he could build right up to the heavenly abode of deity."[14]

However, despite assertions such as DeWitt's that "All modern students of Genesis agree that the tower of Genesis 11 is the Mesopotamian ziggurat,"[15] this is not the case. The Hebrew term used of the tower *(migdol)* is usually used of a military tower or of a fortress, and not of a temple structure.[16] Waltke's solution to this semantic problem is tenable, though not absolute: "Here with reference to Mesopotamia, which did not have the defensive stone watch towers of Canaan, it designates the Mesopotamian ziggurat."

Literary Structure of the Narrative

The book of Genesis is not only a historical work, but a literary masterpiece. Genesis 11.1–9 is an excellent illustration of the pervasive and profound literary artistry of the book of Genesis.[17]

There are several word plays in this story. First, several of the words used are bound together by their similar sound: "let us make bricks" *(nilbenah lebenim),* "bake them thoroughly" *(nisrefah lisrefah);* "tar" and "mortar" *(hemar* and *homer).* Also, there is alliteration between "brick" *(lebehan)* and "for stone" *(le'aben).* Other repeated words sound alike: "the place" *(sham)* is what the rebels use as a base for storming "heaven" *(shamayim)* in order to get a "name" *(shem)* for themselves. But God reverses the situation because it is "from there" *(misham)* that He disperses them.

Indeed, the literary structure of this account is emphatic that this is a story of reversal. "Fokkelman lists the numerous words and phrases that appear in the story with the consonant cluster *lbn,* all referring to the human rebellion against God. When God comes in judgment, He confuses *(nbl)* their language. The reversal of the consonants shows the reversal that God's judgment effected in the plans of the rebels."[18] And the reversal is also shown in Fokkelman's analysis of the chiastic structure of the story.

---

[14]Phil Roberts, "City of God," *The Gospel in the Old Testament: Florida College Annual Lectures,* 252.

[15]Dale S. DeWitt, "The Historical Background of Genesis 11.1–9: Babel or Ur?" *JETS* 22 (1979): 20.

[16]Phil Roberts, "City of God," *The Gospel in the Old Testament: Florida College Annual Lectures,* 252.

[17]The following literary analysis is taken from Fokkelman *via* Longman's *How to Read Genesis* (119–121) and is found in most modern commentaries of Genesis.

[18]Tremper Longman III, *How to Read Genesis,* 120.

A   11.1 (unity of language)
  B   11.2 (unity of place)
    C   11.3a (intensive communication)
      D   11.3b (plans and inventions)
        E   11.4a (building)
          F   11.4b (city and tower)
            X   11.5a (God's Intervention)
          F'   11.5b (city and tower)
        E'   11.5c (building)
      D'   11.6 (counter plans and inventions)
    C'   11.7 (communication disrupted)
  B'   11.8 (disruption of place)
A'   11.9 (disruption of language)

"Unity of language (A) and place (B) and intensive communication (C) induce the men to make plans and inventions (D), especially to building (E) a city and a tower (F). God's intervention is the turning point. He watches the buildings (F') people make (E') and launches a counter plan (D') because of which communication becomes impossible (C') and the unity of place (B') and language (A') is broken. [This] shows on a small scale what is true on a large scale: Genesis is an artfully constructed piece of literature."[19]

11.10–26, These are the generations of Shem. Here, the line of Shem—the line of the Messiah—receives a more full treatment. This genealogy is parallel to the genealogy in chapter five in that it is a list of ten names, ending with a man who had three sons. In both instances the son listed first is not the oldest, but the most prominent of the three: the one who carries the Messianic blessing.

Growth of the Seed: The Messianic line continues through Shem.

---

[19]*Ibid.*, 120–121.

Abraham

Having spent just eleven chapters covering hundreds, if not thousands, of years of history, the narrative "slows nearly to a halt. The next ten chapters trace events that occurred during a brief twenty-five-year period in the life of a single individual, Abraham."[1] And the remainder of the book of Genesis will cover only three more generations.

Abraham, as we shall see, is not without faults in his life. The inclusion of these faults in his history goes a long way toward comforting those who feel like they could never live up to a faith like his when God calls them. Not only are his faults instructive to us, but they were instructive to him as well. It was the constant honing of character—the lessons learned in his mistakes—that led Abraham to be the great man of faith who stood at Moriah with his knife raised in the air, ready to strike the promised seed without further question.

Ultimately, Abraham becomes the quintessential model of faith. "The writer of Hebrews... normally devotes one verse to each [hero of faith]; to Moses he devotes six. However, to Abraham the author gives a full twelve verses (Heb 11.8–19). Abraham and the other heroes of faith in Genesis—Isaac, Jacob, Joseph and Judah—are the holy root from which the Lord Jesus Christ sprouts and of the tree into which the Gentiles have been grafted (Rom 11.17–21). Abraham is the father of all who believe (Rom 4.16–17)" (Waltke).

---

[1] David A. Dorsey, *The Literary Structure of the Old Testament*, 56.

Historically speaking, Abraham was as real as they come: "His actions are set against a well-authenticated background of non-biblical material, making him a true son of his age who bore the same name and traversed the same general territory, as well as living in the same towns as his contemporaries. He is in every sense a genuine Middle Bronze Age person, and not a retrojection of later Israelite historical thought, as used to be imagined."[2] Further, "Some of the place names that survived in the area of the Balikh River appear to have originated with the ancestors of Abraham. The cities of Serug, Terah, and Nahor were all located in the vicinity of Haran, and the Mari letters mention the city of Nahor, the home of Rebekah, quite often, speaking of it as Nakhur, a flourishing locality where some of the Habiru lived."[3]

---

[2] R.K. Harrison, "Abraham," *ISBE,* 17.

[3] R.K. Harrison, *Old Testament Times,* 72. Harrison earlier identifies the Habiru as the people from whom the Hebrews come. See *ibid.,* 66.

Structure and Pattern in Genesis
The Abraham Cycle: Concentric Pattern

A   Genealogy of Terah (11.27–32)

   B   Promise of a son and start of Abraham's spiritual odyssey (12.1–9)

      C   Abraham lies about Sarah; the Lord protects her in foreign palace (12.10–20)[4]

         D   Lot settles in Sodom (13.1–18)

            E   Abraham intercedes for Sodom and Lot militarily (14.1–24)

               F   Covenant with Abraham; annunciation of Ishmael (15.1–16.16)

               F'   Covenant with Abraham; annunciation of Isaac (17.1–18.15)

            E'   Abraham intercedes for Sodom and Lot in prayer (18.16–33)

         D'   Lot flees doomed Sodom and settles in Moab (19.1–38)

      C'   Abraham lies about Sarah; God protects her in foreign palace (20.1–18)

   B'   Birth of son and climax of Abraham's spiritual odyssey (21.1–22.19)

A'   Genealogy of Nahor (22.20–24)

11.27, Terah fathered Abram, Nahor, and Haran. We follow the position that Abram is listed first because of prominence rather than primogeniture. "Lest one dismiss this... approach as artificial and rationalistic harmonization, observe that the immediately preceding chapters of Genesis provide a parallel to sons being listed in an order unrelated to their age. Genesis 5.32 lists the three sons of Noah in this sequence: **(1)** Shem, **(2)** Ham, **(3)** Japheth. But this cannot be the order of their birth, for 9.24 identifies Ham as the youngest son of Noah" (Hamilton).

It is worth noting, however, that this position is not without opposition. Kidner, for example, follows the Samaritan text which lists Terah's age of

---

[4]We are unsure as to whether the Lord protected her in this instance. See comment on 12.19.

death at 145. "Abram would scarcely have made the exclamation of 17.17 had his own father begotten him at 130."[5]

Wenham, understanding Abram to be the firstborn writes: "Terah died at the age of 205, when Abraham was 135 (11.32; *cf.* 11.26). Yet Abraham was only two years older (137) when his wife Sarah died (23.1; *cf.* 17.17). In other words, Terah was alive and notionally head of the family throughout most of the period covered by the Abraham cycle." At this point, he has to explain why, if this is the order of events, Terah's death is recorded so early.[6] This arrangement, however, falters when it is considered against the words of Stephen: "And *after* his father died, God removed him from [Haran]" (Acts 7.4, my emphasis).

Young argues against accepting the Samaritan Pentateuch, a 'spiritual death' solution (as Wenham suggests), and a contradiction between Genesis and Stephen. He suggests that Stephen might be referring to "the order in which the events are narrated in Genesis. Hence, upon this view, his words 'after the death of his father' would simply be the equivalent of 'after the account of the death of his father.'"[7]

Any suggested solution has its obstacles. The simplest solution—and the one that falls in line with the pattern of Genesis—remains that Abram was not Terah's oldest son. His statement in 17.17 would seem to have as much to do with Sarah giving birth at her age as it does him fathering a child. It was not too many years before this when he sired Ishmael through Hagar. Further, Terah began having sons at 70 and had them spanning 65 years. This is clearly not the same thing as Abraham and Sarah not being able to have any children up to that point.

11.28–32, Haran died… in the land of his kindred. …Terah died in Haran.
After fathering Lot, Haran died. Lot then travels with Terah as the sole representative of Haran's line. After Terah dies, he travels with Abram, perhaps as an heir to Abram.[8]

---

[5]Waltke also argues in favor of the Samaritan Pentateuch, saying it is unlikely that Terah was 130 at Abram's birth, because it accords badly with the rest of the genealogy of Shem to Terah, who have their firstborn in their early thirties and that there would be nothing exceptional in Abraham fathering Isaac at 100 years of age. This seems to argue, however, that Terah had his firstborn earlier—not necessarily that Abram is the oldest.

[6]If this arrangement is to be accepted, one explanation to this problem is probably the symbolic significance that Wenham notes: "True life is to be found only in Canaan, and Terah, who set out for Canaan but settled in Haran, died there."

[7]Edward J. Young, *Thy Word is Truth*, 178.

12 *1, Now the* LORD *said to Abram, "Go…to the land that I will show you."* Abram is told to leave his homeland. It is helpful to remember that Abram is not a fresh-out-of-college twenty-something who would be ready to leave his father's house and homeland. He's already 75 years old. "Ten years beyond modern retirement, Abram begins his new venture" (Waltke). And he's expected to pick up and move *to the land that I will show you. Canaan* is not specified. This certainly seems to indicate that Abram did not know where he was going, though it is safe to say that God guided him along the way. Here, the promise of the land to Abram is implicit. It is clarified in 13.15, after Abram and Lot separate.

By this point in history, idolatry and wickedness had again sprung up. In Ur and Haran, they worshipped the moon god (Waltke, see also Hamilton). Some of this family had fallen into the trap of idolatry. Terah and those fathers who lived beyond the Euphrates are specifically noted as serving other gods (Josh 24.2). Nahor's wife, Milcah, had a name that may have been derived from the title of the goddess Ishtar, daughter of the moon god Sin (Waltke).

Thus it is evident why God wanted to separate Abram and his family. "If God's identity was to be preserved upon the earth, He must act again. But having promised never again to cleanse by flood, God chose another way—separating from the world a faithful family in order to bring into the world an eternal answer to wickedness, a dying savior."[9] And so God called Abram to make a great sacrifice: to leave home and family and go to a place where he had never been. If Abram was to be God's friend, he must forever be separated from idolatry. Further, faith can only become strong through testing. Cut off forever from the support of country and family, Abram would now have only God to trust.

The call of Abram serves as an example for those who would be his seed in faith. "All through our earthly lives, God through His gospel message calls us to venture from the land of our birth to a land to be revealed. Our start, like Abram's, involves sacrificial separation. We, too, must leave the land of our birth with its contaminating idols and be separated to God. …[And] while it does not always mean physical separation from coun-

---

[8]See EXCURSUS E.

[9]John M. Kilgore, "Abraham: The Friend of God." *Things Written Aforetime: Florida College Annual Lectures,* 14.

try and relatives, it does mean a spiritual separation from anything that would supplant God as the center of our love and service."[10]

12.2, "And I will make of you a great nation." A nation refers to "a political unit with common land, language and government" (Mathews). This would have come as a surprise to Abram, a 75-year-old man with no children. "Abram's industry could have obtained for himself a land, wealth, and fame, but in the acquisition of children by Sarai, he was helpless without God" (Mathews). Though the promise will later be extended to other nations which he fathers (*cf.* 17.5), this promise is not referring to all of the peoples that would come from Abram's various descendants, but to the nation of Israel. It would be a large nation, but that is not all there is to this promise. God does not count greatness by numbers, so certainly *His people's* greatness would not be limited to that. "The reference is both to numbers and significance" (Waltke). The greater facet of this nation is told more fully in the last portion of this promise: it would be the nation to carry the Messianic line.

But though this promise refers specifically to Israel, it is ultimately fulfilled to an even greater degree. Paul argues in his writings that the the ultimate *great nation* of Abraham is the community of the faithful, whether circumcised or not (Rom 4.9–12; Gal 3.7–9, 25–29).

"And I will bless you." "'Bless' in Genesis describes primarily two benefits: progeny and material wealth. Here 'bless' indicates material wealth for Abram, since the promise of a populous nation had already been made" (Mathews). Abram began as a wealthy man (12.5), and continued to grow in wealth (12.16), until his amassed possessions became an area of contention between his servants and Lot's servants. By chapter 14, he has 318 trained servants who were born in his house.[11]

"And make your name great." Waltke says, "In the ancient Near East, a name was not merely a label but a revelation of character. Thus, a great name entails not only fame but high social esteem 'as a man of superior character.'" And Mathews: "The naming of 'Abraham' best explains [this promise]; Abraham will be revered as 'father' by a host of peoples whom he will influence throughout the centuries. The telling reality of

---

[10]*Ibid.*, 16.

[11]See comment on 14.14.

this promise is that Judaism, Christianity, and Islam 'look to Abraham' (Isa 51.2) as their spiritual progenitor."

This promise finds its closest parallel in 2 Samuel 7.9, where David is promised *a great name*. Also, Psalm 72.17 offers a prayer for the king to have a name that endures forever. "This is clearly royal language, and Abram is to be viewed as a regal figure. ...Abram is promised that 'kings' will come from him (17.6). ...In 23.6 Abraham is referred to as a 'prince' by the Hittites" (Hamilton).

And this promise is something of an irony. Previously, the people of Babel had tried to make a name for themselves. Here, God takes a no-body and promises to make his name great. "Whereas chapters 1–11 de-pict the folly of human efforts to obtain wisdom (3.5) and fame ('name,' 6.4...) by unlawful means, the patriarch receives a 'name' by divine grant" (Mathews). And Hamilton: "If his name is ever to become great it will not be because of any self-initiated effort. The great name will be a gift, not an achievement."

"So that you will be a blessing." This phrase has received much attention. It is an unusual construction, occurring only in two other passages (Isa 19.24; Zech 8.13), and has been interpreted in a variety of ways ranging from *you shall be blessed* to *you will be the embodiment of blessing* to *he will be a source of blessing to others* to the imperative *be a blessing*. Hamilton notes: "This is the middle [phrase of God's initial speech to Abram], and perhaps for that reason a... pivotal [statement]. The blessings of God are not all to be turned in on Abram. ...Abram must be more than a recipient. He is both a receptacle for the divine blessing and a transmitter of that blessing."[12]

12.3, "I will bless those who bless you, and him who dishonors you I will curse." As the object of God's attention and promise, anyone who dishon-ors Abram will, in effect, dishonor God. Those who honor Abram, by ex-tension, honor God. It is interesting to note that the parallel phrases jux-tapose a plural against a singular *(those* vs. *him)*. Though it is surely only for poetic effect (Mathews), it shows "God's gracious desire to bless rather than curse" (Waltke), and that, "Divine grace presupposes that there will be *many* that wish Abram well" (Leupold).

---

[12]A different viewpoint on this difficult phrase is suggested by Wenham: "The most likely inter-pretation is that suggested by Zechariah 8.13, 'As you have been a byword for cursing among the nations... so will I save you and you shall be a blessing.' In other words, people will say, 'May God make me as blessed as Abram.'"

It is also interesting to note that the two words usually translated *curse* are different Hebrew words. The first word is rightly translated by the ESV: *dishonor*. According to Mathews, it means *to declare insignificant, to ridicule*. The second word is the common word found in Genesis for curse. Some have argued that this indicates that even the slightest word of ridicule against Abram would bring down the full weight of God's curse. Mathews, however, argues that the parallel effect of the language supersedes any lexical difference in nuance. This may be supported by the repetition of this promise to Jacob (27.29), where the usual word for curse occurs in both instances.

"And in you all the families of the earth shall be blessed." Wenham says, "Not every individual is promised blessing in Abram but every major group in the world will be blessed. The subsequent stories in Genesis illustrate these principles in action. Groups well disposed to Abram and his descendants prosper: those that oppose them do not." Beyond an extension of the previous statement, this promise certainly has Messianic overtones, especially when read in concert with 22.18, where this universal blessing is to be through his offspring. The apostles and New Testament writers identify Jesus as the fulfillment—the blessing to all who believe.

It is significant to note that a specific offspring to Abram is not yet promised. "Mesopotamian law-codes allowed for the adoption of an heir in the case of childlessness."[13] At this point, Lot stands in this position.[14] It is not until Lot rejects the Promised Land that a son is specifically promised to Abram.[15]

12.4–5, So Abram went… and Lot went with him. In obedient faith, Abram went as he was directed. Lot traveled with him, either as his heir or as a possible alternate heir to Terah. Sarai is barren and Terah's only other grandchildren are daughters. "That leaves Lot to perpetuate his grandfather's family. …That Lot went with Abram may be termed, as far as plot is concerned, 'the teasing motif of the presumed heir'" (Hamilton). Lot's accompaniment was not an early failure of Abram to obey and

---

[13]Larry R. Helyer, "The Separation of Abraham and Lot: Its Significance in the Patriarchal Narratives," *JSOT* 26 (1983): 82.

[14]This, of course, is not specifically stated, but can be reasonably inferred. After the separation of Abram and Lot, the heir to Abram is his servant, Eliezer of Damascus (15.2).

[15]See Excursus E.

depart from his kindred; rather, Lot accompanied him because Lot was a *righteous man* (2 Pet 2.8).

And all their possessions that they had gathered, and the people that they had acquired in Haran. Also, they took all of their moveable possessions as well as their servants. Slavery was common in these times. "This was not the sort of chattel slavery later practiced in North America. These slaves had certain limited rights, could be given great responsibility, and were not thought to lose their personhood" (Alter). In this introductory remark, the wealth of Abram—which will become manifest as the story continues—is first hinted at.

12.6, Abram passed through the land. As a wanderer and a sojourner, Abram did not travel looking for the place to stop, but awaiting direction from God to do so. God had told him to go to a place that He would show him and Abram traveled on until he heard the word.

At that time, the Canaanites were in the land. His promised land was already inhabited. If he had entertained any ideas of an easy life in his new home, they were quickly dispelled. We will see, as we continue, that during the first ten years in his new land Abram wandered about, living in a tent as an alien and stranger while confronted with hostile inhabitants, famine, family division and war. Abram's faith is characterized by obedience, even when it flew in the face of common sense (leaving home to travel to an unknown land) and natural love (sacrificing his son). But Abram's faith is also impressive because of its endurance. It is one thing to begin an adventure with all the initial exhilaration and expectations (though few would find enough exhilaration to begin at 75!), but it's quite another to continue that commitment after the honeymoon is over, so to speak, and the realities of the struggle start to settle in.

12.7, Then the LORD appeared to Abram. The Lord's appearance to Abram marked when he was to stop his travel. Until this point, he traveled in silent faith. Further, this is the first recorded appearance of the Lord to a patriarch. According to Patrick, the shift from speaking to appearing is not incidental. "A theophany is a way of augmenting an audition to heighten its dramatic force, and reinforce the claim that a divine intervention has occurred" (qtd. in Hamilton).

"To your offspring I will give this land." This may also have come as quite a shock to Abram. Although God never specifically promised the

land to Abram himself, it could be argued that it was implied in God's original statement. Abram now learns that he has traveled all this way to a land that would never be his, but his descendants'. Rather than being upset by this turn of events, Abram worships God (v 8). Here it first becomes clear that Abram did not obey for what he could get out of obedience; rather, his obedience was due to his understanding of who God is.

Hamilton argues that this promise to his offspring eliminates Lot as the presumptive heir. We, however, are not so sure about this. As already noted, Mesopotamian law allowed for the adoption of an heir in cases of childlessness. With Abram's heir being Eliezer after his separation from Lot (15.2), it is probable that Lot stood in that place prior to their separation. Thus Lot traveled with Abram, not as a potential heir to Terah, but as a potential heir to Abram. It could, however, be argued that the use of *zera* renders this possibility unlikely, as it is also the word used for semen and may imply a seed from the loins of Abram.

12.8, Pitched his tent… built an altar. "There is force in the contrast between *pitched* and *buil[t]* (v 8), the one for himself, the other for God. The only structures he left behind him were altars: no relics of his own wealth" (Kidner).

12.9, And Abram journeyed on. Even though Shechem marked his stopping point, it is clear to him that his journey is not over. This land was to be given to his offspring. He would continue to dwell in it, but his life would be that of a nomad. Interestingly, the word for *journeyed* derives from a term for the pulling up of tent stakes. "The progressive form in which it is cast is a precise indication of movement through successive encampments" (Alter).

Negeb. Negeb is the Hebrew word for south. The southern regions of the land had gained their own identity—similar to how The South has become a proper noun in our culture.[16] "The brief itinerary of Abram described in verses 5–9 takes him from the northern to the southern border of the land. He not only sees what has been promised to him; he walks through it, and he lives and worships in it. Symbolically he has taken possession of it" (Wenham).

---

[16]Harrison disagrees: "During and after the Middle Bronze Age this southerly region was known as the Negeb, which is rather inaccurately translated 'The South' in some English versions. In point of fact the Hebrew term *negeb* means *dry* or *arid*, and referred originally to climatic conditions rather than to a specific geographical region." *Old Testament Times*, 83.

12.10, Now there was a famine in the land. "Its fluctuating rainfall made it susceptible to food shortages until the advent of modern methods of irrigation, and Egypt was the standard refuge in this situation, as the Nile provided a much more certain food supply" (Wenham).

So Abram went down to Egypt. "Abram has no sooner entered Canaan than he finds the land unable to support him. ...The solution which occurs to Abram is straightforward. There is food in Egypt, so why not go down to Egypt for a while?"[17]

"It is striking that Abram is said to have gone to 'settle in' Egypt, to be an immigrant there. To live as an immigrant... suggests the intention of long-term settlement, which is somewhat alien to Abram's wandering lifestyle. It also comes as quite a surprise to hear that Abram is ready to settle in Egypt so soon after he has been promised 'this land'" (Wenham). This proves to be a mistake which God specifically forbids Isaac from following (26.1–2). Jacob, having learned this lesson, will need divine reassurance before traveling to Egypt (46.1–4). See Excursus I.

Alter suggests that this episode foreshadows the later sojourn to Egypt and subsequent exodus: initiated by famine, an encounter with a Pharaoh, and sent away because of plagues.

12.11–13, "Say you are my sister." The lie was planned. This was not a spur-of-the-moment mistake, but a premeditated sin.[18]

Technically, this was a half-truth (20.12). Part of its motive probably stemmed in the "esteem in which the Hurrians (influential at Haran) held the wife-sister relationship: a husband would even legally adopt his wife as sister to increase his authority and the status of the marriage" (Kidner). This esteem is seen clearly in other events where the brother has tremendous say over the sister's marriage (*e.g.*, Laban with Rebekah, 24; Jacob's sons with Dinah, 34). Perhaps Abram hoped that he would have the right to reject any suitor's requests to be Sarai's husband.[19]

---

[17]Iain M. Duguid, "Hagar the Egyptian: A Note on the Allure of Egypt in the Abraham Cycle," *WTJ* 56 (1994): 419.

[18]This is the first of three wife-sister episodes (*cf.* chapters 20 and 26). Critics are quick to attribute these to one story that was somehow repeated throughout. A simpler explanation is that it was family custom (20.13). For a fuller discussion of these episodes, see Mathews.

[19]This custom is now held in some question (see Wenham and Hamilton). The examples with Rebekah and Dinah, however, seem unquestionable.

Waltke notes that this is more properly translated as a request—*"Please say"*—rather than an order, but also points out that Sarai pragmatically consents: "Their philosophy is 'Better defiled than dead.' This is not a philosophy that establishes God's kingdom in a pagan world."

"You are a woman beautiful in appearance." This sin came about because of her beauty (v 11). As she lived to be 127, she is middle-aged at 65. Kidner argues that the lifespan of the patriarchs seems to have been a special providence: "Their continued vigor shows that this was no mere postponement of death but a spreading-out of the whole life process. …Sarah's sixties would therefore presumably correspond with our thirties or forties." Even if that is granted, how many times does a wealthy and powerful man with no morals and every option chase after the middle-aged? This is especially difficult to understand in a society where older men regularly took younger women—even girls in their early teens.[20]

Leupold sees it as a political move: "On Pharaoh's part the taking of a woman into his harem may be largely a political expedient to enhance his influence." At the height of Abraham's wealth and power, he and Lot were too large to share a single portion of land (ch 13), he conquered kings (ch 14), and his son brought fear in others (ch 26). It is conceivable that, even at this point, Pharaoh may have sought to marry Sarai for this reason—though it fails to help to explain the Egyptians' acknowledgement of her beauty (vv 14–15): "The narrative insists that this is not merely the opinion of a neurotically jealous husband, for the Egyptians heartily concurred" (Wenham).

Perhaps her beauty was that of a comparable sort: "She might easily appear very beautiful in the eyes of the Egyptians, whose wives, according to both ancient and modern testimony, were generally ugly, and faded early" (Keil).

And other suggestions have abounded: "Calvin observed that childless women preserve their beauty longer than mothers. Gunkel suggested there was a natural tendency to glorify the national mother figure (*cf.* 24.16; 29.17.) Cassuto argues that if Sarai could bear her first child at 90, the narrator must have believed she was still pretty at 65. Finally, it should be borne in mind that ideas of feminine beauty in traditional societies differ from ours: well-endowed matronly figures, not slim youthful ones,

---

[20]"Ironically, when Abram tries at a later point in his life to perpetrate the same ruse (20.1ff), he makes no remarks about his wife's beauty! In this second situation she is eighty-nine. …Is her pulchritude waning?" (Hamilton).

tend to represent their ideal of womanhood" (Wenham). Also, Mathews notes that in this period, "beauty was measured by one's eyes and form." Or maybe, as Waltke so succinctly argues, "Sarai retains her beauty."

"Then they will kill me, but they will let you live." We find the ultimate motive for the lie in verse 12: fear of death. Apparently, this fear was not baseless. "Marriage was respected sufficiently that men felt they must dispose of the husband before they could take his wife. Egyptian parallels prove that men had no hesitation about committing murder in an effort to secure their object" (Leupold). The irony is thick enough to slice: a culture that respected marriage enough that they wouldn't just take someone else's wife—they would only take her after they killed the husband! But of course, pagan cultures do not hold the market on this type of thievery: "That Abram's fears were probably well founded may be seen in David's abduction of Bathsheba and the murder of her husband Uriah" (Mathews).

Also note that Abram only mentions that she will not be killed, without raising the possibility that they will take her to be a wife. "Maybe that possibility never entered his mind, if for no other reason than that his concern is with his own fate, not Sarai's" (Hamilton). Or, maybe it is just because saying as much would be an eminent statement of the obvious.

A final note on the lie: It is easy to pontificate from a passage like this that all half-truths are the same as lies. But we must be wary in doing so, as this passage also teaches that *not* all half-truths are lies. This statement was not a lie because it was only half true, but because it was used to deceive. Imagine all of the times that Abram introduced Sarai to someone as his wife *without* including that she was also his half-sister. Certainly, those times—just as much half-truths as this time—were not lies. It is the motive that makes the lie.

12.14–16, The Egyptians saw that the woman was very beautiful. Abram was correct in his expectation. "At first, Abram's plan works well. As he anticipated the Egyptians noticed her beauty… and nothing untoward happened" (Wenham).

They praised her to Pharaoh. "But then an unforeseen complication occurred: her beauty was reported to the Pharaoh. His advances could not be staved off, and Sarai 'was taken into Pharaoh's house'" (Wenham). Clearly, Abram expected Sarai's beauty to be noticed—but he could not have supposed that word would have traveled all the way to the palace. While he may be able to fend off a peasant suitor, he was helpless against the Pharaoh.

Pharaoh. "This is actually a title meaning 'Great House,' not a personal name; it is a metonymn, like 'Crown' for the British monarch" (Waltke).

Was taken into Pharaoh's house. See comment on verse 19.

For her sake he dealt well with Abram. "It is quite likely that the bounty bestowed on Abram represented [bride money], though it may have been simply a mark of Pharaonic goodwill toward Sarai's 'brother'" (Wenham). There is some question as to how much of the things listed here were given by Pharaoh and how much Abram already possessed. "When, then, the things are listed that Abram possessed, the sense of the passage cannot be that Pharaoh's gift included all these elements but rather that, partly as a result of Pharaoh's gift, Abram's wealth was made up of the constituent parts listed here" (Leupold).

And this is a common theme in the three wife-sister stories: "Each of the wife-sister episodes has the motif of the patriarch's enrichment in connection with his deception (20.14–16; 26.12–13). However, in this first story the Pharaoh enriches Abram after the matriarch's abduction; in the case of Abimelech and Sarah, the Philistine rewards Sarah to compensate for his wrong (20.14–16); in the case of Abimelech and Rebekah, the Lord blesses Isaac (26.12–14). In spite of the patriarchs' failure of faith, God extends them grace and plunders the real criminal, who we may presume would have killed Abram to gratify his lust" (Waltke).[21]

12.17, But the LORD afflicted Pharaoh…great plagues. "Comparatively speaking, Pharaoh was in the right… for Pharaoh had acted in good faith, and Abram had practiced deception" (Leupold). That Abram lied, however, does not make Pharaoh a worthy recipient of divine mercy; ignorance does not justify sin.

"Though the nature of the diseases is unexplained, it probably pertains to sex so as to suggest to Pharaoh that Sarai is their cause" (Waltke).[22] This interpretation, though probable, is not necessary. "This term refers to skin disease in Mosaic legislation (Lev 13), and the verbal form describes the leprous judgment by the Lord against Uzziah" (Mathews). Wenham notes that these diseases "were generally regarded as the consequence of serious sin."

---

[21]For detailed comments on each of the items given Abram, see Waltke

[22]See comment on verse 19.

His house. This probably refers to "the members of his royal court, including his harem, as with King Abimelech (20.7, 17)" (Mathews).

12.18, "What is this you have done to me?" Here the patriarch of Israel, the 'father of the faithful,' receives a moral rebuke—and a well-deserved one, at that—from the mouth of a polytheistic pagan who neither acknowledges nor worships Yahweh. Leupold suggests that he stands silently and receives it perhaps shows his awareness that it is deserved.

Upon learning she is married, Pharaoh returns her to Abram. "The Egyptian emerges rather saintly, but Abram, the one in whom the Egyptians and other nations are to be blessed, appears rather sinister. This Egyptian monarch does not operate by the principle of the divine right of the kings. Unlike Jezebel (1 Kgs 21), he will not kill to get what he wants" (Hamilton).

12.19, "I took her for my wife." The KJV and NKJV translate this passage with a *might*. But there is nothing in the Hebrew to indicate a subjunctive mood in this sentence.[23] Thus, this passage indicates clearly that Sarai was taken into Pharaoh's harem. It is highly doubtful that she was taken as his wife without the marriage being consummated. If this is the case, their lie forced Sarai into adultery. "This is doubtless a case of actual adultery between Pharaoh and Sarai, rather than the potential adultery such as we find in 20.3–4" (Hamilton).[24] And Wenham: "That plagues were sent seems to indicate that Pharaoh did actually commit adultery."

Most commentators are quick to dismiss this as a remote possibility, if that, arguing in verse 13 that her *being taken into his house* would not necessarily or even probably include any sexual relationship, while offering little comment on this verse. Some have suggested that he may have taken her into the harem but had not yet gotten to her (though if she were as beautiful as is reported, this would be difficult to imagine). Others suggest that God's protection of Sarah in chapter 20 indicates that He did the same here. A few go so far as to suggest the plagues were some kind of "genital disorder preventing intercourse" (Alter). We are convinced, with Hamilton and Wenham, that this sin *did* include adultery.[25]

---

[23]Perhaps the translators' intention in using *might* was to convey the meaning *was able to.*

[24]See Hamilton's footnote for further reading on this matter.

[25]At the very least, the lie put her in a situation where adultery would have been committed had God not intervened.

12.20, And Pharaoh gave men orders concerning him. Abram left with a Pharaoh-appointed escort. Perhaps this is to ensure that Abram and Sarai left Egypt (Mathews, Wenham). Or it is to ensure their safe travel to the borders of Egypt. God had made it plain that His favor rested on Abram—perhaps Pharaoh was afraid that he would be further punished if any evil befell Abram while he was in the land of Egypt (Leupold, Hamilton). Or maybe it was a little bit of both.

"Considering that he had feared death at Egyptian hands and that his dishonesty had involved the king in adultery, which was regarded throughout the ancient world as the 'great sin' deserving the death penalty, the royal leniency is remarkable. Pharaoh implicitly acknowledges that God is protecting Abram, and he therefore takes no revenge on him" (Wenham).

Growth of the Seed: God makes covenant promises to Abram (vv 2–3); the birth of the covenant child is delayed due to adultery(?)[26]

---

[26]See comment on verse 19.

13 *1, So Abram went up… into the Negeb.* Many translations render *Negeb south*, which leaves the question as to how one may be said to go *up into the south*. *Negeb* was used both of the direction and the south-country of Palestine, "always so called from the standpoint of central Palestine" (Leupold). Their travel, thus, was not in a southerly direction, but into the portion of land known as—as we would render it—the South. To put it into our terms, a flight from Cuba to Alabama would be 'up into the South.' Or, perhaps this was simply meant to be understood as his journey from Egypt to Canaan—a trip always described as *up*.

And Lot with him. Lot has not been mentioned in a while, because he was peripheral to the Egypt journey's themes (Hamilton). Because this chapter is a turning point in the story of Lot, we are reminded that Lot journeyed with Abram down into Egypt and back up into the Negeb. His placement in the list may indicate that relations among the family are already growing apart. Sarna says, "By placing [Lot] last in the list, after Abram's possessions, the text hints at a degree of estrangement" (qtd. in Waltke).

13.2–3, Now Abram was very rich. Abram's wealth is enumerated for the first time. And he is wealthy beyond the normal standards of wealth. Wealth was largely measured in livestock and servants (both of which Abram had), but it was rare to find someone with silver and gold—especially someone who was a nomad. "Only the livestock can be attributed to the gifts of Pharaoh. By the mention of silver and gold, the narrator inferentially points to the Lord as the ultimate Blesser, though the immediate cause may have been various sorts of commercial transactions. Precious metals afford a measure of security and protection in times of famine" (Waltke). Wenham, by contrast, suggests that the gold was acquired in Egypt, as it is not mentioned before this and that this may be intended to foreshadow the exodus, as "the Israelites were also given silver and gold before leaving Egypt."

Interestingly, the same word used for *rich* is translated *severe* in chapter 12 as a description of the famine. "The use of the same term… invites the comparison of his situation at the beginning of the two episodes" (Wenham).

And he journeyed on. The Hebrew indicates a journey by stages (Waltke), which is what you would expect of a wealthy nomad with many herds—from one watering hole to the next; slow and laborious to ensure the animals are not overdriven.

13.4, Abram called on the name of the LORD. Upon completing his journey, Abram stops to worship. This wording echoes chapter 4 where men first called on the name of the Lord and "indicates...that there was a continuum between the roots of authentic worship and the practice of Abram" (Mathews). His physical return to the Promised Land is accompanied by a spiritual return to his faith in God, which had lapsed in Egypt. "This time he does not need to build an altar: the old one is still there, perhaps implying that the promises still stand too" (Wenham). This is the second time such an incident is noted in his life (*cf.* 12.7), and it is the beginning of a pattern which will pervade his life: worship in every place he goes. Even when he knows that he has made a mistake, he returns to God.

13.5–7, Lot also had flocks and herds and tents. Having been re-introduced into the story, we learn that Lot is also a wealthy man—"Abram mediates blessing to those with him" (Waltke). And Lot is so blessed *that the land could not support both of them.* On top of there not being enough land for both of these men and their herds, *the Canaanites and the Perizzites were dwelling in the land.* All of these factors led to *strife between the herdsmen of Abram's livestock and the herdsmen of Lot's livestock.* In addition to their presence taxing the capability of the land, "they can scarcely afford such divisiveness when they are surrounded by potential enemies" (Alter).

There is some question as to the identity of the Perizzites. "The Perizzites are not listed as descendants of Canaan (10.15–18). Rather than an ethnic term, it probably denotes a social class of Canaan's descendants, a section of the population...living in the open country. If so, the Canaanites may represent the citizens connected with the walled cities. Together, they composed the indigenous population that restricts the pasturage and watering holes, making it impossible for the kinsmen to sustain the fertility of their flocks and herds grazing together" (Waltke). Keil disputes this point of view, suggesting instead that the Perizzites be understood simply as not descending from Ham. Wenham also understands this to be an ethnic grouping.

13.8–9, "If you take the left hand." Abram's offer is beyond gracious. "The manipulation that Abram formerly manifested [in Egypt] now gives way to magnanimity. Lot, unlike Sarai, is given a free hand" (Hamilton). As the older,[1] the leader of the family, and the one to whom the land was promised, he could have easily insisted on his rights and taken the first choice. But, "The social superior humbles himself before the inferior to preserve peace, thereby proving himself the spiritual superior. Abram's faith gives him the freedom to be generous" (Waltke). Among other things, this passage serves as an excellent illustration of the contrast between faith and sight.

"Left... right." Helyer points out that in an east-oriented culture (*i.e.,* direction is determined by facing east), the left and right would indicate the north and south. "For Abram, the 'whole land' [v 9] is the land of Canaan. ...Abram had set before Lot the option of choosing whether to pasture his flocks in northern Canaan... or to graze the southern Canaan region. ...In other words, Abram desired that the land of Canaan *should be partitioned* between himself and Lot."[2]

It is also noteworthy that Abram offers Lot his choice of the whole land, which should be somewhat surprising since the Canaanites occupied the land. "This... reflects Abram's early confidence in the Lord's promise of possession. Abram spoke proleptically as if the land were his to distribute to whomever he chose" (Mathews).

13.10, The Jordan valley was well watered everywhere. The area is compared to the garden of the Lord and to Egypt.[3] To the eye of sight, the Jordan valley was like those two places that were watered by rivers and never had lack. "By contrast, the central ridge where Bethel and Hebron are located depend upon the Lord to send rain (see Deut 11.10–12)" (Waltke).

Mathews points out that this account has similar terminology as both the fall (ch 3) and the pre-flood wickedness (ch 6)—eyes, saw, watered, destroyed, garden, chose, *etc.*—which would have caused this to be immediately foreboding to the original readers.

13.11–12, And Lot journeyed east. Abram had given him the choice of the left or the right, the north or the south. But *Lot journeyed east.* These four words ring increasingly ominous as the story continues. But notice, even here, the distinction that is made between Abram who *settled in the land of Canaan* and Lot who *settled among the cities of the valley.* "It is

---

[1]*Probably* the older. See Excursus E.

[2]Larry R. Helyer, "The Separation of Abraham and Lot: Its Significance in the Patriarchal Narratives," *JSOT* 26 (1983): 79.

[3]On Egypt, see Excursus I.

clear from verse 12 that the territory chosen by Lot lies outside the borders of Canaan" (Hamilton). Further, *east* has already become synonymous with trouble. Adam and Eve journeyed east after their sin; Cain settled in Nod, east of Eden; the people of Babel migrated from the east. As Armstrong notes, "The easterly direction had come to symbolize distance and exile from the divine presence, and without the sacred there could be no blessing" (in Waltke). And Wenham: "The very direction Lot takes suggests divine judgment." How stark is the contrast: Abram's tent is pitched in Bethel, at the altar to God; Lot's camp is eastward, toward the ungodly city of Sodom.

The precise location of these cities has been debated through the years and has ranged from sites north or southeast of the Dead Sea to the southern basin of what is now under the sea. "The southern locations, especially the southeastern plain of the Dead Sea, have generated more support based on literary and archaeological analysis. More information is required before scholars will achieve a consensus on their identification" (Mathews).

13.14, The LORD said to Abram, after Lot had separated from him. It is no accident that the renewal of the promise is expressed on this occasion with special emphasis placed on his offspring. Abram's heir had just been separated from him.[4]

"Lift up your eyes and look." Alter notes: "The location between Bethel and Ai is in fact a spectacular lookout point, and already the implicit contrast between Abram and Lot is extended—Abram on the heights, Lot down in the sunken plain."

13.15–17, "I will give [the land] to you and to your offspring forever." Keil turns this into a spiritual application: "Through Christ the promise has been exalted from its temporal form to its true essence; through Him the whole earth becomes Canaan"; however, such an interpretation is not necessary. The Hebrew *olam* was never understood as meaning forever in the sense that moderns use it. Rather, it refers to "indefinite continuance into the very distant future" and does not contain the idea of endlessness, as "shown by the fact that sometimes it is thought desirable to repeat the word."[5]

---

[4]See EXCURSUS E.

[5]Allan A. Macrae, "Olam," *TWOT,* 672–673.

"The dust of the earth." Before this, reference to Abram's offspring was vague—12.7 assumes descendants, but that is about the extent of it. Here, at the parting of Lot, the promises regarding his offspring are made more explicit and concrete, even to the point of saying that his descendants would be innumerable. But it is still not specified that his offspring would come from Sarai. This, of course, sets the stage for the Hagar incident.

"Walk through the length and the breadth of the land." This act was to symbolize his legal acquisition of the land. "Walking around the perimeter of a piece of property was a common legal ritual in the ancient Near East for taking final possession" (Alter). Waltke offers several parallel instances of this custom, including the carrying of Yahweh's throne around Jericho for seven days "presumably to stake out their claim."

13.18, The oaks of Mamre. "Some twenty miles south of Bethlehem,[6] became the chief centre of Abram's movements, near which he would purchase his only property, the burial cave of Machpelah" (Kidner). Mamre, the person, later arrives. He is the Amorite who seeks security in an alliance with Abram (14.13, 24).

There he built an altar to the LORD. Yet again, Abram's priority in arriving in a new location is the acknowledgement of God and worship of Him.

Growth of the Seed: Lot rejects the Promised Land and is thus rejected by God;[7] the covenant is renewed with Abram (vv 14–17).

---

[6]Mathews marks it two miles north of Hebron.

[7]See Excursus E.

Excursus E: The Separation of Abram and Lot

Why is there so much about Lot in the Bible? As we said in the introduction, the events recorded in Genesis are there for the purpose of letting us know the people from whom Jesus descended and why He came from those people. How does Lot fit into this category? If our thesis on the purpose of Genesis is true, then it must be possible that Jesus could have come through Lot.

Lot as Abraham's Heir

Abraham and Sarah were childless for many years. In chapter 15, we learn that a servant of Abraham's household, Eliezer of Damascus, was positioned to be Abraham's heir. And, indeed, "Mesopotamian law-codes allowed for the adoption of an heir in the case of childlessness."[1] We can reasonably assume, then, that Abraham viewed Lot as his heir until they were separated. After their separation he made Eliezer his heir; after God promised a son, he took Hagar and fathered Ishmael.

But could Lot have been the heir? It is important to remember that Isaac is not specifically promised until chapter 17. Further, it is important to remember that Lot was faithful to God. When God said for them to get up and leave their wicked homeland, Lot went—just as quickly and faithfully as Abram did. Peter calls Lot *that righteous man* (2 Pet 2.8).

If Lot had remained faithful, God would have used him.

Lot and Abraham as Co-Heirs

A second possibility is that Lot and Abraham were co-heirs of Terah, because it is possible that they were near the same age or even that Lot was older. This possibility does require some hypothetical thinking, so bear with us.

First, Abraham wasn't the oldest son of Terah. We have taken the position that Abraham was sixty years younger than Terah's firstborn son.[2]

Haran, the father of Lot, died first. Perhaps that was because Haran was the oldest. If that is the case, and Lot was born in the first 60 years of Haran's life, Lot would have been older than Abraham. If Lot was born any time in the next ten years, Abraham and Lot would have grown up together. (Again, we acknowledge that this is hypothetical, but it certainly isn't outside the realm of possibility.) If Terah's deceased firstborn's son is as old as or older than Abraham, it is not a stretch to suggest that they were co-heirs of Terah. If Lot and Abraham were co-heirs, it probably means that the blessing would have come through

---

[1] Larry R. Helyer, "The Separation of Abraham and Lot: Its Significance in the Patriarchal Narratives," *JSOT* 26 (1983): 82.

[2] See INTRODUCTION.

either Abraham or Lot—whoever was faithful. The unfaithful one would be cast out of the Messianic line.

But what about the fact that the promise had already been made to Abraham? The easy answer to this question is that all of God's covenants are conditional. If Abraham was not faithful, the covenant would be voided, and God would be able to offer it to a more faithful person. In addition—although we would not press this point—God does not technically enter a covenant relationship with Abraham until chapter 15, after Lot is no longer an option.

Whichever position is taken—Abraham's heir or co-heirs with him— it is evident why so much space in the Bible is taken up telling of Lot. He was positioned to be in the Messianic line.

So What Went Wrong?

Why did Isaac become necessary and Lot find himself removed from the promise? This brings us back to chapter 13: *"Lot chose for himself all the Jordan valley, and Lot journeyed east… Abram settled in the land of Canaan, while Lot settled among the cities of the valley"* (vv 11–12).

By choosing outside the land of Canaan and associating himself with the wicked cities of the valley (13.13) he showed his focus to be more worldly than spiritual. More importantly, by rejecting the land of Canaan, he rejected the promise of God.

The separation of Abraham and Lot not only set the stage for Abraham's subsequent rescue of Lot (ch 14) or the narration of Sodom and Gomorrah's downfall (ch 19). The separation of Abraham and Lot is vital to the story of Genesis because it explains why Abraham was chosen, why Isaac was necessary, and why Lot was eliminated from the Messianic line.

14 *1–9,* The number of parentheticals throughout this section gives us an idea of how obscure these names and places are—even to its original audience thousands of years ago. Moses first uses the old name, for the sake of history, before using the modern name which would be recognizable to his listeners. It would be analogous to the following statement: 'Some of the early settlers founded the colony of New Amsterdam (which is now New York).'

This does, of course, lead naturally to anachronisms in the text, such as *the country of the Amalekites* in verse 7. The Amalekites descended from the grandson of Esau—whose father was still several years from being born (*cf.* 36.12). It should be clear that Moses intends the reader to understand the subtext: *The country that is **now** the land of the Amalekites.*[1]

The antiquity of this document, as well as the some of its topographical details and words, have led many to think that this was an extract or adaptation of a foreign document. While critical scholars would jump on this as an opportunity to reinforce their documentary hypothesis, Kidner argues, "If [this is a foreign document], it is an independent witness to Abram's historicity."

14.2–4, These kings made war. The chapter begins with the list of kings who went to war with each other. This is the first time that biblical events are expressly coordinated with external history—as well as the Bible's first mention of war—but to date, none of the kings listed has been definitely identified in extrabiblical sources. That each city would have a separate king is not surprising; this is, in fact, "quite in harmony with the condition of Canaan, where even at a later period every city had its king" (Keil).

"Their names suggest a very wide area from the Black Sea to the Persian Gulf, the whole Mesopotamian Valley, all of what later is Babylon and Asher. One explicitly comes from Elam (part of modern Iran) and another from Shinar (modern Iraq). The other two are probably from Turkey. The historical situation of several powers, rather than one, only fits the Middle Bronze Age, Abram's horizon" (Waltke). Kidner also dates this to the Middle Bronze Age (*i.e.,* the early second millennium BC), but does so based on "some of its words and topographical details" giving this chapter "its own character and the stamp of great antiquity."

---

[1] Many modern scholars have solved the problem alternately, equating these Amalekites with a different group of people (see Wenham).

Bera king of Sodom, Birsha king of Gomorrah. Wenham notes that the names of these two kings are compounded with the Hebrew words for *evil* and *wicked*, a trait fitting for kings of these two cities.

The Salt Sea. "The Dead Sea is called the Salt Sea because its average 32 percent saline content is about ten times more than the three percent average of the oceans" (Waltke).

They rebelled. Here we find the motive for the war. After serving Chedorlaomer for thirteen years, they rebelled. Waltke suggests that this rebellion was the refusal to pay an annual tribute, which would have been required as they *served [him]*. This is furthered by Wenham's assertion that "This verse implies that the Dead Sea kings had been defeated in battle."

14.5, The kings who were with him. This verse makes it clear that Chedorlaomer is the leader of the eastern coalition of kings (*cf.* v 9). That the other kings accompanied him speaks either to a peace-time alliance between him and neighboring kings, or to Chedorlaomer's influence by power: that, as Leupold suggests, he compelled them.

14.7, They… defeated all the country of the Amalekites. The kings *came* (vv 5, 7)—from the east; this narrative reads from a Westerner's perspective—and conquered four peoples on their way. "Description of their itinerary and impressive victories over the inhabitants in the region heightens the narrative's excitement as the foreboding army of Chedorlaomer makes its way toward Sodom" (Mathews).[2]

14.8, The king of Sodom… went out. Here, the verb changes, indicating the first sign of resistance; these kings are *going* to meet those who are *coming*. "The verb is singular, suggesting that the king of Sodom heads the Dead Sea Coalition" (Waltke).

They joined battle. Translations vary on this verse. The NIV's *drew up battle lines* indicates a traditional battle, "matching strength against strength, five kings on the home ground against four kings far removed from their homeland. The contrast underscores the might of the eastern kings" (Waltke). And the might of the eastern kings made quick work of the Dead Sea kings: "Although verse 8 describes the battle lines being drawn and verse 10 the rout, there is no account of the fight itself, perhaps suggesting that it was over very quickly" (Wenham).

---

[2]For more details on the geography of their journey, see Mathews or Wenham.

14.10, Bitumen pits... some fell into them. The precise meaning of this is uncertain. Often this word, when used in war, simply means to die. It can, however, indicate a purposeful falling—*threw themselves into.*[3] It could mean, then, that they tried to hide in the pits.

If it is to be read as parallel to the following line, *the rest fled into the hill country,* then we should understand it as meaning that they hid themselves in the pits. If, however, it is to be read in contrast, it should be understood as indicative of their demise. If the latter is the case, Waltke's words are worth considering: "The forces of nature under the invisible hand of Providence also conspire against the wicked men of Sodom to bring them down in defeat." Leupold, however, sees a problem with this view, because the subjects expressed are the kings of Sodom and Gomorrah. "The assumption [that they perished] would create a difficulty in verse 17 where the king of Sodom is still alive. ...So we have the somewhat disgraceful situation of a number of defeated kings hastily crawling into bitumen pits, and their defeated armies taking refuge in the mountains." A final possibility is that "it is a general comment on the troops of Sodom and Gomorrah, that they are the ones who fell in and perished there, though as verse 17 makes plain, the king himself survived" (Wenham). This is the least likely possibility, as the natural reading of the Hebrew connects the verb *fell* with the subject *the kings.*[4]

14.12, They also took Lot... who was dwelling in Sodom. Our last encounter with Lot had him leaving the Promised Land for the plain of the Jordan. Then, we learn that he pitched his tent *toward* Sodom. Now, we learn that he was living in the city. By chapter 19, he is a respected citizen of the city and has a difficult time leaving—although admittedly not as difficult as his wife. In this verse, we find a physical consequence of his departing the Promised Land in addition to the spiritual consequence already noted. Hamilton notes: "Both Sarai and Lot are abducted while staying outside the land of promise (in Egypt and Sodom, respectively)."

"The taking of Lot proves to be Chedorlaomer's undoing. ...As the account emphasizes, Lot was 'Abram's nephew' (v 12). ...As in chapter 13, which portrays the blessing Lot enjoyed in accord with the promises made to

---

[3]"Genesis 24.64 refers to Rebekah who 'lowered herself' [lit., 'fell!'] from her camel" (Hamilton).

[4]See Mathews' footnote.

Abram (12.3), Chedorlaomer's mistreatment of Lot, which was tantamount to opposing Abram, results in his destruction (12.3, 'curse')" (Mathews).

14.13, Then one… came to Abram the Hebrew. It is striking that Abram, even though he had no property, would be well-known enough to be the immediate destination of an escapee. Perhaps it is simply "the invisible hand of providence" (Waltke).

Interestingly, this is the only place where Abram is referred to by his race. "It is clear that [Hebrew] is only invoked in contexts when Abraham and his descendants stand in relation to members of other national groups" (Alter). So also Mathews: "Reference to Abram 'the Hebrew' distinguishes him from Mamre 'the Amorite.'"[5]

The use of *the Hebrew* is one of the indicators that this chapter may have originally been an independent document (Kidner).[6] Wenham notes: "This is not a term used by Israelites of themselves, but only by non-Israelites of Israelites (39.14; 41.12)."[7]

Mamre… Eschol… Aner. These were allies of Abram. The names seem to be listed only as indicators of where Abram lived. The descriptor *allies* may indicate why Abram lived near them. That there is an alliance will later explain (v 24) why they joined Abram in this rescue operation. "The three brothers were probably the heads of aristocratic families in Hebron. Since their own kinsmen are attacked, they too have reason to uphold their treaty with Abram" (Waltke).

14.14–16, He led forth his trained men, born in his house, 318 of them. Here is where we first begin to get a picture of the wealth and prominence of Abram. To have 300 servants indicates great wealth. To have 300 *trained* servants—"practiced in arms" (Keil)—indicates an extraordinary wealth.[8]

---

[5]For more on the meaning of the word, see Waltke.

[6]See comment on verses 1–9.

[7]This, of course, raises the question as to what Abram would call himself, or what Moses would call him. Clearly, he was not an *Israelite* either.

[8]As this is the only time this term appears in the Bible, it is questioned whether this term carries with it a connotation of skilled fighters as Keil suggests. Waltke notes: "The meaning of the unique Hebrew term is derived from an Egyptian cognate meaning 'retainer,'" but Mathews says, "It refers to 'armed retainers' by Canaanite chieftains in second-millennium texts." And Hamilton: "Here in particular *[yalid]* is applied to a slave or servant whose major function is to provide military assistance. They are not shepherds who grabbed a spear or a sling and headed north for some 125 miles."

But to have 300 trained servants who were *born in his house*—as opposed to those more recently acquired—speaks to wealth and prominence beyond our typical understanding of this sojourner. In light of this, Leupold suggests, "This points to a body of servants easily numbering a thousand and gives us some idea of the size of the flocks as well as of the influence of the man."

And he divided his forces against them by night. Abram's battle strategy is described. Even his wealth and power described in the previous verse would be a pittance in comparison to the armies of these four kings. Clearly, with a 318-soldier army, he was undermanned.

And defeated them. "No foreign king can exercise power against the blessing of God."[9]

Then he brought back... Lot. The other possessions are listed as well, but the primary purpose of his warring was to regain the safety of his kinsman.

14.17, The King of Sodom. Unless they had already chosen another king, or had a hierarchy or replacement in place, this would seem to indicate that the King of Sodom did not die in the bitumen pits. Here, he comes from hiding—or, if enough time had passed, from his home—to meet with Abram.

14.18–20, Melchizedek. Like most kings in the ancient world, Melchizedek also served as the priest of his people. See Excursus F.

Salem. This is the shortened name for Jerusalem. The same form appears in Psalm 76.2.

Bread and wine. Waltke suggests, "'Bread' probably means 'food.' The combination is a merism for a full dinner, a royal banquet (see 2 Sam 17.27–29; Prov 9.5)."[10]

God Most High. This name given to God is somewhat perplexing. The two Hebrew words *El Elyon* refer to two distinct pagan Canaanite deities, but the Hebrew terms also mean, quite simply, *God Most High*, "and elsewhere are used separately or (once) together[11] as designations of the God

---

[9]Eugene F. Roop, *Genesis,* 107.

[10]"It is indeed noteworthy that one of the things that is said about Melchizedek in the Genesis narrative is passed over by [the author of Hebrews] without mention—his bringing forth of bread and wine for Abraham's refreshment. Few typologists of early Christian or more recent days could have resisted so obvious an opportunity of drawing a Eucharistic inference from these words!" F.F. Bruce, *The Epistle to the Hebrews,* 134–135.

[11]Psalm 78.35.

of Israel" (Alter).[12] But because of its Canaanite correlations, many question whether Melchizedek was a monotheistic Yahweh worshipper. It is, however, clear from the rest of Scripture—and Abram's use of the same terminology in verse 22 in conjunction with the name Yahweh[13]—that the Bible considers him to be such. Kidner offers: "Whatever *[el elyon]* meant to his predecessors and successors, [it] meant to him the true God, self-revealed in measure, as his next words show."

And he blessed him. Three times *barak* is used, which "looks back to 12.1–3 where Abram was promised that he would be a blessing and that all families would find blessing in him" (Wenham).

Possessor. Or creator.[14]

And Abram gave him a tenth of everything. "Giving the tenth was a practical acknowledgement of the divine priesthood of Melchizedek; for the tenth was, according to the general custom, the offering presented to the Deity" (Keil). And Waltke: "Melchizedek celebrates Abram as God's warrior and blesses him. Abram recognizes Melchizedek as the legitimate priest and king of God."

14.21, "Give me the persons, but take the goods for yourself." With little bargaining room, the king of Sodom makes a plea for the freedom of his people, 'generously' offering Abram the spoils of the war that he had already taken. "What is wrong with the king of Sodom's proposal is his audacity and his attitude. The victor, not a defeated king, has the right to stipulate the disposition of the spoils of war" (Waltke).

14.22, "I have lifted my hand." Abram had made an oath that he would not keep any of the Sodomites' possessions, lest their name become associated with his. He did not extend this compulsion to his allies (v 24—and one must wonder how much each of them took), but his primary concern was the return of Lot and keeping himself distinct from the wicked cities of the plain.

It is interesting to ponder why he felt so strongly about this, yet took

---

[12]"It is difficult to say that the El Elyon of Genesis 14.18 is a Canaanite deity simply on the basis that 'El Elyon, creator of heaven and earth' corresponds to no actual deity in the Canaanite pantheon. This pantheon has a god El whose grandson is Elyon" (Hamilton).

[13]"For Abram the significance of the name *El Elyon* was the sovereign lordship of his God over creation and also the nations, as shown by the defeated kings of the east" (Mathews).

[14]For a fuller treatment of this word's range of meaning, see Hamilton or Mathews.

gifts from Pharaoh in chapter 12. Perhaps it is due to his change in attitude since he returned to the Promised Land—if he is already lying and causing Sarai to commit adultery, what is the harm in taking a pagan's money? Or, perhaps, the renown of the Sodomites was already such that the pagan ways of the Egyptians paled in comparison. Leupold suggests: "No doubt, Abram knew the king of Sodom to be just such a character who would afterward distort the facts of the case in such a fashion to claim: 'I made Abram rich.'" And Waltke: "Abram anticipates that, were he to accept the offer, the king of Sodom would claim that he disadvantaged himself in order for Abram to be advantaged."

In addition to the contrast between the king of Sodom and Pharaoh, there is a clear contrast between the king of Sodom and the king of Salem. "Sodom brought nothing, whereas Melchizedek brought out bread and wine. Melchizedek blessed Abram. Sodom makes a short, almost rude demand of just six words: 'Give me people; take property yourself.' There is none of the customary courtesy. The word order (note how he mentions 'giving' before 'taking') reflects Sodom's ungracious self-centeredness" (Wenham).

"A thread or a sandal strap." "Reference to a narrow and a wide strap is a merism and synecdoche for all the plunder" (Waltke).

14.24, "The young men… the men." The word for *young men* "also has a technical military sense of picked fighters" (Alter). Here it seems that it is used to distinguish his own fighters *(young men)* with his allies *(the men)*.

Growth of the Seed: The results of rejecting the Promised Land; Melchizedek typifies the Messiah (vv 18–20; *cf.* Heb 7.1–3; See Excursus F).

Theological Reflection: Going to War with 300 Men
There's an interesting connection between Abraham and Gideon. Each of them took about 300 men to fight a much larger army and each returned victorious.

After Lot's capture in Genesis 14, Abraham takes 318 of his trained servants and went in pursuit of the kings of the East. We aren't told much about the battle, but it seems that there was some strategy involved. More than that, of course, is that God was involved.

Gideon went through a much more arduous process. He started with a large army and had to take several steps to whittle the army down. Ultimately, he had an army of three hundred. Though more of the details of his battle are told, it is essentially the same as Abraham's, except with lights, pitchers and horns. And again, the final reason he won is that God was on his side.

The obvious point in looking at the two events is that military might is not what matters with God. Or, to make it more applicable, *spiritual* might *is* what matters with God. Essentially: you and God are a majority, regardless of how outnumbered you are—this is the lesson that Elisha's servant learned in an exciting way when his eyes were opened to the angelic chariots on the hillside (*cf.* 2 Kgs 6.15–17).

But there's another lesson that we can draw from comparing the two men and their two fights. Notice how they approached their wars. With Abraham, all it took was the word of one man to send him off with full assurance that God was with him. Upon being told that Lot was captured, he gathered his servants and went into battle.

Gideon, on the other hand, required much more coaxing. The man who was initially found threshing grain in a winepress had to be gently boosted in his faith time and again—'Do a miracle, God, and I'll believe…Okay, now do it in reverse' are the most familiar two, although even on the night of the battle, he needed additional reassurance.

But ultimately, both Abraham and Gideon won their wars. And they both won to the utmost. Gideon didn't partially win while Abraham fully won. And Abraham didn't win easily while Gideon had to fight extra long to make up for his slow-developing faith. They both won. And, when you scan Hebrews 11, both of them are forever memorialized as men of faith.

And there was never a point in Judges where God expressed any frustration with Gideon or doubt as to whether or not he would eventually get where he needed to be. Never once did He tell Gideon that He was tired of bolstering Gideon's faith and that he needed to hurry things along.

Perhaps you're someone for whom faith doesn't come as easily as it did for Abraham. Or for your friends. Or for your parents. That's okay. It isn't as easy for some people as it is for others. God understands that and is patient. As long as the faith eventually comes and results in obedience, how long it took you to get there is of no consequence. As long as you get there.

Gideon won despite his shortcomings. And, even if it takes you longer than it takes someone else, you can be assured that, with faith, you will win too.

Excursus F: The Priesthood of Melchizedek

Melchizedek arrives on the scene with no warning and departs as quickly as he came. He is mentioned once again, in Psalm 110.4, as being a priest of the order in which the Messiah would come. If nothing else, this should be enough to make us want to examine him more closely.

Who was Melchizedek?

Melchizedek was, first, a priest of God Most High. This description of God is an uncommon one, yet not one without significance. "[It] draws attention to the exalted character of God. Any priesthood is evaluated according to the status of the deity who is served, which means that Melchizedek's must have been of a highly exalted kind."[1] That Abraham would later use this term signifies that *El Elyon* is to be identified with Yahweh.

That a priest of God would come from a Palestinian city is something of a surprise.[2] Kaiser suggests: "Evidently God was also calling out a people for his own name from among the Gentiles even though the text rarely pauses in its pursuit of the promise-plan of God through the Hebrew people to reflect on this phenomenon."[3] And Pickup: "It may be that the reader is expected to infer that [the iniquity of the Amorites not yet being complete (*cf.* Gen 15.16)] was due in part to Melchizedek's efforts to promote the worship of Yahweh in Salem."[4]

Melchizedek's appearance, however, is something of an enigma. The Hebrew author would later pick up on this and use it as evidence of his enduring priesthood. This has led others, however, to suggest that he was an angel or a Christophany. But these suggestions are without warrant. "It is not suggested [in the text] that he was a biological anomaly, or an angel in human guise."[5] And Kaiser: "There can be little doubt that the text treats him as if he were a real historical character who touched the life of the biblical patriarch at a very crucial time in his service for God."[6] Further, the Greek used in Hebrews makes it untenable to view Melchizedek as a pre-incarnate appearance of Christ. "A major obstacle to [this being an appearance of the Logos] is the statement that Melchizedek resembled (Gk. *Aphomoiomenos)* the Son of God (Heb 7.3). The

---

[1] Donald Guthrie, *The Letter to the Hebrews: An Introduction and Commentary*, 155.

[2] "That 'Salem' was a designation for Jerusalem is confirmed by its use in Psalm 76.2... in synonymous parallelism with 'Zion.'" D.W. Burdick, "Melchizedek," *ISBE*, 313.

[3] *Hard Sayings*, 120.

[4] Martin Pickup, *From the Prophets to the Son*, 157.

[5] F.F. Bruce, *The Epistle to the Hebrews*, 137.

[6] *Hard Sayings*, 120.

verb *aphomoioo* always assumes two distinct and separate identities, one of which is a copy of the other. Thus Melchizedek and the Son of God are represented as two separate persons, the first of which resembled the second."[7]

Jewish scholars found difficulty in Melchizedek being greater than their patriarch, and sought to alleviate that tension by identifying him with another historical character. "That Melchizedek should be greater than Abraham, as Genesis 14 so clearly indicates, constituted a problem for Jewish exegetes. Some of them identified him with Shem, whose life, according to MT, overlapped Abraham's—he survived the Flood by some 500 years (Gen 11.11)."[8] And Edersheim has slightly modified this proposal: "We stand here at the threshold of two dispensations. The covenant with Noah had, so to speak, run its course, or rather was merging into that with Abram. At the commencement of the New Testament, John gave testimony to Jesus, and yet Jesus was baptized by John; so here Melchizedek gave testimony to Abram, and yet received tithes from Abram. If we add, that in our view Melchizedek was probably the last representative of the race of *Shem* in the land of Canaan, which was now in the hands of the Canaanites, who were children of *Ham*, as well as that he was the last representative of the *faith* of Shem, in the midst of idolatry—being a 'priest of the most high God,'—the relation between them will become more clear."[9]

Can we put any credence in suggestions that Melchizedek was Shem or the last of his descendants in Canaan? We find it speculative, at best, to link Melchizedek with Shem. If he is to be identified with another Bible character, the Bible does not make that connection clear. Although it is possible that Melchizedek is one of Shem's descendants, he is one who did not make the genealogy or was known by another name (*cf.* Gen 11.10–26). It seems better, rather, to understand Melchizedek as someone who knew of God from other means, and was thus appointed to be His priest.

Melchizedek Before the New Testament
Although the Old Testament is silent about Melchizedek after his brief appearance (save the Psalm already mentioned), people remembered him.[10] "There is some evidence that the Hasmonean priest-kings of Judah (164 BC–63 BC),

---

[7]D.W. Burdick, "Melchizedek," *ISBE*, 313.

[8]F.F. Bruce, *The Epistle to the Hebrews*, 139.

[9]Alfred Edersheim, *Bible History: Old Testament*, 61.

[10]Does the Bible subtly mention him again? "Some scholars point to the sudden appearance of the Zadokite line of priests after David captures Jerusalem, suggesting that they descended from Melchizedek (the ZDK in Zadok and Melchizedek are forms of the same root) and merged with the Aaronic line." *Hard Sayings*, 684. *Cf.* 2 Sam 8.17; 15.24–36; 17.15.

from which the Sadducees probably came, looked to Melchizedek for a precedent of a person who was both a priest and a king."[11] Further, "[A Qumran fragment] saw Melchizedek as playing a significant role, standing in the assembly of God among the angelic beings. There he is depicted as executing divine judgment, which is somehow related to the Jubilee Year. He also seems to be involved either as the one who atones for the sins of the people or as the priest who mediates atonement to them."[12] It seems evident that Melchizedek's brief cameo in the Genesis narrative had made quite an impression on subsequent generations.

The Priesthood of Melchizedek

David says that the Messiah was to be of the same order of priesthood as Melchizedek. But what exactly is the order of Melchizedek?

The author of Hebrews seeks to extrapolate this very thing by making a comparison of Melchizedek and the Messiah. He compares his name (translated King of Righteousness, Heb 7.2) with the Messiah's position as the king of righteousness. "This type of exegesis would possess special force for Jewish readers, for whom names were significant, because it was accepted that names denoted the nature as well as the identity of the person."[13] This, with the subsequent title, king of Peace (Heb 7.2), helps to identify Melchizedek and the Messiah as the same type of priest-king.

But the most significant aspect of their priesthood that marks them as being of the same order is the ascension to it and the duration of it. The author of Hebrews notes that Melchizedek has no genealogy. This is not intended to convey that he had no parents and, thus was an angelic being, but that he did not come to his position through any sort of birthright. A parallel example may help illustrate this point. An inscription about an Assyrian king, who assassinated Ben Hadad and usurped the throne, calls him the "son of nobody." "The point of the inscription is that this man did not inherit the kingship through succession; he was not of the royal lineage."[14] And Guthrie: "Unlike the Aaronic priests for whom Levitical descent was essential for eligibility to hold office, the order of Melchizedek is a wholly different kind. There is no account of his father or children. He stands mysteriously apart from all need to establish his genealogy."[15] Pickup summarizes: "Melchizedek's lack of priestly ancestry

[11]*Hard Sayings*, 684.

[12]D.W. Burdick, "Melchizedek," *ISBE*, 313.

[13]Donald Guthrie, *The Letter to the Hebrews: An Introduction and Commentary*, 156.

[14]Martin Pickup, *From the Prophets to the Son*, 164.

[15]Donald Guthrie, *The Letter to the Hebrews: An Introduction and Commentary*, 156.

is noteworthy in light of the fact that hereditary succession was an integral element of Old Testament Judaism. The entire Jewish system was predicated upon it. …According to the Law of Moses the Jewish priesthood was a hereditary right, based solely upon genealogical succession," ultimately concluding, "Scripture was silent about his ancestry since it was extraneous to his priesthood. Melchizedek's priesthood originated with Melchizedek himself."[16]

The duration of Melchizedek's priesthood—and the Messiah's—is said to be eternal (Heb 7.3; *cf.* Psa 110.4). Guthrie explains: "What makes Melchizedek's order perpetual is that Scripture says nothing about the succession."[17] And Bruce: "Nowhere is it related that Melchizedek lost his priestly office by death, whereas we have the record, generation after generation, of Levitical priests who died and had to hand on their dignity and duty to their heirs."[18]

That their priesthood is forever need not imply that Melchizedek still functions as a priest. The Hebrew word used for *forever* speaks simply of futurity in an indefinite manner. Thus, "All three priesthoods could be described appropriately by this language. But the difference between the Levitical priesthood and the other two priesthoods was this: with the Levitical priesthood, it was the *priestly succession* that was promised to be forever; Aaron himself was never promised perpetual priesthood, nor was any single Levitical priest. But the Messiah and Melchizedek were themselves designated priests forever. The point the Hebrew writer is making when he says that Melchizedek abides a priest forever is that Melchizedek personally fulfilled the full duration of that priestly service. He himself was a priest forever, not he and a priestly succession. This fact precisely foreshadowed the priesthood of the Messiah. The Messiah would personally function as a priest forever, for the full duration of his required service, and he would never pass on that office to a successor."[19] Thus, *forever* would imply not the time involved in the priestly function, but the exhaustive nature of it.

Finally, the author of Hebrews shows the eternal nature of this order of priesthood by pointing out that Melchizedek did not die (Heb 7.3). Again, this is not to be understood as a literal never-ending life, but that there is no record of his death. "Scripture never presents Melchizedek as dying and passing on his office to a successor. His priesthood was not of that type. Scripture's portrayal of Melchizedek only as alive, with no account of his death, high-

---

[16]Martin Pickup, *From the Prophets to the Son,* 167,169.

[17]Donald Guthrie, *The Letter to the Hebrews: An Introduction and Commentary,* 157.

[18]F.F. Bruce, *The Epistle to the Hebrews,* 141.

[19]Martin Pickup, *From the Prophets to the Son,* 176.

lights the fact that his office was not one that required successors; it was carried out solely by this one man himself whose own life was sufficient to fulfill the office. So it is, the Hebrew writer argues, with the priesthood of Christ. He will be succeeded by no one, for He Himself will fulfill His high priestly role till the end of time."[20]

To summarize, Melchizedek's priesthood was one held by himself alone: "The information Scripture was silent about regarding Melchizedek was information indispensable to the Levitical priesthood. ...Therein lies the major point of similarity between the Melchizedek priesthood and the priesthood of Christ. Christ's priesthood was solely His own. He neither inherited it from a predecessor, nor would He pass it on to a successor."[21] His role as a priest of God was one which He performed exhaustively, needing no heirs.

It is this, we believe, that marks the order of Melchizedek. A priesthood—and kingship—where one person fully exhausts the priestly role (*cf.* Heb 7.23–24) and never passes the office on to a successor.

---

[20]*Ibid.*, 174.

[21]*Ibid.*, 173.

15 *1, After these things.* Critical scholars suppose that these words do not refer to chapter 14, as it seems to be of separate origin. "But the events of that chapter followed convincingly those of chapter 13, and Abram's fine renunciation in 14.20b–24 makes the promise of this verse doubly apt" (Kidner). "Coming on the heels of the battle, the Lord's word to Abram...has the character of a royal grant to an officer for faithful military service" (Kline qtd. in Waltke). And, "God's reward takes the place of the spurned booty" (Waltke).

The word of the LORD *came to Abram in a vision.* "Since the chapter presents itself as a unit, one part naturally attaching itself to the other, the statement at the head, that this revelation came in a vision, covers the entire chapter" (Leupold). And Keil: "The expression 'in a vision' applies to the whole chapter. There is no pause anywhere, nor any sign that the vision ceased, or that the action was transferred to the sphere of the sense and of external reality." And Hamilton: "The emphasis in verses 1–6 is that Abram had a vision of Yahweh in which the following action and dialogue took place."

It is interesting to note that this is a formula that is characteristic of the prophetic books, not of the patriarchal accounts. To that end, "It is noteworthy that in Genesis 20 God refers to Abraham as a 'prophet'" (Alter).

"Fear not." The context *(i.e., after these things)* may suggest that Abram feared some sort of retaliation from the eastern kings whom he had ambushed (Waltke); however, the remainder of this chapter—indeed, everything from here through 18.21—is about his childlessness. Perhaps the events of chapter 14, followed by Lot's return to Sodom (*cf.* 18.22–19.1), reinforced that Lot was not to be his heir. A third alternative, based on the frequency with which this phrase occurs in the context of a divine oracle, is that God is simply calming Abram as He speaks to him, since God's appearance to man historically brings terror to the recipient of the vision.

15.2, "The heir of my house is Eliezer of Damascus." His place as the heir of Abram's household is most likely due to Lot's departure.

Kidner argues that Abram's response to God displays more faith than doubt. If he had no faith in God's original promise, he would have had no desire to question why he had no familial heir. "He has set his heart on the original vision and call. ...His spirited response opens the way to the explicit pledge of verses 4 and 5 and the informed faith of verse 6."

15.4–6, "Your very own son shall be your heir." Until this point, the promise had not been this specific, and it is still not as specific as it will later be (17.16). Because the Old Testament does speak of a legal heir as 'son' (*cf.* Ruth 4.17), it is emphasized that Abram's heir would be his very own son. "From this point onward, Abram is enabled to see clearly that when God speaks of Abram's offspring, He means the term very literally" (Leupold). Many translations render this verse as a son that would come from his own loins. The point, of course, is exactly the same. "Abram will have a real son, not simply a legal heir" (Wenham).

"Number the stars, if you are able to number them... so shall your offspring be." Here is an analogy that is lost to urban culture. A visit to a country field, unobstructed by light pollution, would help the average reader to better understand God's point. Modern astronomy will tell us approximately how many stars are visible to the naked eye, but of course, that is not the point. An average person scanning the night sky finds the stars innumerable—this is the purpose of the illustration.

There is a close comparison between this analogy and that given in 13.16: *the dust of the earth*. Both assume a family beyond numbering, but the change from sand to stars may reflect even more: "The comparison now stresses not only numbers, but a noble sort of multitude that God will bring into being" (Leupold). And Alter: "This is a complementary image to that of the numberless dust in chapter 13 but, literally and figuratively, loftier, and presented to Abraham in the grand solemnity of a didactic display, not merely as a verbal trope to be explained."

And he believed the LORD. According to Waltke, "The Hebrew is better translated 'trusted.' Abram considers God true, reliable and trustworthy." And according to Leupold, the Hebrew uses a "device [that indicates] the permanence of this attitude is to be stressed: not only: Abram believed just this once, but: Abram proved constant in his faith."

15.7–8, "I am the LORD who brought you out." We find this phrase for the first time in a passage that goes on to foretell the bondage to the Egyptians and exodus. This is almost certainly no accident, as this phrase is most well known in the Old Testament with the added prepositional phrase *of Egypt*.

"How am I to know?" It would seem odd for a man whose faith was attested just moments earlier to already be asking in doubt. Rather, it is better understood as "desire for the confirmation or sealing of a promise"

(Keil). This understanding of Abram's motive explains the covenant proceedings which follow. Ultimately, this indicates that, instead of doubt, "Abram's request for a sign is motivated by faith. ...Complaint and faith are not antithetical; complaint is based on taking God seriously" (Waltke).

15.10–11, And he brought him all these, cut them in half, and laid each half over against the other. The first important matter to understand is that this is not a sacrifice. That he did not burn the animals nor have an altar should clarify that at once. Rather, this fits clearly with the ancient custom of covenant rituals. "Covenants in which the two parties step between cloven animal parts are well attested in various places in the ancient Near East. ...The idea is that if either party violates the covenant, his fate will be like that of the cloven animals" (Alter).[1]

Birds of prey. Keil suggests: "The birds of prey represented the foes of Israel, who would seek to eat up, *i.e.,* exterminate it." And Waltke: "Here the noun may be singular or collective... and accordingly represents either Pharaoh or the Egyptians who will threaten the emergence of the nation." This would be apt, as birds of prey are unclean. If this is the case, Abram's driving them away may symbolize God's protection of the nation, or may simply show Abram's desire to protect his progeny. It does, however, seem difficult to make the divided animals representative of the later Israelites as this interpretation would do. But assuming that this is part of the vision,[2] it would seem odd if these birds and Abram's reaction to them were not indicative of something.

Alter, who sees this section as not being a part of the vision, renders this phrase *carrion birds*, a preferable translation if this is not part of the vision; birds of prey would be uninterested in dead animals.

15.12, A deep sleep fell on Abram. If the position posited above is true, this would refer to a deeper level of the vision: "The vision here passes into a prophetic sleep produced by God" (Keil). On the other hand, this could signify a new vision. If that is the case, this chapter contains two visions (1–6; 12–16) with the preparation for the covenant ceremony following the first vision and the actual ritual following the second. Interestingly, this is the same word used of Adam's sleep (Alter).

---

[1] See comment on verse 17.

[2] See comment on verse 1.

Dreadful and great darkness fell upon him. We are not told exactly what this darkness is or represents,[3] but perhaps it describes Abram's feeling throughout this portion of the vision. Leupold suggests an interpretation based on the difference between the participle and verbal form of *fall* in its two instances in this passage, *i.e.*, the darkness fell as a single act, but the dreadful darkness kept falling. If this is correct, it would show this phrase to be a descriptor of Abram's emotional state through the vision. Thus, "The 'terror and the great darkness' that fall upon him are the terror which the ancestor experiences in the vision at the revelation of the sufferings which his descendants must endure" (Leupold).

15.13–14, "Sojourners… servants… afflicted." It is not difficult to see why a dreadful and great darkness fell upon Abram as he heard this.

"400 years." "Compare the 120-year delay before the flood… God's people must learn to live with delay (2 Pet 3.8–10)" (Waltke). See Excursus G.

"But I will bring judgment on the nation that they serve." God reminds Abram that, as creator of all, He is also the judge of all. Unlike the false, pagan, local deities, all are ultimately accountable before Yahweh, the one true God.

"They shall come out with great possessions." They will live as afflicted slaves, but they will leave as a wealthy nation (*cf.* Exod 12.35–39).

15.15–16, "As for yourself." The natural question for Abram—whether he asked it aloud, we do not know—is: *When will this happen?* or, perhaps, *In my lifetime?* God answers this, perhaps putting his mind to ease.

"You shall go to your fathers." This is the standard Old Testament euphemism for death. It is important to note that, although we know little of how much the patriarchs understood about the afterlife, they had some belief in it. This phrase cannot be understood strictly as the burial in a family tomb.[4]

"The iniquity of the Amorites." As the largest tribe in the region of Canaan, *Amorites* often stood for the entire land as it does here (*cf.* Josh 24.15; Jdg 6.10). "They were nearing the point where the divine tolerance could bear with them no longer, but they had not yet arrived at this point"

---

[3]Waltke suggests that the darkness represents Israel's enslavement and mistreatment in Egypt.

[4]See comment on 25.8.

(Leupold). In this statement, God again affirms that all are subject to His judgment. "This... articulates the idea that the fixing of times is conditioned not on necessity but on morality" (Hamilton).

They shall come back here in the fourth generation. By the typical measure of a generation, the Israelite sojourn in Egypt greatly exceeds four generations.[5] Within the context, specifically that of a 400-year sojourn, it is better to understand *generation* here to mean *life-span* or *time-span*. Thus, a generation would stand for 100 years; four generations would equal 400 years. Albright understands this not as a difficulty, but as "the translation of archaic terminology into classical Hebrew" (qtd. in Hamilton).

15.17–18, A smoking fire pot and a flaming torch. While Alter is correct that this particular rendition of smoke and fire is peculiar to this chapter, we must disagree with his position to not interpret symbolism into these images. The context of the vision demands that these symbols be understood as God who passes between the animals. God's later use of smoke and fire (*cf.* Exod 13.21)—albeit without the fire pot or torch—would seem to verify this interpretation.

Passed between these pieces. Previously, Abram had arranged for a covenant ceremony, but God did not fulfill the ritual before telling Abram what was in store for his offspring. Here, the covenant is completed. *The* LORD *[cut] a covenant with Abram.*[6] This wording, plus the ritual described echoes Jeremiah 34.18, "which speaks of the people passing between a dismembered calf. This act is then interpreted as an enacted curse. 'May God make me like this animal, if I do not fulfill the demands of the covenant.' ...[Here], it is God himself who walks between the pieces, and it is suggested that here God is invoking the curse on Himself, if He fails to fulfill the promise" (Wenham).

"Since Abram does not walk through the pieces, he is not under obligation to the Lord to realize the promises" (Mathews). Further, there is nothing that Abram could have done to ensure this covenant was brought about: mankind's fate is wholly in the hands of God. That does not mean, of course, that nothing is required of Abram: faithful obedience is a con-

---

[5]The only way to make four literal generations fit is to hold to a position of a 215-year bondage in Egypt, which has other difficulties. See Excursus G.

[6]The Hebrew word for *cut* is invariably used when describing a covenant being made. Most translations obscure this by using *made* in its place.

sistent requirement of the human participants in a covenant relationship with God (*cf.* ch 22). It indicates that the promise was to come first, and foremost, through the working of God. This is manifestly evident in Abram's encounters with Pharaoh and Abimelech (chs 12; 20).

15.18–21, "*To your offspring I give this land.*" The promise of the land receives a greater level of specificity, as the promise of the seed had earlier in this chapter. The ESV footnotes a perfect tense of the verb—*I have given*—an action that can be considered already completed. "This small grammatical maneuver catches up a large narrative pattern in the Abraham stories: the promise becomes more and more definite as it seems progressively more implausible to the aged patriarch" (Alter).

Growth of the Seed: God renews covenant promises with Abram through covenant ceremony (vv 4–7; 18–19).

Excursus G:
The Duration of the Egyptian Bondage

Problem: There are three figures for the duration of Israel's sojourn. How long, exactly, was the Egyptian bondage? Does the Bible give conflicting details? Can these differences be resolved?

Passages mentioning 400 Years: Genesis 15.13, 16; Acts 7.6
Passages mentioning 430 Years: Exodus 12.40–41; Galatians 3.17
Passages mentioning 450 Years: Acts 13.17–20 [1]

Hoehner offers three suggestions to solving this dilemma.[2] We will follow his three suggested durations, summarizing his points and suggested weaknesses to each position, then offer our own comments.

Suggestion 1: An Egyptian Bondage of 215 Years
The 430 years mentioned in Galatians 3.17 begin with the call of Abraham and end with the Exodus. The 400 years has reference to the period from the weaning of Isaac until the Exodus. Therefore, one would have a 215-year sojourn in the land of Canaan and another period of 215 years in Egypt, making a total of 430 years for the sojourn. Also, it was prophesied that they would return to Palestine in the fourth generation. Four generations fits into 215 years more easily than it does into 430 years.

Hoehner's Objections to Suggestion 1
1. Both Genesis 15.13 and Acts 7.6 say that they will be in a land that is not theirs and be oppressed for 400 years.
2. Galatians 3.17 measures the 430 years from the confirmation of the Abrahamic covenant (not Abraham's call) until the Sinaitic covenant.
3. To say that Isaac was weaned at five is a guess. Children did wean much later in ancient times, but this position puts a lot of weight on estimation.
4. With regard to the *fourth generation* promise, it would seem evident that this has reference to the 400 years mentioned in the same context: *i.e.,* each generation stands for 100 years. Joseph saw his third generation before he

---

[1]This is generally accepted as an estimation based on an understanding of 400 years: 400 years of bondage, 40 of wandering, about 7 for conquest, thus 'about 450 years.' The question it leaves is why Paul would write 430 in Galatians 3 and estimate from 400 in Acts 13. Further, some question remains about this reference due to manuscript differences found here. The KJV and its followers find a reading that places the 450 years after the exodus until the time of the judges. Such a New Testament textual critical question is outside the scope of this study, though we must at least acknowledge it.

[2]Harold Hoehner, "The Duration of the Egyptian Bondage," *BSac* 129 (1969): 306–316.

died (Gen 50.23); ten generations are listed between Jacob and Joshua (1 Chron 2.2; 7.20–27).[3]

5. An increase in national population from 70 or 75[4] to more than 2 million (on the basis that there were 603,550 men of arms, *cf.* Num 1.46; 2.32) would need more than 215 years.

We do not have any further objections to offer to this suggestion or responses to his objections.

Suggestion 2: An Egyptian Bondage of 430 Years

The 430 years refers to the length of the Egyptian bondage. Four hundred years is just a round number. This is the standard suggestion that is held by many conservative scholars to this day (*e.g.*, Waltke, Hamilton, Finegan as well as some of the scholarship from a generation or two before: Young, Leupold, Keil, *etc.*).[5]

Hoehner's Objections to Suggestion 2

1. "This view does not adequately explain the difference between the 430 years and the 400 years. To pass the 400 years off as only a round number seems to do an injustice to the text. The proponents of this view do not cite any other examples of such a phenomenon" (*e.g.*, the proponents of this view take literally the 300 years in Judges 11.26).

2. The advocates of this view have little or no discussion of the 430 years in Galatians 3.17.

3. Why would Paul give a figure of 430 years in Galatians 3 and 400 years in Acts 13? One would think that he would be consistent.

4. How do you reconcile the 430 years (if it's the exact number) with the *about 450* which includes the wilderness wandering and the conquest time? Certainly *about 450 years* could not be stretched to 477 years!

5. "If one holds any sort of doctrine of inspiration, it seems difficult to pass off the 400 years as a round number. Would not this allow great liberty in interpreting other numbers in the Scriptures?"

In response to Hoehner's objections: The first two and last are weak, at best. First, whether or not the proponents of this view take the 300 of Judges 11 lit-

---

[3] See comment on 15.17.

[4] On how many went to Egypt, see comment on 46.8–27.

[5] Although it cannot be considered as evidence, the continuance of modern scholarship to assert this view speaks some confidence in it. (See James R. Battenfield, "A Consideration of the Identity of the Pharaoh of Genesis 47," *JETS* 13 [1970]: 77–85.)

erally has no bearing on whether or not this instance is an estimation. While we make no claims at being an expert in biblical numerology (if it may be so designated), numbers are often filled with symbolic meaning, and this one—40 X 10—would fit perfectly into that category. Second, that those scholars who argue this do not discuss the 430 years of Galatians has no bearing on whether or not it is an accurate assessment. Finally, the doctrine of inspiration also has no bearing on whether or not this is an estimate: that inspiration excludes estimation is purely conjecture—especially if God Himself first gave the 400 year estimate when talking to Abraham! All of these objections are irrelevant.

Objections three and four go together—*i.e.,* why was Paul not consistent in his own reporting of the elapsed time? This objection is a difficult one with which proponents of the second view must come to terms. We have not found a clear answer to this objection in any scholarship, nor are we able to provide one of our own.

Suggestion 3: An Egyptian Bondage of 400 Years

The Egyptian bondage refers to the 400-year period stated in Genesis 15 and Acts 7. The 430 years is that period of time from the confirmation of the Abrahamic covenant to the Mosaic covenant (Gal 3). The *about 450 years* began in Egypt (Acts 13), included the 400 years of bondage, 40 years of wandering, and about 7 to conquer land. This position accounts for all three different numbers without any estimation, except where one is obviously used in Paul's own words.

On a superficial level, this is clearly the most attractive option, as it offers a solution to all of the different numbers (400, 430, 450). Unfortunately, as this is Hoehner's view, he offers the fewest objections to it of any of the options and quickly backpedals from the one objection he gives.

Hoehner's Objection to Suggestion 3

Exodus 12.40–41 states that their Egyptian bondage was 430 years, not 400.

Hoehner's Rejoinder to the Objection

First, Exodus and Galatians do not say that the *bondage* was 430 years, but the *sojourn.*

Second, notice how the various translations render the relative pronoun *asher* in Exodus 12.40. ASV and RSV translate it *that,* referring to the time; KJV translates it *who,* referring to the Israelites. So, a question remains as to whether it says that the children of Israel were a group of people who sojourned for 430 years, or that they were a people who sojourned *in Egypt* for 430 years. Since the Hebrew relative pronoun is indeclinable and its antecedent may be singular or plural and of either gender, there is great latitude in how it can be translated. Hoehner suggests that *children of Israel* is a better choice for its antecedent since it is closer in position and since the ASV and RSV chose the English word *time* based on a secondary meaning of *movoshab*. This is the only place (out of 44 occurrences) where the ASV and RSV translators translate it with *time*, including an occurrence in the same chapter (Exod 12.20). Essentially, basing this suggestion's downfall on that one verse, when it is possible (if not probable) to translate it in a way that aligns with this suggestion is questionable.

Finally, the LXX of Exodus 12.40 reads: *Now the sojourning of the Children of Israel, who dwelt in the Land of Canaan and in the land of Egypt was 430 years.* This seems to imply that the 430 years were not intended to include the Egyptian bondage only.

Further Objections to Suggestion 3

In order for this suggestion to bear out, it must follow that the time began with the confirmation of the covenant. This, of course, is allowable—if not preferable—from the Galatians passage. But for this to work, the counting must begin with the last recorded confirmation of the covenant before going into Egypt— the confirmation given to Jacob in Genesis 35. That this would be the designated starting point of the stopwatch, rather than the original promise in chapter 12, the making of the covenant in chapter 15, the giving of the sign of the covenant in chapter 17, or any number of other confirmations of the covenant—except that it is the only one that fits Hoehner's suggestion—is perplexing.

Finally—and again, we acknowledge that this objection is far from conclusive—we find it curious that in the nearly 40 years since Hoehner's view was first published in a major biblical studies journal, not one noteworthy scholar has adopted his view. While the lack of corroborating support among biblical scholarship does not seal the case against Hoehner's view, it should make the student think twice before adopting it as his own without any reservation or further study of the matter.

16 In this account, the story shifts its point of view so that each of the women involved is the focal point of half of the chapter: Sarai for the first half; Hagar for the last half. "In both cases the women are distraught over their position in the household: Sarai is embarrassed by her barrenness, and Hagar faces the life of an outcast" (Mathews).

Inside the larger structures mentioned at the head of the various sections, many smaller narrative devices exist. The following (taken from Waltke) is just a sampling of the rich literary style found throughout the book of Genesis.[1]

A Sarai proposes (1–2a)
  B Abram agrees (2b)
    C Sarai's action (3)
      D Hagar's reaction (4)
A' Sarai proposes (5)
  B' Abram agrees (6a)
    C' Sarai's action (6b)
      D' Hagar's reaction (6c)

16.1, Now Sarai, Abram's wife, had borne him no children. Sarai's barrenness, foreshadowed (11.30) and forgotten, now comes to a head. "The complication of the seed now resembles the complication of the land" (Waltke).

A female Egyptian servant whose name was Hagar. Hagar was most likely obtained during their Egyptian sojourn (*cf.* 12.16).

There are conflicting beliefs as to what her relationship with Sarai was. Waltke says, "A maidservant is a personal servant owned by a rich woman, not a slave girl answerable to the master. Hagar's relationship to Sarah resembles Eliezer's to Abram" (also Mathews). But Alter argues, "The tradition of English versions that render this as 'maid' or 'handservant' imposes a misleading sense of European gentility on the sociology of the story. The point is that Hagar belongs to Sarai as property, and the ensuing complications of their relationship build on that fundamental fact." Thus, Alter renders Hagar's position as *slavegirl*.

At the root of this debate is whether the Hebrew *ama* and *schiphcha* are to be understood as two different categories of servants (as Waltke would argue) or synonymous (Alter).

---

[1]See David A. Dorsey, *The Literary Structure of the Old Testament.*

Wenham may offer the best solution: "In some contexts 'maid' is interchangeable with 'slave-girl.' …However, 'slave-girls' usually seem to be answerable to a master as opposed to mistress," and, "That Hagar is under Sarai's control is emphasized in the following story by the personal adjectives, 'my maid,' 'her maid.' Sarai gives Hagar to Abram, and even afterwards Abram states, 'As the maid is under your authority' (vv 2,3,6)."

16.2, "Go in to my servant; it may be that I shall obtain children by her." More literally, this passage reads *"be built up through her."* The Hebrew of *built* and *son* sounds strikingly similar and is to be understood as a play on words (Alter) and is a Hebraism for *obtain a son* (Waltke). "It was a serious matter for a man to be childless in the ancient world, for it left him without an heir. But it was even more calamitous for a woman: to have a great brood of children was the mark of success as a wife; to have none was ignominious failure. So throughout the ancient East polygamy was resorted to as a means of obviating childlessness" (Wenham).

Notice how impersonal all of this is. "Sarai never speaks directly to Hagar or speaks her name; Hagar is a tool to relieve Sarai's embarrassment. Yet Sarai never claims Ishmael as her son (cp. Rachel, 30.6; Leah, 30.20)" (Mathews).

"The LORD has prevented me from bearing children." Though God is often the last place to look in times of success, He is the first place to look when casting blame. But the explanation of this statement may lie in something more than disparaging God: "Sarai's words reflect an OT perspective that Yahweh is the ultimate source behind all of life's experiences, from the exhilarating to the annoying and depressing" (Hamilton). Whatever the motivation, in this instance, Sarai was right. God *had* restrained her from bearing children. If the Egyptian sojourn had resulted in adultery, a time for purifying before the coming of the promised seed would have been in order. Mostly, however, it seems that God's restraining was to teach faith and patience.

16.3, So after Abram had lived ten years in the land of Canaan. It has been ten years since the family's arrival in Canaan. The promised seed has not come and Sarai has passed her childbearing years.

Hagar the Egyptian. See EXCURSUS I.

Gave her to Abram her husband as a wife. The word used is not the word for concubine and modern translations that render it such miss the point of the narrative. "The terminological equation of the two women is surely intended, and sets up an ironic backdrop for Sarai's abuse of Hagar" (Alter). That literary point made, God still sees a distinction between the two women and their place in the family.[2] It is also interesting that although she is called a wife here, 25.6 uses the standard Hebrew word for concubine when speaking of her and Keturah, who is also initially called a *wife* (25.1).

And what a reversal of roles we find! "Just as Abram gave Sarai to Pharaoh, now Sarai gives Hagar to Abram. Abram the donor becomes Abram the receiver, and Sarai the pawn becomes Sarai the initiator" (Hamilton).

"The institution of surrogate maternity to which she resorts is by no means her invention, being well attested in ancient Near Eastern legal documents" (Alter). Thus, although this was an acceptable practice in their custom, it is obvious that the negative consequences far outweighed the positive—or, to use Kidner's words, "The present story and chapter 30 are proof of its unwisdom." Further, it clearly falls outside God's ideal for marriage, which was taught from the beginning. It was Sarai's idea, but Abram listened to her; Hagar apparently didn't protest (and we cannot know how much good it would have done her had she protested). So who was ultimately at fault? It would seem most likely that everyone holds a little of the responsibility: none are exonerated from the long-lasting effects of this arrangement.

The primary problem with Sarai's idea—outside its defilement of the marriage relationship—is that "it involved the employment of human devices seemingly to bolster up a divine purpose" (Leupold). "Her complaint condemns her for seizing the initiative from [God's] hands" (Waltke). This passage—and many others—fly in the face of the manmade doctrine that 'God helps those who help themselves.' While this is sometimes true, other times it clearly is not. The Bible teaches that God helps the faithful. And sometimes, even that cannot be seen.

Interestingly, Hamilton defends this arrangement: "It is difficult to determine whether this is an obligation or a privilege for Sarai. Both the biblical text in Genesis 16 and the extrabiblical texts are ambiguous enough to support either conclusion. But given the emphasis on the indispensability of (male) progeny to perpetuate the family line, I am inclined to think that Sarai's action was obligatory, and that no ignominy was attached to

---

[2]See comment on verse 9.

such a procedure." Harrison clarifies the 'extrabiblical texts' mentioned by Hamilton: "The Nuzu tablets indicate that the institution of marriage was regarded as a means of procreation rather than a device for human companionship. The marriage contract provided that if the wife remained childless for any reason, she was obliged to give a handmaid to her husband, so that children might be born into the family circle."[3]

Gave... took... went in to. Many commentators note how closely this passage parallels The Fall. Wenham summarizes this point nicely: "The sequence of events is similar in both cases: the woman takes something and gives it to her husband, who accepts it." What's more significant is that it seems to indicate the author's perception of this act: "By employing quite similar formulations and an identical sequence of events in Genesis 3.6b and 16.3–4a, the author makes it clear that for him both narratives describe comparable events" (Berg qtd. in Wenham).

16.4, She looked with contempt on her mistress. After the plan was successful (*i.e.,* Hagar conceived), we begin to see the evil results of this evil beginning. Appropriately, Sarai, the initiator of the plan, is the first to feel these results (Keil). This passage is also translated *became dishonorable in her eyes* or *lightly esteemed in her eyes.* The idea is that Hagar felt a boastful feeling, perhaps to the point of looking down on Sarai: 'God has given me what he did not give you,' she says. Waltke notes that the same word is translated *curses* in 12.3. Perhaps she felt that her pregnancy exalted her to a position ahead of Sarai in the familial pecking order. "Sarai reads Hagar's action as a threat against her place in the household" (Mathews).

16.5–6, And Sarai said to Abram. Sarai's anger leads to impaired judgment. Further, Hagar's wrong leads Sarai to do a further wrong. First, she blames everything on Abram, although it was initially her idea. Then, after casting the blame on Abram, she admits to her part—while still blaming him! It is amazing what someone led by emotions and wounded pride will say.

"May the LORD judge between you and me." The same ancient legal codes that allowed surrogate marriages offered protection to the first wife—Hamilton notes that the slave must not claim equality with her mistress. (He makes a distinction between that and *showing contempt.* We are more inclined to view this as the vehicle by which she showed contempt.) Ap-

---

[3] R.K. Harrison, *Old Testament Times,* 76.

parently, Abram had not protected Sarai; he allowed this situation to develop. "If Abram will not offer the legal protection to which she is entitled, Sarah hopes confidently that the Lord will" (Waltke).

"In your power." The ESV loses something of the impact made by the wordplay both here and in its rendering of *embrace* (v 5). More literally, *embrace* is *in your arms* and this verse reads *in your hands*. They are to be understood as playing off one another. "Putting Hagar 'in your [Sarai's] hands'… rectifies the charge 'in your arms'" (Mathews).

"Do to her as you please." While Abram's response may seem harsh[4]—especially in light of Sarai's current temperament—it is an entirely appropriate response, as she was Sarai's servant, not Abram's. One must assume, however, that Abram is not condoning any sort of violence. "[He] does not give her to Sarai to do whatever she pleases; rather, she is to treat Hagar as she sees 'best' (*hattob*, 'the good'). Abram directs his wife to treat the handmaiden the right way" (Mathews).

Then Sarai dealt harshly with her. The vagaries of this statement leave some question as to just what Sarai did. The word has a variety of nuances, which does not help clarify the meaning. It should be noted that the text does not say that Sarai did something that was unjustifiable. Further, Hagar had done wrong and required correction. Perhaps, Sarai proceeded to offer some corrective discipline (*e.g.,* demotion to living with other servants,[5] performing menial tasks, *etc.* have been suggested by some commentators) which did not sit well with Hagar. Of course, this term does not necessarily mean something so congenial and could refer to physical abuse. Interestingly, the same term is used to describe the suffering endured by the Israelites in Egypt. Perhaps there is seen in this passage "a foreshadowing of the Israelites' exodus experience—only in reverse."[6]

She fled from her. Whatever the case, Hagar refused the correction (or abuse) and fled. "Thus, instead of securing the fulfillment of their wishes, Sarai and Abram had reaped nothing but grief and vexation, and apparently had lost the maid through their self-concerted scheme" (Keil).

---

[4]Hamilton calls it "at best, lame and passive."

[5]This suggestion probably stems from the Code of Hammurabi, which forbids the mistress from selling the servant, but would allow her to be marked with a slave mark and counted among the slaves (Waltke).

[6]Iain M. Duguid, "Hagar the Egyptian: A Note on the Allure of Egypt in the Abraham Cycle," *WTJ* 56 (1994): 419.

16.7, The Angel of the LORD. Here is the first mention of the Angel of the Lord in the Bible. This character—the angel of Yahweh—shows up repeatedly throughout the Old Testament and clearly is not to be understood as just *any* angel of God, but a specific messenger who portrays God and often speaks as God Himself. Hagar understood this to be God Himself, even if only in the message (v 13). See EXCURSUS H.

Found her. That He would come specifically to Hagar is a huge honor. Perhaps this is to indicate that she also has faith in Yahweh. The chief servant, Eliezer, will later display great faith. Perhaps Hagar, the chief maid—if she may be so labeled—also has come to believe in Abram's God.

Shur. The exact location of Shur is unknown, though most place it somewhere on the outskirts of Egypt, between there and Palestine. "Shur means 'wall' in Hebrew, and scholars have linked the name with the line of fortifications the Egyptians built on their northern border" (Alter). Such a location for Shur makes sense, as Hagar would naturally flee to her homeland. And there may be a little more to this location's name also: "The same word could also be construed as a verb that occurs in poetic texts, 'to see' (or perhaps, more loftily, 'to espy'), and may relate to the thematics of seeing in Hagar's story" (Alter).

16.8–9, "Hagar, servant of Sarai." The Angel of Yahweh first points out Hagar's rightful place—Sarai's servant. "Her flight has not altered her position or her duty, nor has her state of pregnancy caused any such alteration: Hagar is still 'Sarai's maid'" (Leupold).

"Where have you come from?" The Angel who knew Hagar's name and position without any introduction must ask about her origin and destination!? Clearly, this question is rhetorical and may be compared with the questions that God asked Adam (3.9) and Cain (4.9). That this is "the first time the Lord has asked someone their whereabouts since Genesis 4...emphasizes the parallel between this story and those earlier ones" (Wenham).

"I am fleeing from my mistress." Hagar recognizes and admits that her position remains.

"Return... and submit." Before she can accomplish anything else, Hagar must correct the wrong in her life. In this case, she must resume her proper position of servitude to Sarai (*cf.* Onesimus and Philemon). "Plain dutiful submission in the fulfillment of her duties is sufficient for Hagar" (Leupold).

16.10–12, "I will surely multiply your offspring." God's blessing of nations to Abram finds its first fulfillment through Hagar and Ishmael. "It is striking that Hagar is the first woman to receive a birth annunciation…from the Lord" (Mathews).

"You shall call his name Ishmael." "Hagar already knows she is pregnant. …The novel information given to her now is that she is carrying a male" (Hamilton). His name, *God hears,* will be a constant reminder of this occasion when God spoke with and reassured her.

"He shall be a wild donkey of a man." Though Hamilton sees this description as "derogatory and derisive," he seems to be alone in this assessment. The wild donkey enjoys an unrestrained liberty (*cf.* Job 39.5–8). "The fearless and fleet-footed Syrian onager is a metaphor for an individualistic lifestyle untrammeled by social convention" (Waltke)—"and also anticipates his desert residence" (Mathews). "The freedom his mother sought will be his one day" (Wenham). And, "Ishmael's descendants, the Arabs, roving over the wide expanses of the desert lands adjacent to Bible lands, are still characterized by this trait" (Leupold). Kidner concludes, "To her mind, lacking the questing faith of Abram, the promise might well offer all she could wish, though it said nothing of blessing for the world or of a promised land. Enough that Ishmael would multiply, and be at nobody's beck and call."

"His hand against everyone." He will be continually at odds with other peoples. "[These words] describe most truly the incessant state of feud, in which the Ishmaelites live with one another or with their neighbors" (Keil).

"He shall dwell over against all his kinsmen." The Ishmaelites would be surrounded by, yet independent from, the rest of Abraham's seed. Kidner points out that the phrasing used is something of a double entendre: "It can have equally a local and a hostile sense (lit. 'to, or against, the face of'), and both were to be true of these cousins of Israel." Abram became the progenitor of the Muslim world through Ishmael and, through Isaac, the Jewish and Christian world. To this day, the conflict prophesied to Hagar rages on.

16.13–14, "You are a God of seeing." This is the only recorded instance of a person giving a name to God, "Hagar gives God a name that expresses His special significance to her. …She no longer gloats that she is pregnant but marvels at the Lord's care for her" (Waltke). The name she gives, *El-Roi,* could mean either *the God who sees me* (which fits the context) or *the God I see* (which fits her explanation). "The former speaks of His care for her; the latter, of her experiences of God's manifestation (Waltke).

184 | *The Growth of the Seed*

"Truly I have seen him who looks after me." Or, following the Hebrew (ESV margin), *Have I really seen him here who sees me?* Her question as to seeing God can be interpreted in one of two ways: either she was surprised that she saw Him and remained alive or she was surprised that He would appear to her at all. We would guess that Hagar's thoughts were not theological (*i.e.*, 'No one can see God and live, but I am still alive; how can that be?'), but practical (*i.e.*, She had been thinking: 'Does God see me? Does God care?' Here, God provides her an answer).

The well was called Beer-lahai-roi. "'The well of the living-one, my seer.' So the name commemorated the abiding rather than the transient element in the experience" (Kidner). "Note the difference between Hagar's exclamation in verse 13 that she has seen (something of) God, and the name given to commemorate the place where this Theophany occurred. This name focuses on the fact that God showed Himself to her. She does not call it 'the well belonging to the Living one whom I have seen.' Hagar is the object, not the subject. In effect, then, *Beer-lahai-roi* focuses on the graciousness of God who manifested Himself to a pregnant woman in the wilderness, rather than on any special status accorded to Hagar" (Hamilton).

16.15, Abram called the name of his son, whom Hagar bore, Ishmael. Abram follows the will of God in naming the child. It is assumed that either Hagar conveyed the message of God's prophecy or God spoke to Abram as well. "That Ishmael was born in Abram's house and named by Abram himself indicates that he is to be fully reckoned as Abram's son" (Hamilton).

This is strikingly different from other instances where the wife names the child of her servant through her husband (*cf.* 30.3–13). "The absence of Sarai is noteworthy. The child was intended to be Sarai's, but three times the text says 'Hagar gave birth to a son for Abram'" (Wenham). The plan devised at the beginning of the chapter has failed.

16.16, Abram was eighty-six years old. Eleven years have passed since Abram and his entourage left Haran. "Continued attention to the ebbing sands of time makes the birth of a son to the elderly couple only increasingly unlikely, magnifying the miracle of the child Isaac" (Mathews).

Growth of the Seed: Abram and Sarai seek to help the promise through Sarai's maidservant; Ishmael is born, the father of an Abrahamic nation.

Excursus H: The Angel of the Lord

Who exactly is this Angel of the Lord who appears so frequently in the Old Testament (58 times; *Angel of God,* 11 times)? Is he merely a messenger sent in God's name or is he a theophany, a visible appearance of God? "To this many answers have been given, of which the following may be mentioned: **(1)** This angel is simply an angel with a special commission; **(2)** he may be a momentary descent of God into visibility; **(3)** he may be the Logos, a kind of temporary preincarnation of the second person of the trinity."[1] We will follow Wilson's three suggestions in examining this question.[2]

An Angel with a Special Commission

"Since the root meaning of *angel* is 'messenger' or 'one who is sent,' we must determine from context whether the word refers to the *office* of the sent one or to the *nature* of created angels as finite beings."[3] Thus, it is linguistically possible for this being to simply be a messenger of God. Waltke notes: "In the ancient Near East the royal messenger was treated as a surrogate of the king. ...So also the Lord's messenger is treated as God and yet as distinct from God, as God's angel." And Payne: "The explanation that some have offered is that the Angel simply acts for God and speaks in God's name, just as did the prophets (*cf.* Isa 1.2)."[4][5]

Is the answer that simple? "Initially, some contexts of the term 'angel of the Lord' appear to refer to nothing more than any other angel. ...But as the narrative progresses, that angel transcends the angelic category and is described in terms suited only to a member of the Trinity."[6]

First, the angel is equated with God. The people who encounter this angel link him to God (*e.g.,* Hagar, Gen 16.13; Jacob, Gen 48.15–16). The angel of the Lord claims to be God (Exod 3.2–6) and the text of the Bible verifies that claim (v 4).

Second, he carries the name of God. In Exodus 23.20–23, God sends His angel ahead of the Israelites in the wilderness and warned that they must obey

---

[1]J.M. Wilson, "Angel," *ISBE,* 125.

[2]Positions 2 and 3 are differentiated by the person of the Godhead who descends, not that one is God and the other is not.

[3]*Hard Sayings,* 191.

[4]J. Barton Payne, *The Theology of the Older Testament,* 167.

[5]An interesting suggestion from Waltke: "If we may equate him with the *angelos kyriou* [Gk., angel of the Lord] of the New Testament, he announces the birth of John the Baptist (Luke 1.11) and of Jesus (Matt 1.20,24; Luke 2.9) and identifies himself as Gabriel (Luke 1.19)."

[6]*Hard Sayings,* 191.

and not rebel against this angel. "The reason was a stunning one: 'Since my Name is in him.' God would never share His memorial name with anyone else, for Isaiah 42.8 advised that He would never share His glory with another."[7]

Third, the Angel of the Lord has divine qualities, prerogative and authority: the power to give life (Gen 16.10); to see and know all (Gen 16.13; Exod 3.7); to forgive sin (Exod 23.21); to perform miracles (burning bush, Exod 3.2; plagues, Exod 3.20; calling for fire, Jdg 6.21; ascending the flame of the altar, Jdg 13.20). "Finally, this angel commanded and received worship from Moses (Exod 3.5) and Joshua (Josh 5.14). ...[Yet] when John attempted to worship an angel in Revelation 19.10; 22.8–9, he was corrected quickly and told not to do it."[8]

And so, we stand with Payne: "The evidence from the Mosaic period renders it impossible to view the Angel as a mere representative of deity."[9]

A Momentary Descent of God into Visibility

We summarize this position with the following quotes: "A study of the Angel of the Lord passages... leaves no room for doubt that the term denotes God Himself as seen in human form; what should be added is that 'Angel', by its meaning 'messenger', implies that God, made visible, is at the same time God *sent*" (Kidner). And Hamilton: "The angel of Yahweh is more a representation of God than a representative of God," going on to say that this angel is "essentially indistinguishable from Yahweh Himself." But will this position bear out?

Payne is staunchly against it, offering three examples of distinction made between the Angel of the Lord and Yahweh.

"If, as an alternative explanation, it is suggested that the Angel might be simply Yahweh, the Father Himself, in some temporary manifestation, [Exodus 3.4] proceeds to declare: 'And when Yahweh saw that he [Moses] turned aside to see, Elohim called unto him out of the bush.' That is, the Elohim-Angel is, in the text, differentiated from Yahweh."[10] Second, Exodus 23.20–21 "describes the Angel as sent by Yahweh (and so, distinct from him); but it then goes on to state that God's name (Person) is in Him."[11] Finally, "Zechariah describes the angel of Yahweh as distinct from Yahweh (1.12), and yet giving orders to ordinary angels (1.11; 3.4); and as pleading for the elect before God (1.12), and yet sitting in God's place (3.1, 2) and forgiving sins (v 4)."[12]

---

[7]*Ibid.*, 191.

[8]*Ibid.*, 192.

[9]J. Barton Payne, *The Theology of the Older Testament*, 168.

[10]*Ibid.*, 168.

[11]*Ibid.*, 168.

[12]*Ibid.*, 169.

Payne's point is not, of course, to argue that this Angel is less than deity, but to note a clear distinction between the Angel and Yahweh—between one person of deity and another.

The Logos

The Logos is, of course, the preincarnate designation for Jesus (*cf.* John 1.1–4). This is the position traditionally held by Christian exegetes through the centuries. And there is little left: clearly this being is God (*e.g.*, he accepts worship as God does); yet, just as clearly, he is, in some way, distinguished from God (*e.g.*, he pleads for the elect before God). It would seem that the best solution is that he is a different person of the Godhead.

This solution may find its final verification in Malachi. Malachi speaks of *The Angel of the Testament* (Mal 3.1), the one who will accomplish redemption by serving as the historical testator. His coming is further identified as preceded by that of God's messenger, Elijah (Mal 4.5), namely John the Baptist (Matt 11.14). Clearly, the Angel of the Testament is the Logos who would become flesh (John 1.14). If a conclusive connection between these two beings could be shown, the case would be made. Unfortunately, there is no clear connection made between this Angel of the Testament and our Angel of the Lord.[13]

Kaiser boldly says, "It is clear from this abundance of evidence that the angel of the Lord in the Old Testament was a preincarnate form of our Lord Jesus Christ, who would later permanently take on flesh."[14] While we would lean toward the same interpretation, we do not see the same "abundance" that Kaiser does and hesitate at his boldness. We would say, rather, with Wilson: "It must be remembered that these are only conjectures that touch on a great mystery."[15][16]

---

[13]To briefly argue against this position, it is odd, as Waltke notes, that the New Testament never identifies this principal Old Testament character with the principal New Testament character, if such identification is to be made.

[14]*Hard Sayings*, 192.

[15]J.M. Wilson, "Angel," *ISBE*, 125.

[16]See J. Barton Payne, *The Theology of the Older Testament*, "The Angel of the Testament," (167–170) for fuller discussion of other occurrences of this phrase.

17 Fundamental to this chapter is understanding that the covenant spoken of is not a new covenant, but an advance in the covenant previously made (15.18). "The things previously guaranteed are now foretold as finally coming to pass" (Leupold).

17.1, Abram was ninety-nine years old. We are now 24 years after Abram left Haran and at least 13 since the last chapter: "Thirteen years in which Sarah's inability to bear children has been further demonstrated. Thirteen years in which Abram's hopes of an heir have focused on Ishmael" (Wenham). Verse 24 retells his age, but as *Abraham* instead of *Abram*.

God Almighty. Heb., *El Shaddai.* "The most probable [meanings] are (1) 'The Powerful, Strong One'…and (2) 'The One who suffices'" (Waltke). Kidner notes: "More recently Shaddai has been equated with 'mountain' (*cf.* the common Old Testament term 'rock' for God); but there is no universal agreement. …[Its use] confirms the familiar emphasis on might, particularly over against the frailty of man (it is a favorite divine title in Job). In Genesis it tends to be matched to situations where God's servants are hard-pressed and needing reassurance." Regardless of its precise meaning, its uses in context seem to indicate, as Wenham says, "Shaddai evokes the idea that God is able to make the barren fertile and to fulfill His promises." Or Delitzsch: "The God who compels nature to do what is contrary to itself, and subdues it to bow and minister to grace" (qtd. in Leupold). These clearly are not to be understood as a lexical definition of the Hebrew, but they fit the way this title is used of God, especially in this case.[1]

"Walk before me." This represents a God-conscious life of the best sort; sound spiritualism. "This phrase usually expresses the service or devotion of a faithful servant to his king, be the latter human…or divine" (Hamilton). And Waltke: "To walk before God means to orient one's entire life to his presence, promises and demands."

"And be blameless." Here is described a faithful observance of all duties; conscientious conduct. "The Hebrew word signifies a wholeness of relationship and integrity rather than no sin" (Waltke).

When seen together, to *walk before God* is the soul of true religion; to *be blameless* is to practice true religion (Leupold).

---

[1] See EXCURSUS B.

17.2–3, "That I may make my covenant between me and you." "God's command for Abram to walk blamelessly is but a means to an end. If Abram so conducts himself, God will multiply him abundantly" (Hamilton). Again, this is not a different covenant than the one which was previously made. Rather, this makes operative and brings into effect the one already in existence. "God is simply assuring Abram that the time has now come to let the promised things begin to take place" (Leupold).

"The three divisions of this covenant—'As for me...' (4–8), 'As for you' (9–14), and 'As for Sarai' (15–16)—recognize the obligations of all the partners. God promises commitment to Abram and his offspring (4–8, 15–16); they follow His commands (9–14)" (Waltke).

Then Abram fell on his face. Abram worshipped. It is not God's appearance alone that brings Abram to the ground. If that were so, this verse would have immediately followed verse 1. "It is a combination of the theophany and the divine word of directive and promise that follows that produces awe in Abram" (Hamilton). And so, "Abram, in a gesture more powerful than words, shows his humility before God and his willingness to listen" (Wenham).

17.5–6, "Your name shall be Abraham." Father of a multitude.[2] But what a misnomer it must have seemed! A 99-year-old man with only one son being called the father of a multitude. Abraham must have felt much like the 6'5", 350 lb. man everyone calls *Tiny*.

"I have made you the father of a multitude of nations... I will make you into nations." Abraham will not be the father of only one nation, but many. Further, he will not be the father of a multitude of small nations, but he will be *exceedingly fruitful*, or *prolific*. Part of Abraham's progeny will also turn into a royal line, as *"kings shall come from you."*

Keil writes: "The whole of the twelve sons of Jacob founded only the nation of Israel, with which [Yahweh] established the covenant made with Abraham... so that Abraham became through Israel the lineal father of one nation only." Although Keil makes this point to emphasize a great truth—"the posterity of Abraham... extends beyond this one lineal posterity, and embraces the spiritual posterity also"—it is evident that Abraham *did*, in fact, become the lineal father of many nations, the fountainhead of which were Ishmael and Esau, as well as his sons through Keturah

---

[2] See Waltke for a more detailed description of this name's meaning.

(25.2). Indeed, "The Ishmaelites and the sons of Keturah, as well as all Israelites acknowledge him as father" (Leupold).

17.7–8, "An everlasting covenant." The Hebrew *(olam)* does not denote non-ending, but "into the hidden future" (Leupold)—or, as we might say, 'We don't know when it will end.' This word is used in some contexts to mean eternal, while in others its duration does not last longer than an individual's life. It is, therefore, suspect to exegete from this one word that God's covenant with the Jewish people remains today.

"And I will give... the land of your sojournings." The land promise is renewed after the nation promise is renewed. Shortly, the seed promise is also renewed, completing the reiteration of God's promises to Abraham. To have all these promises specifically renewed under the context of the covenant seals up everything together for the faith of Abraham.

"An everlasting possession." Again, *olam* does not mean *everlasting* in a modern sense. "Long endurance of this possession is guaranteed by this expression but not eternal possession" (Leupold).

17.9–10, "Keep my covenant." God "imposes the duty upon Abraham and all his descendants to live in a manner befitting those bound by God's covenant" (Leupold). Wenham writes, "Whereas inaugurating the covenant was entirely the result of divine initiative, confirming it involves a human response, summed up in verse 1 by 'walk in my presence and be blameless' and spelled out in the demand to circumcise every male."

"Every male among you shall be circumcised." Here, God clarifies exactly what He wants Abraham to do. It should be pointed out that circumcision is not, in itself, the covenant. "The designation of circumcision itself as a covenant is a synecdoche for covenantal obligation: 'this is [the aspect of] my covenant you must keep'" (Hamilton). The covenant, of course, is the agreement that God made with Abraham, symbolically sealed in chapter 15. Circumcision is the sign of the covenant (v 11). "[It] is God's brand" (Kidner). It is the part of the covenant which Abraham and his descendants are to keep that show him to be in covenant relationship with God.

17.11–14, "You shall be circumcised." God proceeds to give detailed instructions about this process. This, of course, is consistent with how God conducts business in the Old Testament (see Leviticus). Verse 11 answers the 'what' *(circumcised in the flesh of your foreskins)* and the 'why' *(it shall be a* *sign of the covenant between me and you).* Verse 12 gives the 'when' *(a child at eight days old)* and the 'who' *(every male... born in your house or bought with your money from any foreigner who is not of your offspring).* Verse 13 then repeats the 'who' question with an emphasis on it being for everyone. Finally, verse 14 answers the 'what if' *(any uncircumcised male... shall be cut off from his people).*

For whom is this covenant a sign? Clearly it is not to be a sign for non-Israelites as clothing would cover it up, and many other nations also practiced circumcision. Rather, it is a reminder to God's people that they are a part of God's covenant: "Thus interpreted, circumcision is a mnemonic sign, reminding God's people of who they are... from what they have been delivered, and by whom they have been delivered" (Hamilton).[3]

Alter offers the following on why circumcision is chosen for the sign of the covenant: "A covenant sealed on the organ of generation may connect circumcision with fertility—and the threat against fertility—which is repeatedly stressed in the immediately preceding and following passages. The contractual cutting up of animals in chapter 15 is now followed by a cutting of human flesh."

17.15–16, "Sarah shall be her name." Sarah is also given a new name, though there is some question as to how different this name was than Sarai. "It appears that Sarai and Sarah are only older and newer forms of the same word 'princess'; but the re-naming was a landmark and brought her specifically into the promise in her own right" (Kidner).[4] Ultimately, her name change isn't as important as her being specified as a part of the covenant. The seed would be *her* child—not an adopted heir like Lot or Eliezer; not a surrogate son like Ishmael.

"She shall become nations." With Abraham, her seed will turn into nations and even *kings... will come from her.*

17.17–18, *Then Abraham fell on his face and laughed.* This passage is typically interpreted in one of two ways (which will affect the interpretation of the next two verses as well): (a) that Abraham fell on his face in laughter

---

[3]Hamilton also offers the following: "It is equally possible that circumcision is a sign to God, as was the rainbow in chapter 9. God will see the circumcised penis of the Israelite before and during sexual congress, and will then 'remember' His promise to Abraham and to all his descendants to make them very fertile."

[4]Alter says, "[Sarai] reflects an archaic feminine suffix, [Sarah], the normative feminine suffix."

at how far-fetched this sounds (Alter, Kidner, Mathews, Waltke, Wen-ham[5]); (b) that Abraham fell on his face (in reverence) and laughs (in joy) (Keil, Leupold and Speiser[6]). We are not given a clear answer in the text, and either can be supported by the context.

And then there are those who seek to blur the lines. Calvin writes: "Not that he either ridiculed the promise of God, or treated it as a fable, or rejected it altogether; but, as often happens when things occur which are least expected, partly lifted up with joy, partly carried out of himself with wonder, he burst into laughter" (qtd. in Keil). And Delitszch: "The promise was so immensely great, that he sank in adoration to the ground, and so immensely paradoxical, that he could not help laughing" (qtd. in Keil). Though these responses are tidy, they do little to help the understanding of what follows.

For our part, we are more inclined to follow *a*. The indicator seems to be the correlation in what he says (v 17b) with what Sarah says after her laughter (18.12–13). If their thoughts and words surrounding the laughter are precisely the same, this is a fairly strong suggestion that their motivation in laughing was the same. It could be argued against *a* that it interprets the same act (falling on his face) as worship in one place (v 3) and completely differently here.[7] In either event, we would be wise to refrain from teaching our young ones that Isaac was named *laughter* because of Sarah's laughter—especially since the name is God-given at the time of Abraham's laughter, not Sarah's.[8]

Though we follow *a*, we do not leave Abraham as utterly faithless. We would stand with Kidner: "[The laughter] was a first, incredulous reaction... but open to correction. On such genuine struggles of faith God is never hard."

---

[5]Wenham writes, "The very word... 'and laughed' spells 'and Isaac.' So in laughing at God's promise, Abraham unwittingly confirms it."

[6]Though for different reasons. Speiser, a critical scholar, argues that this depiction of Abraham would be outside the keeping of P's character.

[7]Waltke's suggestion may solve this dilemma: "Is his humble posture (see 17.3) a cover-up for his inner skepticism?"

[8]Kidner suggests that his name is not to be understood as an indictment against Abraham or Sarah, but expressing a prayer. As Ishmael means *May God Hear*, Isaac would then mean *May he smile (upon him)*. Yet, of course, "To those who were in the secret it spoke of the laugh."

A further point to be made is that while Abraham laughed in the presence of God, Sarah knew not that the three visitors were from heaven. Also, she laughed *to herself* and in the tent.

"Oh that Ishmael might live before you." Following interpretation *a*, this plea to accept Ishmael should be interpreted as suggestion of a substitute. "Abraham reacts...not with joy and celebration, but with consternation: it is a complication in his life."[9] Those who would follow interpretation *b* would argue that this is simply a father looking out for his son's welfare, realizing that he is not to be a part of the promise: "When he observes that God's new promise passes by Ishmael completely, he seeks a favor from God for him, that he too might have God's good will directed toward him" (Leupold).

17.19–20, "No, but Sarah your wife shall bear you a son." There is some question as to whether God's retort should be translated as *no* or *most assuredly*. If *no* is the proper translation, God is refusing Abraham's request (which certainly cannot be, then, to look after Ishmael, as God twice does—chapters 16, 21—and here assures Abraham that He will). Thus, verse 19 represents God refusing Abraham's request for Ishmael's standing in the Messianic line and verse 20 indicates that Ishmael will not be left without hope—though He will not count Ishmael as the blessed child, He knows of Abraham's concern for him. This translation would be the final exegetical clue that the proper interpretation is *a*.

If, however, *most assuredly* is to be preferred, we find God prophesying about Isaac in verse 19 and granting Abraham's request in verse 20. This interpretation is more ambiguous, though it would seem to support an interpretation of *b*—"Since nothing in Abraham's remark suggests a substitute suggestion, God has nothing to reject" (Leupold).

"As for Ishmael, I have heard you." It is interesting that in this response, God highlights the etymology of Ishmael's name, perhaps intending to remind Abraham that He had already promised as much. God will not leave Ishmael without hope. He will father twelve princes corresponding to Israel's twelve tribes. "In rehearsing this for Israel, Moses is reminding the Jews that the Arab nations had a common father with them. And in saying Abraham was willing to settle for Ishmael (17.18) rather than look for some future promise, Moses would undermine any grounds for elitism in the Jews. And in rehearsing that God gladly heard Abraham's prayers on behalf of the Ishmaelite connection, Israel is being told that God is very much concerned about nations other than Israel."[10]

---

[9]Eugene F. Roop, *Genesis*, 124.

[10]Jim McGuiggan, *Genesis and Us*, 127.

17.21, "I will establish my covenant with Isaac." The three-part covenant is to be passed on through the son who was still yet to come, and whose promise evoked laughter from both of his parents. "Isaac represents the living God's triumph over barrenness. By his own sovereign counsel the Lord elects Isaac, not Ishmael. The Lord's chosen race will not come by natural generation but by supernatural grace at the ordained time" (Waltke).

17.22–23, When he had finished talking with him God went up from him. "It is God who closes the conversation, as it was He who opened it, a fact that will be particularly marked and significant in the intercession passage of 18.16ff" (Kidner). And Wenham: "To draw attention to God's dramatic exit, the end of his speech is described much more fully than usual. Usually nothing is said about God ceasing to speak or going away: He just stops and the next event is described (*cf.* 18.33; 35.13)."

He circumcised the flesh of their foreskins that very day. Abraham's obedience was immediate, as he shows himself to be a faithful covenant partner. "Biblical faith is never simply a cerebral exercise. What is said and thought is also done" (Hamilton). In reckoning Abraham's faith, it is helpful to remember that this would not have been an easy task. Some have estimated that Abraham's household included as many as 1,000 when he went to war with the kings of the east—and that number was some fourteen years prior to this.

Further, his obedience was complete: "He carried out the circumcision in exact accord with divine instruction ('as God told him'). ...The narrative description (vv 23, 27) of their circumcision corresponds to the earlier language of instruction (vv 10–14). The paragraph repeatedly points to the inclusiveness of the rite, 'all, every' (v 23, *kol* [3x]; v 27)" (Mathews).

17.24–25, Abraham was ninety-nine years old when he was circumcised. Something is to be said of the degree of faith Abraham had in order to perform this procedure on himself at this age with the crude medical tools and complete lack of anesthesia among the ancients.

This verse is, in large part, a repeat of the first verse, except with *Abraham* instead of *Abram*. "'Abram' may have had questions in his heart about the heir at the start, but by the end of the theophany 'Abraham' readily undergoes the pain of the knife" (Mathews).

Ishmael was thirteen years old when he was circumcised. Though Ishmael is excluded from the line of the promised seed, he is not excluded from the blessings which God will bring. Interestingly, "The Arabs even now defer circumcision to a much later period than the Jews, generally till between the ages of 5 and 13, and frequently even till the 13th year" (Keil).

17.26–27, That very day. The repetition of this phrase emphasizes the significance of Abraham's immediate obedience and the importance of this event.

All the men of his house... were circumcised with him. Abraham's obedience was complete.

Growth of the Seed: God renews the covenant (vv 4–8), gives covenant names (vv 5, 15), gives the sign of the covenant (vv 10–11); Ishmael is rejected from the Messianic line (vv 18–19); Isaac is specifically promised (v 19).

18 **1,** *And the* LORD *appeared to him by the oaks of Mamre.* This first sentence is a summary of the rest of the chapter. Yahweh Himself appears to Abraham here, though in the form of a man. "The narrator at once apprises us of the divine character of Abraham's guests, but when Abraham peers out…what he sees from his human perspective is three 'men'" (Alter). The end of this chapter and chapter 19 reveal that these men are Yahweh and two of His angels.

Heat of the day. The time when most people would take a break, because the heat is dangerous to them (Leupold). This is also the time of the day when most travelers would seek shade and rest.

18.2, *Three men were standing in front of him. Standing in front of* is equivalent to our *knocking.* They were politely waiting to be acknowledged and would not come closer until they were invited. "There can be no thought of drawing nearer until the one standing has been invited to do so" (Leupold).

"Older Christian interpreters seized upon the number *three*…and identified them with the Trinity. Obviously, such a statement reads a considerable amount into the text, and forces on the text an interpretation the text itself will not yield" (Hamilton).

He ran from the tent door to meet them. Abraham immediately seeks to provide for his guests.

Bowed himself to the earth. Keil suggests that his bow is due to his perceiving that this is God,[1] but such perception would be amazing. That he proceeds to treat them as travelers in need of sustenance and respite would seem to argue against such perception. "Had Abraham at once discerned His divine character, he could not have offered food" (Leupold). We would suggest that this is not an act of obeisance as before God, because he did not know their identity (*cf.* Heb. 13.2). "These gestures express both the warmth of Abraham's welcome and his deep respect for his visitors" (Wenham).

18.3, *"O Lord."* The word is not Yahweh rendered LORD, but the word for *master (adonai,* the same word which Sarah will use later of Abraham, v 12). Although one of these men is in fact Yahweh (v 1), Abraham does not know this yet.

---

[1]See also Waltke.

It is interesting that Abraham's address is in the singular (to one of them), rather than the plural (to all three).[2] Though such does not necessitate that he knows one is God and the other two are not, it seems to indicate that one of them stood prominent as the obvious leader.

"If I have found favor in your sight, do not pass by." Hospitality was viewed far differently then than it is now. Rather than an inconvenience, it was viewed as a privilege. Rather than inviting the men in because he felt compelled, Abraham almost begs for the honor of providing for these strangers. "Extending hospitality, as the subsequent contrasting episode in Sodom indicates, is the primary act of civilized intercourse" (Alter).

18.4–5, "Water… wash your feet… rest yourselves… a morsel of bread, that you may refresh yourselves." Abraham sought to provide for all the needs of his guests: food, drink, washing, rest, and refreshment. His offering seems simple, but it shows itself to be generous.

"Since you have come to your servant." The KJV reads, *"For therefore you have come."* Perhaps, Abraham saw the fact that they came by his tent as a providential opportunity to display courtesy (Leupold).[3]

18.6–8, "Quick! Three seahs of fine flower! Knead it, and make cakes." A *seah* is two gallons of a grain (Waltke). Abigail made sufficient provisions for David and his band of outlaws with five seahs of parched grain (1 Sam 25.18). This will provide more than enough food for these three men.[4] Further, Abraham went to the herd to get a calf, *tender and good.* He also gave them curds and milk. "That Abraham provides a *calf* shows either his relative prosperity and social standing, or his desire to give his best to his guests, or both" (Hamilton). And Mathews: "The tornado of activity ('hurried,' vv 6, 7; 'quick,' v 6; 'ran,' v 7) reinforces the picture of Abraham as the extraordinary host."

What Abraham offered *(a morsel of bread)* and what he provided (a full meal) are two different things—out of his generosity and wealth he gave

---

[2]See Alter for further discussion; see Hamilton for a discussion of the eight shifts from singular to plural in this narrative.

[3]Arguing against this wording—although Leupold's comment would probably still represent a truth of Abraham's character—the same Hebrew phrase in 19.8 is rendered *since* (as the ESV follows here) or *for* (Kidner).

[4]"What is left over can be disposed of with ease by the servants of so large an establishment as the one Abraham had" (Leupold).

to these strangers. This is not to say, of course, that Abraham deceived his guests; rather, "Abraham promises modestly, a little water and a morsel of bread, while hastening to prepare a sumptuous feast" (Alter). "Had he disclosed what a feast he was going to put on, they might have felt they were imposing on him and declined his invitation. So he only mentions part of what he will provide. Such understatement is characteristic of generous people in Scripture" (Wenham).

And he stood by them… while they ate. The implication is that he stood by to be of service. "He is both waiter and host" (Hamilton).

But why are these spiritual beings eating? Certainly they would not need to eat in order to receive sustenance. It is also doubtful that God and the two angels arrived on the earth miles away and walked in human form the distance, requiring then some sort of rest. Rather, as Leupold suggests, "The friendliest and most intimate contact among the sons of men are oft made over a friendly meal." Thus, God sought "to draw near to Abraham in intimate contact."

18.9, "Where is Sarah your wife?" The question is rhetorical, as God knows where Sarah is. But they brought a message for her. God had already told Abraham of their coming son. The purpose of this visit was to reveal the news to Sarah. "The question… secures Sarah's attention for the announcement" (Waltke).

It may surprise us to find that these men knew of Abraham's marriage and his wife's name, but Abraham is not surprised. As the food was being prepared, she may have come up in conversation. This unexplained knowledge (even if it is easily explainable) may be a literary device: "Perhaps the narrator makes a deliberate contrast between the three men who know who Sarah is and Abraham who does not know who they are" (Hamilton).

"She is in the tent." This is where a wife usually would have been when guests were outside.

18.10, "Sarah will have a son." The promise previously given to Abraham is now repeated for Sarah's benefit. This may have been the first indication to Abraham of the identity of his guests.

18.11, So Sarah laughed to herself. "Her derision suggests that either Abraham had not yet told her of the promise (17.16, 19) or that he had failed to convince her" (Kidner). The latter suggestion would better explain the necessity of a divine visit, unless the former means to say that Abraham had not yet told her and was not planning to. Further, that she is referred to by the name *Sarah* would seem to indicate that Abraham had informed her of God's message. Kidner suggests, "God's rebuke [v 15]... points to the latter, *i.e.*, that Sarah was persisting in unbelief, not merely reacting in astonishment."

It is worth noticing the difference in her laughter and Abraham's. Abraham fell over and laughed; Sarah laughed *to herself* and *behind him*, where he would not be able to see her smile. Abraham knew he was speaking with God; Sarah only knew that there were three strangers outside. "Sarah's display of shock is not as skeptical as that of her husband. At least she does not fall on her face, laughing. Her response is more of a bemused reflection after she overheard the visitor announce her forthcoming pregnancy to Abraham" (Hamilton).

His laughter certainly seems to be the worse, yet hers is the more notorious. Perhaps this is due to what follows the laughter. Ultimately, Abraham faithfully obeyed God's command and circumcised himself and his entire household on that same day, proving that he believed God's message. Sarah, on the other hand, was afraid because her innermost thoughts were known and she denied laughing. Though we do not mean to cast any aspersions on Sarah's level of faith, the immediate change in Abraham upon hearing the further oracle of God makes his laughter fade to the background more quickly, whereas Sarah's denial and God's abrupt dismissal allows her laughter to echo. If Kidner's suggestion is accurate— that she persisted in unbelief—it would explain further why this secret laughter has been treated more harshly than Abraham's open laughter.

The way of women had ceased to be with Sarah. According to Waltke, "The Hebrew literally reads, 'Sarah no longer experienced the cycle of women.'" Sarah, having reached menopause, was beyond the point of being able to bear children.

18.12, "After I am worn out and my lord is old." Not knowing that this is God speaking (and possibly not having been told of the promise by Abraham), her response is a natural one. But if Abraham had told her of God's promise and these three men arrive bringing the same news, Kidner's comment should be considered: "Her purely sensual comment (v 12b) adds to the impression that her interest in the covenant and promise was still shallow."

In discussing the proper conduct of a godly wife, Peter notes that Sarah calls Abraham lord (1 Pet 3.6). Although this certainly is not the only occasion in which this occurred (as such submissiveness was her normal manner of conduct), it is the only recorded occasion of such. It should be noted, then, that Sarah not only called him lord to his face, but she did so when she spoke of him within herself. Even when she could get away with calling him whatever she wanted, she maintained the proper attitude.

"Shall I have pleasure?" The precise meaning of this term is somewhat obscure. It is translated variously: *conception* by an ancient Aramaic translation; *lust* by *HALOT*; *delight* by *NIDOTTE* (Waltke). Alter argues that it is cognate with *Eden* and probably suggests sexual pleasure, as does Mathews, who adds, "Her inner thoughts poignantly confirmed that the couple had not engaged in sexual relations for years."

18.13–15, "Why did Sarah laugh?" Sarah must have felt a shock when this stranger who could not see her knew that she laughed. "Sarah's position in the tent, 'behind Him' (v 10b), and her internal monologue, 'to herself' (v 12a), indicate that by unusual means the visitor knew her heart, not having seen a facial expression or heard a chuckle" (Mathews). And Hamilton: "Sarah has overheard the anonymous visitor talking to her husband. Now the tables are turned—the visitor overhears Sarah talking to herself."

But Sarah denied it, saying, "I did not laugh." Afraid and befuddled, Sarah seeks to cover herself by lying to the one who knew of her laughter and read her heart. This is most likely the reason why her laugh is more widely known than Abraham's: "The condemnation of one was equally a condemnation of the other. The text focuses on Sarah's unbelief because she went on to deny it." [5]

"No, but you did laugh." God's brief rebuttal stamps her response as unworthy of further consideration. "The definitive tone of His answer ended the matter" (Mathews).

18.16, Then the men set out from there, and they looked down toward Sodom. Having completed the first part of their journey (*i.e.*, assuring Sarah of her impending pregnancy), the men set out on the second portion of their mission: to inspect the cities of the Jordan valley. God will remain behind and talk to Abraham, while the angels travel to Sodom (*cf.* 19.1).

---

[5] *Hard Sayings*, 123.

"The strangers effect beginnings and endings as the messengers of hope and life to Abraham and Sarah and of judgment and death to the people of Sodom and Gomorrah" (Waltke).

And Abraham went with them to set them on their way. "By detailing Abraham's accompaniment of the departing guests, the narrative completes its portrait of the perfect host" (Mathews).

18.17–19, The LORD said. Divine soliloquies are not often recorded. This one is not, of course, God trying to determine what He plans to do, but an explanation of why He revealed this to Abraham. "He reflects for a moment on the nature of His covenantal relationship with the patriarch and what that dictates as to revealing divine intention to a human partner" (Alter). Further, "This dialogue between the Lord and Abraham is for Abraham's benefit, to challenge him to act wisely and nobly for justice" (Waltke). The following scene, where Abraham dares to be Sodom's intercessor before God, plays off of this scene where God dares to adopt Abraham as His confidant.

"For I have chosen him." The Hebrew reads *known*, using the same word which describes the sexual relationship between Adam and Eve. Clearly, that is not the relationship being described, but the use of the same word does speak drastically to the level of intimacy between God and His saints. Leupold suggests that it connotes, "to acknowledge one as an intimate friend" (also Kidner).

"Verse 19 shows particularly clearly how grace and law work together, for it opens with grace *(I have known him)* directed towards the firm discipline of law *(command… way… justice and judgment)* through which eventually grace may reach its goal *(that the Lord may bring… what he has promised,* RSV)" (Kidner).

"That he may command his children and his household." Ultimately, the purpose of God's telling this to Abraham is to ensure that Abraham would teach his children about the righteousness of God and the perils of wickedness, "so that they might become partakers of the promised salvation, and not be overtaken by judgment" (Keil). Understanding that God was behind the cities' destruction and understanding His motivation for destroying them would serve as an object lesson to Abraham's family as to the need to do righteousness and justice (v 19).

"Righteousness and justice." "Procksch… distinguishes between these two terms, making the former signify inner, the latter outer righteous-

ness" (Leupold). Waltke distinguishes them differently and in relation to a life within a community: "A righteous person rightly orders community, and a just one restores broken community, especially by punishing the oppressor and delivering the oppressed." Alter notes that these words are largely played upon in the following dialogue and subsequent narratives: "*Tsedeq* and *mishpat* [righteousness and justice] will continue to reverberate literally and in cognate forms through Abraham's pleas to God on behalf of the doomed cities, through the Sodom story itself, and through the story of Abraham and Abimelech that follows."

Interestingly, this is the first time that the fulfillment of the promise is made contingent on moral performance (*so that*, v 19). "Election means election to an ethical agenda in the midst of a corrupt world of Sodoms" (Wright qtd. in Mathews).

18.20–21, "The outcry against Sodom and Gomorrah is great and their sin is very grave." To say that sin is crying out to heaven is an emphatic way of saying that they are calling for divine intervention (Leupold). The word used is often associated with the shrieks of torment of the oppressed (Alter). "Like the blood of Abel, unpunished sin cries out to heaven for vengeance" (Wenham).

"I will go down to see." It is certain that God did not need to go down to the cities (*i.e.*, send His angels to bring a report) to know the level of wickedness therein, though this follows what He did before His last instance of divine judgment (*cf.* 11.5, 7). Instead, God chooses this procedure to display that "He, as just judge of all the earth, does nothing without first being in full possession of all facts" (Leupold). Waltke agrees: "This is the narrator's figurative way of saying that God always thoroughly investigates the crime before passing sentence." And MacKenzie: "He is shown as having the qualities of an ideal judge. He is merciful by preference, not hasty to condemn; He will investigate and know for certain. But if it is indeed so, then He will act, and drastically."[6] He does not *need* to gather evidence: He has already said that the facts of the case have come up before Him; rather, He does this to illustrate this point to Abraham, and ultimately, to us. Further, "The subsequent experience of the angels in Sodom displays the moral state of Sodom more effectually than could many an explanation besides" (Leupold).

---

[6] R.A.F. MacKenzie, "The Divine Soliloquies in Genesis," *CBQ* 17 (1955): 165.

Again, we find taught the sovereignty of God. "There is no suggestion that the inhabitants of the Pentapolis knew or worshipped Yahweh—rather the contrary. Yet Yahweh alone is concerned to judge and punish them."[7] As with the flood and the Babel tower, Yahweh alone is the judge of mankind—whether or not one acknowledges Him as such.

18.22, *So the men turned from there and went toward Sodom, but Abraham still stood before the LORD.* This verse, read with 18.2 and 19.1, make it evident that the three journeymen were God and two angels. "Appropriately, two go to confirm the crime, as later in Mosaic law two witnesses are needed for capital punishment" (Waltke). God, however, does not depart. Though the MT has Abraham standing before the Lord (as does the ESV above), according to scribal notes, the text originally read: *The Lord remained standing before Abraham* (Hamilton). This indicates how large a part God played in the following discussion—but by His passiveness. He brought the subject up (v 17) and then waited for Abraham's plea (v 22). "It suggests that the Lord is challenging Abraham to play the role of a righteous judge" (Waltke). Ultimately, "The whole passage displays His approachability to such a servant" (Kidner).

18.23, *"Will you indeed sweep away the righteous with the wicked?"* God has not yet said that He would destroy the cities—only that He was going to see if the report of their wickedness was true. Abraham, however, drew that conclusion based on his knowledge of God and his knowledge about Sodom and Gomorrah. "If the outcry has reached heaven, surely it had been heard by Abraham at nearby Mamre!" (Mathews). The extent of their wickedness was most likely known to the whole region. It is not insignificant that Abraham understands the righteousness of God. "Bear in mind that he's still wandering and heirless after twenty-five years despite God's promises. *Still* Abraham knows God can be relied on to do what's right."[8] And that He will always do the merciful and loving thing.

Abraham proceeds "in a spirit of faith… of humility… and of love, demonstrated in his concern for the whole city, not for his kinsmen alone" (Kidner). And Mathews: "He rests his argument upon the twin pillars of divine

---

[7]*Ibid.,* 166.

[8]Jim McGuiggan, *Genesis and Us,* 133.

justice and divine mercy." Roop says, "Abraham...[proposes] that the future of everyone be determined not by the wicked ones in the midst of the community, but by the righteous ones."[9] And this is what God always does (*cf.* Rahab, Josh 2; Assyria, Jonah 3–4; and Israel, Ezek 14.12–20).

"This is Abraham's second intervention for Sodom (*cf.* 14.14): it anticipates the blessing the whole world was to enjoy through him (12.3), and something of the self-giving which must be its means" (Kidner).

18.24, "Suppose there are fifty righteous in the city." And so Abraham begins one of the most famous scenes in the Bible: a man bargaining with God over how many righteous people it would take for Him to spare the city. Abraham moves down to forty-five, then to forty, to thirty, to twenty, and finally to ten. At each instance, God agrees not to destroy the city if there are that many righteous people in it.

One must ask why Abraham would do this. Was Abraham really concerned that God would do unjustly? Did he think, perhaps, that he was more compassionate than God was? Was he only concerned with Lot and his family? Or was he simply participating in the customary bargaining process of his time? Just what prompted Abraham to bargain with God?

We feel that the answer to each of the above questions is *no*. Perhaps the closest one to the truth is his concern for Lot, though this was not his only concern. Instead, "He pleads the case of God's love over against God's righteousness" (Leupold).

The answer to the question of why Abraham would bargain with God lies in the fact that Abraham was made in God's image. A righteous man, made in God's image, would seek to do the things that God would do. To use Kidner's terminology: "Abraham's spirit of love and justice derived from God as surely as it strove with Him." Abraham, however, is not privy to all the information that God is (specifically, how few righteous there were in Sodom), so he must be shown the answer that God already knows.

It is also important to see the free address of faith in this. Abraham does not hold back when it comes to his relationship with God. He says what is on his mind. It would have done him no good to hold back, as God already knew his thoughts. If he had tried to hide it from God, he would have only been dishonest with himself and with God. (This may also be

---

[9]Eugene F. Roop, *Genesis,* 130.

a good explanation of why he laughs openly when God tells him about Isaac's imminent birth.)

But here before our eyes is unfolded a plea that stands without parallel in all history. The world's best car buyer couldn't pull this kind of deal off on the world's worst car salesman.

So why did God let this happen? The most important thing to understand is that God is not being influenced by Abraham. God isn't being worked over like a bad salesman as the number gets lower and lower. *The righteousness of God did not change from the beginning of this discussion to the end.* Abraham does not know the specific wickedness of these cities as God does. In this discussion, God's position is not being altered. He is, in fact, proving Abraham's statement of verse 25 true: He is not an unjust God—here, He goes to great lengths to show that truth. And it's important to see that God is not displeased with Abraham. He does, after all, grant Abraham's petition each time.

This type of reasoning (*i.e*, 'not for just one less') could go on until the number was down to one. Why, then, does Abraham stop at ten? Though the answer to this question is not clear, there are a couple of plausible possibilities. Perhaps Abraham knew enough about the righteousness of God to know that anything below ten is no longer an act of mercy to those few righteous who remain. Perhaps Abraham had enough knowledge of the flood—where only *eight* were saved—to know that God had already 'made it a policy' to not spare the wicked for less than ten. Or perhaps Abraham knew that any number lower than ten would have "degraded a worthy intercession into narrow plea for one's relatives only" (Leupold).[10]

18.33, *And the* LORD *went his way… and Abraham returned to his place.* "The report of a character's returning to his place or home is a formal convention for marking the end of an episode in biblical narrative" (Alter). Keil suggests that God simply vanished. Leupold adds, "There is no need of saying where Yahweh went. Everyone knows that." And Alter on Abraham: "This minimal indication has a thematic implication here—the contrast between Abraham's 'place' in the nomadic, uncorrupted existence in the land of promise and Lot's location in one of the doomed cities of the plain."

---

[10]Alter notes that ten is "the minimal administrative unit for communal organization in later Israelite life."

Having established now that the judgment on Sodom and Gomorrah is just, God leaves. "The Lord investigates the accusations thoroughly (18.22), ensures two objective witnesses, involves the faithful in His judgment, displays active compassion for the suffering, and prioritizes divine mercy over indignant wrath (*i.e.*, not to be destroyed if even ten are righteous)" (Waltke).

Growth of the Seed: Isaac is specifically promised to Sarah (v 10); The promise line receives an object lesson in God's mercy and judgment (v 19).

19 The book of Genesis is a history of the chosen people; more than that, it is a history of the Messianic line. It is a fair question, then, to ask why this episode, which has nothing to do with either, is included. The clearest answer is that it was to teach the chosen people a lesson (*cf.* 18.19).[1] Beyond that, it is a type of the final overthrow of the wicked and deliverance of the righteous in the final judgment (*cf.* 2 Pet 2.6–9; Jude 7). Finally, this explains the origin of the Moabites, through whom came Ruth, through whom came Jesus.

19.1, Lot was sitting in the gate of Sodom. The gate of a city was where the elders of the city met. At the gate "legal matters [were] adjudicated, transactions closed, bargains made, and affairs discussed" (Leupold).[2]

Finding Lot at the gate may show the progression of his worldliness. First, he chooses the plain of the Jordan over the Promised Land. Then, he moves into Sodom itself. Now, we find him in and among the leaders of the city. "His place *in the gate* proclaimed him a man of standing in Sodom" (Kidner). Yet, in a short time, the citizens will spurn him as an alien. Kidner writes, "His public ineffectiveness must be balanced against the influential careers of Joseph and Daniel, whose high office was a vocation; the difference lay there." It may be said, in his defense, that it was during his time in Sodom that he is called a righteous man (2 Pet 2.7) and he seems to use his time at the gate to protect visitors from the wicked Sodomites.

19.2–3, "Turn aside to your servant's house." "Lot has exchanged his tent, formerly pitched *near* the city for a house in Sodom" (Waltke). Even so, he does not forsake the duty of hospitality.

"We will spend the night in the town square." The town square was an enlarged area within the city gate. It typically served "as a market place and for the concourse of all manner of people" (Leupold). In general, it was not a strange thing for visitors to a town to stay in its square. But this response from the visitors would be surprising to Lot. "If oriental convention dictated that one should offer strangers a bed for the night, it just as firmly dictated the acceptance of such offers (*cf.* 24.23, 54; Jdg 18.2; 19.4–20)" (Wenham).

---

[1] Notably, in each case where an individual is rejected from the Messianic line, God gives a brief history concerning the rejected one: previously, Cain, Ham and Japheth; later, Ishmael and Esau; here, Lot.

[2] *Cf.* Genesis 23.10, 18; Deuteronomy 21.19; 22.15; 25.7; Ruth 4.1ff, 11; 1 Kings 22.10; Job 5.4; Psalm 127.5; Proverbs 31.23; Amos 5.10, 12, 15.

But he pressed them strongly. Lot's response displayed that he was different than the people of Sodom. There is no reason to believe that Lot understood the visitors to be angels, but he clearly understood the Sodomites.

So they turned aside to him and entered his house. "They yielded to Lot's entreaty to enter his house; for the deliverance of Lot, after having ascertained his state of mind, formed part of their commission, and entering into his house might only serve to manifest the sin of Sodom in all its heinousness" (Keil).

Unleavened bread. Unleavened was the bread of choice when haste was required. Its use "shows that this was no leisurely feast like that of chapter 18 (*cf.* Exod 12.39)" (Kidner).

19.4–5, But before they lay down, the men of the city… to the last man, surrounded the house. The verbal forms used convey a hostile intention. To convey that nuance, Speiser renders this verse *they closed in on the house* (Hamilton). "They first surrounded the house before addressing those inside, showing their hostile intentions from the beginning" (Mathews). Further, everyone was involved: young and old, to the last man. Abraham's concern that the righteous would perish with the wicked is clearly not a possibility—there were no righteous.

"Bring them out to us that we may know them." In addition to the sin of homosexuality, they had a complete disregard for the duty of hospitality. It is not that they did not know of their responsibility in this regard; rather, they failed to keep it due to their sexual perversion. "The enormity of the prevalent vice was indicated by the fact that the sacred duty of hospitality was so completely replaced by the eagerness to practice vile lust that even strangers would be scarified to wholesale abuse—a treatment most likely to terminate in death" (Leupold). And Waltke: "The men of the city cry not just for homosexuality but for rape."

Regarding the sin itself, Kidner writes, "At this early point in Scripture the sin of sodomy is branded as particularly heinous. The law was to make it a capital offence, grouped with incest and bestiality (Lev 18.22; 20.13), and the New Testament is equally appalled at it (Rom 1.26–27; 1 Cor 6.9; 1 Tim 1.10)." Those who would argue that the verb *know* in this instance is not used in reference to sexual activity will have a hard time explaining why Lot would offer his two virgin daughters to the crowd as a substitute. There, "It becomes clear that the issue is intercourse and not friendship" (Hamilton).

19.6–8, Lot went out to the men. Facing this mob alone shows the courage of Lot and his desire to fulfill his duty to protect his guests, even at his own peril.

Shut the door after him. Lot *shuts the door* here; the angels *shut the door* when they save him. "Figuratively, 'door' conveys multiple meanings. The door is in effect the boundary between the saved and the condemned; it is symbolic of the line between the righteous and the wicked, the civil and the vulgar" (Mathews).

"I beg you, my brothers, do not act so wickedly." His first attempt at dissuading them is to plead with them. He begins by addressing them kindly to win their good will, but he can hardly be sincere in his address—Lot, a brother of *these* men?

"I have two daughters." After his kind entreaty did not work, Lot seeks to protect his guests by offering the mob his daughters—as Delitzsch has said, "seeking to avert sin by sin" (qtd. in Keil). Although there was an exaggerated emphasis on hospitality, this suggestion is still patently wrong. Some have suggested that Lot knew they would refuse his offer, but that raises the question of why he would make it. "Lot could hardly have anticipated with a certain shrewdness that the Sodomites were so bent on this particular form of vileness as to refuse any substitutes" (Leupold). More likely, he was terrified and befuddled and said the first thing that came to mind, as the sacredness of the host-guest bond took precedence over all other obligations (Alter). But even granting that, one must ask if it would have come to mind if he had not been living in Sodom. At the very least, there would have been no opportunity for it to come to mind if he had remained in Palestine.

"For they have come under the shelter of my roof." Finally, Lot appeals to the men's sense of duty to hospitality in an attempt to convince them that their plan was wicked. "To violate this custom would (and did) brand the city lawless" (Mathews).

19.9–10, "This fellow came to sojourn, and he has become the judge." Lot's time in Sodom has not been a complete waste. Their reaction is most likely not to this event only, but to a continual attitude of Lot—he has been playing the part of judge since he arrived.

"Now we will deal worse with you than with them." They are prepared to salve their desire with Lot. "They will take Lot himself as a substitute sex partner rather than his daughters" (Hamilton).

But the men reached out their hands and brought Lot into the house with them. Lot is saved by the angels' hands. "The townsmen put forth their hands against Lot (v 9). But now *the men* extend their hands, pull Lot back inside the house, and slam the door" (Hamilton).

Shut the door. This hearkens back to the flood account where God closed the door of the ark in order to ensure its safe passage (7.16). Here, God's messengers close the door of Lot's house in order to ensure their safety.

19.11, And they struck with blindness the men... so that they wore themselves out groping for the door. While this may have included physical blindness, it probably was more than that. Surely, a town's worth of men already gathered around a house could find a door, even if they were blind. Keil compares this with 2 Kings 6.18 (where the same Hebrew word is used—not the usual Hebrew word for blindness) and calls this "mental blindness, in which the eye sees, but does not see the right object." Kidner agrees, calling it a "dazzled state, as of Saul on the Damascus Road." And Hamilton: "The problem is not that they are blind, but that their vision is faulty—it does not correspond to reality."

The men groping for the door is almost laughable. "Yet in another way it surprises us. Why did they not go home as soon as they were struck with blindness? Is this another hint of how deeply rooted their sin was? Divine judgment is supposed to induce repentance (*cf.* Amos 4.6–12); here it does not, so yet greater calamities must be expected" (Wenham).

19.13, "For we are about to destroy this place." The mission of the angels is now complete: there are now two witnesses to the wickedness of the city. And so now, the angels reveal themselves and their purpose to Lot.

19.14, So Lot went out and said to his sons-in-law. Sons-in-law? But his daughters were virgins (v 8). Either they were sons-in-law to be (betrothed and considered a part of the family already, as the ESV indicates: *who were to marry his daughters,* also NASB, RSV, NIV; *cf.* Keil, Kidner, Hamilton) or Lot had other daughters who had married men of Sodom (*who married,* ASV, KJV, NKJV, Leupold, Alter). "The ambiguity of the participle (married/to marry) makes both interpretations viable" (Wenham).

But he seemed to his sons-in-law to be jesting. This is the same verb (though in a different conjugation) used of Sarah's laughter in the previous chapter. "It is, of course, a wry echo—the laughter of disbelief of those about to be divinely blessed, the false perception of mocking laughter by those about to be destroyed. The common denominator…is skepticism about divine intentions" (Alter). And Kidner: "The mob of Sodom had had no ears for any appeal (v 9); Lot's closest associates had none for any warning. This was the temper of the city: not even the desperate visit by night could be taken seriously."

And so, the sons-in law "are types of all such as have had all sense of justice and of judgment erased by growing callous in sin. The nearer the judgment comes, the less will men believe it to be impending" (Leupold). If he had other daughters, they were just as disbelieving, as only the virgin daughters escaped (vv 16, 30–38). How aptly this foreshadows our society, which has lost all sense of justice and judgment, and for whom the judgment of God is a joke.

19.15–16, *As morning dawned, the angels urged Lot.* Though still a righteous man, Lot is not who he once was. At the word of God, he left Ur with Abraham to travel to an unknown land. Here, he needs to be urged by the angels to leave Sodom. Assuming that the mob event and relaying the message to his sons-in-law had not taken all night, he had decided to wait until morning in spite of the angels' warning of impending doom.

"Take your… two daughters who are here." As opposed to the daughters who are not here? This would seem to indicate that his sons-in-law were not 'to be' but that he had other daughters in the city.

But he lingered. After receiving an initial warning, he delays through the night. Now, upon receiving a second warning, he continues to delay. Clearly, he lacks the decisiveness of his youth. How powerful is the grip of 'this present evil world.'

So the men seized him… and they brought him out and set him outside the city. "For a second time, then, his visitors grab him. First they grabbed him and pulled him inside his house (v 10). Now they grab him and pull him *outside the city*" (Hamilton).

19.17, *And as they brought them out, one said.* The speaker here attributes the destruction of the city to himself, which is later attributed to God (v 24), but there is no indication that God had rejoined the two angels. Keil offers, "Lot recognized in the two angels a manifestation of God…and the angel who spoke addressed him as the messenger of [Yahweh] in the name of God."

"Escape for your life. Do not look back or stop anywhere in the valley. Escape to the hills, lest you be swept away." Four specific instructions are given to Lot all for the same purpose—*lest you be swept away:* (1) *Escape for your life.* Run; leave; get out. (2) *Do not look back.* Utmost haste is of absolute necessity. They cannot be slowed down by lingering any longer, even if it is one last glance at their home. (3) *Do not stop anywhere in the valley.* The entire area is going to be destroyed. They cannot afford to stop before they reach their destination. (4) *Escape to the hills.* Run. Don't look back. Don't stop nearby. Keep going until you get to the mountains.

19.18–20, And Lot said to them, "Oh, No, my Lords." Lot's plea is presumptuous. Essentially, he asks to go precisely where the angels have just instructed him *not* to go. He bases his plea on the mercy that has already been shown him, his supposed physical inability to reach the hills, and his fear that the evil he is being delivered from would overtake him. He instead proposes a flight to a city of the valley, claiming that it is near enough to reach and small enough to be worth sparing. "It almost taxes the reader's patience to bear with this long-winded plea at a moment of such extreme danger" (Leupold)—imagine how God must have felt! And Kidner: "The warning to 'remember Lot's wife' (Luke 17.32) gives us reason to see ourselves potentially in the lingering, quibbling Lot himself, wheedling a last concession as he is dragged to safety."

19.21–22, "I grant you this favor also." Perhaps because of time constraint (v 22), God allows Lot's request in a spirit of remarkable patience. Until Lot reaches Zoar, the angel will not act.

19.24–25, Then the LORD ... from the LORD out of heaven. "The twofold use of the tetragrammaton reinforces the fact that the disaster that struck Sodom and its environ was not a freak of nature. Rather, it was sent deliberately by Yahweh Himself" (Hamilton). It is also noteworthy that this verse indicates the Lord's position as being in heaven. The last two chapters have shown God as moving on the earth. "Now suddenly Yahweh, from His heavenly position, unleashes a catastrophe on Sodom" (Hamilton).

Rained. That this judgment was *rained* may draw a further connection between this divine judgment and the flood. "In each case, God wipes out a whole population because of epidemic moral perversion, marking one family for survival" (Alter).[3]

Sulfur and fire. The ESV renders the more familiar *brimstone* with the more understandable *sulfur.* Most likely, this does not refer to two different substances falling, but is a hendiadys for *burning sulfur* (Keil; Hamilton). It is worth noting that the ground of this area contained asphalt or bitumen pits (*cf.* 14.10). Likely, the ground caught fire and burned the cities away below the ground level—this may account for the shallow southern end of the Dead Sea. It is doubtful that the entire sea was a result of this event, but it is possible that the burning of the bitumen pits lowered the ground level enough for the waters of the northern section to fill in the burned-out area.[4] This understanding is based on the local tradition which favors a site at the southern end of the Dead Sea (Hamilton).[5]

And he overthrew those cities, and all the valley. God, who will always do what is merciful and loving, wiped these cities off the face of the earth. How wicked they must have been that the only loving thing that God can do for mankind as a whole is to destroy them!

And what grew on the ground. The vegetation is also highlighted, reminding the reader of Lot's original choice of the land that was like Eden and Egypt. "Genesis implies that the present desolate aspect of the Dead Sea plain goes back to this act of divine judgment" (Wenham).

Some look to passages such as this to distinguish between the 'God of the Old Testament' and the 'God of the New Testament,' arguing that the Bible does not paint a clear picture of one God. This one is angry and judgmental, while the New Testament portrayal is loving and merciful. But we cannot read accounts such as these as if God was gleefully seizing the chance to burn the ungodly into ashes. The 'God of the Old Testament' does not take pleasure in the death of the wicked (Ezek 18.22–23). In Jesus' lament over Jerusalem, He speaks of how God—in the Old Testament—longed to bring them under his wing (Matt 23.37–39). Hosea depicts God as a forlorn lover, whose spouse persists in infidelity, yet He repeatedly forgives. Those who think that God sits back "after each judg-

---

[3]A further connection may be seen in the idiom *to keep alive seed* and the male survivors' subsequent drunkenness and sexual violation by his offspring (Alter).

[4]While the southern end—presumably created by this event—is usually between three and four feet in depth, and never deeper than 12 feet, the northern end reaches a maximum depth of 1,200 feet. See Leupold.

[5]"Sodom's connection with Zoar supports a site in the south, for Zoar is in the Jordan Valley (Deut 34.3) near Moab (Isa 15.5; Jer 48.34)" (Hamilton).

ment with a smile of satisfaction…haven't been listening to Him weep (Luke 19.41–44)."[6] And just as God grew weary with wickedness in the Old Testament, so He will again (*cf.* Col 3.5–6). Our God of 'love and mercy' will come again in fiery judgment (*cf.* 2 Pet 2; Jude).

19.26, But Lot's wife, behind him, looked back. She may have looked back from a longing for what was left behind (Keil)—this would certainly make sense if she was a Sodomite.[7] Or this may indicate that she was not making a determined effort to escape. "She lost her life for only one reason: because she overtly ignored the directive of verse 17" (Hamilton). She turned back toward Sodom and was overtaken by God's judgment. Although no longer *in* Sodom, she was still clearly *of* Sodom. "Almost escaped, she allowed her vigilance to relax. So she became a warning example to all who do not make a clear-cut break with the life of wickedness as Jesus' remarkable warning designates her" (Leupold).

And she became a pillar of salt. If we are to assume that Lot did not also look back (to see her), we are probably to understand that they came back and found her after the overthrow of the cities. This has led some to suggest that she was not transformed into salt, but—like the rocks and land surrounding the Dead Sea—was so encrusted with salt that she appeared to be a pillar of it (Leupold; Mathews). *Became* does not necessitate an immediate transformation (Hamilton). That she became *salt*—whether in content or in appearance—is in itself significant: "In the biblical world, a site was strewn with salt to condemn it to perpetual barrenness and desolation (Deut 29.23; Jdg 9.45; Psa 107.34; Jer 17.6)" (Waltke).

19.28, The smoke of the land. This seems to indicate that the ground itself burned.

19.29–30, God remembered Abraham and sent Lot out of the midst of the overthrow. This verse, which summarizes the entire chapter, indicates that Lot was spared for the sake of Abraham. One must wonder if God's patience with Lot in his fickleness and petulance would have lasted as long had it not been for his righteous uncle.[8]

---

[6]Jim McGuiggan, *Gensis and Us,* 142.

[7]There is no mention of her prior to chapter 19. Perhaps, this is because Lot was not married until his arrival in Sodom.

[8]On God remembering, see comment on 7.1.

Lot went up out of Zoar and lived in the hills…for he was afraid to live in Zoar. Lot departed Zoar, perhaps for fear that the same fate would befall Zoar as the other cities (Leupold) and dwelt in the hills—from the place he begged to go to the place God originally told him to go.[9] After saying that he could not reach the hills and being assured that God's mercy would extend to Zoar, Lot loses faith that the city would be spared and does travel to the hills. "The restlessness of fear is classically illustrated. …Fear had driven him there (vv 19ff); fear blindly drove him out again. It had brushed aside the call and now the pledge of God (vv 17, 21)" (Kidner).

So he lived in a cave. "Lot's cave is a bitter sequel to the house (v 3) which had dwarfed his uncle's tent" (Kidner). Lot and his two daughters in a cave: how far this is from his state in chapter 13 where he is so wealthy as to require separation from Abraham.

19.31–32, "Our father is old." Waltke says, "She presumably means that Lot is too old to remarry and have sons by whom they could have children (*cf.* Ruth 1.12–13)."

"There is not a man on earth to come in to us." Certainly this is not to be understood literally—as if they had believed the destruction of Sodom to be a worldwide calamity such as the flood. How long they had lived in Zoar is not recorded, but surely they were there long enough to have seen other people. Rather, their fear is that they will not be able to find anyone to continue their lineage.

"Let us make our father drink wine." How far Lot has come from his choice of the land that was like Egypt! "The end of choosing to carve out his career was to lose even the custody of his body" (Kidner)

"We will lie with him, that we may preserve offspring from our father." Hamilton points to the irony in this situation: "Earlier the father was willing to use his daughters for sexual purposes without their consent. Now they will use their father for sexual purposes without his consent." Here, where "drunken Lot unwittingly takes the virginity of both of his daughters, suggests measure-for-measure justice meted out for his rash offer" (Alter).

The results of living in the wicked city are evident: Lot's family is corrupt. After his wife (and other daughters?) dies because of her attachment to Sodom, these daughters show a lack of faith in God, and "to off-

---

[9]Another possiblility is that the residents of Zoar blamed the destruction of Sodom on him, the sole survivor. If so, he may have fled for fear of them.

set the deficiency [they devise a scheme] worthy of the depraved Sodomites" (Leupold).

19.37–38, Moabites…Ammonites. The descendants of these incestuous offspring become two of the nations which frequently come into contact with the Israelites and would produce "the worst carnal seduction in the history of Israel (that of Baal-Peor, Num 25) and the cruelest religious perversion (that of Molech, Lev 18.21). So much stemmed from a self-regarding choice (Gen 13.10ff) and persistence in it" (Kidner).

Their names speak of their mothers' sin: *Moab*—from the father; *Ben Ammi*—son of my kinsman. "The Moabites and Ammonites were rejected by God, however, not because of their questionable lineage but because of their mistreatment of Israel (see Deut 23.3–6). Yet from this lineage will come Ruth, and so Jesus Christ (see Ruth 4.18–22; Matt. 1.5)" (Waltke).

Keil concludes, "Lot is never mentioned again. Separated both outwardly and inwardly from Abraham, he was of no further importance in relation to the history of salvation, so that even his death is not referred to."

Growth of the Seed: The results of rejecting God's covenant; the origin of the Moabites, one of whom (Ruth) would continue the Messianic line.

20 Critical scholars point to this chapter (as well as Isaac's reprisal, 26.6–11) as evidence that Genesis was composed in a piecemeal fashion and the same story was somehow placed in the narrative three times, though slightly different each time. Kidner writes, "Critical scholars reckon the story a duplicate of 12.10ff, ultimately on the ground that a man does not repeat a lapse of this kind. But it is easier to be consistent in theory than under fear of death." The simpler explanation is that its repetition shows it was the standard procedure of Abraham and Sarah (v 13)—and that Isaac learned his father's bad habits.

20.1, From there Abraham journeyed. Because Abraham is a sojourner who owns no land, he is constantly moving from place to place. In context, *from there* must refer to the place from which Abraham viewed Sodom (19.27–28).

And he sojourned. The same pair of verbs *(journeyed, sojourned)* are used to introduce the Egypt narrative of chapter 12, hinting to the reader that this event may follow a similar path as the previous one.

Gerar. Gerar is on the southeast border of Canaan (10.19).

20.2, "She is my sister." Abraham, not having learned from his Egypt experience, reverts to lying about his relationship with Sarah. "He is without excuse for acting out of fear rather than faith. God has pledged that the promised seed will be through Sarah, a bond now even more firm than when they had traveled to Egypt" (Waltke).

Abimelech. Abimelech is evidently a throne name, as Pharaoh was for the Egyptians.[1] Abimelech translates: 'The king is my father.' In a world where the reigning king was believed to be the son of the local deity, it may carry the connotation 'God is my father.'

Took Sarah. This does not imply adultery (*cf.* v 4). Though this word is the common one for taking in marriage, it does not necessarily mean that and here context demands that it must simply mean *to take into his harem.*

It should be remembered that this is 25 years after the first incident when Sarah is taken because of her beauty. At 90—and no longer in Egypt (whose women were known for their ugliness)—the motive for this attempted marriage is probably different than the previous. At this point, Abraham is extremely wealthy and powerful. And Gerar is hardly the em-

---

[1]Chapter 26 brings another Abimelech, and Psalm 34 gives this title to Achish (*cf.* 1 Sam 29).

pire that Egypt was when Abraham and his entourage sojourned there. Thus, Abimelech most likely "sought to create an alliance with this influential nomad and so increase his following" (Leupold).[2] And Kidner: "It is significant that… there is no mention of her beauty. To Abimelech she was marriageable for her wealth and for the alliance that would be cemented with her 'brother,' as Abimelech's further approach to Abraham for a covenant, when this move had failed, suggests in 21.22ff."

20.3, But God came to Abimelech. It is rare for God to appear to someone who was not among His chosen people. When He does, as in this instance, it is a dream of warning (*cf.* 31.24; 40.5; 41.1; Dan 4.1ff). That He does not reserve His word for His people indicates that God's people do not have a monopoly on divine revelation.

20.4–5, "Lord, will you kill an innocent people?" "As titular head of his people, the king's behavior determines the future of his subjects" (Hamilton). Thus, Abimelech pleads for the well-being of his kingdom. In this plea, he shows full confidence in God's justice—that He does not punish indiscriminately. "If God would spare the evil city of Sodom for ten righteous people, how much more an innocent nation?" (Waltke).

"Did he not himself say to me… and she herself said." Abimelech rests his defense on his being deceived—both parties involved lied to him. Sarah's words are not recorded in the previous narrative, but it would seem odd that a man pleading a case of innocence before God would concoct a lie in his defense.

Integrity of my heart. Abimelech claims a pure inner motive.

Innocence of my hands. Abimelech claims that his outward deed was proper (considering what he was told).

20.6–7, "Yes, I know that you have done this in the integrity of your heart." God confirms Abimelech's inward innocence, but stops short of saying that his deed was pure. Ignorance does not excuse sin.

"It was I who kept you from sinning against me." "Interestingly, God says to Abimelech that adultery would have been a sin against God, not against the husband" (Hamilton) (*cf.* 26.10; 39.9b).

God's prevention of adultery on this occasion was primarily concerned with the immediately preceding promise of Isaac's birth. "On the brink of

---

[2]*Cf.* 26.28–29.

Isaac's birth-story here is the very Promise put in jeopardy, traded away for personal safety" (Kidner). It may also be because God knew that Abimelech's heart was innocent that He prevented Abimelech from sinning against Him. Evidently there is something different about Abimelech than his contemporaries. His efforts to make restitution (vv 14–16) seem to indicate this, as does God's statement to him (v 4), which clearly implies that he understands the honor and sanctity of marriage.

In addition to this appearance, God may have physically prevented Abimelech from adultery, as he was in need of healing (v 17).

"I did not let you touch her." "The verb *touch* (Heb. *naga*) may reflect an interesting double entendre. In the first wife-sister story *naga* was used with man as object and meant 'to afflict (with plagues)' (12.17). Here, with woman as object, it means 'to approach sexually.' It will not be necessary for God to send any *negaim* (plagues) on Abimelech, for Abimelech has not *naga* (touched) Sarah" (Hamilton). This would seem to further the case that Pharaoh (ch 12) did *touch her.*[3]

"Return the man's wife." Abimelech has been spared because of his inward innocence. But now he has the responsibility to act on his full knowledge of the situation and return to Abraham his wife.

"For he is a prophet, so that he will pray for you." "This is the first use of *prophet* in the Bible. The role of the prophet here is that of intercessor: he *will pray for you*" (Hamilton). Kidner says, "In heathen religion the holiness of *a prophet* was nearer magic than morality (*cf.* Num 22.6); so the reader can see better than Abimelech how far short of his title Abraham had just fallen. …He can also note how God stands by His servants, retrieving Abraham from his folly."

"And you shall live." This refers to physical life (as made evident by the following contrast), but it may also extend to include the healing which the prayer will bring (*cf.* vv 17–18). Because God had closed the wombs of the women, the line of Abimelech would eventually pass away—even if God did not kill him on the spot, he would have no progeny and would thus die.

"You shall surely die." This warning began God's speech (v 3) and lingers until repentance, even though God has exonerated Abimelech. Thus, God is not predicting "an inexorable doom but was declaring what Abim-

---

[3]See comment on 12.19.

elech in reality had merited and what would of necessity follow if Abimelech failed to give heed to the divine injunction" (Leupold). And Hamilton: "He has not committed adultery, and he is no kidnapper. But if he refuses to return her, he *will certainly die.*"

20.8, So *Abimelech rose early in the morning.* He immediately obeys.[4]

And called all his servants and told them all these things. Further, he shows great humility in telling his servants when he could have done this quietly and avoided the embarrassment. "His willingness to be open and tell the truth contrasts with Abraham and his subterfuge" (Hamilton).

And the men were very much afraid. "This comment shows how unjustified Abraham was to allege that there was no fear of God in this place (v 11)" (Wenham).

20.9–10, "*What have you done to us?*" The 'friend of God' is again being reprimanded by a pagan king—though at least this one is righteous in motive. Abimelech lays full blame for this situation at Abraham's feet. "Abimelech's speeches are not simply harsh condemnation. Rather, they mix moral indignation with a sense of shock, and Abraham's lame replies tend to increase our sympathy for Abimelech" (Wenham). Further, the questions "make it clear that Abraham had only asked himself 'What will this do for me?', stifling the reflections 'What will it do to them?' 'What do they deserve?' and 'What are the facts?' (Kidner).[5]

And Abimelech said. Abraham says nothing, which must be interpreted as an admission of guilt. But Abimelech, wanting more than a silent admission repeats his question.

20.11–13, "*I did it because I thought.*" His trouble began when he based his action on an unsubstantiated supposition.[6]

"There is no fear of God at all in this place, and they will kill me because of my wife." His assumption was that the fear of God was lost here, as it was in the rest of Canaan where he sojourned. "With the respect for God gone, men would hardly respect the rights of their fellow-men" (Leupold): apart from God, there is no ethical standard.

---

[4]See comment on 21.14.

[5]For a comparison of Abimelech's and Pharaoh's discourses, see Wenham.

[6]For the possibility that this is based on observation, see Hamilton.

Waltke distinguishes between 'Fear of God' and 'Fear of Yahweh' saying, "The latter refers to respect for the special revelation of Scripture, while 'fear of God' involves general revelation, moral standards known by humans through conscience and accepted by them out of fear of God's judgment." Thus, Abraham does not indict them for not being in covenant relationship with Yahweh, but he supposed that they did not even know *Elohim*.[7]

"Besides, she is indeed my sister." This answer sounds juvenile: 'I wasn't really lying.' As they shared a father, Sarah was his half-sister.[8] But his lie was not excused because it was based on the truth.

Abraham probably hoped that his rights as a brother would prevent any suitors.[9] As it failed in Egypt, it did so here as well.

It is worth noting again that we must not use instances like this to make a blanket statement that all half-truths are lies. Indeed, all half-truths *used to deceive* are lies—for that matter, full-truths used to deceive are lies. But no one would accuse Abraham of lying when he said to his visitors in chapter 18 that his wife was in the tent, rather than saying, 'Well, you should know, she's my half-sister too.' There is no deceit in a half-truth given because the other half is irrelevant. It is the motive of the speaker which makes the half-truth a lie.

"When God caused me to wander." He now incriminates God. "The verb use for *wander*... means to wander about hopelessly and aimlessly, often in a hostile environment" (Hamilton). Kidner also notes that this verb is never used in a good sense and calls this statement, "The language and wry attitude of the pagan; one man of the world might be speaking to another."[10]

"At every place to which we come, say of me, 'He is my brother.'" Abraham and Sarah had a standing agreement since they left Ur that this is the story they would tell everywhere they went—an arrangement that has lasted at least 25 years. One must wonder how many other times this happened that are not recorded! Or, perhaps Abraham was successful in preventing would-be suitors in those other instances.

---

[7] See Excursus B.

[8] Assuming Abraham was telling the truth—we are given no genealogical record to verify this claim and it is mentioned nowhere except in this excuse.

[9] See comment on 12.11.

[10] By contrast, Leupold argues that this can hardly be understood as a complaint, but a simple statement of fact. "He knew that his lot was to be that of a sojourner. He accepted that lot with open eyes."

20.14–16, *Then Abimelech took sheep and oxen... and returned Sarah his wife to him.* Abimelech gave gifts to Abraham as well as restoring his wife to him. In addition to his stated motive (below), these lavish gifts show the respect he has for Abraham's power—or, at least the power of Abraham's God. Also, he may have sought to ensure Abraham's intercession. Surely, it is not because he happily accepted Abraham's given excuses. "Pharaoh gave gifts to Abraham *before* he found out who Sarah was (12.16). Here Abimelech gives gifts to Abraham *after* he finds out Sarah's true identity. This point gives the impression that Pharaoh's gifts are a bridal price, and those of Abimelech are compensation" (Hamilton).

"My whole land is before you; dwell where it pleases you." He also gave Abraham the choice of land for his sojourn, which suggests a 'no hard feelings' approach—perhaps for fear, because Abraham was a prophet of God. This is quite different from Pharaoh who sends Abraham and Sarah out of Egypt with an armed escort.

"Behold, I have given your brother a thousand pieces of silver." Wenham says, "Fifty shekels was the maximum ever asked for in bride money (Deut 22.29); the typical old Babylonian laborer received a wage of about half a shekel a month. This gives an indication of the scale of Abimelech's compensation." The Babylonian worker would have had to work 167 years to earn this sum![11] Continuing, Wenham adds, "But note the barbed 'I am giving... to your *brother*'—not 'to your husband.' Despite his prompt obedience to God's instructions and his display of magnanimity toward Abraham, Abimelech still resented Abraham's behavior."

"It is a sign of your innocence in the eyes of all who are with you, and before everyone you are vindicated." The motive behind these gifts is to indicate to everyone present Sarah's innocence. Hamilton translates this *"a foil to everybody who is with you,"* noting that the word is literally *a covering of the eyes.* "The eyes of any of Sarah's acquaintances will be blind to any sexual misconduct on her part."

20.17–18, *Then Abraham prayed to God.* "In offering the compensation Abimelech owned his error (though the term *thy brother* re-emphasized his innocence), and in accepting it Abraham acknowledged the matter as settled" (Kidner).

---

[11]Leupold suggests that the value of the previously mentioned gifts was a thousand pieces of silver, rather than this being in addition to those gifts.

God healed Abimelech. "That Abraham's intercession means Abimelech 'shall live' [v 7] and that 'God healed' him suggests he suffered a fatal illness" (Mathews). Or perhaps a better understanding, in the context of the barren women, is that God struck the people with an epidemic of sexual impotence (Alter). Whatever it was almost certainly prevented him from approaching Sarah (v 4).

And also healed his wife and female slaves so that they bore children. The irony is thick: "Abraham can pray, and as a result barren Philistine women are able to conceive. Yet his own wife has not yet been able to become pregnant" (Hamilton).

Because of Sarah, Abraham's wife. Waltke notes the further irony: "When Sarah is among them they become barren; when she leaves, wombs are opened but she remains barren." And her barrenness is fitting: Abraham and Sarah claimed a brother-sister (*i.e.*, non-sexual) relationship; they got the results of such a relationship.

Growth of the Seed: God intervenes and protects Sarah due to the proximity of the promised child's birth (v 3).

Theological Reflection: She's My Sister
In Abraham's failure there are many lessons to learn. Here are a few of the more apparent ones.

Half-truths are lies. Any time you practice deception, you lie. Even if you are telling the complete truth, if your intention is to deceive, you have lied. Certainly Satan intertwines the truth with deception (*cf.* Gen 3; Matt 4). How often have you been deceived by someone only to be told, 'I wasn't *really* lying' (*cf.* 20.12)? But their truth or partial-truth was told with the intent of leading you to a conclusion that wasn't true. You certainly understand when you've been lied to this way. Likewise, if you use truths and half-truths with this intent, you have lied to another.[12]

Ignorance does not justify sin. This is expressly apparent in that Abimelech and Pharaoh are both punished for what they did, even though they weren't aware of the sin. God makes this clear to Abimelech in their dialogue: *"In the integrity of my heart and the innocence of my hands have I done this." Then God said unto him in the dream, "Yes, I know that you*

---

[12]We would not argue that *all* half-truths are necessarily lies. See comment on verses 11–13.

224 | The Growth of the Seed

have done this in the integrity of your heart" (20.5–6). Abimelech points to the integrity of his heart and the innocence of his hands. Here, the heart represents the inner motive and the hands represent the outer deed (*cf.* Jas 4.8 for similar usage). Abimelech says that he is innocent in motive and deed. God, however, corrects him in the next verse by omitting *the innocence of his hands*. By silence, He says, 'No, Abimelech, you're only innocent in motive... not in deed.'

Your lie can cause someone else to sin. The only thing worse than separating ourselves from God by sinning is when our sin takes someone else down with us. Abraham's sin did just that. According to 12.19, Pharaoh took Sarah as his wife. Most likely, that marriage was consummated. And that God plagued Pharaoh also seems to indicate he committed adultery, even though Genesis does not come out and give us the sordid details.[13] By lying, we can cause someone else to sin.

Your lie judges another. When you lie, you are casting judgment upon the person to whom you are lying. When Abraham told Pharaoh and Abimelech that Sarah was his sister, he was saying (if we may paraphrase), '*Listen, I know you're the kind of scumbag lowlife that would kill me and take away my wife. Since I know I can't trust you any farther than I can throw you, I'll just lie to you to protect myself.*' And the same is true when we lie to someone today. When you feel it necessary to withhold the facts from someone, you have judged them unworthy of the truth. Perhaps your judgment may not be as offensive as Abraham's was, but you have still judged the character of that person, which is certainly not righteous judgment.

Sometimes the hard decisions are the easiest. We are constantly amazed by how Abraham picked up and left everything to wander around for a lifetime or how he was prepared to offer his only son as a burnt offering. Yet, here we find him telling 'a little white lie.' The same is true with Noah: he spent his life building an ark and walking with God, yet ended up drunk and ashamed (9.20–25). Or Moses, who led the people out of Egypt, parted the Red Sea, and delivered the Law to the people, but couldn't find it within himself to speak to the rock instead of striking it (Num 20.8–12).

Sometimes it is easier to muster up the faith for a big, life-altering decision than to constantly, always obey God in your day-to-day life. Perhaps that's why Paul says, *I discipline my body and keep it under control, lest after*

---

[13]See comment on 12.19.

preaching to others I myself should be disqualified (1 Cor 9.27). He understood that even though he had made the big, hard decisions, many of the 'easy' ones were still to come—the easy ones which were so difficult that he felt it necessary to *discipline his body* to *keep it under control.*

In Genesis 13, upon Abraham and Sarah's return to the land of Canaan, we find Abraham stopping to worship God. In spite of the terrible sin he had just committed—and caused Sarah to commit—he stopped to worship. Even though he had just made a mistake, he still sought to come into the presence of God.

Every now and then when we are evangelizing, we come across someone who won't come to God because they think they're not good enough to come to Him. But no one is. That's exactly why we must. And, perhaps more than anything, that's what we learn from Abraham's mistakes in Genesis 12 and 20: even the greatest on the earth aren't good enough to come to God; yet, through His love and grace, He provides a way for the most sinful to enter the Most Holy.

21 **1–2, The LORD *visited… as he said… and… did to Sarah as he had promised.*** "The birth of Isaac is predicted twice (17.16–21; 18.10–15), and here the fulfillment of the promise is mentioned twice" (Wenham). "'Visited' is a common metaphor conveying the intervention of God in nature and the affairs of humanity" (Mathews). Isaac represents a clear type of Christ, beginning here (*cf.* Matt 1.18, 20; Luke 1.35).

At the time of which God had spoken to him. One year after the promise (17.21; 18.10).

21.3–5, *Called the name of his son… Isaac. And Abraham circumcised his son Isaac.* Abraham names his son as God had instructed him (17.19) and circumcises him as the covenant stipulates (17.10–12). "God's precise fulfillment of his promise is matched by Abraham's exact obedience" (Wenham). And Mathews: "Abraham's doubting laughter is transformed into obedient faith."

A hundred years old. "Abraham's earlier question of 17.17—'can a child be born to a centenarian?'— is now answered by the narrator" (Hamilton). The birth of Isaac was fully the working of God's mercy.

21.6–7, *"God has made laughter for me."* Their son was named Isaac *(he laughs)* because of the faithless laughing of Abraham at the promise of his birth (17.17). The appropriateness of the name was reinforced when Sarah reprised Abraham's laughter at the later promise (18.12). Here, Sarah shifts the focus of the name from being about their lack of faith to God's good blessing. "The name, potentially a reproach, now conveys only joy" (Kidner), as "Sarah's doubting laughter is transformed into joyous faith" (Mathews). The reproach of a lifetime has been removed from Sarah.

"Everyone who hears it will laugh over me." The name reflects not only their joy, but that all who hear her story will rejoice with her, amazed over the blessing of God.[1] Also, *who hears* is similar to *Ishmael (God hears)* in sound and "may be another jab at the rival mother and child, calling them to rejoice with her over the birth of the rightful heir" (Mathews).

"Who would have said?" Sarah expresses her joyous disbelief in a statement of how remarkable God's work is. Yet this statement may also betray her: "God had said several times to Abraham that his wife would bear a son. Sarah was aware of that promise" (Hamilton).

---

[1] Hamilton understands this second use of *laugh* to be the laughter of ridicule, so that Sarah is afraid that she will become the butt of sarcasm and sneer.

21.8–9, And the child grew and was weaned. Children were usually weaned at three years of age in the ancient Near East. Waltke cites an Egyptian text that speaks of "the mother's breast in your mouth for three years."

A great feast. "In a society where infant mortality was high, to reach the age of two or three would be regarded as a significant achievement. …From now on Isaac looks relatively certain to be Abraham's heir" (Wenham).

Sarah saw. "From her experience with Hagar (see Gen 16), Sarah perceives the significance of Ishmael's disdain for Isaac and his threat to her son's inheritance" (Waltke).

The son of Hagar the Egyptian. It is not insignificant that he is so designated here, rather than by name.[2] Also, the absence of his name may signify his secondary position to Isaac. Waltke notes that his objectification by the other characters is common: to Sarah, he is the *son whom Hagar… has borne* or *that slave woman's son* (21.9–10). To Abraham he is *his son* or *the boy* (21.11, 14). To God he is *the boy* (21.12, 17, 18, 20).

Laughing. Here, the play on Isaac's name is directed toward him. The *piel* stem of this Hebrew verb, used absolutely as it is here, is only found in a few places (*e.g.,* Exod 32.6; Jdg 16.25), "each time with nasty overtones, usually of someone being mocked" (Wenham). "Isaac, the object of holy laughter, was made the butt of unholy wit or profane sport. …The little helpless Isaac a father of nations!" (Hengstenberg qtd. in Keil). Leupold calls the Hebrew here a frequentative participle and argues that it denotes a repeated action. He thus translates: *"[Ishmael]… was always mocking."* And Kidner: "The discord… came from a fundamental rift which time would disclose and the New Testament expound as the incompatibility of the natural and the spiritual (Psa 83.5–6; Gal 4.29 and context)." This incompatibility of the natural and the spiritual indicates further enmity between the seed of the woman and the seed of the serpent.

Another suggestion about Ishmael's action understands the play on Isaac's name differently. Rather than Ishmael mocking Isaac in laughter, he is 'Isaac-ing,' that is, "Sarah sees Ishmael presuming to play the role of Isaac, child of laughter, presuming to be the legitimate heir" (Alter). Many older commentators suggested that it might indicate some sort of sexual activity (as the RSV's *fondling* implies), though most reject this now.[3]

---

[2] See Excursus I.

[3] Although this interpretation is unlikely, it may find support in the same word being used of Isaac *laughing with* Rebekah (26.8). For further arguments for this position, see Hamilton.

21.10–11, "Cast out this slave woman with her son." Sarah's solution is to send Hagar and Ishmael away, though she refuses to speak of them by name. Interestingly, this is the same verb used in the casting out of Adam from Eden and Cain to Nod (Hamilton).

This is not simply a repeat of chapter 16. There, Hagar fled from Sarah, but was not sent away by the family. Further, in that instance, Sarah acted wholly in anger. Here she acts in spiritual understanding. Her request is "to disinherit Ishmael so he will never share in the inheritance (see 25.5–6)" (Waltke).

"The son of this slave woman shall not be heir with my son Isaac." Perhaps there is some anger involved, but we would hesitate at calling it vindictive cruelty as some have. Rather, she understood that the scoffer of the promised son could not share in his inheritance. Had he stayed, he would have had legal right to the inheritance under ancient law (Hamilton). What's more: God supports her position, including the underlying truth that Ishmael would not inherit with Isaac (v 12).

The thing was very displeasing to Abraham. This is most likely an understatement. "Elsewhere, men explode in anger when they are merely 'displeased' (*e.g.*, Num 11.10; 1 Sam 18.8). When God is 'displeased' with something, death often follows (*e.g.*, Gen 38.10; 2 Sam 11.27). Only here is anyone said to be '*very* displeased.' Quite what Abraham said and did to express his displeasure is left to the imagination. The narrator is content to give the reason 'for his son's sake'" (Wenham).

On account of his son. *Cf.* 17.18–19. This move would disinherit his son. Ancient law-codes stipulated, "If a slave bears children and the father then grants freedom to her and her children, 'the children of the slave shall not divide the estate with the children of their (former) master'" (Waltke).

21.12–13, "Whatever Sarah says to you, do as she tells you." God stands behind Sarah's decision to cast out Ishmael. God's people must be set apart from worldly people (*cf.* 16.11–12).

"Because of the boy." It is interesting that God refers to Ishmael as a *na'ar* (lad) rather than a *yeled* (child) as Abraham and Hagar do. "The latter word denotes a biological relationship. The use of the former word by God minimizes Ishmael's relationship to Abraham as son" (Hamilton).

"For through Isaac shall your offspring be named." *Cf.* 17.18–19. Ishmael cannot remain as a backup to the child of promise. Abraham must put his faith fully in God's working through Isaac. "On this anvil there was no escape from the final hammer-blow of the next chapter, and Hebrews 11.18–19 shows that Abraham's faith was brought to perfection by this very means" (Kidner).[4]

"I will make a nation of the son of the slave woman also." "As Cain suffered both banishment from the divine and protection by the divine, so Ishmael is both loser and winner, cut off from what should be his [legally] but promised a significant lineage" (Hamilton). There are few Bible characters who had a promise concerning them repeated as often as Ishmael (twice to Abraham: 17.20; 21.13—not counting the more general promises of 12.2; 15.4–5; and 17.6—and twice to Hagar: 16.10; 21.18). It should be no surprise that he grew up to be a wild man whose descendants were faithless to God—everyone around him was constantly in doubt and needed to be reminded of God's promise. Here, "God overcomes Abraham's hesitation on two grounds. Abraham's lineage will be reckoned through Isaac, and Ishmael's descendants will become a great nation in spite of his expulsion" (Waltke).

"Because he is your offspring." Abraham was to be the father of many nations. Ishmael, as one of his sons, would help fulfill this promise. "Because of God's great love for Abraham, even his natural children, who will not directly participate in the redemptive kingdom, are blessed on earth (see 17.6). Since Abraham cannot provide for Ishmael, God will provide for him" (Waltke).

21.14, So Abraham rose early in the morning. *Cf.* 19.27; 20.8; 22.3; 26.31. This may indicate the mindset of those who "[face] a hard task resolutely" (Kidner). He would not be any more indifferent to this event than he was to offering Isaac in chapter 22. "In both cases the author depicts the father as dutifully carrying out the Lord's directions, relying on God to fulfill his promises" (Mathews).

Bread and a skin of water and gave it to Hagar, putting it on her shoulder, along with the child. The ESV wording, though it follows the Hebrew word order, is unfortunate, as it almost indicates that Ishmael was put on his mother's shoulder along with the bread and water. This would certainly be unlikely at his age—17 or older. Rather, *the child* is the object of *he gave* (Mathews). "The word order delaying the mention of 'the child'… until

---

[4]See Excursus I.

the last possible moment conveys Abraham's great reluctance to part with Ishmael, a point already made explicit in verse 11" (Wenham).[5]

The limited provisions have led some to suggest that Abraham's intention was to make sure Hagar could not go too far. This, however, conflicts with his prompt obedience. "And his use of the name Hagar rather than 'slave-wife' [as she is designated in the chapter to this point] suggests he is treating her with consideration" (Wenham).

And she departed and wandered in the wilderness of Beersheba. It is interesting that she wanders. When she fled from Sarah (ch 16), she took a direct course to Egypt, stopping in Shur. Here, she does not so travel but instead wanders, seemingly aimlessly, until she runs out of provisions. Perhaps emotions have overtaken her (as she was kicked out instead of fleeing on her own will) and she has lost her path. Or perhaps she was trying to stay nearby (*cf.* vv 31–32) in the hope that the family would take her and Ishmael back.

21.15–16, She put him under one of the bushes. Again, we are not to see in this a mother taking her child off her shoulder and setting him down under a bush. Rather, a young man whose unseasoned strength falls short is helped along by his mother until she determines that it is hopeless. "'To throw' signifies that she suddenly left hold of the boy, when he fell exhausted from thirst" (Keil). Also Kidner: "The word *cast* suits the exhausted action of one who had half supported, half dragged her son towards the shade of the bush." The same word is used of Joseph, who at 17 is thrown into the pit (37.20, 22, 24).

About the distance of a bowshot. "According to a concise simile very common in Hebrew, as far off as archers are accustomed to place the target" (Keil), *i.e.,* close enough to be able to see him, but far enough so as not to see him clearly. As Ishmael is later a bowman (v 20), this figure may be a hint that Ishmael will be saved (Mathews).

"Let me not look on the death of my child." Her action betrays her comment, as one can see farther than the range of a bowshot. "She sits at a distance, so that she cannot hear the crying of her child which tears her heart, and to allow herself to weep freely" (Jacob qtd. in Wenham).

---

[5]Hamilton, who argues that *child* is the direct object of *put,* does not see it necessary that Abraham put Ishmael on his mother's back, for this word also means *commit* or *entrust.* "Abraham places the physical provisions on her back and entrusts their son and his welfare to Hagar's care."

21.17–20, And God heard the voice of the boy. It is interesting that it is Ishmael God heard rather than Hagar. "Ishmael provoked their plight; his prayer now leads to their salvation" (Waltke). Of course, we do not know if his calling to God was a sincere part of his daily life (which is possible, as he grew up with Abraham), or a last-ditch effort (as even some atheists will call to God in the face of death).

"What troubles you, Hagar?" 'Have you so soon forgotten the last visit of God's angel and the promise which came with it? Have you so soon forgotten the God who, as you said, *looks after me?'* (*cf.* 16.11–13).

"I will make him into a great nation." Again, the promise concerning Ishmael is repeated, though this is the first time Hagar hears of the nation that will come.

Then God opened her eyes, and she saw a well of water. This is, most likely, not the miraculous creation of a well that was not previously there, but God "providentially guiding her search for water" (Whitelaw qtd. in Leupold). In the wilderness, wells are generally covered to protect from excessive evaporation and thus are hidden from those who do not know their location.

And God was with the boy. God's many promises concerning Ishmael were fulfilled. Even as he grew up, God was with him.

An expert with the bow. The Hebrew contains a doubling of the professional designation (literally *archer-bowman*). Alter understands it "as an indication of his confirmed dedication to this hunter's calling, or his skill in performing it" and thus renders it *a seasoned bowman.*

21.21, His mother took a wife for him from the land of Egypt. As the responsibility of finding a wife should fall on the father, Hagar shoulders this full responsibility, the parent's final obligation to a child. She chooses a mate for Ishmael from her homeland, but in so doing chose a woman who did not know or fear God. "In this respect she does not display the wisdom used by Abraham in choosing, as he did, a god-fearing wife for his son" (Leupold).[6]

Aside from his assistance at Abraham's burial (25.9), Ishmael is never mentioned again. Mathews provides a fitting conclusion: "The picture of Ishmael as the rejected son is complete: he is the son of a slave wom-

---

[6]Wenham, however, sees this in the opposite light: "Later Abraham will send to his homeland in Mesopotamia for a wife for Isaac. Thus although separated from her husband Abraham, we find Hagar acting in the best tradition of his faith and practice."

an, married to an Egyptian, lives outside normal social bounds, and is remembered for his hostilities."

21.22–24, Phicol the commander of his army. "'Phicol' may, if it be a Hebrew word, mean 'mouth of all,' and so the captain of the army may have occupied a post as representative of the people" (Leupold). If so, it may be a positional title, as *Abimelech* seems to have been[7] or a family name. Thus, when Phicol returns with Abimelech 26 years later, we need not assume either is the same man as the Phicol and Abimelech found here.

"God is with you in all that you do." Abimelech saw the evidence of this in how prominent and influential the sojourner had become. But surely, this also was brought about by his own personal experience with Abraham's God (20.3–7).

"Swear to me here by God that you will not deal falsely with me." Currently, there was good will between Abimelech's people and Abraham's entourage. He sought to secure permanently the friendly relations that now exist. Perhaps their previous encounter encouraged Abimelech to secure Abraham's honesty by an oath to God.

"Or with my descendants or with my posterity." The covenant was to last beyond the rule of Abimelech, so that his descendants would also be protected against this powerful sojourner. This indicates that "Abimelech believes that Abraham will have an enduring posterity" (Waltke).

"As I have dealt kindly with you." Cf. 20.14–15. Abimelech's kind dealings were done to ensure Abraham's intercession, but it does seem clear that he went beyond the bare minimum in making restitution.

"I will swear." Abraham agrees at once.

21.25–26, Abraham reproved Abimelech about a well of water that Abimelech's servants had seized. It is significant that Abraham agrees to peace before making this objection. Had he acted in the other order—perhaps the natural order—it would have shown him as reluctant to take the steps that would guarantee peace. Rather, Abraham agrees to peace first and then seeks to iron out the difficulties (Leupold), though it could also be said that the covenant is not finalized until the difficulties are ironed out (v 27). Abraham's claim to the well was probably based on his digging the well (though such is not expressly stated) and Abmilech's invi-

---

[7]See comment on 20.2.

tation to dwell in the land (20.15), which would require the use of the land's water (Mathews).

"I do not know who has done this thing." Abimelech assures Abraham that it was not done with his knowledge, much less his blessing. On the other hand, "This comment may also be a negotiating tactic. It seems just as probable that a keen ruler would know about the activities of his servants. In fact, the tensions between his servants and Abraham might have prompted his request for a nonaggression pact" (Waltke).

"You did not tell me." This may cast a little blame back on Abraham, who should have had enough confidence in Abimelech (so he thought) to complain before this day (Leupold), though Kidner argues that the verb used "suggests that Abraham had to make his complaint several times; perhaps Abimelech was adept at evasive tactics." It is never said clearly, but we should understand that Abimelech immediately returned the well to Abraham.

21.27, Sheep and oxen... and the two men made a covenant. Cf. 15.9–11.

21.28–31, Abraham set seven ewe lambs of the flock apart. Abraham gave Abimelech an additional seven lambs as *a witness for me that I dug this well.*

Beersheba. Beersheba translates *well of the seven.*[8] There was, however, probably a play on words involved as well: "The fact that 'to swear' is from a similar root would not pass unnoticed" (Kidner).

21.33–34, Abraham planted a tamarisk tree. "The planting of this long-lived tree, with its hard wood, and its long, narrow, thickly clustered, evergreen leaves, was to be a type of the ever-enduring grace of the faithful covenant God" (Keil). And Waltke: "The planting of this small tree of the Negeb probably serves as a landmark of God's grace, a pledge that Abraham will stay in the land, and perhaps as a symbol of God's shading presence."

Called there on the name of the LORD. Abraham worshipped, as always.

The Everlasting God. *El Olam.* "The name is one of a series that includes *El Elyon* (14.18), *El Roi* (16.13), *El Shaddai* (17.1), *El-elohe-Israel* (33.20), *El-Beth-el* (35.7), each an aspect of God's self-disclosure" (Kidner).[9]

---

[8] Waltke and Mathews are among the few who add *or well of the oath* and allow for the pun to go the opposite way.

[9] See Excursus B.

Abraham sojourned many days in the land of the Philistines. This covenant with the king and his military commander assured Abraham of peace and a safe dwelling place.

The *Philistines* were not yet on the scene, making this use anachronistic. "The writer may mean merely to refer casually to this rejoin in geographic terms familiar to his audience" (Alter).[10]

Growth of the Seed: The promised child is born; the Messianic line continues through Isaac; Ishmael receives assurance that he will become a great nation.

---

[10]Hamilton argues that there may have already been Philistines in Palestine, though it is more likely that they are 'Philistines' because they live in the land that the Israelites would later know as Philistia. Kitchen writes: "Those in Genesis live around Gerar, and under a king, not in the 'pentapolis' (*i.e.,* Gath, Gaza, Ashkelon, Ashdod, Ekron) under 'lords.' ...They are relatively peaceable, not forever waging wars, despite having an army commander. It is therefore more prudent to compare the Philistines of Abraham and Isaac with such people as the Caphtorim of Deuteronomy 2.23" (qtd. in Wenham). These 'Philistines' were probably displaced by the nation who would become such a thorn in the side of the Israelites during the time of the Judges and Kings.

22 *1, God tested Abraham.* Not a temptation to fall (*cf.* Jas 1.13), but a proving of the faith (1 Pet 1.5–7). "Abraham's trust was to be weighed in the balance against common sense, human affection, and life-long ambition" (Kidner). "This information is imparted to the reader, not divulged to Abraham, in order to remove any possible misunderstanding that God requires human sacrifices as such. …Now the reader knows that the son will not be slaughtered" (Sarna qtd. in Waltke).

22.2, "Take your son, your only son Isaac, whom you love." Notice how the proverbial knife is twisted as Abraham listens—each phrase specifying more and reaching a more intimate and personal level: *your son… your only son… Isaac… whom you love.* "With this fourfold characterization of Isaac, the whole poignant tale of Isaac so far, the promise, the delay, and the miraculous fulfillment, is summed up" (Wenham).

["Please"]. The Hebrew includes the particle *na*, which is usually translated *please*, but often omitted when spoken by God, or assigned a strengthening function, rather than the usual meaning of kind request. Hamilton notes that it is a term used more than 60 times in the book of Genesis alone, but God only speaks it five times in the entire Old Testament: "Each time God asks the individual to do something staggering, something that defies rational explanation or understanding. Here then is an inkling at least that God is fully aware of the magnitude of His test for Abraham."[1]

"Go to the land." Leupold includes *to/for/by yourself* found in the Hebrew and renders this *go for yourself* calling *lekha* a dative of interest, which "rules out the idea of others sharing in the test: Abraham must fight this problem through alone." Waltke succinctly says, "Faith is a lonely pilgrimage."

"Moriah." Moriah is the mountain on which Solomon built the temple (2 Chron 3.1), which has generated the Jewish tradition, still followed by some scholars, that the temple was built on the site where Abraham was to offer Isaac.[2] This location, however, has been questioned by some. A trip from Beersheba to Jerusalem would hardly take three days (although three full days is not required in Jewish reckoning—a part of a day would

---

[1]Waltke, by contrast, follows Lambdin in understanding the particle used with *hinneh* to denote that the command in question is a logical consequence. "The particle, then, conveys the consequential nature of Abraham's attentive and receptive response; in other words, 'Since you are ready to obey me, take your son.'" We are more inclined to follow Hamilton.

[2]See Waltke for this position.

count as a whole), and it seems odd that the Chronicler would not draw this connection if it were so apparent. Further, the temple was built on Mount Moriah, but this passage speaks of a region (see Mathews). It is evident in this context that only God knew the way to this place *("I will show you")*; perhaps it is still best to suggest that God alone knows the way to the land of Moriah.

Moriah is the first of six plays on the Hebrew verb for seeing.[3] Laniak notes: "In the Old Testament, faith is sometimes described as a form of sight," and cites Uzziah who was commended for, "literally, 'learning how to *see* God'" (2 Chron 26.5). He also notes that prophets were most commonly called *seers,* as they were people "who could see divine things, and could see earthly things from a divine perspective."[4] Though faith is the conviction of things not seen (Heb 11.1), it is interesting that in this chapter, the ultimate test of the 'father of the faithful,' there is a clear emphasis on things being revealed to Abraham by sight.

"Offer him there as a burnt offering." "The son given to Abraham was to be given back to God without reservations of any sort" (Leupold). And this is not a contradiction of moral law, "because the firstborn always belongs to the Lord (Exod 13.11–13)" (Waltke). But notice: "It wasn't a matter of simply resigning himself to Isaac's death—he himself had to build the fire, bind the boy, raise the knife, look in his eyes, and plunge it in his defenseless body. It wasn't enough that he had to suffer the loss—he was being compelled to carry out the process."[5]

God ultimately stopped the sacrifice, showing that it was not the slaying of Isaac he wanted, but Abraham's complete surrender. "Nevertheless the divine command was given in such a form that Abraham could not understand it in any other way... because there was no other way in which Abraham could accomplish the complete surrender of Isaac, than by an actual preparation for really offering the desired sacrifice" (Keil).[6]

---

[3] The other five: Abraham lifting up his eyes and seeing the place God was taking them (v 4); Abraham's answer to Isaac that God will provide (more literally, reveal) the offering (v 8); Abraham lifting up his eyes and seeing the ram (v 13); the name of the place: "The LORD will provide" (more literally, see) (v 14); the explanation of the name: it shall be provided (seen) (v 14). For alternatives on Moriah's meaning, see Hamilton.

[4] Tim Laniak, "Believing is Seeing," *Basics of Biblical Hebrew,* 204.

[5] Jim McGuiggan, *Genesis and Us,* 157.

[6] On the necessity of this event, see THEOLOGICAL REFLECTION, below.

22.3, Abraham rose early in the morning. Abraham's obedience is immediate and without question.[7] "The bargainer falls silent: no debate (unlike
with Ishmael [Gen 17.18] or with Lot [18.22–33]), only movement, hur-
rying, saddling, taking, splitting, arising, going" (Waltke).

Saddled his donkey. This does not indicate a saddling for riding, but for
carrying a load, "for the beast must have been taken along to carry the
rather sizeable load of wood sufficient to make a fire adequate for a burnt-
offering" (Leupold). Levitical law (*cf.* Lev 1) would later specify a burnt
offering "as the only one to be completely consumed (except for the hide)
on the altar" (Hamilton).

Cut the wood. It interesting that we find Abraham twice doing the work
that would normally be done by the servants who were at hand (*i.e.*, saddling the donkey, cutting the wood). It is also strange to find such details
in a narrative that is "famous for its rigorous economy in reporting physical details" (Alter). Perhaps this is to indicate that Abraham sought to stay
occupied to avoid thinking about what was to come even while preparing
the very items which would be used.

The order of the events—saddled the donkey, gathered the servants,
cut the wood—seems strange. "It would have been more sensible to cut
the wood first. The illogical order hints at Abraham's state of mind. Is
he so bemused that he cannot think straight, is he quite collectedly trying to keep everybody in the dark about the purpose of his journey till
the last possible moment, or is he trying to postpone the most painful
part of the preparation till last? ...All these interpretations are possible,
indeed are not mutually exclusive, and need to be borne in mind as the
narrative unfolds" (Wenham).

22.4, On the third day. Not only did Abraham have to physically go
through all the steps to kill his son, he had plenty of time to think about
it. "In the flush of passion we can all do heroic (or nearly heroic) deeds,
in the heat of combat very ordinary people can do extraordinary things.
Abraham's test wasn't over in a flash—he had three long days to talk himself out of obeying; three long days to come up with good reasons why this
shouldn't be obeyed. To his everlasting credit, the delay between the order
and the execution made no dent in his willingness to obey!"[8]

---

[7]See comment on 21.14.

[8]*Ibid.*, 159–160.

22.5, "Stay here with the donkey." The servants are left behind. It was Abraham's task to complete, not theirs—nor could they understand the impending sacrifice. "This is their function, a very strange one in any narrative, characters who are introduced solely in order to take no part in it. It compounds our sense of Abraham's isolation" (Landy qtd. in Waltke).

"[We] will... come again to you." Though the ESV closely follows the Hebrew word, its failure to include the pronoun implied in the first, plural verb obscures the faith of Abraham: *We will come again to you.* The author of Hebrews indicates that Abraham's faith was based in his knowledge that God had power over death (Heb 11.19).

22.6, *Abraham took... and laid... and took.* The details increase as the sacrifice draws nearer, giving the narrative the feeling that each successive step was an added agony for Abraham (Leupold).

Laid it on Isaac his son. This gives us some indication of Isaac's age at this point: he was able to carry a load of wood up the mountain. Abraham, unable to carry the burden of the wood at his age is left to carry the two means of destruction: *the fire* (a container with live coals) and *the knife* with which he would kill Isaac. "*Genesis Rabbah*, the Jewish midrash, comments that Isaac with the wood on his back is like a condemned man, carrying his own cross" (Wenham).[9]

So they went both of them together. And again in verse 8. The companionship of father and son are twice recorded, framing this scene, "suggesting both their isolation and their companionship as they climb alone up the mountainside" (Wenham). Although Abraham had faith that God would raise Isaac, this statement would seem to make it clear that he cherished these last moments.

22.7–8, "Where is the lamb?" Isaac knows that they are off to worship and is old enough to understand what was required—and what was oddly missing. He may also have noticed something weighing on his father's mind. Thus, he asks a natural question—yet the very question that Abraham dared not answer. We cannot know if he has figured out precisely what was going on, but he knew that something was not right.

"God will provide for himself the lamb." Abraham's answer is remarkable—a combination of considerate love and anticipative faith. In it, "He

---

[9]See comment on verse 9.

spares Isaac undue pain and leaves the issue entirely in the hands of God, where in his own heart he left them throughout the journey" (Leupold).

The structure of this dialogue is interesting: Isaac's question consists of six words (in Hebrew) and Abraham's answer is also six words; Isaac begins his question with *father* and Abraham ends his answer with *son*.

22.9, Abraham built… laid… bound… laid. Again, the details increase as the sacrifice draws near.

Notice Isaac's submission. If he was old enough to carry the wood up the mountain, he would surely be old enough to overpower his geriatric father. That he allowed himself to be bound "is an act of supreme faith in God and of full confidence in his father. …If it were not for the even more marvelous faith [displayed by] his father, [Isaac's submission] could justly be classed as among the mightiest acts of faith" (Leupold). In this respect, Isaac represents a clear type of Christ: the only son, taken up a hill, bearing his own cross, to be slain by the father, to please God, while he silently submits—except no one stayed the hand of God when Jesus was killed. Yet how much clearer are the words of Abraham when looking at Jesus' cross: *The Lord will provide.*

22.10, Abraham… took the knife to slaughter his son. Abraham's faith is unfaltering; his commitment to God is not superficial, nor has it been superseded by his love for Isaac.

22.11–12, The angel of the LORD. See Excursus H.

"Abraham, Abraham!" "The repetition connotes the urgency (*cf.* Gen 46.2; Exod 3.4; 1 Sam 3.10; Acts 9.4)" (Waltke).

"Do not lay your hand on the boy." In Abraham's heart, the necessary surrender had been made: he would allow nothing to stand between him and God. His faith shown, God prevents the death of Isaac.

"Now I know." Is this merely anthropomorphic speech? Is it a confusing way of saying 'Now *you* know that you fear me'? Or can it be said that, in free will, God has made a rock too large for Him to lift? Is the ultimate display of God's power that He made a creature with such freedom that even He cannot determine what it will do—or does this impugn the might of God? Leupold suggests that it indicates knowledge by experience, and the statement would thus indicate that Abraham has proven that he loves God. And Waltke: "[The narrator] focuses on the reality that

God does not experience the quality of Abraham's faith until played out on the stage of history."

"That you fear God." Here is shown the apex of true God-fearing: complete subjection to God's sovereign will. Anything less is not to fear Him at all. Mathews compares Abraham with Job (who *feared God and turned away from evil,* Job 1.1) noting, "If Abraham is the model of faithfulness to *Yahweh* in Israel, Job represents the nations whose integrity is put to the test."

22.13, *A ram, caught in a thicket by his horns.* As Abraham has said, God provided for Himself the burnt offering.

22.14, *That place.* If this is as opposed to 'this place,' it may indicate that the name was given after they left, even though this verse shows them still at Moriah (Leupold).

"The LORD will provide." As Abraham had said to Isaac on the way up, so God did in such a way that clearly displayed His divine providence. "The name does not draw any attention to Abraham's role in the story. Thus his part in the story is not memorialized; rather, it is subordinated to that of Yahweh. The name highlights only the beneficent actions of Yahweh. The reader [is to] come away from this story more impressed with God's faithfulness than with Abraham's compliance" (Hamilton). [10]

22.16–18, *"By myself I have sworn."* An oath was not necessary to ensure God's faithfulness, but *an oath is final for confirmation. So when God desired to show more convincingly… the unchangeable character of his purpose, he guaranteed it with an oath* (Heb 6.16–17), and, *since he had no one greater by whom to swear, he swore by himself* (Heb 6.13).

"I will surely bless you." God repeats the promises to Abraham, emphasizing the significance of Abraham's obedient faith, and adding two new elements *(sand that is on the seashore* and *possess the gate of his enemies).*

"Your offspring shall possess the gate of his enemies." "Since the gate was the keypoint in [controlling] a city, 'to possess the gate' was the equivalent of gaining control of or capturing a city" (Leupold). His descendants would be successful in battle with their enemies.

---

[10]Is there any significance to Abraham using Elohim in his first statement and only using Yahweh after Isaac is spared? Did he, perhaps, feel that God had violated the covenant by demanding Isaac's sacrifice, and thereby refrained from using the covenant name?

"All nations of the earth shall be blessed." The promise was never intended to be restricted to the Jewish people. From the beginning, it had universal appeal. The prophets also clearly and repeatedly speak of the nations entering into God's kingdom.

22.20–24, "Milcah has also borne children to your brother Nahor." Connection with the family in Mesopotamia has been lost until this point, where a report comes to Abraham that Nahor had family as well. This (especially v 23) sets the stage for chapter 24, where Abraham sends his servant to his homeland to find a wife for Isaac.

Growth of the Seed: The Messiah is typified; the covenant is renewed.

Theological Reflection: Why Would God Ask This?
Although we generally think of Abraham at the peak of his faith, at this point he is still growing. He openly laughed when God told him that Sarah would bear a child and asked instead that Ishmael receive the blessing (17.17–18). He had participated in a lifetime of using a planned lie (12.10–13; 20.13). He had balked at the thought of sending Ishmael away and relying solely on God's promise through Isaac (21.10–12). Though he had shown himself to be a faithful man, he was not yet the mountain of faith we often think of him as (notice how God responds to his passing of this test: 22.12).

Another possible answer to the question points us to Abraham's love for Isaac. Abraham had waited long for the arrival of Isaac who was the object of remarkable promises. But strong love such as this—as good and right as it is—can, over a period of time, crowd aside the higher love for God. Perhaps his love for Isaac was slowly overtaking his love for God in ways he did not even realize (Leupold). Such a danger needed to be faced and worked through. The love of God must consciously be put first.

Aren't you glad that God doesn't call on us to do the same thing? Doesn't he? *"Whoever loves his father or mother more than me is not worthy of me, and whoever loves his son or daughter more than me is not worthy of me"* (Matt 10.37).

We can liken Abraham's testing to a game of poker. In poker, if you have a lousy hand, but are good enough, you can 'bluff' your way to winning. The idea is that you pretend you have a good hand until everyone else 'folds' and you win. If, however, you get 'called' when you're bluffing, you lose. Abraham got called. Did he really love God more than he loved his son? A test of this nature would surely show the answer.

Likewise, we have been commanded to love God more than family. Are we bluffing? What would happen of God called us on it? Would we pass the test as Abraham did? It isn't that love of family is improper and that God expects us to diminish it. It must, however, be consciously put in its proper place. It must be directed and purified.

And Abraham did pass the test. The next morning, he awoke immediately and without delay set out on the road for Moriah. He simply obeyed. He understood that God's commands aren't to be questioned, but obeyed— even after three days of thinking about it (v 4).

Though the testing of our faith may not be as open and horrific as Abraham's test, our faith *will* be tested and God requires of us the same thing he required of them. As Isaac was required, so we must put also put our complete faith in God, regardless of the circumstance. As Abraham was required, so we must also love God more than our family. Though we may not be called on it, if we are bluffing, God will certainly know. And there will come a day where we will all lay our cards down.

Excursus I:
The Role of Egypt in the Life of Abraham

On three occasions, the nation of Egypt finds its way into the narrative of Abraham's life: in his flight to Egypt during the famine (12.10–20); in a description of the plain of the Jordan (13.10); in the person of Hagar, the Egyptian servant (16.1–4, *et al.*). Although each of these occurrences may seem innocuous enough on its own, the three share a startlingly common element—and one that would have great meaning to a nation who had just left Egyptian bondage and was traveling toward the Promised Land.[1]

The Allure of Egypt in the Abraham Narrative

Egypt first shows up, interestingly enough, in the chapter where the Abraham narrative begins—chapter 12.

"Abram has no sooner entered Canaan than he finds the land unable to support him… the solution which occurs to Abram is straightforward. There is food in Egypt, so why not go down to Egypt for a while?"[2]

Egypt then shows up in a seemingly insignificant reference which makes a rather odd comparison. In this description of the plain of Jordan, it is compared not only to the Garden of the Lord, *but the land of Egypt* (seeming to place Egypt on even a higher plane than the garden). More importantly for the theme we see developing, the plain of the Jordan that Lot chooses is *outside the Promised Land* (13.12).[3] Ultimately, "The eye of sight chooses the well-watered, apparently fruitful location, which is like Egypt, over the apparently less attractive land of promise."[4]

Finally, Egypt shows up in the person of Hagar.[5] Again, the factor initiating

---

[1] Full credit for the concept found in this excursus belongs to Iain Duguid, whose short article "Hagar the Egyptian: A Note on the Allure of Egypt in the Abraham Cycle" pointed me in this direction. Conceptually, the following differs only slightly from his article. Anywhere I fail to attribute something to him is an oversight.

[2] Iain M. Duguid, "Hagar the Egyptian: A Note on the Allure of Egypt in the Abraham Cycle," *WTJ* 56 (1994): 419.

[3] See comment on 13.11–12.

[4] *Ibid.*, 420.

[5] The book of Genesis shows more than just a passing interest in Hagar's home country. She is introduced as *an Egyptian servant* (16.1). Her ethnic origin is emphasized in 16.3. When she runs from Sarai, the Angel of the Lord finds her *on the way to Shur*, which borders Egypt. When she shows up again in chapter 21, she is reintroduced as *Hagar the Egyptian* (21.9). She is the one who introduces the Egyptian daughter-in-law into the family (21.21). And, finally, in the listing of Ishmael's descendants, she is once again called *Hagar the Egyptian* (25.12). That Hagar was Egyptian is clearly important to the author.

the crisis is the apparent barrenness of the object of promise. Instead of the Promised Land, however, it is the promised mother who is barren (16.1). "Again the solution appears to be to turn to the Egyptian option for help, in this case to Hagar, the Egyptian slave-girl of Sarai. She proves to be fruitful and conceives at once."[6]

In each of these instances, we see contrasted the apparent fruitfulness of Egypt with the apparent barrenness of God's promise.

Consequences of Choosing Egypt

In each case, however, choosing the fertility of Egypt over faithfulness to the promise leads to disastrous consequences.

The first choosing of Egypt results in nearly losing Sarai into Pharaoh's harem—without God's intervention, Abram may have never gotten his wife back. In addition, it is possible—indeed, probable—that this lie forced Sarai into adultery, which may have pushed back the time table of the promise.[7]

Lot's choice of 'Egypt' also had great consequences. The more obvious ones include his being carried away as a captive (ch 14) and his near destruction in the overthrow of Sodom and Gomorrah (ch 19), not to mention whatever ill effects living in that wicked place had on the upbringing of his family (19.30–38). But perhaps the most important effect of this choice is his rejection from the Messianic line.[8]

Finally, the results of using Hagar to continue the family line have had some of the most long-lasting detrimental effects. To summarize: Hagar's son, Ishmael, is a continuing problem for Abraham and Sarah; his descendants were a continual thorn in Israel's flesh; what's more, it is a portion of his descendants who are a thorn in the side of Jews and Christians to this day.

"The Egyptian option, while apparently attractive, always leads to disaster in the long run."[9]

Lessons to Learn

For Abraham:[10] Understanding this theme sheds additional light on the need for Hagar and Ishmael to be driven away from Abraham and Sarah in chapter 21. Ishmael represents a second string in Abraham's bow; a backup, a reserve to the child of promise.

---

[6]*Ibid.*, 420.

[7]See comment on 12.19.

[8]See Excursus E.

[9]*Ibid.*, 420.

[10]Much of the application to Abraham is quoted from Duguid, 421.

Isaac was a mere babe at this point, and infant mortality rates were high. Perhaps Abraham comforted himself with the thought that if anything happened to Isaac, there would still be Ishmael. He had already suggested to God that, as far as he was concerned, Ishmael would do perfectly well as the promised child (17.18). In chapter 21, *the son of Hagar the Egyptian* is a strong, healthy lad; a built-in 'Egyptian option,' should anything happen to the child of promise.

So, when Sarah suggests casting out Hagar and Ishmael, we should not be surprised to find Abraham unhappy at the thought. But God intervenes and supports Sarah, because Abraham must turn his back on the Egyptian option once and for all, and place his faith in the promise that it is *"in Isaac that your seed shall be called"* (21.12). Abraham must burn all bridges behind him, choosing the apparent weakness of the promise over the apparent strength of Egypt. It is a necessary preliminary step before the ultimate test of chapter 22, when he is called upon to offer up the child of promise as a sacrifice. Only when the Egyptian option has been abandoned can his faith genuinely be tested to the limit.

For Isaac and Jacob: The lessons continued for the next two generations. Isaac was prone to follow in his father's footsteps—in both the good and bad (*cf.* ch 26), even to the point of desiring to flee to Egypt during a famine. God, however, did not want this for Isaac and forbade his journey, emphasizing that he must stay in the land of promise (26.2–3). The lesson finally seems to have sunk in for Jacob. After his early years of rebellion, he knows better than to walk away from God's promise and rely on the abundance of Egypt. Although he seeks food from the Egyptian storehouses, he will not take his family there to sojourn until he seeks God's counsel and is directed by God to make that journey—and is assured that God will be traveling with him (46.3–4).

For the Israelites: The necessity of emphasizing this lesson to a generation who have recently left Egypt and are on the verge of entering the Promised Land is immediately apparent. In the wilderness, they quickly grew tired of manna and wanted to return to the more eclectic diet of Egypt (Num 11.5–6, 18–20). Their first response when the spies returned with a bad report was a call for return to Egypt (Num 14.3). And when there was no water to drink, they again expressed their preference for Egypt (Num. 20.5; 21.5). "To such people, in the face of the difficulties experienced in possessing the land of promise, the apparent prosperity of Egypt must have been a magnet."[11] Moses' generation—the people to whom Genesis was written—certainly needed to learn the lesson of not looking to Egypt.

And this wasn't the last generation for whom this was true. In the prophets, the Israelites are warned time and again not to rely on the strength of Egypt

---

[11]*Ibid.*, 421.

(Isa 30.1–3; 31.1–3; 36.6–9; Jer 42.13–22, *etc.*). "The clear message was that God's people were to remain in the land of promise no matter what the impediments. This principle is neatly summed up in the dictum of Deuteronomy 17.16: *'You shall never return that way again.'"* [12]

Theological Reflection

Certainly, there is application for us in this as well, although our Egyptian option isn't a physical one. Egypt represents security and stability: those things that look good when following God appears fruitless. Surely Satan hasn't forgotten the art of making things of the world appear more promising than God's promises.

Perhaps that is exactly why Jesus preached so much about the cost of discipleship. There can be nothing that divides our loyalties, whether money, possessions, social standing, or family. There can be nothing that represents a second string in our bow. We must burn all of our bridges behind us and come to Christ without reservation—for to come partially is not to come at all. There are no 'reserves' in God's army. His military enrolls no 'weekend warriors.' Only when our Egyptian options have been eliminated can our faith be tried, proven, and found true.

The way of Egypt *always* leads to disaster. The way of Egypt *always* leads to destruction. But the promises of God lead home.

---

[12]*Ibid.*, 421.

23 The previous chapter reaches the climax of the Abraham narrative. Everything built up to that moment; now, things gradually taper to the conclusion. Only a few matters of importance still need to be reported. This chapter, recording the death and burial of Sarah, is one of those. This event certainly could have been recorded much more succinctly; however, upon closer inspection, we find in it another great act of faith displayed by Abraham.[1]

23.1, Sarah lived 127 years. Sarah dies 37 years after the birth of Isaac. Interestingly, she is one of the few women in the Bible whose death is recorded—the only one whose age at death is recorded. The precise reason for this is unknown, though Keil suggests it is because she is the matriarch of the promised seed and is seen as the mother of faithful women (*cf.* 1 Pet 3.6).

23.2–3, Hebron. Though Abraham's location has changed, we are not told when or under what circumstances, as is usual in Genesis. "The narrator [does not record] the precise relationship and movement of the patriarchs with reference to Beersheba (21.34; 22.19), Hebron (23.2), and the Negeb (24.62)" (Waltke).

Abraham went in. The precise meaning of the verb is somewhat uncertain, and could indicate that he entered her tent, that he traveled from Beersheba to Hebron, or it could be an idiom meaning "to proceed" (Waltke). Wenham suggests that it refers to the mourning rites, which were carried out in front of the corpse, thus, that he went into the tent.

Mourn. This is a light translation of the word, which means to *bewail* and often was displayed by beating one's breast and lamenting (Leupold). Wenham adds, "The use of both terms together [mourn and weep] suggests that Abraham did not just weep aloud but carried out other traditional mourning customs, such as rending his garments, disheveling his hair, cutting his beard, scattering dust on his head, and fasting." Having been married for at least 70 years—and probably much longer—Abraham was understandably affected by his wife's death.

Hittites. Literally, *Sons of Heth.* "Whether these are actually Hittites who have migrated from Anatolia into Canaan or a loose Hebrew desig-

---

[1]An alternate interpretation is to see this chapter in the light of the previous one as a further test of faith. "First the promise of seed seems threatened in the command to sacrifice Isaac; then the promise of the land seems to be mocked in Abraham's need to bargain with these sharp-dealing Hittites for a mere gravesite" (Alter).

nation for non-Semitic Canaanites is unclear" (Alter). If they are the former, Kidner suggests that they settled there in the course of trade. Waltke disconnects them from the Hittite Empire to the north, citing that they did not practice the same customs as the Hittite Empire, they have Semitic names, and that Abraham could converse with them without a translator.[2]

23.4, "Sojourner." A *sojourner* is a "foreigner in a strange land possessing no property and having no fixed habitation" (Leupold). Kidner adds, "A resident alien with some footing in the community but restricted rights."

"*Foreigner.*" This is distinguished, albeit slightly, from the previous term. A *foreigner* is a visitor who "has a permanent dwelling, but no property in the form of land" (Leupold).

These two words—probably a hendiadys: *a sojourning foreigner* or *resident alien*—aptly describe the life of Abraham in Canaan since he arrived. Sometimes he settled down in one location for a few years; sometimes he wandered as a nomad.

23.6, "You are a prince of God among us." It is obvious to these men that he follows God, that God has raised him up, and that God's favor has been bestowed on him—an "expression far too graphic to be a greeting of formal courtesy" (Hamilton).[3] Their estimation of him is far from his self-description in the previous verse. Roop notes: "Abraham has put himself at the bottom of the social ladder, and they put him at the top."[4]

"*The choicest of our tombs.*" Note the shift from Abraham's words, *property for a burial site.* Waltke says, "While the Hittites are willing to grant this mighty prince the right to bury his dead on their land, they are reluctant to give him a permanent possession there."

23.8–9, "Ephron the son of Zohar." "Abraham's rejoinder, naming an individual, made skillful use of the fact that while a group tends to resent an intruder the owner of an asset may welcome a customer" (Kidner).

"*At the end of his field.*" "Abraham wants to make it clear that he will not need to...encroach on the rest of the Hittite property" (Alter).

"*For the full price.*" The offering of the Hittites (v 6) was not meant to be

---

[2]For a fuller discussion of the Hittites, see R.K. Harrison, *Old Testament Times,* 89–92.

[3]They probably would have meant the more literal of the Hebrew plural: *a prince of the gods.*

[4]Eugene F. Roop, *Genesis,* 154.

accepted by Abraham, but a form of generosity intended to start the bargaining process. People in the ancient Near East offered as a gift whatever one admires; however, they do not expect that he will take it.

23.10–11, The gate. See comment on 19.1. The agreement was made "before the legally responsible citizens who validated the agreement as witnesses," whose approval was necessary because Abraham, as a sojourner, would not ordinarily be entitled to buy land.[5]

Of his city. Perhaps Ephron was the ruler of the city (Keil), but any resident can refer to a home as 'his town.'

"I give you the field." Ephron repeats the offer made by the Hittites to give his cave as a gift to Abraham. "The seller's offer to give the property to the buyer is a natural part of such procedures and conceals neither a reluctance to sell nor a desire to be rid of the property."[6] Nor is the offer expected to be accepted by the buyer. "This 'bestowal' is really a maneuver to elicit an offer from Abraham" (Alter). Another alternative is suggested by Wenham: "Abraham can use his grave but… he does not intend to sell the land in perpetuity. Land merely 'given' is land on loan. A gift, as opposed to a sale, places the recipient under obligation to the donor."

23.13, "I give the price." Abraham again offers full price. Leupold argues that Abraham's declining of the offer went beyond customary bargaining practices, because if he had, "Abraham would really have been ready to receive from a heathen man what in reality he had already received from a higher hand. …To receive from man what had been given by God would have called in question whether God's gift was true and valid." Though such a theology sounds good on the surface, it would invalidate much of what was given 'by man' to the Israelites through the remainder of the Old Testament.[7]

"Of the field." Abraham originally sought the cave only, but agrees to buy the field as well. Lehmann suggests that he purchases the field in order to avoid the feudal duties. He concludes that the negotiation recorded is not

---

[5]Gene Tucker, "The Legal Background of Genesis 23," *JBL* 85 (1966): 77.

[6]*Ibid.,* 78.

[7]*E.g.,* The freedom to rebuild the temple given by Cyrus, *cf.* Ezra 1.1–4. Though not stated so clearly, could not Ephron have been acting as an agent of God in imparting this small portion of Canaan to Abraham?

about price, but it "concerned the question of who would render the services due the king as a result of principal ownership of the land."[8] Although this may be the case, it is not necessarily implied in the text. "Rather, this passage is an account of normal legal negotiations which were conducted with elaborate hospitality and exaggerated politeness [polite expressions and gestures abound: *bowed*, verses 7, 12; *mighty prince*, verse 6; *my lord*, verses 6, 11, 15; *hear me* or *hear us* signifying polite entreaty: verses 6, 11, 13, 15]."[9]

23.15–16, "Four hundred shekels of silver." An amount that should be of no consequence to the wealthy Abraham. The custom of ancient Near Eastern sales was to begin with a free offer, not expecting it to be accepted. Then, the seller would claim to fix a modest price to the item, which was really an exorbitant price, though understood to be the starting point to bargain (Leupold).[10] "Perhaps the story of Abraham's purchase of the land serves as a model to later Israel that the taking of their land will also be costly. Nothing will come easily or automatically. ...But the cost will be moral, not monetary. Abraham's descendants will gain possession of the land...by obeying Yahweh and his decrees" (Hamilton).

Abraham weighed out for Ephron the silver that he had named. "That the transaction is legitimate and permanent is the point of the verse; it describes Abraham counting out the purchase price in the eyes of numerous witnesses, adding that the silver met the proper standard" (Mathews). Further, Abraham shows himself to be above haggling price on a matter so serious. Perhaps we should ask ourselves when haggling for price if our motive stems from frugality in order to be a good steward or from the love of money.

Tucker notes that these last verses "resemble the style and schema of the written dialogue documents much more closely than it does a strictly oral contract, such as that in Ruth 4, which is concluded with statements by the parties and witnesses."[11] Perhaps, Moses had access to and

---

[8]Qtd. in *Ibid.*, 78. This explanation is based on two ancient Hittite laws, which may or may not apply here. For the text of those laws, see Hamilton or Harrison, R.K. *Old Testament Times*, 89.

[9]*Ibid.*, 78.

[10]We cannot know for certain whether or not this is an exorbitant price. "Jeremiah paid only seventeen shekels for a field (Jer 32.9), and David fifty for a threshing floor and oxen (2 Sam 24.24). On the other hand David paid 600 gold shekels for the whole temple site (1 Chron 21.25), and Omri bought the virgin hill of Samaria for two talents (6,000 shekels) of silver (1 Kings 16.24). Without details of these properties or current prices no certainty is possible" (Kidner).

[11]*Ibid.*, 82.

concluded the chapter with the actual purchase contract for the cave and field at Machpelah.

23.17–18, So the field… was made over to Abraham as a possession. This documents the details of the contract. Excavated contract tablets read similarly to these verses.

To the east of Mamre. This explains why Abraham wanted this particular piece of land. When dwelling near Hebron, Abraham lived near the terebinths of Mamre. Thus, Abraham wanted the place of burial to be as near as possible to his place of residence.

23.19, Abraham buried Sarah. "Even if Ephron did overcharge Abraham, the price paid suggests Sarah's burial ground was quite extensive. As befits the mother of the nation, her grave was impressive, a worthy memorial to a great woman" (Wenham).

Growth of the Seed: Abraham displays faith in the promises of God as noted below.

Theological Reflection: Buying the Promised Land
Abraham's faith is shown in his purchase of this land. He desired that his wife's remains rest in the land that had been promised to him and his descendants. Abraham knew that he would never possess the land. He also knew that his descendants would have to wait another 400 years before they would possess the land (15.13). He desired, however, for his wife—and eventually himself—to be laid to rest in the land that God would one day provide. "By leaving their bones in Canaan the patriarchs gave their last witness to the promise" (Kidner). The presence of this tomb in the land, when the Israelites came so many years later, was an eloquent testimony to them all that Abraham was sure of God's promises.

In addition, in this purchase, he conclusively rejected Ur and Mesopotamia. Burial in one's homeland was, and still is, important (*cf.* Gen 49.29–31; 50.25). Though Abraham never owned land—and though he lived with a 'this world is not my home' attitude (*cf.* Heb 11.13–16)—he showed that his home dwelt in the promises of God: Canaan.

24 **1, Now Abraham was old.** At least 137, *cf.* 23.1.

The LORD had blessed Abraham. This effectively marks the conclusion of the Abraham narrative. "Abraham's life is lived out between the promise of divine blessing (12.2) and the actualization of that promise (24.1). The future 'I will bless' is now completed with *Yahweh had blessed.* Prospect has become reality" (Hamilton).

24.2, Abraham said. This interchange contains the last spoken words by Abraham in the Bible. Thus, the scene is analogous to the deathbed scenes of Jacob and Joseph (Wenham). In each of those scenes, however, the son is made to swear; here, the oath is required of the servant. This may be a foreshadowing of the seemingly passive nature of Isaac throughout the Old Testament narrative.[1]

His servant, the oldest of his household, who had charge of all that he had. The most common assumption for this servant's identity is Eliezer (*cf.* 15.2), though it would be odd for Eliezer to go unnamed. Leupold suggests that for Eliezer to hold the position he had in chapter 15, he would have already served Abraham for about 20 years. If so, he would have offered Abraham more than 80 years of service by chapter 24, which would put his age near 100. Assuming that he is still alive, it would seem strange that Abraham would send such an aged man across the known world to find a wife for his son. If still alive, Eliezer would certainly have been *the oldest of his household*; however, the Hebrew used does not necessarily indicate age. BDB says that the term is used more than 100 times in the Bible as a technical term referring to people having authority. "The importance of the assignment is heightened by the stature of the servant Abraham selected; he is the senior administrator… of the entire household" (Mathews).

Kidner summarizes this particular servant: "This chief steward is one of the most attractive minor characters in the Bible, with his quiet good sense, his piety (vv 26f, 52) and faith, his devotion to his employer (vv 12b, 14b, 27) and his firmness in seeing the matter through (vv 33, 56). If he is the Eliezer of 15.2–3, his loyalty is all the finer in serving the heir who has displaced him, almost as John the Baptist to his Master (*cf.* John 3.29–30)."

"Put your hand under my thigh." The *thigh* in this context is widely understood to be a euphemism for the genitals.[2] Keil calls this "a bodily

---

[1]See Wenham for further discussion.

[2]This is implied "in light of passages such as Genesis 46.26 and Exodus 1.5, where a man's children

oath." And Waltke: "When facing death, the patriarchs secure their last will by an oath at the source of life (see Gen 47.29)." The significance of the thigh or loins is that it is the "seat of procreative power" (BDB qtd. in Leupold). Thus, "The form of oath has particular regard to the descendants and is taken in reference to them" (Leupold).[3]

24.3–4, "You will not take a wife for my son from the daughters of the Canaanites... but will go to my country and to my kindred." The advantage for Isaac would have rested in marrying a Canaanite. Such would have given Isaac a foothold in the land—and should he marry the right woman, powerful connections and social standing. But Abraham did not want this for Isaac.

No clear answer is given to Abraham's motivation for this concern, though we would address a perceived fallacy in the common explanation and offer a viable alternative. The standard explanation for this oath is that it shows the faith of Abraham. Take Leupold: "The patriarch's chief concern was to find a wife for Isaac who with him knew and believed in Yahweh and so would share with her husband a common faith." This position, however, does not bear out: God specifically tells Abraham to leave Mesopotamia to be separated from his pagan homeland. The brother and niece of the woman Abraham sends the servant to find—Laban and Rachel—each prove to be idolatrous (31.19).

We suggest that the motivating factor for Abraham was his knowledge of the future of the Canaanites. God had told Abraham that they would be removed by his descendants when the proper time came. A marriage among them would compromise that task by intermingling the lineages. Waltke says that Abraham set the example for his offspring "to secure wives from the blessed Semites, not the cursed Canaanites."

24.5, "Perhaps the woman may not be willing to follow me back to the land." The servant's concern is a valid one: 'How can I know that a woman from

---

are said to come from his thigh" (Hamilton).

[3]Keil says that early Jewish commentators thought that the oath was connected with the rite of circumcision. Hamilton suggests that this may simply be a way in which the servant reassures Abraham that he will honestly carry out his master's wish, noting: "Words such as *testimony, testify, attest* have their origin in Latin *testes,* suggesting the possibility that Roman society had some kind of symbolic gesture of touching (some)one's genitals when an oath was taken."

over there will be willing to leave home and family to cross the desert and marry someone she's never met?'[4]

"Must I then take your son back to the land from which you came?" The solution seems simple to the servant, though he first seeks Abraham's approval: take Isaac back to her if she will not come to him.

24.7–8, "'To your offspring I will give this land.'" The author may intend to highlight the faith of Abraham in God's promises by including in his last recorded words a quotation of the promise, even as he ensures Isaac's continued dwelling there.

"See to it that you do not take my son back there. …Only you must not take my son back there." Abraham is emphatic on this point, beginning and ending his answer with the prohibition. The Lord had taken him from Mesopotamia to inherit Canaan. Isaac returning there would be a step in the wrong direction. Further, he was certain that God would be with the servant in this mission. Finally, in order to set at ease the mind of the servant, Abraham declared him free from the oath if she would not return. "While Abraham acts on the basis of God's promises, he does not presume upon them, freeing the servant of his oath if the Lord does not prosper his mission. Abraham enters and leaves history on the basis of the divine promise" (Waltke).

24.10–11, Ten of his master's camels… choice gifts from his master. The camels were, in part, to carry the gifts to Mesopotamia, which would serve as the dowry for the bride. "The details of the camels and the servants (see 24.32, 59) underscore Abraham's wealth and faith in the journey's success" (Waltke).

And he made the camels kneel down… by the well. "The picturesque description of kneeling camels at the well fits the mood of repose and prayer, but it also possesses by 'kneel' *(barak)* a sound play on the popular term 'bless' *(barak)* of the chapter. Indeed, the setting for blessing is ready" (Mathews).

The time when women go out to draw water. The servant was looking to complete his task.

---

[4]Of course, in the days of prearranged marriages, this would have been less a concern than it might seem to modern society. This is not to say, however, that the brides had no say in their marriages (see comment on vv 57–60).

24.12–14, "O LORD… please grant me success." A prayer of simple faith follows, which speaks of Abraham's example to his servants. Interestingly, it is the first recorded prayer for specific guidance in Scripture. The servant is not prescribing to God what he thinks ought to happen; rather, he shows earnest desire in his words: 'O that it would please you for this to happen.' Ultimately, his prayer is unselfish: in it, he shows regard only for his master Abraham.

"Today." "This request is impressive in its immediacy. …This is the first passage of many in Scripture where the urgency of a prayer, an appeal, or a command is qualified by 'today'" (Hamilton).

"God of my master." This phrase is not intended to dissociate the servant from God, "but stresses the covenant with Abraham… to which the household was pledged by circumcision" (Kidner).

"Steadfast love." The word used is translated *kindness* in most versions and, in other places, *grace*. It "entails loyalty to a covenant relationship. The inferior party depends on the kindness of the superior to meet desperate need. God's reliable kindness to His needy people is the basis of the covenant relationship (see Isa 54.10)" (Waltke). And Mathews: "By appealing to God's 'kindness,' the servant alludes to the divine promises and their provision for Abraham; he interprets his task as an extension of the promises, making his prayer a corollary to Abraham's faith in the Lord's adequacy."

"'I will water your camels.'" Hospitality is so emphasized in this culture that it is the determining factor in finding the wife, even before beauty and chastity (v 16). "Since a camel could drink twenty-five gallons, the servant's sign is sagacious; it is a test of the woman's kindness, hospitality, industry, and willingness to help a stranger" (Waltke). Sternberg says, "What touchstone could be more appropriate than the reception of a wayfarer to determine a woman's fitness to marry into the family of the paragon of hospitality? And it is a stiff test, too, since it would require far more than common civility to volunteer to water 'ten' thirsty camels" (qtd. in Waltke). Further, "It was customary for women, particularly unmarried girls, to be responsible for drawing the water and herding the flocks (*cf.* 29.10; Exod 2.16; 1 Sam 9.11) but, as the actions of Jacob and Moses show in a similar situation, quite in order for men to water the animals" (Wenham). Thus, it would be highly improbable for the wrong girl to accidentally fulfill the servant's request.

24.15–16, Before he had finished speaking. Though the servant is to be commended for his faith, Rebekah would have been found without his prayer. Although He accommodates the servant's prayer, God was directing this before the servant arrived at the well.

Very attractive in appearance, a maiden whom no man had known. In addition to meeting the qualifications of the servant's prayer, the woman who comes to him is beautiful, marriageable, and chaste. The word used for *maiden* speaks to being of a marriageable age: "approximately a teenager" (Wenham).[5]

24.17–20, The servant ran to meet her. Eager to discover if God had so quickly answered his prayer, the servant seeks to know if she will pass the prescribed test.

"Drink, my lord." She immediately fulfills the first part of the test, though such is not a surprise in a culture that so valued hospitality. To allow him a drink would be common courtesy.

"I will draw water for your camels." The second part of the test—volunteering to water his ten camels—would prove to be what would set her apart from anyone else. Leupold notes: "Travelers claim to have witnessed the same procedure many a time, but none tell of the second offer which Rebekah made."

Alter notes that Rebekah is presented in this scene "as a continuous whirl of purposeful activity. In four short verses (Gen 24.16, 18–20) she is the subject of eleven verbs of action and one of speech."[6] And Hamilton: "In her behavior she is reflecting the quick and hospitable actions of her father-in-law-to-be. Abraham, when visited by three men, 'ran' from the tent door to meet them (18.2), then 'hastened' into Sarah's tent and told her to make ready 'quickly' three measures of fine meal (18.6), while he himself 'ran' to the herd to fetch a calf for the meal (18.7)."

24.21, The man gazed at her in silence to learn whether the LORD had prospered his journey or not. Though his prayer had been answered fully and immediately, the servant was still not certain that this was the right

---

[5]It should be noted how different the marriage customs were in ancient times than they are now. In addition to arranged marriages and dowries, teenagers would regularly marry 40-year-old men (*cf.* 25.20; 26.34).

[6]Robert Alter, *The Art of Biblical Narrative*, 53–54.

woman. One last qualification needed yet to be met: a wife from Abraham's kindred (v 4). [7]

24.22–24, A gold ring... two bracelets. The servant offered her these gifts either as gratitude for her service, or in faithful anticipation of a positive answer to the next question (*i.e.*, as a bridal gift). Verse 47 clarifies that this was a nose ring. "The nose ring was a sign of wealth and beauty (Prov 11.22; Isa 3.21; Ezek 16.12); a woman's nose was a physical feature valued for its elegance (Song 7.4[5])" (Mathews).

"I am the daughter of Bethuel... whom she bore to Nahor." The beautiful virgin who fulfilled the previous prayer was also from Abraham's family.

24.26–27, The man bowed his head and worshipped the Lord. The servant shows gratitude to God for His answered prayer. As his master Abraham would have, he worships. "He that will make his [worship] as freely and openly as does this man is both a devout and courageous soul" (Leupold).

"Blessed be the Lord, the God of my master Abraham." The servant does not worship a local deity, but understands that Abraham's God is Yahweh, the creator of all.

"Who has not forsaken his steadfast love and his faithfulness toward my master." God has, without exception, followed a course of treating Abraham with divine kindness. This incident was merely one more token of God's consistent mercies. Further, this speaks to the servant's faith and understanding of the covenant: "Only a man in fullest spiritual sympathy with the spiritual heritage of Abraham's household could have stated the case so properly" (Leupold).

"As for me." "Success, which inflates the natural man, humbles the man of God. This servant's first thought is for the Lord, his second for his employer (27b), and his final one, with unaffected delight, for himself: 'he led me—*me*—straight to the house'" (Kidner).

---

[7] "This is the first of three narratives in the Pentateuch where woman meets man at the well, and a marriage is eventually consummated. The other two are 29.1–14 and Exodus 2.15–21. The parallels in all three are that a man visits a land other than the one in which he is living. By a well he meets a girl who comes to draw water. She runs home to tell, and shortly a marriage occurs. A feature that Genesis 24 shares with Genesis 29, but not with Exodus 2, is that the land where the woman lives is the original home of the man; and the woman he marries is a relative. Unique to Genesis 24 is the representation of the husband-to-be by proxy, and the absence of anything heroic by the servant. He does not roll away the stone at the well, as did Jacob (29.10); nor does he drive away any nasty shepherds, as did Moses (Exod 2.17)" (Hamilton).

24.28, The young woman ran and told her mother's household. The women had separate tents (or separate 'compartments' of the same tent) from the men, which forced Rebekah to choose a parent to tell. In a place where bigamy was becoming increasingly common, the bond to the mother would probably be stronger than the bond to the father (Leupold). Further, with sons being the child of preference, it would only be natural for the bond between a mother and daughter to be stronger than the bond with her father.

24.29–31, Laban. On Laban's role, see comment on verses 50–51. His name, "which means 'white' and is used elsewhere as a poetic metonym for the moon (Isa 24.23; 30.26; *cf.* Song 6.10), is perhaps another indication of his family's connection with the lunar cult" (Waltke).

As soon as he saw the ring and the bracelet. The gifts were significant enough to impress anyone who saw them. Waltke sees Laban's reaction as being beyond merely impressed: "Whereas Rebekah innocently rushed to show hospitality to a stranger, Laban instead is gripped by greed. This picture of Laban racing after gold foreshadows his dealings with Jacob." And Alter: "His sharp eye on the precious gifts surely invites us to wonder about him."

Standing by the camels. Wenham points to this as another indication that Laban was consumed with greed—what he noticed about the servant was the obvious prosperity, as camels were "a rare and luxurious type of transport." While this may be true of Laban's character, it may also be said that Wenham's point about the scarcity of camels could indicate another reason why Laban would notice that: it was not an everyday occurrence to see a man standing with ten camels.

"Blessed of the LORD." We find out later that Laban was not a monotheistic Yahweh worshipper (31.19). The polytheistic mindset, however, will allow the acknowledgment of other gods. Apparently, he had gathered from Rebekah's words that Yahweh was the God of Abraham. His words to the servant—even though he is an idolater—would be natural. If his concern, as Waltke suggests, is material concern, his words seem hollow.

24.32–33, So the man came to the house. As with Abraham and Lot, the emphasis on hospitality is evident: a place to stay for him and his camels, straw and fodder, water to wash his feet, a meal.

The men who were with him. Here we first learn that the servant brought other servants with him. This, of course, would be necessary with ten camels and a dowry large enough to require ten camels. "In keeping with the rigorous economy of biblical narrative, these are not mentioned until now, when they become requisite participants in the hospitality scene" (Alter).

"I will not eat until I have said what I have to say." When God and the angels came to speak to Abraham and then to Lot (chs 18, 19), the meal preceded the business that was to be discussed. The servant, however, sees his business as so urgent as to waive the customary formalities. "This break with the leisurely tempo of polite custom gave uncommon urgency to his words" (Kidner). And Leupold: "He takes his commission so seriously that he cannot eat until he has delivered the message and ascertained whether the girl… will actually follow him."

24.34–36, So he said. With this, he begins to recount his mission and journey (through v 48). "Hebrew storytellers are usually very sparing with their words, so the fullness of the servant's recapitulation of events shows it has a most important function. The first account shows how the servant discovered Rebekah and became convinced that she was Isaac's chosen bride. But now he has to persuade her family that it is right for her to marry Isaac. His whole approach is pitched with this end in view, and it is important to read the second account in the light of the first to see how the servant appeals to the interests of Laban, in particular to convince him that Isaac is a worthy match for Rebekah" (Wenham).[8]

Most of this account is a simple retelling of what has already been said, though a few things require additional comment.

"The LORD has greatly blessed my master and he has become great." After this general statement, the servant proceeds to enumerate more specifically the blessings of God on Abraham. The servant is not bragging or merely 'catching up' with family; rather, as a representative of Abraham and Isaac in this marriage proposition, "it is essential that he make an accurate and complete statement of his master's standing and of his master's son's financial prospects" (Leupold). Thus, the servant gives a condensed account of Abraham's wealth—attributing its source as God. Further, "By mentioning his master's request that Isaac marry within his own family and his refusal to allow marriage with the Canaanites, the servant assures them that Rebekah's children will be the sole heirs" (Waltke).

---

[8] See his comments on this section for a further description of this 'salesmanship.'

"Sarah my master's wife bore a son to my master when she was old." There would naturally be some question as to why the children-to-wed were off a generation (Isaac was Terah's grandson; Rebekah, his great-granddaughter). This statement would clear up any question in that regard.

24.40, "'The LORD, before whom I have walked.'" The servant diplomatically omits the part about God removing Abraham from his family (v 7)— "a notion the family, to whom God has not deigned to speak, might construe as downright offensive" (Alter).

24.49, "Now then... tell me." All of the facts of the case have been presented in a simple and straightforward fashion. Now the family must decide. Notice that the servant never asks that Rebekah come back; rather, he tells them how he sought God's will and lets the facts speak for themselves.

"Steadfast love." This key word of covenantal relationship recurs, as the servant seeks to know whether Rebekah will enter into God's covenant with Abraham and Isaac.

24.50–51, Laban and Bethuel. It is not insignificant that Laban, Rebekah's brother, is mentioned alongside her father in this instance. "That Rebekah's brother Laban should have taken part with her father in deciding, was in accordance with the usual custom (*cf.* 34.5, 11, 25; Jdg 21.22; 2 Sam 13.22), which may have arisen from the prevalence of polygamy, and the readiness of the father to neglect the children (daughters) of the wife he cared for least" (Keil). And Mathews: "In the ancient Near East the elder brother played a conspicuous role in the household and is known to have overseen marriage agreements for his sister."

"We cannot speak to you bad or good." The figure of speech (merismus) covers the whole range of possibilities by listing the two extremes. Thus, it means, *We cannot say anything.* God had done the speaking; there was nothing left to be said. The family sees the leadings of God's providence as manifestly as the servant did (Leupold).

24.52–54, Bowed himself to the earth before the LORD. The servant immediately worships again. It is obvious that his master's practice of frequent worship has been thoroughly ingrained in him as well.

The servant brought out jewelry of silver and gold. The servant delivers the dowry to Rebekah's family, as was customary for the bridegroom (or his representative) to do upon the agreement of marriage. "The bride price was payment for the loss of the bride's services and her potential offspring" (Waltke). Also, this gave proof of financial competence (Leupold). These gifts would have been of the richest sort, corresponding to Abraham's actual wealth.

"Send me away to my master." On the morrow, the servant sought to return to Abraham immediately. Knowing of Abraham's desire to know the outcome of the servant's journey, he is anxious to be on his way and asks for permission to leave that very morning.

This entire story is one of rapid motion: the servant *ran* to meet her (v 17); Rebekah *ran* to the well to draw water (v 20); she then *ran* to her mother's house to tell her (v 29); Laban *ran* out to meet them (v 29); the servant delayed the meal until after his mission was completed (v 33); the servant seeks to leave the next morning (v 54).

24.55–58, "Let the young woman remain with us a while." Naturally, such a sudden departure is too soon for the family. It is doubtful that Laban is trying to stand in the way of God; rather, the family "wanted a couple of days to grow accustomed to the thought of separation" (Leupold).

"At least ten days." Literally, the phase is *days or ten*. Some argue that days in the plural may mean a year (*cf.* Lev 25.29 for a clear illustration of this usage). If so, Laban could mean anything from ten days to 'a year or so' to ten years. Any interpretation given clearly foreshadows Laban as one who bargains with time (*cf.* 29.27).

"Do not delay me, since the LORD has prospered my way." The servant does not want to be slowed in completing his mission. God's will has already been shown; delaying the parting will make the separation harder, and will be an act against God's providence.

"Send me away." Or *"Dismiss me."* The servant kindly seeks the permission of his hosts to go and complete his journey.

"Let us call the young woman and ask her." If she was willing to go, that would settle the matter. Though it may seem odd to ask the bride's opinion in an arranged marriage such as this, Hurrian marriage contracts specified that the bride's consent was "an important counterpoise to the family's initiative" (Kidner). Wenham says, "Presumably, Laban calculated that attachment to home and respect for her mother's opinion would surely make her ask for a delay."

"I will go." Rebekah immediately shows her faith in God by not delaying to fulfill His will that had been so clearly displayed at the well. "Seem-

ingly against her father's wishes, she complies with the Lord's direction, matching Abraham's faith to leave the family" (Waltke).

24.59–61, Her nurse. Deborah (*cf.* 35.8). "She probably accompanied Rebekah to provide some solace for the young girl so far away from her homeland. Deborah is a memento of the past kept by Rebekah" (Mathews). [9]

And they blessed Rebekah. It was customary to bestow such blessings on brides. This one is recorded as it is so literally fulfilled.

Rebekah and her young women arose and rode on the camels. The gifts dispatched, the camels now find their second purpose: transporting Rebekah and her entourage back to Palestine. Three years have passed between the last time marker and now (*cf.* 23.1; 25.20). It is not clear whether the servant's journey takes three years, if three years pass before his journey, or if it is a combination of the two.[10]

24.63, Isaac went out to meditate in the field. "While his servant is absent on business vital to himself, Isaac at home stimulates devotion and engages in earnest prayer" (Leupold). Keil suggests, "The object of his going to the field to meditate was undoubtedly to lay the question of his marriage before God in solitude." And Mathews: "That Isaac was meditating at the moment of Rebekah's appearance also fits well with the providence-prayer motif of the chapter." If so, this would indicate that the servant's prayer at the well was not the only cause of God's blessing of the journey.[11]

24.64–66, She dismounted from the camel. "To this day, when in the Near East a woman riding meets a man, courtesy demands that she dismount" (Leupold).

She took her veil and covered herself. "Rebekah's veiling symbolizes to Isaac that she is the bride. Israelite women were not normally veiled (see

---

[9]Why Deborah is unnamed here we cannot know for certain. Hamilton suggests that her anonymity is to balance the unnamed servant and his companions.

[10]See also footnote to verse 66.

[11]The verb translated *meditate* is found only here and its precise meaning is unknown. Interestingly, the LXX renders this *in order to gossip.* Some modern translations vary as well. If verse 65 is meant to paraphrase his purpose, then we see Isaac as simply going for a walk; Alter renders the verb in verse 63 *to stroll*—the purpose of this passage would most likely then be to indicate God's providence at work again: after all this time, Isaac is out in the field to meet his new bride as she arrives. See Waltke. Mathews notes that an alternate meaning is *complain, lament,* which may find support in Isaac's later consolation over his mother's death (v 67).

12.14; 38.14). It was customary, however, to veil the bride in the marriage ceremony" (Waltke).

The servant told Isaac all the things that he had done. Thus, Isaac would know what sort of woman Rebekah was, why he was back so soon,[12] and how remarkably God had answered the prayer. And notice the shift from Abraham as master and head of the household to Isaac as being in that position—the servant reports to Isaac—even though Abraham lives another 35 years (see 21.5; 25.7, 9). "By this editorial choice, Isaac is presented as lord and successor of Abraham even as Rebekah is presented as mother and successor of Sarah" (Waltke). And Mathews: "The omission of the senior patriarch has a literary function, demonstrating the passage to the next generation."

24.67, Isaac brought her into the tent of Sarah his mother. This act shows three things: Isaac's courtesy by immediately taking her to a tent; his tact by taking her to a woman's tent; his honoring of her by taking her into the vacant tent of Sarah—the matriarch of God's chosen people (Leupold).

She became his wife. Cf. 25.20.

So Isaac was comforted after his mother's death. Fox writes, "As the story opened with [Isaac's] father in his last active moments, it closes with the memory of his mother. [Isaac] is on his own."[13] And Mathews: "This final verse shows that the objective of the search is now complete."

Growth of the Seed: Abraham secures a bride for Isaac, ensuring the continuance of the Messianic line.

---

[12]His return was quick, relatively speaking; Hamilton notes that half of the roundtrip journey would have taken at least a month; if chivalry surpassed the desire for a quick return, the trip home likely would have taken longer.

[13]Everett Fox, *Genesis and Exodus: A New Rendition with Commentary and Notes,* 101.

25 *1, Abraham took another wife, whose name was Keturah.* Two main questions arise regarding Keturah. First, why is this told when it has nothing to do with the history of the lineage of Christ or the Israelites? In response, Abraham's children by Keturah continue to fulfill the promise that he would be the father of many nations. Beyond that, it helps illustrate an important point about genealogy: relation to a faithful person does not ensure blessing. Most of Abraham's descendants fell into paganism and were not blessed (*cf.* Rom 9.6–7). Even Abraham's descendants are just another heathen group if they fail to keep God's promises (Leupold). To the original audience, this would serve as a stern warning.

The second question that arises is when this occurred. Its place in the text would indicate that it took place after Sarah's death when Abraham was in his later years. Verse 6 implies, however, and 1 Chronicles 1.32 clearly states that she was merely a concubine, which has caused some to suggest that Abraham had taken her as such prior to Sarah's death. Some point to Abraham's vitality as evidence that he must have been at a younger age (*e.g,* Kidner). Further, it is evident that the Genesis record is not intended to be strictly chronological. If it were, the death of Abraham would need to be placed after the births of Jacob and Esau (21.5; 25.7, 26).

Although this interpretation is possible and perhaps likely, it is not necessary to make sense of the text: she may be listed as a concubine because the writers of Genesis and Chronicles did not place her on the same level as Sarah. Sarah was his first wife, his wife of the longest marriage, and the mother of the child of promise and the Israelites. To the descendants of Abraham, Isaac, and Jacob, Keturah would have been merely a concubine—even if she was, in reality, a later wife. Second, although his vitality may point to a younger age, God had blessed him with children at 100; there is no reason to suggest that He could not do such again at an even later age. Ultimately, we do not know when Abraham married Keturah; ultimately, it does not matter. The significant point is documenting the fulfillment of the promise and issuing a warning to future generations of Abraham's offspring.

25.2, *She bore him Zimran, Jokshan, Medan, Midian, Ishbak, and Shuah.* "Fertility, one of God's choicest blessings to his own, is minimally manifested with Sarah and Hagar, but maximally manifested in the life and womb of the relatively obscure Keturah" (Hamilton).

25.5–6, Abraham gave all he had to Isaac. Abraham had pled for Ishmael to be acceptable as the child of promise (17.18). Abraham became upset at the prospect of sending Ishmael away (21.11), but was told by God, *"Through Isaac shall your offspring be named"* (21.12). Although Abraham could be a slow learner (*cf.* 'She's my sister'), he eventually learned what God would have him know. This short verse provides the evidence.

The sons of the concubines. Presumably this refers to the sons of Hagar and Keturah, though it is conceivable that Abraham had other concubines who are not mentioned in the text.

He gave gifts. "Sons of full wives could expect a definite share (Deut 21.15–17; *cf.* Num 27.1–11). Sons of concubines were completely dependent on their father's goodwill" (Wenham). And Waltke: "Since he is probably not legally required to give them gifts, his gifts are a gesture of goodwill. The result of this gesture, if not its purpose, probably wins their goodwill toward Isaac until the time of the conquest."

He sent them away from his son Isaac. "One might compare Abraham's actions with the sons of his concubines, especially Keturah's…with wife Hagar and her son Ishamael (ch 21)" (Hamilton).

25.7, 175 years. Abraham lived 100 years in the land of Canaan (*cf.* 12.4).

25.8, Abraham breathed his last… and was gathered to his people. Those who would argue that the Old Testament has no teaching of an afterlife must explain passages such as this. This passage uses the phrase *gathered to his people* in a way that cannot be limited to burial. Abraham was not *gathered to his people* in any literal sense by being buried: his body was never returned to Mesopotamia, and Sarah's corpse in Machpelah could hardly be defined as *people*. Jacob also provides as compelling a case: he was *gathered to his people* several days before he was buried (49.29–33, 50.12–13), hundreds of miles from the family burial plot. This phrase is here "distinguished from death (v 8a) and burial (v 9), and accordingly suggests the reunion of the deceased with his forefathers" (Hamilton). And Kaiser: "The event of being 'gathered to one's people' is always distinguished from the act of burial, which is described separately."[1] Thus, Keil says that this phrase "denotes the reunion in Sheol with friends who have gone before, and therefore presupposes faith in the personal continuance of a man after death."[2]

---

[1]*Hard Sayings*, 128.

[2]On Sheol, see Excursus M.

It seems clear from other passages, in fact, that the ancients did believe in an afterlife (*e.g.,* Job 3.13–14). Their understanding of it was not as clear as ours, as they had not received the extent of revelation that we have,[3] but they did understand that there was more to life than just this world. Though some object that such concepts are too 'developed' for the primitive times and Old Testament minds, "We need only to remind each other that life after death was already the overriding passion of the Egyptian culture."[4]

25.9, Isaac and Ishmael his sons. Any hard feelings between the brothers were put aside at the death of their father (*cf.* 35.29).

25.11, God blessed Isaac. "The theme of inherited blessing that is central to the Abraham narrative appears in [this] verse. ...The blessing does not die with the favored patriarch; it is an eternal promise rooted in the will of God (13.15; 17.7–8, 13, 19)" (Mathews).

Isaac settled at Beer-lahai-roi. This is the location where the Angel of the Lord had appeared to Hagar and where Ishmael was subsequently born (16.14). "That Isaac settles in the place where Ishmael was born indicates that, geographically, Isaac is indeed the one son chosen by Yahweh to be blessed, and that Ishmael is to be either displaced, or more likely, replaced" (Hamilton).

25.12, These are the generations of Ishmael. The genealogy which follows shows that the promises made to Hagar and Ishmael are fulfilled (*cf.* 16.10; 17.20; 21.13, 18).

25.18, He settled over against all his kinsmen. Cf. 16.12.

Growth of the Seed: The birth of children to Abraham through a second wife fulfills the *many nations* promise; Ishmael's genealogy shows the fulfillment of God's promises to Abraham and Hagar.

---

[3]We would argue that even we do not know as much as we often presume to know about the afterlife—only the pictures that God has seen fit to share in obviously figurative and anthropomorphic terms.

[4]*Ibid.,* 128.

Isaac and Jacob

Structure and Pattern in Genesis
The Jacob Cycle: Concentric Pattern

A Oracle sought; struggle in childbirth; Jacob born (25.19–34)

   B Interlude: Rebekah in foreign palace; pact with foreigners (26.1–35)

      C Jacob fears Esau and flees (27.1–28.9)

         D Messengers (28.10–22)

            E Arrival in Haran (29.1–30)

               F Jacob's wives are fertile (29.31–30.24)

               F' Jacob's flocks are fertile (30.25–43)

            E' Flight from Haran (31.1–55)

         D' Messengers (32.1–32)

      C' Jacob returns and fears Esau (33.1–20)

   B' Interlude: Dinah in foreign palace; pact with foreigners (34.1–31)

A' Oracle fulfilled; struggle in childbirth; Jacob becomes Israel (35.1–22)

Although Isaac is the second of the great patriarchs of faith, the information given about him is limited, and usually he is in the background scenes of his father's story (ch 22), his servant's story (ch 24) or his son's story (ch 27)—the one exception is chapter 26, and even there, to a large degree, he is merely following in his father's pattern.

From a literary standpoint, Isaac is a non-entity. If the *toledot*[1] of a person indicates that it is the history of his descendants, there is no section of Genesis specifically dedicated to him. Terah's *toledot* (11.27) tells of Abraham (11.27–25.18); Isaac's *toledot* (25.19) tells of Jacob (25.19–37.1); Jacob's *toledot* (37.2) tells of Joseph and Judah (37.2–50.26). Abraham does not have a *toledot;* Isaac does not have a story.

For the sake of convenience, we have included him in the narrative of Jacob, as this section of Genesis contains the only chapter where Isaac takes the lead role.

25.21, Isaac prayed to the L*ORD *for his wife. This is the first record of such intercession. "As Abraham's servant secured Isaac's wife by prayer, so also will Isaac obtain his offspring" (Waltke). Wenham adds, "Elsewhere this term…involves a request to remove some serious ill; it occurs most frequently in Exodus of Moses entreating God to send away the plagues." And Hamilton: "Isaac's handling of his wife's infertility is distinguished from Abraham's handling of a similar situation. Abraham's prayers result in the opening of the wombs of Philistine women (20.17), but never did we read that Abraham prayed for Sarah when she was incapacitated. In order to alleviate barrenness God visited Sarah (21.1–2) and remembered Rachel (30.22). But no verb is used with God as subject and Rebekah as object. Instead, the urgent prayer of Isaac is highlighted."

Unlike Sarah, Rachel and Leah, Rebekah does not resort to concubinage to solve her barrenness; Isaac is the only monogamous patriarch.

Because she was barren. For the second time, the mother of the promised seed is barren. Again, it is emphasized that the completion of God's plan comes by divine grace, not human working. Although the time passes quickly in the narrative, Rebekah remains barren for 20 years (25.20, 26).

25.22–23, The children struggled together within her. This is an early foreshadowing of the life that is to be led by Jacob and Esau. Her following question indicates that this is not the average 'kicking' of an unborn child, as is even more evident by Wenham's translation that they *smashed themselves together inside her.*

"Why is this happening to me?" More literally, *"Why am I?"* or *"Why this, I?"* Because it is such a difficult passage, it has been variously interpret-

---

[1] On *toledot,* see pages 20–21.

ed. Keil understands it to mean: "Why am I alive?" (also Wenham).[2] And Leupold: "For what am I destined?" Mathews writes, "She interpreted the bizarre behavior of the children... as an omen of animosity, and she pondered what this would mean for her and her children. In effect she is asking, 'What good is my pregnancy?' 'Will the children survive?' 'Will I survive?'" And Kidner: "The context of answered prayer (v 21) and further enquiry (v 22b) rather suggests her disquiet that God's frown had so suddenly replaced his smile"—thus the basic meaning of the question is something like *'If all is well, why am I like this?'*

The Lord said. "This prefacing of each 'family history' with a word from God thus serves to highlight that every stage of the patriarchal history was guided by God. Despite the appalling mistakes of these fallible men, God's purposes were ultimately fulfilled" (Wenham).

"The one shall be stronger than the other, the older shall serve the younger." There may be no clearer instance of divine election in the Bible. It is important, however, to note that even here, it is not the one *individual* who is elected while the other is rejected; the verse makes it clear that *nations* are under discussion. This prophecy does not indicate that Jacob was to be blessed while Esau was to be cursed—both sons were blessed (*cf.* Heb 11.20); rather, God chooses Jacob for a particular blessing and role from which Esau is excluded. God did not choose the nation of Israel merely to bless it. He chose Israel to be His instrument of blessing to the whole world, including Esau and his descendants.

25.24–26, There were twins in her womb. "Their descriptions poke fun at both: a hairy monster and a heel-clutcher" (Waltke).

The first came out red. But have you ever seen a baby come out who wasn't red? Such is the nature of the birthing process! It is doubtful that his hair was red, as such is not common in Semitic people; rather, the noting of the red seems to simply foreshadow the later significance of 'red' and his later name 'Edom' (*cf.* v 30).[3]

All his body like a hairy cloak, so they called his name Esau. The mention of this explains both his name, which means *hairy,* and the later need

---

[2] This interpretation most likely follows the Syriac, which adds *alive* to Rebekah's question.

[3] The notion that there was something red about Esau beyond the birthing process need not be wholly dismissed. David would later be described with the same word, translated *ruddy* there (1 Sam 16.12; 17.42)

for Jacob to disguise himself with animal skins. "The Hebrew word also sounds like Seir, where Esau will live (see 32.3; 36.8)" (Waltke).

His brother came out with his hand holding Esau's heel, so his name was called Jacob. Jacob's name means *he takes by the heel,* and carries the connotation of cheating. This position may also be "a sign of his future attitude toward his brother" (Keil). And Wenham: "Here the second twin is seen trying desperately to catch up with the first. The pattern for the rest of the story is set." Further, his name foreshadows the life he will live on this side of the Jabbok.[4]

25.27–28, Esau was a skillful hunter, a man of the field, while Jacob was a quiet man, dwelling in tents. As the sons grew up, the differences between them became apparent. Esau was a man of the open country; Jacob was a milder man. Interestingly, Esau's description is similar to Ishmael's, who became a bowman and was a wild man. Is this intended to foreshadow his fate?

Isaac loved Esau because he ate of his game, but Rebekah loved Jacob. This is the first of two clear illustrations regarding the folly of choosing favorites among children (Jacob's favoritism toward Joseph being the latter example). "We should not conclude that the parent felt animosity toward the disfavored son; rather 'loved' means each showed a strong preference toward one (*cf.* 37.3–4)" (Mathews).

Esau was a perfect father's son—a hunter and outdoorsman; he brought his father game and prepared it. Besides that, it may be that "the more passive Isaac finds himself attracted to the more active and bold Esau just because he himself lacks these qualities" (Leupold). *Because he ate of his game* is literally *for the game in his mouth.* "It is unclear whether the idiom suggests Esau as a kind of lion bringing home game in its mouth or rather bringing game to put in his father's mouth. The almost grotesque concreteness of the idiom may be associated with the absurdity of the material reason for Isaac's paternal favoritism" (Alter).

It is striking that no reason is given for Rebekah's favoritism of Jacob, though most suppose it was because he was a homebody. Alter, on the other hand, suggests that the absence of a listed motive implies that "her

---

[4]Although Jacob is a complex character whose personality grows and changes throughout his life, it is just before crossing the Jabbok, when he wrestles with God, that his life makes the most drastic turn. See comment on 32.22–32.

affection is not dependent on a merely material convenience that the son may provide her, that it is a more justly grounded preference."[5] If so, her favoritism may stem from God's promise that the younger son was chosen.[6]

25.29–30, *[Esau] was exhausted.* Having come in from a day of hunting, Esau was tired and hungry. The word is translated by some *famished*, which is in the realm of possibility and made more likely by the context. Waltke stands alone in arguing that it is not hyperbole.

"Let me eat some of that red stew." The ESV cleans up the Hebrew, which reads more like: *"some of the red, that red."* His words are expressive of an uncontrolled hunger—the first hint at the underlying character of Esau. Further, the ESV's translation of the verb is a poor choice. He does not ask to *eat* the stew, but to *swallow it* or *gulp it down* (Hamilton). "The verb he uses for gulping down occurs nowhere else in the Bible, but in rabbinic Hebrew it is reserved for the feeding of animals" (Alter).

Therefore his name was called Edom. Esau is never called Edom in Genesis, though his descendants are known to the Israelites as the Edomites. In all likelihood, this became a derogatory nickname for his descendants— "The play on the name is not complimentary, since it brings to mind Esau's ineptness in dealing with the artful Jacob" (Mathews)—a reminder their forefather lost the birthright for 'some red stuff.' This phrase may simply serve to explain to the Israelites the origin of their cousin-nation's name.

25.31, *"Sell me your birthright now."* It would seem as though they'd had this discussion before; perhaps, "Esau had made some derogatory remark about its value, or had even spoken about his own readiness to part with the privilege" (Leupold). At the very least, Jacob had long been thinking of a way to obtain it. Otherwise, one is hard pressed to explain why such a notion would suddenly come to Jacob's mind. Jacob is often seen in a poor light—conniving to take something that did not rightly belong to him— but the blame should be squarely placed on Esau.

---

[5]Robert Alter, *The Art of Biblical Narrative*, 44.

[6]Wiesel notes a different interpretation, offered by Rashi, an eleventh century French Jewish commentator, who is said to be "citing the sages": "Pregnant with twins, [Rebekah] felt them stirring in different places inside her. When she passed before a house of study, Jacob wanted to come out. Before a place consecrated to idols, it was Esau who hastened to be born" ("Esau," *BR,* 26). Although this makes excellent drama, it is hardly substantiated by any biblical text.

The birthright was the double-portion of inheritance.[7] Many commentators see it as one-and-the-same as the blessing, though it seems to us that this passage coupled with chapter 27 clearly distinguishes between the two: the birthright concerns the physical inheritance; the blessing concerns the spiritual inheritance (*cf.* 1 Chron 5.1–2).[8] "It may be significant that ['birthright'] is an anagram of 'blessing' [in the Hebrew], the subject of chapters 26–27 and a key theme in Genesis. What Esau is prepared to forfeit here will pave the way to his greater loss, the loss of the blessing, in chapter 27" (Wenham).

25.32, "I am about to die." If this is true, he made a good deal. It remains, however, unlikely that another hour without food would have led to the death of Esau. "Esau is hardly such a big baby. Sturdy hunter that he was, he must have been somewhat inured to privations" (Leupold). Surely a manly hunter such as Esau could have waited long enough to prepare his own food. Further, his continued talking shows how far from death he is. "Esau prattles on, showing he is far from being on the point of death and exhibiting a careless indifference to a privilege that the ancient world held dear" (Wenham).

Some have instead sought to interpret this as more of an existential statement: 'I'm going to die eventually, anyway.' In addition to assigning Esau more philosophical insight than is due him, it still leaves Esau with the same problem: he is wrapped up in the sensual enjoyment of the present and tangible.

25.33, "Swear to me now." Jacob capitalizes on this opportunity by sealing it with an oath. This phrase effectively bookends Jacob's life (*cf.* 47.31), though its use is far different in each occasion. "In the first Jacob is in control, he is master of the situation—he will dictate the terms. In the second he is a helpless, elderly man, totally dependent on the will of somebody else to expedite his last wish" (Hamilton).

25.34, [Esau] ate and drank and rose and went his way. After filling his belly, Esau walked away unconcerned. Thus, Esau begins to show himself

---

[7] The inheritance was divided by one more than the number of sons. The firstborn would receive two portions and the remaining sons would receive one each.

[8] This also seems to be true of Jacob's later action with his children, where Judah receives the blessing (the Messianic line) and Joseph the birthright (the double-portion of the land of Canaan).

to be a person who is concerned with the temporary and fleeting, rather than the eternal. Kidner writes: "If Jacob is ruthless here, Esau is feckless... embracing the present and tangible at any cost, going through with the choice and walking away unconcerned." Keil speaks to the implications of Esau's actions: "The frivolity with which he sold his birthright to his brother for a dish of lentils rendered him unfit to be the heir and possessor of the promised grace." And Mathews: "By this incident the author implies that Esau's decision regarding his religious heritage disqualified him to succeed his father."

Thus Esau despised his birthright. This statement is the key to understanding Esau as the culprit rather than Jacob; Jacob did not steal Esau's birthright—Esau despised it and was quick to part with it for a bowl of stew. "The chapter does not comment 'So Jacob supplanted his brother'... and Hebrews 12 shares its standpoint, presenting flippant Esau as the antithesis of the pilgrims of Hebrews 11" (Kidner).

Growth of the Seed: The preeminence of Jacob/Israel is prophesied (v 23); Esau shows faithlessness (confirming God's choice of Jacob?[9] vv 29–34).

---

[9] The point of God's choosing Jacob *in utero* is, of course, that God chooses whomever He wants however He wants (*cf.* Rom 9.10–13). It is at least noteworthy, however, that Jacob goes on to develop faith (Heb 11.21)—however difficult it might have been for him—while Esau becomes the ultimate example of faithlessness (Heb 12.16).

26 Although Isaac is certainly a man of strong faith, he is not the prominent, aggressive man whose faith demands attention as way Abraham's did. With Abraham, many distinct advances were made in God's covenant relationship with man: separation from the wicked, relocation to the Promised Land, making of the covenant, reception of the covenant's sign. To use Leupold's terminology, these advances were "guarded" by Isaac. Primarily, he kept the faith and stayed true to the covenant. But he did little else. Thus, little needed to be said of him.

This chapter contains the only scenes in the Bible where Isaac is the chief character, and even here, he only offers echoes of his father's life. This chapter speaks primarily of two things: the influence of the father on his son and the meekness of Isaac's character.

26.1–2, Now there was a famine in the land. Many problems of the patriarchs and the Israelites to whom this was written stemmed from a lack of food—more accurately, a lack of faith in the One who provided the food.

Besides the former famine that was in the days of Abraham. Critical scholars lump this chapter into a group of accidental repetitions of the same story (12.10–20; 20.1–18), even though the text clearly distinguishes it from the famine of Abraham's day. Either they cannot accept the testimony of the text, or they find it impossible to believe that a famine could have occurred twice in a 90-year time span and that a son would have learned from his father's behavior.

To Abimelech. Approximately 80 years has passed since our last encounter with the king of the Philistines. Either he was a very young king in Abraham's day or, as we suggested, Abimelech is a throne name for the Philistine kings as *Pharaoh* was for Egyptian monarchs.[1]

"Do not go down to Egypt; dwell in the land of which I shall tell you." As with his father before him, the famine compelled Isaac to leave Canaan. God, however, intervened ensuring that Isaac would stay in the Promised Land and not rely on the strength of Egypt. "By not escaping to Egypt, the patriarch must endure the famine, trusting that the Lord will deliver him" (Mathews). See Excursus I.

26.3–5, "I will establish the oath that I swore to Abraham your father." This

---

[1]See comment on 20.2. Another possibility, if it was his given name, is that he was named after his father or grandfather, as is common among dynastic rulers. See Kidner's footnote on 26.26 discussing papponymy.

instance of divine promise is filled with firsts. The promises are affirmed to Isaac for the first time.

"I will be with you." This is the first instance of the specific promise of God's abiding presence with the patriarchs. "This promise makes Isaac's behavior even more unconscionable; the promise of divine companionship is not adequate to deter Isaac from engaging in duplicity" (Hamilton).

"To you and to your offspring." Previously, the promise of the land had been solely made to the offspring of Abraham. Here, for the first time, the promise includes this patriarch.

"All these lands." "'All these lands' (vv 3–4) contrasts with the term 'land' in the singular (vv 1, 2, 3, 12, 22). ...'Lands' must include those areas possessed by any number of different neighboring groups. The language corresponds to the comprehensive description of 'all the land that you see' promised to Abraham during his strife with Lot (13.15)" (Mathews).

"Because Abraham obeyed my voice." Abraham's faith may have wavered at times; he certainly made his share of mistakes. Yet he *always* obeyed the commands of God. Isaac is told that these blessings have come upon him because of his father's obedience, carrying with it the clear implication that continued blessing is contingent on his continued obedience.

"And kept my charge, my commandments, my statues and my laws." God makes the covenant conditional on the obedience of the covenant recipient. Although the covenant is carried out solely by God's grace, it also requires man's participation. It is not insignificant that Abraham was not under a system of law; everything he was and had was due solely to the grace of God. Yet even then, when there was no written law, God's grace required man's obedience.[2]

26.6, *So Isaac settled in Gerar.* Isaac obeyed God's command and did not go to Egypt. "In faith, Abraham went out (12.4). In faith, Isaac now remains. Just as Abraham, Isaac meets the conditions of blessing" (Waltke).

26.7, *"She is my sister."* Like father, like son.

Thinking, "Lest the men of the place should kill me because of Rebekah." A lie is a judgment on another's character, even if it is not as clearly de-

---

[2]Waltke suggests that this could be a reference to the whole law of Moses. "Genesis is a part of the Pentateuch and should be interpreted within that context. In Deuteronomy 11.1 the same list of terms refers to the whole law of Moses. The text shows that the person of faith does not live by law but keeps the law."

liberated as this was. Kidner writes: "Typically human, Isaac mixes faith and fear, an incompatible combination which can give a special quality of meanness to the sins of the religious." And Hamilton: "The shortage of food in the land is an appropriate context for the shortage of truth in Isaac. The famine caused by a food shortage he leaves behind, but the famine of truth, caused by a preference for expedience over conviction, persists at Gerar." The beauty of his wife and fear of his neighbors showed a chink in the armor of Isaac's faith. That Isaac would follow in his father's steps in this regard is most puzzling, "for Isaac must have known how the matter turned out in the case of his father. But then, for that matter, sin is never logical" (Leupold).

26.8, *When he had been there a long time.* Unlike Abraham's encounters with Pharaoh and Abimelech, Isaac remains in the land under this lie for a long time without Rebekah being taken by any of the Philistines. This may suggest that this event may be out of chronological order. "The fact that they could live a long time in Gerar without anyone realizing that they were man and wife indicates that this episode precedes the birth of Esau and Jacob" (Wenham). Also, this "demonstrates that the danger to Rebekah was more imagined than real. …Thus Isaac's act is repugnant in that it was not only deceitful but also unnecessary" (Hamilton). This may also serve to explain what happens next. Alter cites Rashi as suggesting that "Isaac became complacent with the passage of time ('From now on I don't have to worry since they haven't raped her so far.') and allowed himself to be publicly demonstrative with Rebekah."

Isaac laughing with Rebekah his wife. The translations vary *(e.g., showing endearment, caressing, etc.).*[3] The ESV follows the school of thought that renders the Hebrew in a non-sexual sense, but such an interpretation is without warrant: although the precise nature of what was going on is not known, the implication of their action is very clear—as Abimelech presently spells out.[4]

26.9–11, *"Behold, she is your wife."* Whatever it was, it was not something that siblings do together!

---

[3]Interstingly, the word used comes from the same root as Isaac's name, making this an obvious play on words. Mathews notes that this could be rendered *Isaac was Isaacing.*

[4]The Hebrew word does not inherently carry with it a sexual connotation, though it can be used in that way. *Cf.* 17.17; 18.12, 15; 19.14; 21.6 for other uses.

"What is this you have done to us?" Once again, the forefather of God's chosen people receives a stern rebuke from a pagan king. Abimelech shows himself to be more righteous than Isaac had judged him to be; this Abimelech has retained at least some of the morality of the previous king.

"You would have brought guilt upon us." Hamilton argues that *guilt* is too weak. "It is not just the potential immoral behavior of the Gerarites that concerned Abimelech but the consequences of that behavior." Further, "Abimelech understands the solidarity of a group. One person's action affects the whole community" (Waltke). Thus, from Abimelech's perspective, Isaac endangered an entire nation by his effort to protect himself from danger.

So Abimelech warned all the people. He seeks to make sure his people know that this woman is not to be touched. It seems that he wants his people to be as morally upright as he is.

26.12–13, Isaac sowed in that land and reaped in the same year a hundredfold. Isaac did some farming, which is not recorded of Abraham. His harvest is unheard of—"the yield even in very fertile regions is not generally greater than from twenty-five to fifty-fold" (Keil). Also, this bounty "is to be contrasted with the famine in Canaan that precipitated the whole affair. A wasteland is only a few miles away, but here is Isaac, now a farmer, harvesting a bountiful crop" (Hamilton). And Wenham: "It confirms that the Lord is indeed looking after Isaac; he did not need to enter Egypt to escape the famine." And so it is evident: *The LORD blessed him.*

26.14–17, The man became rich. As his father before him, the Lord blessed Isaac with prosperity in the land as well. Interestingly, no camels or donkeys are listed with Isaac's wealth, as they regularly were in describing Abraham's wealth. It is unclear whether he no longer had need of them, or if they are omitted for another reason.

Now the Philistines had stopped and filled with earth all the wells that his father's servants had dug in the days of Abraham his father. Because of their envy (v 14b) and fear (v 16), the Philistines sought to rid themselves of Isaac by cutting off his most basic supply. "The statement that they were wells that Abraham had first dug…clearly establishes Isaac's claim to these wells" (Leupold). And Waltke: "Wells were given names to establish proprietary rights. By giving them the same names as his father had, Isaac aims to make his ownership incontestable." And this is no mere inconvenience; it is a serious attack on Isaac's livelihood and, quite possibly, his life. Further, this is an instance where his wealth would do more to hurt him than to help him—"Isaac's living riches, far from cushioning him against reality, threw him back on his basic resources all the harder" (Kidner)—the servants, herds, and plants all need water as much as Isaac and his small family.

Abimelech said to Isaac, "Go away from us." It becomes apparent (v 29) that Abimelech was not behind the stopping of Isaac's wells (unless he is lying and Isaac feels no compulsion to note such). Nor was he stopping his people from doing it—a point which Isaac certainly could have called him on. Abimelech was apparently moral enough to command his people not to touch Rebekah, but allowed them to touch Isaac's wells to his detriment. Fueled by envy and fear, the otherwise-moral king turned a blind eye to the actions of his citizens in order to expedite Isaac's departure.

So Isaac departed. Isaac leaves as he was asked. Although he had enough might to inspire fear, he did not wield it against the Philistines. Power was safe in the hands of Isaac (Leupold)—this may be the best definition of meekness. As is often said, being meek is not equivalent to being weak. It would have been no feat for Isaac to have refrained from destroying his enemies if he could not have possibly done so. But he could have—and he didn't. Likewise, it is no feat for someone who is much more powerful to destroy someone who is much less powerful. But to have strength and the opportunity to use it, but refrain; therein lies true power—therein lies meekness. Power was safe in the hands of Isaac.

26.20–21, The herdsmen of Gerar quarreled with Isaac's herdsmen, saying, "The well is ours." Although Isaac was meek and left at the word of the king, trouble followed him. After leaving, Isaac re-dug his father's wells (v 18), and dug new wells (v 19), but the locals claimed those wells as their own.

Isaac had left the Philistine land as he was asked; certainly he would not stop to dig in a place that he knew would cause strife. It seems that these people followed him for the express cause of stirring up trouble. Further, they have no just claim to the wells. He and his servants dug all the wells under debate; that he calls them by the same names Abraham gave further indicates that they are his.

Then they dug another well, and they quarreled over that also. Meekly, Isaac gives up what is his and moves on. The Philistines follow him there also, and quarrel over that well.

26.22, He moved from there and dug another well, and they did not quarrel over it. Rather than turning his manpower on this group of bandits, he moved again. Apparently, this time he moved so far that they could not possibly lay claim to the wells he dug.

"For now, the LORD has made room for us." Again, the influence of Abraham on his son is clearly seen, though this time his influence for good.

"We shall be fruitful in the land." Isaac is fully aware of the promises involved in the covenant, including that of numerous descendants. This statement subtly shows full faith in God's will being done in his life. It is no accident that it is on the heels of this display of faith that God reaffirms His continued presence, specifically confirming that aspect of the promise.

26.24–25, "I am with you." Having been run out of the country where God had told him to go (v 2), Issac probably needed an encouraging word from God. God reassures Isaac that as He promised to be with him (v 3), so He was.

"For my servant Abraham's sake." "Both times the point is made that Isaac is so honored because of Abraham (vv 5, 24b). God is not initiating anything with Isaac. He is perpetuating what he started with Abraham" (Hamilton).

So he built an altar there and called upon the name of the LORD. Like father, like son.

26.26–27, Phicol. Phicol also reappears (*cf.* 21.22), which leads us to believe that it is also either a positional title for the captain of the Philistine army or a family name.

"Why have you come to me, seeing that you hate me and have sent me away from you?" Their inconsistency is evident. First, they drive him out; then, they follow him to make a treaty of friendship and good will. Also, Isaac's words imply that he had done nothing to earn their hatred; the entire breach in their relationship was of their doing.

26.28–29, "We see plainly that the LORD has been with you." By making a similar statement at the end of their speech, it becomes clear that the thrust of their fear in Isaac is that he was blessed of Yahweh. "They do not think it safe to be on bad terms with one who so manifestly stands in Yahweh's favor" (Leupold).

"We have not touched you and have done nothing but good." Abimelech and his people were true to his decree (v 11). See comment on verse 16.

26.30–31, So he made them a feast. In his meekness, Isaac agrees to Abimelech's terms. "This meal is not simply a courtesy extended by Isaac to Abimelech as host to visitor. It is, rather, an integral element of the covenant-making process, in which, in a sense, the individual offering the meal admits the other individual to his family circle" (Hamilton).

In the morning they rose early. See comment on 21.14.

And exchanged oaths. Cf. 21.31–32. Like father, like son.

26.32–33, *The same day Isaac's servants came and told him… "We have found water." He called it Shibah.* On that very day, the well they dug yielded water. Perhaps they were reopening Abraham's old well at Beersheba; perhaps they were digging a new one.[5] As Isaac renewed the covenant made with the Philistines, he also renewed the name of the location which symbolized the oath.

26.34–35, *[Esau] took Judith… the Hittite to be his wife, and Basemath… the Hittite.*[6] Esau further shows his incapacity for spiritual values in his choice of wives. "When Abraham's intense concern that Isaac should on no account marry a Canaanite is recalled, it is somewhat unexpected that Esau should marry two" (Wenham). But Esau was not concerned with the spiritual direction of the family or the future of the Canaanite inhabitants. Ultimately, by these marriages he offered further proof of "how thoroughly his heart was set upon earthly things" (Keil). That this note precedes the blessing of Isaac reinforces Esau's unworthiness to be Isaac's heir.

They made life bitter for Isaac and Rebekah. This may be in some part due to his foregoing the practice of arranged marriages. His inability to wait for a proper marriage may also show his earthly nature and inability to restrain himself. Unfortunately, this does not trouble Isaac enough. In spite of this, he plans to bless Esau. When parental favoritism comes into play, logic, reason—and, very often, spiritual concerns—flee.

Growth of the Seed: God extends the covenant to Isaac (v 24); Esau shows lack of spiritual discernment (confirming God's choice of Jacob? v 34).[7]

---

[5]Keil reports that two wells exist in that location today and distinguishes between *Beersheba* and *Shibah* as the two different wells.

[6]These verses should probably stand with chapter 27, as Esau's marriages frame this section of Scripture (*cf.* 28.6–9).

[7]See footnote on previous GROWTH OF THE SEED.

27 This chapter is the third round of the struggle between Jacob and Esau. The first was at birth (25.21–28) and the second over the birthright (25.29–34). The third is over the blessing (Hamilton). From a theological standpoint, "This chapter offers one of the most singular instances of God's overruling providence controlling the affairs of sinful men and so disposing of them that the interests of God's kingdom be safeguarded" (Leupold).

In this chapter, Jacob has often been vilified and Esau seen as wholly innocent. This interpretation fails to take into account Esau's lack of interest in spiritual things, his affection for what satisfies his momentary desire, and God's already-announced will that the blessing would be imparted to Jacob.

27.1, *When Isaac was old*. Some cross referencing and a little math places Isaac's age at 137 on this occasion.[1] The giving of the blessing is typically a deathbed occasion, and although this is an advanced age, Isaac will not die for another 43 years (35.28). Fourteen years earlier, however, Ishmael died when he was 137 (25.17), which might have given Isaac the motivation for blessing his sons at this point (see his words in v 2).

***His eyes were dim so that he could not see*.** This will become an important part of the story as it develops. Further, "Isaac's blindness functions at the metaphorical level for the man's spiritual condition when he preferred Esau for his tasty cuisine" (Mathews). His inability to see (both physically and spiritually) may be intended to contrast with the emphasis on faith and sight in Abraham's test in Moriah.[2]

***He called Esau*.** Isaac's plan was contrary to God's. Certainly Rebekah had told him of God's announcement (25.23). Moreover, he could not help but know of Esau's desire for instant gratification—that he placed physical satisfaction above all else. That he calls Esau singularly would seem to indicate that his plan is surreptitious: "Elsewhere in the OT, it

---

[1]Keil writes: "When Joseph was introduced to Pharaoh he was thirty years old (41.46), and when Jacob went into Egypt, thirty-nine, as the seven years of abundance and two of famine had then passed by (45.6). But Jacob was at that time 130 years old (47.9). Consequently Joseph was born before Jacob was ninety-one; and as his birth took place in the fourteenth year of Jacob's sojourn in Mesopotamia (*cf.* 30.25, and 29.18,21,27), Jacob's flight to Laban occurred in the seventy-seventh year of his own life, and the 137th of Isaac's." Waltke, on the other hand, holds that this is in the same year as Esau's first marriage, making Isaac 100.

[2]See comment on 22.2. In light of this metaphor, it is hard to find plausible Hamilton's suggestion that he may have forgotten God's oracle.

is normal for a dying man to summon all his close male relatives and to bless them publicly and in this way to organize the succession (*cf.* Gen 49; 50.24–25). It is, to say the least, irregular for Isaac to summon merely one of his sons, especially since Jacob and Esau were twins" (Wenham).

His older son. The mention of Esau being the older son may indicate that Isaac's plan went beyond satisfying his palate to fulfilling the custom of primogeniture, though it may only highlight the blessing going to the younger (Mathews).

Although his selling of the birthright did not necessitate the forfeit of the blessing,[3] God had already made that decision. Esau was not rejected because of his worldliness (even though Esau thoroughly proved himself to be unfit for the blessing). Likewise, Jacob was not blessed in spite of his deception. Rather, God had made the choice long before, *in order that God's purpose of election might continue, not because of works but because of his call* (Rom 9.11). In this, it is vital to remember that Jacob is not being singled out for a single blessing, but the nation of Israel is being chosen, that the world might be blessed through Jacob.

27.4, "Prepare for me delicious food… so that I may eat." Although important occasions called for celebratory meals, this does not seem to be the motive for Isaac's request on this occasion. "The word *game* is repeated eight times and *tasty food*, six times. The narrator's repetition of these terms in conjunction with the phrase 'tasty food that I like' and its variants (27.4, 9, 14) suggests that the narrator's focus is on Isaac's sensuality, not the role the meal played in the blessing ritual" (Waltke). And Kidner: "The real scandal is Isaac's frivolity: his palate had long since governed his heart (25.28) and his tongue (for he was powerless to rebuke the sin that was Esau's downfall); he now proposed to make it his arbiter between peoples and nations (v 29)."

"That my soul may bless you." Blessings were common among ancient families. "In effect they were the last will and testament of the person who uttered them, and as such they were legally binding, whether they were committed to writing or not."[4] Typically, it was just a pious wish of good fortune to follow the son, with prayers to God (or the gods)

---

[3]See comment on 25.31.

[4]R.K. Harrison, *Old Testament Times*, 78.

to be with the child. But, "The blessings of… the patriarchs had anoth-er valuable element in them: they were prophetic in character. Before his end many a patriarch was taught by God's Spirit to speak words of great moment, that indicated to a large extent the future destiny of the one blessed. In other words, the elements of benediction and prediction blended in the final blessing" (Leupold).

27.5–6, Now Rebekah was listening when Isaac spoke. Rebekah was eaves-dropping. "The family is not working together but conspiring against one another because the patriarch offers no spiritual leadership. Unlike Abra-ham and Sarah, who listened to the spiritual counsel of one another re-garding the inheritance (see 16.5–6; 21.8–14), Isaac and Rebekah are not communicating" (Waltke). And although Isaac sought to bless Esau, Re-bekah had plans of her own. Perhaps her deed stemmed from memory of God's promise and the desire to make sure it happened as He had spo-ken. It is unlikely, however, that this is the only motivation, considering the narrator's words.

His son Esau… Her son Jacob. Clearly this instance is not about Isaac trying to thwart God's will or Rebekah majestically trying to save it. Rath-er, this instance is about parental favoritism playing itself out, even in the most serious of occasions. Isaac sought to bless Esau in spite of God's wish-es; Rebekah sought to have Jacob blessed, in spite of Isaac's wishes. Both, for their own desire, rejected the one who had the position of headship. Even if Rebekah is seen in the best light possible—trying to preserve God's will—it is wholly unnecessary. God's will needs salvation from no man. God's plan will be accomplished, and although He can use human schem-ing, He surely would have preferred to accomplish it without the sin.

27.7, "I may… bless you before the LORD.'" Rebekah adds this to Isaac's ac-tual words, "thus heightening the sense of the sacred and irrevocable char-acter of the blessing she wants Jacob to steal" (Alter). This might suggest that Rebekah understands that God is controlling the situation. "This will be an act in which covenant issues are involved, issues so momentous that whether Isaac believes it or not, Yahweh will be present to direct and con-trol all, as He, Yahweh, does always regulate all that bears upon the de-velopment of the kingdom and the promises upon which the kingdom is built" (Leupold). The question to answer would then be: If Rebekah be-lieves this of Yahweh, why does she feel the need to help Him achieve His purpose? "Long afterwards Jacob would learn, as he blessed Ephraim and Manasseh, with what simplicity God could order such affairs" (Kidner).

27.9–10, "Bring me two young goats, so that I may prepare from them delicious food for your father… and you shall bring it to your father to eat, so that he may bless you before he dies." Her plan is to deceive the old, blind Isaac. She will prepare the food while Esau is hunting; Jacob will go into the tent in Esau's stead and receive the blessing Isaac plans to give to Esau.

27.11–13, "Behold, my brother is a hairy man, and I am a smooth man… perhaps my father will feel me." Jacob's concern lay not with the lie, but with being caught! "If it backfires by Isaac's discovery of the ploy, Jacob will subject himself to the worst of all fates—his father's curse. Such could be the case for anyone who misleads the blind (Lev 19.14; Deut 27.18) or dishonors his parents (Exod 21.15, 17; Deut 21.18–19; 27.16)" (Mathews). Jacob knew—probably by living with a blind father—that the blind often rely on the sense of touch. Rebekah may be able to fool his sense of taste. And because a brother's voice is often similar, with care Jacob could fool Isaac's sense of hearing. But if anything should arouse his suspicion, his sense of touch would not be so easily fooled.

"Let your curse be on me, my son." If nothing else, Rebekah shows herself to be decisive throughout the Genesis narrative. Even though she does not seem to have a plan now, she continues to move forward, perhaps believing enough in the justice of her cause that she is ready to receive whatever curse Isaac may give (Leupold). We are never told how Isaac reacts to Rebekah after this incident, though some hints are given. She "ominously disappears… after this scene. The narrator memorializes Deborah, her nurse, not Rebekah (35.8) and makes no notice of her death (*cf.* 23.1–2). At the end of Genesis, however, he notes that she was given an honorable burial with the other patriarchs and matriarchs in the cave of Machpelah (see 49.31)" (Waltke).

27.14–16, So he went. "Rebekah easily answered Jacob's objections and silenced him. He who is later capable of wrestling with God wrestles little with his mother or with his conscience. He did what he was told to do" (Hamilton).

His mother prepared delicious food, such as his father loved. After 90 years of marriage, this would be an easy task. Some have suggested that there may be a touch of irony intended—had Rebekah long been stung by her husband's preference for Esau's cooking? (Kidner).

Then Rebekah took the best garments of Esau her older son. As Esau was an outdoorsman and Jacob was not, there would be a unique scent to each of them. Wearing Esau's clothes would cover the sense of smell. This is tested, apparently, when Isaac asks his son to kiss him (vv 26–27). "The extent of Rebekah's cunning is thus fully revealed: one might have wondered why Jacob needed his brother's garments to appear before a father incapable of seeing them—[later] we realize she has anticipated the possibility that Isaac would try to smell Jacob: it is Esau's smell that he [will detect] in Esau's clothing" (Alter).

The skins of the young goats she put on his hands and on the smooth part of his neck. This last sense—touch—is the biggest concern. If she did not previously know how she would fool Isaac in this regard, the solution came to her as she was preparing the meal for Isaac. "Rebekah must believe that her husband is extremely incapacitated, for he will not be able, she thinks, to distinguish between human hair and goatskin. She really thinks she can pull the wool over Isaac's eyes" (Hamilton). Now, with everything prepared and every concern accounted for, she gives the food to her disguised son and sends him off. Alter suggests that the elements "point forward to the use of a garment to deceive first Jacob, then Judah, with the tunic soaked in kid's blood combining the garment-motif and the kid-motif."

27.18–20, "My father." Jacob certainly would have been doing his best to imitate Esau's voice and speech patterns—a task made somewhat easier by familial vocal similarities, but more difficult by a father's knowledge of his sons' voices.

"Who are you, my son?" Although Jacob had tried to sound like his brother,[5] he was unable to fully deceive his father. There was enough of a difference—combined with the quick return—for Isaac to question the speaker's identity.

Jacob said to his father. Jacob's answer was thorough and drawn out. "Jacob recognizes that hesitation or curt responses will arouse further suspicion and prove fatal to his enterprise, and so somewhat volubly he talks right on" (Leupold). In fact, "he nearly gives himself away by talking too much and overasserting his identity with Esau. ...After Isaac says, 'The

---

[5]See comment on verse 31.

voice is Jacob's, but the hands are Esau's,' Jacob only speaks once to say one word 'I (am)' (v 24)" (Wenham).

In his answer, Jacob tells three clear lies: he claims to be Esau; he claims to have carried out Isaac's orders; he claims that the goats from the flock are game that he killed.

"Because the LORD your God granted me success." And then Jacob told the real whopper. "Jacob is subtly claiming divine confirmation of the impending blessing, tying the success of his hunt to the God of the patriarchal blessing" (Mathews). While this bold lie succeeded in quickly disposing of Isaac's question, it is one of the most flagrant instances of the abuse of God's name recorded anywhere in Scripture. "Ironically, though, the assertion is not too far off the mark in one sense: the will of God as revealed in the birth oracle (25.22–23) was achieved after all by the sinister actions of Rebekah and Jacob" (Mathews).

Notice that he refers to Yahweh as Isaac's God. "This is consistent with Jacob's language elsewhere (31.5, 42; 32.9). Not until his safe return from Haran did he speak of the Lord as his own God (*cf.* 28.20–22; 33.18–20). The God of the patriarchs is not his own until he experiences the divine protection for himself" (Waltke).

27.21–24, "Please come near, that I may feel you." Isaac's concerns still were not alleviated, so he calls on his sense of touch to solve the issue—how correct Jacob's concern had been!

"The voice is Jacob's voice, but the hands are the hands of Esau." Jacob's ruse at imitating Esau's voice had not been successful. But voices change. And parents have been known to confuse their children by voice alone. Skin, however, does not change. So Isaac, though perplexed, is convinced.

And he did not recognize him. Jacob is often characterized as a wholly deceitful person. This instance, however, seems to prove that categorization incorrect. This entire lie hinged on Jacob being essentially trustworthy. If Jacob had a long history of dishonesty, Isaac would have known at once that something was wrong, and would not have been so easily fooled.

He said, "Are you really my son Esau?" He answered, "I am." One last lie brings the tally to five and pacifies Isaac's lingering doubt.

27.26–27, "Come near and kiss me, my son." So he came near and kissed him. And so, again, Isaac typifies Christ, although this time in being betrayed by a kiss (Matt 26.49; *cf.* 2 Sam 20.8–10).[6] Mathews writes: "His betray-al with a kiss for personal gain was superseded in Scripture only by Judas's famous kiss of Jesus for silver." [7]

27.28–29, "May God give you of the dew of heaven and of the fatness of the earth and plenty of grain and wine." The first part of the blessing is con-cerned with physical provisions. *The dew of heaven* would refer to rain for crops;[8] *the fatness of the earth,* abundance in harvest.[9] "'Dew' and 'fertile places' as a cause should yield the result of 'grain' and 'new wine,' the es-sentials of food and of drink" (Leupold). The Hebrew for *grain* and *wine* are, interestingly, names of two local gods. *Dagan* (grain) was a Philistine deity and *Tirosh* (wine) was a Canaanite god. This may be to indicate to the Israelites who were about to take the land of Canaan that it was the God of Jacob who "will provide Jacob with all the ingredients of fertility that were thought to be given by the Canaanite gods" (Hamilton).

"*Let peoples serve you and nations bow down to you. Be lord over your brothers.*" From the physical, Isaac turns his focus to the political. In spite of God's pre-birth prophecy, Isaac seeks to bless Esau with dominance over Jacob, seeking "to annul and invalidate God's original verdict in ref-erence to the relationship of these children" (Leupold). Although much time has passed to this point, God's will has not changed. "Since Re-bekah is not known to have other sons, the plural 'brothers' is a poetic convention—not to be taken literally in Jacob's case. ...Or, alternatively, the word... here may be merely 'relatives,' which the word may often mean" (Mathews). It also may refer to the descendants of the sons (Waltke).

"*Cursed be everyone who curses you, and blessed be everyone who bless-es you.*" This line ties the entire blessing back to the blessing given to Abraham (*cf.* 12.2–3).

It is interesting that although Isaac gives to Esau (he thinks) the bless-

---

[6] There may also be a foreshadowing in the bread Rebekah makes as a sop for the meal (v 17). Of course, there is a clear distinction in these foreshadowings—if they be such at all—in that Jesus was not deceived by Judas (*cf.* John 13.11).

[7] On why Isaac would ask that Jacob kiss him, see comment on verse 15.

[8] "Dew from westerly and northwesterly Mediterranean winds plays an important role in the irriga-tion of crops in many parts of Palestine" (Waltke)

[9] An alternate explanation for this is offered by Waltke, who argues that "oil of the earth" is a meton-ymy for rain. Thus, the two parts would be the dew and the rain, which would provide for the crops during the dry and rainy seasons, respectively.

ing of land and nation, he stops short of blessing him with the seed. Either he understands that it is God's to give, or he knows that it is too sacred to be tampered with.

It is also important to understand that although Isaac was deceived, God was not. The blessing came to whom God chose. Jacob lied to get it, but the evil of man will not keep God from being faithful and carrying out His purposes. And Jacob would pay for his deceit—we need not think Jacob was rewarded for his treachery. After he leaves, he never sees his mother again. He leaves a position of means and influence in this prominent family to a position of rigorous service for 20 years. Also, his deceit is cruelly reversed, when Laban has his older daughter impersonate the younger in chapter 29. Finally, Jacob, the deceiver of his father, was even more cruelly deceived by his sons, who sold Joseph into slavery and claimed that he was dead.

27.30–31, *As soon as Isaac had finished blessing Jacob, when Jacob had scarcely gone out from the presence of Isaac his father, Esau his brother came in.* God did indeed bless Esau with a quick catch. It was not, however, quick enough to foil the blessing of the proper son. Although the two brothers nearly cross paths at Isaac's tent door, Jacob has left just before Esau arrives.

"Let my father arise and eat… that you may bless me." Esau spoke words similar to Jacob's when he came into Isaac's presence. "For one thing, that shows at least how carefully Jacob had planned his deception; he knew about what Esau would say when stepping into his father's presence" (Leupold).

27.32–33, *"Who are you?"* Esau must have been shocked to hear this question. He had been sent out to catch game for his father; here, he arrives announcing that it is done, but his father does not know who he is. His response, *"I am your son, your firstborn, Esau,"* probably had a tone of surprise.

Then Isaac trembled very violently. Even this is an understatement of the Hebrew. "The Hebrew employs three devices to convey the desired emphasis, piling one upon the other: the cognate object, the modifying adjective, the adverbial phrase, 'He trembled a trembling, a great, unto excess.' …What a pitiful sight to see the venerable patriarch under the stress of so violent an emotion" (Leupold).

"Who was it then?" Even as Isaac asks the question, he knows the answer. Perhaps, he "pretends not to know who it is that has deceived him, find-

ing it easier to let Esau name the culprit himself. Isaac must of course realize at once who it is that has taken the blessing because he already had his doubts when he heard the son speaking with the voice of Jacob" (Alter).

"Yes, and he shall be blessed." His refusal to retract the blessing shows something of his character—which has suffered in the narrative to this point. Even a bad lawyer could have voided a contract that someone was deceived into signing. Yet Isaac has now accepted God's purpose and will no longer try to thwart it. These words, coupled with verse 27 and Isaac's 'blessing' of Esau, make sense of what would be an otherwise confusing summation given by the Hebrew author—*By faith Isaac invoked future blessings on Jacob and Esau* (Heb 11.20). As Leupold notes, what the Hebrew author writes makes full sense "if we but bear in mind that the erring saint had been corrected by God in the midst of his attempt to transfer the blessing. He had accepted the correction and repented, and so in the end what he did was an act of faith after all."

27.34–36, [Esau] cried out with an exceedingly great and bitter cry. "He who never aspired after higher things now wants this blessing as though his future hopes depended all and only on the paternal blessing" (Leupold). The blessing of Isaac seemed to be the one thing of the whole spiritual heritage that impressed Esau. This may indicate that Esau had placed a superstitious value on it: it mattered not what he did with the rest of his life or how faithlessly he lived, as long as he received this blessing, he would be successful.

"Is he not rightly named Jacob? For he has cheated me these two times." Esau then blames Jacob for things which he did not do. Jacob did not steal the birthright; Esau freely gave it away, having despised it. Nor did Jacob steal the blessing. Although he did deceive Isaac in order to receive it, it had already been given. How often carnal people seek to blame others for their short-comings.

27.39–40, "Away from the fatness of the earth shall your dwelling be." Esau continues his crying for a blessing until Isaac finally speaks. When he does, it is not a blessing that comes from his mouth. First, he speaks of the dwelling of Esau. Edom was a bleak, rocky, barren land. It was not fertile like that promised to Jacob. Keil writes: "The idea expressed in the words was that the dwelling-place of Esau would be the very opposite of the land of Canaan, *viz.,* an unfruitful land."

"By your sword you shall live." Esau's lot was to be one of violence and continual conflict. "Deprived by paternal pronouncement of political mastery, he must make his way through violent struggle" (Alter).

"You shall serve your brother; but when you grow restless you shall break his yoke from your neck." He will be in continual subjugation to his brother. "After a long period of independence at first, the Edomites were defeated by Saul (1 Sam 14.47) and subjugated by David (2 Sam 8.14); and, in spite of an attempt at revolt under Solomon (1 Kgs 11.14ff), they remained under Judah until the time of Joram, when they rebelled. They were subdued again by Amaziah (2 Kgs 14.7; 2 Chron 25.11ff), and remained in subjection under Uzziah and Jotham (2 Kgs 14.22; 2 Chron 26.2). It was not until the reign of Ahaz that they shook the yoke of Judah entirely off (2 Kgs 16.6; 2 Chron 28.17), without Judah being ever able to reduce them again. At length, however, they were completely conquered by John Hyrcanus about BC 129, compelled to submit to circumcision, and incorporated into the Jewish state" (Keil). In New Testament times, they were known by the Greek name *Idumeans*. It is from the Idumeans that the Herods came.

27.41, Now Esau hated Jacob because of the blessing. Esau's whining has become bitter hatred; his despair has turned into vengeance. All of his thinking is continually on the lost blessing, and eventually he decides that he will kill his brother. The reader of Genesis is already familiar with this story—older brother being rejected from God's blessing and killing the younger brother.

"The days of mourning for my father are approaching." Esau suspects that his father will die soon, and he will wait until then to kill Jacob.

"I will kill my brother Jacob." This phrase drives home the reason why Esau was wholly unfit for the blessing. "The murder in Esau's heart (fratricide) identifies him as the seed of the Serpent as surely as it marked out Cain and Lamech (3.15; 4.8, 23; John 8.44)" (Waltke). As the enmity between the seed of the woman and the seed of the serpent continues, Esau shows himself to among be the latter.

27.42–45, But the words of Esau her older son were told to Rebekah. Someone learns of Esau's plan and tells Rebekah.

"Flee to Laban my brother in Haran and stay with him a while." Laban is chosen because he is known to Rebekah and will provide safe refuge for

Jacob. In addition, it will be easier for Rebekah to construe his flight there in a different light to ensure the plan's acceptance by Isaac (vv 46–28.2). There is, of course, irony in this destination, "for he will also flee Laban when deceiving him" (Mathews). She anticipates that his stay will be *for a while,* which is more literally *for a few days.* It seems that she expects his stay in Mesopotamia to be brief, *until your brother's fury turns away.* In reality, his sojourn there will be long and arduous, and she will never see her son again. Also, "As subsequent chapters in Genesis reveal, Jacob is not at all sure, even twenty years later, of his mother's favorable forecast. Jacob knows too well that memories, especially painful memories, die only too slowly, if at all" (Hamilton).

"Why should I be bereft of you both in one day?" There are several possible interpretations of her words. She could refer to Jacob and Isaac: Esau will wait for Isaac to die and then kill Jacob, leaving Rebekah bereft of both husband and son.[10] Or she refers to Jacob and Esau: bereft of Jacob physically and Esau spiritually; or bereft of both physically, should someone take vengeance on account of Jacob's murder (Waltke, Hamilton); or bereft of both physically, if this is to be understood in light of Cain's expulsion after the murder of Abel (Mathews). And Alter suggests, "Although a physical struggle between the two would scarcely be a battle between equals, in her maternal fear she imagines the worst-case scenario, the twins killing each other." In spite of her best efforts, her worst fear is eventually realized: "Upon his return to Canaan, he reconciles with 'his father Isaac' (35.27), but there is no mention of Rebekah except her burial (49.31). She does in a sense lose both her sons on that regretful day" (Mathews).

27.46, "I loathe my life because of the Hittite women." Esau's wives made life bitter for Isaac and Rebekah (26.35). Many times, certainly, they had discussed this matter. Perhaps they had even discussed what they would do concerning Jacob. Rebekah uses Esau's wives and Jacob's continued bachelorhood to secure his safety. "Yet [Jacob] must not go as a fugitive, but with his father's backing and to the shelter of her family—and Isaac must preferably suggest the idea himself. For this, her broaching the subject of Jacob's marriage was a masterstroke: it played equally on Isaac's self-interest and his principles. The prospect of a third Hittite daughter-in-law and a distracted wife would have unmanned even

---

[10]The primary problem with this view is, as Waltke notes, that Isaac is not a near antecedent of *you.*

an Abraham. Rebekah's diplomatic victory was complete; but she would never see her son again" (Kidner).

Growth of the Seed: God accomplishes His purpose to have Jacob blessed.

28 This is a poor chapter break: the first nine verses of this chapter belong with the section that began in 26.34. The first scene continues the last scene of chapter 27 and verses 6–9 serve as the end of the *inclusio* begun by Esau's first marriages.

28.1–2, "You must not take a wife from the Canaanite women." Isaac's speech is not merely for the benefit of his wife. The wives that Esau chose were also displeasing to him (*cf.* 26.35; 28.8). Agreeing with the sentiment that his wife had expressed—even if her purpose was not fully revealed—Isaac decides to send Jacob off for a wife.

"*Go to Paddan-aram… and take as your wife from there one of the daughters of Laban your mother's brother.*" There is similarity and distinction between Isaac's method and Abraham's method of securing a wife for their respective sons. They both received a wife from the family stock in Mesopotamia and were forbidden from marrying a Canaanite. Isaac, however, seems content to send Jacob where Abraham forbade Isaac from going—was he also aware of Esau's intentions? The emphasis on Laban's relation to Rebekah (*i.e., "your mother"*) "may well reflect on Jacob's closeness to his mother and shows how Isaac encouraged Jacob to leave home" (Wenham).

28.3–5, "God Almighty bless you." Jacob is sent off with a blessing from God—this time an intentional blessing. "Now Isaac, whatever misgivings he may have about Jacob's act of deception, knows that his younger son has irrevocably received the blessing, and he has no choice but to reiterate it at the moment of parting" (Alter).

"*And make you fruitful and multiply you.*" In addition to repeating this aspect of the Abrahamic blessing, this is a fitting blessing as he is sent off to find a wife.

"*A company of peoples.*" Waltke says, "In 35.11 the expression means a community of nations coming from the patriarch. …The blessing will be reversed against Israel under judgment, when she is attacked by a community of peoples (see Ezek 23.24; 32.3) rather than being blessed and joined by them. The fulfillment is found in Christ and his church."

"*May he give the blessing of Abraham to you and to your offspring with you.*" Although this phrase links this blessing to the Abrahamic blessing and may refer to the entirety of it, it lacks the offspring portion of the blessing. That the other two portions (land and nation) are specifically included may or may not not imply that *the blessing of Abraham* is meant to cover what Isaac does not specifically mention. Of course, that raises the question of why he would leave it out. At the very least, "Isaac publicly recognizes Jacob as the true heir of Abraham's blessing" (Waltke).

"That you may take possession of the land of your sojournings." God's blessing is to the end that he will take possession of the land that was promised to him. That this is the purpose of God's blessing in Isaac's mind may indicate that the Promised Seed was probably not in mind in the previous phrase (Mathews).

Jacob and Esau. Having secured both the birthright and the blessing, Jacob now receives 'top billing' from the narrator (*cf.* 25.9).

28.6–9, Now Esau saw. For what might be the first time in his life, Esau is paying attention to what is going on around him. He sees Isaac's blessing of Jacob, he hears Isaac's command to Jacob, and he observes Jacob's obedience to Isaac. This all leads him to the conclusion he should have come to a long time ago: *the Canaanite women did not please Isaac his father.*

Esau went to Ishmael. Waltke notes: "Esau is a figure of tragic irony" quoting Roop, who calls him, "a marginalized family member who deeply wanted to belong." The irony is even deeper, as his journey parodies Jacob's. "For the purposes of the author, the connection of Esau and Ishmael is a fitting end to this slice of the narrative, for it matches the actions of the two outcast sons who form an ancestral bond (36.3)" (Mathews).

And took as his wife, besides the wives he had, Mahalath the daughter of Ishmael. Before this point, Esau seems to be among the ranks of those who are so 'in love' with their significant other that they cannot tell everyone else hates that person. Finally realizing this, he goes to Ishmael's house to find another wife, hoping to satisfy his parents by marrying within the family. "There is no indication of his father's response to this initiative, but the marriage is an echo in action of his plaintive cry, 'Do you have but one blessing, my Father? Bless me, too, Father'" (Alter).

There are, however, a couple of problems with his solution. First, "To take a third wife, even though an Ishmaelite was better than a Hittite, was hardly the way back to blessing" (Kidner). Greater still, "He failed to consider that Ishmael had been separated from the house of Abraham and family of promise by the appointment of God; so that it only furnished another proof that he had no thought of the religious interests of the chosen family, and was unfit to be the recipient of divine revelation" (Keil).

28.10–11, Jacob left Beersheba and went toward Haran. Jacob reverses the long trip that Abraham originally made. "His situation, however, is even more precarious than that of his grandfather. Back in Beersheba, Esau lies in wait like an angry lion. Ahead in Haran, Laban waits with his spider web to trap and suck the life from his victims" (Waltke).

The sun had set. Jacob stopped; he could no longer travel due to nightfall. The symbolism is rich. "Sunset and sunrise are common images of distress and deliverance (*cf.* 15.12, 17; 19.1; John 13.30). The sunset begins Jacob's dark journey to Paddan Aram, through which he must struggle with humans and God. The true 'daybreak' for his soul will not come until the end of his twenty-year exile (32.26)" (Waltke).

Taking one of the stones of the place, he put it under his head and lay down in that place to sleep. Some older translations render the word *pillow*. As Leupold notes, the word "does not actually mean 'pillow' but 'head place'—a proper distinction, for pillows are soft, 'head places' not necessarily so." Others note that it does not even necessarily mean that he laid his head on the stone. "Passages like 1 Samuel 26.11–12; 1 Kings 19.6, where the same phrase 'round his head,' appears, suggest the stones were placed round his head to protect him rather than to lie on" (Wenham).

Stones will become Jacob's personal motif: "From the stone at his head to the stone marker, to the stone upon the well he will roll away, and the pile of stones he will set up to mark his treaty with Laban" (Alter).

28.12, And he dreamed, and behold there was a ladder.[1] "The ladder was a visible symbol of the real and uninterrupted fellowship between God in heaven and His people upon earth. The angels upon it carry up the needs of men to God, and bring down the assistance and protection of God to man" (Keil). The point, of course, is not that there is an invisible ladder upon which angels work all the time, but to emphasize the continual

---

[1] The precise meaning of the term is unknown. Waltke notes that the context, an Akkadian cognate, and the LXX would seem to indicate that "it signifies either a ladder or a flight of steps, such as on the slopes of a ziggurat (*cf.* Gen 11.1–9). A flight of steps would more readily accommodate angels ascending and descending than a ladder." Also we find the phrase *gate of heaven* (v 17) in this context, a phrase associated with the Mesopotamian ziggurats, may indicate that *ladder* is not the intended meaning. Hamilton calls this a modern and rationalistic concern rather than a linguistic one, saying, "If we wish to be completely modern and rationalistic, then we need to isolate the issue in terms not of 'ladder' versus 'stairway,' but why angels would need either one!" But, of course, the precise nature of the apparatus is immaterial to the meaning of the dream.

communion of God with man.[2] Jesus will later say that He is the ladder—the ultimate mediator between heaven and earth (*cf.* John 1.51).

Set up on the earth and the top of it reached to heaven. Waltke says that the Hebrew is literally *placed toward the earth* rather than the ESV's *set up on the earth*. Unlike the tower which men sought to build to the heavens (Gen 11.4), "Here the stairway is represented as stretching from heaven down to earth" (Waltke). Houtman says, "The impression is made that the narrator wishes to express that the communication between heaven and earth is established by an initiative from on high, on the part of God. The contact between heaven and earth exists by the grace of God" (qtd. in Waltke).

And behold, the angels of God were ascending and descending on it! Angels accompany Jacob's departure from and return to Canaan (*cf.* 32.1). "The angels suggest that the Lord who makes his presence known at Bethel will also be present to Jacob through the angelic messengers" (Waltke). And Wenham: "This vision of the angels is an assurance of God's protection of Jacob even though he is leaving home."

*28.13–15, Behold, the L*ORD* stood above it and said.* For the first time, Jacob receives the promises that had been given to his father. In addition to the land and nation, which Isaac had blessed him with, God bestows on him also the blessing of the promised seed. If Isaac's *the blessing of Abraham* (v 4) was intended to convey the entirety of the blessing, God is here clarifying and establishing precisely what that blessing entails.

*"I am the L*ORD*, the God of Abraham your father and the God of Isaac."* It may be surprising that God does not censure Jacob for his behavior. "Far from fulminating against Jacob, Yahweh bestows on Jacob a *catena* of unconditional promises. In this respect, Jacob joins Isaac and Abraham in that all three are relatively free from censure by God for patently scandalous behavior" (Hamilton). Yet there may be, in this particular statement, an indirect rebuke. As Hamilton goes on to say, "He is the God of the first generation. He is the God of the second generation. Will he be the God of the third generation?"

"I am with you and will keep you wherever you go." The promises given span across time and space, "a stream of assurances flowing from the central 'I am the Lord,' to spread from the past (v 13a) to the distant future,

---

[2]It is noteworthy that the Bible does depict angels as regularly working on the earth, *cf.* Zechariah 1.10ff; Job 1.6ff.

from the spot where Jacob lay (v 13b) to the four corners of the earth (v 14) and from his person to all mankind (v 14b)" (Kidner). This shows the omnipresent and eternal nature of God, and the universality of His blessing that was to come. Because of God's omnipresence, He can go with Jacob to protect him, even while remaining with the family in Palestine. "[Jacob's] travels cannot outdistance the safekeeping of God" (Mathews).

"Will bring you back to this land." Although Jacob will sojourn in Mesopotamia for several years, he will know throughout that it is not to be his permanent home. He is to return to the land to which God had taken his grandfather. "His parents prompted his departure from Canaan; Yahweh will determine and direct his return to Canaan" (Hamilton).

28.16–17, "Surely the LORD is in this place, and I did not know it." Having awakened, Jacob realizes the point of the vision and finally understands God's presence throughout the earth.[3]

He was afraid. Jacob's reaction is different than Abraham's and Isaac's reaction to divine revelation (*cf.* 12.1; 15.1; 17.1; 22.1; 26.1). "Perhaps his fear is prompted by his realization that he has wronged his father and brother. Adam also feared God's presence after he had sinned. ...This fear is also an appropriate contrast to his fleeing for his life. There are greater forces than his brother—personal and spiritual issues of faith and righteousness—that must be reckoned with" (Waltke).

28.18–19, Jacob took the stone... and set it up for a pillar. That is, to set it up that it would stand out as a marker of the place. This is not intended to convey setting it up for idolatrous purposes (see Waltke). Even so, this type of pillar will later be forbidden by the Law of Moses (*cf.* Exod 23.24; 34.13; Deut 16.21–22; 1 Kgs 14.22–23). "That patriarchal religious practice does not everywhere conform to later pentateuchal law is one sign of the antiquity of the Genesis tradition" (Wenham).

And poured oil on the top of it. The anointing by oil was a sign of consecrating and dedicating the place.

Bethel. Bethel means *house of God* (*cf.* v 17).

---

[3]We disagree with Leupold's comment: "Of course he knew that. Any true believer's knowledge of God involves such elementary things as knowledge of His not being confined to one place. Such crude conceptions the patriarchs never had. To suppose that the account is trying to picture Jacob as on a lower level than Abraham in spiritual discernment is misunderstanding." The picture of Jacob to this point is one of someone with less spiritual discernment. It is *because* of this vision that his spiritual discernment begins to grow.

28.20–22, Then Jacob made a vow. "The vow reorients Jacob's journey. The journey had originated as flight to avoid assassination and a trip to find a wife suitable to his parents. Now, however, Jacob's journey becomes a pilgrimage with theological content. He goes to the same place for much the same purpose, but now he travels as a carrier of God's promises with divine assurance of aid. ...The promise and the vow transform Jacob's journey as surely as an encounter with God changes a stony place into a sanctuary."[4]

"If God will be with me... then the LORD shall be my God." The if/then language used is the mode of covenant speech; Jacob is not placing conditions on his obedience (Kidner). Because Jacob's words echo the promises made in verse 15 (with food and clothing added), "Jacob's prayer is thus based on the divine promise" (Wenham).

"And this stone... shall be God's house." Jacob plans to establish in this place a sacred spot or sanctuary upon the completion of this vow (*cf.* 35.6–7).

"Of all that you give me I will give a full tenth to you." This is the second reference in Scripture to a pre-Mosaic tithe to God (*cf.* 14.20). "Jacob's promise of a tithe marks an important moment in his transformation—no longer grasper but giver" (Waltke).

Growth of the Seed: The Messiah is typified (v 12; *cf.* John 1.51); God establishes covenant with Jacob (vv 13–15).

---

[4]Eugene F. Roop, *Genesis*, 187.

29 *1, Then Jacob went on his journey.* Having been promised protection by Yahweh, Jacob continues his trip with full assurance of divine guidance.

29.2, He saw a well in the field. This was not the kind of well that we usually conjure up in our minds when we think of a well. Rather it was most likely "a cistern dug into the ground…probably so constructed that after the stone had been rolled away the flocks could be driven to the edge to drink" (Keil). A large stone covered the opening to the well, to keep thieves out and help prevent evaporation. This particular well was the well where his kin would come and water their flocks. Jacob knew which direction he was going, but could not have known which specific well to look for. That this happens on the heels of God's promise of guidance would clearly indicate that this is not merely coincidence or blind luck.

29.3, When all the flocks were gathered there. Due to the size of the stone, watering the flocks was not done individually, but as a group. All of the shepherds would come, together roll away the stone, water the flocks, and then return the stone to its place.

29.4–6, "Where do you come from?" It is possible that Jacob was not aware of his precise location. He had not traveled this way before and we cannot know what sort of map or directions he had. By asking this question, he could ascertain the nearest town and get a better idea of exactly where he was.

"Do you know Laban?" It turns out that they are from Laban's own town. Since he is trying to locate Laban, this question follows naturally.

"Is it well with him?" Again, this question follows naturally on the heels of the previous question. The shepherds respond that Laban is well and that his daughter is approaching.

Each of his questions are met with "rather surly responses by the shepherds, suggesting their suspicion of this…foreigner" (Wenham).

29.7–8, "Behold, it is still high day." Having learned that his cousin is approaching, Jacob seeks to clear the other shepherds out. He appeals to the good grazing time left in the day, admonishing them to not waste it. There may be some concern for the welfare of the sheep, but the context would suggest that his larger concern is privacy to meet his kin.

"It is not time." "This is a striking display of providence. At what appears to be the wrong time, Jacob meets the right people and the right girl" (Waltke).

"We cannot until all the flocks are gathered together." This is the first of Jacob's questions to receive a substantial response, yet it falls flat. "They are shirkers, as Jacob has insinuated. ...Moreover, they are not about to break their lazy work habits" (Waltke).

29.10, As soon as Jacob saw Rachel...Jacob came near and rolled the stone from the well's mouth. The stone that took a group to roll away, Jacob moved by himself! Clearly, he was not the 'mama's boy' that some portray him to be.[1] "Further, he knows how to present his actions to the best advantage, capping the feat of strength with one of service, and this in turn with the dramatic announcement. It is a superb entry" (Kidner).

"Unlike his stone pillar that commemorates God's encounter with him at Bethel (28.16–19) and the stone heap that bears witness to his treaty with Laban in the sight of God (31.42–45), the stone in this scene is not connected to God either by Jacob or the narrator. The contrast suggests that Jacob is unaware of obvious Providence" (Waltke).

29.11, Then Jacob kissed Rachel and wept aloud. The order of events is somewhat strange: surely it would have been expected of Jacob to introduce himself first! "This unusual sequence of actions...portrays a man swept along by the joy of meeting his cousin" (Wenham).

Those who see this through the lens of a Hollywood love story would portray this as 'love at first sight' (see Leupold). It would seem better to interpret it in the context of the emotional upheaval through which Jacob had just gone. He had left homeland in fear of his life and journeyed through an unknown wilderness. Having unexpectedly arrived at his destination, he finds himself overjoyed and weeps.

What seals the interpretation that it is not, in fact, love at first sight is the text's insistence that Jacob watered the flocks not for Rachel's beauty, but because they belonged to Laban, Rebekah's brother (v 10). "This suggests that Jacob's prime motive at this stage is to ingratiate himself with

---

[1] In all fairness, Jacob probably had an advantage over the shepherds. Leupold writes: "If a girl like Rachel tends her father's flock...then others of the shepherds may well have been young men, in fact, quite young men, who would require their united strength, or at least that of some two or three of the lads, to remove the stone." This explanation seems preferable than Hamilton's, which attribute's Jacob's strength to the divine presence being with Jacob, much like it was with Samson.

his uncle" (Wenham). Certainly he saw her beauty on this occasion also, but it is too much to call it love when a simpler, contextual answer will suffice. That said, it is clear that it did not take long for infatuation with Rachel to develop (v 18).

29.13, *As soon as Laban heard the news about Jacob... he ran to meet him.* Is Laban excited to meet a family member or is he "recalling that the last time someone came from the emigrant branch of the family in Canaan, he brought ten heavily laden camels with him" (Alter)? Or, perhaps, having heard of Jacob's feat of strength, he already envisions the sort of service that he might give. Fokkelman writes: "Tricky Laban knows, even before he has seen Jacob, that a workman is on his way who is worth his weight in gold" (qtd. in Waltke).

And embraced him and kissed him. "Laban's kiss proved to be as incongruous with his treatment of Jacob as the patriarch's own beguiling kiss of his father (27.27)" (Mathews).

Jacob told Laban all these things. What precisely he told him is of some debate. Did he tell him *everything* that had happened, including his deceit of Isaac and Esau's bitter hatred or did he just tell him everything that had happened since Isaac commissioned his journey to find a wife? Some have argued that a penitent Jacob would have included a report on everything, lest he stay there under false pretenses (see Leupold).

29.15, *"Should you therefore serve me for nothing? Tell me, what shall your wages be?"* Laban will show himself to be a selfish person over the next few chapters. We may, in fact, already begin to see some of those motives at work.[2] He already knew of Jacob's purpose for coming and probably of his feelings for Rachel—he could tell by the way Jacob looked at her. Further, he knew that Jacob could not afford a dowry, and would work for an extended period of time to get her. Thus, he seeks to exploit Jacob by inviting him to make an offer. Also, he may have already planned the daughter switch, knowing that he could get double work out of Jacob. In any event, "Their relationship for the next twenty years is that of an oppressive lord over an indentured servant paying off a bride price, not of an uncle helping his blood relative" (Waltke).

---

[2]Hamilton points out that Laban's offer to Jacob for remuneration for his work is only *after* he has worked a month for him.

Others have suggested wholly good motives in Laban: that he would bind a relative to himself and help out his kin; that he would arrive early at a definite arrangement to avoid future misunderstandings. As the elder, he would naturally be the one to propose such an arrangement, so his suggesting this is not necessarily a reason to suspect him. It is, however, hard to see Laban this way in the light of his character revealed throughout the remainder of this narrative. As Wenham asks, "Should family relationships be reduced to commercial bargaining?" Waltke adds: "What Laban should have done as a loving relative is to help Jacob get a start on building his own home, as Jacob asks of Laban in 30.25–34. …Instead, Laban keeps Jacob as nothing more than a laborer under contract, as Jacob bitterly complains in 31.38–42."

29.17–18, Leah… Rachel. "Their names, meaning 'cow' and 'ewe,' respectively, were appropriate in a shepherding family, but, sadly, Laban actually treats Leah and Rachel like shepherds' animals, commodities for bargaining and trading. Later, the women use business language to describe how they understood their father's treatment [*cf.* 31.14–15]" (Waltke).

Leah's eyes were weak. Leah had weak or delicate eyes. The precise meaning of this is unknown. Some have suggested that they were weak in strength and she had a squint. Others have argued that they were weak in color—not the dark, lustrous eyes with "that clear-cut brilliance that Orientals love" (Leupold). In either event, beauty was often judged by the eyes, as they were often all that was seen. An alternate explanation is that this adjective is used to indicate a good quality about her eyes. This, by contrast, would suggest that Leah had one asset to her appearance, whereas Rachel was more fully beautiful (see Alter). Hamilton also argues this, saying, "Leah may be older, but her eyes are the beautiful eyes of a person who looks much younger."

Rachel was beautiful in form and appearance. She had a beautiful face and body. The very thing that sensible parents warn their children against marrying for, Jacob uses as his motivation to marry Rachel. This contrasts starkly with the action of Abraham's servant who constantly sought God's guidance in prayer when he sought a wife for Isaac. This is, incidentally, the only good thing that the Bible says about Rachel. See Excursus L.

Jacob loved Rachel. If we are correct in interpreting Jacob's emotional response at their meeting as something other than 'love at first sight,' it only took him a month for that feeling to grow. But, "Just as Esau, an older brother, stands between Jacob and the blessing, here an older sister stands between Jacob and his true love" (Hamilton).

"I will serve you seven years for your younger daughter Rachel." This would serve as his dowry, meaning that Jacob is effectively not receiving wages from Laban after all (v 15). Laban agrees quickly, seeming to indicate that he is prepared for this particular request. (That he went through all of this before—a family member returning from Palestine for a wife—may also have prepared him for Jacob's request.) Further, it is probably more than Jacob needed to spend, as Jacob did not want to risk a refusal.[3]

At his departure, Rebekah told Jacob that she would call for him 'soon,' yet Jacob agrees to work for seven years. Perhaps his love for Rachel was such that he was prepared to forsake his mother's call for him for a few years, if needed. Or maybe he was well aware that Esau's anger would not blow over so quickly.

29.19, *"It is better that I give her to you."* This may indicate an already-existent plan of Laban to deceive Jacob: he never says who *she* is. The context would certainly demand that it be Rachel. "But in light of Jacob's very precise request to marry 'Rachel, your younger daughter,' it may be no coincidence that Laban never names the daughter he intends to give Jacob" (Wenham).[4] Waltke adds: "The prayerless patriarch is not discerning enough to either see through his uncle's character or to detect the ambiguity of 'her.'"

29.20, *They seemed to him but a few days because of the love he had for her.* This is interesting, because usually anticipation makes time seem slower—the whole 'watched pot' thing. Perhaps this statement is not intended to indicate the passing of time, but the worth or cost of his labor (Kidner). For instance, something that may cost thousands of dollars does not seem so expensive to someone who greatly values the purchase; likewise, the spending of years would only seem like the spending of days to Jacob,

---

[3]Levitical law set a maximum marriage gift at 50 shekels (Deut 22.29), "but typically the gifts were much lower" (Wenham). As casual laborers were paid between one-half and one shekel a month, Jacob's named price—somewhere between 42–84 shekels—was certainly an over-payment.

[4]Wenham also suggests: "Maybe he was keeping his options open, perhaps hoping that someone else would come along to marry Leah before Jacob had completed his seven years of service for Rachel," although this seems far too kind an estimate of Laban, given the character he consistently shows through the Genesis narrative.

regardless of how the time seemed to pass. Incidentally, "It should be observed that 'a few days'... is exactly the phrase his mother had used in advising him to go off to stay with her brother" (Alter).

29.21, "Give me my wife that I may go into her." This is quite a brash thing to say to a father-in-law-to-be. Perhaps seven years of working for Laban had revealed his character. Although *go into* is typically colloquial for sexual relations, it may simply mean *marry*. If not, it "contains another sad irony for Jacob, since it is the moment of ultimate deceit" (Mathews).

It also may be surprising to find Jacob referring to her as *my wife* rather than *your daughter*. "His relationship to Rachel must be akin to Joseph's relationship with Mary in the NT. The couple are husband and wife, but the marriage has not yet been physically consummated" (Hamilton).

29.23, He took his daughter Leah and brought her to Jacob. This switch is Laban's legacy. The question we must face is how he could have accomplished such a ploy. In considering this, some things must be kept in mind: Leah was brought in under darkness *(in the evening)*; when she was visible she was, no doubt, veiled; she was probably similar in size and stature as her sister; wedding night conversations are not known for their great depth or length—much would have been whispered, especially in a tent with family within earshot; there may have been wine at the feast, numbing Jacob's perception; Jacob had no reason for suspicion.

Leah may be at fault, in some part, but it is likely that she had little say in this trickery.

This deceit in darkness is the first portion of poetic justice served to Jacob for his deceit of his blind father.

29.25–27, "What is this you have done to me?" Jacob's accusation is wholly laid at Laban's feet, seeming to exonerate Leah.

This trickery further shows the power of God's providence. Regardless of what Laban thought he was getting away with, God would have the last word. As God had previously used man's wicked actions to accomplish His purpose, so He will again. It would be through Leah that the priestly line would come (Levi) and the Messianic line would continue (Judah). Further, the polygamy of Jacob would hasten the fulfillment of God's promise to make a great nation out of Abraham's descendants. This furthers the irony of the situation: "The deceiver Jacob was deceived, and the despised Leah was exalted" (Kidner).

"It is not so done in our country, to give the younger before the first-born." Laban's response is "a perfectly worthless excuse; for if this had really been the custom in Haran... he ought to have told Jacob of it before" (Keil). Had he always planned to make this deception in order to secure extra work from Jacob? One must also wonder if there is a barbed, underhanded dig in Laban's specification that such was not done *in our country* (Wenham). This may have had "the effect of touching a nerve of guilty consciousness in Jacob, who in *his* place acted to put the younger before the firstborn" (Alter).

"Complete the week of this one." The week of the wedding is what is under question. "Syrians still term this the 'king's week,' the time during which bridegroom and bride are respectively addressed as king and queen" (Leupold), a week that would serve a role close to our modern honeymoon. Laban tells Jacob that he can marry Rachel after completing Leah's week—a week that would "toast Laban's wit and the humiliation of Jacob and of Laban's daughters" (Waltke)—but he would then be required to work an extra seven years following the second marriage. "By his treachery, Laban achieves two favorable outcomes: first, he ensures that both daughters marry, for Jacob's love compels him to marry Rachel; and second, he ensures another seven years labor from his industrious nephew" (Mathews).

29.30, So Jacob went into Rachel also. Levitical law forbids marrying sisters (*cf.* Lev 18.18). It is interesting that the father of the nation was the motivation for this law.

He loved Rachel more than Leah. Although this is how the relationship began, we do not believe that it ended as such.[5]

29.31–30.24, Our comments on this section of the text can be found in Excursus L.

Growth of the Seed: A bride is secured for Jacob, ensuring the continuance of the Messianic line.

---

[5]See Excursus L.

30 *25–26, As soon as Rachel had borne Joseph.* Different commentators reckon the time span of the births of Jacob's sons differently. It would seem, however, that Joseph's birth coincided with the ending of the second period of seven years.[1] Thus, we would understand that the births of his sons are not recorded chronologically, but simply grouped by the mother (*i.e.,* Leah bore first; sometime while bearing the first four, Bilhah bore; then Zilpah; Leah again; finally, Rachel).

"Send me away, that I may go to my own home and country." The significance of this decision coming after the birth of Joseph is that it bound Rachel to him by child. "Evidently the women could make a choice to leave or not to leave with Jacob (30.26; *cf.* 31.1–16). Perhaps Laban would have tried to keep his disgraced, barren daughter from going with Jacob and Leah" (Waltke). So, with his family complete, he seeks to return to his homeland. His choice of words "expresses the desire of an underling for release from duty. ...The same language appears in Deuteronomy's description of the released servant who had sold himself into service (15.12–13, 18)" (Mathews).[2]

More importantly, however, his words express a desire to fulfill his vow (28.20–22). "This blessed but flawed man has always had faith and been committed to the land and to the God of Abraham and Isaac (see 28.4, 13; 31.13)" (Waltke). Further, as Wenham notes, "There could be another dimension to his description of it as '*my* land.' The land is his by promise (28.4, 13), so he must go back to claim his inheritance."

"Give me my wives... for you know the service that I have given you." Jacob seeks Laban's acknowledgment that he had fulfilled the contract. This would be given by allowing him to depart with his wives and children. His appeal is based on his record of service. His work would "bear the closest scrutiny and must be acknowledged to be a faithful performance of his own part of the agreement" (Leupold). As before, Jacob is blunt with Laban (*cf.* 29.21), which may indicate that he had learned of his character from their time together.

---

[1] Whitelaw has summarized the births in this manner: "The six sons of Leah may have been born in the seven years, allowing one year's complete cessation from pregnancy, *viz.* the fifth; Bilhah's in the third and fourth years; Zilpah's in the beginning of the sixth and seventh; and Rachel's toward the end of the seventh, leaving Dinah to be born later" (qtd. in Leupold).

[2] Mathews also notes that it echoes the words of Abraham's servant (24.54, 56) and looks ahead to Jacob's struggle with the Lord (32.26).

30.27–28, "I have learned by divination." If it were not clear before, it becomes apparent here that Laban is an idolater. By appeal to his gods, Laban shows himself to not be a follower of Yahweh, even though he acknowledges Yahweh's blessing extending onto him because of Jacob—something that he did not need divination to see.[3]

"Name your wages, and I will give it." The sentence every employee longs to hear! "Laban is ready to go to almost any limit to retain a man whose services have been so advantageous to himself" (Leupold)—a fact that may also say something about his character. Although the line between 'good business' and 'selfish' can be fine, Laban shows himself to be on the selfish side when this agreement begins to cost him (*cf.* 31.7).

And as welcome as these words may seem, they would certainly have sounded suspect coming from Laban's tongue: "His statement has haunting echoes of the first deal he offered Jacob. The reader should anticipate that he intends to deceive Jacob again" (Waltke) And Wenham: "Laban owed Jacob nothing, because he already had two wives promised in exchange for his fourteen years of labor. This he had only just completed, so he could not demand anything more at this stage. Therefore, if Jacob wants to go with anything more than Leah and Rachel, he will have to work longer. A neat reply." Nonetheless, Jacob changes his mind. The ball is in his court, and he now has the opportunity to build himself a nice 'nest egg' to provide for his family, rather than returning to Canaan penniless.

30.29–30, "You yourself know." Apparently, Laban had never admitted that he owed his newly-won prosperity to Jacob's work until Jacob was going to leave—a point which Jacob emphasizes, adding how poorly Laban's flock had done prior to Jacob's arrival. As livestock was the primary measure of a man's wealth in the ancient Near East, Jacob had made Laban a wealthy man—beyond the value of the dowry he could not pay—and his work had not been acknowledged.

"The LORD has blessed you wherever I turned." Cf. 12.3. This reads, more literally, *at my foot*, indicating that wherever he went, God's blessing followed him and spread to Laban.

"But now when shall I provide for my own household also?" Jacob was not too quick to play his hand. He did not jump on Laban's offer to name

---

[3]Several commentators note that *divination* makes little sense here, especially since it is used to see something in the future, not the past (Hamilton). Alter suggests, instead, understanding this by its Akkadian cognate and translates: *"I have prospered and the Lord has blessed me because of you."*

his wages; rather, he seized Laban's admission and reiterated the gain that Laban received by his service. Now, "by his rhetorical question, Jacob insists that he deserves the opportunity to enrich himself" (Mathews).

30.31–34, "What shall I give you?" Laban's response is an admission that Jacob is justified in asking for a substantial flock for himself, and he seems willing to give it on the spot.

"**You shall not give me anything.**" The Hebrew word order emphasizes the negative by bringing it to the front of the sentence. Although Jacob will continue to serve Laban, he will not be subservient to him as he was in their previous arrangement.

"**Let me pass through all your flock today, removing from it…**" Jacob will take the spotted and speckled sheep, the brown lambs, and the spotted and speckled goats from Laban's flock as his wages. "In the east the goats, as a rule, are black or dark-brown, rarely white or spotted with white, and the sheep for the most part are white, very seldom black or speckled" (Keil). Thus, Jacob was taking the *exceptions* as his wages,[4] putting the possibility of acquiring wealth entirely in the hands of God—a remarkable act of faith on Jacob's part.

"**So my honesty will answer for me later, when you come to look into my wages with you.**" Anything not spotted or speckled will be considered stolen. The issue was clear-cut. Deceit was clearly out of the question. Jacob fully expects inspection, but knew that his righteousness will speak for itself. Laban agrees to Jacob's terms.

Some have argued that Jacob is tempting God by expecting Him to work a miracle for Jacob. We are in agreement with Leupold that this is not the case. God had promised to be with him and bless him, and Jacob had seen evidence of that very thing. Now, he relies on God to bless him in this regard. This would seem more like faith being manifested than Jacob presumptuously expecting an undue miracle.

30.35–36, But that day Laban removed the male goats… and put them in charge of his sons. And he set a distance of three days' journey between himself and Jacob. Although Jacob had been nothing but trustworthy since his arrival and had created an agreement that could not be violated without

---

[4]"Normally the hire of a shepherd is 20 percent of the flock, and rarely, if ever, would the speckled population be such a large percentage" (Waltke)

notice, Laban showed distrust in him by these three things: he separated Jacob's flock, although the agreement stipulated that Jacob would; he put his sons in charge of Jacob's flock; he separated his flock from Jacob's by a three-day journey. Those who are least trustworthy always doubt the veracity of others. Although Laban does all of these things to limit Jacob's acquisitions, it will ultimately work "for Jacob's advantage, for it will allow Jacob to carry out his crossbreeding in relative privacy, without Laban or his shepherds spying or checking on him" (Hamilton).

30.37–39, Jacob took fresh sticks of poplar... and peeled white streaks in them. ...He set the sticks that he had peeled in front of the flocks in the troughs. ...The flocks bred in front of the sticks and so the flocks brought forth striped, speckled, and spotted. As Jacob pastured Laban's flocks, he sought to increase his own flock. It is believed in many cultures that, "particularly in sheep, whatever fixes their attention in copulation is marked upon the young" (Keil). Some commentators say that this works; that it works for Jacob may be further evidence of that (although, as Kidner notes, the intention of narrative is to state the sequence, not to pronounce cause and effect—the Hebrew lacks *so* in verse 39). Other commentators, however, discount this, saying it was only God's intervention that brought forth the spotted and speckled young.[5]

In a sense, this practice may be compared to the casting of lots. Many ancients believed that casting lots was divinely controlled, although most would argue that its outcome was random chance. On some occasions, however, it is obvious that God controlled those circumstances (*e.g.*, Achan, Josh 7.14–18; Jonah, Jon 1.7; Matthias, Acts 1.26).[6]

A further question that must be considered is whether this manifested a lack of faith in Jacob. He had laid everything in God's hands; now, he seeks to secure his fortune by his own devices. This is a difficult question, especially considering how frequently Jacob seemed to rely on his own cunning. It is also difficult, however, to see how this is different than a Christian couple seeking a fertility doctor's help when they are unable to conceive: would we also call them faithless? Ultimately, Jacob testifies that it was God, not the sticks, that brought the desired results (*cf.* 31.9–12).

---

[5]It is interesting that the Hebrew for *white* is *laban*. "As Jacob took over Edom (*i.e.*, red) by red stew, so he takes over Laban by white branches" (Waltke).

[6]*Cf.* Prov 16.33: Does God *always* control it?

Finally, we must address the commentators who argue that this was just another one of Jacob's schemes. While appearing to be honorable in his dealings with Laban, he only sought to undo him by craftiness that was outside the agreement. "Yet the passage does not indicate that Jacob's plan involved 'deceit' or 'stealth,' which are descriptions commonly used when narrating deceitful actions (*e.g.*, 27.35–36; 29.25; 31.20, 26–27; 34.13)" (Mathews). Further, that he ultimately attributed his success to God's working seems to indicate that he was not merely leaning on his own cunning as he had in the past.

30.41–42, Whenever the stronger of the flock were breeding, Jacob would lay the sticks in the troughs. In order to increase the strength of his flock as well as the number therein, Jacob would only lay the sticks in the troughs when the stronger sheep were breeding. When the weaker ones bred, Jacob would not lay the sticks in the troughs, *so the feebler would be Laban's and the stronger Jacob's.*

30.43, Thus the man increased greatly. Cf. 12.16; 26.13–14. The Lord fulfills His promise and blesses the one whom He had promised to bless.

Growth of the Seed: Leah shows knowledge of Yahweh;[7] Judah is born; through wives and concubines, the groundwork is laid for Israel to become a nation.

---

[7] See EXCURSUS L.

31 *1–3, "Return to the land of your fathers."* Verses 1–3 explain the motivation for Jacob's sudden departure. First, Laban's sons had developed animosity toward Jacob due to his acquiring Laban's wealth (v 1). Second, Jacob could see that Laban no longer regarded him with favor (v 2). Finally, the Lord directed Jacob to leave (v 3). "Unlike Laban's change of favor, God's attitude had not altered toward him" (Mathews).

The first two reasons do not seem to be the sort of thing that could happen without Jacob noticing. Thus, it is likely that for some time, Jacob had been aware of the change in the emotional climate. He did not act, however, until he received word from the Lord that it was time to act. "Since he had been living under God's direct guidance ever since the time of the Bethel vision, Jacob would not presume to return unless God so directed" (Leupold). Although Jacob is still not the man of faith he will later become, he is not entirely faithless.

"To your kindred." This divine direction is quite different than the one given to Abraham. Abraham was told to leave his kindred while Jacob is told to return there. Further, "What was an unknown land to Abraham (12.1) has now become the land of the fathers" (Waltke).

31.4–5, So Jacob sent and called Rachel and Leah. Having been told by God to leave Haran and return to Canaan, he calls his wives to let them know of the plan.

Into the field. That he calls them into the field is the first indication that he plans to leave surreptitiously. Jacob would later explain his secret departure as motivated by fear (v 31), but such fear was not necessary. Shearing was done at the end of the herding cycle (*cf.* v 19), which would also match the end of the contract period.[1] Thus, Jacob's departure was not a breach of contract. More important, his departure was sanctioned by God; he should feel no need to sneak away. "If the separation from Laban was permissible and right, and God has even sanctioned it, then it should have been carried out openly as the honorable thing that it actually was" (Leupold). Although we cannot go so far as to say his mode of departure was sinful, it was certainly unnecessary, inadvisable, and lacked wisdom.

"I see that your father does not regard me with favor as he did before."

---

[1] See Martha A. Morrison, "The Jacob and Laban Narrative in Light of Near Eastern Sources," *BA* (Summer 1983): 158.

Jacob is not just telling Rachel and Leah *that* they are leaving, but *why* they are leaving. This, most likely, is an effort to ensure their loyalty to him over their father—a loyalty that would not be difficult to obtain (*cf.* vv 14–15). In the Hebrew, *I see* is a participle and placed first in the sentence for emphasis. This would seem to indicate that his conclusion is not drawn on one or two observances of this fact, but that it was a fixed attitude of Laban that he had seen for some time (Leupold).

"The God of my father has been with me." "Jacob's speech begins, continues, and ends with God's victories over Laban: Laban is against him, but God is with him (31.5); Laban cheated him, but God did not allow harm (31.6–7); Laban changed wages, but God changed flocks (31.8–9)" (Waltke). And the contrast is not only between Laban and Yahweh, "but also between 'your father' and 'return to your father's land' and 'my father's God.' One father is repugnant; the other father is inviting" (Hamilton).

Is Jacob saying that Yahweh is not *his* God too—that He is only the God of Isaac? Although there may be something to Jacob not speaking of Yahweh as *his* God until after the wrestling match at Peniel (32.24–31), that is hardly the point of this statement. His point, rather, is that God has shown proof of His faithfulness to Jacob as He was also faithful to his father. He is claiming to be the heir of Isaac's (and Abraham's) powerful God with all the blessings attendant.

31.6–9, "You yourselves know." Jacob bases his argument on what his wives knew by their own experience and witness: he was a faithful worker for Laban, but Laban had cheated Jacob.

"Your father has cheated me and changed my wages." The contract stipulated that Jacob was to receive all of the unusually colored of the flock (30.31–34). Laban, however, sought to distinguish among the unusual sheep (v 8). "The two men had agreed on Jacob's wages, but Laban's words were empty promises" (Mathews).

"Ten times." This may not be intended to be an exact count. If it is symbolic, it would express the idea of completeness and mean *as much as he could* or *constantly*, which may make ten either hyperbole or fewer times than Laban actually changed his wages. Apparently, Jacob had enough trust in God to go along with these absurd changes in the contract. At this point, the sticks (30.37–39) most likely were no longer used. Even if Jacob believed that they were originally producing the variation, "no device could be calculated to produce such nice differentiations in coloring

as the new contracts made necessary. So, without a doubt, Jacob himself was led to ascribe all success he had to God's providence" (Leupold).

"Thus God has taken away the livestock of your father." Jacob attributes his herd to God rather than to his devices. In this, he is not withholding the truth from his wives; rather, he realized over time where the real power lay and ascribed his success to the proper source. "He is making clear to them that he did not dupe Laban out of his flocks by magic or trickery. Had he done so, then Leah and Rachel might have been sympathetic toward Laban. Rather, God is responsible for Jacob's prosperity" (Hamilton). The verb for *has taken away* is not the usual Hebrew word for *take,* but "is a common word [that] usually indicates deliverance or salvation from physical harm. ...Jacob may be implying that as God had plucked the animals from Laban's clutches, He will deliver their family from injury. That God had delivered the animals proved his resourcefulness to rescue them" (Mathews).

"And given them to me." Surely, not every sheep and goat owned by Laban was now in Jacob's possession. Enough time had passed, however, for much of Laban's original flock to be replaced and Jacob's flock to have grown to the point that it seemed that he had taken the entire flock of Laban. It certainly appeared that way to his sons (v 1).

31.10–13, "I lifted up my eyes and saw a dream." Finally, Jacob tells his wives that they are to leave because God commanded it. Reporting the dream also shows that he rightly attributed his success to God.

"The angel of God." See Excursus H.

"'The God of Bethel.'" God's reference back to Bethel would remind Jacob of the dream there and the promises He made. Essentially, God is telling Jacob that He had fulfilled His word and now it was time for Jacob to fulfill his (28.15, 20–22).

31.14–16, Then Rachel and Leah answered. That Rachel is placed first indicates that she took the initiative in speaking (Leupold). That Leah also answered indicates her agreement to depart, but may or may not indicate agreement with everything said.[2]

"Is there any portion or inheritance left for us? ...Are we not regarded by him as foreigners? For he has sold us, and... devoured our money." "Laban's

---

[2]Rachel is also placed first in verse 4, which is most likely due to her place as favorite. This may be the case here as well, although her later theft of the gods would seem to indicate that she was the sister primarily concerned with the inheritance, which is the main thrust of the argument here.

capitalizing of his daughters had not escaped their notice" (Kidner). Like foreigners, "They are exploited in the same way as Jacob, rather than being treated as members of Laban's clan" (Waltke). Their *portion* that is distinct from the *inheritance* may refer to the dowry. "In a socially decorous marriage, a large part of the bride-price would go to the bride. Laban, who first appeared in the narrative (ch 24) eyeing the possible profit to himself in a betrothal transaction, has evidently pocketed all of the fruits of Jacob's fourteen years of labor" (Alter). And Wenham: "They are agreeing that their father has indeed cheated their husband of his due and thereby has cheated them."

It is noteworthy that the focus of the response is not on agreement to God's decree, but on the material possessions—or lack thereof—that they would receive from their father.

"All the wealth that God has taken away from our father belongs to us and our children. Now then, whatever God has said to you, do." 'These riches are ours anyway, so let's go ahead and do what God says.' The tone and focus of this response seem to imply that they "consent to what God commands because their best material interests are not being served by the present arrangement" (Leupold), rather than a response of faith as Kidner suggests. It almost makes you wonder what the response would have been had the wealth lay in Laban's hands! Nothing more is said about Leah in regard to this, but shortly we see more evidence of where Rachel's interests lay regarding material things.

Their speech makes a further point. Calling to attention their children "evidences the women's zeal for their own heirs, distinguishing their family from that of their father and brothers. The line in the sand is drawn, and their allegiance is solely to their husband and children" (Mathews).

31.18, He drove away all his livestock... to go to the land of Canaan. Haste was what Jacob sought. Although flocks cannot be driven too hard, Jacob aimed to put as much distance between himself and Laban as possible. "This long catalogue of all his retinue, however, slows the narrative down drastically. It suddenly reminds us that this move was a major undertaking. Jacob has become very wealthy, so fleeing from Laban was more difficult than fleeing from home" (Wenham).

31.19–21, Laban had gone to shear his sheep. Because the flocks were separated by a three-day journey (30.36), this was the perfect opportunity to get a head start (v 20).

And Rachel stole her father's household gods. Rachel, however, saw it as a perfect opportunity for pilfering, which speaks poorly of Rachel's character.[3] The possessor of the household gods had claim to the inheritance (Keil) and "held the paternal authority of the head of the house."[4] Harrison adds, "Nuzu law recognized as the leader of the family the one who had possession of the household idols."[5] [6] Rachel had already shown the inheritance to be a primary concern (v 14), and here may have sought to ensure whatever portion remained. Assuming that Jacob had shared with his wives his faith and the promises given to his family,[7] it shows that Rachel lacked faith and understanding in God's covenant with Jacob. In addition, this may indicate that she was a daughter of her father: an idolater. Even if all other suggestions are rejected, it shows that Rachel was, at the very least, a thief.[8]

Jacob tricked Laban... he intended to flee. The Hebrew idiom translated *tricked* is more literally *stole the heart of,* which implies deceit.[9] Thus, Jacob's life on this side of the Jabbok is again marked by deceit and flight. Previously, he had deceived his father and fled from his brother; here, he deceives Laban and flees from him. "Ironically, he flees to the homeland that he first fled in search of safety" (Waltke).

---

[3] "The ancient reader would not miss the sarcasm in this story, for here is a new crime—'godnapping'!" (Hamilton).

[4] Martha A. Morrison, "The Jacob and Laban Narrative in Light of Near Eastern Sources," *BA* (Summer, 1983): 161.

[5] R.K. Harrison, *Old Testament Times,* 78.

[6] It has also been suggested that the household gods were "worshipped as givers of earthly prosperity, and also consulted as oracles" (Keil). Part of her motive for theft then may have been to prevent them from revealing to Laban that Jacob's household had fled. Another suggestion is that Rachel sought the household gods in order to give her son priority over Leah's in their family. Finally, some have suggested that Rachel stole the gods out of greed (for their monetary value, see Mathews) or spite (see Hamilton).

[7] This does not seem like a stretch, given Leah's development of a relationship with Yahweh, see EXCURSUS L.

[8] Those who would argue that Rachel is only trying to right a wrong against her—*i.e.,* reclaiming her inheritance—have a difficult case. As the gods gave one the position of head of the household, her desire to possess the gods of Laban "could only mean that she wished Jacob to be recognized as paterfamilias [rather than Laban's sons] after Laban's death" (Greenberg). Thus, Rachel is seeking something that, as daughter of Laban, she had no right to possess. See Moshe Greenberg, "Another Look at Rachel's Theft of the Teraphim," *JBL* 81 (1962): 243–244.

[9] Unlike our culture where the heart represents emotion and love, to them the heart was considered the organ of attentiveness or understanding (Alter).

The Aramean. This is the first time that Laban is so designated (*cf.* 29.10, 14). "The ethnic identity underscores the total alienation of Jacob and Laban; they represent two distinct groups of people" (Waltke).

31.23, He took his kinsmen with him and pursued him. Laban's intentions were obviously malicious. "By assembling a host of kinfolk, Laban's actions suggest that he had harm in mind, or at least intimidation, requiring God's intervention to deliver Jacob. 'Pursued' often describes trailing armies with hostile intentions (*e.g.*, 14.14–15; Exod 14.9; Jdg 8.12). Laban's later boast implied that Jacob's small band of servants was of no consequence (v 29). This bravado even in the face of God's forewarning gives credence to Jacob's fears (vv 31, 42). One can only imagine what havoc Laban would have committed if the Lord had not restrained him" (Mathews).

For seven days. Even with a three day head start, Jacob, his family, and flocks could not travel fast enough to outrun Laban. After just a few days, Laban drew near to Jacob.

31.24, But God came to Laban the Aramean in a dream. God intercedes in a dream to protect Jacob (*cf.* 20.3–7).

"Be careful not to say anything to Jacob, either good or bad." The Hebrew figure is intended to cover the whole range of possible speech by naming the extremes. Its thrust, thus, is: *Do not say anything to Jacob.* This is not, however, to be understood as a prohibition against all speech *to* Jacob (for he obviously fails in that regard), but to forbid any speech *against* Jacob—"anything to influence Jacob to return, or... anything by way of bitter reproach" (Leupold); "not to exceed his authority" (Mathews); "God has corked the bottle of his aggressiveness" (Fokkelman qtd. in Hamilton). This warning is surprisingly brief, considering the intentions of Laban. This may be "due to the author's assumption that the reader recalls the fuller message delivered to Abimelech [in chapter 20]" (Mathews).

31.25, And Laban overtook Jacob. Following God's message to Laban, he catches Jacob. And if he had not been nasty already, the following dialogue shows even more clearly the deplorable character of Laban.

Jacob... Laban with his kinsmen. The contrast "effectively distinguishes the Aramean band from Jacob and his 'relatives' who are primarily to be found in Canaan" (Mathews).

31.26–28, "What have you done?" It is only natural for Laban to ask Jacob's motivation for leaving the way that he did. His next statement, however, shows that his motive is not only curiosity, but a desire to put sole blame on Jacob, casting his actions in the worst possible light.[10]

"You have… driven away my daughters like captives of the sword." Their departure may seem this way, but this is overstatement even for a concerned father. His choice of simile contains "ominous military implications, suggesting that Jacob has behaved like a marauding army that seizes the young women to serve as sexual and domestic slaves" (Alter). But more to the point, Laban was no concerned father. The daughters' own testimony was that he devoured their inheritance, sold them, and treated them like foreigners (vv 14–15). Jacob had not, in fact, driven them away like captives.

"Why did you… not tell me, so that I might have sent you away with mirth and songs, with tambourine and lyre?" This must be seen only as an empty lie that Jacob does not even dignify. Laban has worked to keep Jacob there from the beginning. "In accordance with Jacob's agreement to count all the normally colored stock as 'stolen,' Laban repeatedly attempted to put Jacob in the position of owing livestock at the end of the year. …Thus, Jacob would have become… through debt and dependence on the livestock owner, affiliated with his family permanently."[11] The idea was to keep Jacob bound to work for him in perpetuity. There would have been a festive farewell party for Jacob, indeed.

"And why did you not permit me to kiss my sons and my daughters farewell?" Again, Laban feigns concern and love for his daughters that has never existed prior to this point.

31.29–30, "It is my power to do you harm. But…" The empty boast of a lifelong bully who has been beaten at his own game. "His braggadocio endeavored to convince his audience that Jacob was not the better man" (Mathews). One must wonder if anyone was daft enough to believe him.

---

[10]Waltke writes, "Although his rhetoric may have impressed his kinfolk, his speech is a classic example of dramatic irony. He is unaware of what the audience already knows. He pictures his daughters on his side against Jacob, whereas in fact we know the aggrieved daughters have disassociated themselves from their father in favor of their husband. The silence of Rachel and Leah in this scene bears witness against him. However, he is so self-righteous that he fails to note their silent shout. As a result, he does not expect his daughters to deceive him and make an even greater fool of him."

[11]Martha A. Morrison, "The Jacob and Laban Narrative in Light of Near Eastern Sources," *BA* (Summer, 1983): 161.

"But why did you steal my gods?" Either those who had reported Jacob's departure to Laban also knew about the missing household gods or Laban stopped by the homestead before pursuing Jacob. In either event, Laban was surprised—and upset—that Jacob had stolen his idols. In Laban's mind, this marks a contrast between their behavior: "Laban respected Jacob's God, but Jacob has not respected Laban's gods" (Hamilton).

31.31–32, "Because I was afraid, for I thought that you would take your daughters from me by force." Jacob's motive for the secret departure was in an effort to protect Rachel *and* Leah. It is interesting that even this early, Jacob was concerned about Leah.[12] This of course does not answer the question of why he left, part of which Laban surely already knew, since he was the one cheating Jacob. Perhaps Jacob had already spoken to Laban about the promises made by God and his eventual plan to return to Canaan, so God's word to him needed no repetition. Or perhaps because Laban was an unbeliever, it warranted no mention. In either event, Jacob only answers the question that was asked and volunteers no further information.

"Anyone with whom you find your gods shall not live." A monotheist and an honorable man, Jacob would not permit either thievery (*cf.* 30.33) or idolatry. This may have been partly based on Hammurabi's code which held that one who stole the property of a god or temple would die. Obviously, as the text states, Jacob did not know that Rachel had stolen the idols. Interestingly, Rachel's next appearance in the Genesis narrative documents her death (35.16–20). "If he is not unwittingly condemning Rachel to death, his preemptory words at least foreshadow her premature death in childbirth" (Alter).

31.33–35, Laban went into Jacob's tent. The Hebrew stem indicates a thorough search as opposed to a brief perusal of what the eye could see. Laban searched the individual tents of Jacob, Leah, and the two servants before finally turning to Rachel. The slowed pace of the narrative heightens the tension. "That he inspected the women's tents shows that Laban did not truly believe they were innocent parties to Jacob's scheme" (Mathews).

Laban felt all about the tent. The verb matches the one used of Isaac feeling Jacob to determine which son was before him (*cf.* 27.12, 21–22).

---

[12]See Excursus L.

"He who was once touched, searched by his father, now has his tent and Rachel's tent touched, searched by his father-in-law" (Hamilton).

Now Rachel had... put them in the camel's saddle and sat on them... and she said to her father... "I cannot rise before you, for the way of women is upon me." Having hidden the idols and sat upon them, Rachel claims that her menstrual cycle prevents her from rising before Laban. Either for a desire not to further add to her discomfort or because there was an issue of uncleanness, he does not make her stand. And so Rachel shows herself to be a match to her father in cunning.[13] We cannot know, of course, whether Rachel's words were technically a lie. If they were true, it was awfully convenient. But even if the words she spoke were truth, they constitute misused truth of the worst kind. Her motive was clearly devious and filled with deceit.

31.36–37, Then Jacob became angry and berated Laban. Years of pent up anger—having been cheated at the hands of Laban—finally spill forth into words. Here, in Jacob's eyes, is another attempt by Laban to pull something over on him before he leaves. Jacob, having been justified by the idols not being found, speaks the words that have been in his heart for at least two decades.

"What is my offense? What is my sin that you have hotly pursued me?" Jacob begins by protesting his innocence, declaring that nothing has been found to warrant such a pursuit. One must also wonder if Jacob's question is not only about Laban's immediate pursuit of Jacob's caravan, but his 20-year pursuit of Jacob's slave labor.

"You have felt through all my goods; what have you found? ... Set it here before my kinsmen and your kinsmen, that they may decide between us two." He challenges Laban to bring out his evidence before the eyes of all the witnesses to prove that Jacob had done something wrong. Having no evidence, Laban could only stand silent and take Jacob's verbal barrage.

31.38–42, "These twenty years I have been with you." Jacob details his twenty years of faithful, quality service to Laban, reminding him that he never lost a sheep or goat to miscarriage, that he never ate of the flocks,

---

[13] Alter suggests that the monotheistic author of Genesis may also be presenting a "satiric glance... on the cult of figurines, as necessity compels Rachel to assume this irreverent posture toward them."

that he bore the loss to wild animals himself,[14] and that he served Laban in the elements and with little sleep.

"And you have changed my wages ten times." 'What is my reward for all of this work?' Jacob asks. 'Trickery and deceit.'

"If the God of my father... had not been on my side, surely now you would have sent me away empty-handed." Jacob knows who is protecting and caring for him. He does not claim that his own cunning or schemes brought him success; rather, he attributes it to God.

"The Fear of Isaac." This name for God (*cf.* v 53) is unique in the Bible. Mathews says, "'Fear' probably is a metonymy, substituted for 'God,' in which the effect ('fear') is placed for the cause ('God'). The cryptic name refers to God as the One of Isaac, who brings about terror in the hearts of others. This interpretation corresponds to the impact that Laban's dream created, preserving Jacob from danger."

31.43–45, "All that you see is mine. But what can I do for these my daughters?" Laban, again, resorts to empty claims and vain attempts to cast Jacob as the antagonist. Certainly, he does nothing to answer Jacob's accusations. He dodges the real issue—that he had treated Jacob unfairly from the beginning—and petulantly whines that there is nothing he can do (to avenge himself?).

"Come now, let us make a covenant, you and I." We would not suggest that Jacob's words "cut Laban to the heart with their truth, so that he turned round, offered his hand, and proposed a covenant" (Keil). Rather, now knowing the hostility that Jacob feels toward him and how he would react under similar circumstances, Laban seeks to make a covenant of peace with Jacob. His seeking this covenant to prevent any kind of vengeance taken by Jacob is, in effect, a silent acknowledgment of his wrongdoing. "When foreigners seek to make covenants or oaths with the patriarchs, it is an acknowledgment of the latter's superiority. *Cf.* 21.22–24; 26.26–31. Laban now feels he must protect himself from the power and blessing that evidently rests on Jacob; hence, he asks for a covenant" (Wenham).

So Jacob took a stone and set it up as a pillar. Jacob is ready and willing to preserve the peace even though Laban does not deserve it (*cf.* 26.27–31).

---

[14] "Both biblical and other Near Eastern codes indicate that a shepherd was not obliged to make good losses caused by beasts of prey and thieves, where no negligence was involved" (Alter). Thus, Laban requiring Jacob to bear these losses was further evidence of his unfair treatment of Jacob.

Although the covenant is made at Laban's suggestion, Jacob is the one who is seen taking the initiative to seal the treaty he probably resented.

31.48–50, "*This heap is a witness between me and you today. …The LORD watch between you and me. …If you oppress my daughters.*" Laban takes this one last opportunity to draw Jacob as the villain. The stones were *witnesses*—as if a witness was needed to verify Jacob's word. The Lord would *watch* them—as if he needed watching. Finally, and most insultingly, he bestows a fatherly warning against mistreatment of Rachel and Leah. It is one thing for a father to warn a groom-to-be. It is quite another to warn your son-in-law of thirteen years—especially when Laban was the one who had mistreated them. "It is an effort to slander a good man and do it with the sanctions of apparent piety—in other words, it is wicked hypocrisy" (Leupold).

"*If you take wives beside my daughters.*" This is standard verbiage in ancient marriage contracts, although this setting clearly does not fit that picture.[15] "There is an element of irony in his demand that Jacob should not take any extra wives beside his daughters. …It was Laban who had forced bigamy upon Jacob in time past!" (Wenham).

31.51–53, "*See this heap and the pillar, which I have set between you and me.*" Having added a scolding and condescending lecture to the covenant, Laban now takes credit for the covenant's witness (*cf.* v 45).

"*I will not pass over this heap to you, and you will not pass over this heap and this pillar to me, to do harm.*" Still concerned about Jacob's potential vengeance, Laban draws a line in the sand that neither of them is to cross. As is typical, one man assumes of another what he would likely do if he had the chance.

"*The God of Abraham…judge between us.*" Laban already knew that Yahweh was protecting Jacob (v 24). Now, he sought to ensure that same protection for himself.

"*The God of Nahor.*" Does this indicate that, after all, Nahor and his family were Yahweh-worshippers—*i.e.*, is Laban indicating that the God of Abraham and the God of Nahor are the same God? Although this is conceivable, it is hardly likely. Nahor was of the family that God called

---

[15]It is interesting that not once in this entire narrative does Laban refer to Leah and Rachel as Jacob's wives; rather, each instance, he calls them "*my daughters.*"

Abraham from and Abraham forbade Isaac's return to. Further, if Nahor had served Yahweh, it is not reflected in the lives of his descendants. More likely, this is referring to each of their respective gods, although "Laban, according to his polytheistic views, placed the God of Abraham upon the same level as the God of Nahor and Terah" (Keil). Thus, "In Laban's mind a god on each side was invoked, as in political covenants" (Kidner). That the plural form of the verb *judge* is used seems to be a clear indication that more than one god is under question—even though there is really only one God under question.

So Jacob swore by the Fear of his father Isaac. Jacob only swore by Yahweh,[16] omitting *the God of Nahor.*

31.54, Jacob offered a sacrifice in the hill country. Jacob follows in the steps of his father and grandfather, worshipping upon his success brought by God's hand.

31.55, Early in the morning. See comment on 21.14.

Laban arose and kissed his grandchildren and his daughters and blessed them. "He gives a kiss and a farewell blessing to his grandsons and daughters, but not to Jacob. Laban appears to ignore him. This last encounter with Jacob contrasts vividly with their first meeting, when Laban 'ran to meet him, and embraced him, and kissed him' (29.13)" (Hamilton).

Growth of the Seed: Jacob begins his return to the Promised land; Rachel proves to be a thief and an idolater.[17]

---

[16]See comment on verse 42.

[17]See Excursus L.

32

1–2, *The angels of God met him.* This is the second occasion where Jacob sees angels. He saw them first when he was departing Canaan in the vision of the ladder. "Just as the angels ascending and descending had represented to him the divine protection and assistance during his journey and sojourn in a foreign land, so now the angelic host was a signal of the help of God for the approaching conflict with Esau" (Keil). As Ross notes: "Jacob's sojourn in Aram is deliberately bracketed with supernatural visions."[1] That the angels appeared to him at his departure and at his return suggested "their accompaniment of the patriarch during the entirety of his travels" (Mathews).

Jacob was barely removed from the danger that threatened him from Laban when he is immediately faced with another danger: Esau. When Abraham journeyed from Haran to Canaan, his journey was marked by faith because he did not know where he was going. Jacob's journey is also marked by faith, but because he *did* know where he was going!

"This is God's camp!" "As Bethel was the gate of heaven (28.17), Mahanaim is God's camp on earth" (Waltke).

Mahanaim. *Mahanaim* means *double camp.* His own camp was being watched by another (*cf.* 2 Kgs 6.15–17). "The narrator employs the number two throughout the scene: two camps, two families, two meetings—one with God and Esau—and two brothers" (Waltke).

32.3–4, Jacob sent messengers before him to Esau. Rebekah told Jacob that she would send for him when Esau's anger subsided (27.45). She never sent for him. For all Jacob knew, his anger had never subsided. He had no way of knowing Esau's intentions; that God sought to reassure him seems to make his fear legitimate.

In the land of Seir. Esau had already moved from Canaan into what would become the land of Edom. "Esau during the twenty years of Jacob's exile has already dispossessed the Horites at Seir or is in the process of doing so (Deut 2.12), suggesting his military might" (Waltke).

"My lord Esau… your servant Jacob." Jacob first seeks to win Esau's favor by petitioning him as a servant. Although he is well aware of his preeminence in God's eyes and his familial preeminence from the blessing of Isaac and purchased birthright, Jacob is ready to concede every outward

---

[1] Allen P. Ross, "Studies in the Life of Jacob, Part 1—Jacob's Vision: The Founding of Bethel," *BSac* 142 (1985): 226.

advantage for the sake of peace (Leupold). "Like Abraham with Lot, Jacob takes the first step toward giving up the rights of his election to the blessing (13.1–12), trusting God to fulfill the promise" (Waltke).

"I have sojourned with Laban and stayed until now." Leupold renders this *"I was detained,"* indicating that "his stay had become more protracted than he had at first intended that it should be." Hamilton also translates this way, saying, "Jacob is careful to emphasize the reason for the delay of his return, and he cautiously avoids any reference to the alacrity of his departure in the first place."

32.6, "There are four hundred men with him." Esau receives Jacob's servants without hostility, but sends no word back. Rather, he is coming to meet Jacob—with four hundred men and silence. "Nothing could be more ominous than Esau's silence and his rapid approach in force" (Kidner). It is all the more unnerving, as four hundred men is the standard number for a militia (Waltke).

32.7–8, He divided the people who were with him. ..."If Esau comes to the one camp... then the camp that is left will escape." Jacob seeks to provide safety to at least half of his household by dividing into two groups. "It is over-facile to condemn his elaborate moves as faithless, for Scripture approves of strategy when it is a tool rather than a substitute for God (*cf.* Josh 8.1c, 2c; Neh 4.9ff)" (Kidner). See THEOLOGICAL REFLECTION, below.

Two camps. "A law of binary division runs through the whole Jacob story: twin brothers struggling over a blessing that cannot be halved, two sisters struggling over a husband's love, flocks divided into unicolored and [multi]colored animals, Jacob's material blessing now divided into two camps" (Alter).

32.9–12, And Jacob said. Having made preparations, Jacob sought God's counsel and protection in prayer. In many ways, this could serve as a model prayer. It rests its confidence securely on the foundation of the covenant, as it both begins and ends with reference to it; it shows a true spirit of worship in wonder at God's mercy; requests are withheld, in spite of impending danger.

"O God of my father." Jacob prays, focusing on the relationship that God had with Abraham and Isaac. In doing so, he recalls both the covenant relationship and God's faithfulness to his family.

"O LORD who said to me, 'Return to your country... that I may do you good.'" Jacob is not seeking to remind God of His own command; rather, he approaches God as all ought to in prayer: standing firmly on God's promises and God's word. Praying according to God's will does not imply praying apologetically as if we ought not to ask. We have every right to have the utmost confidence in our prayers if we are taking a stand on God's promises.

"I am not worthy." Jacob humbles himself before God, confessing his impurity and acknowledging his total dependence on God's mercy. "Jacob's confession indicates that a spiritual transformation is taking place in Jacob: he submits to Esau and recognizes his unworthiness before God, casting his lot with the weak" (Waltke).

"Please deliver me from the hand of my brother." Having made his stand on God's word and properly humbling himself in the light of God's mercy, Jacob finally gets to the heart of the matter: his upcoming encounter with Esau.

"But you said, 'I will surely do you good, and make your offspring as the sand of the sea.'" "The only ground upon which godly men can take their stand in times of distress is God's Word. ...Naturally, there is a certain boldness about holding God's promises before Him and taking one's stand on the ground of them; but such an attitude distinctly belongs to faith" (Leupold).

32.13–15, From what he had with him he took a present for his brother Esau. Jacob further sought to prevent Esau's anger by sending ahead a peace offering—550 head of livestock. "In an attempt to appease Esau's anger, Jacob encircles Esau with gifts so he has no place, psychologically speaking, to move" (Waltke). And this gift was significant. According to Morrison, the value of one sheep "equaled approximately three months of average grain rations."[2] And some of the animals given—cattle, donkeys, camels—would have been more valuable than sheep, increasing even further the value of this gift. Of course, Jacob would be willing to give extravagantly in order to preserve his life, but the real significance is to see exactly how much wealth God had blessed him with—even after giving this much away, he had enough to separate into two parties.

---

[2]Martha A. Morrison, "The Jacob and Laban Narrative in Light of Near Eastern Sources," *BA* (Summer, 1983): 159.

32.16–20, These he handed over to his servants, every drove by itself. The gift went to Esau piece by piece. The idea was to slowly overwhelm Esau with good will as what would have seemed a large gift—the first drove alone—was doubled, then tripled, and so forth. Finally, the next day, Jacob would arrive as the climax of the procession.

"'Whose are these ahead of you?'" Each servant was to follow the flock. This arrangement is the reverse of what is typically done: the shepherd usually goes before his herd. Perhaps the hope was for the size of each drove to impress Esau before the message got to him that it was meant as a gift to him.

"I may appease him." According to Waltke, the language resembles religious sacrifice. This should not be shocking. "It is no less appropriate to pacify an offended brother than to appease an offended God" (*cf.* Matt 5.23–24).

32.22, The same night, he arose… and crossed the ford. Having appealed to God and taken every precaution, Jacob confidently moves on, trusting that God will protect him.

His eleven children. "The obvious omission of Dinah must be understood as the author's interest in Jacob as Israel, whose sons' descendants constituted the nation" (Mathews).

Jabbok. The name of the river is related to the Hebrew word for wrestle. Most likely, it was named after Jacob's upcoming wrestling match, and its use is anachronistic. "This river in eastern Canaan flows through deep-cut canyons into the Jordan about 23 miles north of the Dead Sea. It is approximately 50 miles long and descends from its source at 1900 feet above sea level to about 115 feet below sea level where it meets the Jordan" (Hamilton).

32.23–24, He took them and sent them across… and Jacob was left alone. Having sent his family and possessions across the river, Jacob remained behind. "The natural thing for the master of the entire establishment to do is to stay behind to check whether all have really crossed or whether some stragglers of this great host still need direction" (Leupold). Also, it seems likely that he sought to be alone to further meditate—many commentators agree that the wrestling originated and continued through a time of fervent prayer.

A man. The man is not named, although it is understood to be God (vv 28, 30). The Bible will later identify the man as an angel (*cf.* Hos 12.4), but this does not contradict our understanding that it was God. If Hosea's identification is to be understood as The Angel of the Lord, he is confirming what Jacob believed about this encounter.[3] That this is Hosea's point seems to be confirmed by the parallelism seen between verses 3 and 4.

From His words in verse 26, it seems that the man attacked during the night to conceal His identity. "Had the assailant come in the daytime, Jacob would have recognized the man's special authority (v 29) and identity (v 30b). If Jacob had perceived whom he [had] to fight, he would never have started the fight, let alone continued with his peculiar obstinacy."[4]

Wrestled with him until the break of day. "The image of wrestling has been implicit throughout the Jacob story: in his grabbing Esau's heel as he emerges from the womb, in his striving with Esau for birthright and blessing, in his rolling away the huge stone from the mouth of the well, and in his multiple contendings with Laban. Now, in this culminating moment of his life story, the characterizing image of wrestling is made explicit and literal" (Alter).

Interpretations of this event have varied widely throughout the generations. Josephus understood it as only a dream, while Philo and Clement of Alexandria each saw it as an allegory—a spiritual conflict in literal terms. Jerome saw it to be long and earnest prayer. Other Jewish literature saw it as a physical fight, but understood it to be the angel of Esau with whom Jacob wrestled.[5] Ultimately, long discussions about the nature of the fight fail to understand the true point. As Ross notes, "The fight is but the preamble to the most important part—the dialogue."[6] If all of our discussion focuses on the specifics of this unique encounter with God, we fail to see the true significance of the event: the renaming of Jacob.

32.25, When the man saw that he did not prevail against Jacob. Jacob fought

---

[3]See Excursus H.

[4]Allen P. Ross, "Studies in the Life of Jacob, Part 2—Jacob at the Jabbok, Israel at Peniel," *BSac* 142 (1985): 344.

[5]Miles interestingly argues that Jacob wrestled with Esau himself, supposing that Esau sneaked over to Jacob's camp, remembering the physical advantage he previously had over Jacob. Miles seeks to support this interpretation with Jacob's statement to Esau in 33.10: *"I have seen your face, which is like seeing the face of God."* See "Jacob's Wrestling Match," *BR* (Oct 1998): 22. While this would make good drama, it falls apart at the word of Hosea.

[6]Allen P. Ross, "Studies in the Life of Jacob, Part 2—Jacob at the Jabbok, Israel at Peniel," *BSac* 142 (1985): 343.

his assailant to a draw. "Humbling himself, God has come to Jacob on some type of even terms" (Waltke). See Excursus J.

He touched his hip socket, and Jacob's hip was put out of joint as he wrestled with him. Just a touch was enough to dislocate Jacob's hip.[7]

32.26, "Let me go, for the day has broken." One cannot see God and live (*cf.* Exod 33.20). This also explains "why Jacob was unaware of his foe's identity and indeed took him on. Had he realized that his enemy was divine, he would never have engaged him in a fight" (Wenham). And Hamilton: "Already Jacob had passed one night in his life close to somebody, a somebody whose true identity he learns only in the morning. Might not 'and in the morning, behold, it was Leah' now become 'and in the morning, behold, it was Elohim'?"

"I will not let you go unless you bless me." "Jacob is physically broken but will not give up. Now it is a battle of words, and Jacob clings for a blessing. ...Jacob prevails with prayer, not with natural strength. This is the change of Jacob to Israel" (Waltke). Further, "This request provides a clue that the real nature of the man is dawning on Jacob as day breaks, for the inferior would solicit a blessing from the superior" (Hamilton).

32.27–29, "What is your name? ...You shall no longer be called Jacob, but Israel." Having fought to a stalemate, the assailant finally shows His superiority. That He is able to demand the name of Jacob and change it—while refusing to give His name—indicates this.

The question may call to mind the time when Isaac asked the same question and Jacob answered, "Esau." But more to the point of this narrative is the implied confession in giving his name: "Here the 'heel-catcher' was caught and had to identify his true nature before he could be blessed."[8] Leupold adds, "This question is addressed to Jacob not for information's sake but to center Jacob's attention upon what was about to come and upon the thought his name connoted." And Waltke: "The ques-

---

[7]Hamilton offers a different—and somewhat surprising—suggestion: "Given the other references to 'thigh' in the patriarchal traditions, it is inconceivable that any later Israelite would have missed the national import of this verse. Jacob, the ancestor of Israel, had his thigh struck, and it was from that thigh that Israel would come forth (Exod 1.5)." See his commentary for further discussion on the possibility of this interpretation.

[8]Allen P. Ross, "Studies in the Life of Jacob, Part 2—Jacob at the Jabbok, Israel at Peniel," *BSac* 142 (1985): 345.

tion forces Jacob to own up to his devious past and be purged from it by embracing his new name."

Jacob had asked for a blessing. "But instead of merely blessing him, his opponent changes Jacob's name, thus announcing Jacob's new character and destiny. Similarly, Abram's name was changed to Abraham and Sarai's to Sarah to presage the long-awaited fulfillment of the promise of the birth of a son (17.5, 15). Here Jacob's rebaptism as Israel is equally significant, for Israel is of course the name of the nation, and in granting it, Jacob's opponent reveals the true import of the encounter" (Wenham).[9] See Excursus J.

"Why is it that you ask my name?" This question most likely carries an undertone: 'Why do you ask? Don't you know who I am?' At the same time, however, the context indicates why God was unwilling to give His name. The giving of the name implies submission and allows the other power over the name. "He was unwilling to release His name for Jacob to control."[10]

"You have striven with God." Although chosen by God in the womb, Jacob did not realize his destiny without strife. For much of his life, he relied on his own cunning, rather than in the might of the Lord. "Jacob had to struggle to become the chosen one. Apparently, election means more than just sitting and waiting for God to make His decision; it has to do with assertive action on the part of the elected."[11]

There he blessed him. "The crippling and the naming show that God's ends were still the same: He would have all of Jacob's will to win, to attain and obtain, yet purged of self-sufficiency and redirected to the proper object of man's love, God himself" (Kidner).

32.30, Peniel. Peniel means *face of God.* The Hebrew is an abbreviated form of what Jacob says next: *I have seen God face to face.*

---

[9]Hamilton does not see this name change with the same significance as most commentators: "The explanation says nothing directly about any repentance by Jacob, or even about any shedding of distasteful character traits. The new name does not carry any guarantees that from this point on Jacob is transformed. What it highlights is Jacob's success in wrestling with God and his success with people. Accordingly, one is led to conclude that the change of name from *Jacob* to *Israel* focuses on Jacob's assertiveness, his ability to cling to his stronger assailant despite his injury, his insistent desire for his opponent's blessing."

[10]Allen P. Ross, "Studies in the Life of Jacob, Part 2—Jacob at the Jabbok, Israel at Peniel," *BSac* 142 (1985): 348.

[11]Frederick C. Holmgren, "Holding your own against God! Genesis 32:22-32 (In the Context of Genesis 31–33)," *Interpretation* 44 (1990): 5.

"I have seen God face to face, and yet my life has been delivered." The traditional understanding is that Jacob is amazed that, having wrestled with God, he remained alive. Hamilton, however, argues a different meaning: "Such an interpretation misses the thrust of the double use of ['preserve'] in this chapter. Earlier, Jacob had prayed 'Preserve me... from my brother (v 11). Now he says: *my life has been preserved.* ...In other words, Jacob's recognition that none other than God himself stands before him gives Jacob the assurance that Esau shall not destroy him. Jacob's earlier prayer for deliverance is now answered by God in this encounter. Jacob shall be 'preserved' from Esau, for God has 'preserved' him. In this verse Jacob moves, in his own words, from a proclamation of revelation... to a statement of testimony... that is, he shifts from awe to relief." And Ross: "His prayer for deliverance (vv 9–12) was answered by God in this face-to-face encounter and blessing. Meeting God 'face to face' meant that he could now look Esau directly in the eye."[12]

32.31, *The sun rose upon him as he passed Penuel.* In addition to the historical note that Jacob forded the river at sunrise, having fought all night, this may be seen symbolically in two ways. First, it represents a new day of light dawning for Jacob, after a long night of deceit and self-sufficiency. This is the spiritual awakening of Jacob. Second, it bookends Jacob's time away from Canaan as a period of darkness. The sun set on him as he departed the Promised Land (28.11), having stolen the blessing that God intended to give him. Here, as he returns, the sun rises. Perhaps the greatest truth can be seen in combining the two views. As Jacob left Canaan, he was deceitful and filled with self-sufficiency—and the sun set on him. At that point, he received his first vision from God and slowly began an uphill climb from that point to this one, where he reaches a new plane in his spiritual development, just as he returns to the Promised Land.

Limping because of his hip. A dislocated hip is a difficult injury to overcome and often has lasting effects. It is likely that Jacob would carry with him a physical reminder of this night throughout the remainder of his life, "witnessing to the reality of his nocturnal encounter and showing that although in one sense he was victorious, God had left His mark on him. He was not totally self-sufficient" (Wenham).

---

[12]Allen P. Ross, "Studies in the Life of Jacob, Part 2—Jacob at the Jabbok, Israel at Peniel," *BSac* 142 (1985): 349.

Growth of the Seed: Jacob is given covenant name (v 28); he 'sees the light' (v 31).

Theological Reflection: Preparing for the Storm

Many commentators have argued that Jacob twice shows a lack of faith in this account: first, by preparing his strategy before bowing in prayer (and after God had shown him a vision of reassurance); then, by sending a gift after his prayer.

As a Floridian, I tend to understand Jacob's action. Although we pray for safety as a hurricane approaches, we still take precautions against the storm—board the windows, secure loose objects, and even evacuate, if necessary. There is a vast difference between faithlessly helping oneself (*cf.* 16.1–4) and using prudent judgment and acting with wisdom. Although Jacob understood that God was with him, he still took precautions to be ready for any trouble that might come along.

Also, there are some situations that require action first and prayer second. Consider a second illustration: if a known murderer was standing on your lawn, you might find yourself locking the door before kneeling to pray. Such does not render you faithless, but prudent.

Is there faithlessness, then, in Jacob's gift after the prayer? We would argue that there isn't. Prayer does not result in inaction. Having locked the door and said a prayer, you wouldn't just sit around as the murderer approached your house; certainly, you would call the police.

It is easy to call Jacob faithless from the security in which we stand. Yet if there was someone nearby who, last we knew, wanted to kill us, we would find ourselves acting in very much the same way—if not displaying even more 'faithlessness.'

Excursus J: Wrestling with God?

This account brings up several questions, the first of which concerns Jacob's victory over God in the wrestling match. The text says, *[God] saw that he did not prevail against Jacob* and later God says, *"You have striven with God... and have prevailed."* At best, however, Jacob fought to a stalemate. Even then, it was *his* hip that was dislocated and *he* was the one who was compelled to give up his name and have it changed. In what way, then, did Jacob prevail against God?

It would seem evident that the sense in which Jacob prevailed does not refer to the physical fight. For that matter, any success Jacob had in the physical fight would only be as God allowed. But the physical fight, of course, is symbolic for the greater struggle of Jacob's life—and it is in that greater struggle that we can discern how Jacob had prevailed against God.

Leupold sees in the physical wrestling a spiritual significance in relation to prayer. "This statement does not impugn God's omnipotence, but it does effectively portray the power of prayer. God does allow the prayer of men to be mighty in His sight. At the same time there is a certain measure of truth to the idea that God is the opponent of believing men as they pray. God is not pretending. But God must oppose because the sinful will of those that pray often is not yet reduced to full accord with the divine will. As the will of man learns ever more perfectly to submit to God's will, God can no longer 'prevail' against such a one." In other words, Jacob prevailed by aligning himself with God's will.

Curtis suggests, "Jacob was ready to receive the promise, but his entire life had been characterized by his determination to seize the promise and the blessing for himself. The contrast between the work of God and the work of man that is evident at various points in the narrative seems to come to a focus for Jacob at this point with respect to his occupation of the land. The incident at Jabbok brought him to the awareness that the fulfillment of the promise must be the work of God rather than the work of Jacob. ...God struggles with Jacob, and in the process Jacob prevails—not in the sense that he overcomes God, but in the sense that by recognizing his dependence on God he is now able to receive the promise and the blessing of God to Abraham."[1] Thus, similar to Leupold's suggestion, Jacob's prevailing is a reference to him realizing that he must trust in God.

Ross also follows closely: "What he had surmised for the past 20 years now dawned on him—he was in the hands of One against whom it is useless to struggle. One wrestles on only when he thinks his opponent can be beaten. With the crippling touch, Jacob's struggle took a new direction. With the same

---

[1]Edward M. Curtis, "Structure, Style and Context as a Key to Interpreting Jacob's Encounter at Peniel," *JETS* 30 No. 2 (1987): 135.

scrappy persistence he clung to his Opponent for a blessing. His goal was now different. Now crippled in his natural strength, he became bold in faith."[2]

Finally, Boice offers the following: "With men Jacob had contended successfully... and lost. He cheated Esau of the blessing but lost Esau's good will. He outwitted his blind and ailing father but lost his good name. None of these victories had brought satisfaction, and now on the banks of the Jabbok he is bottled up between enemies. He even has God for his antagonist. However, in his battle with God Jacob suffers a reversal of his fortunes which is actually his victory. He loses his wrestling match with God; God touches his hip and he is permanently wounded. But, in the divine logic, which is beyond our full comprehension, this loss is Jacob's victory. He wins by losing and is now able to go on in new strength as God's man."[3] And each step thereafter would serve as a reminder of the victory he won on the banks of the Jabbok.

Changing of His Name
A second point of interest in this event is the changing of Jacob's name. As noted above, the forced 'confession' implicit in giving his name naturally led to the rebirth of Jacob in the giving of Israel.

Ross notes that this was a turning point in the spiritual development of Jacob. "The object was to contrast the old name with the new. When one remembers the significance of names, the point becomes clear: a well-established nature, a fixed pattern of life must be turned back radically! In giving his name, Jacob had to reveal his nature. This name, at least for the narratives, designated its owner as a crafty overreacher. Here, the 'heel-catcher' was caught and had to identify his true nature before he could be blessed."[4]

And Keil: "Whilst by the dislocation of his hip the carnal nature of his previous wrestling was declared to be powerless and wrong, he received in the new name of *Israel* the prize of victory, and at the same time directions from God how he was henceforth to strive for the cause of the Lord. By his wrestling with God, Jacob entered upon a new stage in his life. As a sign of this, he received a new name, which indicated, as the result of this conflict, the nature of his new relation to God." He had exited Canaan as Jacob, self-sufficient and crafty enough to make his own way. Through twenty long years, that person

[2]Allen P. Ross, "Studies in the Life of Jacob, Part 2—Jacob at the Jabbok, Israel at Peniel," *BSac* 142 (1985): 350.

[3]Qtd. in Edward M. Curtis, "Structure, Style and Context as a Key to Interpreting Jacob's Encounter at Peniel," *JETS* 30 No. 2 (1987): 134–135.

[4]Allen P. Ross, "Studies in the Life of Jacob, Part 2—Jacob at the Jabbok, Israel at Peniel," *BSac* 142 (1985): 345.

had slowly changed. Now, he must be completely done away with. Instead, Israel, the man who had striven with God and prevailed, is the one who must return to Canaan.

The question that arises is why, unlike Abraham and Sarah, is he still referred to as Jacob sometimes? Why is his new name not permanent?

Leupold sees the answer as a distinction between a personal change and a divine blessing: "Since it represents a personal achievement rather than a divine destiny, as by way of contrast 'Abraham' does, it is used interchangeably with Jacob, according as the older or the newer type of character predominates. In this respect the use of the name Peter in the Gospels is a close parallel." Wenham notes several things about the name change. *Jacob* is used more frequently than *Israel* (31x vs. 20x), arguing that "since Jacob is the normal form, it is the exceptional appearance of Israel that needs to be explained." He also notes that, in prose, Jacob always refers to the historical individual while Israel sometimes refers to the people (46.8; 47.27; 48.20). When Israel is used of the individual, it seems to allude to his position as clan head (43.6, 8, 11; 46.1; 48.2), while Jacob seems to be used where his human weakness is most obvious (*e.g.*, 37.34; 42.4, 36; 47.9). "So Jacob turns into Israel when his strength revives (45.28; 48.2)." In contrast, Alter sees it as a straightforward synonym, citing later Old Testament use: "The narrative continues to refer to this patriarch in most instances as 'Jacob.' Thus, 'Israel' does not really replace his name but becomes a *synonym* for it—a practice reflected in the parallelism of biblical poetry, where 'Jacob' is always used in the first half of the line and 'Israel,' the poetic variation, in the second half."

33 *1, And Jacob lifted up his eyes… and behold, Esau was coming.* No sooner had he finished wrestling with God and crossed the river than he encounters Esau. Imagine the conflict of emotions that may have been aroused in Esau's heart as he marched to meet his brother. With 400 men flanking him, he was conscious of his greatness; with the memory of Jacob's treachery, he was thirsting for revenge; with the memories of his twin with whom he was raised and spent many years, he longed to see his brother.

So he divided the children. Jacob's actions do not mirror the previous plans of 32.7. There, he divided the family strategically to save half of them, in case of attack by Esau. Here, he simply divides them into three groups of mothers and children, with the two concubines forming a single group, for introduction to Esau (vv 6–7).

33.3, He himself went on before them. This action "shows us the new Israel triumphing over the old fear-dominated Jacob" (Wenham). Previously, Jacob had insisted on staying behind the party; now, he leads them.

Bowing himself to the ground seven times. Seven bows was a token of respect customarily given to kings, according to the Amarna tablets and other Ugaritic documents. This could simply be a showing of extra respect to Esau, or, if Esau had already conquered the region of Seir, Jacob could be bowing to him because of his high position.

33.4–5, Esau ran to meet him and embraced him. It is possible that all three emotions—pride, anger, affection—at once swelled within Esau, but the conflict of emotions was brought to a climax upon seeing Jacob; fraternal love won out. Kidner writes: "Guilt and forgiveness are so eloquent in every movement of the mutual approach (33.4), that our Lord could find no better model for the prodigal's father at this point than Esau (*cf.* v 4 with Luke 15.20)."

Esau's *running* to meet him may be meant to contrast with Jacob's limp.

And they wept. The other terms are normal ways of greeting relatives in the Bible. "But note here 'and *they* wept.' When Jacob joins in weeping with Esau, the ice is broken; the brothers are reconciled, and verbal communication can begin" (Wenham).

"Who are these with you?" Esau first asks about Jacob's family. In twenty years, Jacob had acquired quite an entourage. Jacob attributes his success to God, but mentions only the children in his response. "Perhaps he feels

that mentioning [the wives] would only resurrect in Esau's mind Jacob's departure some twenty years ago from Canaan to get a wife from Paddan-aram and Esau's involvement in that event. The more the past remains entombed, the better for Jacob" (Hamilton). [1]

33.8–9, "What do you mean by all this company that I met?" Esau next asks about the gifts that Jacob had sent ahead. Esau's question was not meant to learn information: certainly, the servants had done their job of relaying Jacob's message. Rather, his tone is that the gift should not have been given—he could not be the recipient of so great a gift.

"I have enough." Esau is also a wealthy man. He does not need Jacob's gift. But, "According to Isaac's blessing, he acquired it by war, not by farming or shepherding. …Both sons, each in his own way, have been blessed" (Waltke).

"My brother." "It is striking that he addresses Jacob as 'my brother'—the familial term…is generally a form of *affectionate* address in biblical Hebrew—while Jacob continues to call him 'my lord,' never swerving from the deferential terms of court etiquette" (Alter). And Hamilton: "Now that they are reunited, Esau desires a fraternal relationship, but Jacob is unable to move beyond a formal relationship."

"Keep what you have for yourself." "This is perhaps a double entendre for 'keep the droves' and, more subtly, 'keep the birthright and blessing'" (Waltke). If so, Esau would be indicating that he is no longer concerned about what caused the rift in their relationship.

33.10–11, "No, please." "Jacob is as insistent with Esau as he was with the man at Peniel. His 'I will not let you go unless you bless me' now becomes, in effect, 'I will not let you go unless you accept my gift'" (Hamilton).

"If I have found favor in your sight, accept my present from my hand." Jacob's gift is not just for show, but a sincere offer to Esau. Esau's acceptance, then, would be the surest sign that he had forgiven Jacob and they were reconciled to one another. The words *accept* and *present* are both important terms used for sacrifices and God's acceptance of them (*e.g.*, Lev 1.4; 7.18; 19.7 for *accept*; Gen 4.3–5; Lev 2.1, 3–7 for *present*). Thus, "Jacob's argument is that since you have received me with forgiveness as God has, so

---

[1] Hamilton also suggests that any declaration about the wives may start an autobiography with humiliating details: "Nor will he make a fool of himself by sharing with his brother how he was duped into polygamy. Not a word about that wedding night!"

you must accept my 'present'… as God would" (Wenham). And Mathews: "For Jacob the transformation of his moral character would be incomplete if he did not also experience reconciliation at the human dimension."

"For I have seen your face, which is like seeing the face of God." In Esau's face, Jacob saw a reflection of divine mercy. Esau held over him the power of life and death, and Jacob was spared. Curtis suggests: "The acceptance of Jacob which he saw on the face of Esau recalled for him the events at Peniel and confirmed for him that it was God who had changed Esau's heart to make it friendly."[2] And Waltke: "Jacob treats Esau as one who stands in God's stead. He bows down, pleads for grace, identifies Esau's pacified face with the pacified face of God, and offers tribute when he finds favor."

"Accept my blessing." Jacob changes the word for the gift. *Present* (v 10) would express the humility in the gift; *blessing,* here, expresses the good will in the offering (Kidner). Waltke suggests, "Jacob subtly makes reparation by offering a 'blessing' to Esau in exchange for the 'blessing' he had taken from him."

"Because I have enough." The Hebrew is different than what Esau says in verse 9. "Esau says he has plenty; Jacob says he has everything—on the surface, simply declaring that he doesn't need the flocks he is offering as a gift, but implicitly 'outbidding' his brother, obliquely referring to the comprehensiveness of the blessing he received from his father" (Alter).

And he took it. "By not offering a gift in exchange, Esau indicates that he accepts the gift as payment for the wrong done to him" (Waltke).

33.12–15, "Let us journey on our way, and I will go ahead of you." As an expression of good will, Esau suggests that they travel together. Perhaps there was in his mind the thought of the brothers joining together and engaging in great exploits. They had both been successful over the past twenty years; now, they can join together and enjoy even greater success.

"The children are frail… all the flocks will die." Jacob declines, quite honestly, because the children and cattle could not take the pace set by Esau's army—and, surely, the army would be somewhat annoyed by the slowed traveling pace. The animals were already overdriven in Jacob's escape from Laban; now, caution must be used lest they die. Perhaps, there was also in

---

[2] Edward M. Curtis, "Structure, Style and Context as a Key to Interpreting Jacob's Encounter at Peniel," *JETS* 30 No. 2 (1987): 136.

Jacob's mind the need for his camp to remain distinct from the one outside the blessing.

"Let my lord pass on ahead of his servant, and I will lead on slowly." Jacob suggests, sensibly, that each party travel at the pace best suited to their company.

"Until I come to my lord in Seir." … *But Jacob journeyed to Succoth.* Some have suggested that Jacob has already reverted to deception (*e.g.*, Kidner, Hamilton), but such is not necessarily the case. Jacob neither says nor implies that he will journey to Seir immediately. Surely, Esau would understand—and perhaps expect—that Jacob would seek to care for his hard-driven family and flock before he came to visit. Besides, we have no way of knowing that Jacob did not go visit Esau—he may have gone to visit several times in the parts of his life not detailed in Scripture. "The text has been candid heretofore about deception and obfuscation by Jacob, and its silence here implies that Jacob's action is not a violation of the peaceful intention agreed upon by the brothers" (Mathews). And Waltke: "The narrator implies that Esau bears him no grudge, for he draws this book to conclusion with the brothers in peace together burying their father (35.29)." Thus, it is presumptuous and speaks on thin evidence to say that this statement is Jacob reverting to old habits.

"Let me leave with you some of the people who are with me." Esau kindly suggests a guard to accompany his brother's company. Jacob replies that there is no need (*cf.* 32.1–2), and that Esau's good will is sufficient for him (to paraphrase: 'I'm just glad that you didn't kill me!').

33.16, Succoth. Succoth means *booths.* The name is derived from the action that Jacob took there (much like Jabbok).

And built himself a house. Jacob stops short of Bethel, which is his intended destination (*cf.* 28.19–22; 31.13). We do not know how much time he spends in Succoth, but that he builds a house and booths indicates that he plans for a lengthened stay. At the very least, sufficient time passes for Dinah to have aged enough to go out to *see the women of the land* by 34.1. "Succoth was a backward step, spiritually as well as geographically [*i.e.*, North]: it is difficult to reconcile the call to Bethel with the prolonged stay involved in building cattle sheds… and a house, east of the Jordan" (Kidner).

33.18–20, Jacob came safely to the city of Shechem. This note sets the stage for the events of the next chapter.

Which is in the land of Canaan. However long he stayed in Succoth was time that he remained outside the Promised Land. "In reality the land of Canaan was not reached till the Jordan was crossed" (Leupold).

He bought… the piece of land on which he had pitched his tent. This piece of land would later become the burial plot of Joseph (*cf.* Josh 24.32). Further, "This purchase showed that Jacob, in reliance upon the promise of God, regarded Canaan as his own home and the home of his seed" (Keil).

There he erected an altar. Jacob's return to Canaan ends the same way as Abraham's journey: settling in Shechem and worshipping (*cf.* 12.6–9). "Although purchasing the land and erecting the altar were acts of faith, Jacob errs in settling into the land. He made a vow to worship in Bethel when he returned to the Promised Land, but it takes him at least ten years to fulfill this vow. The idle years near the Canaanite city reflect a general spiritual passivity on Jacob's part that has horrendous consequences" (Waltke).

Growth of the Seed: Jacob continues return to the Promised Land.

34 *1, Now Dinah the daughter of Leah.* That the Old Testament would trace a person's lineage through the mother *(i.e., the daughter of Leah)* is unusual (see Hamilton). Here, "The importance of Dinah as 'the daughter of Leah' is her full-blood relationship to Simeon and Levi... this connection is emphasized by the author in verse 25 ('Dinah's brothers')" (Mathews).

Went out to see. This is the beginning of Dinah's problem. Family history alone should have told her that it was unwise to go among the Palestinians as an unwed woman: "She should have known that Egyptians and Canaanites (12.15; 20.2; 26.7) regarded unmarried women abroad in the land as legitimate prey and should not have gone about unattended" (Leupold). Although we are not told what her intentions were, it isn't a far stretch to suggest that she may have been looking for trouble—such would certainly match her brothers' estimation of this event (*cf.* v 31). This would certainly be the correct understanding if Hamilton's translation—*to be seen among the women of the land*—is followed.[1]

The women of the land. "This is another critical comment on Dinah's behavior. The lifestyles of Canaanite women repulsed Abraham, Isaac, and Rebekah" (Waltke).

Most estimate Dinah's age to be around 14 or 15 at this point.[2] This may seem young to a modern mind, but it was prime marrying age in the ancient Near East.

34.2–4, And when Shechem the son of Hamor the Hivite, the prince of the land, saw her, he seized her and lay with her.

As the son of a prince, Shechem assumed that he could have anyone he wanted, anytime he wanted.

Humiliated her. This is a better translation of the Hebrew than any rendering that implies rape *(e.g., NASB: lay with her by force)*. Although the

---

[1]Two further arguments could be made to this end. Wenham notes that an Akkadian cognate of the verb "describes a housewife who conducts herself improperly outside her home" and also notes that "the targums translate 'cult prostitute' as 'one who goes out in the countryside.'" Second, ancient Jewish interpretation made a connection between Leah's mention here and Dinah's action, noting that Leah *went out* to allure Jacob (30.16), thereby condemning Dinah's action.

[2]Keil writes, "There is no ground for supposing her to have been younger [than 13]. Even if she was born after Joseph, and not till the end of Jacob's 14 years' service with Laban, and therefore was only five years old when they left Mesopotamia, eight or ten years may have passed since then, as Jacob may easily have spent from eight to eleven years in Succoth. ...But she cannot have been older [than 15]; for, according to 37.2, Joseph was sold by his brethren when he was 17 years old, *i.e.*, in the 11th year after Jacob's return from Mesopotamia."

word used can mean rape, it does not always mean so—context must determine the meaning. See Excursus K.

And his soul was drawn to Dinah. ...He loved the young woman and spoke tenderly to her. ..."Get me this girl for my wife." Alter notes: "The psychology of the rapist is precisely the opposite of Amnon's in 2 Samuel 13, who, after having consummated his lust for his sister by raping her, despises her." Alter may well have written that the psychology of Shechem is precisely the opposite of *all rapists.* Indeed, this would be odd, unparalleled behavior for a rapist.

34.5, Defiled. Waltke notes: "The word tips the hand of the narrator's evaluation of the incident. This was an act not of mere guilt but of defilement (*i.e.,* ritual uncleanness, an outcast state)."

[Jacob's] sons were with his livestock in the field, so Jacob held his peace until they came. As has been previously noted, brothers played a significant role in a sister's marriage. Jacob, meanwhile, remains strangely silent. Mathews offers: "The narrative suggests by these differences between Jacob and the other participants' involvement that Jacob has lost the respect of the community and his household, revealing the ascendancy of his sons, as he helplessly stands by and witnesses concomitantly their growing moral corruption."

34.7, The men were indignant. The word translated *indignant* is translated elsewhere *shocked* or *hurt,* indicating its effect on the brothers. Waltke notes that the word "is found elsewhere only for God's reaction to human wickedness. ...These proper emotions are assigned to the brothers, not Jacob." Of course, what began as proper emotions quickly turned to deceit and murder.

He had done an outrageous thing. This phrase is often used in the Old Testament for "crimes against the honor and calling of Israel as the people of God, especially for shameful sins of the flesh (Deut 22.21; Jdg 20.10; 2 Sam 13.12, *etc.)*" (Keil).

In Israel. The precise meaning of this phrase in context is not clear. It could have been solely used for Moses' original audience as he sought to emphasize the necessity to marry within the race. It may signify that the growing family already considered themselves to be *Israel* from which the nation would continue to develop. Or it could be intended to mean *against* Israel.

34.8–10, Hamor spoke with them. Again, notice the brothers' part of the process of negotiating a bride price/wedding arrangement. *(cf. 24.50).*

"The soul of my son Shechem longs for your daughter." Although he seems to be addressing Jacob *(daughter)*, the pronoun is plural indicating that the brothers are still in consideration, "recognizing that the brothers took a paternal stance toward their sister (*cf.* 24.50; 2 Sam 13.20, 32; Song 1.6)" (Mathews). Hamor doesn't seem to think that anything improper has happened. If it *was* a rape, he has either been left in the dark by his son or is experiencing the ultimate case of parental blindness to a wicked son's actions.

"Make marriages with us. ...You shall dwell with us." "They feel that Jacob's clan should feel honored at the proposal of a matrimonial alliance with their own princely line. Or at least they anticipate that a financial adjustment may smooth out all misunderstanding" (Leupold). But to intermarry with them would be against everything that the fledgling nation stood for. Waltke points out an interesting dilemma now faced: "The narrator does not spell out precisely how Jacob's children should have secured spouses in the land of Canaan. After the hostilities between Jacob and the Arameans, the option of returning to Paddan Aram is essentially ruled out. Probably, since they had four different mothers, they could have married among themselves even as Esau married the daughters of Ishmael. Moreover, they could have honestly insisted upon the circumcision and religious purity of males who married their daughters, and their males could have married Canaanites such as Tamar and Rahab, who embraced their lifestyle and worldview."

34.11–12, Shechem also said… "Let me find favor in your eyes, and whatever you say to me I will give. Ask me for as great a bride price and gift as you will, and I will give whatever you say to me. Only give me the young woman to be my wife." Shechem further shows how far his mindset is from that of a rapist by imploring the brothers to like him and indicating that he loves Dinah so much that he is willing to pay whatever price they name—a willingness the brothers will take full advantage of.

34.13–17, The sons of Jacob answered Shechem and his father Hamor deceitfully. Jacob's sons—Simeon and Levi, in particular—devise a plan to exact revenge. There are, of course, a couple of moral problems in these verses. The most obvious problem is their deceit and plan to murder the

Shechemites. Beyond that is the fact that Jacob silently agreed. It seems as though he didn't know of their plan (v 30); he did, however, seem perfectly agreeable to allow Dinah to intermarry if they were but circumcised. Jacob—who still has not made it to Bethel or purged the idols from his household (*cf.* 35.1–3)—seems to have slipped in this matter.

Although it is not enough to rectify the entire situation, some good can be said of this—little though it may be. It does show that Jacob had taught his sons about God and being in a covenant-relationship with Him. They knew enough to know that circumcision was important—so important that marrying an uncircumcised man would *"be a disgrace to us."* Indeed, Jacob's sons were right in saying that Dinah could not marry an uncircumcised man. But outward circumcision alone would not put the Shechemites in covenant relationship with God anymore than someone merely saying he believes means he has saving faith or being dunked under water means he has been born again. "They sacrilegiously and reprehensibly empty the holy covenant sign of its religious significance, commitment by faith to Abraham's God, and abuse it to inflict vengeance" (Waltke).

Of course, circumcision was not the brother's real plan anyway—but it seems to have been enough to satisfy Jacob.

"Become as we are by every male among you being circumcised." In order for the clans to merge by intermarriage (v 16), everyone in the town would need to conform to the Israelites' customs. A demand such as this need not be considered odd. Religious rites such as this would often be required in order for such a contract to be negotiated (Kidner). Alter suggests that this would be "a physical sign of their collective identity, but also the infliction of pain on what is in this case the offending organ." And Sarna: "The part of the body used by Shechem in his violent passion will itself become the source of his own punishment!" (qtd. in Waltke).

"If you will not… be circumcised, then we will take our daughter and we will be gone." The brothers make a strong demand of Shechem—all or nothing. Perhaps they hoped that not everyone could be convinced. But even if that was their original intention, they still practiced deceit, as they never had any intention of letting Dinah stay among them.

Those commentators who are befuddled by Hamor and Shechem holding Dinah hostage (*e.g.,* Waltke) would find their problem resolved if they would accept an interpretation to this chapter other than rape. If she was seduced, as we believe, she is staying in Shechem's house at her own volition, not under duress. Then, if no marriage terms could be agreed upon, the father and brothers would have the right to take her back to their clan.

34.18, The words pleased Hamor and Hamor's son Shechem. The suggestion was pleasing to Shechem since he wanted, above all, Dinah's hand. He had told the brothers to name their price; now, he shows that he was serious in that offer. And the words pleased his father, because he wanted the happiness of his son. Or, as Mathews succinctly says, "Shechem would gain his wife and Hamor a business interest." Now, they just needed to make it appealing to everyone else.

34.19–24, [Shechem] was the most honored of all his father's house. A good starting point for Shechem to convince the people is that he was well liked. Some leaders have the quality about them that makes people willing to follow wherever they lead. That Shechem was the most honored in his father's house would make the proposal much more palatable. "Another young man less respected than Shechem might not have been heeded by the villagers in the proposition on which his marriage hinged" (Leupold).

The gate of their city. See comment on 19.1.

"These men are at peace with us." The story reaches its ironic peak.

"The land is large enough for them." Their intermingling will not cause any property disputes; there is plenty of land for all of them and all of us.'

"Will not their livestock, their property and all their beasts be ours?" It was evident even to these people that Jacob was extremely wealthy, and that making a pact to intermarry with Jacob's family was a wise choice from a perspective of financial gain. Also, they expected this family to blend in with their people. Leupold says, "The Hivites apparently predominated in numbers, and so there was no danger that they would become submerged in the process"— thus, these things would have become theirs.

Notice what is left out of their speech to the villagers. They do not mention the personal vendetta (*i.e.*, Dinah), nor do they mention the financial benefit that the Israelites stand to gain. Hamor and Shechem are politicians of the finest form! "Like other political leaders in the world, they make their own lust appear to be in the interest of the community" (Waltke). And Wenham: "Certainly this disclosure of Hamor and Shechem's double-dealing and the avarice of their fellow citizens tends to reduce our shock at the fate that is about to overtake them."

34.25, On the third day, when they were sore. The lack of medical technology—anesthetics, instruments that would make the procedure the least painful, and post-procedure pain killers—would have led to a more painful circumcision and a longer recovery time. Also, wounds of this nature are at their worst on the third day. "In this instance it was known to be the third day when a man was incapacitated in a very special sense" (Leupold). And, "The fever that would develop as a result of the operation would only make the condition of the recently circumcised more intolerable" (Hamilton).

Simeon and Levi. Dinah's full brothers.[3]

Took their swords and came against the city... and killed all the males. It is noteworthy that they *took* their swords, as this word has shown up repeatedly through this narrative. "That Simeon and Levi 'took' swords (v 25) and 'took' back their sister (v 26) directly answers the crime of Shechem who 'took' Dinah (v 2)" (Mathews).

Some have sought to excuse their actions by citing the necessity to remain separate from the nations or to take vengeance. There is, of course, a problem with both of those suggestions. Murder was not necessary to remain separate from the nations. Second, if vengeance was the motive, murder of that magnitude was not necessary—if vengeance was even called for. Even under the law of Moses, their sin only required marriage (*cf.* Deut 22.28–29).

Took Dinah out of Shechem's house. Was she being held as a hostage or had she been seduced by Shechem, wooed by his words spoken to her heart, and stayed by her own choice? Did they, perhaps, *take* her because she did not *want* to go, or is that just the word chosen for *rescue?*

34.27–29, The sons of Jacob came upon the slain and plundered the city. Either *the sons* is intended to be understood as still referring to Simeon and Levi or the sons who did not participate in the killing now participated in the looting. Most commentators prefer the latter interpretation.

All their little ones and their wives. Most likely, they were made slaves.

34.30, "You have brought trouble on me by making me stink to the inhabitants of the land." Here is Jacob's only strong reaction in the entire chap-

---

[3]Reuben and Judah do not take part in this, presumably because they have something of a moral compass (*cf.* 37.22; 44.18–34). Issachar and Zebulun either share their morality or are still too young for a murderous rampage.

ter and it is more focused on the social issues than the moral ones. It may be argued, as Keil does, that this social focus was because "this was the view most adapted to make an impression upon his sons." His final say on this event (49.5–7) "is proof that the wickedness of their conduct was also an object of deep abhorrence" (Keil). Mathews says, "Their crime from Jacob's viewpoint shamed their father. …This was in effect an attack on his patriarchal position; their conduct could be likened to the sin of Reuben, whose incest challenged the integrity of Jacob and his household. The cohesion of the family is crumbling, and Jacob is impotent to stop it." Waltke points out the change from *your daughter* (v 1) to *our sister* (v 31), calling it "another symbol of the terrible family split."

"My numbers are few." Has he forgotten the double camp and the angels who have watched his journey? Has he forgotten his wrestling match that indicated that Esau and his men were no cause of concern? What has happened to the faith of Jacob? Jacob's fear of the inhabitants was not without basis, but he should have known that God would protect him (*cf.* 35.5).

34.31, But they said, "Should he treat our sister like a prostitute?" The brothers are impatient with Jacob's rebuke and snap back with their assessment of what had gone on—and their self-justification. Although Jacob allows them the last word for now, he will ultimately have the final say regarding this argument (*cf.* 49.5–7).

And their assessment passes judgment on their sister. If she had been the victim of rape, these words are the most insensitive and cruel—not to mention inaccurate—thing they could have possibly said.[4]

Growth of the Seed: Simeon and Levi are rejected from the Messianic line due to their wrath (*cf.* 49.7).

---

[4]For those interpreters who prefer to understand this as rape, a plausible alternative to this interpretation is offered by Mathews: "By offering them money for Dinah's hand, the brothers interpreted this as prostitution." It seems more likely that they understood Shechem's gift for what it was—a bride price—and the impetus of their words falls on Dinah.

Excursus K: Was Dinah Raped?

This event is usually referred to as the rape of Dinah. Every commentary we have consulted understands it to be rape. Virtually all of the paraphrase-Bibles say that Shechem *raped* Dinah. Even the NASB says that *he took her and lay with her by force.* This last phrase of verse 2 is what raises the question of whether she was raped or not: *he humbled her.* Therein lies the heart of his issue: was Shechem's humbling of Dinah a rape?

Evidence from the Hebrew

Something that we must consider is how Moses uses this word *(anah)* in other places. Deuteronomy 22.23–29 contains laws regarding sexual crimes. As Bechtel notes, this serves as excellent inter-biblical commentary on Moses' use of the word *anah*.[1]

In verses 23–24, a woman was to be stoned along with the man for not crying out for help when a man *humbled (anah) her.* The woman was executed because she was a participant in the guilt; clearly, this is not an instance of rape.

In verses 28–29, the same word is used. Here the man *humbles (anah)* a virgin. For doing this, he is to pay a dowry and marry the woman. Although some commentators would not agree, we would suggest that this is not rape either. At the very least, it is beyond our comprehension to suggest that a girl marry her rapist—or that a rapist would desire to marry his victim.

Nestled between those two laws is one that clearly pertains to rape (vv 25–27). Here, only the man will die, because *she has committed no offense punishable by death. For this case is like that of a man attacking and murdering his neighbor because he met her in the open country, and though the betrothed young woman cried for help there was no one to rescue her* (26–27). Interestingly, the one instance where rape is unquestionably being addressed, our word—*anah*—is nowhere to be found.

Although Moses' use may imply that rape is not meant, this alone does not prove that the word itself cannot mean rape. In fact, there are some places in Scripture where it clearly *does* mean rape (*e.g.,* 2 Sam 13.12–14; Lam 5.11). It does, however, indicate that *anah* does not *always* mean rape. It would seem that a good working definition for this word would be "the 'humiliation' or 'shaming' of a woman through certain kinds of sexual intercourse including rape, though not necessarily."[2] The context must determine whether or not rape is the intended meaning. The context of this chapter does not lead to that conclusion.

---

[1] See Lyn M. Bechtel, "What if Dinah is not Raped?" *JSOT* 62 (1994): 25–27.

[2] *Ibid.,* 24.

348 | *The Growth of the Seed*

Evidence from Shechem's Action
Shechem's soul was drawn to Dinah. He loved her and spoke to her heart (v 3), a phrase that connotes reassurance, comfort, loyalty, and love. He immediately went to his father to ask for Dinah as a wife (v 4). He sought favor in the eyes of Jacob's family (v 11). These are all things which are irreconcilable with a rapist's mindset. Such behavior would be unprecedented in a rapist. By contrast, psychological and sociological studies have conclusively proven that rape is about hostility, hatred and power, not love and devotion.

Evidence from Dinah's Action
It could be argued that although he did not think it to be rape, she did. The problem with this interpretation is that it seems she was sufficiently enamored by Shechem that she was in no hurry to leave. Even after the men were too incapacitated to fight for their lives, she is still in Shechem's house and her brothers have to *take* her out of it (v 26). Kidner suggests: "It was not a casual liaison, but one with a view to marriage, for Dinah remained in Shechem's house."

Further, as noted in the comments above, it may be that her original intent was less than pure.[3]

Evidence from the Brothers' Words
We learn more from the brothers' response to Jacob: *"Should he treat our sister like a prostitute?"* (v 31). This also seems to imply that they understood it was not rape. Prostitutes are known more for seeking trouble than they are for being raped. Perhaps this explains verse 1. She must have known, especially after Abraham and Isaac's experiences, that single women were eagerly taken by Palestinian men (*cf.* Gen. 20, 26). The brothers' estimation of her as being treated like a prostitute may point back to her intent in going out. Bechtel writes: "By saying that Dinah has become like a harlot, the sons of Jacob show that they do not regard Dinah as having been raped. Instead, they are pointing to the fact that she has become a marginal figure by engaging in sexual activity outside her society."[4]

Evidence from Jacob's Reaction
We cannot find much evidence in Jacob's reaction as to whether Dinah was raped or seduced. For that matter, there doesn't seem to be much reaction on Jacob's part at all. He held his peace until his sons came. Beyond that, his only reaction is directed toward the revenge taken by Simeon and Levi, not the action

---

[3]See comment on 34.1.

[4]*Ibid.*, 31.

of Shechem. While it would not be prudent to build an entire case on Jacob's in-action, it seems odd that a father would not react at all to his daughter's rape.

Conclusion

Thus, we conclude from the context that Dinah was not raped, but seduced. Her humiliation was something in which she willingly took part. "Ironically, if there is a rape in this story, it is Simeon and Levi who 'rape' the Shechemites. It is their behavior that is violent and hostile, carried out for the purpose of exploitation."[5] [6]

---

[5]*Ibid.*, 34.

[6]For those who would interpret this as a rape and seek to do so on contextual grounds, the best argument to that end is based the linguistic pun made between Jacob's sons reply to Shechem and Shechem's action against Dinah—the verb for *replied* (v 13) has the same Hebrew consonants as the word for *humiliated* (v 3) (Hamilton). The original audience may have been intended to see a play on the words and understand from Simeon and Levi's rape of the Shechemites that Shechem had also raped Dinah. A lesser argument may be made from the statement that Shechem *spoke tenderly to her.* Hamilton notes: "The expression occurs ten times in the OT, always in less than ideal situations, where there is a sense of guilt or repentance, where A attempts to persuade B of his feelings." This, however, could just as easily point to Shechem seeking forgiveness for a non-forced, illicit sexual relationship with Dinah.

35 *1, "Arise, go up to Bethel."* "Jacob's life has been one of 'rising and going.' Such a directive came from his mother (27.43), from his father (28.2), and from the 'God of Bethel' (31.13). It is now the God of Bethel who summons Jacob back to Bethel" (Hamilton). It took a second call from God (*cf.* 31.3) to get Jacob to finish the journey that he had vowed to make. He had come back from Haran, but he had not yet made it to Bethel. Instead, he had allowed some ten years to pass without performing the vow he had made, even though it was called to his mind when he began his return (31.11–13).

"Make an altar there." Cf. 28.18–22. God would allow this neglect no longer. His call to Jacob to return to Bethel and build the altar marked the end of a beginning, bringing to a close this period of Jacob's life. Interestingly, this is the only instance of God commanding a patriarch to build an altar. Is it because Jacob had failed to do so under his own volition?

35.2–3, "Put away the foreign gods." Jacob's neglect went beyond his lack of return to Bethel. Even after the spiritual height he reached at Jabbok, he had not fully purified his household from idolatry. God's call to him stirred him to perform what had been neglected. "It is to Jacob's credit that he himself is responsible for suggesting the extirpation of the gods. That was not a part of God's directive to Jacob in the previous verse. He intuitively senses that the continued presence of these gods is irreconcilable with the new life he has found in Yahweh. The whole incident must be read as an illustration of Jacob's religious maturation" (Hamilton). See Theological Reflection below.

"Purify yourselves and change your garments." Before moving along at God's word, his household needed a thorough repentance and purging. "Chapter 34 is dominated by the theme of defilement; this chapter opens with the subject of purification" (Sarna qtd. in Alter). And Wenham: "Worship, which brings one into the presence of a holy God, demands inward and outward purity, the latter being seen as an expression of the former."

"Then let us arise and go up to Bethel." The decision to go almost seems too resolute. But, as Waltke notes, "It takes courage for the militant family to travel through hostile territory. They had been known as peaceful shepherds, but now they are known for their violent acts."

"Who answers me in the day of my distress and has been with me wherever I have gone." Cf. 28.20–21. Jacob remembers the precise reason he is returning to Bethel: God had kept the vow.

35.4, So they gave to Jacob all the foreign gods that they had. Jacob's command was kept to the letter. But this must have also included a terribly dramatic scene that goes unmentioned. Surely, *all the foreign gods* included the household idols that Rachel had stolen from her father. Does he immediately hear his own words: *Anyone with whom you find your gods shall not live* (31.32)? Does he wish he could recant his outburst of righteous indignation following Laban's failed search (31.36–37)? Can he ever look at Rachel the same way again? Tucker, among others, believes that Jacob carried with him a burden after this—that he felt, in effect, that his words led to Rachel's untimely death: "It is, indeed, in the very next scene, immediately upon leaving Bethel, that Rachel goes into labor and dies in childbirth."[1] Whether or not Jacob's curse upon the thief was the cause of Rachel's death is unknowable. It is not, however, a stretch to believe that Jacob would rue those words for the rest of his life.

In addition to the household gods that Rachel had taken, idols may have come from the servants acquired while in Mesopotamia and any idols obtained during the plundering of Shechem.

And the rings that were in their ears. "As archaeology has abundantly discovered, earrings were often fashioned as figurines of gods and goddesses" (Alter).

The terebinth tree that was near Shechem. Jacob's journey parallels Abraham's original journey (*cf.* 12.6; see comment on 32.1–2; 33.20), though his relation to this tree is different than his grandfather's.

35.5–7, A terror from God fell upon the cities... they did not pursue the sons of Jacob. God gave them safe passage, presumably against revenge (*cf.* 34.30).[2]

He and all the people who were with him. The first time Jacob came to Bethel, he came alone. Now he returns with a great company—God was beginning to fulfill his promise (28.14)

There he built an altar. Finally, having purged his household, Jacob fulfills his vow.

---

[1] Gordon Tucker, "Jacob's Terrible Burden in the Shadow of the Text," *BR* June (1994): 25–26. Tucker also suggests that Jacob may have felt responsible for Joseph's supposed death, since he was in the tent with Rachel. And if she was already pregnant with Benjamin, he would have been in the tent also, which would explain "Jacob's refusal, even at the risk of starvation, to allow Benjamin to leave him and journey with his brothers to Egypt" (27).

[2] Hamilton notes an interesting contrast: "Throughout his life Jacob has had to contend with his own fears—fear of God (28.17), fear of Laban (31.31), fear of Esau (32.7, 11). Nobody has been in fear of him. Angry, yes; fearful, no. On Jacob's travels from Shechem, that all changes."

El-bethel. Hamilton explains the change of names: "Jacob's memories of two experiences at Bethel (chapters 28 and 35) will recall for a long time to come the God Jacob encountered there, rather than recall Bethel as a divine residence, a holy site. 'The God of the House of God' rather than simply 'The House of God.'"

35.8, Deborah, Rebekah's nurse, died. The record of this event is something of a surprise, especially since Rebekah's own death is not recorded. It seems that Deborah had joined Jacob at a later date (after the death of Rebekah?). Mathews writes that her death is included "to symbolize the end of the prior generation; she represents the older generation, as does Isaac (vv 28–29)," though this does not explain why she is used for this purpose rather than Rebekah. Waltke's suggestion may have merit: "Scripture memorializes the death of the aged, faithful nurse of Rebekah (see 24.59), not the matriarch herself, probably because she deceived Isaac and because Jacob was not present when she died."

Of Deborah, Luther wrote: "She was a wise and godly matron, who had served and advised Jacob, had supervised the domestics of the household and had often counseled and comforted Jacob in dangers and difficulties" (qtd. in Leupold). Undoubtedly, Luther's assertion is somewhat speculative, though we would not be surprised if much of it were true. At the very least, we may firmly agree with Keil: "The mourning at her death, and the perpetuation of her memory, are proofs that she must have been a faithful and highly esteemed servant in Jacob's house." McGuiggan compares her with the better-known Deborah of the Bible, saying, "Deborah the prophet undoubtedly served Israel more *conspicuously* but hardly more significantly than Deborah the nurse,"[3] ultimately pointing to the practical truth that all in God's kingdom play important roles, even if they are not seen by the masses.

35.9–10, God appeared to Jacob again… and blessed him. The former promise to Jacob was to be with him while he was in Haran. That promise complete and the vow kept, God extends the promise to the remainder of Jacob's life. "Just as Abraham's three-day pilgrimage to sacrifice on Mount Moriah climaxed in the most categorical reaffirmation of the promises in his career, so, too, Jacob's sacred journey is crowned with the strongest

---

[3]Jim McGuigan, *Genesis and Us*, 241.

statement of the promises that he ever heard, summing up and adding to what had been said to him on earlier occasions" (Wenham).

"No longer shall you be called Jacob." God confirms the renaming of Jacob. If there had been any doubt in Jacob's mind as to the identity of his opponent in wrestling, this would certainly have confirmed it. Moreover, this offers a different viewpoint to the renaming: "In the first naming, the context of chapters 32–33 focused the reader on the patriarch's transformation, from 'Jacob' the trickster to 'Israel' the one blessed of God. Here the context highlights the national and royal importance of the name, shown by the new character of the promises in verse 11 and the first formal listing of his twelve tribal descendants (vv 23–26)" (Mathews). And Alter: "In this instance, moreover, the new name is a sign of Jacob's glorious future rather than of the triumphs he has already achieved." But perhaps Hamilton's comments are the most apt: "Jacob is reminded that he returns to Canaan not as Jacob but as Israel. He is not only to bury the foreign gods, but he is to bury what has become for all practical purposes a foreign nature—a Jacob nature. He who earlier instructed the people to change their garments must live up to his own change of name."

35.11–12, *"I am God Almighty."* God identifies himself to Jacob as He had identified Himself to the other patriarchs, indicating clearly that He was the same God.

"Be fruitful and multiply." As Jacob seems to have already done his part in this, this command most likely has his children in view. This is supported by God's next words: a great nation coming from Jacob.

"A nation shall come from you. …The land that I gave to Abraham and Isaac I will give to you." Interestingly, only two parts of the three-part promise are repeated. Why is the seed not mentioned? Could it be, as Leupold notes, "This most prominent part of the blessing had been laid hold upon by the faith of Jacob so decisively and retained so firmly that it required no repetition"? While we would regard Leupold as overstating his case, we have no alternate theory to propose.

35.14-15, *Jacob set up a pillar.* Verses 14–15 reproduce almost exactly his original act in 28.18–19. " 'New perils past, new sins forgiven' separate the two occasions, to make the second inwardly richer than the first. God's repetitions, if this is a sample, are turns of a spiral rather than a wheel" (Kidner).

35.16–20, Then they journeyed from Bethel. No reason is given for their journey. Presumably, it was to *"come again in to my father's house in peace"* (28.21).

Rachel went into labor. ... So Rachel died. "No sooner has Jacob finished with one funeral [Deborah's] than he is involved with a second one—Rachel's. ...It is ironic that Rachel, who earlier had proclaimed she would die if she had no children (30.1), and who gave to her firstborn the name Joseph, implying a yearning for another son (30.22–24), dies at the birth of this avidly looked-for second son" (Hamilton).[4]

35.22, Reuben went and lay with Bilhah his father's concubine. The motivation for this act is not given, nor whether Bilhah was a willing participant or was raped.[5] But this event serves to explain why Reuben is never respected as the family leader, either among the brothers or by Jacob.[6] It also prepares the reader for the blessing—or lack thereof—that Reuben will receive (*cf.* 49.3–4).

It seems as though all of Jacob's post-return woes are neatly packaged up into two chapters: Dinah's defilement; Simeon and Levi's vengeance; Deborah's death; Rachel's death; Reuben's incest. But the hardest trial—the deceit of his sons as they sell Joseph into slavery—is yet to come.

35.22b–26, Now the sons of Jacob were twelve. The family and history of Isaac complete, this is the ideal place to list the family in order.

35.29, Isaac breathed his last, and he died. "From that time onward Jacob enters into the full patriarchal heritage, having at last attained to a spiritual maturity which is analogous to that of the patriarch" (Leupold).

Was gathered to his people. See comment on 25.8.

His sons Esau and Jacob buried him. If Jacob had deceived Esau as some suppose (*cf.* 33.13–17), there is no lingering strain on their relationship. Either the death of their father cures all wounds, or Jacob had not acted as deceitfully as some would suggest.

---

[4]See EXCURSUS L and comment on 35.4.

[5]Various suggestions have been made for Reuben's motive. Mathews presumes the motive to be "A grasp for power, a symbolic action indicating his claim to his father's place. That this was a customary gesture of royal usurpation is attested in Israel's history (*e.g.,* 2 Sam 12.8,11; 16.20–21 with 20.3; 1 Kgs 2.22; 20.3–7). Since Bilhah was the maidservant of Rachel, the favorite wife of Jacob, his affront was a pointed claim to Jacob's place." And Waltke: "By defiling Bilhah, he makes certain that with Rachel's death her handmaid cannot supplant Leah as chief wife."

[6]See contrast of Judah and Reuben in EXCURSUS N.

Growth of the Seed: Jacob completes his return to the Promised Land; his covenant name is renewed (v 10); the covenant is renewed with Jacob (vv 11–12); Reuben is rejected from the Messianic line (v 22; *cf.* 49.3–4).

Theological Reflection: Jacob's Repentance
Jacob's exorcising of the family's idols serves as a model of repentance to all followers of God after him. Jacob called his family together and gave them three pieces of instruction which they needed to follow to make their repentance complete. His words closely parallel what Paul would later tell Christians about this same process: *Put off your old self, which belongs to your former manner of life and is corrupt through deceitful desires, and… be renewed in the spirit of your minds, and… put on the new self, created after the likeness of God in true righteousness and holiness* (Eph 4.22–24).

God's desire for His people in repentance has not changed in the thousands of years since Jacob instructed his family. Though the law may have changed, and with it the way we go about serving Him, God has not. In Jacob's message to his family, there is much we can learn about how God would have us repent.

Put away the foreign gods, or as Paul says, *put off your old self.* The first step needed to make a true repentance is to put the wickedness away. One certainly cannot make an honest effort to change if he is trying to drag the sin around with him, keeping it as close as possible while trying to not cross that line.

Purify yourselves. Here, Paul says, *be renewed in the spirit of your minds.* In both wordings, the message is the same. Change your heart. Once one has put away the outward act of sin, it is time to look inside. An illness is not overcome by treating the symptoms, but by getting to the root of the problem. Likewise, one can never overcome sin if he does not get to the root of the problem—the heart.

Change your garments. *Put on the new self.* One must be clothed with something once he has removed the old self and renewed the mind. If he does not put on new garments, he will quickly retake the old ones. Time must be filled with spiritual things, not the same worldly things that used to fill it.

These are the steps that God requires the penitent sinner to take in restoring a right relationship with Him. It has never been enough to make a superficial apology while secretly planning the next sin (*cf.* Joel 2.12–13).

Excursus L:
Rachel or Leah: The True Love Story of Jacob

The great love story of Jacob is familiar: he saw the beautiful Rachel, immediately fell in love with her, and was willing to work seven years for her hand in marriage—years that flew by because he loved her so much. Then, upon being deceived by Laban, he was willing to work *another* seven years—14 total—to be the husband of the woman he loved so dearly (though he was allowed to marry her *before* the second set of seven years, 29.27–30). The love story of Jacob and Rachel has the kind of plot that Hollywood thrives on. It is rare, however, that Hollywood love stories represent the kind of love stories that God would want His people to live. We propose that the great love story told in Jacob's life is not his great love for Rachel, but that he learned to love Leah—and, in the end, it was Leah who had the greater hold on his heart.

This excursus will take us through the development of character in Rachel and Leah as Genesis tells the story, and how character led Jacob to his ultimate choice.[1]

The Naming of Children: Hints of Character (29.31–30.24; 35.16–18)
The first thing that we read about after the marriages of Jacob is the births of his children. Rachel and Leah both play a prominent role in this section of the story, as they name the children. The meanings of the children's names, what their mothers say at the naming, and their actions surrounding the births of the children shed much light on the hearts of these women and help show their character.

Leah's First Four (29.31–35): Yahweh saw that Leah was not loved as Rachel was, so He opened her womb to bear children.

Her first son is born and she names him Reuben *(Look, A Son!),* saying, *"Because [Yahweh] has looked upon my affliction; for now my husband will love me."* She acknowledges Yahweh's gift and displays hope that this will change Jacob's attitude toward her.

Simeon *(hearing, heard, famous)* is born next. At this time, she says, *"Because [Yahweh] has heard that I am hated, he has given me this son also."* Again, she acknowledges Yahweh in the naming of this son.

Levi *(joined/attached to)* is born next. *"Now this time my husband will be attached to me, because I have borne him three sons,"* Leah says at his birth. Here she does not attribute the child to Yahweh, but her attitude is one of optimism and hope that Jacob will change his outlook toward her.

---

[1]Parts of this excursus have come from the work done by Dene Ward in her teacher's manual for *Born of a Woman: Woman's Place in the Scheme of Redemption.*

Judah *(praised)* is her fourth child. *"This time,"* she says, *"I will praise [Yahweh]."* Notice that she no longer speaks of her yearning for the love of Jacob. Either Jacob has started to show her more affection or she has realized it is futile to fight for this, and has decided to just commit the issue into the hands of Yahweh, simply praising Him and being thankful.

The common feature in the names and statements surrounding the births of Leah's first four children is her attribution of them to Yahweh, and her hopefulness for Jacob's love.

Bilhah's Two Sons (30.1–8): After seeing that she still could bear no children, Rachel gives her handmaid Bilhah to Jacob as a wife, that *"she may give birth on my behalf"* (v 3).

Bilhah's first child is named Dan *(judge, judgment),* and Rachel says, *"God has judged me, and has also heard my voice and given me a son."* What case has God judged? Contextually, it would seem that she is referring to the ongoing sibling rivalry between herself and Leah. Rachel is saying that God has judged in favor of her, and the birth of Dan through Bilhah is evidence of the verdict. Finally she has a child she can call her own, and in naming him, she gives no glory to God—she simply uses Him to boast about a supposed victory over her sister.

Next, Bilhah gives birth to Naphtali *(my wrestling).* At his birth, Rachel says, *"With mighty wrestlings I have wrestled with my sister and have prevailed."* Again, she fails to acknowledge God in the birth of this son, using his naming only as an opportunity to boast of a victory over her sister.

Zilpah's Two Sons (30.9–13): Leah was not immune to the sin of envy and discontent. Seeing that Rachel has obtained children through her handmaid, she seeks to do the same. This was certainly one of the low points in Leah's spiritual development. Though we must not condone what Rachel did, at least she could claim that custom demanded that she give her handmaid if she could not conceive. Leah had no plea but envy.

Zilpah first gives birth to Gad *(fortune* or *troop).* Leah's words were either *"good fortune has come"* or *"a troop comes"* depending on which meaning you take for Gad. *Fortune* seems to fit the context better, especially considering the name of the second son through Zilpah.[2] In this birth, she rejoices to have more children.

Then, Zilpah gives birth to Asher *(happy* or *fortunate)* and Leah says, *"Happy am I! For women have called me happy."*

In the names of these two sons, we find no reference to Yahweh. Perhaps that is fitting, since these sons were born in polygamy, as Leah strove to outproduce her sister. Though polygamy was regulated, and thus allowed, under

---

[2]Interestingly, *troop* fits better in the context of 49.19.

Mosaic Law, Jesus makes it clear that such an arrangement has never been pleasing to God (*cf.* Matt 19.4–9). In each of the names, however, there is a reference to happiness and the continued optimism that constantly shone through Leah's character.

Leah's Next Two (30.14–21): Leah then bears two more children.

Issachar *(reward* or *wages)* is born next. At his birth, she says, *"God has given me my wages because I gave my servant to my husband."* Here, Leah seems to be totally off base, supposing that God has rewarded her for her humility in giving Zilpah to Jacob. Though we would suggest that she is wrong in that supposition—for God would not reward such an act—Issachar *is* a result of God hearing her prayer (v 17).

Zebulun *(dwelling* or *neighbor)* is the last of Leah's sons. At his birth, Leah says, *"God has endowed me with a good endowment; now my husband will honor me, because I have borne him six sons."* And again, we see the prevailing pattern of Leah being displayed: acknowledgment of God in naming of the son with a word of hope that Jacob would esteem her more highly.

Rachel's Two Sons (30.22–24; 35.16–19): Finally, God blesses Rachel with her own sons.

At the birth of Joseph *(may He add)*, Rachel says, *"God has taken away my reproach. …May [Yahweh] add to me another son."* Finally she gets the son she's wanted for so long and the best she can do is ask for another. While it is understandable that she would anticipate and desire more children, such a request is unseemly; her gratitude is virtually invisible. Her acknowledgement of God seems more concerned with *her* reproach than with *His* act of kindness.

Ultimately, God does give her another son, as she requested. This son, however, would cost her life. There is irony in Rachel's statement to Jacob, *"Give me children, or I shall die"* (30.1). It is the gift of children that ultimately killed her. She names this son Ben-Oni *(son of my sorrow)* as she dies. Jacob would mercifully rename this son Benjamin *(son of my right hand)*; however, the character of Rachel stands clear in the naming of this son. She gave him a name that would remind him and everyone else that his mother died giving birth to him. In essence, she named him 'I killed mom,' a deplorable and inexcusable act.

Hints at their Character: Leah is always grateful to God, happy and optimistic. Rachel is always self-serving and immature, not satisfied with what she has (the love of Jacob), but wanting the one thing that Leah has alone, constantly searching for evidence in the children's births that she has prevailed. When God, in His mercy, does give Rachel a child, she immediately asks for another. The answer to that request culminates in her death where she memorializes the event by naming that son 'You Killed Me.'

In naming their children, we find hints of the character of Leah and Rachel. Certainly these names and statements alone are not enough to hang an entire case upon, but they lay the groundwork for the rest of the story the Bible tells of these two sisters and their husband.

Rachel's Failings

In addition to the hints of character we find in the naming of the sons, Rachel had other failings that stand out in the text.

Attempted Pregnancy (Genesis 30): When Rachel saw that she could not bear children, she did not immediately look to God for help. First, she demands children of Jacob (30.1), as if it is his fault that she cannot bear children (obviously, it was not—Leah had no problem conceiving). Then, she gives Jacob her handmaid (30.3—which Jacob, knowing the history of Hagar and Ishmael, should have immediately rejected). Next, she attempts the use of mandrakes (30.15).[3] Finally—only after these things haven't worked—does she appeal to God (30.22: *God heard her*). Only as a last resort does she look to God for help.

Theft of the Teraphim (31.19, 34–35): When Jacob was ready to part company with Laban, Laban was out shearing his sheep. As Jacob uses this opportunity to get a head start, Rachel uses the opportunity to steal the household gods (*i.e.*, teraphim). According to customs of the time, the possessor of the teraphim had claim to the inheritance (notice Rachel's previous concern with the lack of inheritance, 31.14).[4] God had already promised an inheritance to Jacob beyond anything mere man could leave for him. Certainly, after 13 years of marriage, Jacob, a man of faith, had told Rachel of the promises given to him by Yahweh. Rachel, however, lacked the faith in this inheritance and sought to secure for herself the inheritance of her father.[5] It is also possible that Rachel was a daughter of her father and believed in these idols as he did, though we cannot know that for certain.

After Laban chases Jacob's company down, he demands to search for the teraphim. Having searched the entire camp, he comes to Rachel's tent, where she has hidden them in her camel's saddle and is sitting on them. *"Let not my lord be angry that I cannot rise before you,"* she tells her father, *"for the way of women is upon me"* (31.35). She claimed that she was having her monthly period, ensuring that Laban would not touch her. We do not know whether or not she was techni-

---

[3]Mandrakes were a fruit that was thought to be an aphrodisiac and increase fertility.

[4]See comment on 31.19.

[5]Other studies have argued that the possession of the teraphim did not guarantee inheritance rights (see comment and footnotes on 31.19). However, this does not exonerate her theft, which could have only been due to theological convictions and idolatry if not inheritance rights.

cally telling the truth in this instance. Yet even if she was relaying a fact to her father, she was doing so in the spirit of deceit—in an effort to get away with theft.

At the very least, Rachel was a thief and a liar. At the most, she was a thief, an idolater, a liar, and had a lack of understanding of, or faith in, God's word. The truth may be somewhere between those extremes.

Leah's Virtues

The naming of children gave us hints as to the virtues of Leah. She is a woman who seeks to give glory to God and who always has an optimistic outlook on things. Leah's virtues, however, become even more evident on closer study

Use of God's Name: One of the themes running through the book of Genesis is the use of the Hebrew words *Yahweh* (usually translated *the Lord*) and *Elohim* (translated *God).* Thematically, Yahweh is used when the covenant and/or the personal relationship with God and man is being emphasized. After the covenant was established with Abraham, *Yahweh* is used almost exclusively when covenant issues are being discussed. *Elohim* ('deity') is used in reference to the creative power of God or His power over nature. In short, Yahweh is the 'covenant God.' Elohim is the 'creator-God.'[6]

When Leah gave birth to her first four children, she attributed them all to *Yahweh.* This displays her understanding of the covenant and her faith in it. Rachel always spoke of *Elohim.* The only time she used the personal name of God was when she was demanding from Him another child. Rachel's failure to use God's covenant name could further the case that her theft of the teraphim was a lack of faith in God's promises, as well as lend support to the supposition that she was an idolater. Keil writes: "It is to be noticed, that Rachel speaks of *Elohim* only, whereas Leah regarded her first four sons as the gift of [Yahweh]. In this variation of the names, the attitude of the two women, not only to one another, but also to the cause they served, is made apparent."

A Prayer Life: Whereas Rachel used God as a last resort in bearing children, Leah looked to Him almost immediately. *"Yahweh has looked on my affliction,"* she says at the birth of Reuben and *"Yahweh has heard…"* at the birth of Simeon. Both of these statements imply that she called to God and He answered. It is stated even more clearly at the birth of Issachar, where we are told that God listened to Leah. Leah, understanding the true nature of the covenant God, developed a prayer life almost immediately.

Not Perfect: Leah was far from perfect. Whatever part Leah played in the deception of Jacob at their wedding (presuming she had a choice in the matter)

---

[6]See Excursus B. The Bible makes it clear that *Yahweh* and *Elohim* are both referring to the same God; Genesis does not support polytheism. But by using different terms, Moses distinguishes the different aspects of God's relationship with man.

certainly deserves censure. In addition, her imitation of Rachel in giving her handmaid to secure more children is deserving of a rebuke (though Jacob deserves some blame for taking both handmaids). The envy in her heart during the sibling rivalry should not be condoned, and her explanation for the birth of Issachar seems to be based on a faulty premise. What stands out about Leah, however, are her virtues—especially her understanding of Yahweh and the covenant that He had made with Jacob and his fathers—just as what stands out about Rachel are her failures.

Yahweh's Choice

Ultimately, what matters is the choice that Yahweh makes. As with all the accounts in the book of Genesis, Yahweh is choosing which person the Messianic line will continue through. The faithful is kept in the line; the unfaithful is rejected. Though in most instances this involves a choice between men, here the women are central.

Ultimately, the choice is Leah. Leah is the wife through whom the High Priesthood came. She was the wife through whom the kings came. She was the wife through whom the Messiah came. By withholding sons from Rachel for so long, while blessing Leah with so many, Yahweh virtually assured that the blessing would come through one of the sons of Leah. Even though the choosing of God revolves around the faithfulness of the individual and the free will of the sons could have excluded them from the blessing, giving Leah six children before Rachel's two almost guaranteed that one of Leah's would be the one to carry the Messianic line. "The fact that these four sons formed the real stem of the promised numerous seed, she was proved still more to be the wife selected by [Yahweh], in realization of His promise, to be the tribe-mother of the greater part of the covenant nation" (Keil).

Jacob's Choice

Jacob never lost that special love for Rachel. That is displayed best in the favoritism that he showed toward her sons. Jacob, however, did come to love Leah through the years (notice his concern for both of them in 31.31 and 32.11), and ultimately, his love for Leah eclipsed his love for Rachel.

In chapter 35, Jacob calls for all the idols to be brought out, and he buried them under the terebinth tree by Shechem. This was probably where he first learned that Rachel had stolen the teraphim from Laban. After this, we never hear about Jacob's great love for Rachel again. One must wonder if this moment was an epiphany for him: confronted with the complete lack of character in Rachel, he realized that he had allowed his flesh to rule in his love.

More important for us to notice is that just after this, Rachel dies. And upon her death, Jacob buried her where she fell. It would have taken only a day's journey—15–20 miles—to bury Rachel in the cave at Machpelah. Certainly that was nothing compared to the journey Jacob expected his sons to make to bury him there—about 300 miles from Egypt (49.29–30). So, burying Rachel where she died was not a matter of the trip to Machpelah being inconvenient. Rather, it was a decision made by Jacob that Leah would be buried at Machpelah. Though Rachel was his preferred wife at first, Leah was God's preferred wife—and Jacob's covenant wife. Notice what Jacob says as he concludes his instructions for his burial: *"There they buried Abraham and Sarah his wife. There they buried Isaac and Rebekah his wife, and there I buried Leah"* (49.31). Leah was Jacob's ultimate choice. Leah was the wife whom he laid in the family tomb, with the other patriarchs and matriarchs. Leah was the wife Jacob wished to lie next to after this life had passed.

It is possible that Jacob's love story is the greatest in the Bible. It is not great, however, in the way that it is often told. Instead, it is a great love story because it is culminated in *real* love, not superficial love: the kind of love that is learned and based on a mutual faith in the promises of God.

36 "The brotherhood of Jacob and Esau, living on in the nations of Edom and Israel, is never forgotten in the Old Testament. The present chapter, with its painstaking detail, is a witness to this sense of kinship, which will later come to surface in contexts of diplomacy, law and national feeling (see, respectively, Num 20.14; Deut 23.7; Oba 10–12)" (Kidner).

36.2, Esau took his wives… Adah the daughter of Elon the Hittite, Oholibamah the daughter of Anah the daughter of Zibeon the Hivite and Basemath, Ishmael's daughter. This is something of a surprise. The Canaanite wives were previously recorded as Judith and Basemath (26.34) and Ishmael's daughter as Mahalath (28.9). Basemath seems to have changed families, and the other two wives are not mentioned at all previously.

Three solutions may be found to this problem. Kidner suggests two: "The simplest explanation is that the lists have suffered in transmission; but there may also have been some alternative names (like Esau's own nickname Edom)." Perhaps an even simpler explanation lies in the truth that Genesis does not claim to be an exhaustive history of Esau. There is no reason to believe that Esau did not have more wives than those listed in chapters 26 and 28 and, for whatever reason, they are omitted from this genealogy while later wives were included.[1]

36.6–7, He went into a land away from his brother Jacob. Even after making peace with one another, Jacob and Esau do not dwell together in the Promised Land. "Esau, in keeping with his loss of birthright and blessing, concedes Canaan to his brother and moves his people to the southeast" (Alter).

For their possessions were too great for them to dwell together. The land of their sojournings could not support them because of their livestock. Here, we find the motive for Esau's move—the reason they could not dwell together in Canaan (*cf.* 13.5–9). "Although Esau is outside the covenant promise, God's blessing extends to him in two ways: children (vv 4–5) and prosperity (vv 6–7). …He departs from Canaan with an amiable, commonsense view of things, not in anger or resentment" (Hamilton).

36.11, Eliphaz… Teman. "The conjunction of the names *Eliphaz* and

---

[1]It must be conceded that this suggestion does little to solve the problem of Basemath changing families, unless it is further hypothesized that Basemath was a common enough name that Esau could have married two women of different nationalities with the same name—a hazardous leap, we admit.

Teman in verse 11 points to Edom as the probable setting of the book of Job, where an 'Eliphaz the Temanite' is prominent" (Kidner).[2] This supposition is also supported by Esau's later descendant, *Uz* (v 28).[3]

36.12, *Concubine…Amalek.* Waltke notes: "As the offspring of a concubine, Amalek does not come under the umbrella of Edom's protected status with Israel (Deut 23.7–9). The Amalekites are punished for their treacherous, unprovoked aggression against Israel during her Exodus journey from Egypt to the Promised Land (Exod 17.8–16; *cf.* Jdg 3.13; 6.3–5, 33; 7.12; 10.12). Samuel commands Saul to annihilate the Amalekites. …When Saul spares Agag their king, Samuel himself slays him (1 Sam 15). It remains for Mordecai, another descendant of Kish (1 Sam 9.1; Est 2.5), to destroy Haman the Agagite (Est 3.1, 10; 8.3, 5; 9.23–25), presumably an Amalekite, as identified by Josephus."

36.15, *These are the chiefs.* That is, the tribal chiefs (Waltke). Some have suggested a meaning of *clans*, but "most of the occurrences of the term elsewhere in the Bible clearly indicate a person, not a group" (Alter).

36.20, *The sons of Seir the Horite.* Previously, Anah's family had been identified as Hivite (v 2). The change "either indicates that the terms overlap, or that Hivite may be, here and elsewhere, a copyist's error for Horite. The term Horites usually seems to denote the Hurrians, a non-Semitic people widely dispersed in the Ancient Near East; the Semitic names in these verses however suggest that the Horites of mount Seir were of different stock" (Kidner).

36.24, *He is the Anah who found the hot springs in the wilderness.* This is an interesting family history note, and the only anecdote in the genealogy. Presumably, it would have had meaning to the Israelite audience familiar with the terrain. The precise nature of what he found is, however, under some debate by linguistic scholars who have also rendered this *hapax legomenon* as *mules, vipers,* or *water,* though many seem to be leaning toward *water* (*e.g.,* Alter, Hamilton, Wenham, *etc.*). Alter writes: "Discovery of any water source in the wilderness would be enough to make it noteworthy for posterity."

---

[2]*Cf.* Jeremiah 49.7.

[3]Also, in Lamentations 4.21, the daughter of Edom dwells in the land of Uz, *cf.* Job 1.1.

36.31, Before any king reigned over the Israelites. Does this indicate a late date for this genealogy or is it a scribal addition that has made its way into the text? Of the two, we would lean toward the latter, though there is no need to subscribe to either view. Moses himself spoke of the time when Israel would have a king (Deut 17.14–20). And clearly, there were kings in Edom during Moses' life (Num 20.14).

Growth of the Seed: Esau, outside the blessing, dwells outside the Promised Land. Even so, his descendants multiply, further fulfilling the *many nations* promise made to Abraham.

Judah and Joseph

Chapters 37–50

The *toledot* of Jacob tells of the development of his children, with its primary focus on two: Joseph and Judah. Hamilton argues that the story is about Joseph and everything else—those things told of Simeon, Judah and Benjamin, in particular—are told "only as they relate to Joseph." We are not convinced. In fact, it could just as easily be argued in reverse: the story is only about the development of Judah's character, and those things relating to Joseph are only told as they are an explanation of how the bearer of the promised line will come to live in Egypt. In reality, however, it seems that the focus is on both of these characters, though in different regards.

With the explanation already given of why the older three are bypassed in the blessing (34.25–31; 35.22), we are now left to witness the development of Judah's character (esp. ch 38) and leadership ability as he will be the blessed child of Jacob's twelve. Although Joseph receives the majority of the press, Judah's story is an intriguing one—especially when contrasted with Reuben[1]—and should not be overlooked, if no other reason than because he is the son through whom the Messiah would come.

Joseph's story is quite different. As the privileged son of the favorite wife, he is lavished with gifts and attention until he is so hated that his brothers stop just short of killing him and sell him into slavery. God uses their wickedness to develop the character of Joseph as he rises in power to

---

[1]See Excursus N.

368 | *The Growth of the Seed*

the end that Egypt is well prepared for the famine that would come. Ultimately, the family reunites and, at the invitation of Joseph and Pharaoh, they move into Goshen, where God will grow this family into a nation.

The structure of the Joseph cycle can be broken down in several ways,[2] which shows the literary richness of this particular section of the book of Genesis. We have chosen to show two of the patterns before entering the narrative.[3]

Structure and Pattern in Genesis
The Joseph Cycle: Concentric Pattern

A Introduction: beginning of Joseph story (37.2-11)
  B Jacob mourns 'death' of Joseph (37.12–36)
    C Interlude: Judah signified as leader (38.1–30)
      D Joseph's enslavement in Egypt (39.1–23)
        E Joseph savior of Egypt through disfavor at Pharaoh's court (40.1–41.57)
          F Journey of brothers to Egypt (42.1–43.34)
            G Brothers pass Joseph's test of love for brother (44.1–34)
            G' Joseph gives up his power over brothers (45.1–28)
          F' Migration of family to Egypt (46.1–27)
        E' Joseph savior of family through favor at Pharaoh's court (46.28–47.12)
      D' Joseph's enslavement of Egyptians (47.13–31)
    C' Interlude: Judah blessed as ruler (48.1–49.28)
  B' Joseph mourns death of Jacob (49.29–50.14)
A' Conclusion: end of Joseph story (50.15–26)

---

[2]See David A. Dorsey, *The Literary Structure of the Old Testament*, 59–63.

[3]The first, as the previous structures have been, is taken from Waltke. The second from Dorsey, 59.

Structure and Pattern in Genesis
The Joseph Cycle: Parallel Pattern

A   Trouble between Joseph and his brothers (37.2–11)

A'   More trouble between Joseph and his brothers (37.12–36)

    B   Sexual temptation involving Judah (38.1–30)

    B'   Sexual temptation involving Joseph (39.1–23)

        C   Joseph interprets two dreams of prison mates (40.1–23)

        C'   Joseph interprets two dreams of Pharaoh (41.1–57)

            D   Brothers come to Egypt for food (42.1–38)

            D'   Brothers again come to Egypt for food (43.1–44.3)

                E   Joseph has some of his family brought to him (44.4–45.15)

                E'   Joseph has all of his family brought to him (45.16–47.12)

                    F   Prospering in Egypt: Joseph in ascendancy (47.13–26)

                    F'   Prospering in Egypt: Blessings on Jacob's sons (47.27–49.32)

                        G   Death of patriarch: Jacob (49.33–50.14)

                        G'   Death of patriarch: Joseph (50.15–26)

37 *1–2a, Jacob lived in the land of his father's sojournings, in the land of Canaan.* After an entire lifetime away from the Promised Land, Jacob has returned to stay. With his father having died, "Jacob had now entered upon his father's inheritance, and carries on the patriarchal pilgrim-life in Canaan" (Keil). This is most likely meant to contrast with the preceding verse, regarding the settling of Esau's lineage outside the Promised Land (36.43).

These are the generations of Jacob. This statement prepares us to hear the story of Jacob's sons. Interestingly, the generations of Jacob are characterized by far fewer divine revelations than any of the generations hitherto.

37.2, Being seventeen years old. Jacob will, in turn, live with Joseph the last seventeen years of his life (47.28). "Such symmetry reveals God's providence" (Waltke).

He was a boy. The Hebrew usually refers to age, but often carries the meaning of servant. As his age has already been given, its use in relation to his brothers probably refers to his status (Kidner), *i.e.*, they were the shepherds, he was their helper.

With the sons of Bilhah and Zilpah. Not all of the brothers were present at this point.[1] No reason is given. We may speculate that as the sons of the concubines, they were given the harder work and assigned the favorite son as a helper.

And Joseph brought a bad report of them to their father. There are two possible interpretations to this passage. First, Joseph may have been simply reporting back to his father as part of an assigned duty (*cf.* v 14). If so, his first duty was to his father, and reporting their deeds was wholly appropriate. An alternate interpretation is suggested by the word used. Waltke notes that the Hebrew used for *report* "denotes news slanted to damage the victim" and concludes by referring to Joseph as "a pestering, tattletale little brother." Wenham agrees with this estimation of the Hebrew, saying that it "is always used elsewhere in a negative sense of an untrue report." That it is qualified as a *bad report* would cause it to seem likely that "Joseph misrepresented his brothers to his father, his father believed him, and his brothers hated him for his lies" (Wenham). To this end, Hamilton translates the word *maligned*.

---

[1]An alternate explanation is that all the brothers were present, but he was only assigned specifically to the sons of Bilhah and Zilpah (Kidner).

37.3, Now Israel loved Joseph more than any other of his sons. Should we expect any less from a man who learned parental favoritism from childhood and had shown favoritism among his four wives? It is noteworthy that this comment is made on the heels of Joseph reporting on his brothers.

Because he was the son of his old age. The reason given, however, is surprising. "Jacob did not love Joseph the most because he had loved Rachel more than Leah. Jacob is still kicking against primogeniture" (Waltke). Even so, this report is strange, because Benjamin is the final son of Jacob and, in the truest sense, the son of his old age. "Of course, Joseph's birth to Jacob by Rachel is the only instance of a birthing incident involving Rachel that has a happy ending" (Hamilton).

And he made him a robe of many colors. The Hebrew here is difficult. Its translation as a *robe of many colors* traces back to the LXX. A cognate Aramaic term, however, means *palm of the hand,* which has led many to render it *a long-sleeved robe.*[2] If this latter interpretation is to be taken—a robe extending to the wrists and ankles—"It was not... a garment adapted to work but suitable to distinguish a superior, or an overseer. By this very garment the father expressed his thought that the son should have preeminence over the rest" (Leupold). That said, it may have been multi-colored, too. Archaeological discoveries of Mesopotamian artwork have revealed that many such long-sleeved robes were, in fact, multi-colored. The point of the text, however, seems to indicate the status it gave Joseph rather than the appearance of the robe.[3]

37.4, When his brothers saw that their father loved him more... they hated him. Jacob's favoritism resulted in family strife—as if the family didn't already have enough problems. And if favoritism wasn't enough, the gift has promoted Joseph from being a helper in the field to being the supervisor of his older brothers in the field—as well as remaining the informant for his father.

Their hatred is typically understood as being directed toward Joseph, which may well be the case. One must wonder, however, if their hatred is also, in part, directed to their father, the one who showered Joseph with gifts and love. As Hamilton says, "[Joseph] had not placed an order for

---

[2] For a fuller discussion of the meaning of *pas,* see Waltke. For a full discussion of the translation options, see Hamilton.

[3] The same terminology is used to describe the robe worn by a king's daughter in 2 Samuel 13.18.

the garment. In no way had he been solicitous of his father's time and gifts." They had already shown their relationship with their father to be weak (*cf.* 34.30–31) and their later revenge on Joseph has Jacob as a clear second target. It is not dubious to suggest that their hatred at this point was at least partly reserved for their father.

And could not speak peacefully to him. As *shalom*—peace—was the common greeting, this verse may indicate that they brothers would not even greet Joseph.

37.5, Now Joseph had a dream. "The account of the dreams, coming at the outset, makes God, not Joseph, the 'hero' of the story: it is not a tale of human success but of divine sovereignty" (Kidner). God is in control of the events of the subsequent chapters.

He told it to his brothers. A question that comes to the mind of every reader of Genesis at this point is, *Why?* Three potential reasons stand out: he may have thought that, as the favorite, he was untouchable and sought to rub it in; he may have been naïve and not realized that his brothers hated him or what relating the dream would do to their anger; finally, he may have merely been excited (notice the threefold repetition of *behold!* v 7), and, not realizing the extent of their hatred toward him, thought that they would share in his excitement—or "self-absorbed, blithely assuming everyone will be fascinated by the details of his dreams" (Alter).

They hated him even more. Their hatred intensified because of the dream.

37.7–8, "My sheaf arose and stood upright. And behold, your sheaves gathered around it and bowed down to my sheaf." Joseph's dream could only be interpreted as him having an unequivocal preeminence over his brothers, a point his brothers did not miss (v 8).

"This is the first dream recorded in Genesis in which the voice of God does not speak, thus removing it from the category of a theophany" (Hamilton). The dreams, while showing God's providence in retrospect, were not prophetic *per se*. He is not informing Joseph, or anyone else, of the things that were to come, "yet God so controlled the dream that later it was seen to be in conformity with fact" (Leupold). But it is only in looking back that connection is made clear. This may be part of the distinction between prophecy and providence.

Some have sought to make the binding of the sheaves specifically prophetic, as Joseph was in charge of the food supply when the brothers would later bow to him (42.6ff). But such an interpretation is a stretch. First, binding sheaves was so common a job that it might be compared, if a modern comparison may be made, to typing on a keyboard. Such a common task could hardly be seen as prophetic! Further, though Joseph *was* in charge of the food supply, he probably was one of the very few who *wasn't* binding the sheaves.

"Are you indeed to reign over us?" The brothers were indignant. Although Joseph may have been the favorite to Jacob, they refused to believe that they would ever bow before him.

So they hated him even more for his dreams. Bookending the dream, this phrase emphasizes the degree of hatred that the brothers felt for Joseph at this point.

And for his words. Was Joseph so oblivious (or cruel) as to not only tell a dream with obvious implications but then spell out its interpretation as well? "They hated him both for having such dreams and for insisting on talking about them" (Alter).

37.9, Then he dreamed another dream. "The doubling of a dream is a sign that what it portends will really happen" (Alter). *Cf.* 41.32. In addition, the Joseph narrative "is characterized by pairing: Joseph's two dreams, Judah's two slain sons, Judah's twin sons through Tamar, two temptation scenes with Potiphar's wife, two dreams of two prison mates, two dreams of Pharaoh, Joseph's two sons, *etc.*"[4]

And told it to his brothers. Is Joseph still naïve? "Caution and discretion should have taught Joseph to keep silence about this dream in the presence of his brethren, for he must have noticed how the former dream had displeased them" (Leupold). Is this, then, meant to instruct us that he was, in fact, a spoiled brat?

"The sun, the moon, and eleven stars were bowing down to me." This dream was essentially the same, though a different scene and two added elements: his parents.

37.10–11, His father rebuked him. Without any explanation, Jacob realized immediately the implication of the added characters in this dream. And this rebuke is not intended to be understood as a mild one. The word used indicates screaming or a sharp rebuke (Leupold).

---

[4]David A. Dorsey, *The Literary Structure of the Old Testament*, 61.

"Shall I and your mother and your brothers indeed come to bow ourselves to the ground before you?" The emphasis in Jacob's rebuke was most likely on the part of him and Joseph's mother bowing, and less on the brothers bowing, though so much is not said. Had Jacob, by the coat, not already implied that they would bow?[5]

Jacob's question seems to render moot Wenham's suggestion that the moon's presence in the dream "is included just to complete the picture of the heavenly bodies." There is some question, then, as to who is intended by *your mother.* Although some would suggest that it was Rachel, "who was neither forgotten nor lost" (Keil), the more sensible answer is that it referred to Leah, the matriarch of the family. To a lesser degree of probability, it could refer to Bilhah, Rachel's handmaid, if she had taken over any of the mother's duties at her death (so supposes *Genesis Rabbah).* Suggestions that this is an account out of chronological order—*i.e.,* before Rachel's death—must be rejected on account of the eleven stars: Benjamin had already been born.

But his father kept the saying in mind. As dreams were a recognized means of revelation—a medium which Jacob had personal experience with—Jacob's response was with something of an open mind and humility (in spite of the sharp rebuke), keeping the matter in his heart (*cf.* Luke 2.19), a stark contrast from the envy, skepticism and hatred of the brothers. He had now learned to allow for God's hand in man's affairs (Kidner).

It has been suggested that the different approaches taken illustrate the attitudes that divide people even today upon hearing God's word. Some react hastily and solely on an emotional plane, where the message often tears before it heals and strikes before it binds up (*cf.* Hos 6.1–3). Others, however, take the message to heart and meditate on it, allowing it to work on the inner man and, ultimately, produce a changed person (Kidner).

37.12–14, His brothers went to pasture their father's flock. We learn later that this is not only the concubines' sons (as in v 2), but Leah's sons as well (*cf.* vv 21–22, 26).

Near Shechem. That they would pasture the flock near Shechem is surprising, given the family history there (*cf.* ch 34). Although we cannot be sure precisely why this land was chosen, various suggestions have been made. Perhaps a *terror from God* was still on the land (*cf.* 35.5). Or may-

---

[5] See comment on verse 3.

be the brothers sought a thrill from living on the edge of danger. Or—an even simpler explanation—they were using the plot of land which Jacob still owned (*cf.* 33.19; John 4.5). Or, if we should attribute to them scheming, perhaps they were seeking to place distance between themselves and their father in order to harm Joseph (though such would presume that they knew Joseph would be sent across the countryside to visit them).

"Are not your brothers pasturing the flock at Shechem?" It would seem that, whatever their motive, Jacob was not completely comfortable with this arrangement.

"See if it is well with your brothers… and bring me word." Because Joseph has shown himself to be a reliable source, Jacob sends him to make sure all is well with the flock. It is interesting that Jacob would send Joseph alone to meet his brothers. His later lack of suspicion of the brothers seems to imply that he was not aware of any hatred they harbored for Joseph. One must wonder if the brothers had so well concealed their hatred of Joseph that Jacob was unaware of it, if this lack of knowledge is further evidence of Jacob's poor parenting, or if he just never thought that they would go so far with a *brother.*

From the Valley of Hebron. The journey from Hebron to Shechem is about 50 miles, more than one day's journey. The continued trip to Dothan (v 17) would be another 15 miles.

37.15–17, A man found him wandering in the fields… "I am seeking my brothers." It should not be considered odd that a stranger would at once know who Joseph's brothers were. Indeed, after the Dinah incident, everyone in the countryside would know them! Ironically, "Joseph, alone and vulnerable, is safer with a Shechemite than with his brothers" (Waltke).

Some have seen a connection between this unnamed man and the unnamed man of Jabbok (32.24–32). While such a suggestion is not without merit,[6] it is unnecessary to the narrative; indeed, the providence God holds over this story is usually worked through human hands. "Since the 'man' intercepted Joseph, overheard the private conversation of the brothers, and correctly directed Joseph to discover his brothers at Dothan, the passage conveys the theological orientation of the narrative as a whole.

---

[6]It is clear that angels did sometimes appear as men (*cf.* 18.2) and that they often watched over Abraham's seed (*cf.* 16.7–13; 28.12–17; 32.1–2; 35.5).

Whether the 'man' is an angel or human, the unseen hand of the Lord is apparent here" (Mathews).

"They have gone away, for I heard them say, 'Let us go to Dothan.'" Not only did this man know the brothers; it seems as if he was assigned a specific task of keeping an eye on them while they were in the area.

Kidner suggests that Dothan marks the two extremes of God's providential workings. In this narrative, Joseph calls out for help in Dothan, but no one answers (*cf.* 42.21). At a later time, Dothan will be the place where at a single word, Elisha's servant's eyes are opened and he sees a mountain filled with the angelic army (2 Kgs 6.13–17).

37.18–20, They saw him from afar, and… they conspired against him to kill him. They were able to see him from afar, presumably because his coat was recognizable even from a distance (*cf.* v 23). If this is the first group conspiracy, it would seem that their motive to shepherd in Shechem was not to put distance between themselves and their father.

"Here comes this dreamer." The text literally reads *the master of dreams,* a common idiom for someone who specializes in something—obviously used in a mocking tone. With this moniker, the brothers reveal which of Joseph's 'faults' they hate him for most. "It is his dreams that their plan will sabotage" (Hamilton).

"Let us kill him." Whether knowingly or not, the brothers seek to follow in the cursed footsteps of Cain, the seed of the serpent.

"And throw him into one of the pits." The pit was most likely a dried cistern (v 24). Cisterns "are large bottle-shaped pits hewn out of rock for retaining water. They range from six to twenty feet in depth. A dried-out cistern makes an excellent dungeon (*cf.* Gen 40.15; Jer 38.6)" (Waltke).

"Then we will say that a fierce animal has devoured him." The murder is coldly planned. Obviously, this is a plausible alibi, as Jacob believes it when it is presented (*cf.* 1 Sam 17.34–35).

"We will see what will become of his dreams." In retrospect, this line must be considered the height of irony in the story. The result of these very actions is precisely what they are trying to prevent.

37.21–22, When Reuben heard it, he rescued him out of their hands. Reuben—either because he was the eldest and felt responsible or because he was a pacifist (notice that he took no part in the massacre at Shechem)—rescued Joseph from death.

"Cast him into this pit here… but do not lay a hand on him." Reuben's suggestion seems to be without any conclusion—were they to leave him in the pit until he starved to death?—which will allow Judah to come up with an alternate plan. Most likely, they planned to leave him in the pit until he died, thus allowing themselves to satisfy their thirst for blood without getting their hands bloody.

That he might rescue him out of their hand. His plan was without conclusion, because he planned to return at a later time and rescue Joseph (v 29).

To restore him to his father. Was Reuben's motive for saving Joseph an attempt to find a way back into his father's good graces? (*cf.* 35.22).

37.23, They stripped him of his robe. "Only now do we learn that Joseph has the bad judgment to wear on his errand the garment that was the extravagant token of his father's favoritism" (Alter). And Hamilton: "Wearing it in Dothan is like waving a red flag in front of a bull." The brothers immediately removed from him the object that had earned him both his special place of preeminence and their special hatred. "They dethroned the royal son" (Waltke).

The mention of the cloak may have a literary purpose as well. "The bestowal and removal of Joseph's attire signified change in his social standing. The stripping of his garment by his brothers and the seizure of his cloak by Potiphar's wife (39.12–13) represented his descending status—from favored son to slave, from slave overseer to prisoner. The snatched garments were used in both cases to bolster false claims against Joseph. The clothing and accessories he received from Pharaoh, on the other hand, announced his superior role as courtier (45.22)" (Mathews).

37.25, Then they sat down to eat. Calloused to their actions by their intense hatred, the brothers show no remorse whatsoever for what they had done. Calmly, they sit to eat. Waltke notes: "Their next meal in Joseph's presence will be with Joseph at the head table (43.32–34)."

37.26–28, Then Judah said to his brothers. It is already at the word of Judah, not Reuben, that the brothers act. "His speech to his brothers at the climax of this scene stands in contrast to the ineffective speeches of Reuben before (37.21–22) and after (37.30)" (Waltke). [7]

---

[7] See comparison of Reuben and Judah in EXCURSUS N.

"What profit is it if we kill our brother?" Unlike Reuben's motive, Judah's is not noble at all. Though he will come to be the leader in the family (*cf.* 44.18–34), his actions here are completely self-absorbed and without any moral merit. His motive seems to be less "the feeling of horror… at incurring the guilt of fratricide" (Keil) than it does a desire for profit.

"Let us sell him." Traders passing by must have sparked this idea in Judah's mind. Rather than killing him and having blood on their hands, they could sell him, make a profit, and still be rid of him.

"To the Ishmaelites." Joseph was sold to the rejected branch of the covenant family.

"Let not our hand be upon him, for he is our brother, our own flesh." How noble Judah sounds—as he sells Joseph into slavery for 20 shekels of silver. "It is… a dubious expression of brotherhood to sell someone into the ignominy and perilously uncertain future of slavery" (Alter). Hamilton adds: "Both later biblical law and cuneiform law prohibit what Judah and his brothers did to Joseph. It is a crime that is considered a capital offense."

Midianite traders passed by. This is not a contradiction with the previous verse. Ishmaelites and Midianites come from the same ancestor—Abraham (16.15; 25.2)—and may have intermarried (*cf.* 25.17–18). Also, Midianites are elsewhere called Ishmaelites (Jdg 8.22–28). "It appears from this that 'Ishmaelite' was an inclusive term for Israel's nomadic cousins (Ishmael was the senior offshoot from Abraham), somewhat as 'Arab' embraces numerous tribes in our way of speaking, and can alternate with one of their names without awkwardness" (Kidner). Or it may have been that both groups were in the same caravan. "The Ishmaelites may have been the dominant faction, the Midianites the more numerous. In such a case both designations would be suitable" (Leupold). A final suggestion, made by Hamilton, is that *Ishmaelite* here is "a catchall term for nomadic travelers" rather than an ethnic term; *Midianite*, then, would be the ethnic term.

37.29–30, When Reuben… saw that Joseph was not in the pit, he tore his clothes. The sale of Joseph had taken place while Reuben was away—either as a coincidence or because the other brothers had come to realize that he would interfere with their plans. Where Reuben went cannot be known with any degree of certainty, though some have speculated that he left at this time so it would not seem odd for him to leave later (to rescue Joseph, *e.g.,* Leupold), though he may have just gone to watch the sheep. It has been suggested that, in addition to Judah making the suggestion, Simeon played a large part in this. With Reuben gone, he was the next oldest, had experience in cruelty (*cf.* 34.25–26), and would later receive a special punishment from Joseph (42.24).

And returned to his brothers and said. Reuben, distraught over Joseph's apparent death, later seems to have been left in the dark with Jacob as to what happened while he was gone (*cf.* 42.22).

"They boy is gone, and I, where shall I go?" Already in Jacob's doghouse for sleeping with Bilhah, Reuben has now let the favorite son be killed under his watch. Their lack of surprise must have at once informed him that they were responsible for his disappearance.

Reuben is easy to view as the would-be hero of this narrative. But whatever good graces he earns with the reader must be tempered by a clear weakness: he resorted to scheming to save Joseph rather than simply standing for what was right. Clearly, to do so would not have been easy in the face of the other brothers, and may have earned him a trip to Egypt as well, but before he is placed on a pedestal for his morality, let us remember that it was a morality shrouded in deceit—and, sadly, ineffective deceit at that.

37.31–32, They took Joseph's robe and slaughtered a goat. The irony runs deep. Jacob deceived his father with a slaughtered goat and Esau's clothing. Here, his sons use a slaughtered goat and Joseph's robe to deceive Jacob (*cf.* 27.9, 15).

And dipped the robe in the blood. They created evidence to support their alibi (v 20), making Jacob believe that Joseph was dead. In so doing, they would double their revenge—having already taken revenge on Joseph for being the favorite and the dreamer, they now extend their revenge to Jacob for favoring him (and his mother?).

And they sent the robe… to their father. Having created an escape, they did not complete the plan themselves. Rather, they sent it with a message—*"Is this your son's robe?"*

37.33, "It is my son's robe. A fierce animal has devoured him." With no prompting other than the planted evidence, Jacob reaches the desired conclusion. "Jacob's paternal anxiety turns him into the puppet of his sons' plotting. Not only does he at once draw the intended false conclusion, but he uses the very words of their original plan" (Alter).

37.35, All his sons... rose up to comfort him. The audacity! Even if prompted by guilt, it would take some nerve to comfort their father in this regard.

And all his daughters. Other than Dinah, we do not know of any daughters—though that does not mean that he had no other daughters. If there were any daughters-in-law at this point, they would be included among this number (*cf.* Ruth 1.11).

He refused to be comforted. Is this because he feels, in some part, responsible for Joseph's death?[8]

"No, I shall go down to Sheol to my son, mourning." The Hebrew term *Sheol* can mean either the grave or the realm of the dead, depending on the context. Here the meaning probably does not simply refer to the grave, as Jacob expects to go down to Joseph in Sheol "and Joseph he imagined to be devoured, or at best unburied. Sheol must therefore mean simply *death.* ...Jacob's words about being with his son in Sheol thus seem to indicate the patriarch's belief in a conscious reunion some day with Joseph."[9] See Excursus M.

37.36, Sold him to Potiphar, an officer of Pharaoh, the captain of the guard. Keil notes that this is literally "captain of the slaughterers, *i.e.,* the executioners," which would make him the "commanding officer of the royal body-guard, who executed the capital sentences ordered by the king." Some, however, have understood *slaughterers* in a different context and supposed Potiphar to be the Pharaoh's chief cook.

Growth of the Seed: God begins His plan to move the covenant family to Egypt where they will be preserved from famine and grow into a nation.

---

[8] See comment on 35.4.

[9] J. Barton Payne, *The Theology of the Older Testament,* 445. Whether or not it means a conscious reunion is debatable. It most likely excludes it from simply referring to the grave, but it may be an extension of that same thought and mean *death* in a broader sense.

Excursus M: Sheol

Jacob's mention of going down to Sheol brings up one of the more debated questions in Old Testament scholarship. Just what did Old Testament characters believe about life after death? A full discussion to that end is beyond the scope of this work, but we would posit that the ancients had some concept of an afterlife.[1] Though a full discussion of the debate is beyond us, we will here discuss in some more detail the concept of Sheol.

There are several perspectives regarding Sheol. Stuart lists six different opinions: the grave "to which all people, good or bad, go after death... and where no conscious existence is lived"; "a shadowy, semi-conscious continuing life of some sort in a place where all people go after death"; the next world, divided into two compartments, to one of which everyone goes upon earthly death; a place where only bodies go, as opposed to souls—at least those of the righteous, which go to heaven; a Nether World "inhabited by demons and some or all of the dead, who live an existence divorced from and, for demons, in opposition to the purposes of God and those who live on the earth"; Sheol is used two different ways, one simply being death/grave and the other being the next life.[2]

The wide variety of views should make it immediately clear that this question is difficult. Consider the following opinions:

On What It Is

- "Since the word in its 65 occurrences in the OT never takes the definite article, however, it often is a proper name denoting the netherworld, which, in essence, was an extension of the grave" (Hamilton). And Waltke: "The prepositions frequently accompanying it indicate that it is a place below the earth, 'the underworld.'"
- "Sheol is the place of the dead in the OT, where the spirits of the departed continue in a shadowy and rather unhappy existence (cf. Isa 14.14–20) and where relatives could be reunited with each other (cf. 2 Sam 12.23). Though Sheol is not beyond God's power (Amos 9.2), the psalmists pray for deliverance from Sheol, and it is possible that the OT believer hoped for something better than life in Sheol in the world to come (cf. Psa. 16.10; 30.3–4; 49.15–16)" (Wenham).
- "In every one of the sixty-five instances of *Sheol* in the Old Testament, it refers simply to 'the grave,' not the shadowy region of the netherworld."[3]

---

[1]See coment on 25.8.

[2]D.K. Stuart, "Sheol," *ISBE*, 472.

[3]*Hard Sayings*, 128.

382 | *The Growth of the Seed*

- "On the physical level it refers to the grave; on the metaphysical, to the realm of death as distinct from the realm of life. The emphasis is on the awfulness of death in comparison to life" (Waltke).

On Who Goes There

- "Because Sheol is so often pictured in the OT in a decidedly negative fashion and is frequently cited as the destiny of the wicked (Num 16.30, 33; 1 Kgs 2.6, 9, *etc.*), it would be proper to infer that Sheol is the ultimate and final abode of the wicked. Genesis 37.35; 42.38 (both spoken by Jacob); and 44.29, 31 (Judah's quoting of Jacob to Joseph) are among the rare passages that speak of a righteous person descending to Sheol. It is likely that in these Genesis passages, all involving Jacob, one should consider Sheol as denoting the state or condition of death into which the dejected Jacob will enter, without the sphere of that existence being any more definitely defined than that to which one 'descends,' much like our equally vague 'the great beyond' or 'afterworld'" (Hamilton).
- "When 'sheol'... is used in a local sense with reference to the righteous, its meaning is consistently that of 'the grave.'"[4]

Descriptions of Sheol

Sheol has a mouth (Psa 141.7) which it enlarges (Isa 5.14), and is never satisfied (Prov 27.20; 30.16). It is so powerful that none escapes its grip (Psa 89.48), and no one can redeem another from it (Hos 13.14; *cf.* Psa 49.7). It is likened to a prison with bars (Job 17.16). Here corruption is the father and the worm the mother and sister (Job 17.13–16). It is a land of no return (Job 7.9), an abode where socio-economic distinctions cease. Rich and poor (Job 3.18–19), righteous and wicked (Job 3.17), wise and fools (Psa 49.10), and Israelite and foreigner lie together. It is a land of silence (Psa 94.17), darkness (Psa 13.3), weakness and oblivion (Psa 88.10–18) (Waltke). Yet Waltke goes on to say: "One errs to take such figurative descriptions of the grave as literal depictions of an intermediate state."

The Word Itself

What does the word itself mean? Its etymology is difficult. Payne says that it "is presumably derived from the root... which means to 'ask.' Its basic reference would thus be to the never satisfied grave (Prov 30.16; *cf.* 1.12),"[5] though Stuart calls this conjecture "speculative at best."[6]

In two passages, the New Testament quotes the Old Testament where Sheol

---

[4]J. Barton Payne, *The Theology of the Older Testament*, 447.

[5]*Ibid.*, 445.

[6]D.K. Stuart, "Sheol," *ISBE*, 472.

is used (Acts 2.27; 1 Cor 15.55). "In the first case the passage is used to support the bodily resurrection of Christ from the grave, in the second, the resurrection of the believers."[7] It would seem then that, at least in these two passages, the basic meaning of Sheol is *the grave*. Harris also notes that outside the Old Testament, the word does not occur at all, except once in the Jewish Elephantine papyri, where it means *grave*.

What, then, is Sheol?

Harris, with Kaiser, believes that Sheol means *the grave* on every occurrence. He says that the descriptions found in the Old Testament "[give] us a picture of a typical Palestinian tomb, dark, dusty, with mingled bodies and where 'the poor lisping stammering tongue lies silent in the grave.' All the souls of men do not go to one place. But all people go to the grave."[9]

But is that all that it ever means? Certainly, words and definitions evolve with use. Payne argues: "By a natural extension of meaning, the noun *sheol* does come to identify death in the abstract."[10] Is it any stretch of the imagination, then, to further argue that a second natural extension would refer to the place souls go at death? After all, the Old Testament already has another word for grave, *qever*, and the word for pit, *bor*, often functions as its synonym.

Can we, then, say conclusively that it refers to a place for all the dead (Wenham) or for just the wicked (Hamilton)? Harris sees a problem with the former option: "One problem with [Sheol meaning the underworld] is the theological one. Does the OT teach, in contradiction to the NT, that all men after death go to a dark and dismal place where the dead know nothing and are cut off from God?"[11] And Stuart notes a problem with the latter: "Nowhere in the OT is Sheol described as a place of torment or punishment for the wicked. At most it is a place of confinement away from the land of the living."[12]

Where then are we left? Certainly, the safest option is to understand Sheol as simply referring to the grave in every instance and seek evidence of a belief in the afterlife in other places, such as the report of the patriarchs being gath-

---

[7]R. Laird Harris, "Sheol," *Theological Wordbook of the Old Testament*. Chicago: Moody Bible Institute, 1980, 892.

[8]*Ibid.*, 892.

[9]*Ibid.*, 893

[10]J. Barton Payne, *The Theology of the Older Testament*, 445.

[11]R. Laird Harris, "Sheol," *Theological Wordbook of the Old Testament*. Chicago: Moody Bible Institute, 1980, 892.

[12]D.K. Stuart, "Sheol," *ISBE*, 472.

ered to their people, a reunion of the family which Payne calls, "the Bible's first generalized revelation concerning the immortality of the soul."[13]

We find it difficult, however, to believe that during the thousands of years over which the Old Testament was written and *sheol* was used, its meaning did not evolve. It certainly is understandable, if not expected, that with time it would come to refer to death, in general, as Payne supposes. Whether or not it came to mean more than that—are Job's, and others', words merely poetic descriptions of an average tomb or their literal suppositions of an afterlife?—will be left to the scholars to debate.

---

[13]J. Barton Payne, *The Theology of the Older Testament*, 446.

38 This chapter has been the source of much consternation, as it seems to be a break in the Joseph narrative. Such is to be expected when these chapters are approached as 'The Joseph Narrative' rather than the *'Toledot* of Jacob.' As these chapters tell of the descendants of Jacob, it is only natural that there would be some focus on his other sons, particularly the one that would carry the family blessing. And that, really, is the crux of the matter. Joseph receives such attention primarily because his story explains to the original audience how they got to Egypt in the first place. Judah's story, however, must be told as it continues the theme of Genesis: tracing the Messianic lineage.

This chapter is an excellent illustration of the Genesis chapters not always following a strict chronological order. If this sequence of events began at the time of Joseph being sold into slavery (v 1), it will not end until the events of chapter 42. Joseph is in Egypt for about 22 years before his brothers arrive (13 years until his promotion, seven years of plenty, two of famine); the events of this chapter cover 20–22 years (assuming his sons marry in their mid-to-late teens) ending just as Judah returns to the family and travels with the brothers to Egypt.

38.1, It happened at that time. These events began immediately after Joseph was sold.

Judah went down from his brothers. Judah left the family, though under vastly different circumstances than did his brother Joseph. Some have speculated that he departed from them due to their wickedness in regard to Joseph and hypocrisy in regard to their father. This seems unlikely, as the sale of Joseph was *his* idea and the text does not at all indicate that he was a horrified onlooker as his brothers comforted Jacob.

38.2–5, He took [Shua's daughter] and went in to her. Judah turned aside from the family to marry a Canaanite woman—precisely what Isaac and Jacob were not to do, and what Esau did that caused his family such grief. Indeed to do so was dangerous to the family (*cf* ch 34). The family could be drowned out—a minority assimilated into the more dominant element. This would be especially dangerous, considering it was God's plan to destroy the Canaanites. Among other things, this chapter may show the need of the family to move to Egypt to prevent such intermarrying as the family grew. Unlike the Canaanites, the Egyptians typically stayed away from strangers, especially shepherds (*cf* 46.34). If the family was to grow into a pure nation, they would need to do so in a location where intermarrying would not be a temptation (Leupold).

The combination of *saw* and *took* in this verse may carry implications. Previous use of this phraseology has "overtones of illicit taking (*cf.* 3.6; 6.2; 12.15; 34.2; *cf.* Jdg 14.1–2), suggesting Judah's marriage may have been based on mere lust" (Wenham). Hamilton says, "Their relationship to each other is conveyed by six verbs: three for him (he meets her, marries her, and has intercourse with her, v 2), and three for her (she conceives, bears a son, and names the child, v 3). Judah and his wife relate sexually, but the text says nothing else about their relations."

Er… Onan… Shelah. Judah's wife bears him three sons.

38.6, A wife for Er… Tamar. Nothing is said about Tamar's background, though it would seem that she is a Canaanite, since there is no mention of an Israelite connection. "Conversely, one could argue that the identification of Judah's wife as a Canaanitess (v 2) means that the silence of the text for Tamar's ethnicity implies that she was Israelite" (Mathews).

38.7, But Er… was wicked in the sight of the LORD, and the LORD put him to death. No explanation is given as to what Er's wickedness was that earns him notoriety as the first individual in Scripture whom God kills. Alter says, "Given the insistent pattern of reversal of primogeniture in all these stories, it seems almost sufficient merely to be the firstborn in order to incur God's displeasure: though the firstborn is not necessarily evil, he usually turns out to be obtuse, rash, wild, or otherwise disqualified from carrying on the heritage."

There is also a play on words in this verse. In Hebrew, *wicked* is *Er* spelled backwards, a pun that Wenham attempts to capture in his translation: *Er erred.*

38.8–10, Then Judah said to Onan, "Go into your brother's wife and perform the duty of a brother-in-law to her, and raise up offspring for your brother." As per the levirate custom,[1] Onan was to father a child with Tamar, who would be considered Er's son. This would become law under Moses, but even now was a widespread custom.

But Onan knew that the offspring would not be his. Here is Onan's motivation for his following action. "Each of the three Old Testament refer-

---

[1] See Mathews for an extended discussion of levirate customs.

ences to this regulation (*cf.* Ruth 4.5f) shows that it could be most unwelcome, chiefly through the very fact that the donor himself set great store on family inheritance—but his own" (Kidner).

So whenever he went into his brother's wife he would waste the semen on the ground. That this happened *whenever* he lay with Tamar indicates that it was a repeated, not a one-time occurrence. And though he repeatedly had sex with Tamar, he refused to perform his duty. He used the levirate arrangement for sexual gratification, but not for its intended purpose: siring an offspring for his dead brother. "As Simeon and Levi desecrated circumcision (see 34.15), Onan desecrates a sacred duty. He abuses his brother and his wife" (Waltke).

What he did was wicked in the sight of the LORD, and he put him to death also. "It is noteworthy that Judah, who invented the lie that triggered his own father's mourning for a dead son, is bereaved of two sons in rapid sequence. In contrast to Jacob's extravagant grief, nothing is said about Judah's emotional response to the losses" (Alter).

38.11, Then Judah said to Tamar... "Remain a widow in your father's house, till Shelah my son grows up." It seems from this that Judah was committed to protecting Tamar's rights by ensuring that the next son would perform the levirate duties. But, for now, Shelah was too young—at least, that was Judah's cover story. What is said next clarifies that this is just a convenient excuse.

For he feared that he would die, like his brothers. In reality, Judah refused to give Shelah to Tamar because he seems to believe that Tamar was bad luck—everyone who was with her died![2] —"a kind of superstitious notion worthy rather of a heathen Canaanite than a member of the chosen family" (Leupold). At this point in his life, Judah was so spiritually imperceptive that he refused "to connect the evil conduct of his sons with their early demise."[3] Coats summarizes: "The crisis of the story thus arises from a violation of basic justice. And the violation hinges on Tamar's rights within the levirate custom, and Judah's determination not to fulfill those rights through his third son."[4]

---

[2]Coats says, quite colorfully, "When a father loses two sons on the same battlefield, he does not readily sacrifice a third one to the same cause." See "Widow's Rights: A Crux in the Structure of Genesis 38," *CBQ* 34 (1972): 463.

[3]Stigers, qtd. in Steven D. Mathewson, "An Exegetical Study of Genesis 38," *BSac* 146 (1989): 378.

[4]George W. Coats, "Widow's Rights: A Crux in the Structure of Genesis 38," *CBQ* 34 (1972): 463.

38.12–14, Shua's daughter died. When Judah was comforted, he went up to Timnah to his sheepshearers. These two facts indicate to the reader why this would be such a tempting time for Judah. First, his wife had died. Now comforted from his sadness,[5] but still single, he would be more susceptible to sexual temptation. Second, shearing sheep was hard and dirty work that was known for the rowdy parties which accompanied it, including heavy wine drinking (Leupold). In addition, there was in the region a Canaanite cult which encouraged fornication as fertility magic (Kidner). Judah would be going to the sheepshearing, because he was the owner of flocks (*cf.* 31.19; 1 Sam 25.2; 2 Sam 13.23–24).

When Tamar was told... she took off her widow's garments and covered herself with a veil... and sat at the entrance to Enaim. Everything was perfectly aligned so that Tamar could seduce Judah and receive from him the duty he kept his son from doing. "No doubt Tamar calculated that the flavor of this festival and the sexual unfulfillment that resulted from being a widower would make Judah quite susceptible to sexual temptation."[6]

The word for *prostitute* in verses 21–22 suggest that Tamar disguised herself as a cult prostitute. "The *veil* of verse 14 seems to confirm this, since... no prostitute except a (married) cultic one might wear it. Such was the world into which Judah married" (Kidner).[7] In everything to this point, Tamar has been a passive object that was acted upon by Judah and his sons. Here, however, "A clear perception of injustice done her is ascribed to Tamar (v 14), and she suddenly races into rapid, purposeful action."[8]

For she saw that Shelah was grown up, and she had not been given to him in marriage. Judah was temporariliy able to keep Shelah away from Tamar on the basis of his youth, but that ploy would no longer work. "Tamar is wholly concerned with her right as matriarch of Judah's eldest line" (Kidner). As such, "She is determined to secure offspring if she can, and if her father-in-law has thwarted her, she purposes to thwart him" (Leupold). Such action—though shocking—is not without parallel in the Old Testa-

---

[5] "The contrast between the conclusion of Judah's bereavement and the widow's clothing of Tamar points out Judah's irresponsibility" (Mathews).

[6] Steven D. Mathewson, "An Exegetical Study of Genesis 38," *BSac* 146 (1989): 378.

[7] Hamilton argues that it is not the veil, but her positioning herself at Enaim that makes her appear to be a prostitute.

[8] Robert Alter, *The Art of Biblical Narrative*, 8.

ment: Esther exploited Ahasuerus' sexual desires for the achievement of her aim; Naomi played on Boaz's appreciation of Ruth's beauty.

38.15–19, He said… she said… We cannot know for certain whether or not Judah had engaged in this type of activity before, but the dialogue does not suggest that he's a nervous first-timer. "He seems to know altogether too well how to carry on a transaction of this sort" (Leupold). Of course, it is quite a jump from this to make Judah a regular john.

"Come, let me come into you." He is brutally direct in his solicitation of Tamar. "Judah's sexual importunacy becomes a background of contrast for Joseph's sexual restraint in the next chapter" (Alter).

"A young goat from the flock." This is the customary fee for such a transaction (*cf.* Jdg. 15.1). As she was disguised as a cult prostitute, it would make sense to give her a goat, which could then be used as an offering to the idol—if this is the case, it would further show how far Judah had traveled from Yahweh worship.

"If you give me a pledge, until you send it." Tamar asks for a pledge to make sure he is good to his word. He obliges by giving her his signet and cord, and his staff. The signet is either a large seal or a ring that is personalized. The cord seems to clarify for us that it was a seal hung around the neck "which was part of the dress of any man of substance" (Kidner). The staff was his walking stick, but it was more than that. This staff would have had "his mark of ownership etched on top of it. Scepter heads incised with names have been found throughout the ancient Near East" (Waltke). Essentially, Judah surrenders his ID card, "something like taking a person's driver's license and credit cards in modern society" (Alter)—"which he expects to be quickly redeemed, but which Tamar retains for her own purposes."[9]

38.20–23, When Judah sent the young goat. Waltke notes the irony: "He has the honor to keep his obligation to a prostitute but not to his daughter-in-law!"

He did not find her. His friend was unable to find the cult prostitute. We cannot know why his friend was sent to pay the debt. Leupold suggests: "A certain shame may have led him to choose a less sensitive Canaanite to pay his whorish debts," though it may have simply been to further distance himself from his shameful act.

---

[9]Vawter, qtd. in Steven D. Mathewson, "An Exegetical Study of Genesis 38," *BSac* 146 (1989): 379.

"Let her keep the things as her own or we shall be laughed at." Judah calls short the search, lest he advertise his deed, and become the butt of a joke—primarily that he would give "such valuable objects for a fleeting pleasure" (Alter). Wenham says, "Judah's fear was well founded, for if he was not already a joke, in three months he certainly would be!"

38.24–25, About three months later. Enough time for her pregnancy to begin to show.[10]

"Tamar... has been immoral. Moreover, she is pregnant by her immorality." "Judah is the head of the family and responsible for all that transpires in it. So even his former daughter-in-law, or, as she may be called, his potential daughter-in-law comes under his jurisdiction" (Leupold).

"Bring her out, and let her be burned." "Tamar was regarded as the affianced bride of Shelah, and was to be punished as a bride convicted of a breach of chastity" (Keil). Perhaps Judah also saw it as a convenient release from his obligation of giving Shelah to her.

"By the man to whom these belong, I am pregnant." Tamar was prepared for such a response and provided Judah's personal identification to reveal the father of her baby. Does this remind him of his past (*cf.* 37.32)? Alter notes that this connects perfectly with the previous story of the deception of Jacob: she sends the evidence to argue her case; she confronts the father figure with *"Please identify"*; and like his father, Judah must acknowledge recognizing what was brought to him.[11]

38.26, "She is more righteous than I, since I did not give her to my son Shelah." This passage has been one of debate. What is being compared exactly? Are there differing degrees of sin? Before putting too much theological stock in Judah's words, we should remember that we are dealing with someone who has long been apostate from a relationship with Yahweh.

One possible solution is that she was more righteous as her sin was single, but Judah's was three-fold: while she committed fornication, Judah committed fornication, failed to give her Shelah, and forced her into such a position. Further, her actions were not motivated by lust, while his were.

---

[10]See Hamilton for a comparison of this event with the David–Bathsheba liaison.

[11]Clifford notes other similarities between Judah and Joseph: both *went down* from their brothers (38.1; 39.1) and married foreign women, fathering two sons who became rivals for firstborn status (38.27–30; 48.17–21). See Richard J. Clifford, "Genesis 38: Its Contribution to the Jacob Story," *CBQ* 66 (2004): 521.

An alternate solution is to look at *righteous* as being more concerned with legality than with morality, as the word used covers both functions.[12] If this is the correct interpretation, we would then understand Judah to simply be saying: 'I didn't do my duty, so she did it for me.' Tamar was more righteous because she was trying to keep the law while Judah was trying to subvert it. "However strange her deed, Tamar has carried out the will of God while he has not."[13]

And he did not know her again. This statement "may have more than a legal, historical referent. Throughout most of the narrative Judah has not really known Tamar. She is a brother's wife (v 8), a daughter-in-law (v 11), a widow (v 11), a prostitute (v 15), and a woman (v 20). Most conspicuously he did not 'know' Tamar as Tamar when he thought he was consorting with a prostitute. ...Now that he knows her, the need for further knowledge is over" (Hamilton).

This event marks the moment of enlightenment for Judah and his repentance.[14] And how quick was his change from ignoring his evil to open confession of it! At this point, apparently, he returns to the family and becomes the leader of it. And so we read of these events happening in the middle of the Joseph narrative because they explain Judah's actions throughout the remainder of Genesis: what transpired to change him and send him on the right track. Clifford sees this change as "indispensable for a proper understanding of the larger story; for Judah was the first of Jacob's sons to recognize how God brought good out of evil in guiding the family (38.26), enabling him to give the speech (44.18–34) that led his brother Joseph to a similar recognition (45.4–8)."[15]

38.27–30, When the time of her labor came, there were twins in her womb. Twins in the womb and the struggle between them reminds the reader of Jacob and Esau. Zerah's arm came out first and a ribbon was tied on

---

[12]Even when it is functioning in moral terms, it carries a certain undertone of the legal term, since morality in the Old Testament was concerned with keeping the law. Thus, Alter argues that it is strictly a legal term. Mathewson, more convincingly, argues that its basic meaning "is conformity to a standard, whether ethical or moral. The standard in this case would be the accepted social custom and duty of levirate marriage" ("An Exegetical Study of Genesis 38," *BSac,* 380).

[13]Richard J. Clifford, "Genesis 38: Its Contribution to the Jacob Story," *CBQ* 66 (2004): 530.

[14]For a further study of this chapter in the context of Judah's life, see Anthony J. Lambe, "Judah's Development: The Pattern of Departure–Transition–Return," *JSOT* 83 (1999): 53–68.

[15]Richard J. Clifford, "Genesis 38: Its Contribution to the Jacob Story," *CBQ* 66 (2004): 520.

it. Perez, however, was born first. We learn in a later genealogy that Perez was the carrier of the Messianic seed, pointing us to a different lesson this chapter teaches: "God will carry out his purpose(s) despite His people's unfaithfulness and its tragic consequences on their lives. His purposes will not be frustrated, even if He has to use means other than His people to accomplish them,"[16] even if He had to use a Canaanite woman—acting like a cult prostitute!—to do it.

Growth of the Seed: Judah repents; Perez will carry the Messianic line (*cf.* Matt 1.3).

Theological Reflection

Judah, as everyone in the Messianic line to this point, had some growing to do before he was the righteous bearer of the seed. The Bible consistently acknowledges the failings of the faithful, a point which both gives us hope when we falter and emphasizes the truth of the biblical record: it doesn't glorify God's people at the expense of the truth.

---

[16]Steven D. Mathewson, "An Exegetical Study of Genesis 38" *BSac* 146 (1989): 392.

39 The events of this chapter serve two purposes for Joseph while it documents his rise to power. "In Potiphar's household, he becomes familiar with Egyptian life in general and with the elements of a successful business administration. In the humiliation of the prison, however, Joseph is seasoned so that he is later able to endure being placed in an exalted position without danger of falling into conceit" (Leupold).

Also, this chapter shows a stark contrast with the previous chapter. In the previous chapter, we encountered Judah who was contaminated by the Canaanites' lack of moral character. Here, we find Joseph keeping a moral character in spite of temptations. This contrast is most clearly illustrated in Judah seeking out a prostitute while Joseph turns down an open invitation.

39.1, Potiphar, an officer of Pharaoh. The word used for *officer* is the word which usually translates *eunuch.* Either some eunuchs had wives, as Potiphar did, or the meaning of this word had evolved to a term synonymous with prominent court officials.[1]

The captain of the guard. This position was one that would have made him very close with Pharaoh (*cf.* v 20). Keil understands it to mean the chief executioner.

Had bought him. This note makes it clear that this chapter picks up where the narrative left off in 37.36. "At the end of chapter 37 Joseph is 'sold'…and here he is *purchased.* …This semantic shift reinforces the shift in the story from the brothers and the Midianites to Joseph and Potiphar" (Hamilton).

From the Ishmaelites. See comment on 37.28.

39.2, The LORD was with Joseph. His sufferings were not unknown to God. That this is told at the outset makes it evident that the success Joseph experiences is not due to his own work. This chapter is the only place in the Joseph narrative where *Yahweh* is used. "The name Yahweh occurs here at what is the most uncertain moment in the life of Joseph. His future hangs in the balance. He is alone in Egypt, separated from family, vulnerable, with a cloud over his future. Or is he alone? …The narrator… tells us, no less than five times, that in a very precarious situation, Joseph is not really alone. Yahweh is with him. …Joseph may be over Potiphar's household, but he is under Yahweh's blessing and guidance" (Hamilton).

He was in the house. As opposed to being a field hand. "Semitic slaves in

---

[1]Hamilton suggests that it is a borrowed word from Akkadian that means *he who belongs to the king.*

Egypt by their ability often received better positions than the less intelligent Egyptian *fellahin*, were employed about the house as domestics... and could rise to positions of trust under their masters."[2] Of course, the narrative makes it clear that the ultimate cause behind Joseph's placement was the Lord, not his ethnicity.

39.3–4, *His master saw that the LORD was with him.* His success was observed by Potiphar and even Potiphar could tell that his success was traceable to more than Joseph's ability.[3] "Precisely what he achieved and how it came to his master's attention is unstated, although 'blessing' in Genesis typically involves material wealth (*e.g.,* 24.35; 26.12; 30.27, 30). We may surmise that the household operated smoothly and Potiphar increased in his holdings. This role presages his future status as second to Pharaoh by accumulating unprecedented wealth for the king (41.49; 47.15–26)" (Mathews).

And he made him overseer of his house and put him in charge of all that he had. Potiphar was no fool! He saw Joseph's ability and that the hand of the Lord was with him in all that he did, so he put Joseph in charge of everything he had. This position may have had the connotation of being Potiphar's personal attendant.[4] As such, he had authority over the household and personally attended to Potiphar's needs.

39.5–7, *The LORD blessed the Egyptian's house for Joseph's sake.* God continues to bless Joseph and the blessing extends outward to Potiphar, who had treated Joseph well (*cf.* 12.3).

So he left all that he had in Joseph's charge. His trust in Joseph was full. Nothing was withheld from his trust to the extent that *he had no concern about anything but the food he ate,* which most likely was because of ritual separation at mealtimes (Hamilton).[5]

Now Joseph was handsome in form and appearance. Apparently, *all that he had* includes his wife. Thus, this note prepares us for what comes next in the narrative. "A young unmarried man... who is left alone with a wife

---

[2]K.A. Kitchen, "Joseph." *ISBE*, 1127.

[3]Does Joseph tell Potiphar of his God? (*cf.* 40.8; 41.16).

[4]See Hamilton for an argument against this position.

[5]Mathews suggests that *food* may be a euphemism for Potiphar's wife (*cf.* Prov 30.20); Waltke suggests that it is a figure of speech for his private affairs.

who has been virtually abandoned by her husband spells potential trouble" (Hamilton). Alter suggests that it is a "signal of warning in the midst of blessing that Joseph may suffer from one endowment too many."[6]

After a time his master's wife cast her eyes on Joseph. Previously, she had not noticed Joseph. But now he was in a prominent position, dressing to that position, and carrying the authority due it, he stood out to her. "She, the mistress of the house, is a slave to her lust for her husband's slave!" (Sarna qtd. in Waltke).

"Lie with me." She boldly approaches him with her desire. "Egyptian women were noted for their lascivious and unfaithful ways" (Leupold).

39.8–10, But he refused. Joseph's response is unmistakable. There is no waffling or giving it any thought. And his refusal is a stark contrast from her proposition. She speaks to him two words (in Hebrew); he responds with 35. "It is a remarkable deployment of the technique of contrastive dialogue repeatedly used by the biblical writers to define the differences between characters in verbal confrontation" (Alter).

"Nor has he kept back anything from me except yourself." His master had put unlimited trust in him, which he could not betray. She was the one thing that he could not have. It may be noteworthy that she was *kept back,* a very active term. Perhaps the motivation for this is not just concern for *Joseph's* behavior, especially if Egyptian women were as unfaithful as Leupold suggests.

Joseph was unsupervised; in his youth, he had risen to power quickly; his master had put unlimited trust in him; she was the only thing he could not have. All of these reasons—which Joseph used as motivation to spurn the temptation—are the very things which some would use as motivation *to* sin (Kidner).

"How then can I do this great wickedness and sin against God?" Ultimately, Joseph refused the temptation because he understood that yielding would be a transgression against God.

She spoke to Joseph day after day. "The shameless hussy was not in the least impressed by any of the higher considerations that Joseph had sought to drive into her conscience" (Leupold). She continued to pressure him daily.

---

[6]Robert Alter, *The Art of Biblical Narrative,* 108. Interestingly *beautiful in form and appearance* are the exact words used to describe Joseph's mother (29.17).

He would not listen to her… lie beside her or be with her. Joseph refused to be taken in by her constant pressure. He ensured his loyalty to his master and his God by not even being alone with Potiphar's wife.

39.11–12, One day, when he went into the house to do his work. The basic idea conveyed by *one day* is that this was his normal routine. "The narrator, besides explaining the daily routine of Pharaoh's household, makes it plain that at this critical juncture Joseph was guilty of no reckless or provocative action, but was attending normally to his regular business" (Honeyman qtd. in Hamilton).

None of the men of the house were there… she caught him by his garment, saying, "Lie with me." Here, she uses a third approach to temptation. Previously, she had sought to tempt him with flattering and startling words (v 7). Then, by a long, drawn-out process of leaving the temptation open for the taking (v 10). Now, she ambushes him and all is won or lost in a moment (Kidner). But why was Joseph alone with her? It is doubtful that it was his fault. He had made precautions against this very thing. It seems that he was in the house for his usual work, something of which she would have been well aware. Given her character, it is not too speculative to suggest that she sent the other men out of the house to arrange this very situation.

But he left his garment in her hand. For the second time Joseph is stripped of his garment and it is used to purport a lie. See comment on 37.23.[7]

And fled and got out of the house. Joseph made absolutely certain that he would not be taken into her sin (*cf.* 2 Tim 2.22).

39.13–15, As soon as she saw… she called to the men of her household. Joseph's coat left in the house would arouse as many questions about her as it would about him—especially if he had been seen fleeing. To point suspicion to him, she quickly calls a household meeting and accuses him of attempted rape, explaining both his clothes on the floor and his hasty exit.

"He has brought among us a Hebrew to laugh at us." At least three things are noteworthy in this short sentence. First, she refers to her husband neither by title nor by name as she casts blame on him (*cf.* 3.12). Second, the verb—*to laugh*—"can mean sexual dalliance or mockery, and probably

---

[7]There is some debate as to whether this refers to the outer garment (Waltke) or a different garment, which would leave him nearly naked as he fled (Alter and Hamilton). Wenham writes: "To pull either of these garments off against the wearer's will must have involved surprise and violence, perhaps suggesting that the woman was working according to a premeditated plan."

means both here" (Alter). Finally, that she refers to Joseph by his nationality "is an obvious attempt on her part to enlist their sense of Egyptian solidarity. She is probably suggesting that the very supremacy of this foreigner in the household is an insult to them all" (Alter).

39.16–18, She laid up his garment by her until his master came home. She kept the evidence to use against Joseph as soon as Potiphar arrived, and tells Potiphar the same story she had told the men of the household.

"The Hebrew servant, whom you have brought to us, came into me to laugh at me." Just how much of an indictment this is against Potiphar is subject to interpretation: Alter explains that it could mean either "the slave came to me—the one you brought to us—to dally with me" or "the slave came to me, the one you brought to us to dally with me." [8]

"He left his garment beside me." "Instead of saying that Joseph left the garment 'in her hand' (v 12), she says he left it 'beside her,' thus insinuating that he had disrobed quite voluntarily as a preliminary to rape" (Wenham).

39.19–20, As soon as his master heard the words that his wife spoke to him… his anger was kindled. And Joseph's master took him and put him into the prison, the place where the king's prisoners were confined. This is a shocking turn in the story. The penalty for Joseph's alleged act was death;[9] instead, Joseph is tossed into the nicest prison around.[10] Why is this? Kitchen says, "That Joseph was not immediately put to death but simply imprisoned may be a hint that Potiphar doubted his wife's story, or at least perhaps intended to inquire more closely into the matter at leisure."[11] It could very well be that Potiphar knew the truth, but was in a bind. He could not disprove his wife's statement, nor could he take the foreign slave's word over his wife's word. He could not let the situation continue to brew, lest the whole countryside know of the situation in the house of the captain of the guard! And notice that we are not told the object of Potiphar's anger. It never says that he was angry *at Joseph*. If he was, certainly

---

[8]Robert Alter, *The Art of Biblical Narrative*, 110.

[9]Keil writes that an attempt at adultery was punished by 1,000 blows, and rape upon a free woman still more severely.

[10]Leupold points out that this shows the importance of Joseph's position: "The chief servant of the captain of the bodyguard was as important a man as the king's prisoners."

[11]K.A. Kitchen, "Joseph," *ISBE*, 1128.

he would have brought about the appropriate punishment for the attempted rape. Could it be that Potiphar's anger is kindled because he is losing the best thing that has ever happened to his household?

Into the prison. This is, more literally, *into the house of the prison.* Mathews notes that it indicates the stark contrast in Joseph's state with the beginning of the chapter—there, he was *in the house of his Egyptian master.* How different is this from the parallel account in Judah's life! "Judah's sexual license results in an expanded family; while Joseph's righteousness results in undeserved imprisonment."[12]

39.21, But the Lord was with Joseph. This minor setback was not outside God's plan.

And gave him favor in the sight of the keeper of the prison. The prison in which Joseph was put was most likely a prison under the oversight of Potiphar (*cf.* 40.3; 41.10)—the keeper of the prison, then, a subordinate of Potiphar (Keil). That favor is found *in the sight of* the prison keeper provides a contrast from Joseph *in the sight of* Potiphar's wife. Hamilton says: "She saw a male figure to satisfy her sexual lust; he saw a reliable, model prisoner who could be trusted with responsibilities."

39.22–23, The keeper of the prison put Joseph in charge of all the prisoners. …Whatever was done there, he was the one who did it. If we are correct in understanding Potiphar to have believed Joseph and this prison to be one under his oversight, we would further suggest that in addition to God's working (or, perhaps, as the method of God's working), Potiphar had something to do with Joseph's ascent in the prison. Ultimately, he received a position of similar authority as he had in Potiphar's house.

He paid no attention to anything that was in Joseph's charge. His trust in Joseph was complete.

Whatever he did, the Lord made it succeed. This, in a nutshell, is the story of Joseph's life in Egypt: God blesses; an Egyptian takes notice; Joseph is promoted. All of this is part of the preparation for him to see God's hand at work in his life—to build him into the kind of leader that would be fitting for the responsibility he would be given.

Growth of the Seed: God's plan to preserve the Israelites in Egypt continues; the promise to Abraham is repeatedly confirmed (vv 3, 5, 23; *cf.* 12.3a).

---

[12]David A. Dorsey, *The Literary Structure of the Old Testament,* 63.

40 **1–3, Some time after this.** We cannot know precisely how much time Joseph spent in prison before this event, because we do not know how long he served in Potiphar's house. He was sold to Egypt when he was 17 (37.2) and rose to rule over Egypt 13 years later at age 30 (41.46). Two years pass between the end of this chapter and the beginning of the next, indicating that Joseph was 28 years old at this time.

The cupbearer and the baker of the king of Egypt. As they were in charge of Pharaoh's food and drink, both would have been valued officials. They were also, of necessity, *trustworthy* employees: "Both had close access to the Pharaoh, and both could play a sinister role in a conspiracy against him" (Waltke). Nehemiah, the cupbearer to Artaxerxes, provides a parallel of a cupbearer being a man of influence and ability (Neh 1.11–2.8). Kitchen writes: "[Cupbearers] (often foreigners) became in many cases confidants and favorites of the king and wielded political influence" (qtd. in Waltke).

Committed an offense against their lord. The terminology used implies actual guilt, in contrast with Joseph's imprisonment. They were not just thrown into prison on a royal whim.

He put them in custody of the house of the captain of the guard… where Joseph was confined. They were sent to the royal prison to await a sentence from the Pharaoh, where Joseph also was confined and now working as the steward of the prison (39.21–23).

40.4, The captain of the guard. Presumably Potiphar (*cf.* 37.36; 39.1).

Appointed Joseph to be with them. Because he knew Joseph's work, he knew Joseph could be trusted to be with these two important prisoners.

To attend to them. Note that Joseph's position is not to watch over them, but to *serve* them. And so we see another downward turn in Joseph's path. From favorite in the family, he was sold into slavery; then, from master of Potiphar's house to the prison; now, having risen to authority in the prison, he finds himself serving the prisoners. Poor, frustrated Joseph could have never guessed that this would be his way out![1]

This raises the question why these prisoners would get a servant. The answer is that these are no ordinary prisoners. And in every age, prisoners of high rank are not treated like every other prisoner. "These two pris-

---

[1]Hamilton disagrees: "What he did for Potiphar, and may continue to do for Potiphar, he now does for the cupbearer and baker. Certainly Joseph's responsibilities to Potiphar included anything but menial, tedious, chorelike activities. The same would be true of his responsibilities to these two."

oners had occupied important places in the court, and Pharaoh may yet pardon them, so it makes perfect sense that they should be singled out for special treatment in prison, to be attended personally by the warden's right-hand man" (Alter). Potiphar knew that he would not have been doing himself a favor to have them mistreated should they be released and regain their position of prominence.

40.5, *And one night they both dreamed.* Unlike others who dreamed, knowing that God was speaking to them (*cf.* 15.1–6; 28.10–17), these dreams were not clear messages from God and their meanings were lost on these men. Clearly, these dreams are not to be equated with the patriarchal visions, though they do fit into a pervading theme of the Joseph narrative.

Each his own dream, and each dream with its own interpretation. The dreams had something in common: they happened on the same night and each had a meaning. But they were also distinct: different dreams, each with a unique meaning. As with Joseph's dreams, they are stated at the outset to indicate that God is in charge throughout—what will later happen is no mere coincidence. Waltke observes: "Here is knowledge that lies outside of imperial power."

40.6–8, *[Joseph] saw that they were troubled.* Joseph was a good worker in whatever he did, paying attention to the smallest detail.

"We have had dreams, and there is no one to interpret them." Leupold writes, "The manner of statement of these high officials indicates that on general principles they believed in dreams and would, had they been at liberty, at once have resorted to some acknowledged interpreter." Mathews adds, "In Pharaoh's court such dreams received the consideration of professional counselors, but they are cut off from the expertise that they had probably often witnessed." And Hamilton: "Few would have had their insights and explanations prized as highly as those of the king's professional dream interpreters. A dream without an accompanying interpretation is like a diagnosis without a prognosis."

"Do not interpretations belong to God?" Joseph understands that when dreams foretell something, no man can be sure of its interpretation, save through God (*cf.* Dan 2.28). "Joseph's attitude is consonant with the OT's rejection of occult practices and its reliance on prophecy as a means of discovering God's will (Deut 18.10–22)" (Wenham).

"Please tell them to me." Joseph's request is indeed a bold one. We can-

not know exactly what motivated him, though various suggestions have been made. Most commonly, this is seen as an act of faith, though some have seen it as mere presumptuousness. It is also possible, though speculative at best, that God had told him that He would give him interpretations of dreams. "Ironically, the slave in his Egyptian masters' houses exercises by his gifts and character an authority over Pharaoh's chief cupbearer and chief baker" (Waltke).

40.9–11, So the chief cupbearer told his dream to Joseph. Convinced by Joseph, though we cannot know why, they, in turn, share their dreams with him.

"In my dream…" The cupbearer's dream was of a grape vine quickly going through its process of growing and bearing fruit. The cupbearer held Pharaoh's cup in his hand, which he filled with the juice and gave to Pharaoh.

40.12–13, "The three branches are three days. In three days Pharaoh will lift up your head and restore you to your office." As the dream describes his job, Joseph tells him that he will have his job restored to him. His head will be *lifted up*, which contrasts verse 7, where he is *downcast*. The number three is prominent in the dream. Three actions follow the three branches (*budded…blossomed…ripened*). Also, Pharaoh's cup is mentioned three times and is followed by three actions (*took…pressed…placed*). "The recurrence of the number three confirms the dream and the three days" (Waltke).

40.14–15, "Only remember me when it is well with you." Although the traditional interpretation—that Joseph is asking for a favor in turn for his interpretation—is still standard, Leupold suggests that he is not asking the cupbearer for immediate assistance, but telling him that a time will come when he does remember him. This would change the sense of the next phrase—*please do me the kindness to mention me to Pharaoh*—from a request for immediate help to a request for help at the appropriate time. Though this explanation better fits what happens (41.9–13), it is hard to reconcile it with verse 23, which seems to indicate that Joseph's anticipation was immediate help. "Just as the cupbearer is unable to interpret his own dream, Joseph is unable to make his own defense before the pharaoh. Each needs the help of the other" (Hamilton).

"Remember me… do me the kindness… and so get me out of this house." Cf. Exodus 2.24; 20.2,6. "His plea seems to foreshadow the ultimate redemption of all Israel from Egyptian slavery" (Wenham).

"I have done nothing that they should put me into the pit." Though Joseph would not be the last prisoner to claim innocence, "if a prisoner lays claims to liberation, he must offer some explanation for his right to be liberated" (Leupold). In addition to the favor he did for the cupbearer, Joseph tells him that he has been wrongly imprisoned.

40.16–17, When the chief baker saw that the interpretation was favorable.
He is excited to share his dream now. The cupbearer had just received a great interpretation and he knew that there were similarities between his dream and the cupbearer's: both related to official duty; both had the number three prominent in them. But although there were some similarities, the baker missed the clear distinctions between the two dreams that should have given him pause. "In the baker's dream Pharaoh is not seen, the baker is not performing his duty, and there is nothing in the former dream corresponding to the birds of prey. …Since Pharaoh did not receive the baked goods prepared by the baker, unlike the dream of the cupbearer, the picture conveyed impending doom" (Mathews).

"I also had a dream…" In his dream, he carried baskets of baked goods on his head to the Pharaoh, but the birds ate out of the baskets. As bizarre as this may seem, it would have been quite sensible to them: Egyptian men regularly carried baskets on their head; as a baker, he would have often carried baskets of bread and other baked goods. In that process, of course, birds would try to eat from the baskets. That he would not try to preserve the king's bread, however, does not bode well for the baker (*cf.* 15.11).

40.18–19, "The three baskets are three days." The fulfillment of this dream will also come in three days.

"Pharaoh will lift up your head." Like the cupbearer, so will the baker's head be lifted up.

"From you!" All similarities end here. While the cupbearer's position was to be restored, the baker was to be decapitated.

"And hang you on a tree. And the birds will eat the flesh from you." Decapitations were sometimes followed by impalement on a stake, where birds of prey and carrion eaters would dispose of the carcass. Mathews writes: "The impalement of a corpse was commonly enough practiced and was considered frightfully ignominious (*e.g.*, Deut 21.22–23; Josh 8.29; 10.26; 2 Sam 4.12; 21.12)." Wenham adds, "This treatment was designed to prevent his spirit from resting in the afterlife." And Waltke: "The se-

vere punishment of an ignominious and defiling death, rather than a decent burial, probably entails that, unlike the cupbearer, he has committed a grave crime that demands public censure."

40.20–22, On the third day… as Joseph had interpreted to them. Everything comes to pass, just as Joseph had said it would. "The exact accordance with the fulfillment… showed that as the dreams originated in the instigation of God, the interpretation was His inspiration also" (Keil). And Hamilton: "One gets the impression that the presence of God with Joseph, spoken of eloquently in the previous chapter, is still a reality."

 Which was Pharaoh's birthday. This may not be the celebration for his physical birth, but the celebration of his accession as the son of Re. "That accessions of new kings included the release of prisoners may give the background for Pharaoh's release of the cupbearer (*cf.* Jehoiachin, 2 Kgs 25.27)" (Mathews). Waltke suggests *anniversary* instead of *birthday* and Wenham notes that amnesties were often granted on the anniversaries of his accession.

40.23, Yet the chief cupbearer did not remember Joseph, but forgot him. It is highly unlikely that this was merely a slip of the mind—especially not after everything happened just as Joseph said it would. Rather, it would seem likely that he intentionally forgot Joseph. Perhaps he had no desire to help Joseph. Or perhaps he was waiting for a more convenient time— when *"it is well with you"* (v 14)—as opposed to seeking a favor immediately after being pardoned, a request that would take more nerve than most men have. And so, Joseph is left in prison. "The ingratitude of the Egyptian cupbearer prefigures the later national experience of the Israelites in Egypt (*cf.* Exod 1.8)" (Sarna qtd. in Waltke).

 "For sharing his sense of divine destiny Joseph finds himself sold by his brothers to some caravaneers going to Egypt (ch 37). For refusing to compromise his moral standards and sense of duty to his superiors, he is falsely accused and cast into prison (ch 39). In spite of the fact that he helps a fellow prisoner, that prisoner refuses or forgets to reciprocate when he has the chance to help Joseph. Here is a chain of three aggravating setbacks for Joseph" (Hamilton).

Growth of the Seed: God's providence continues.

41 This chapter focuses solely on Joseph's rise to power, and is filled with foreshadowing. Roop writes, "The pilgrimage of Joseph from slave to vice-regent parallels the journey of Israel as escapees from Egypt to the nation under Solomon, the life of David from shepherd's helper to king, and the story of Jesus from manger to the right hand of God. ...The presence of God brings life in the place of death, honor instead of humiliation, and fertility over sterility. ...The story depends not on the prowess of the people, but on the presence of God."[1] And Waltke: "Joseph prefigures Moses at the founding of Israel and Daniel at the end of Israel's monarchy. All three, oppressed captives in a hostile land, come to power by pitting God's wisdom against the wise of this world and displaying the superiority of God's wisdom and His rule over the nations. They prefigure Christ, God's wisdom, who astonishingly is raised from the cross to rule the world (1 Cor 1.18–2.16; Rev 12.1–5). As all were commanded to bow before Joseph (Gen 41.43), so 'at the name of Jesus every knee should bow' (Phil 2.10)."

41.1, After two whole years. This sets the time frame of the chapter: Joseph has remained in prison for two years since the cupbearer was released.

Pharaoh dreamed. Dreams continue to play a prominent role in the Joseph narrative. That Pharaoh has a dream immediately cues the reader that Joseph's services will soon be required. And that Pharaoh dreamed would have been significant to the original audience: "Kings, especially Egyptian Pharaohs, stood very close to the divine realm, and so they are often credited with revelatory dreams in ancient oriental texts" (Wenham).

The Nile. The Hebrew reads *the river*, but it obviously refers to the Nile. So also verses 3–4, 17–18.

41.2–4, There came up out of the Nile seven cows attractive and plump. There would be nothing remarkable about this detail of the dream. As do modern cows, ancient cows would submerge themselves in water to keep cool and bug-free (Kidner). That they *fed in the reed grass* would also be natural and is probably only noted to contrast the second set of cows. That there were seven cows, however, is noteworthy: "Cows were not simply the typical farm animal of ancient Egypt, but they symbolized Egypt, the primordial ocean, and one of the gods, Isis, among other

---

[1]Eugene F. Roop, *Genesis*, 260.

things. Throughout the ancient world, 'seven' was a sacred number, sometimes symbolizing fate" (Wenham).

Seven other cows, ugly and thin, came up out of the Nile. These cows are meant to stand in direct opposition to the first set of cows: ugly and thin rather than attractive and plump.

And the ugly, thin cows ate up the seven attractive, plump cows. This is odd, indeed—a vegetarian cow becomes a carnivorous cannibal. Verse 21 adds that eating the fat cows did not make them any fatter.

And Pharaoh awoke. The dreams were so strange that they jarred Pharaoh to consciousness.

41.5–7, And he fell asleep and dreamed a second time. The second dream indicates that the meaning is fixed by God (v 32). Also, the Joseph narrative is characterized by pairs.[2]

Seven ears of grain, plump and good. The previous dream is repeated, though this time with grain instead of cows. "Egypt, breadbasket of the Roman Empire, was as famous for its grain as for its cattle" (Wenham).

Blighted by the east wind. "This wretched wind, called to this day the *chamsin*, utterly wilts all green things upon which it blows" (Leupold).

Behold, it was a dream. The interjection, *behold* (Heb. *hinneh*), indicates surprise on the part of Pharaoh (as opposed to some translations, which render the word *indeed*, indicating confirmation, rather than surprise). As often happens, no matter how strange or unrealistic a dream may be, the dreamer thinks it real until awakening. Pharaoh, though confused, seems relieved to find that it was only a dream.

41.8, His spirit was troubled. Pharaoh is disturbed by these strange dreams. "In contrast to Pharaoh's troubled spirit, Joseph has the spirit of God (v 38)" (Waltke).

He sent and called for all the magicians of Egypt and all its wise men. Dream interpretation was considered a weighty matter in Egypt (*cf.* 40.8). The word used for *magicians* is an Egyptian-based word; "It appears to be part of a composite title for those who were expert in handling the ritual books of priestcraft and magic" (Kidner).

---

[2]See comment on 37.9.

There was none who could interpret them to Pharaoh. A pagan interpreter cannot decipher a message from Yahweh.[3] This is especially noteworthy, as the dream should have been relatively easy to interpret. As cows were revered as a symbol of earth's productive power, and grain was the primary source of food, "If…God wished to show Pharaoh that seven years of plenty were approaching, this announcement could hardly have been made plainer in the language of dreams than by showing to Pharaoh seven well-favored [cows] coming up out of the bountiful river to feed on the meadow made richly green by its water" (Dods qtd. in Leupold). Yet, as easy as this dream should have been to interpret, God wished to use His own instrument in its interpretation.

41.9–12, Then the chief cupbearer said to Pharaoh, "I remember…" The cupbearer remembers Joseph. Even if we grant to the cupbearer a period of time for things to return to normal before seeking a favor, two years is excessive. Now, however, he cites Joseph's interpretation of the dreams in prison and suggests that Pharaoh consult him (a strategic ploy to win more favor with the Pharaoh?).

"My offenses." Whether he is referring to forgetting Joseph or his offenses that landed him in prison is debated. In reality, he has done both Joseph and Pharaoh a disservice by not bringing Joseph to Pharaoh sooner (*cf.* 39.3, 5, 23; 41.38–41; 47.20–21, 25–26).

"A young Hebrew was there with us, a servant of the captain of the guard." Jewish interpreters have seen this description as somewhat disparaging. "Certainly the description is meant to suggest that Joseph was quite insignificant and that therefore it is not surprising the cupbearer had not mentioned him to Pharaoh before. But placed here, this comment accentuates the change in Joseph's position as dramatically as possible: one minute a forgotten imprisoned slave, the next on his way to the top of Egyptian society" (Wenham).

41.14–16, They quickly brought him. Learning the interpretation of these dreams was foremost on Pharaoh's mind.

When he had shaved himself and changed his clothes. "The utmost of meticulous cleanliness was essential for those who were to be presented to the

---

[3]It is doubtful that the magicians offered no interpretation at all. More likely, they could not offer a *satisfactory* interpretation.

Pharaoh" (Leupold). Thus, he was cleaned and put in proper attire. That he needed to be shaved is not to point out his neglect in prison, but to contrast Egyptian and Semitic etiquette (Kidner)—"Egyptians were usually clean shaven...while Asiatics usually wore beards" (Waltke).

"When you hear a dream you can interpret it." More literally, this phrase reads, *"You hear a dream to interpret it,"* which may imply, *"For you to hear a dream is to interpret it"* (Leupold). If this is the case, it indicates just how easy dream interpretation was for Joseph—a point juxtaposed against the difficulty faced by the Egyptian magicians. The Egyptian method of interpreting dreams would include much ceremonial arm-waving, dancing, and the like. Joseph, on the other hand, simply heard the dream and knew its meaning. See comment on verse 25.

"It is not in me; God will give Pharaoh a favorable answer." Joseph deflects credit from himself to God, just as in 40.8 he had pointed the two prisoners away from himself to God. And his deflection is done in haste and with grammatical emphasis. His denial—*it is not in me*—is just one word in the Hebrew; the position of *God* in the next sentence emphasizes the proper object of focus. Kidner, noting this, concludes that Joseph's abruptness contrasts with the polished speech of Daniel to the same effect (Dan 2.27–30). "Though Joseph is being humble about himself, he is at the same time offering something better, divine interpretation of the dreams" (Wenham). See THEOLOGICAL REFLECTION, below.

41.17–24, Then Pharaoh said to Joseph... Pharaoh's retelling of the dream adds a few details that are not in the original telling: verse 19 adds an extra adjective *(poor)*; verse 21 adds that there was no change in the weight of the thin cows; verse 23 adds an extra adjective *(withered)*.

41.25, "The dreams of Pharaoh are one." The two dreams have the same meaning; in essence, there is only one dream. "Joseph, it should be observed, doesn't miss a beat here. The moment he has heard the dreams, he had everything in hand: the meaning of all their details, and the explanation for the repetition" (Alter).

"God has revealed." The dream and the interpretation are from God.

"To Pharaoh what he is about to do." Such a revelation to a pagan king is rare, though without Joseph's interpretation, it would not have been known. This revelation must be understood as a means to retrieve Joseph from prison and put him in a position to save the family from the famine,

fulfill his own earlier dreams, and relocate the family to a place where they can grow into a nation. That this phrase is twice repeated (vv 28, 32) emphasizes Pharaoh's need to act on the issue. To this end, Joseph will offer advice (vv 33–36).

41.30, "All the plenty will be forgotten." Just as the skinny cows ate the fat ones and Pharaoh could see no evidence that the fat ones ever existed, so will the seven years of famine devour the seven years of plenty.

41.32, "God will shortly bring it about." Not every prophecy to a pagan king is a judgment against that nation. This is not an edict to repent, but a precautionary warning given so that the king would follow the measures needed to ensure survival in the midst of the famine. Here, God is using nature (famine) to guide Israel to Egypt, not punishing Egypt.

41.33–34, "Let Pharaoh select a discerning and wise man, and set him over the land of Egypt." Joseph not only interprets the dream, but offers the Pharaoh counsel regarding how to manage the upcoming famine. A chief administrator is needed, someone who has insight and wisdom—the same word used of the magicians who could not interpret the dream. "Pharaoh has already consulted with [Egypt's cleverest magicians] and they failed him miserably. Let the pharaoh not make the same mistake twice!" (Hamilton). While this word choice may indicate a sarcastic indictment of Egypt's wisdom, it is doubtful that Joseph had himself in mind for the position.[4]

"Appoint overseers over the land." Middle management: those who will make sure that the administrator's orders are followed from place to place.

"Take one-fifth of the produce of the land of Egypt during the seven plentiful years." The people would give a double-tithe. This would not have been excessive during years of plenty. If this excess was not collected and stored, it would have likely been wasted.

41.35–36, "Under the authority of Pharaoh." Of course, all things would be done with Pharaoh in charge.

"In the cities." The cities are the obvious locations for the storage, as they are central locations of the population, where they could more easily be *kept* or *guarded.*

---

[4]See comment on verse 36.

"That food shall be a reserve for the land against the seven years of famine." The end of this plan is, of course, the preservation of the people during the famine. Storing thusly during the years of plenty will provide enough food to keep the people through the years of famine.

"So that the land may not perish through the famine." The word used for *perish* is in a verbal stem that often gives it the meaning of being *cut off* from the community for violation of community standards. "Joseph does not say that Egypt will 'die (of starvation),' but rather Egypt 'will be cut off.' The consequence for rejecting Joseph's counsel is judgment. This moves Joseph's words to Pharaoh out of the category of option and into the category of mandate" (Hamilton).

Although it is easy to read this back into Joseph's advice, it is highly doubtful that Joseph had himself in mind for this position (unless God had already made him aware of this part of His plan). Most likely, he never would have even thought of himself: he was a foreigner—and a Hebrew shepherd at that (*cf.* 43.32; 46.34); he had never held an office of state; he was still a prisoner; and since his birth into the promised family, he had gone nowhere but down the ladder of importance. He certainly would not have expected a promotion to the office second only to Pharaoh in Egypt; his best hope would have been to be set free.

41.37–38, This proposal pleased Pharaoh and all his servants. Believing Joseph's interpretation to be true, the Egyptians saw the wisdom in his plan. "Though Joseph had given a gloomy interpretation of the dream, this did not prejudice the Pharaoh against him, for he too had viewed the dream as threatening. And because Joseph had followed up his interpretation with very positive suggestions about how Pharaoh should act to avert the disaster, his ideas were warmly received" (Wenham).

"The Spirit of God." Clearly, this statement is tainted by Pharaoh's polytheism. Keil sees it referring to a "spirit of supernatural insight and wisdom," not an acknowledgement of Yahweh. Even so, the Egyptians show enough spiritual discernment to see the supernatural at work.

41.39–41, "Since God had shown you all this." Pharaoh remembers Joseph's protestation (v 16). See Theological Reflection, below.

"You shall be over my house. …I have set you over all the land of Egypt." Pharaoh's thought: 'The god who revealed this to you will surely equip you with the ability to make it work.' The position to which Joseph is pro-

moted has been compared to prime minister; Joseph's position was one of real power—he was not just a figurehead. Even Pharaoh's assertion of his own ultimate power (v 40) is not an aggressive one; rather, "He does so to show again how expansive the rule of Joseph is, for the king is the sole exclusion to abiding by Joseph's decrees" (Mathews). Leupold says, "Only a man like Joseph, schooled by adversity and sorrow, could meet a sudden elevation like this without pride or self-exaltation. His rigorous training enabled him to encounter success without succumbing to its blandishments." And certainly, as he had acknowledged God in his interpreting of the dreams, so he would in his gain of authority.

This appointment has parallels with Joseph's past: it is the third *house* in which—and over which—Joseph has been placed. Also, as with his position in Potiphar's house, only one thing is withheld from him, though this time it is the throne of Egypt.

41.42–43, Then Pharaoh took the signet ring from his hand and put it on Joseph's hand. These verses indicate the ceremonial aspect of Joseph's appointment. The signet ring was "the predominant sign of his reign" (Mathews) and would give Joseph the authority to sign documents with Pharaoh's authority.

Garments of fine linen. The most elegant clothes—those fit for his new position. Hamilton says, "Clothing once again enters into the Joseph story, recalling Joseph's coat, which his brothers removed from him (ch 37), and his shirt, part of which Potiphar's wife ripped off him (ch 39)."

Gold chain. A general symbol of authority—only those in high places had such and they were "usually worn in Egypt as a mark of distinction" (Keil).

His second chariot. "A vehicle sufficiently splendid to be recognized as second only to Pharaoh's" (Leupold). And Hamilton: "For a second time Joseph goes for a ride. The first was to Egypt (ch 37); the second is throughout Egypt. The first was as kidnapped victim; the second is as exalted hero."

And they called out before him, "Bow the knee!" A public ceremony was given in honor of Joseph's appointment. Every appropriate outward sign was performed for a person of this authority.

41.44, "I am Pharaoh, and without your consent no one shall lift up hand or foot in all the land of Egypt." With the full authority of who he was—Pharaoh, a son of the gods—he bestows complete control and rule of Egypt on Joseph.

41.45, And Pharaoh called Joseph's name Zaphenath-paneah. This, along with giving Joseph an Egyptian wife, was done "in order that Joseph might be perfectly naturalized" (Keil). No agreement exists on the meaning of the name. Kidner says, "Egyptian-based interpretations have been offered as diverse as 'God has spoken and He lives' (G. Steindorff), 'He who knows things' (J. Vergote), and '(Joseph), who is called Ip'ankh' (K.A. Kitchen)." Efforts to better understand his Egyptian name are moot: the name never reappears in the narrative and is shown to be wholly insignificant when Pharaoh himself refers to Joseph by his Hebrew name (v 55; *cf.* 45.16, 19).

And he gave him in marriage Asenath, the daughter of Potiphera priest of On. Joseph receives an Egyptian wife. This may have been, in part, an attempt to set the Egyptians at ease over a foreigner being in a high position. "Much as the Egyptians may have felt an aversion to foreigners, yet to be introduced to one under such auspicious circumstances, to one who besides has contracted so favorable a matrimonial alliance, ought to cancel all prejudice" (Leupold). Also, "That he married into a priestly caste, which was a commanding influence in Egyptian life, further enhanced his power" (Mathews). *Potiphera* is the full form of the same name of Joseph's old master, Potiphar, "but evidently refers to a different person, since Potiphar was identified as courtier and high chamberlain, not as priest. *On* is not a deity, but the name of a city, later designated Heliopolis by the Greeks because of the sun worship centered there" (Alter).

41.46, Joseph was thirty years old. Thirteen years after he was sold into slavery (*cf.* 37.2).

And Joseph... went through all the land of Egypt. He takes a personal tour of the land that he is now ruling and must plan to sustain through the famine. This action would also have "symbolized the establishment of his rule, actualizing what the king had only declared" (Mathews).

41.47–49, During the seven plentiful years the earth produced abundantly. As before, Joseph's interpretation of the dream is correct. His plan is enacted, and the stored grain becomes so great that they cannot count it.

Like the sand of the sea. "The language here is strongly reminiscent of the covenantal language in the promise of progeny to Abraham and thus provides a kind of associative link with the notice of Joseph's progeny in the next three verses. Upon the birth of Ephraim, Joseph himself will invoke the verb for making fruitful that is featured in the repeated promises of offspring to the patriarchs" (Alter).

41.50–52, Two sons. See comment on 37.9.

Joseph named. "The names of both sons praise God, first for His preservation and second for His blessing. The names celebrate Joseph's new life: the end of the old, the potential of the new" (Waltke). And Hamilton: "Joseph's experiences are going in the opposite direction of Egypt's. Egypt has been experiencing prosperity; but famine and leanness are ahead. Joseph has been experiencing famine and leanness since he was seventeen; but he is now entering years of fruitfulness and prosperity."

Manasseh. "For," he said, "God has made me forget all my hardship and all my father's house." In naming Manasseh, he praises God for delivering him from his sorrows. More significantly, he mentions *all my father's house.* This brings to mind and may answer an interesting question: Why does Joseph not use his newfound authority and rule to return to his beloved father?

It is noteworthy that Joseph never knew about the lie his brothers perpetrated. We can only presume that he lay awake at night in Potiphar's house waiting for his wealthy and powerful father to come rescue him from his slavery. McGarvey writes: "Joseph must have had one thought to bear him up, at least for a time. 'My father loves me more than he does all my brothers. He is a rich man. When he hears that I have been sold into Egypt, he will send one hundred men, if need be, to hunt me up; he will load them with money to buy me back. I trust in my father for deliverance yet.'"[5] But as the years pass, he never hears anything from his father. Not knowing that his father thought him dead, how Joseph's feelings toward his father and his family must have changed! Now, he has the chance to visit his father and he does not—and at the birth of his firstborn, he exalts God for being able to forget his father's house.

Ephraim, "For God has made me fruitful." See comment on verse 49.

41.54–57, There was famine in all lands. As Palestine was watered by rain and the Jordan, and Egypt by the Nile, it would have been a rarity for there to be a famine in both places (Kidner). But as this famine was divinely constructed, it defied the bounds of normalcy. "That the famine

---

[5]J.W. McGarvey, "Divine Providence: Joseph," *McGarvey's Sermons Delivered in Louisville, Kentucky, June – September 1893,* 224.

threatens…the whole earth permits the famine of the Joseph story to function as a counterpart to the flood in primeval history. Joseph is an antitype of Noah, building storehouses just as Noah built his ark. The storehouses of Joseph, however, are for the survival of the masses" (Hamilton).

In all the land of Egypt there was bread. Joseph's plan works.

"Go to Joseph. What he says to you, do." Pharaoh has placed his full trust in Joseph; Joseph's plan is enacted without any royal oversight.

Joseph opened all the storehouses and sold to the Egyptians. It was not long before the Egyptians had run out of their own reserves and came to Joseph.

All the earth came to Joseph to buy grain. The famine was universal. This statement sets the stage for the reunion of Joseph and his family in the next chapter.

Growth of the Seed: Joseph is promoted to a position that will allow him to preserve the covenant family.

Theological Reflection: Making a Difference

After being forgotten in prison for two years, Joseph is finally brought out to stand before Pharaoh. Having been cleaned to their custom, he stands before the king who says, 'So, I hear that you can tell me what my dream means.'[6]

And so Joseph stood there—before the most powerful man in the world—with the perfect opportunity for personal gain, and says, 'No, but God can.' Joseph turns down the chance for personal gain to confess God to someone who already had a plethora of gods.

And that little confession made a difference. After Joseph's interpretation and advice, Pharaoh says, *"Can we find a man like this, in whom is the Spirit of God?"* Then Pharaoh said to Joseph, "Since God has shown you all this…" (38–39). Certainly, Pharaoh's confession is tainted by his polytheism: he attributes this to deity in general *(elohim)*, not Yahweh specifically. Yet he has enough spiritual discernment to see a supernatural hand at work (which is more than can be said for many today!), and he doesn't have to be reminded of Joseph's confession. There is no point at which Pharaoh commends Joseph and Joseph has to say to him again, 'No, Pharaoh, it was God, not me.'

---

[6] See comment on verse 15.

It is doubtful that Pharaoh ever changed from his idolatrous ways, but the fact remains that Joseph's confession made a difference in the way he thought about things.

There would have been nothing sinful in his words had Joseph initially said, 'Yes, Pharaoh, I've interpreted dreams before.' There is no reason to believe that Joseph would have been smitten had he not immediately said, 'No, Pharaoh, it's God, not me.' But Joseph understood where credit was due and gave it. He took what was a rather small and seemingly insignificant moment, confessed God, and made a difference in someone's life.

42 Beginning here, the story shifts from Joseph's slavery, imprisonment, and rise to power to the reuniting of the family. The fact that as much of the narrative focuses on this as on Joseph would seem to indicate that the thrust of the Joseph narrative has as much to do with the relocation of the family as it does with Joseph himself.

42.1–2, When Jacob learned. This is, more literally, *When Jacob saw*, which is meant to stand in contrast with his sons not seeing—looking at one another, not knowing what to do.

"Why do you look at one another?" There is famine in the land of Canaan and food in Egypt; yet everyone in Jacob's house seems to be sitting around waiting for someone else to make the next move. Jacob's words have since been paraphrased by countless fathers to countless sons: 'Don't sit there like a bump on a log; go do something.' Wenham notes, "Here Jacob's authority is apparent: though old, he is still head of the family, and his grown sons do as he bids. His dithering procrastination at the beginning of chapter 43 stands in marked contrast to his decisiveness here." And Mathews: "His sons failed to notice what was obvious to Jacob. That Jacob could 'see' despite his encroaching blindness (48.10) heightens the disparity."

"That we may live and not die." The famine is already so severe that acquiring food in Egypt is a matter of life and death.

42.3–4, Joseph's brothers. This shift in designation (from *Jacob's sons* in v 1) is designed to prepare us for the eventual reuniting of the family (Hamilton).

But Jacob did not send Benjamin. Benjamin was to remain behind. This action has found different interpretations. Kidner suggests that it implies Jacob had figured out that the brothers had done something to Joseph,[1] while Leupold just sees it as parental concern for the favorite and, perhaps, a little paranoia after the loss of Joseph. Whatever the case, it seems to indicate that Benjamin had replaced Joseph as the favored son.

42.5–6, The sons of Israel. Their designation has shifted again. "The narrator identifies them by their national designation to number them among the ethnic groups inhabiting the land of Canaan that go to Egypt for grain" (Waltke).

Now Joseph... was the one who sold to all the people of the land. This is not to imply that Joseph handled every detail of every sale, but that

---

[1] Is this suggestion supported by Jacob's words in verse 36?

he was the superintendent of sales: while personally handling some, he oversaw all sales "and was at hand particularly to give personal attention to all extraordinary cases, especially those that had to do with the sale of grain to foreigners" (Leupold).

Joseph's brothers came and bowed themselves before him. "The killers of the dream unwittingly begin to fulfill the divine dream" (Waltke).

42.7–8, Joseph... recognized them, but he treated them like strangers. The Hebrew for *treated them like strangers* is a form of the same word translated *recognized.* "Both uses pick up the thematically prominent repetition of the same root earlier in the story: Jacob was asked to 'recognize' Joseph's blood-soaked tunic and Tamar invited Judah to 'recognize' the tokens he had left with her as security for payment for sexual services" (Alter).

And spoke roughly to them. This is the point where interpretations on Joseph and his brothers split: why does Joseph treat them the way he does? One school of thought argues that it is part of a plan to redeem his brothers from their evil ways, to test and humble them and to bring about spiritual changes in them. The other extreme is that Joseph cared nothing about them and only sought vengeance for what they had done to him. "By failing to explain Joseph's conduct explicitly, the narrator leaves the reader to surmise and fill the gap himself, and this allows the creation of a multidimensional image of Joseph" (Wenham).

The former suggestion seems somewhat contrived and Pollyanna-ish, especially since this is Joseph's initial reaction to seeing his brothers for the first time since they sold him into slavery. That the last time Joseph's family was mentioned he praised God for being able to forget them would also seem to argue against the former interpretation. It seems more likely that, at this point, Joseph was punishing them by giving them a taste of their own medicine: "as they had threatened him with death and imprisonment, now he threatens them with the same" (Waltke). It is plausible, however, that Joseph's feelings toward them soften throughout the next several chapters, ultimately culminating in his complete forgiveness at Judah's speech (44.18–45.3).[2]

But they did not recognize him. It should not be surprising that his

---

[2]Some who take the latter view hold that all of Joseph's actions through the next several chapters are merely vindictive until Judah's speech where his heart is pricked and he makes a wholesale change of attitude. See J.W. McGarvey, "Divine Providence: Joseph," *McGarvey's Sermons Delivered in Louisville, Kentucky, June – September 1893*, 215–231.

brothers did not recognize him. Because of his younger age, he would have changed more in thirteen years than his older brothers had. Also, they had never seen him in his Egyptian clothes, nor would they have expected him to be clean shaven. Further, the harsh tone and foreign language would have disguised his appearance. And most significantly, they would have never expected him to be a high-ranking Egyptian official. Even if it had crossed one of their minds—'Hey, this guy reminds me of Joseph'—he never would have given it a second thought.

42.9, And Joseph remembered. Though God is often reported to *remember* something (*e.g.*, 8.1; 9.15–16; 19.29; 30.22), such is not commonly said of a person. This use is most likely to be understood as standing in contrast with the last word Joseph spoke regarding his family: praising God for *forgetting* them (41.51). "Despite his zeal to 'forget' his difficult past, he cannot escape it. It is facing his painful past that leads the way to his deliverance from the past" (Mathews).

The dreams. "The present scene fell short of their full promise, and perhaps moved Joseph to press for the presence of the whole family, which he now proceeded to do" (Kidner).

"You are spies; you have come to see the nakedness of the land." Joseph's accusations are to get them to talk. It seems from what follows that Joseph's plan, at this point, is to get Benjamin to Egypt. But first, he needed to learn that Benjamin was still alive. His absence in the entourage, coupled with their history, may have suggested to Joseph that the brothers had done something to him, too. As they defend against his accusations, they give him the information he needs to further his developing plan.

42.10–11, "Your servants have come to buy food." They assure Joseph that they are there for the same reason as everyone else, and that his suppositions are not true. They could not know that they were receiving any harsher treatment than anyone else who came to Egypt for food—for that matter, *we* cannot know how different their treatment was from anyone else who came to buy food.

"We are all sons of one man." Little did they know how much truth they spoke: this statement included the man interrogating them! But why this line of defense? "By affirming their brotherhood, they hope to rebut the charge of spying, for spies would surely not travel together and risk the whole family by one of them being caught" (Wenham).

"We are honest men." This may be the ironic peak of the Joseph narrative. One must wonder how Joseph kept a straight face.

42.12–13, "No, it is the nakedness of the land that you have come to see." Joseph pushes the brothers until he receives the information he seeks.

"We, your servants, are twelve brothers." Finally, they crack, and they tell Joseph their life story. There is no need to divulge all of this information, but pressure can make people talk when they should remain quiet, and say things of no relevance in a grasping effort to preserve themselves. "They think that adding details makes them more credible; in reality, they are giving Joseph the information he wants" (Waltke).

"One is no more." Again, the irony is thick: they tell Joseph he is dead.

42.14–17, "It is as I said to you. You are spies." Is Joseph still merely adding pressure on the brothers, or have their last words about him—and the memories stirred—incensed him? In either event, "He rejects the reasoning of their pleas of innocence just as they had once rejected his plea from the pit (42.21)" (Mathews).

"By this you shall be tested." Joseph remains 'unconvinced,' and further develops his plan to 'test' his brothers. They will be thrown in prison while one returns home to bring Benjamin back. If he returns, their story is corroborated, and they will be released. If he does not return, they will be left in prison. If it is supposed that Joseph is merely seeking vengeance, one must wonder if he had any intention of releasing the brothers. Perhaps his only intention was to rescue his younger brother from the family, keep the ten in prison, and leave his father all alone, as he supposed his father had left him.

And he put them all together in custody for three days. "To show that he is serious, Joseph has his brothers incarcerated for three days. …The adding of a jail sentence to the test is Joseph's way of convincing his brothers that he really thinks they are spies" (Hamilton).

42.18–19, "I fear God." Joseph, of course, meant Yahweh when he spoke these words, but the brothers would have had no way of knowing that, since he said *Elohim;* after all, all of the Egyptians feared *their* gods. In any event, this is Joseph's way of showing the brothers that he is a man of his word—if they do what he says, he will do as he had said. And in this statement, "A powerful contrast is set up. Here stands one (Joseph) whose word is reliable (for he fears God) before a group (Joseph's brothers) whose word may be quite unreliable and who fear Joseph" (Hamilton). And Mathews: "The implication one might draw from Joseph's protestation is that he was a person of integrity and the brothers were not. That the brothers immediately acknowledged their sin suggests strongly that they recognized the deeper meaning of his challenge to their integrity. From their perspective, the Egyptian lord presumably did not know their family secret, but in the ears of their conscience his words were the judgment of God against them."

"Let one of your brothers remain confined." Having left the brothers in prison for three days, Joseph now alters the plan. Rather than one brother returning for Benjamin, one will remain in prison while the rest return for Benjamin. This is, as Joseph says, to facilitate their return home with the food—one traveling alone certainly could not take the necessary food back to the family.

42.21–22, "In truth we are guilty concerning our brother." The punishment and confinement had done what their brother's and father's tears had been unable to do: touch their hearts and elicit a confession (Kidner). That they presume this is a result of their sin tells us two things: first, there was already some guilt in their consciences over what they had done—it was not the first time they had thought back to their actions; second, this is the first really bad thing to happen to them since they had sold Joseph into slavery.

"Did I not tell you not to sin against the boy?" Reuben's words have often been seen as righteous indignation, though they are little more than a glorified 'I told you so.' Hamilton says, "Reuben has a good memory, but he is not very helpful." Most likely, Reuben's argument was "that he should be excused from [being the one to stay behind] because he opposed harming Joseph in the first place" (Waltke).

"So now there comes a reckoning for his blood." It seems that the brothers never told Reuben that they sold Joseph into slavery (because they believed that he would have revealed this to Jacob?), and Reuben believed Joseph to be dead.[3]

---

[3]An alternate explanation to Reuben's words is that he understands kidnapping to be a capital crime, as it is in the Law of Moses (*cf.* Exod 21.16) and the code of Hammurabi. See R.K. Harrison, *Old Testament Times*, 59.

42.23–24, They did not know that Joseph understood them. Joseph was standing by during this conversation. Because he had been speaking through an interpreter,[4] they had no way of knowing that he spoke and understood Hebrew.

He turned away from them and wept. Joseph recognized repentance in them. If his original intention was only to retain Benjamin, it may have changed here to a plan to see the precise level of change in the brothers (*cf.* ch 44). "For all his apparent harshness toward his brothers, this action proves that he still loves them and that if they continue to show a change of heart, reconciliation will be possible ultimately" (Wenham).

And he took Simeon from them. To the brothers, whom he chose would have had little significance. But Joseph would have to make the choice. Simeon was chosen as the brother who would remain behind. Perhaps he had planned to keep the oldest until he learned of Reuben's stand against the brothers.[5] Now, he chooses the next oldest and the one who, with a history of violence, may have been a ringleader of cruelty on the day he was sold.[6]

Bound him before their eyes. This action is further designed to "impress on the brothers how serious [he] is" (Hamilton).

42.25, And Joseph gave orders… to replace every man's money in his sack. In addition to sending the brothers away with grain, he sends them away with the money they used to buy it. We are not told why this is, but commentators have made various suggestions. Leupold suggests that it is simple generosity and a desire to be kind to the family, though Hamilton says that such would be naïve, "unaware that what he does out of love for his brothers will cause a great emotional trauma to his brothers." Gunkel sees it as punishment—to further make them squirm. Von Rad and Sternberg see it as a redemptive act (Waltke). Or he may be merely setting up a trap: now he knows that he can prove them to be dishonest.

Regardless of the motive, doing this forced the brothers to face their

---

[4]Mathews notes a Jewish tradition identifying Manasseh as Joseph's interpreter, although this is doubtful as Manasseh was a child at this point.

[5]Joseph likely would have kept in prison—*a pit*, 40.15—the brother who originally suggested Joseph be thrown in *a pit*, 37.22.

[6]It has also been suggested that the second-born of Leah is detained "while the remaining nine brothers return to Canaan to bring down to Egypt Benjamin, the second-born son of Rachel" (Hamilton).

past. Previously, they had placed more value on money than life (*cf.* 37.26–27); now, he is testing their loyalty to Simeon—and how much harder it would be to return for Simeon when they appeared to be thieves (Waltke). If we are to understand Joseph's plan as changing when he heard them confess, this last option seems to be preferred.

42.27–28, He saw his money in the mouth of his sack. After a day's journey *(at the lodging place),* one of the brothers opens his sack to feed his donkey and finds the money. Most likely, only one sack needed to be opened to feed the animals, and finding the money there, the rest were hesitant to open their own sacks. "It is most likely that the brothers drew the conclusions that money was in their sacks too. But they were afraid to look lest they see the incriminating evidence. Then, when they reached their father, they all opened their sacks, and alas, their worst fears were realized" (Hamilton).

Their hearts failed them. As the heart was the center of thought to Hebrews, this most likely means that they did not know what to think (Wenham). What could they do now? In the eyes of the one who accused them of being spies, they would now appear to be thieves as well.

"What is this that God has done to us?" They believe that this chain of events is divine punishment for what they had done to Joseph, following the rationalistic mindset that all good is a reward for righteousness and all evil is punishment for wickedness.

42.29–34, They told him all that had happened. The brothers recount their stay in Egypt, though they did not really tell Jacob *all.* They left out being imprisoned for three days and finding money in one of the sacks, left ambiguous the state of Simeon, and changed the threat of life or death to a promise that they could trade in the land.[7] The narrator's report that they told him *all that had happened* is most likely to be understood as contrasting with their last report to their father (37.32), rather than a note that this report was exhaustive (Mathews).

42.35–36, Every man's bundle of money was in his sack. Apparently, the others did not check their sacks after the first brother found the money. And now, they *all* look like thieves. "Each time (chs 37 and 42) Jacob's sons have left home, they have returned to their father minus a brother

---

[7]See Hamilton for a full discussion of discrepancies between their account and the narrator's.

(Joseph, Simeon), but with extra silver in their possession" (Hamilton). Is this to be understood as the cause of his following outburst?

"You have bereaved me of my children." Jacob, distressed, begins and ends his speech with self-pity. But here, he speaks more truthfully than he knows regarding Joseph: they *had* bereaved him—how their already-sensitive consciences must have stung to hear those words.

"Simeon is no more." Jacob has no intention of sending anyone back for Simeon; he was as good as dead.[8]

All this has come against me. "His self-pity is understandable but not excusable. What about Simeon! And what about the affliction he inflicts on his family by holding back Benjamin?" (Waltke).

42.37–38, Reuben said to his father, "Kill my two sons if I do not bring [Benjamin] back to you. Put him in my hands and I will bring him back to you." "This accusation that somehow the brothers have contrived the loss of both Joseph and Simeon prompts the reckless and otherwise inexplicable outburst of Reuben. The brothers are trapped by their past lies and their presently aroused consciences" (Wenham). And so Reuben steps up in an attempt to lead the family. Just as in his previous attempts, he fails to garner any followers. "Reuben, as usual, means well but stumbles in the execution" (Alter). Although his offer may make sense in one regard—'I'll match your dead sons with my dead sons'—it is not particularly compelling. What good would two dead grandsons do Jacob on top of three dead sons? If Reuben is so noble, why does he not offer himself as a pledge (*cf.* 43.8–9)?

Reuben shows that, since his sin with Bilhah, he has lost his place of leadership in the family. His efforts to lead the brothers failed (ch 37) and now his effort to lead the family fails. By contrast, Judah shows that he is the one whom the family follows: the brothers follow his word and sell Joseph (ch 37); in the next chapter, Jacob will heed Judah's words and place Benjamin under his care. Finally, it is Judah who will act as the spokesperson of the family before Joseph (ch 44).

"My son shall not go down with you." Alter notes: "The extravagant insensitivity of Jacob's paternal favoritism continues to be breathtaking. He speaks of Benjamin as 'my son' almost as though the ones he is addressing

---

[8] Or, as Alter suggests, "Despite his protestations of grief, he clings to the hope that Joseph, like Simeon, is absent, not dead."

were not his sons. This unconscious disavowal of the ten sons is sharpened when Jacob says, 'he alone remains,' failing to add, 'from his mother.'"

"For his brother is dead, and he is the only one left." Jacob clearly expresses why Benjamin will not go to Egypt: he is the last remaining child of Rachel. "Jacob is of course fearful of another dreadful accident like the one in which he believes Joseph was torn to pieces by a wild beast. There is, then, an ironic disparity between Jacob's sense of a world of unpredictable dangers threatening his beloved son and Joseph's providential manipulation of events, unguessed by his father and brothers" (Alter).

Sheol. See Excursus M. This comment reveals that Benjamin is now as precious to Jacob as Joseph once was (Wenham).

Growth of the Seed: Joseph's brothers begin repentance and make strides toward family reconciliation; the covenant family makes its first trip to Egypt.

43 *1–2, Now the famine was severe in the land.* Any hope that Jacob had that the famine would relent and they would not have to return to Egypt has not been realized. We cannot know exactly how long has passed since their last trip to Egypt, except that it has been less than two years (*cf.* 45.6).

"Go again, buy us a little food." They have exhausted their prior purchase. "Jacob casually requests his sons return to Egypt to get *a little more corn*, as if Egypt is a tad down the road, a place where one can make a quick trip to purchase odds and ends" (Hamilton). Also, he may specify *a little* food, because the Egyptians were only selling the food in limited quantities and any amount would be *little* compared to the need (Leupold). Jacob's failure to mention Joseph's edict could hardly be due to forgetting it as Simeon's absence would be a constant reminder of what was required to retrieve him.

43.3–5, But Judah said. Judah now takes on the role of spokesperson for the family, "since Reuben's leadership had diminished to complaining (42.22) and his influence with his father was exhausted (42.37–38). A tell-tale sign of lost influence is a failed leader's gasping protestation, 'I told you so!'" (Mathews). Judah had already become the leader of the brothers (*cf.* 37.26–28); now, he assumes that role to a larger degree.

"The man solemnly warned us, saying." Judah understands that the man with whom they dealt is not someone to be trifled with.

"'You shall not see my face unless your brother is with you.'" Judah reminds Jacob of Joseph's ultimatum, not found in the previous chapter (*cf.* 42.15, 20). He is either paraphrasing Joseph's words, embellishing his warning to convince his father of the need to send Benjamin, or quoting words of Joseph not previously recorded.

Judah's history made him perfectly suited for this speech. His own family experience (ch 38) had educated him in this very matter: that to unwisely protect the youngest—action out of emotion, rather than reason—endangers the survival of the entire family.[1]

"If you will not send him, we will not go down." If they do not go back with Benjamin in tow, there is no reason to return. It is evident that Judah has no plans of forcibly taking Benjamin to Egypt, thereby usurping his father. Instead, he lays the survival of the family at Jacob's feet.

---

[1] Anthony J. Lambe, "Judah's Development: The Pattern of Departure–Transition–Return," *JSOT* 83 (1999): 53–68.

43.6–7, *"Why did you treat me so badly?"* Jacob seeks to avoid the inevitable by scolding his sons for volunteering information about Benjamin.

"The man questioned us carefully about ourselves and our kindred." *Cf.* 42.9–13. Judah proceeds to list questions Joseph asked that the narrative did not previously record. Different options have been suggested to smooth over this apparent contradiction. Leupold suggests that the account of chapter 42 is more of a summary, while here more details are given. Keil, on the other hand, acknowledges that he had not made direct inquiries, "but by his accusation that they were spies, he had compelled them to give an exact account of their family relationships." Whatever the case, "They are not doctoring the story to excuse themselves, because in 44.19 Judah says the same thing to Joseph, who knows the facts and holds their fate" (Waltke).

"Could we in any way know?" Here is the real thrust of Judah's argument: 'How could we possibly have known that he was going to demand *this?*'

43.8–10, *"Send the boy with me."* If it was not evident already, it is now clear that Judah is the leader of the family.

"That we may live and not die." Jacob is worried about something happening to Benjamin. But if they do not take Benjamin with them, *all* of them—including Benjamin—will die.

"I will be a pledge of his safety. From my hand you shall require him. If I do not bring him back to you and set him before you, then let me bear the blame forever." Unlike Reuben's extravagant and foolish guarantee, Judah's is thought out and inspires confidence. Rather than pledging the lives of his sons for the life of Jacob's son, he pledges himself. For a second time, Judah shows himself to be the superior leader.

"We would now have returned twice." Here is the confidence with which a leader speaks.

43.11–15, *"Carry a present down to the man."* Jacob, having acquiesced, now seeks to do everything within his power to ensure the safety of Benjamin and the success of the trip. First, he arranges to send a gift down to Joseph: a little of the best of what they had. A gift such as this would have been a customary way to demonstrate respect to a superior, "an almost indispensable courtesy in approaching a person of rank" (Kidner). The gifts he sends are significant, because some of these items were not indigenous to Egypt (Leupold), while others would have been useful for embalming[2] or for other medicinal purposes (Waltke).

"Take double the money with you." Second, Jacob seeks to show complete honesty in their financial dealings: they will send back the money that was returned to them in their sacks. Whether this refers to the specific bundles of money—had no one touched it since they found it in the sacks? (Leupold)—or just an identical amount of money cannot be known for certain. There is also some debate as to exactly how much money was taken. While many have understood it to simply mean double the money (what was brought back and what is needed to buy more food), it has also been understood to mean double the money *plus* what was sent back, thus three times the money. If the latter is to be understood, it may have been motivated by fear that the price of food had risen with the continuance of the famine.

"Take also your brother." Third, Jacob agrees to send Benjamin. While the gift was a *nice* thing to do and the return of the money the *right* thing to do, sending Benjamin was the *necessary* thing to do.

"May God Almighty grant you mercy." Finally, Jacob prayed for God's blessing on the venture, using specifically the designation *El Shaddai* (*cf.* 17.1; 28.3; 35.11; 49.25). "In each of these passages… [El Shaddai] is a deity who is blessing, making promises and covenants, and revealing Himself. How appropriate it is, then, for Jacob to use the name El Shaddai when he is in the circumstances he is in, and appealing to a God of mercy" (Hamilton).

"May he send back your other brother and Benjamin." His respective designations for Simeon and Benjamin show where his real concern lay.[3]

"If I am bereaved of my children, I am bereaved." Jacob's final words almost sound like a resignation of defeat in the matter; however, coupled with his prayer of faith, it must be understood as a resignation to God's will: 'If this is what God intends, so be it.' "The wheel seems to have come full circle. The plot movement that started with a brother leaving home in all innocence to join his brothers, only to find himself the property of a trading caravan bound for Egypt, now presses for closure

---

[2]See Howard F. Vos, *Genesis*, 173.

[3]Interestingly, some Jewish commentators have suggested that the vague reference—*your other brother*—is an unwitting prophecy referring to Joseph (Wenham).

once the brothers leave home in a caravan to rescue a brother in Egypt" (Sternberg qtd. in Wenham).

And Benjamin. Benjamin being tacked onto the end of the list is, perhaps, an intentional literary device. "The 'and Benjamin' hangs like the resigned sigh of a father trapped between the need to live and the possibility of a life made utterly empty through another loss" (Humphreys qtd. in Hamilton).

43.16, When Joseph saw Benjamin. The placement of this at the head of the events "implies that all Joseph did next was prompted by Benjamin's arrival" (Wenham). In one regard, the issue is now settled in the mind of Joseph: Benjamin had not been treated by his brothers as he was treated by them; all that they had said had now been shown true. The test for the brothers, however, is not yet over.

"Bring the men into the house." "Their last encounter with Joseph in Canaan, more than two decades earlier, was in an open field, where he was entirely in their power. Now, crossing the threshold of his house, they will be entirely in his power—whether for evil or for good they cannot say" (Alter).

"For the men are to dine with me at noon." This would have been strange indeed—for a man in Joseph's position to invite a group of foreigners into his home for dinner. The servant, however, does not question his master; he simply does what he is told.

43.18–19, And the men were afraid because they were brought to Joseph's house. First, Joseph had confused and frightened his brothers by his severity (42.7); now, he does so by his invitation (Procksch qtd. in Leupold). This is far more than they wanted—"all they hoped for was Simeon's release and fresh food supplies" (Wenham)—and they overreacted, construing the invitation to be something in the nature of a judicial summons, linking it, in their minds, to the returned money. "It never dawns on the brothers that Joseph has enough authority to have them arrested on the spot without having to resort to a dinner invitation" (Hamilton).

"So that he may assault us and fall upon us and make us servants." Thieves were sold as slaves (*cf.* Exod 22.2–3). Once again, the irony is thick (*cf.* 37.23–24, 28).

"And seize our donkeys." Kidner sees this remark as a hint of naiveté in the brothers' fear—that Egypt, "like some petty clan," would want their

donkeys. "It highlights the contrast between the tent-dwellers and their novel surroundings."

So they went up to the steward of Joseph's house. Afraid for their lives and their freedom, they approach Joseph's steward and plead their case, assuring him that the replaced money was an accident—they had no idea how it was returned to their sacks—and that they would gladly repay the money (vv 20–22).

At the door of the house. They were hesitant to enter into this trap without at least pleading their case. "Pointedly, their actual sitting down at Joseph's table is prefaced by a literally liminal moment: they stand at the entrance, expressing their anxiety to Joseph's steward" (Alter).

43.23–24, "Peace to you." He assures them that God had returned their money. But this does not sound much like an Egyptian reponse. Vos suggests that "some of Joseph's piety had rubbed off on him";[4] more likely, Joseph had prompted him (*cf.* 44.4).

Then he brought Simeon out to them. This alone would have relieved their fear. "The narrator links the restoration of Simeon to the restoration of the money, not to the return with Benjamin. The unexpected connection validates the interpretation that Joseph placed the money in their sack to test their fidelity to a brother" (Waltke).

Given them water, and they had washed their feet, and when he had given their donkeys fodder. The brothers are not being treated like thieves at all; rather, they are being treated as honored guests.

43.26, They… bowed down to him. The first dream is now fulfilled; all ten brothers are bowing to Joseph.[5] There is no place in the narrative where Jacob and Leah bow to Joseph, fulfilling the second dream; however, the repeated references to Jacob as *your servant* (*e.g.,* 43.28) may be intended to serve that purpose.

43.27, "Is your father well… is he still alive?" Joseph's first question is about his father. Whatever hard feelings he had harbored for Jacob (if any) have

---

[4]Howard F. Vos, *Genesis,* 173.

[5]Interestingly, this is not mentioned when they first arrived, which they most certainly would have done upon arrival (v 15). Waltke suggests that this delay is intentional, so the first bowing recorded is with all eleven brothers (*i.e.,* after Simeon's release) in order to highlight the fulfillment of the dream.

melted at the sight of Benjamin. Surely, he would have asked in as casual a manner as possible—*"the old man of whom you spoke"* seems to indicate this effort. But any questioning along these lines at all would have made the brothers nervous, not knowing where they might lead (*cf.* v 7). Joseph's inquiry about Jacob remaining alive, however, is most likely more than polite conversation. "In times of natural catastrophes the highest casualties are among the very young and very old. Has Jacob been able to tolerate the effects bought on by famine?" (Hamilton).

43.29–30, [He] saw his brother Benjamin, his mother's son. Having learned about Jacob, he turns his focus to Benjamin. His identification as *his mother's son* is meant to distinguish him from the half-brothers.

"Is this your youngest brother?" Surely, Joseph knew the answer to this question (v 16), but at the same time it had to be asked, both for formality, and because Joseph would have hardly recognized him. Though we do not know Benjamin's age the last time they were together, it is certain that he would be virtually unrecognizable to Joseph now.

"My son." Joseph's designation of Benjamin as *"my son"* is more to continue the royal façade than to indicate that Benjamin was yet a child, "though 'my brother' is hiding in the word he uses" (Alter).

Joseph hurried out... and he sought a place to weep. This is the first of three times Joseph had to step out of the room as his emotions overcame him.[6] His ability to come and go enabled him to keep up the charade.

43.31–32, "Serve the food." Sarna points out the irony: "Joseph hosts a meal for his brothers, who years before had callously sat down to eat while he languished in the pit" (qtd. in Waltke).

They served him by himself, and them by themselves, and the Egyptians who ate with him by themselves. Their dining arrangements were set up according to the Egyptian caste system, "which neither allowed Joseph, as minister of state and a member of the priestly order, to eat along with the Egyptians who were below him, nor the latter along with the Hebrews as foreigners" (Keil). And Hamilton: "For a second time Joseph is separated from his brothers at meal time. ...But he is no helpless occupant of an empty cistern this time. At the first meal separation he was the victim. Here he is the victor."

---

[6]Mathews says, "If Jeremiah is the so-called 'weeping prophet,' Joseph is the 'weeping patriarch.'"

An abomination to the Egyptians. Waltke notes: "Herein lies a clue to the rationale for the Egyptian sojourn. Whereas the Canaanites are willing to integrate and absorb the sons of Israel, the Egyptians hold them in contempt. Judah's intermarriage with the Canaanites in Genesis 38 shows the danger that syncretistic Canaanites present to the embryonic family. The Egyptian segregated culture guarantees that the embryonic nation can develop into a great nation within their borders."

43.33, They sat before him, the firstborn according to his birthright and the youngest according to his youth. Joseph arranged for the brothers to sit according to their age, from the oldest to the youngest.

And the men looked at one another in amazement. This "impressed them with the idea that this great man had been supernaturally enlightened to their family affairs" (Keil) and "increase[ed] the brothers' uneasy sense of exposure to divine intervention" (Kidner).

43.34, Benjamin's portion was five times as much as any of theirs. Joseph further tests the brothers to see if they would envy and hate Benjamin because of this distinction as they had formerly treated Joseph. Benjamin, of course, would not have been required to eat the excess of food that was given to him; rather, this was a customary way of distinguishing someone as honored at a meal (Leupold).

Drank and were merry. More literally, this reads *drank and got drunk*. "Spirits are abundant and spirits are high" (Hamilton). While this may be a colloquial expression for *drank and became fully content* (Waltke), it may be intended to inform us that, even with wine-loosed tongues, they did not mistreat Benjamin.

With him. The antecedent of this pronoun is somewhat vague. Are we to understand this as saying that they enjoyed their time in Joseph's presence or that, in spite of his place of honor, they drank and were merry with Benjamin?

Growth of the Seed: Joseph's brothers continue to show repentance; the covenant family makes its second trip to Egypt.

44 After a successful trip to Egypt, the brothers return to Palestine with full sacks and a full family. Their trip runs into trouble when Benjamin turns up with Joseph's stolen cup. Judah's speech to save Benjamin (and that ultimately proves the brothers' repentance) is one for the ages.

44.1–3, "Put each man's money in the mouth of his sack." Having learned by their return that they would not sell Simeon into slavery,[1] Joseph's puts the brothers to the ultimate test. Will they trade Benjamin for money as they had Joseph? In returning the money, he makes "the brothers feel they are trapped in a network of uncanny circumstances they can neither control nor explain" (Alter).[2]

"Put my cup, my silver cup, in the mouth of the sack of the youngest." This particular cup is put in the sack, most likely because it would have been one of the most valuable things within reach of pilfering at the banquet table. "At least it had to be displayed or stored in a place where the guests had access to it or could observe it, and thus later they could be charged with theft" (Hamilton). Here, then, is the test of the brothers. They returned for Simeon. But now, Benjamin will be framed as a thief and taken back to Egypt. He had just been shown extreme favoritism in their sight; how will they react? If they return for him, they have proven themselves to be wholly changed. If not, then he has rescued Benjamin from the still-evil brothers.

And he did as Joseph told him. The steward follows these strange orders without question.

The men were sent away with their donkeys. Having given his brothers a brief head start, he sends his steward after them to retrieve the 'stolen' cup.

How happy the brothers must have been when they left. They were treated like royalty by the man whom they feared. The money that made them look like thieves was attributed to God's working. Simeon had been freed. And, most importantly, not a finger had been laid on Benjamin. They were sent on their way with sacks filled to the brim with grain. "The weight of the bulging pouches probably gave the brothers the sense of generosity continued from the night before, encouraging a false impression of security" (Mathews).

---

[1] See comment on 42.25.

[2] Alternately, some have suggested that this return of the money was motivated wholly by generosity to his family. We are not convinced of this.

One must ask, after their last experience, why they did not check their sacks this time before they left. Most likely, they could not do so in front of Joseph or the steward, lest they be seen as ungrateful or rude. Perhaps they intended to do so once they got out of earshot, but never had the chance, as the steward overtook them after just a short time. Or perhaps, they were too happy over the outcome of the trip to even think about checking their sacks this time.

44.4–5, "Say to them, 'Why have you repaid evil for good?'" Joseph tells his steward exactly how to interrogate his brothers. The phrase—*repaid evil for good*—"does not describe merely ingratitude but describes malicious exploitation of a person's kindness" (Mathews).

"By this… he practices divination." Divination was a heathen custom practiced in a variety of methods. Some poured clear water into a bowl and then strewed into the water small pieces of gold and silver or precious stones. Some poured oil into the water. Others observed the manner in which light rays broke on the surface. Usually, the resulting designs observed in the water, whether from the particles thrown into it or from the oil, were construed after certain rules in order to draw conclusions as to the future (Leupold).

Was Joseph guilty of divination? A variety of suggestions have been made. Some have suggested that it was simply to add a mystical air to the cup itself: "The intention of the statement may simply have been to represent the goblet as a sacred vessel, and Joseph as acquainted with the most secret things" (Keil). Others have seen it only as part of the act: "Referring to the wine goblet as a divining cup contributes to the ruse" (Waltke). Wenham sees it differently yet: "It is dubious whether this remark by the steward describes Joseph's practice; it is just a threatening comment to stress the gravity of the offense and to explain why he is sure the brothers are guilty." Some, however, have seen it at face value, suggesting that God may have chosen this avenue to work: "It may actually have pleased God to use some such means in order to convey higher revelation to Joseph" (Vilmar qtd. in Leupold). Kidner suggests: "Unless this was part of his pose, Joseph here took his coloring from Egypt, in a matter on which no law was as yet in being." Or, perhaps, "As Vergote points out, the phrase 'whereby he certainly divineth' could be translated 'about this he certainly would have divined.' It is a small difference, but it would give added point to verse 15, where the implication would be, 'Did you think you could be undetected?'" (Kidner).

44.7–10, "Far be it from your servants to do such a thing!" Joseph's brothers respond that they are not the type of people to do something like that. Hamilton suggests that the brothers are swearing to that effect as the word used is "usually used to introduce an oath."

"Behold the money that we found in the mouths of our sacks we brought back to you from the land of Canaan." They cite as proof their return of the money that they found in their sacks. "Their indignant retort is logically sound: thieves don't return merchandise in order to steal. If they were thieves, it would have been self-defeating to return the silver, and since they had, it was irrational for them to steal now" (Mathews).

44.9–10, "Whichever of your servants is found with it shall die." They are so certain of their innocence that they agree for the guilty party to be executed over the theft. Their words are similar to the ones spoken by Jacob to Laban when he sought his household idols (31.32). "It is a teasing parallel with crucial differences: Laban does not find what he is looking for, but the death sentence pronounced on the actual guilty party—Benjamin's mother, Rachel—appears to be carried out later when she dies bearing him" (Alter).

"We also will be my lord's servants." Not only do they volunteer the guilty party for death, but they are so confident of their innocence that the remainder of them will return to be slaves to the steward's master, if the cup is found among them. "Their assurance contrasts with the apprehension of imprisonment they had when first taken to Joseph's house (43.18). Ironically, they condemn themselves to the punishment that they all along feared" (Mathews).

He said, "Let it be as you say." The steward agrees to their terms, but in so doing changes them. Instead of a death penalty for the guilty and slavery for the rest, he proposes slavery for the guilty and freedom for the rest, setting the stage for the test to do to Benjamin what was done to Joseph: sell him into Egyptian slavery. But this time, the price—their freedom—was much more valuable than the 20 pieces of silver they shared for Joseph's sale (Kidner).

44.11–13, Then each man quickly lowered his sack to the ground. They were certain of their innocence and sought to prove it with the utmost haste.

And he searched, beginning with the eldest and ending with the youngest. The scene is played to achieve the utmost suspense. The steward searches through ten bags that do not contain the cup so he might arrive last at Benjamin, where he already knows the cup is hidden. "Laban investigates Rachel's tent last probably because he suspects her the least. The steward searches Benjamin's sack last to give the appearance that he suspects Benjamin the least" (Hamilton). It is interesting that nothing is said of the money that would have been once again found in the sacks. Waltkes suggests, "The narrator blanks what happened to the silver in the mouth of each of the sacks (44.1) because it is overshadowed by the goblet in Benjamin's sack and because it is inconsequential to the reconciliation of the brothers."

Then they tore their clothes. The change in the brothers is complete. No longer are they seeking to rid themselves of Rachel's children. They have now become like their father (*cf.* 37.34). "The narrative conveys again the irony of deserved punishment for the offenders. They were guilty but did not show remorse; now they are innocent and demonstrate deepest agony" (Mathews). And Hamilton: "They no more suspect they are victims of fraud than did their father suspect foul play when he was given the bloodied coat. In neither case is an alternative explanation explored."

And every man loaded his donkey, and they returned to the city. They reject the offering of the stewards—*the rest of you shall be innocent* (v 10)—and return with Benjamin to Joseph's house. "Whereas they had contrived to dispatch Joseph to Egypt, this time they voluntarily return with Benjamin to Egypt" (Wenham).

44.14–16, *They fell before him to the ground.* This does not indicate a prostrating bow, but more literally, they *threw themselves* to the ground. They were desperate, not deferring (Waltke).

"What deed is this that you have done?" In light of the previous day's favor, they were rank ingrates (Leupold). "The brothers had been received as guests, they had shared a meal with the master of the house, and now they had shown outrageous disdain for their host!" (Westerman qtd. in Wenham).

"Divination." "Ironically, this divination cup does not discern Benjamin's innocence" (Waltke). See comment on verse 5.

And Judah said. The leader of the family speaks on behalf of them all.

"How can we clear ourselves?" There is such overwhelmingly evidence against them that it is pointless to claim innocence.

"God has found out the guilt of your servants." Clearly, the brothers see

this as divine retribution for their sin against Joseph.[3] Even though they had stolen nothing from Joseph, twice they have been made to look like thieves before him. God, they thought, was paying them back in kind for selling Joseph into slavery. "The mysteriousness of what happened in just singling out Benjamin seems to impress them all so strongly with the thought that a higher hand is at work" (Leupold). And Hamilton: "They [feel that they] deserve what is happening to them even if they are not guilty of this particular crime. Here is a graphic illustration of the Bible's emphasis on God's justice. The wrongs one does will be repaid, someway, somehow, somewhere."

"Behold, we are my lord's servants, both we and he also in whose hand the cup has been found." Here lies a sense of family and group solidarity that previously had not been found among the brothers.

44.17, "Far be it from me that I should do so!" "His words have double meaning. It is not he who would make his brothers slaves" (Waltke).

"Only the man in whose hand the cup was found shall be my servant." Joseph gives them the perfect out. He protests strongly against the idea of keeping all of them, giving them instead the opportunity to leave behind Jacob's favorite as a slave while they all go free.

"Go up in peace to your father." Just as they had after selling Joseph into slavery. He makes their release seem all the more palatable, by ensuring their safe travel home—they would not be stopped again; their journey would be *in peace.* But Joseph's mention of their father makes them all the more keenly aware of their obligation to him. And these brothers, who were so angry at and indifferent to their father, and so jealous of their brother that they conspired to sell him into slavery, now beg for their father's well being and offer themselves as slaves to save their father's now-favorite child.

44.18–23, Then Judah went up to him and said. Judah now speaks in an effort to win Benjamin's freedom. "Joseph's ostensibly generous offer is met with the longest and most impassioned speech in Genesis" (Wenham). His speech is remarkable and powerful, designed to win the mind of Joseph to release Benjamin for the sake of their father in exchange for himself.

---

[3]It should go without saying that he is not confessing guilt for the theft of the cup, since he just declared innocence of that (v 7).

"My lord asked his servants, saying, 'Have you a father, or a brother?'" Judah begins his speech by arguing that Benjamin was only there at the demand of Joseph. The brothers did not bring him originally, and their father did not want him to go.

"We have a father, an old man, and a young brother, the child of his old age." Judah's report of Jacob and Benjamin emphasizes their ages. "Both the feeble age of Jacob and the youth of Benjamin call attention to their vulnerability" (Mathews).

"His brother being dead." Joseph is again told that he is dead (*cf.* 42.13).

"His father loves him." Previously, this was the sticking point with the brothers (*cf.* 37.4). But now, "This same favoritism is cited as ground for mercy; the other brothers, or at least Judah, have accepted that love for their father must override all other grudges" (Wenham).

"The boy cannot leave his father." Reference to Benjamin as *the boy* is because of his place as youngest, not because of his age, as he is well beyond adolescence at this point (*cf.* 46.21). Perhaps Judah sought to contrast this view of Benjamin with Joseph's—*the man* (v 17).

44.24–31, "As soon as he sees that the boy is not with us, he will die, and your servant will bring down the gray hairs of your servant our father with sorrow to Sheol." Next, Judah appeals to Joseph for the sake of their father. He recounts the conversation that led up to this trip, including the statement that virtually delegitimized himself as a son of Jacob (v 27; *cf.* 42.38). Judah's only concern was for the welfare of Benjamin and their father. On Sheol, see Excursus M.

"'Surely he has been torn to pieces.'" For the first time, Joseph learns why Jacob never came to rescue him. If he had borne any grudge against his father, it would have immediately dissipated at this word.

44.32–34, "Your servant became a pledge of safety for the boy. …Now therefore, please let your servant remain instead of the boy as a servant to my lord." Judah's life has already been given as a guarantee for Benjamin's safety. Here, he acts, offering himself as a slave in Benjamin's place. He has come full circle. He "who conceived the plan of selling Joseph into slavery… offer[s] himself as a slave in place of Benjamin" (Alter). Further, Judah becomes a type of Christ: the first person in Scripture to offer his life for another.

"I fear to see the evil that would find my father." A son who can sincere-

ly say this is a son who genuinely cares for his father and would cause him no grief. "This of course stands in stark contrast to his willingness years before to watch his father writhe in anguish over Joseph's supposed death" (Alter). Judah was a changed man.

Growth of the Seed: Judah illustrates the degree of their repentance and typifies the Messiah by offering his life for another.

45 This is an unfortunate place to break the chapter. The first half of the chapter (vv 1–15) finishes the thought of the previous chapter. The narrative tension and buildup to this moment of climax is sadly stymied by the largely printed '45' on the page. Make no mistake: the first half of this chapter belongs with chapter 44. The second half of chapter 45 (vv 16–28) belongs with chapter 46. The story of Joseph's reunion with his brothers is complete and the narrative focus shifts to the reunion of Joseph with Jacob. Verse 16 is the beginning of the sequence of events which brings that reunion (discussed in chapter 46) to fruition.

45.1–2, *Then Joseph could not control himself before all those who stood by him.* The brothers had passed every test offered by Joseph. They were sorry for what they had done to Joseph; in a similar situation, they did not do the same to Benjamin, even when there was an easy escape for them. Judah had given proof of their new direction by his offer of self-sacrifice to spare Jacob. All of this culminates in Joseph no longer being able to control his emotions. "The imperial power broker who had controlled the course of events in this whole chapter, with only an occasional and very private lapse, suddenly lost control of himself. The man who had been able to keep separate his family and national world could do so no longer."[1]

He cried, "Make everyone go out from me." So no one stayed with him. Joseph clears the room for his self-revelation for at least three reasons. First, this was now purely a family affair. Second, a man of his position ought not to show such extreme emotion in front of subordinates. Finally, clearing the room prevented the airing of such ugly aspects of the relationship of the people of God before unbelievers.[2]

When Joseph made himself known to his brothers. For the past several chapters, the eleven have been referred to as *the men*. Now, in the moment of reconciliation, the narrator returns to describing them as *his brothers* (vv 1, 3–4, 15–16, 24).

And he wept aloud, so that the Egyptians heard it. This is not to indicate that his servants were eavesdropping; rather, they would not get so far away from their master that they could not hear his call to fulfill a command.

---

[1]Eugene F. Roop, *Genesis*, 271.

[2]Howard F. Vos, *Genesis*, 178.

45.3–4, "Is my father still alive?" Although Joseph has already asked this question, previously he asked as a stranger making small talk. Now, he asks as a son—*my father*—genuinely concerned with the truth and expecting the kind of account one brother would give to another (Leupold)—certainly more than they would tell an Egyptian ruler. This may also have served to soften the harshness of the startling announcement—*I am your brother, Joseph*—by an eager, friendly inquiry about their father. Finally, this may be tied up in Judah's speech which comes immediately before this: "Judah had painted such a terrifying picture of the impact on Jacob of the loss of his sons that Joseph was worried" (Wenham). Interestingly, Joseph's question is never answered.

But his… brothers were dismayed at his presence. Their fear and the disconcerting feeling which overcame them is certainly understandable. They are completely in Joseph's power—a man whom they knew (through his Egyptian guise) to be a harsh and cruel man. And a man whom (as Joseph) they had severely wronged.

"Come near to me, please." They had kept their distance, because of his position and their fear of him. His revelation had not inspired them to close the gap, so Joseph sought to do so. This request is to be understood as an invitation to intimate conversation.

And they came near. They obeyed him, but the reader can feel the reticence as they do. Joseph would have to win back their confidence (*cf.* 50.15).

"Whom you sold into Egypt." "No rebuke is intended. He needs to prove his identity (*cf.* 45.12); only Joseph knows their secret. Moreover, with their secret out, they can be freed from suppressed guilt" (Waltke). But this reminder would have probably made the brothers tense with worry, so Joseph quickly assures them that he has no plans for revenge (vv 5ff).

45.5, "You sold me… God sent me." There may be no better summary of providence than found in this sentence. Regardless of what man may do, God's plan will be accomplished. There are two aspects to any event: human mishandling (or, sometimes the blind working of nature) and the perfect will of God. The latter, alone, is of consequence (Kidner). "God's purposes are ultimately fulfilled through and in spite of human deeds, whether or not those deeds are morally right" (Wenham). And Joseph makes certain to explain this point, by repeating it two more times in verses 7–8. Joseph has come to understand God's providence. "He directs the maze of human guilt to achieve His good and set purposes"

(Waltke).[3] "We are not told precisely at what point it dawned upon Joseph that he was a lifesaver sent by God at the most propitious moment, rather than a victim of barbaric men and brutal circumstances. Nothing thus far in the narrative has prepared us for this eloquent and magnificent theologizing on his pilgrimage. We must assume that Joseph perceived bit by bit the hand of God in this nightmare" (Hamilton).

As Judah had done before,[4] now Joseph foreshadows Christ. God had decided that He would—through wicked deeds—sacrifice the life of one for the salvation of others. Also, Joseph is the father's favorite son sent to the brothers who hate him and sell him for a handful of silver pieces. Yet, he becomes their lord (Waltke).

**45.6–8, "*The famine has been in the land these two years."* There remains five years of famine. It is now more than 20 years since Joseph was sold into slavery. "It is comparable with the length of time for Abraham between promise and fulfillment (12.4; 21.5), and for Jacob in the service of Laban (31.41). Each of these delays were fruitful, but no two were alike in form or purpose" (Kidner).

"*God sent me before you to preserve for you a remnant of the earth. ...So it was not you who sent me here."* In retrospect, everything is clear. And Joseph seeks to make it clear to them and comfort them with his forgiving words. He "alleviates the guilt and shame of his converted brothers by placing their crime against the broader picture of God's sovereignty" (Waltke).

Previously, the patriarchs' lying and conniving endangered the promises of God (*cf.* 12.10–20; 20; 26.6–11; 27). Now a famine seeks to do what the patriarchs' failures could not. Joseph's use of *remnant* and *survivors* brings to mind the prophets (*e.g.,* Isa 37.4; Jer 25.20; Amos 9.12), as these words later become "freighted with theological significance. It may well be that... far more is at stake than the mere physical survival of twelve human beings. What really survives is the plan of redemption announced first to [Abraham]" (Hamilton). And it is not a remnant of Israel that will be saved, but a *remnant of the earth.* "If the Jacobites fail to survive, the whole of the human family will die without salvation hope (Mathews)."

---

[3]This may provide another reason the meeting was in private: the Egyptians would have hardly appreciated the peculiar destiny of God's people (Leupold).

[4]See comment on 44.33.

"A father to Pharaoh." This "recognized title of viziers and high officials" (Kidner) carries the meaning of Joseph being his chief adviser (Wenham).

45.9–11, *"Go up to my father and say… 'Come down to me; do not tarry. You shall dwell in the land of Goshen. …There I will provide for you.'"* Joseph invites the entire family down to live nearby where he can provide for their needs more easily. With five more years of famine and a son in charge of the world's food supply, this move is a no-brainer.[5] To Joseph, Jacob is *my father* and his brothers are *your children.* "Thus he conveys intimacy toward his father and distance from his brothers" (Hamilton).

Goshen. There are no references to Goshen in any Egyptian remains;[6] however, "47.11 gives us the name it bore in later times, 'the land of Rameses.' This name, coupled with the fact that the district was fertile (47.6) and *near* to Joseph at court, suggests that it was in the eastern part of the Nile delta, near Tanis" (Kidner). And Wenham: "This area would have been close enough to the royal court in Memphis or Avaris for Joseph to have contact with his family, and later for Moses to conduct negotiations with his Pharaoh (Exod 7–12)."

"So that you and your household… do not come to poverty." Cf. 47.13–26.

45.12–13, *"And now your eyes see."* Joseph's claims are credible. They can verify with their own experience his power and influence in Egypt.

"And the eyes of my brother Benjamin see." "Joseph's words are so incredible that Jacob will need a credible witness. Benjamin is the only brother whose character is beyond reproach and whose testimony is completely credible" (Waltke).

"It is my mouth that speaks to you." Joseph no longer speaks through an interpreter—probably the first Hebrew he's spoken in years.

"You must tell my father of all my honor in Egypt." He must be told these things, so he can know that Joseph can do what he claims to be able to do.

"Bring my father down here." Here, Joseph's words recall those spoken by Jacob and repeated by Judah (42.38; 44.29), though it is to Egypt that Jacob will be *brought down*, not Sheol. "He is going down to life, not to death" (Hamilton).

---

[5]Or is it? See comment on 46.1.

[6]This may be easily explained if Goshen is a Semitic name (*cf.* Josh 10.41; 11.16; 15.51) rather than an Egyptian name (Hamilton).

45.14–15, Then he fell upon his brother Benjamin's neck and wept... and he kissed all his brothers and wept upon them. The family is reconciled. "These authentic gestures of emotion convince his brothers of his good will and finally free them from their stunned silence" (Waltke).

After that his brothers talked with him. Finally, they are comfortable enough with Joseph to talk with him as a brother. Thus the rift of silence that began before he was sold into slavery[7] begins to close.

45.16–18, When the report was heard in Pharaoh's house. More literally, *the voice was heard in Pharaoh's palace* (*cf.* v 2). Word quickly traveled to Pharaoh that Joseph's brothers had come and the family had made reconciliation.

It pleased Pharaoh and his servants. This is the same terminology used of their reaction to Joseph's plan to preserve the kingdom. "The intentional echo of 41.37 shows that the exceptional concessions made by the king to this Asiatic immigration are due to Pharaoh's high regard for Joseph" (Mathews). That not only Pharaoh, but all of his servants approved, attests to the popularity and esteem Joseph held in Pharaoh's house: the things connected with his fortune were a matter of interest to all (Leupold).

And Pharaoh said to Joseph, "Say to your brothers, 'Do this... come to me, and I will give you the best of the land of Egypt.'" Having learned of the brothers' arrival, Pharaoh invites the family to move to Egypt to live off the Egyptian bounty. That his invitation matches Joseph's should be counted as God's providence at work.

45.19–21, "'Take wagons from the land of Egypt for your little ones and for your wives. ...Have no concern for your goods, for the best of all the land of Egypt is yours.'" Pharaoh's offer not only matches, but exceeds Joseph's. Pharaoh was prepared not only to provide them with a living place, but a better means of transporting the women and children. Second, his invitation was not to Goshen, but to *the best of the land* and *the fat of the land* (v 18). Third, Joseph's invitation spoke of the male members of the family (v 10) while Pharaoh explicitly included their *little ones* and *wives*. Finally, they were told not to bring any of their possessions from home, because that would all be replaced with the best of what Egypt had to offer.

Such a magnanimous offer may have come with the risk of other high-ranking officers becoming envious or critical of the Pharaoh. But he en-

---

[7]See comment on 37.4.

thusiastically made the offer. After all, so much of the nation's wealth—not to mention the reason they were all alive—was due to Joseph. Further, this may serve to answer questions about Joseph's background, if any still lingered. If it was public information that Joseph had been a slave, it would have been pleasing for Pharaoh to learn that he came from an honorable family of free nomads who were generally held in high regard (Leupold). But it should be noted that "This free and honorable invitation involved the right of Israel to leave again without obstruction" (Delitzsch qtd. in Keil). This right was, of course, ignored by the next dynasty (Exod 1.8–14; 5.1–9; *etc.*). Further, this invitation is a turning point in the history of God's people. It was "The beginning of a period of isolation (where the family, thoroughly alien, could multiply without losing its identity), and of eventual bondage and deliverance which would produce a people that forever after knew itself redeemed as well as called" (Kidner).

The sons of Israel did so. Joseph and Pharaoh's invitations were accepted, Pharaoh's plan was followed, and the wheels were set in motion for Jacob and his family to relocate to Egypt.

45.22–23, To each and all of them he gave a change of clothes. Once again, clothing comes to the forefront in the Joseph narrative. "Since an article of apparel had featured prominently in the tale of hostility between Joseph and his brothers, it is only fitting that their reconciliation should be marked by a gift of apparel" (Sarna qtd. in Waltke).

To Benjamin he gave three hundred shekels of silver and five changes of clothes. Again, he shows favoritism to Benjamin, though this time it cannot be a test of the brothers. They had passed all of Joseph's tests; this must be sincere favoritism to his full brother. "The regal amount of silver given to Benjamin is the final gesture of 'restitution' for the twenty pieces of silver the brothers took for the sale of Joseph" (Alter).

To his father he sent as follows: ten donkeys loaded with the good things of Egypt, and ten female donkeys loaded with grain, bread, and provision for his father on the journey. In addition to the literary effect of the clothing and silver, the gifts sent back serve a practical purpose. "Joseph demonstrates that he is fully capable of performing the guarantees made to the family throughout the long famine" (Mathews).

45.24, As they departed he said to them, "Do not quarrel on the way." Everything has turned out far better than could have ever been expected.

What is there to quarrel over? Most likely, Joseph understands that now they have to tell their father what they had done. The natural reaction would be to take as little of the guilt as possible. As they were discussing what they would tell Jacob, it would be easy to see what they might quarrel about. It does not take much imagination at all to hear what might be said—*'It was Judah's idea to sell him.' ...'Reuben should have done a better job of making us not do anything bad.' ...'You're the one who flagged down the traders.'* Joseph had tried to impress upon them that all of this was according to God's plan, but that likely would have been forgotten as they tried to get their story straight.[8]

45.26–28, And they told [Jacob]. ...And his heart became numb, for he did not believe them. This reaction is really quite understandable. After twenty long years, a declaration such as this would take some substantial evidence to corroborate. *His heart became numb* is literally *his heart stopped*. Judah had warned that the loss of Benjamin would kill their father because he was the last son of Rachel. But now the shock over the news of Joseph's life—the adding back of the first son of Rachel—nearly does the same.

When they told him all the words of Joseph... and when he saw the wagons that Joseph had sent. They had plenty of evidence to back up their claim. *All the words* must include Joseph's speech on providence, which is used to gloss over the brothers' confession to their father of what they did, a recounting that would have made for an interesting narrative, but is omitted as unnecessary to the story.

The spirit of their father Jacob revived. And Israel said. The distinction between *Jacob* and *Israel* on this side of the Jabbok is not always clear. Here, however, it does make a clear point. *Jacob* was his name prior to his enlightening at Peniel (*cf.* 32.31), and it was often still used of him in his weaker moments. *Israel* is the covenant name: the one who struggled with God and prevailed. It is the name of strength and leadership—"an aggressive combatant in the battle of life, ready to overcome obstacles in the power of God" (Leupold). Since Joseph's 'death,' he had been Jacob, filled with gloom and despair. Now, upon hearing of his life, the crushed spirit and the old *Jacob* again became *Israel*.

---

[8]Alter offers an alternate interpretation, suggesting that the disputed verb does not mean *quarrel* but, since the primary meaning is to *shake*, denotes *fear*; thus, "Joseph is reassuring his brothers that they need not fear any lurking residue of vengefulness on his part that would turn the journey homeward into a trap."

"I will go and see him before I die." The evidence is sufficient. Jacob believes that Joseph is alive. And he declares that they will go see him. Notice, however, that Jacob's words do not imply taking up permanent residence in Egypt, but seem to imply a temporary visit.[9]

Growth of the Seed: Israel will travel to Egypt.

Theological Reflection: Understanding God's Purpose
Joseph had been alone in Egypt for 20 long years before God's purpose became evident. Then, before his brothers, he reveals what God had been planning all along. After long years of ups and downs, Joseph finally sees the picture clearly and explains it to all.

"Do not be distressed or angry with yourselves because you sold me here, for God sent me before you to preserve life. For the famine has been in the land these two years, and there are yet five years in which there will be neither plowing nor harvest. And God sent me before you to preserve for you a remnant on earth, and to keep alive for you many survivors. So it was not you who sent me here, but God. He has made me a father to Pharaoh, and lord of all his house and ruler over all the land of Egypt" (45.5–8).

We must always be patient with God's work in our lives. How many times do you suppose Joseph had prayed that his father would come to Egypt and rescue him while he lay awake in Potiphar's house? And how glad do you suppose Joseph was—after he saw the picture clearly—that his prayer had gone unanswered? Joseph didn't see the work of God clearly for 20 years, but when he did, he knew that God's purpose clearly outweighed whatever suggestions he could have made.

Consider Job. What was the purpose of Job's suffering? Certainly there is more to it than just convincing Satan that Job's service to God was for more than the blessings he received. That Job has been recorded for us as the Bible's only theodicy seems to indicate that the purpose of Job's suffering is for us—that we can read of his life and learn great lessons from it. As far as we know, Job was never given an answer. God never told him about the confrontation He had with Satan in chapter 1. He never told Job about us and the comfort and strength we would get from hearing his story. *Job's questions were never answered.* Does that mean that God's providence was not controlling his life? Certainly not!

---

[9]See comment on 46.1–4.

We don't know when God will reveal to us His purpose for our lives. It may be within the week. But then it may be 20 years from now. Or He may never let us know what He has planned for our lives. But one way or another, He is in control. And His providential power is such that even if we seek to thwart His will, it will be done. Our obedience to Him is not for His benefit, but for our own.

46 Jacob has packed his family onto Pharaoh's carts and they have begun their journey to Egypt. Before exiting Canaan, however, Jacob stops to seek God's approval. We find in this chapter God's assurance of continued fellowship in their journey. This is the last (recorded) appearance of God to man until Moses some 400 years later.[1] For all intents and purposes, this marks the end of the patriarchal period.

At this point, it may be appropriate to note some of the literary bookends of the patriarchal narrative. At the beginning of the patriarchal period, Abraham obeyed the divine revelation to go to the land of Canaan to become a great nation (12.2); at the end of the patriarchal period, Jacob obeys the divine command to leave Canaan to become a great nation. At the beginning, famine drives Abraham to Egypt (12.10); at the end, famine drives Jacob to Egypt (Waltke). And throughout their lives, Abraham and Jacob receive, by far, the most personal visits from God of anyone in Genesis. As Hamilton notes: "God's first talk to Abraham (12.1–3) and final talk to Abraham (22.15–18) are God's promises. Similarly, God's first talk to Jacob (28.13–16) and his last talk to Jacob (46.2–4) are promises."

46.1, So Israel took his journey. It is noteworthy that Israel *journeyed.* "It seems likely that this particular verb, with its etymological background of pulling up tent pegs and moving from one encampment to another, is intended to signal that the beginning of the sojourn in Egypt is to be construed as a resumption of the nomadic existence that characterized the lives of Abraham and Isaac. Thus the clan of Jacob does not head down to Egypt as a permanent place of emigration but as a way station in its continued wanderings" (Alter).

And came to Beersheba. Beersheba was on the border of Canaan. In addition, it was a family place of worship (21.33), and was Isaac's home base (26.23–25, 33). "By worshipping at the altar Isaac built, Jacob shows he worships the same God as his fathers" (Waltke).

And offered sacrifices to the God of his father Isaac. Jacob had every logical reason to proceed without hesitation: survival in Canaan would be difficult; there was food in Egypt; his favorite son was second in command of all the land; he had received an invitation from both his son and Pharaoh; he has already concluded that it was best to go (*cf.* 45.28). And based on this, the family had picked up and traveled to the edge of Canaan. But here,

---

[1]See Excursus G.

in spite of every logical reason to leave the Promised Land and relocate to Egypt, Jacob stops and seeks God's approval—the content of God's reply clarifies the nature of Jacob's petition. And the reason is clear: his grandfather had made the logical choice to avoid a famine by going to Egypt, but found disastrous consequences awaiting him; then, his father was strictly forbidden by God to go to Egypt during a later famine (12.10–20; 26.1–2. *cf.* Excursus I). Moreover, the last word from God to Jacob was to return to the Promised Land (31.13; 35.1). Thus, before this decision—no matter how straightforward it may seem to us—Jacob stopped and sought God's counsel before leaving the land of his inheritance.

46.2–4, God spoke to Israel in visions of the night. This seems to be the typical way that God spoke to Jacob (28.10–16; 31.10–13; 32.24–31; *cf.* 15.4–5, 12–21; 20.3; 31.24). Wenham notes: "To emigrate to Egypt was as momentous a move as Abraham's journey from Ur (12.1–3) or Jacob's flight to Paddan-Aram (28.1–22) or his return to Canaan (31.3–54), all of which were encouraged by visions."

"Jacob, Jacob." Mathews notes: "The dual summons of God…recalls the test of Abraham at Moriah (22.11) and anticipates the call of Moses (Exod 3.4)." Its echo of the Abraham event may be "a suggestion that the sojourn in Egypt is also an ordeal, with an ultimately happy ending" (Alter).[2]

"Do not be afraid to go down to Egypt." Unlike the two previous occurrences, God wanted Jacob to go down to Egypt. This may be explained variously. First, it was promised by God (15.13–14). Second, some of the moral dangers of living in Canaan (*cf.* chs 34, 38) may be avoided by living in isolation in Goshen. Third, this isolation would allow Israel to grow as a nation without losing its sense of identity. Fourth, it will set up the redemption of God's people—an event that will make plain to the Israelites that they were chosen by God. Finally, as Leupold notes, it will give opportunity for faith and hope to be nurtured and grow as they would have to wait on God's promise for them.

"For there I will make you into a great nation." This marks a new aspect of the oft-repeated promise: it is in Egypt that God will make Israel into a great nation. The promise of Canaan remained; Egypt was, in the long run, a step toward it (Kidner).

---

[2] See comment on 22.11.

"I myself will go down with you to Egypt." God offers comforting words to Jacob about his journey: He will journey with him and ensure his safety. Waltke says, "God's presence does not eliminate pain, but it does assure provision and protection in the midst of it (see 28.15, 20; 31.3, 5, 42; 39.2–3, 21, 23). God will be Jacob's escort as he goes south to Egypt, just as He was his escort when he went north to Haran."

"And I will also bring you up again." Then, God offers comforting words to Jacob's descendants—the original audience of this book. He will journey with them as they return to the Promised Land. "In the polytheistic view the theater of activity of a deity was typically imagined to be limited to the territorial borders of the deity's worshippers. By contrast, this God solemnly promises to go down with His people to Egypt and to bring them back up" (Alter).

"Joseph's hand shall close your eyes." This is "a reference to the custom that the eldest son or nearest relative would gently close the eyes of the deceased. Such has remained a time-honored Jewish practice to the present day" (Sarna qtd. in Waltke). Thus, God offers a final, personal comfort to Jacob. "From the great national concerns that have dominated the rest of this announcement, God finally deals with Jacob's most immediate and intimate concern. A frail and elderly man is assured that God will grant his dearest wish" (Wenham). This contrasts sharply with what Jacob had predicted for himself (*cf.* 37.35).

46.5–7, *The sons of Israel.* Or *children of Israel.* This is the first use of this designation for the collective descendants of Abraham, Isaac and Jacob.

Carried Jacob their father. Jacob is old and frail, "no longer an active participant in the journey" (Alter).

They also took their livestock and their goods. This may come as a surprise, since Pharaoh had told them not to take their goods (45.20). But it is doubtful that Pharaoh's words were intended to mean that they were not to take *any* of their goods. At the very least, they would not leave their livestock behind. Further, as godly men, they understood their other possessions to be gifts from God, which they would not rashly abandon (Leupold). These were respectable nomadic shepherds, not freeloaders. It would only have been common sense to take the things that they had *gained in the land of Canaan* with them to Egypt.

All his offspring he brought with him into Egypt. Everyone in the family went. "The Beni-Hasan tableau… depicted the arrival in Egypt of a party of west Semitic nomads of the Patriarchal period, which provides authentic background for the migration of Israel and his sons to Egypt."[3]

That Jacob *brought with him* his offspring is a far cry from his sons who *took their father* by cart (v 5). "The former represents the practical reality; the latter, the ideal social ordering" (Waltke).

46.8–27, Now these are the names of the descendants of Israel, who came into Egypt. The genealogy of those who went to Egypt with Jacob is one of the more interesting lists in Genesis. In regard to women, it counts the granddaughter Serah (v 17), but does not count Dinah or any of the wives. And it includes the deceased (Er and Onan, v 12; *cf.* 38.7, 9–10). Some of the grandsons of Jacob who are listed may not have been born yet (especially the ten listed under Benjamin, who himself could have not been much older than 30 at this point). What's more: this strange list is those who *came into Egypt* (v 26): 66 people in all. But then the very next verse says that 70 came into Egypt.

Clearly, Er and Onan did not come into Egypt. Just as clearly, the women who are not listed did. The number 70 is arrived at by adding the numbers 33, 16, 14, and 7—the descendants of each wife (vv 15, 18, 22, 25).[4] But Dinah must be added while Er and Onan are to be subtracted. Also to be subtracted are Joseph, Ephraim and Manasseh (who are already *in* Egypt). Thus, 66 actually *traveled with Jacob* to Egypt.[5] The 70, then include Joseph, his sons, and Jacob—*all the persons of the house of Jacob* (v 27).[6] But Stephen says that 75 people came to Egypt (Acts 7). This different number comes from the LXX, which Stephen apparently was citing. The LXX adds a son and grandson of Manasseh as well as two sons and a grandson of Ephraim. Certainly this difference in number is not a discrepancy of any magnitude.

But there were more people still. This list does not include wives. Nor does it include servants of the family who made the journey. There were probably also some Shechemite women and children as well (34.29). In all,

---

[3]R.K. Harrison, *Old Testament Times*, 96.

[4]Interestingly, the wives produce twice as many descendants as the concubines.

[5]Those who were not yet born, should such exist in this list, are easily explained as traveling to Egypt by the same logic that Levi tithed Melchizedek: in the loins of his father (Heb. 7.9–10).

[6]*Cf.* verse 4. "One might say that the number accompanying Jacob on this journey is seventy-one, for he has God to guide him and his family to support him" (Hamilton).

there could have been 200–300 people who made the journey, plus their livestock. But genealogies are not always strictly accurate by chronology or an exhaustive listing of every name. Often, genealogies are put together in such a way to emphasize something in particular or to make them easier to remember.[7] This genealogy is designed to arrive at the number 70: seven being the number that marks divine work; ten being the number of completion (Leupold).[8] Thus, the purpose of this genealogy: when it came time for Israel to relocate to Egypt, God had made a complete nation out of Abraham. As He had told Abraham that He would make a nation out of him in Canaan, so He did. Now, it was time for Jacob to leave Canaan for Egypt, where God would make a great nation of Israel.

46.10, The sons of Simeon... Shaul, the son of a Canaanite woman. Because Simeon's Canaanite wife (concubine?) is mentioned, we can most likely infer that she is an exception to the other sons' wives (save Judah, *cf.* ch 38). Presumably, they took wives from Mesopotamia, as Isaac and Jacob had done (Keil), though we cannot know for certain, especially considering the strained relations after Jacob's departure from Laban.

46.18, Whom Laban gave. And again in verse 25. "Why does the narrator remind us at this point of Laban? It is most unlikely he is writing to a people who will be in the dark about Zilpah and Bilhah without further clarification. The resurrection of Laban's name momentarily throws us into the past. It takes us back from a Jacob with seventy kin to a Jacob with no kin. It recalls the similar crisis Jacob faced there. In chapter 31 Jacob was preparing to leave Paddan-aram for Canaan under less than happy circumstances. Here Jacob is preparing to leave Canaan for Egypt under equally unsettling circumstances. In chapter 31 he had to deal with Laban. In chapter 46 he has to deal with a famine. In chapter 31 he fled with his family. In chapter 46 he moves with his family" (Hamilton). And Waltke: "This is a reminder of Jacob's difficult exile in the past from which the ideal

---

[7] See Excursus C.

[8] The number seven pervades this genealogy. In addition to the 70 total offspring, Rachel has fourteen descendants and Bilhah seven. Together they have 21. Leah and Bilhah together have 49. Gad is placed as the seventh son, which is his rightful place by chronology (29.31–30.11), but not where he is usually found (*cf.* 35.23–26; 49.3–19; Exod 1.1–4; Num 26.5–18; 1 Chron 2.1–2). Interestingly, the numerical value of the seventh-placed Gad—who produced seven grandchildren—is seven (Hamilton).

and complete family emerged. Jacob's family will emerge again from what will become a difficult exile in Egypt."

46.20, Asenath. Joseph's wife is the only one named. "Just as the reference to Laban in verses 18, 25 is to distant history, the reference to Asenath is to recent history" (Hamilton).

46.28, He had sent Judah ahead of him to Joseph. Judah, the family leader, went ahead to inquire of Joseph's direction and plan concerning the family, then returned to lead the family into Goshen. Hamilton notes: "It is ironic that Judah is selected to play the lead role, to be the mediator in the forthcoming reuniting of long-separated father from son (37.26ff)." And Sarna: "It is only fitting that Judah, who bore responsibility for separating Joseph from Jacob... should be charged with arranging the reunion" (qtd. in Waltke).

46.29–30, Then Joseph prepared his chariot and went up to meet Israel his father in Goshen. We do not know whether he travels back with Judah to meet the family or waits for them to settle in the land before visiting them.

[Joseph] presented himself to him and fell on his neck and wept on his neck a good while. This is something of an anticlimactic scene. Aside from this note and Jacob's one line, nothing is said of what has been a greatly anticipated reunion. "Joseph appears more concerned about his brothers' forthcoming interview with Pharaoh, for which he coaches them carefully" (Wenham).

"Now let me die." Jacob does not speak this in the sense that he wants to die; rather, he means, *Now I can die in peace* (*cf.* Luke 2.29–30). "The possibility of seeing Joseph again... was the chief reason that Jacob had lived, and likewise Joseph had worried that Jacob might not 'still be alive'" (Mathews). He will, in fact, go on to live seventeen more years (47.28).[9] Almost all of Jacob's words since 37.35 are of death, and continue to be so, but after the turning point of 45.28 the bitterness is largely replaced by a sense of fulfillment and hope (Kidner).

"Since I have seen your face." Hamilton says, "Jacob had a previous experience of seeing a face, the result of which he was never the same again. ...He had seen God's face, yet he continued to live. Having seen Joseph's face, he needs to live no longer."

---

[9]This is the second period of seventeen years Jacob spends with Joseph (37.2).

46.31–34, "I will go up and tell Pharaoh. ... That you may dwell in the land of Goshen." Joseph informs his family that he will tell Pharaoh that they have arrived and that they are shepherds, and tells them to say the same to him. Joseph had already chosen Goshen as the dwelling place for his family (45.10), and though Pharaoh had echoed his invitation, he had not done so this specifically. This was Joseph's plan for Pharaoh to come to the same conclusions.[10] Joseph chose Goshen for his family, because it was a fertile land, known to be good for grazing and thus herding of livestock. As it was not heavily populated, they would be ensured isolation from the Egyptians. Finally, being on the eastern delta would make it easier to leave when it was time to return to Canaan (Leupold).

"For every shepherd is an abomination to the Egyptians." This would be a much-needed piece of information for shepherds moving into Egypt! Most likely it is stated here to explain why this information would ensure their settlement in Goshen: Pharaoh would share the Egyptian customs, but would not want to act rudely to Joseph's family; thus, he would send them to Goshen—virtual isolation, but a perfect place for them to shepherd their flocks. Thus, by emphasizing that they were what the Egyptians hated, Joseph sought "to ensure that Pharaoh's goodwill would be to the family's real benefit, not to their detriment by drawing them into an alien way of life at the capital" (Kidner).

This statement, however, is something of a puzzle, as Pharaoh had his own livestock (*cf.* 47.6) and there is no extrabiblical evidence that Egyptians hated shepherds. "The least convoluted explanation is that the Egyptians, who were by and large sedentary agriculturalists and who had large urban centers, considered the seminomadic herdsmen from the north as inferiors (an attitude actually reflected in Egyptian sources) and so preferred to keep them segregated in the pasture region of the Nile Delta not far from the Sinai border" (Alter).[11]

---

[10] Wenham suggests an alternate explanation for his focus on their occupation: "This seems to be intended to reassure Pharaoh that Joseph is not about to indulge in a bout of nepotism by filling the Egyptian civil services with his relatives. His brothers have been herdsmen from their youth and intend to continue to look after their flocks in the future." And Mathews: "Theirs is not a household of kings, despite Joseph's high office."

[11] There may be in this a reflection of chapter 4. "Cain and the Egyptians are workers of the land. Abel and Joseph's family are shepherds of the flocks. What in Genesis 4 was a fraternal division is in Genesis 46 an international division" (Hamilton).

Growth of the Seed: The covenant is renewed (vv 3–4); the building of a nation is complete;[12] Israel travels to Egypt.

Theological Reflection: *Seeking God's Counsel*

Jacob's stop at Beersheba to seek God's counsel for what should have been an easy decision makes an excellent point about prayer. It's easy to pray about decisions when we aren't sure what we should do. But it is often easy to skip fervent prayer about decisions when our own logic is screaming the obvious answer. Jacob's actions—and Abraham's lack of the same in chapter 12—teach a profound lesson. Even when—*especially when*—something is manifestly sensible and right, we must always consult God in our decision making.

---

[12]See comment on verses 8–27.

47 This chapter is significant in the Genesis narrative for three reasons. First, it bridges the gap between Genesis 12–36 (set primarily in Canaan) and Exodus 1–15 (set in Egypt). It tells us how the people of Israel came to settle in Goshen and how they were able to grow into a nation of an intimidating size to the Exodus Pharaoh. Second, it highlights a theme of the patriarchal narratives: God's people are to be a separate people.[1] They were called from their wicked homeland to the Promised Land of Canaan. And though sojourners, they were never separated in Canaan (*cf.* 20; 26.6–11; 26.34–35; 34; 38). Here in Goshen, they became completely separate, where they could grow uninterrupted as a nation, without interference from outsiders, until they were big enough to return to the Promised Land and occupy it by themselves, again separated—though by conquest. Finally, this chapter displays the blessing of God on Pharaoh. This blessing has a two-fold significance: first, as with Potiphar (39.3–5) and the prison keeper (39.23), it shows a fulfillment of God's promise to Abraham (12.3a): by blessing Joseph, Pharaoh secures a divine blessing for himself. Second, it shows an immediate fulfillment of Jacob's blessing of Pharaoh (v 10).

47.1–2, "They are now in the land of Goshen." Although Joseph has promised them the land of Goshen for a dwelling, Pharaoh has not yet specified the same. Telling Pharaoh that they were already there was the easiest way to receive Pharaoh's confirmation of Joseph's plan; doing this plants the seed in Pharaoh's mind—when he learns they are shepherds, and knows that they are already in Goshen, the decision will be made easy.

From his brothers, he took five men and presented them to Pharaoh. One might wonder why such a presentation was necessary—after all, Pharaoh had promised dwelling and provisions to Joseph's family (45.17–20). "But royalty has often been known to speak generously and afterward to forget what it had promised" (Leupold). Further, Pharaoh's public confirmation protected Joseph against criticism, and legitimized the presence of Israel in Egypt. That Joseph took five of his brothers is also significant, though primarily because it means that he did not take his father. The purpose of this encounter is to beg a favor. Perhaps Joseph has intentionally delayed his father's meeting with Pharaoh so he does not have to lower himself to a pagan king (*cf.* v 7) (Hamilton).

---

[1]See Brian A. McKenzie, "Jacob's Blessing on Pharaoh: An Interpretation of Gen. 46.31–47.26," *WTJ* 45 (1983): 389–390.

47.3–4, "What is your occupation?" Surely, this was not the only thing spoken in the interaction between Pharaoh and the brothers. It is, however, the one matter of consequence and the expected question (*cf.* 46.33–34).

"Your servants are shepherds, as our fathers were." After Joseph's declaration of 46.34, offering this answer may not have been the easiest thing to do. But "The full truth is always the safest course, undiplomatic as it might appear to be" (Leupold). Kidner suggests that their interview with Pharaoh "is a good model of straightforward, peaceable dealings between a pilgrim people and the temporal power (*cf.* 1 Pet 2.11–17)." How starkly this contrasts with Abraham's descent to Egypt during a famine, when he tried to secure his safety through deceit (*cf.* 12.10–20).[2]

"We have come to sojourn in the land." Cf. 15.13. Their intentions were not, as some translations render, to *dwell* in the land, but to *sojourn* or *live here for a while*. The emphasis of their response was the temporary nature of their stay. But that they would sojourn should not be a surprise: the patriarchs never had a permanent home or owned land. More to the point, knowing that they did not plan to stay forever would have made Pharaoh look more kindly on them. To this, they added that they only left their homeland under the utmost necessity: *"the famine is severe in the land of Canaan."* Although their response indicates that they do not intend to remain in Egypt indefinitely, they do appear to be planning a lengthy stay, "since it's likely that Goshen could not immediately support their flocks due to Egypt's own dearth. It is understood that in the interim they will be dependent on Pharaoh's goodwill. They show, however, no interest in or potential of jeopardizing the king's future regime" (Mathews).

"Please let your servants dwell in the land of Goshen." Hamilton notes: "Three times they refer to themselves before Pharaoh as *your servants* (vv 3, 4 [twice]). They never mention that they have come to Egypt because Joseph invited them (45.9ff), or because Pharaoh too invited them (45.17ff). It is need, more than privilege or courtesy, that brings them to Egypt."

47.5–6, "Your father and your brothers have come to you." Here, Pharaoh "delegates to Joseph the authority to accept Jacob's family into Egypt, and to supervise their settlement in Goshen" (Hamilton). Moreover, this clar-

---

[2]To continue the contrast: Abraham's Pharaoh escorted Abraham to the border as he sent him away, while Jacob's Pharaoh invited the family to live on the best land (v 6). Abraham retreats from Egypt, while Jacob makes it his new home. Abraham leaves Egypt alive; Jacob will leave Egypt dead (Hamilton).

ifies Pharaoh's basis for showing them kindness—because they were Joseph's family. How stark a contrast this motive for kindness stands against the later Pharaoh who enslaves the people because he *did not know Joseph* (Exod 1.8) (Mathews).

"The land of Egypt is before you." Pharaoh's answer is an unreserved yes. He gives them Goshen, which he realizes is the perfect place for them. And he gives them care of his own livestock—an opportunity to advance themselves in Pharaoh's royal administration in their own trade, enjoying privileges and legal protection not normally given to foreigners (Waltke). [3]

47.7, Then Joseph brought in Jacob his father and stood him before Pharaoh. It is a token of the respect that he had for his father to present him to Pharaoh. And it is in understanding of his place in God's eyes that he *stood him* before Pharaoh; Jacob does not bow down before the Egyptian king.[4] "The polite relationship Jacob has with Pharaoh differs from the hostilities that Abraham and Isaac endured in foreign lands. The implication is clear: the Lord is with Jacob in this land as He is with Joseph. Egypt is a place of refuge for the Hebrews" (Mathews).

Jacob blessed Pharaoh. What is more surprising: Pharaoh received the blessing (*cf.* Heb 7.7).[5] "Pharaoh, secure in his royalty, is dependent upon Jacob for divine blessing. Jacob, precarious and completely dependent on Pharaoh's goodwill, is the honorable benefactor of divine blessing" (Waltke). Further, Jacob, "a true child of God has more to offer by his blessing than any earthly monarch can offer him" (Leupold). And offering a blessing on Pharaoh is a natural response to Pharaoh's good will to his family. "Pharaoh has enriched Jacob's family. He has promoted son Joseph to a prominent position in Egypt. On several occasions he has sent much-needed grain back to Canaan with Jacob's other sons. He has invited Jacob and his family to Egypt with freedom to settle anywhere. Jacob is profoundly grateful for the assistance Pharaoh has provided. The

---

[3] Hamilton suggests: "An Egyptian Pharaoh requesting the services of Hebrew herdsmen to tend his animals may be compared with a Hebrew Solomon requesting the services of Phoenician craftsmen to help him build a temple. Perhaps shepherding is a vocation that the upper-class Egyptian felt beneath his dignity. In this way, shepherding was an 'abomination' to them (46.34)."

[4] It may also indicate the frailty of Jacob at this point that he had to be taken in and stood; he could not do so by his own power.

[5] By contrast, Moses' Pharaoh refused to acknowledge God.

appropriate response is to bless Pharaoh. 'He has enriched us. May God enrich him'" (Hamilton).

47.8–9, "How many are the days of the years of your life?" The inspiration for Pharaoh's question cannot be precisely known. Perhaps Jacob had blessed Pharaoh with longevity, prompting this question (*cf.* 2 Sam 16.16; 1 Kgs 1.31; Dan 2.4; 5.10; 6.6). Or maybe he was just impressed with Jacob's long life and many children, since the lives of Pharaohs were generally short.

Jacob said. Waltke says, "He does not exalt himself above Pharaoh, but he does not refer to himself as Pharaoh's servant, as his sons did three times."

"My sojourning." None of the three patriarchs had come into actual possession of the Promised Land, but had lived there wandering about, unsettled and homeless, in the land promised to them for an inheritance. And Jacob's life had been even an exaggeration of that: in Canaan, he had as little property as Abraham and Isaac; then, he fled from Esau and dwelt for 20 years in Mesopotamia; his return to Canaan stopped short of its intended destination, only to be moved further along at the word of God; his children didn't play nicely with the neighbors, causing stress and friction during their Palestinian sojourn; and now, the entire family moves to Egypt. There is also, however, a symbolic aspect to his use of this term. It is a figurative representation of the inconstancy and weariness of earthly life (Keil), which is but a pilgrimage to the eternal home where he would no longer stay as a stranger (*cf.* Heb 11.13–16).

"130 years." The ideal and hoped-for life of an Egyptian was 110.[6] "The reference to Jacob's age apparently serves to heighten the significance of [his] blessing. A man whose closeness to God and favor in God's eyes is attested by his attainment of an age greater than any Egyptian dared to hope for blesses Pharaoh."[7]

"Few and evil." The days of Jacob were *few* in comparison to his father and grandfather, as he goes on to clarify. At 130, he was nearly a half-century younger than Abraham or Isaac at their deaths. And Jacob considered the *few* days of his life to have been *evil*. None of Jacob's ancestors had as many hardships as he faced (though many were of his own doing): his brother wanted to kill him; his father-in-law repeatedly deceived and

---

[6]See comment on 50.26.

[7]Brian A. McKenzie, "Jacob's Blessing on Pharaoh: An Interpretation of Gen. 46.31–47.26," *WTJ* 45 (1983): 394.

treated him poorly; he was grieved by the actions of his daughter and the following massacre by his sons; he was deeply pained by Reuben's incest; his life and hope were nearly shattered by the loss of Joseph. Alter says that although he has achieved everything he aspired to, he does not get it in the way he wanted, "and the consequence is far more pain than contentment."

47.11–12, *Then Joseph settled his father and brothers and gave them a possession in the land of Egypt.* In contrast to the brothers' word that they would *sojourn*, Joseph gave them property that they owned. Waltke notes that this was far more than they asked for or expected, and something that, by the end of this chapter, will distinguish them from the native Egyptians (*cf.* vv 20, 26–27). Leupold adds, "They had a more permanent foothold in Egypt than they had had thus far in Canaan."

The land of Rameses. It is doubtful that it was so called at this point, as Rameses had not yet reigned in Egypt, though, as Leupold suggests, it is possible that the king was named after the city instead of the opposite.[8] The simplest explanation, however, is that this is an anachronistic use by Moses—it was called this in his day and he used that name to explain to his audience where Goshen was.[9]

47.13–14, *There was no food in all the land.* The universal lack of food contrasts with the provisions of food for Joseph's family in the previous verse.

The land of Canaan. Canaan is mentioned three times in verses 13–15 alongside *the land of Egypt.* Leupold suggests that the famine was only in the land of Canaan and Egypt. Waltke suggests that it is to remind the readers of Israel's fate had Joseph not saved them. While both of these suggestions have merit, a more compelling explanation is that these are the only two places important to the biblical narrative: the Promised Land and the current residence of the chosen people.

All the money that was found. That the money had to be *found* employs the idea that it had to be diligently sought out. "The sense is that the people fervently rummage for money, bringing every last penny" (Mathews).

Joseph brought the money into Pharaoh's house. Joseph did not keep or

---

[8] "A city may be named after a king; but so may a king be named after a city, or both king and city after some other person or other object bearing a familiar name."

[9] This may seem unnecessary to a generation who lived in Goshen, but it is possible that those to whom Moses wrote were the second generation of Israelites, who, from growing up in the wilderness, had no clear memory of life in Goshen.

pilfer from the money used for purchase of the grain. He was honest in his dealings with Pharaoh.

47.15–17, When the money was all spent. The famine was so severe that the Egyptians ran out of money to purchase grain. And so, with no money, they come to Joseph, to whom they can appeal with confidence, as he has proved to be the nation's savior thus far. No one mistrusts Joseph or his motives.

"Give your livestock." Unlike our entitled society, "It was axiomatic in the ancient world that one paid one's way so long as one had anything to part with—including, in the last resort, one's liberty" (Kidner). Joseph's demand is not unnecessary or merciless; the emergency of the times called for emergency measures.

So they brought their livestock to Joseph, and Joseph gave them food. The livestock brought included *horses, flocks, herds, and donkeys.* That all of these were brought shows how dire the need was. Needless to say, not everyone did this at the same time. Those who began with more money would not have had to do this as soon. Likewise, those with more livestock would not have had to take the next step as soon. Rather than seeing this as a simultaneous exhaustion of money, the universal way in which it is described tells us that, sooner or later, everybody had to do it.

47.18–19, When that year was ended. The food they purchased with their livestock was only sufficient for a year. Now, they approach Joseph again, though this time with nothing but their *bodies and land.*

"Buy us and our land for food, and we with our land will be servants to Pharaoh." As long as there was something to pay with, the Egyptians would pay their way. Those who would cast Joseph as cruel in this ignore that it was not his idea, but theirs. This is, after all, the logical thing to do; the price paid is not too high, for the thing at stake is their very lives.

"And give us seed." Either the famine was nearing its end and they would soon be able to work their lands again or a bit of sowing was attempted every year in a few places where the land might yield slight results (Leupold).

47.20–22, All the Egyptians sold their fields. Again, the emphasis is on the universal nature of the selling rather than the simultaneous action of the people.

As for the people, he made servants of them from one end of Egypt to the other. The ESV follows the MT, while some other versions follow the

LXX, Samaritan Pentateuch, and Latin Vulgate: *he removed them to the cities*. Waltke says that the variant is due to an easy and common scribal error, but it is unclear which way the error originally went. The MT reading seems to better fit the context of the preceding verses. Further, it would seem strange for them to be relocated into the cities, when they are subsequently given seed for their fields (v 24). If, however, relocation into cities is to be followed, the only understandable explanation is that it was for ease in distributing foods (*cf.* 41.35). For our part, we would understand the verse to mean they were made slaves. While being enslaved may seem harsh, "It was in this situation beneficial, for now their food supply was Pharaoh's responsibility" (Wenham).

Only the land of the priests he did not buy, for the priests had a fixed allowance from Pharaoh. Waltke notes that the priests and the Israelites were the only two peoples to escape serfdom in this feudal system; Joseph is related to both: to Israel by blood; to the priests by marriage (*cf.* 41.45).

47.23–25, "I have this day bought you and your land for Pharaoh." Joseph's actions were of no profit to himself. His actions were to increase the wealth and property of Pharaoh. Kitchen writes, "Joseph's economic policy…simply made Egypt in fact what it always was in theory: the land became Pharaoh's property and its inhabitants his tenants" (qtd. in Kidner).

"At the harvests you shall give a fifth to Pharaoh." Things have come full cycle. During the years of plenty, a double tithe was taken from the people to store up. Now, for the privilege of farming on Pharaoh's land and for the starting seed, he levies a 20 percent tax. Most commentators note that this was low by standards of the ancient Near East, where the average tax ranged from 30–50 percent.

"You have saved our lives; may it please my lord, we will be servants to Pharaoh." The Egyptians were grateful to keep 80 percent and be alive. They do not see Joseph as a tyrant, but as a savior. Although we cannot help but view slavery through the lens of the deplorable African slave trade, slavery was not conducted in that manner in ancient times. In ancient society slavery was the accepted way of bailing out the destitute, and under a benevolent master could be quite a comfortable status (*e.g.*, Joseph with Potiphar). Indeed the law envisions some temporary slaves electing to become permanent slaves rather than take the freedom the law entitled them after six years of service. Ancient slavery at its best was more like tenured employment, whereas the free man was more like self-employ-

ment. The latter may be freer, but he faces more risks (*cf.* Exod 21.5–6; Deut 15.12–17) (Wenham).

There is a clear contrast between this and Exodus. In Exodus 1.8–11, Pharaoh makes slaves of the Hebrews and they groan under the misery; here, a Hebrew makes slaves of the Egyptians, and the Egyptians praise Joseph for saving them. The contrast implies both the cruelty of the Exodus Pharaoh and Joseph's wise administration, as well as the difference between a leader who is directed by God and one who is directed by self (Waltke).

47.27–28, *Thus Israel settled in the land of Egypt. ...And they gained possessions in it.* Again, the prosperity of the Israelites stands as a striking contrast to the Egyptian condition.

And were fruitful and multiplied greatly. This note looks both backward and forward. Looking back, it realizes the fulfillment of the promise made to Jacob (*cf.* 46.3). Looking forward, it provides a link to Exodus 1.7 (Waltke).

So the days of Jacob, the years of his life, were 147 years. Jacob lived in Egypt for 17 years. As he spent the first 17 years of Joseph's life with his favorite son, he now spends the last seventeen years of his own life with him.

47.29–31, *"If now I have found favor in your sight."* Typically, this type of language is used by a subordinate to a superior. While this is not the case here, Joseph does hold the legal power and Jacob is fully dependent on Joseph to carry out his wish in this regard (Waltke). From a structural point of view, these death instructions, along with a similar command in 49.29–33, form a frame around the blessing of his sons.

"Put your hand under my thigh." "Before placing his hands on Jacob's eyes (in death), Jacob wants Joseph to place his hand under his thigh (in life)" (Hamilton). Wenham suggests that Jacob was consciously imitating his grandfather (*cf.* 24.2). And Mathews: "The rite of oath and the language of the verse manifestly mimic Abraham and his servant...whose commission from Abraham also pertains to the future of the promises. In that case Isaac could not leave the land, and in this case Jacob cannot be kept from the land."[10]

"Let me lie with my fathers." This request is a testimony to his faith: it is not that he placed some eternal value in physical Canaan, but that his

---

[10]See comment on 24.2.

heart rested in God's promises—his physical body would remain in God's physical Promised Land. Jacob is bound up in God's promises to his fathers. Hamilton summarizes well: "Jacob knows that there is to be no permanent residence in Egypt for his people. Egypt is to Jacob and his family what the ark was to Noah—a temporary shelter from the disaster on the outside. Even if represented only by his decayed remains, he wants to be a part of that redemptive act of God."[11]

"Swear to me." Jacob makes his son directly accountable to God and removes all doubt (*cf.* Heb 6.16) that this will be done. This oath will be important in Joseph's interactions with Pharaoh (*cf.* 50.6).

The head of his bed. The LXX reads *staff* instead of *bed*, a variant that is the result of a different vowel pointing of the Hebrew letters—vowels that were added to the text much later. While many commentators spill inordinate amounts of ink on this question, the reality is that whether Jacob lay back on his bed or leaned on his staff matters very little.

Growth of the Seed: Pharaoh is blessed for blessing Joseph (*cf.* 12.3a); Jacob expresses faith in God's land promise (vv 29–31).

---

[11]Kidner writes: "The ancestral reunion was felt to be only symbolized, not created, by burial in the family place." See comment on 25.8.

Excursus N:
The Sons of Jacob: The Development of Their Story

The *generations of Jacob* (37.2) tell the stories of his sons—stories about the hatred and mistreatment of Joseph, Joseph in Egypt, the failure of Reuben as a leader, the development of Judah as the leader of the family, Joseph's testing of the brothers, the reconciliation of the family under Judah's leadership, Joseph's revelation of his identity to the brothers, and Pharaoh's invitation to the family. Through it all, God's providence reigns supreme. He works His purposes and His will through, and in spite of, the deeds of man.[1]

The Selling of Joseph

Joseph is already disliked by his brothers when we arrive at the events of chapter 37. His father had made him a special coat and treated him as the favorite. Here, however, things get markedly worse. He gives a bad report about the brothers (v 2).[2] He dreams that the family bows down to him. And then he tells them about it. So, his brothers conspire to kill him. Reuben intercedes, suggesting instead that they throw him in a pit (hoping to come back later and rescue him). As soon as Reuben is gone, however, Judah leads the brothers in another direction and they sell Joseph into slavery.

Joseph in Egypt

Joseph's life can be summed up in two paradoxical patterns. First, he is blessed by God as he *rises* in power and responsibility everywhere he goes. But at the same time, he is steadily working his way *down* the ladder of power until chapter 41.

Upon arrival in Egypt he is sold to Potiphar, a prominent and powerful man. God is with Joseph and he becomes successful (39.2). Ultimately, he is placed in charge of everything in Potiphar's house. Later, in prison, God continues to bless him and he rises to a position of authority in the prison (39.22). Finally, Pharaoh sees God's blessing upon Joseph and he rises to second in all Egypt. This pattern can be summarized as follows: Joseph arrives in a new place; God blesses Joseph in what he does; Joseph's Egyptian superior sees God's blessing; Joseph is promoted.

Joseph, however, is also working his way down. He begins as the favorite child in the covenant family. From there he is sold into slavery. As a slave he is

---

[1]Most of what follows has already been said in various places throughout earlier comments. This excursus is an effort to condense the story of the sons of Jacob into a single, brief account. Consequently, citations previously made will not be repeated.

[2]See comment on 37.2, 14.

given great authority (39.5). Then at the word of Potiphar's wife, he is thrown into prison (39.20).[3] There he is again given authority (39.22). Then, he is given the duty of serving the other prisoners (40.4). How frustrating this must have been for Joseph! Every time he seems to make progress, he is knocked down a few rungs, where he starts his way back up, only to be knocked down again. Certainly the humility learned by this constant lowering of position, interspersed with God's blessing and his rising in authority everywhere he goes, prepares him for the big jump in power that God had planned for him.

Reuben and Judah

Reuben seems to be the most moral of the brothers. While Simeon and Levi were massacring the Shechemites, Reuben took no part in it. And he is the only brother concerned with the life of Joseph in chapter 37. Perhaps his responsibility as the eldest is part of the reason for his higher character. Yet though he may have been the moral leader of the brothers, he was never the actual leader.[4]

In chapter 37, Judah shows himself to have already taken the role of leader among the brothers. Though they yield to Reuben's admonition not to kill Joseph, they still act in evil against Joseph as soon as Reuben left. It is, instead, at the word of Judah that they act, selling Joseph into slavery behind Reuben's back (37.26–27), ridding themselves of the brother they hated, ensuring him of a hard life, and garnering a profit for themselves. Though we must not condone the actions of Judah, it is clear that as early as chapter 37, action happened at Judah's word, not Reuben's.

Chapter 38 is a turning point for Judah. Leaving the family and intermarrying with the nations, he reaches a low point (though not any lower than any of the other great patriarchs who had to learn from their mistakes). His sin is comparable to Reuben's (35.22). The difference is that Judah confesses and repents (38.26), coming back to the family, while no such repentance in Reuben is recorded. That Judah became the family leader instead of Reuben is perhaps in large part due to the variance with which they handled their sin. Indeed, God's final verdict in the matter (49.3–4, 9–12, *i.e.*, that the Messiah came through Judah) also seems to indicate the manner in which they handled their sins.

Reuben does not easily relinquish his right as eldest to be the family leader. He rebukes the brothers while in Joseph's prison for the sin they had committed (42.22), and he steps up and offers his sons' lives to Jacob as a surety for Benjamin's safe return (42.37). But Jacob does not allow Reuben to take his youngest son to Egypt. In the next chapter, however, Judah, from his own ex-

---

[3]See comment on 39.19–20.

[4]His moral leadership must be brought under some scrutiny, given his sin with Bilhah (35.22).

perience in how dangerous it is to the survival of the family to be overprotective of the youngest (*cf.* 38.11ff),[5] offers himself as a surety for Benjamin's return (43.9), and Jacob listens (43.3–15). Later, Judah assumes the role of family spokesperson before Joseph and again offers his own life in exchange for the freedom of Benjamin (44.32–34).[6] It is clear that Judah is no longer the leader of only the brothers, but of the whole family.

While Judah's leadership is in part due to how he dealt with his sins, further proof of his superior leadership is seen in a comparison of his words with Reuben's. When Reuben speaks to Jacob, he offers the lives of his sons—*"Kill my two sons if I do not bring [Benjamin] back to you"* (42.37). Though this offer has often been characterized as bold, we see it in a different light. His words are rashly spoken and not well-thought out. What good would it do Jacob to have a dead son *and* two dead grandsons, should harm befall Benjamin under Reuben's watch? Moreover, a truly bold man—and a true leader—is the person who offers not the life of another as a surety, but his own life, as Judah does. Even Reuben's rebuke to the brothers in prison is little more than 'I told you so'—certainly not words befitting a leader in peril.

The Testing of the Brothers
Two different connections are made upon Joseph's recognition of his brothers when they arrive in Egypt (42.7–9).

When Joseph recognizes his brothers, he speaks roughly to them. His immediate reaction, of course, is to punish them for what they did to him. It is this punishment that results in their confession (42.21–22). Certainly this is not the first time that this sin had come to their minds. Their guilt had been building through the years. They had probably been expecting a consequence such as this after what they had done. Now, the evil has arrived, and they are quick to acknowledge what they had done. Joseph's crying out (42.21) had not moved them to confess. Jacob's mourning over his son (37.34–35) had not moved them to confess. The guilt that had grown in them through the years— even the changing of their hearts—had not moved them to confess. This physical punishment manages to do what all of those other things could not. The brothers confess their sin—and, in so doing, they took the first, and perhaps most important step toward becoming new men.

Also, Joseph's recognition of his brothers is linked with his remembering of the dreams. Because this connection is emphasized, it would seem that this ex-

---

[5] See Anthony J. Lambe, "Judah's Development: The Pattern of Departure–Transition–Return," *JSOT* 83 (1999): 63.

[6] On Messianic foreshadowing, see comment on 44.33 and 45.5.

plains his request for Benjamin to come (though his desire to see his full brother would certainly also have come into play).[7] The dream cannot be fulfilled
with only ten of the brothers there. And sending for Benjamin also provides
an excellent opportunity to test the brothers. Having heard them confess, it
seems that Joseph runs them through a series of tests to see if repentance had
accompanied the confession.[8]

Simeon is taken and bound[9] and their money is returned. The return of the
money is important, as it shows that this is more than just keeping Simeon as
a guarantee for Benjamin's coming. Now, appearing to be thieves, returning to
Joseph would be even more difficult. How easy it would be to keep the money,
leave Simeon behind, and think nothing about it had they not changed. Previously, they had valued money over a brother's life (37.28).

Their father delays their return to Egypt, but they do come back for Simeon—
intent on returning the extra money as well. Upon their return with Benjamin,
Joseph treats the brothers as welcome guests, inviting them to a meal in his own
house. There, Joseph shows immense favoritism to Benjamin in word and deed
(43.29, 34). Immediately after this, Joseph recreates the situation in which he was
sold into slavery, offering them the perfect opportunity to re-enact their sin.
Benjamin, having received preferential treatment, is to be kept as a slave, while
the others are free to leave—with sacks full of money. The situation is perfect for
Joseph. If they had not changed, he will have rescued his full-brother from their
continued evil. He would be safe in Egypt to live like royalty away from the family who cared so little for Joseph. If they had changed, they could be forgiven.

The Reconciliation of the Family

The brothers will not repeat their mistake. Instead, Judah makes a speech that
rivals the greatest speeches recorded. Appealing to the emotion of Joseph, he
shows himself a changed man, even offering his own life in place of Benjamin's. The very one who had the idea of selling Joseph offers himself as a slave
to save the youngest—what a change had occurred in Judah's life! It is at Judah's leadership that the family comes together again. The brothers, having
confessed their sins and produced fruits worthy of repentance, are now ready
to take their rightful places. These men, who were so wicked, are now ready to
be the heads of the tribes of Israel—the kingdom of God.

---

[7]See comment on 42.7–8.

[8]Commentators who say that Joseph is trying to lead the brothers to repentance from his first sight
of them in chapter 42 are overstating their case. It does seem clear, however, from what follows that
Joseph is at least curious as to whether they had repented.

[9]See comment on 42.14.

Joseph Reveals His Identity

They have now passed all the tests. They have shown that they are truly sorry for what they had done to Joseph. In a similar situation, they did not do the same to Benjamin, even when there was an easy escape available for them. Judah had given proof of the degree of their change by offering himself in Benjamin's stead, an offer that Joseph would have *never* expected, even had they been truly converted.

Now Joseph, convinced of their changed hearts, *could not control himself* and clears out the room except for his brothers and himself (45.1). Joseph wants privacy for this discussion as it is a family affair and should be kept within the family. Also, the privacy will prevent the airing of ugly aspects of the relationships of God's people before unbelievers. There may also have been some concern for such a great showing of emotion before his subordinates. In addition, the Egyptians would have hardly appreciated or understood the providence of God and the peculiar destiny of God's people of which Joseph was about to speak. And in this condition of privacy he reveals his identity to them.

His first words to them after revealing his identity are to ask if his father is alive. He would already know the answer to this, as he had previously asked this question (43.27). Earlier, however, he asked as a stranger, engaged in 'small talk.' Now, he asks as a son, expecting the kind of account one brother would give to another—more than a simple 'yes.' Also, his request into their father's well-being would soften the blow of learning who he was. Certainly they would have expected him say, 'I am Joseph—and now you will pay for what you did to me!' Instead, he shows concern for the family. But the brothers are afraid—and understandably so. They are completely in the power of someone they knew to be a harsh and cruel man, who they just learned was the brother they had sold into slavery. But Joseph isn't concerned with revenge. He invites them into intimate conversation with him (45.4) rather than standing afar off, addressing him as royalty. They do come near to him, but it is probably more to obey him than to draw near to him in affection or trust.

Now, in an effort to win their confidence, Joseph takes the blame away from them. *"You sold me,"* he says, but *"God sent me before you"* (45.5). Three times in fact, he tells them that it was God who had sent him to Egypt (45.5, 7, 8). He had come to understand the providence of God at work, and by explaining this to them, seeks to assure them that he has no intention of vengeance. There are two aspects to any event: the human mishandling of it and the perfect will of God. The latter alone is of consequence. God's purposes are ultimately fulfilled through, and in spite of, human deeds, whether or not those actions are morally right. He directs the maze of human guilt to achieve His good and set purposes.

Joseph then further seeks to allay their fear by inviting the whole clan to move to Egypt where they would be taken care of. Five more years of famine remain and he wants to be sure the family will survive. His desire for Jacob to be told of his power (45.13) is not boyish pride, as some commentators have suggested, but an effort to add credibility to his claims that he can support the entire family through five years of severe famine. This fits well with the understanding that verse 12 seeks to add credibility to his claim that he is Joseph.

Then he weeps and kisses his brothers one by one, beginning with Benjamin (45.14–15). And finally, after all of these steps to assure them, the brothers' fears are calmed enough that they talk with him (45.15b).

Pharaoh's Invitation

As word gets to Pharaoh that Joseph's brothers have come, Pharaoh offers an invitation to the family to move to Egypt to be safe from the famine. In many ways it repeats Joseph's invitation. This probably speaks to the providence of God, and certainly attests to Joseph's popularity: things connected with his fortune and family are of importance to all. Pharaoh's enthusiastic agreement with Joseph's invitation would also control any negative response other officials might have with Joseph making such a liberal offer to his family during a famine. Pharaoh's invitation, however, was not exactly parallel with Joseph's—in some ways it exceeded it. Pharaoh *commanded* that they take carts to help the family move (45.19). In addition, he told them not to worry about bringing any of their possessions—that the best of Egypt would be given them (45.20).

Pharaoh would have had several motives for inviting Joseph's family to Egypt. As already mentioned, Joseph was universally popular. In addition, so much of Pharaoh's wealth—indeed, the survival of Egypt and the surrounding world—was due to Joseph. Finally, the arrival of the family would answer questions regarding Joseph's background. If it had become public information that Joseph was formerly a slave, there may have been a constant undercurrent of questions as to where he came from and who he was to have such a position of authority (though such questions would not be asked openly). If such were the case, it would be pleasing to Pharaoh to learn that he came from an honorable family of free nomads who were generally held in high regard. Finally, Pharaoh's invitation to Joseph's family is a significant turning point in the history of the people of Israel. It is the beginning of a period of isolation (where the family, thoroughly alien, can multiply without losing its identity) and of eventual bondage and deliverance which would produce a people that forever after knew itself to be redeemed and called. But also, this free and honorable invitation carried with it the right of Israel to leave again without obstruction.

As Joseph sends them along their way, he urges them not to quarrel (45.24).

Upon arrival in Palestine, they would be forced to confess their sin to Jacob. Of course, the natural reaction for them would be to take as little of the guilt as possible. As they traveled and they discussed exactly what they would tell Jacob, it would be easy for an argument to develop. Surely, you can hear them now: 'Well, selling him was Judah's idea… *you're* the one who flagged down the Ishmaelites… well, *you* took the money from them…' and so forth. Even these changed men would want as little as possible to do with their sin when telling Jacob of what happened.

They told their father of Joseph's survival and his position of power. It took some convincing, but Jacob ultimately believes, is revived in spirit, and once again is Israel (45.27–28). At God's word, he moves his family to Egypt (46.1–4), where Pharaoh offers them the best land (47.6) and Joseph gives them land as a possession (47.11). And there, the family begins a sojourn that will last until God redeems them from Egyptian slavery many years later, when He will take them back to the Promised Land of Canaan.

48 The final three chapters—beginning with 47.29–31—are wholly concerned with the future of the chosen family and the Promised Land (Jacob twice instructs his children to bury him in Canaan; he adopts and blesses Joseph's sons; he blesses his sons), clearly displaying his faith, even in a foreign land, even as he was facing his own death.

48.1–2, Joseph was told, "Behold, your father is ill." Joseph's position in Egyptian court probably kept him at some distance from the family. He had not moved to Goshen with his family. Thus, he had to learn from someone else that his father was ill.

So he took with him his two sons. Either Joseph already knew that his father's illness was so severe that he would be ready to impart his final blessing, or "some plan like the one here carried out by Jacob had been discussed between the father and the son on a previous occasion" (Leupold). That he took his sons for blessing is significant: thereby, he "consecrates his sons of an Egyptian mother to the God of Israel and his covenant people" (Waltke).

Manasseh and Ephraim. Manasseh is listed first as he is the elder. Jacob, however, will place the younger before the elder, both in speech (v 5) and in blessing (vv 13–14, 19–20).

Then Israel summoned his strength. Feeble Jacob (v 2) musters his strength and becomes, once again, Israel. "The interchange of the names [Jacob and Israel] is not everywhere so significant as here. Jacob lies down sick, Israel draws himself up" (Delitzsch qtd. in Mathews). In this episode, he deals with issues of the covenant land and in the next (ch 49), he deals with issues of the covenant seed and nation. Thus, in his renewed strength, he takes on the covenant name. Or, as Keil puts it, "Jacob, enfeebled with age, gathered up his strength for a work, which he was about to perform as Israel, the bearer of the grace of the promise."

And sat up in bed. The word for *sat* is the same word used for *lived* in 47.28. "Jacob has deteriorated from 'dwelling' in Goshen… to 'dwelling' in bed" (Hamilton).

48.3, "God Almighty appeared to me at Luz." I.e., Bethel (*cf.* 28.10–19; 35.6–13). Jacob recalls God's appearance to him at Bethel in great detail. Hamilton says, "The only essential element of that Theophany he does not repeat is the name change from Jacob to Israel. In this way, he minimizes his role and maximizes God's role in the event." Thus, the focus is not on what God did for him, but on God and His promises to the family for generations to come.[1]

This, of course, presumes that Jacob had God's appearance in chapter 35 in mind, since he cites the promises of land and nation (v 4), while the appearance in chapter 28 also included the promise of the seed. It would further be fitting for Jacob to be remembering the latter appearance, as it was on Jacob's return to the Promised Land. "Just as Isaac's blessing was ultimately fulfilled when Jacob returned to Canaan, so Jacob hopes his last words will come true when his descendants return there" (Wenham). Of course, this supposition presumes that Jacob distinguishes the promises of God as clearly as the modern reader does and that, in his mind, the two had not blended into one, "since the substance of the divine revelation was both times practically the same" (Leupold).[2]

On *God Almighty*, see Excursus B.

"And blessed me." God's blessing Jacob empowers him to bless the twelve tribes (Waltke).

48.5–6, "And now." Waltke says, "The logical particle shows Jacob has recited God's past blessing on him to validate his present blessing on Joseph."

"Your two sons… are mine." Next, Jacob adopts Ephraim and Manasseh as his own so that they would be counted just *as Reuben and Simeon are.* The fulfilling of this adoption would be found in the dividing of the land of Canaan when the Israelites returned there after the exodus: Ephraim and Manasseh would each receive a tribe alongside ten of the brothers. "By making Joseph's sons Jacob's sons, Jacob is in effect elevating Joseph to the level of himself. That is, both men are now ancestral fathers of the tribes of Israel that will come from them" (Hamilton).

Further, by this adoption of Ephraim and Manasseh, Joseph received the birthright—the double portion of the inheritance (cf. 1 Chron 5.1–2). This is to be understood as distinct from the blessing, which, to the patriarchs, included the Messianic line.[3] Though Joseph receives the birth-

---

[1]Mathews notes that he also omits the mention of kings coming from his body (35.11), "For although this is true of Abraham (17.6, 16) and Jacob, the throne is reserved in Jacob's tribal blessings for Judah (49.10; cf. Psa 78.67–68)."

[2]Waltke suggests an explanation for recalling this incident at this moment: "Jacob's authority to legitimatize Joseph's two sons as numbered among his twelve sons comes from the theophanies given especially to him. Joseph, having never experienced such theophanies, does not have this authority."

[3]See comment on 25.31.

right, the blessing will come through Judah (49.10). Typically, the birthright goes to the eldest son. Although that is not strictly the case in this instance, as Reuben is the eldest, Joseph is the oldest son of Rachel, and "Jacob had naturally destined Rachel to be his only wife. Her sons should have been the first-born" (Leupold).

"Ephraim and Manasseh shall be mine as Reuben and Simeon are." Not only does Jacob here place Ephraim before Manasseh, but he does so in the same breath as naming his own children—*Reuben and Simeon*—chronologically. This subtle hint of what will come slips by Joseph unnoticed (v 13).

"The children you fathered after them shall be yours." This note, distinguishing the remainder of Joseph's children, is for genealogical purposes, which would have been important to the Israelite readers. While Ephraim and Manasseh were to be counted as Jacob's sons, any others Joseph had would be his own.

"They shall be called by the name of their brothers in their inheritance." Any other sons, though counted as Joseph's, would then be under Ephraim or Manasseh's tribe in the inheritance. Either the narrator blanks other sons that Joseph already had, or this is all a provision for future children that he may have. As far as we know, Joseph never had any other sons.

48.7, "To my sorrow, Rachel died in the land of Canaan." Although we hold that Jacob ultimately came to love and respect Leah to a higher degree[4] that is not to be understood as Jacob not loving Rachel or seeking to pay her death honor. This is clear in the favoritism displayed to Joseph and Benjamin. But also, the sons adopted are as Rachel's, taking the place of others she would have borne him had she not died. There is a clear contrast between Joseph's prospect of having more children and Jacob's lack of having more children by Rachel (Waltke). "He thus was giving honor to Rachel… by making three tribes descend from her."[5]

48.8, "Who are these?" Surely he knows Joseph's sons—"he has just proposed to adopt them by name!" (Waltke). Various options exist as to why he would have asked this question. Jacob's vision was failing him (v 10). He may assume that they are Joseph's sons, but wants to verify that im-

---

[4]See Excursus L.

[5]Leon Wood, *Genesis,* 143.

pression. Or he may recall his own deception of Isaac and seek to make sure that the same is not being done to him. Or maybe Jacob had not seen them in a while (Joseph's job kept him away), and was surprised at how they had grown. We speak like this now, when we see children for the first time in years—'Is that little Johnny?'—even though we are well aware that it is. Finally, some have suggested that this was part of the adoption ritual. If so, Jacob did not ask because he needed to learn or verify their identity, but because it was ceremonial, much like we ask the question at weddings, 'Who gives this woman?'

48.9, "Whom God has given me." Cf. 33.5. "Since throughout the Bible children are seen as God's gift (*cf.* Psa 127; 128), this comment seems rather a platitude, but despite the promises of offspring, children came slowly to the patriarchs. So Joseph's remark draws attention to the fulfillment of the promises" (Wenham). And Hamilton: "They are not sons whom his wife, Asenath, has given to him, but sons whom *God* has given him."

 "Bring them to me, please, that I may bless them." Wenham says, "The key word, 'blessing,' is used nineteen times in 27.1–28.9 and nine times in chapters 48–49 out of a total of thirty-seven times in the life of Jacob (chs 27–50). Jacob, who was so anxious at his father's deathbed to acquire blessing for himself, is now just as keen to pass it on to his descendants before he dies."

48.10, *The eyes of Israel were dim with age.* This note about Jacob's health serves to prepare the reader for Jacob's forthcoming reaction and to explain his previous question. As such, it serves as a transition from one part of this scene to the next.

48.11–12, "I never expected to see your face; and behold, God has let me see your offspring also." Though his eyes were dim with age, he sees both Joseph and his sons by God's grace. "God blesses both father and grandfather through these boys. To Joseph they are an incredible gift after years of affliction; to Jacob they are an incredible vision after he had lost all hope of ever seeing Joseph" (Waltke). It is clear that neither father nor son attributes the boys to luck or good fortune. To Joseph, they are sons whom God gave; to Jacob, God has let him see them. "Jacob may lament that his days have been few and evil, and that he has not lived as long or as well as his father and grandfather (47.9). Yet Jacob is the only patriarch in these narratives who meets and has any dealings with his grandchildren. ...In having this privilege, Jacob is exceeded only by Joseph, who saw perhaps three generations beyond him (50.23)" (Hamilton).

From his knees. Placing Ephraim and Manasseh on or between his knees was a ritual gesture of adoption, "symbolizing his giving them birth in place of Asenath daughter of Potiphera" (Waltke). As Jacob was bed-ridden and the boys nearly twenty, if not older, it is most likely that they "stood by their grandfather's bed, near his knees" (Hamilton).

And he bowed himself with his face to the earth. Here, the opposite of the dreams happens. Joseph bows before his father. The one who is second only to Pharaoh "humbles himself before the patriarch who mediates God's promises" (Waltke).

48.13–14, *And Joseph took them both, Ephraim in his right hand toward Israel's left hand, and Manasseh in his left hand toward Israel's right hand.* Joseph arranges his sons so the eldest would receive the higher blessing. The *right hand* is "the position of strength, honor, power and glory (*cf.* Exod 15.6; Psa 89.13; Prov 3.16; Ecc 10.2; Matt 25.33; Acts 2.33)" (Waltke).

And Israel stretched out his right hand and laid it on the head of Ephraim, who was the younger... crossing his hands. Having already named Ephraim first (v 5), Jacob now crosses his hands and blesses the younger above the older. His explanation (vv 15–20) shows that his hands were guided by God. "Jacob may be losing his sight, but he is not losing his insight" (Hamilton). And Sternberg: "The blind patriarch shows an insight into the future denied to his clear-sighted (and occasionally clairvoyant) but for once earthbound son" (qtd. in Hamilton).

48.15–16, *And he blessed Joseph.* *Joseph* is most likely to be understood as a collective term for his two sons (Kidner), though it is also true that in blessing the sons, Jacob also blessed the father (Leupold).

"God before whom my fathers... walked." First, God's covenant relationship with the patriarchs is emphasized, as was the patriarch's part of the covenant: their *walk*. "How appropriate it is for one grandfather, now a father who is blessing his (grand)children, to recall his own father and grandfather" (Hamilton). Implicit in this description is that the descendants must do likewise. "God's covenant promises to Abraham and Isaac are certain because they walked before God. For their heirs to experience the promised blessings, they too must walk before him" (Waltke).

"My shepherd." This is the first of many places that this analogy is used

of God (*e.g.*, Psa 23; 80.1; Isa 40.11; John 10.11; Heb 13.20; 1 Pet 2.25, *etc.*). "Himself a shepherd, Jacob well understood what a measure of tender care the figure involved" and saw it as a fitting parallel (Leupold). This phrase marks the turn of focus from Jacob's father and grandfather to himself. But the change of focus is twofold. Also, "He shifts the emphasis from himself and anything he has done to God and what He has done for Jacob. If Abraham and Isaac walked before God, God has walked before Jacob" (Hamilton).

"The angel who has redeemed me." Although this might seem to be an odd description of God, it is running parallel with two clear descriptions of Him. Further, it ascribes to Him a divine work: redemption from evil. It seems clear, then, that this is also a description of God. This expression "calls to mind God's visible encounters with Him at turning-points in his life, above all at Peniel; and the word *redeemed* expresses the protection and reclamation which a man's... kinsmen provided in times of trouble" (Kidner).[6]

This is the only occurrence of *redeemed* in Genesis, though it is used to describe God's deliverance of Israel from Egypt in Exodus and later refers to the role of a human redeemer who rescues a relative (*e.g.*, Lev 25; 27.13–33; Num 35.12–27; Deut 19.6–12; Ruth 4.7–11). "Thus, the divine [redeemer] is related to His people by covenant and intervenes in the face of dire circumstances to save them where they cannot save themselves. ... The Mosaic community would have understood that the God of redemption whom they served was the same Lord who delivered their ancestor Jacob from his trials in and outside the land when he faced the likes of Esau and Laban as well as the local Canaanite populations" (Mathews).

Leupold sees the trinity in these three descriptions. To do this, he equates the Father with *God*, the Spirit with *shepherd*, and the Son with *angel*. We are not convinced by this approach, as it is quite speculative and highly doubtful that any of the original readers would have understood it as such. Rather than pigeonholing each phrase as an individual in the godhead, it seems better to see each as a varying aspect of the work of God, a distinction that Kidner makes between "naming His attributes" and "recalling His dealings," suggesting that it is the latter that is done here.

"Bless the boys." To paraphrase: 'May this three-fold God continue to

---

[6]See Excursus H.

show these blessings to Ephraim and Manasseh, allowing them to walk before him, shepherding them, redeeming them from evil, that they may be as me and my fathers were to God—in a covenant relationship; God's people.'

"Let them grow into a multitude." The verb used is a *hapax legomenon.* Waltke says that it might be related to the word for *fish* and Wenham translates the verse, *May they multiply like fish.*

Of all that Jacob did in his life, the author of Hebrews chose this as his great act of faith (11.21), probably because "it has the quality, praised in that chapter, of reaching towards the promise, even in the face of death, 'having seen it and greeted it from afar'" (Kidner). Through his ups and downs, even now as he embarks on the unknown, Jacob never lost his confidence in God's power.

48.17–18, When Joseph saw that his father had laid his right hand on the head of Ephraim, it displeased him. …And Joseph said to his father, "Not this way, my father." Joseph waits until now to speak, because he cannot act immediately upon seeing Jacob's mistake. He is listening to what his father has to say, a solemn, prophetic blessing that is not to be lightly interrupted. But as soon as his father had spoken the blessing, he acted to correct the mistake, just as Esau attempted to reverse the blessing given to Jacob.[7]

48.19, "I know, my son." There is a touch of irony in this scene. "Blind Isaac blessed Jacob without knowing it. Jacob, though almost blind, knows and deliberately follows God's unconventional plan. If Isaac's unwitting blessing could not be reversed, how much more this conscious blessing?" (Waltke).

"His younger brother shall be greater than he." Wenham says, "As Esau's protests in 27.34–36 were countered with a reaffirmation of the blessing just pronounced (27.37–40), so here Joseph's attempt to make Jacob change his blessing is rejected" and the blessing is reaffirmed. Ephraim will be a greater nation than Manasseh.

During the time of Moses the number of the two tribes went back and forth. At the first census taken in the second year after the exodus, Ephraim is 20 percent larger than Manasseh; at the second census a generation later, however, Manasseh is larger by 40 percent. It is not until the time of the Judges that Ephraim becomes completely dominant and stays that way. Af-

---

[7] Two alternate possibilities: First, he acted immediately, but it is told after the blessing so it does not interrupt the narrative (Waltke). Second, he is so upset by what he sees his father do that he never hears what his father says (Hamilton).

ter the kingdom divides, Ephraim becomes synonymous with Israel, dominant over all the northern tribes, and in the prophets *Ephraim* is used interchangeably with *Israel*. [8] Perhaps we can see in this comment the faith of Moses to record something that so clearly *hadn't* happened (Leupold).

48.20, "By you Israel will pronounce blessings." They would become so blessed that their names would be linked to blessing

Thus he put Ephraim before Manasseh. This was not without parallel in the ancient world: "The traditions of Alalakh reinforce certain ones in existence at both Mari and Ugarit to show that the father was at liberty to disregard the natural sequences of primogeniture, and instead to choose his own firstborn from among his sons. This custom has obvious bearing upon the case of Manasseh and Ephraim (Gen 48.13–20), the repudiation of Reuben (Gen 49.3f), and the elevation of Joseph (Gen 48.22)." [9]

48.21, "God will be with you and bring you again to the land of your fathers." Jacob leaves Joseph with the assurance that Egypt will not remain their homeland. God in His power will return them to the land of their fathers.

48.22, "I have given to you rather than to your brothers one mountain slope that I took from the hand of the Amorites with my sword and with my bow." We can be nearly certain that the land he is talking about is in Shechem. The word translated *mountain slope* is a homophone of Shechem, and it is later recorded that Joseph receives an inheritance in the land of Shechem (Josh 24.32; John 4.5), if we are to identify that inheritance with this promise.

There is, however, something of a difficulty in making that identification. Joshua specifies that the land in question was one which Jacob purchased from the Shechemite (*cf.* 33.19). But Jacob seems to indicate that it is not that same piece of land, rather one which he had to fight for. There are two views for determining how Jacob came to receive this portion of Shechem *with sword and bow.* Some suggest that it is an event not elsewhere recorded in the Bible. These would argue that it could not refer to the massacre

---

[8]Thus, the northern and southern tribes were Joseph and Judah, respectively. The two sons who dominate the Genesis narrative and receive the greatest blessings from their father, ultimately become representative of the entire nation. Also, of the 603,550 fighting men numbered at Sinai, only two made it to the Promised Land—a Judahite and an Ephraimite.

[9]R.K. Harrison, *Old Testament Times,* 79.

of chapter 34, as Jacob had no part in it and condemned it. Further, "The plundering of Shechem was not followed in this instance by the possession of the city, but by the removal of Jacob from the neighborhood" (Keil).

Others, however, argue that this is to be identified with the massacre of chapter 34. Even if he disowned his sons' actions, any spoils of the victory would still be counted as his (Kidner). So, ultimately, in spite of his distaste for his sons' overreaction, he accepts the reality that through their actions, he conquered and took the city. This, of course, would not be the first or last time that God has used the evil of man to achieve His aims without acquitting the guilty.

Growth of the Seed: Jacob looks forward to the time when the promise of the land will be fulfilled, adopting Ephraim and Manasseh so they will receive an equal inheritance with his own sons.

49 Having adopted Ephraim and Manasseh, thereby bestowing the birthright upon Joseph, Jacob now turns his attention to blessing his own sons.

One may question whether all of this chapter should be called blessings, considering the specific censure of some of the sons and the discouraging words to others. In response, it must be emphasized that although there is censure, there is no cursing, save of the particular sin of Simeon and Levi. Leupold says rightly, "These criticisms are blessings in disguise, for they point out to the tribes involved the sin that the tribe as a whole is most exposed to and against which it should be particularly on its guard. ...Yet, for all that, not one of the tribes is removed from the concord of the blessings laid upon the rest. ...The blessed land is denied to none. The benefits of the covenant of the Lord in which all stood are cancelled for none."

This chapter reveals precisely why the events since chapter 34 have been recorded. They show why Judah was chosen and why the others were rejected: his elder brothers were wicked and impenitent. Judah, though he had a straying moment, returned to the family and to God. This principle, it would seem, is applicable throughout the book of Genesis. Each account tells a 'choosing' of God—one is kept in the Messianic line; one is removed from it.[1]

This blessing also serves a prophetic function regarding the futures of the tribes, thrusting forward the story of the Bible even as Genesis is ending. "The groundwork of the prophecy was supplied partly by the natural character of his twelve sons, and partly by the divine promise which had been given by the Lord to him and to his fathers Abraham and Isaac" (Keil). Thus, "The narrative of Genesis, which began with God's blessing on creation, now ends with Jacob conveying the divine blessing on his children" (Waltke). In this lies an important point: this is God's blessing on them, as much as it was Jacob's. Thus, it was God and Jacob who both pronounced verdicts on actions about which they had previously been silent.

Regarding this chapter's prophetic function: for the most part, the blessing does not contain predictions of specific historical events, but a general portrait of the peculiarities of the different tribes.[2] Some blessings

---

[1]See INTRODUCTION, pages 15–17.

[2]It will become evident as we proceed through this chapter that Jacob often uses the meanings of his sons' names as a part of the blessing.

seem to point to a specific fulfillment (especially in the case of Judah). But if we spend our time looking through the Bible and other ancient records to find specific fulfillments of this chapter, the most we are likely to find is a headache. This is especially true since so many of the prophecies, though they would have had meaning to the audience, have little to do with the story of the Bible and are blanked therein.[3]

49.1, *Then Jacob called his sons and said, "Gather yourselves together."*
Waltke writes: "Unlike Isaac, who transferred the divine blessing behind closed doors, creating rivalry and conniving between parents and siblings, Jacob gives his blessing openly, inviting all his sons to gather round."

"In the days to come." Although some believe this to specifically refer to the Messianic times and thus translate it *the last days*, most feel the Hebrew phrase is much more general as the ESV translates above. This does not, of course, exclude the Messianic future, but does not limit itself to it either. "It points to the future, including the Messianic future" (Leupold). And Waltke: "Here it embraces the entire history of Israel from the conquest and distribution of the land to the consummate reign of Jesus Christ." In any event, we can be assured by this phrase that Jacob's words have a prophetic meaning, as this phrase only occurs in prophetic contexts (Wenham). "It is fitting that Jacob's last words are prophecies, for his life began with a prophecy (25.23)" (Hamilton).

49.2, *"Asssemble and listen... listen."* The double exhortation to hear is most likely a simple parallelism, which may carry the meaning forward somewhat,[4] but would do little other than make the point emphatic. This added emphasis may be due to the fact that his message is "doubly precious, since [it voices] his own best counsel as well as the wisdom imparted by God's Holy Spirit" (Leupold).

Jacob... Israel. Throughout the Old Testament, Israel and Jacob stand next to each other in parallel lines and the occurrence of the name change is most likely understood in that regard. Another possible explanation,

---

[3]When we see specific fulfillments, they generally occur earlier in Israel's history, rather than later: "As to the general period in view, it is mainly that of the settlement of the twelve in their tribal lands" (Kidner).

[4]"As we read the lines of Hebrew poetry carefully, we see that the second phrase is related in meaning to the first phrase. However—and this is important—it always carries forward the thought found in the first phrase in some way." Tremper Longman III, *How to Read the Psalms*, 98.

though less likely, is that one name is used to symbolize *his* thoughts and wishes in the following blessing (*i.e.*, Jacob), while the covenant name (*i.e.*, Israel) is used to symbolize God speaking through him.

49.3–4, "Reuben." Kidner writes: "The heaping of phrase on majestic phrase in verse 3, building up to an ignominious collapse, reflects the exalted hopes that were shattered at Reuben's fall. ...It would be hard to find a more withering contrast between a man and his calling." The building up of verse 3 to the crash of verse 4 excellently illustrates how Jacob must have felt about Reuben. His father lost respect for him when he sinned with Bilhah in chapter 35; his younger brothers had already lost respect for him by chapter 37 and were following Judah's lead.

"My firstborn." The phrase guarantees right to a double portion and leadership (*cf.* Deut 21.15–17),[5] and recalls all of the great hopes any father has for his firstborn. In the ancient Near East, alteration of inheritance was always and only due to serious offense against one's own family (Waltke).

"Unstable as water." "Jacob's long and eerie silence about [Reuben's sin] is broken in one of the fiercest denunciations in Genesis" (Wenham). *Unstable* could also be translated *turbulent* or *seething*. Literally, it means *boiling up*, making it an appropriate descriptor of the lust that led him to his sin with Bilhah. It is also the kind of characteristic that one does not want in a leader. So, because of his instability—because of his sin—his place as firstborn is stripped from him. This also serves as Jacob and God's reaction to and judgment of a deed that was previously not addressed.

"You shall not have preeminence." The original word play is obscured by most translations, though salvaged by the ESV. *Preeminence* is meant to contrast with *preeminent in power* in the previous verse, as they are both from the same verbal root. Thus, "Reuben is deprived of his status because of his misconduct" (Wenham).

This also addresses the long-term result of Reuben's sin and points to the antiquity of this saying. "From the time of the settlement onward, there is no trace of Reuben's original primacy" (Wenham). Not once in Israel's history did Reuben's tribe furnish a leader of any kind. "It earned a name for irresolution in Deborah's day (Jdg 5.15b–16); later it seems

---

[5] The referenced verse forbids a father from transferring the rights of the firstborn by his first wife to the eldest son of a second wife, which Jacob clearly did. "This is one of several examples of patriarchal practice conflicting with later legal theory and is a pointer to the antiquity of these traditions" (Wenham).

to have been overshadowed by Gad and periodically overrun by Moab" (Kidner). Reuben's tribe settled on the east side of the Jordan, demanding their inheritance prematurely. In sum, as Israel develops further as a nation, Reuben becomes increasingly insignificant.

"He went up to my couch." The shift from second to third person reflects "Jacob turn[ing] away from his son as from a stranger in sad reflection" (Leupold), and "expos[ing] him to his brothers: it is a gesture of revulsion" (Kidner).

49.5–7, "Simeon and Levi are brothers." This is not meant to state the obvious or even clarify that they are full brothers rather than half brothers. Instead, it indicates that they are of the same mind and disposition: they are allies or confederates; they are the same in thought and action.

"In their anger they killed men. …Cursed by their anger." Jacob had already condemned their sin, but his rebuke did little good (*cf.* 34.31). In this blessing he does so again, to emphasize the severity of what they did and to explain why they are passed over for the blessing. "Having demoted Reuben from his primacy, Jacob might have been expected to confer the leadership on his next oldest sons, Simeon or Levi. But they too have disqualified themselves" (Wenham).

It is noteworthy that, though their anger is cursed, they are not. "The brothers had flattered and, no doubt, at first prided themselves upon what they had done, as though it had been a deed born out of righteous indignation. But good motives do not produce murder" (Leupold). Instead, their actions follow in the footsteps of Cain and Lamech: the seed of the serpent. And so, Jacob curses their sin and passes over them in the blessing.

"They hamstrung oxen." This detail is not given in chapter 34. Although they seized the flocks of the Shechemites (34.28), the oxen were of no use to them because they were shepherds, not cattlemen or farmers. To *hamstring* something is to cut the leg tendons "a process by which animals were not merely lamed, but rendered useless, since the tendon once severed could never be healed again" (Keil). The brutality of the attack on the Shechemites was both ruthless and senseless; they were more concerned with revenge than plunder. "Thus by merism (human and animal), Jacob condemns their wanton attitude toward life" (Mathews).[6]

---

[6]Wenham notes: "While not kind to cattle, such a comment is an anticlimax after the mention of homicide in the previous line; this is contrary to the conventions of poetry, where typically the second line develops or says something more important than the first line." This has led some to

Or, this could simply be a figurative way of describing their attack on the Shechemites.

"I will divide them." "They had joined together to commit this crime, and as a punishment they should be divided or scattered in the nation of Israel" (Keil). And Leupold: "They who had banded together to their own hurt were to be dispersed for their own good." As implied in these quotes, this phrase most likely refers to the future of the tribes. By the second census (Num 26), Simeon was the weakest tribe. When Moses blessed the tribes before entering Canaan (Deut 33), he omitted Simeon. Their inheritance was *in the midst of the inheritance of the people of Judah* (Josh 19.1). And it did not take long before Simeon was not even recognized as a separate tribe, completely absorbed by Judah. Levi's fate was slightly different, though they also received no land. They took a stand with Moses in Exodus 32, regaining some of their honor and became the religious leaders of Israel and the priestly family. Ultimately, they received 48 cities, spread across the land, where they could do their priestly work for the tribes.

49.8–12, "Judah, your brothers shall praise you." This is the first occurrence of name-play in the blessing. Judah's name means *praised* and Jacob says that the brothers will praise him (*cf.* 2 Sam 5.1–3). "What Jacob raised derogatorily as a possibility with Joseph (37.10) he now affirms with Judah" (Hamilton).[7]

"Your hand shall be on the neck of your enemies." This figure shows an enemy who is defeated. Thus, Judah's tribe would succeed in warfare. In its history, God achieved many victories through Judah. "Earlier, when the brothers were debating the best way to rid themselves of Joseph, Judah protested 'let not our hand be upon him' (37.27). ...Judah refused to put his hand on Joseph, but is praised by his father for putting his hand on his real enemies" (Hamilton).

"Judah is a lion's cub... a lion... a lioness." Each instance of *lion* in this verse is a different word, accounting for three of the seven Hebrew words

---

suggest alternate interpretations to this phrase. The most noteworthy include the suggestion that oxen refers to the leaders of the Shechemites (following the meaning of Hamor's name, *i.e.*, donkey) and that it is a reference back to Jacob, "whose interests in peace and security were put at risk by his son's deeds" (Wenham). See also Calum Carmichael, "Some Sayings in Genesis 49," *JBL* 88 (1969): 435–444.

[7] The mental gymnastics done by Good and Carmichael to make this a curse on Judah are just short of mind-boggling and stands in stark contrast with the text itself. See Carmichael, *ibid.* and Edwin M. Good, "The 'Blessing' on Judah, Gen. 49.8–12," *JBL* 82 (1963): 427–432.

for lion. "There may be a sense of movement or growth by Judah in the verse by the change in lion imagery from a young 'cub' to a 'lion.' This would correspond with the development of Judah in the narrative who emerges from the pack of brothers as their leader and spokesman" (Mathews).

"He stooped down. …Who dares rouse him?" "Judah is likened to a fierce lion that has seized its prey, returned to its den, and here lies daring anyone to challenge it" (Wenham). And Hamilton: "The lion, having recently eaten, has retired to its sleeping quarters to digest its meal. Even while it is reposing, nothing else tries to invade its territory, so powerful is the lion."

"The Scepter shall not depart from Judah." The scepter symbolizes rule and royal power. It is a long staff that the king held in his hand when speaking to public assemblies. When he sat down to arbitrate, it would be *between his feet.*[8] This also hearkens back to 38.18, where Judah leaves his staff and seal with Tamar as a pledge.

"Until tribute comes to him." Or, *until Shiloh comes.* The precise identity of Shiloh is something of a conundrum. "The meaning of the Hebrew is arguably the most debated in Genesis" (Waltke). *Shiloh* seems to be a reference to the Messiah, but it occurs nowhere else in the Old Testament as a Messianic title, the New Testament never cites this verse as being fulfilled, and no one is exactly sure what *Shiloh* means. Mathews writes: "Other than the general tenor of the passage, there is no reason… to identify 'Shiloh' with the Messianic king."

Jewish exegetes sought clarification for this passage from Ezekiel 21.26–27. "They suggested that behind this word lies *shel,* meaning 'which,' and *loh,* meaning 'belongs to him.' Thus understood, the meaning of Shiloh accords with Ezekiel 21.27, 'until he comes to whom it rightfully belongs.'"[9] If that meaning is to be imported to this verse, the *it* in this verse would have reference to either *judgment* (as Kaiser suggests) or *the scepter,* either of which would make the promise mean that the royal Messiah, to whom the throne rightfully belongs, will come through Judah. As Judah is the lion of the tribes, his noblest descendant is the lion of that tribe (*cf.* Rev

---

[8]An older view to *between his feet*—followed by Wenham—is that it is a reference to Judah's descendants. The reasoning is that children come out from *between your feet* and *"feet* are a regular euphemism for the private parts. …In other words, a descendant of Judah will always be a national leader." Other commentators have seen it as a phallic euphemism. But neither interpretation is necessary: "A Persian relief shows King Darius seated on his throne with a ruler's staff between his feet" (Watlke).

[9]*Hard Sayings,* 135.

5.5). This view, however, is based on the alternate Hebrew textual reading. And though Mathews follows it, even he admits that "it does not explain the development of the erroneous [Shiloh]."

Another view is indicated by the ESV text. "This reading fits the parallelism of the verse and eliminates any over-messianizing. Interestingly, the NT ignores Genesis 49.10 and virtually all the ancient versions take [Shiloh] as other than a proper name in this verse."[10] And Wenham: "It produces a good poetic line in parallel with the next line, 'and the peoples obey him': tribute from foreign nations expresses their submission to the Judean king. Furthermore, these two lines take further the leadership promised in the previous two lines, which spoke of a Judean king always heading the nation... [and adds] that the Davidic king was appointed to rule the nations."

The final alternative is to switch the subject and object: *Until he comes to Shiloh*. Hamilton says, "Taking Shiloh as a representative term for northern Israel, the verse would point to the extension of the Davidic kingdom in Judah to include the northern tribes. In other words, the phrase foretells a great future for David and his kingdom. ...The problem with... [this] interpretation is that the people of Israel never did become monotribal although they were for a while a united kingdom." A further difficulty with this interpretation is that it demands this be a non-standard spelling of the town-name Shiloh (Mathews).

It does seem clear that the *until* is used in an inclusive sense. That is, the coming of Shiloh does not mark the limit of Judah's dominion over Israel, for if it did it would constitute a threat and not a blessing (Leupold). Instead, "The idea is that the sovereignty of Judah is brought to its highest point under the arrival and rule of Shiloh."[11] [12] Ultimately, it may be said: "All at least agree that this line is predicting the rise of the Davidic monarchy and the establishment of the Israelite empire, if not the coming of a greater David. And if the primary reference is to David, traditional Jewish and Christian exegetes would agree that like other Davidic promises it has a greater fulfillment in the Messiah" (Wenham).

Until now, the birthright and blessing had come to the same son. Here, it is split between Joseph and Judah. Joseph has already received the birth-

---

[10]D.K. Stuart, "Shiloh," *ISBE*, 478–479.

[11]*Hard Sayings*, 134.

[12]If, however, *until* is taken in an exclusive sense, it may simply refer to Judah being the only tribe left at the arrival of the Messiah.

right, the double portion of the physical inheritance (ch 48); here, Judah receives the blessing, the spiritual inheritance of the Messianic line. Although we may have suspected the distinction between the two by Esau's seeking after the blessing though he had already forfeited the birthright, the blessing on Jacob's sons makes it absolutely clear that the two are not one-and-the-same.

"Binding his foal to the vine and his donkey's colt to the choice vine, he has washed his garments in wine." This is the turning point of this blessing. Until now, the theme has been the fierce domination of Judah. But with the coming of Shiloh, "the scene becomes an earthly paradise such as the prophets foretell in their Messianic poems" (Kidner). The language becomes figurative as Jacob speaks of the golden age of the coming one. He deliberately uses the language of excess. "No one but an incredibly wealthy person would tether a donkey to a choice vine, for the donkey would consume the valuable grapes" (Waltke). [13] And how plentiful wine must be that it could be used for scrub water! [14] Wine and milk would be so plentiful that *his eyes are darker than wine and his teeth whiter than milk.*

49.13, "Zebulun." As is typical in Genesis, the birth order is once again disregarded. If it had remained in sequence, the next son blessed should be either Dan (the first of Bilhah) or Issachar (the fifth of Leah). Zebulun is, however, the sixth and final son of Leah, the tenth overall. This order is also followed in Moses' blessing (Deut 33.18). "In both blessings, Zebulun is the more energetic and prosperous of the two. In fact, Issachar is represented as lazy, submissive, and effete" (Waltke). One must wonder if this character trait is not only a prophecy of Issachar's tribe, but present in him and the reason why he is bypassed by Zebulun.

"Shall dwell at the shore of the sea… his border shall be at Sidon." The ESV does a poor job with this verse, which more literally reads that Zebulun will dwell *toward the shore* and its border will be *toward Sidon.* Although the difference is slight, it is an important one, since Zebulun touched no

---

[13] A more allegorical and fanciful approach sees this as a foreshadowing of the triumphal entry of Christ. "The vine, in accord with Jesus' declaration 'I am the true vine' (John 15.1), represents Christ and the donkey, and its foal bound to the vine is the Gentiles and the Jews who respond to the gospel" (Chrysostom qtd. in Mathews).

[14] Rather than using wine for water, some commentators suggest it refers to the fullness of the wine presses—so full that those who tread the grapes will exit the wine press looking like they had washed their clothes in wine.

sea nor bordered directly on Sidon. The tribe of Zebulun was located in the north, *near* both the Sea of Galilee and the Mediterranean Sea, but touched neither.

Jesus, though a Judean by birth, was a Zebulunite by residence (Hamilton). His time spent on or around the sea is well-documented in the gospels and gives us a clearer picture of what life in the tribe of Zebulun may have been like.

49.14–15, *"Issachar is a strong donkey. …He saw a resting place that was good… so he bowed his shoulder to bear and became a servant at forced labor."* Issachar had the advantage of physical strength, but was lethargic and unambitious. *He saw a resting place that was good.* "The sin is as old as Adam and Eve. The woman saw that the tree was good for food… and the Issacharites saw a resting place that was good" (Hamilton). And because he preferred rest to work, he did nothing, ultimately becoming a worker for others. "Like an idle beast of burden, he would rather submit to the yoke and be forced to do the work of a slave, than risk his possessions and his peace in the struggle for liberty" (Keil). "Issachar is thereby warned against aiming too low, against burying his talent in a napkin" (Leupold).

There is no report of Issachar being such a person to prompt this sort of blessing, and finding a fulfillment is questionable, at best. Wood suggests, "Issachar, which was assigned land in the fertile Esdraelon Plain, did not choose to seize this land from the native Canaanites, but took the easier way of living wherever its people could find a place. It is evident that they were not in their assigned territory, for instance, in Gideon's day, for his battle with the Midianites was fought in this territory and yet Issacharites are not even mentioned as playing a part in Gideon's army (see Jdg 6.35)."[15] Waltke adds, "The tribe is mostly slighted in the book of Judges. It is not mentioned in the inventory of the tribes in Judges 1 or in the prose accounts of the battle against Canaan and Midian (Jdg 4 and 6). This means that it played no significant role, and in fact an inglorious one, during this period."

49.16–17, *"Dan shall judge his people."* Dan's blessing is also a play on his name, which means *judge*. Hamilton suggests that *judge* means *plead the cause, defend* rather than *condemn*. "Hence, verse 16 needs to be read as a statement of praise directed at Dan."

---

[15]Leon Wood, *Genesis,* 146.

"Dan shall be a serpent in the way." Kidner sees verse 17 as contrasting verse 16. Thus, Dan is like Reuben: a tribe with heightened expectations, but failed hopes. It is possible, however, to see verse 17 as being in concert with verse 16. Thus, those who deal wickedly will have to face the judgment of Dan: he will overthrow all who wrongfully antagonize him. "All who wickedly oppose him may find him as deadly an opponent as 'a serpent'" (Leupold).

A serpent in the way has been seen as referring to Dan's lack of moral commitment and tendency to encourage idolatry (*cf.* Jdg 18), and has been cited as the reason his tribe is omitted in Revelation 7.5–8.[16] By contrast, Waltke sees it as a figure representing "the tribe as small and in a vulnerable position" and referring to its future character: "Though small, Dan will be aggressive, dangerous, and strike unexpectedly to overthrow nations… Samson, from this tribe, single-handedly wounds the Philistines." And Hamilton: "Dan, although small, will be quite capable of holding his own. His strength will be greater than his size. As small as he is, he will be able to strike panic into an animal as large as a horse."[17]

49.18, "I wait for your salvation, O LORD." Repeatedly, Jacob has spoken of the strength of the tribes—Judah, the lion; Issachar, the strong donkey; Dan, the serpent—that may lead to self-reliance. But Jacob displays the proper focus of God's children in this prayer that "seems to be a reflection of the difficulties he sees the tribes facing: he prays to the Lord that he will deliver his descendants in the future" (Wenham). Jacob does not expect salvation by means of self-reliance. "Even when men help themselves, they are only truly delivered if God helps them" (Leupold).

An alternate view of this verse should be considered. Many have seen this prayer in direct relation to the preceding blessing on Dan. Wenham writes: "Attached to the blessing of Dan, Jacob's remarks suggest an awareness of the precarious plight of that tribe… the Danites were forced to migrate to the north. And though on the first reading the book of Judges may sound like a celebration of Israel's glorious heroes, it seems likely that the book is really illustrating the nation's political and moral decline in that era." Among those who see it in relation to the preceding blessing,

---

[16] See John J. Davis, *Paradise to Prison,* 300.

[17] "Of the animals named in the Blessing of Jacob, the snake is the only one that lives alone. Dan's move to the far north put it at a great distance from the center of Israel's life" (Mathews).

Mathews may have the best to offer. He sees verses 16 and 18 as forming "the boundaries of the stanza, both pertaining to deliverance from enemies—Dan who defends 'his people' (v 16) and the Lord who is Israel's defender (v 18)."

Interestingly, this is the only place where the word (or any form of the root of) *salvation* is used in Genesis. "Although the illustrations of salvation and deliverance are scattered throughout Genesis, only here is the Hebrew word that most clearly means 'salvation' used" (Hamilton).

49.19, "Raiders shall raid Gad, but he shall raid at their heels." In Hebrew this verse has six words, four of which are a play on Gad's name.[18] The ESV captures well the rich wordplay in the verse. Gad will be pressed hard, but he will, in turn, press hard against those who assail him. The tribe of Gad was east of the Jordan. Throughout history, it was attacked many times by nations such as the Ammonites, Moabites, Armeneans, and Assyrians, all of which is recorded in the Bible or other history. And, "as a consequence of their wars for survival, the Gadites became renowned warriors (*e.g.,* 1 Chron 5.18; 12.8, 14)" (Mathews).

That Gad would *raid at their heels* most likely refers to the tactics which they would need to engage in to be successful in war. "Gad is not big enough to engage in frontal warfare. He must attack from the rear (v 19b). Mobility rather than number is Gad's major asset" (Hamilton).

49.20, "Asher's food shall be rich, and he shall yield royal delicacies." Asher—whose name means *fortunate*—is to dwell in a wealthy land and from the abundance of his land would come foods that would grace a king's table.

49.21, "Naphtali is a doe let loose." This refers to being fleet of foot. Unless we are to understand Barak and the 10,000 of Naphtali and Zebulun as fulfilling this word (Jdg 4), we can find no record of any fulfillment.[19]

"*That bears beautiful fawns."* Some have alternately translated this *beautiful words* and see in it Barak's part in the song of Deborah (Jdg 5).

---

[18]Gad may mean *fortune,* rather than *troop* (see Excursus L), but the words sound enough alike to make this blessing a viable pun. On the other hand, this blessing may indicate the proper understanding of his name and Leah's words in 30.11.

[19]For the variety of translations that this verse has prompted, see Hamilton.

49.22–26, "Joseph." Joseph's blessing can be interpreted one of two ways. Its content may refer to the events that started in chapter 37, progressing through Joseph's time in Egypt, and finally looking forward to the future of Ephraim and Manasseh (*e.g.,* Kidner). Alternately, it has been suggested that since 'Joseph' refers to Ephraim and Manasseh (*e.g.,* as it does in Numbers, Joshua, and the prophets), it cannot refer back to Joseph, but instead looks forward to the future of those two tribes.[20] The former is the traditional view, dating back to the ancient Jewish commentators. The latter is more prevalent in modern commentaries. We will explain how the following phrases are interpreted by each perspective.

"Joseph is a fruitful bough." The reference to a fruitful vine is a metaphor for fertility. Also a well-watered, fruitful, far-spreading vine very well depicts Joseph's depth of character and width of influence. On the other hand, it may portray the fruitful, enduring tribe of Ephraim, and to a lesser degree, Manasseh.

"The archers bitterly attacked him... yet his bow remained unmoved." Neither his brothers, Potiphar's wife, nor the cupbearer destroyed him because *his bow remained unmoved.* By contrast, this may refer to the conflicts awaiting his descendants, in which they would constantly overcome by God's help all hostile attacks (Keil). If the latter is the case, it is difficult to identify any specific fulfillment.

"The Mighty One of Jacob... the Shepherd, the Stone of Israel... the God of your father... the Almighty." Vos writes, "As if to underscore how much God had been on his side, how much He had blessed, and how much He would bless, Jacob heaped up names [and descriptions] of deity."[21] Then, he heaped blessing on top of blessing: *blessings of heaven above... of the deep that crouches beneath... of the breasts and of the womb.* The alternate approach to this verse—that it only looks forward to the tribes—changes little.

It is interesting that there are no great spiritual blessings foretold for Joseph's descendents. Regardless of how faithful their father Joseph was, the tribes of Ephraim and Manasseh never excelled in faithfulness. Jeroboam (an Ephraimite), for example, led the northern kingdom into idolatry, from which it never recovered.

---

[20] The argument that since the context is prophetic, it must only refer to the future, is hard to defend when at least two of the previous blessings—*i.e,* Reuben and Simeon/Levi—clearly look back to past events.

[21] Howard F. Vos, *Genesis,* 193.

"The blessings of your father are mighty beyond the blessings of my parents." This means either that God had blessed him more abundantly than his fathers (Leupold) or that the blessings which Jacob implored for Joseph were to surpass the blessings which his parents transmitted to him (Keil). Or, perhaps, those suggestions are not mutually exclusive, and there is a little of both in Jacob's thought. Kidner writes: "A foretaste of this blessing would come in the award to Ephraim and Manasseh of the pick of all Canaan, with presumably greater things to follow."

"Set apart from his brothers." "He who was once separated from his brothers by spite is now separated from his brothers by blessing" (Hamilton).

49.27, "Benjamin is a ravenous wolf." How stark a contrast this is from the defenseless youngest son we have read about previously in the narrative! This is not intended to be a criticism of Benjamin, but a compliment for his tenacity. "Clearly, the future military exploits of the tribe of Benjamin are in view" (Wenham). Thus, "The animal imagery of Benjamin as a predatory, ravenous wolf who shares his prey matches the tribe's reputation for bravery and skill in war (*cf.* Jdg 3.15–30; 5.14; 20.14–21; 1 Sam 9.1–2; 13.3; 1 Chron 8.40; 12.2–22, 29; Est 2.5; Rom 11.1)" (Waltke).

"In the morning devouring the prey and at evening dividing the spoil." The language fits the character of the beast: defeating early and dividing the spoil later. It also serves the literary feature of merism: morning and evening indicating that Benjamin is continually on the prowl (Mathews) and always successful in defeating his foes (Leupold).

49.28, This is what their father said to them as he blessed them, blessing each with the blessing suitable to him. The threefold use of *bless* "clearly designates what Jacob has said to his sons as blessing" (Hamilton). And, "The blessing each son received was 'appropriate' (lit., 'according to his blessing') to each tribe's role in the nation" (Mathews).

49.29–31, "I am to be gathered to my people." Jacob is "clear both about the distant future of his family and its descendants (vv 1–28), and his own immediate future (28–33)" (Hamilton).[22]

"Bury me with my fathers." Jacob repeats to all the sons the instructions that he has given previously to Joseph alone, though this time with more

---

[22]See comment on 25.8.

specific instructions that he be buried in the *cave of Machpelah... which Abraham bought with the field from Ephron the Hittite to possess as a burying place.* "Like the account of the purchase in chapter 25, he emphasizes the previous owner, the exact location of the property, and the fact that it was acquired as a permanent holding. Thus, at the end of Genesis, legal language is used to resume a great theme— that Abraham's offspring are legitimately bound to the land God promised them, and that the descent into Egypt is no more than a sojourn" (Alter).

49.32, "There they buried Abraham and Sarah his wife. There they buried Isaac and Rebekah his wife, and there I buried Leah." The listing of the patriarchs and matriarchs connect this command with God's blessing and covenant. It is not merely the unimportant whim of a dying man, but a direction with purpose. Even in their deaths, "all three patriarchs wanted their children to have clear testimony that they had believed God's promises" (Leupold).[23]

49.33, He drew up his feet into bed and breathed his last. "Jacob, who fought his way into life, departs just as dramatically. The life of Jacob, which has stretched over half the book of Genesis, has seen the family through moments of trust and betrayal, sterility and fertility, feast and famine, separation and reunion, all within the promise and providence of God." [24]

Growth of the Seed: Judah is blessed to carry the Messianic line (v 10).

---

[23]On his burial of Leah at Machpelah, see EXCURSUS L.

[24]Eugene F. Roop, *Genesis,* 290.

50 **1, *Then Joseph fell on his father's face and wept over him and kissed him.*** These gestures are by now strongly associated with Joseph (*cf.* 42.24; 43.30; 45.2, 14–15; 46.29). "Joseph is at once the intellectual, dispassionate interpreter of dreams and central economic planner, and the man of powerful spontaneous feeling" (Alter).

Certainly all of the brothers were there and mourned. Joseph is listed exclusively, presumably because he had the closest relationship with Jacob, both originally and since being reunited in Egypt. "The great bond between Jacob and Joseph, which has been the mainspring of the story since chapter 37, is at last broken, and a new era is about to begin" (Wenham). Further, Joseph's attendance at Jacob's death had been specifically promised (46.4). Hamilton notes: "All weepings of Joseph thus far have been weepings of joy—he is reunited with his brothers, with Benjamin, then with his father. This weeping is one of sorrow. Earlier, when his father was still alive, Joseph 'fell on his father's neck' (46.29). In Jacob's death Joseph literally 'falls on his father's face.'"

50.2, Joseph commanded his servants the physicians to embalm his father. "Essentially, embalming was designed to retard the normal processes of putrefaction of the corpse. Methods varied from simply wrapping the body in resin-soaked linen to the elaborate procedures of disemboweling the corpse, collecting the organs in containers, and filling the void with linen" (Mathews). It may be significant that Joseph used physicians to embalm his father rather than embalmers. Perhaps it is simply a matter of convenience—he had his own physicians, *his servants.* More likely, it had to do with the practice of embalming. "Egyptians embalmed the honored dead to assist them in the afterlife journey" (Waltke). Thus, to avoid the magic, mysticism, and paganism that went with the embalmers, Joseph used his own group of physicians to carry out the process, a group competent to perform the task without the religious rites (Kidner). And though Joseph did not want the theological baggage that came with the embalming, it was a necessary step in order to fulfill Jacob's wish of burial in Canaan.

50.3, And the Egyptians wept for him seventy days. The first 40 days of the weeping also covered the embalming process (v 3a). After he was embalmed, the weeping continued another 30 days. That the Egyptians would weep for Jacob shows their respect and gratitude for Joseph and what he did for them during the famine, though most likely it was mandated by Pharaoh for this purpose (Hamilton).[1] The level of respect is heightened when it is understood that this fell just short of the mourning period for a Pharaoh, which is 72 days (Kidner).

50.4–6, Joseph spoke to the household of Pharaoh. It is interesting that Joseph does not speak to Pharaoh directly. Perhaps he could not have appeared before Pharaoh during his mourning, unshaven and unadorned (Keil; *cf.* Est 4.2). As Leupold points out, this may seem unlikely as *the days of weeping for him were past*, but Vos suggests that he would have worn the mourning clothes until the burial had occurred.[2] An alternate suggestion is that he was unclean from having been in contact with a dead body.

"My father made me swear." The oath Joseph gave is the strongest part of his argument. Notice that in Joseph's quotation of his father, he omits the references to Jacob's desire not to be buried in Eygpt (*cf.* 47.29–30). "Joseph does not want to make it appear in any way that his father has a disliking for Egypt, or is in any way ungrateful. Egypt has been a great place to live. It just is not the best place to be interred" (Hamilton).

"In my tomb that I hewed out for myself.'" Jacob's desire for burial in Canaan was not merely a rash deathbed wish, but had been previously planned. Most likely, each patriarch dug out his own burial place in the family tomb.

"Go up, and bury your father, as he made you swear." Because of the oath, Pharaoh grants Joseph permission to bury Jacob in Canaan. Notice, "He does not end with 'and then come back to me,' as Joseph said he would. This is another indication of Pharaoh's implicit trust in Joseph's truthfulness" (Hamilton).

50.7–9, With him went up all the servants of Pharaoh, the elders of his household, and all the elders of the land of Egypt. "The grandest state funeral recorded in the Bible was given to Jacob. His life story spans more than half of Genesis and now, as befits the father of the nation, he is laid to rest with all the pomp and ceremony that Egypt could muster" (Wenham). The Egyptians accompanied Joseph and his family as a sign of respect for

---

[1] Such an official period of mourning may be compared to our nation's flying the flag at half staff. It is probably also a sincere mourning, as becomes evident—*great and grievous*—at Atad (v 10).

[2] Howard F. Vos, *Genesis*, 195.

his prominent position, though "the monuments indicate that the Egyptians dearly loved imposing elaborate funeral processions" (Leupold).

All the household of Jacob, his brothers, and his father's household. On the one hand, this foreshadows the exodus of the Israelites. On the other, the escort of Jacob homeward by all of Pharaoh's dignitaries together with chariots and horsemen stands in striking contrast with the Mosaic exodus (Waltke), unless they are to be compared with later chariots and horsemen who pursue Israel as they leave for Canaan (*cf.* Exod 14.9, 17–18, 23–28).

Only their children, their flocks, and their herds were left in the land of Goshen. These could not easily make the journey to Canaan and back, so they were left behind. Further, leaving their children and livestock showed that they were not trying to leave for good—they intended to return to Goshen after Jacob's burial.

Chariots and horsemen. Such a caravan would require food and protection. The chariots, or *wagons,* would carry the needed provisions; the horsemen provided protection for the dignitaries making the journey (Leupold).

50.10–11, When they came to the threshing floor of Atad, which is beyond the Jordan. No one is certain of the precise location, though it is presumably east of the Jordan. There is no reference point in relation to *beyond the Jordan,* but one may safely assume that it is *beyond* in relation to where Joseph was coming from or *beyond* in relation to where the Promised Land—and the cave of Machpelah—was. Generally, in biblical usage, *beyond the Jordan* indicates the territory east of the Jordan.[3] Thus, it seems that they took the long way around, further foreshadowing the exodus. "The reason for this more southerly course may have been the antagonism of certain nations or groups along the northern route" (Leupold).

Abel-mizraim. The name given by the Canaanites to the place either means *mourning of Egypt* or *brook of Egypt,* depending on which vowel points are added to the Hebrew word. It seems unlikely to name a place *the mourning.* If, however, they named it *the brook of Eygpt,* that would serve well to identify the place with the event, while also allowing for the play on words that would help explain why it was named after the Egyptians.

50.12, Thus his sons did for him as he had commanded them. Now, the brothers come to the forefront and "take in hand very properly the more

---

[3]It is possible, though unlikely, that its reference point is the audience of Moses in the wilderness. If so, beyond the Jordan would then refer to the Promised Land itself, west of the river.

intimate part of the burial service, the actual laying of the patriarch in his last resting place" (Leupold). Most likely, the Egyptian funeral procession stopped short at Abel-mizraim and allowed the family to bury their father alone. Their father had laid upon all of his sons a strict charge (49.29). Here we see them fulfilling his wishes. "Joseph is willing to accommodate himself to Egyptian mourning rituals, including embalming, and to contextualize Jacob's burial request in words Pharaoh understands. He does so without compromising Israel's distinctive theology. The journey of Jacob's embalmed body takes him home to the grave of his ancestors in the Promised Land, not to the Egyptian understanding of the afterlife in the presence of their pagan gods" (Waltke).

50.14, *Joseph returned to Egypt with his brothers and all who had gone up with him to bury his father.* This verse marks the transition from the first section of this chapter to the next. Having completed their task, everyone returns to Egypt—Joseph, to continue to rule; the brothers, to continue to live under his watchful care. It is precisely that combination of roles that will prompt the next scene in the narrative.

50.15 *When Joseph's brothers saw that their father was dead.* Clearly, this cannot mean that they saw this for the first time. Rather, it must mean something like "when the full reality of their father's passing dawned on them" (Hamilton). They believed that their father's death changed their situation (*cf.* 27.41).

"***It may be that Joseph will hate us.***" The Joseph narrative began with the brothers hating him (37.4–8), but ends with their suspicion that he will hate them. Although their hatred was real, his was imaginary on their part (Hamilton). Ironically, their mistrust of Joseph's forgiveness is in a context of Joseph fulfilling his word—first to Jacob (vv 5–7); then to Pharaoh (v 14)—and displaying faith in God's word (vv 24–25). Their fear, of course, is based on their guilty consciences, not on Joseph's behavior.

50.16–17, *So they sent a message to Joseph.* They didn't personally convey this message to their brother. We cannot know who conveyed the message, though it would be reasonable to guess that Benjamin carried it (Leupold).

"***Your father gave this command before he died, 'Say to Joseph, Please forgive the transgression of your brothers and their sin, because they did evil to you.'***" They send a message to Joseph, which essentially says, 'If you were only sparing our lives for our father's sake, then you must continue to spare them, because it is what he wanted.' There is no way to know whether Jacob said this or if they made it up to protect their lives. Scholars have taken both positions. If, however, we are to understand them as truly repentant, it would seem audacious to lie in the same breath as they appeal to Joseph as the *servants of the God of your father,* an appeal "not to bloodlines but to spiritual roots and relationships" (Hamilton).

Wenham notes five aspects of this plea in which they "pull out all the emotional stops in an effort to obtain Joseph's mercy." First, they approach him through an intermediary. Second, they say Jacob gave the instructions just before his death. Third, they twice plead for forgiveness. Fourth, they describe their sin in the most comprehensive way: *crime* (twice), *sin,* and *evil*—"three of the four principal OT terms for wicked deeds." Finally, they implore Joseph to act like their father's God, "who is one who 'forgives iniquity, transgression [crime], and sin' (Exod 34.7; Psa 32.1; Mic 7.18)."

Joseph wept when they spoke to him. Those who see the brothers' message as a lie would suggest that Joseph's weeping was due to their transparency. If, however, Jacob had spoken those words—for that matter, even if they *were* lying—Joseph's weeping is better attributed to the arm-length approach and the lack of trust they have toward him now. They doubted the sincerity of his forgiveness, and it is always painful to have sincere motives questioned. "It is as though the whole ordeal has been in vain: if they have learned anything about him beyond externals—and the fear may well have haunted them all those years—the effect has evaporated" (Sternberg qtd. in Hamilton). And Waltke: "After seventeen years of kindness to them that reinforced his original forgiveness (45.7–8), they still misunderstand his goodness and think that he will at last take his revenge."

50.18, His brothers also came... "Behold, we are your servants." After sending word to prepare the way, the brothers follow with an appeal to be Joseph's slaves.

Fell down. More literally, *threw themselves down.*[4] This connects the entire story, hearkening back to Joseph's dreams in chapter 37.

50.19–21, But Joseph said to them. Joseph's response is what Kidner calls a threefold pinnacle of faith.[5]

---

[4] See comment on 44.14.

[5] See THEOLOGICAL REFLECTION, below.

"Am I in the place of God?" Joseph understands that, though second most powerful in Egypt (perhaps in the world), the righting of wrongs was not his to do (*cf.* Rom 12.29; 1 Thes 5.15; 1 Pet 4.19). "There is a considerable contrast between Adam and Eve and Joseph. Genesis begins by telling us about a primeval couple who tried to become like God, and ends by telling us about a man who denied he was in God's place. Adam and Eve attempted to wipe out the dividing line between humanity and deity. Joseph refuses to try to cross that line. Joseph will only be God's instrument, never His substitute" (Hamilton).

"God meant it for good." Joseph saw God's providence in man's malice. This is a comforting truth "because it says that no enemy has power over the called of God. They meant death for him and God used it for life. They meant shame for him and God used it for glory. They meant slavery for him and God used it for power. And this was not only to benefit *Joseph!* The young man makes that very clear. …God used their sin to bless many nations and *them.*"[6]

"So do not fear; I will provide for you and your little ones." Joseph does not only repay their evil with forgiveness, but also repays it with practical affection (*cf.* Luke 6.27ff).

Thus he comforted them and spoke kindly to them. "With (this scene) the goal of not merely the Joseph story, but of the whole patriarchal history is reached: the ideal unity of the sons of Israel has been created. Abraham had two sons but they did not get on together. Isaac had two sons, but they parted forever. Not until Jacob's twelve sons was the future firmly established. But precisely because they were a large number was there a danger of disunity and division. In the event there was dissention among them, so that they hated and persecuted the best of them. But eventually there was a complete reconciliation, not through the arbitration of a third party, but through the inner transformation of those who hated, for which the sufferer had waited and now in brotherly love acknowledges" (Jacob qtd. in Wenham).

50.22–23. Joseph lived 110 years. More than 50 years have passed since Jacob's death before Joseph follows him. The patriarchs' lifespan continues to shorten. It was considered ideal in the Egyptian mind to live 110 years and was seen as a sign of God's blessing, which may be seen as a crowning

---

[6]Jim McGuiggan, *Genesis and Us,* 314. See comment on 45.5, 7–8.

touch to Joseph's honor in Egypt.[7] "This attainment would be regarded as a signal mark of divine favor by his contemporaries."[8]

And Joseph saw Ephraim's children of the third generation. Despite their long lives, Joseph is the first character since the patriarchs to see his great-grandchildren. Such a long life was considered a special blessing from God (*cf.* Psa 128.6; Prov 17.6; Job 42.16). Sarna notes: "A seventh-century [BC] Aramaic funerary inscription from Syria airs the notion that living to see 'children of the fourth generation' is the reward of righteousness" (qtd. in Waltke).

Machir. The most important clan of Manasseh; even identified with the whole tribe. *Cf.* Num 32.39; 36.1–10; Josh 17.1; Jdg 5.14.

Were counted as Joseph's own. Literally, this is *were born on Joseph's knees.*[9]

50.24–25, And Joseph said to his brothers. Either some of Joseph's older brothers outlive him or this is a more general reference to his kindred. The latter seems more likely when compared with the deathbed wishes of the patriarchs.

"God will visit you and bring you up out of this land to the land that he swore to Abraham, to Isaac, and to Jacob." As his fathers had done, Joseph expresses clear faith that the word of God will be fulfilled and they will be returned to the Promised Land (*cf.* Heb 11.22) and that one greater than he would provide for them (*cf.* v 21). This is not a new prediction or revelation, simply the expression of faith in the promise already given to Abraham (15.16).

This is the first mention of Abraham, Isaac, and Jacob together. "That era has passed, but not its hope. Throughout the Torah the cluster is used, as Sarna explains, 'invariably in a context of the divine promises of national territory for the people of Israel'" (Waltke).

Then Joseph made the sons of Israel swear. Based on his confidence in the promises made by God's sworn oath to his forefathers (v 24), Joseph requires the Israelites to *swear* that they would return his remains to Canaan (Mathews).

---

[7] "No less than twenty-seven references to such an age, from all periods, have been collected by J.M.A. Janssen" (Kidner).

[8] K.A. Kitchen, "Joseph," *The International Standard Bible Encyclopedia*. 2. Grand Rapids: Zondervan, 1979. 1129.

[9] See comment on 48.12.

"God will surely visit you, and you shall carry up my bones from here." Unlike Jacob, Joseph does not expect his body to be returned to Canaan immediately. The circumstances are different now than at Jacob's death. "After Joseph's death, there was no man of Israel influential enough to make the needed arrangements" (Leupold). So Joseph would instead later depart with Moses. "In consequence of his instructions, the coffin with his bones became a standing exhortation to Israel, to turn its eyes away from Egypt to Canaan, the land promised to its fathers, and to wait in the patience of faith for the fulfillment of the promise" (Keil).

50.26, They embalmed him, and he was put in a coffin in Egypt. Davis provides an excellent conclusion: "The book of Genesis began with the brightness and glory of God's original creation. All that He did was pronounced good, and the earliest earth was a divine masterpiece. However, sin entered the picture, and the book ends not with man in a beautiful garden but with the bones of Joseph in a coffin. His coffin is a grim reminder of the effects of sin. ...But just as Joseph was hopeful and optimistic when he died, so we rejoice in the redemption which God has provided. While our bones may rest in the wilderness of a cursed earth, they will one day be resurrected, and there will be a new heaven and a new earth."[10] And we, like Joseph, will be carried into the Promised Land with the elect of God.

Growth of the Seed: Joseph expresses his faith in God's Promised Land (vv 24–25).

Theological Reflection: Repaying Evil with Good
Perhaps there is no place in the Bible where a teaching on how to repay evil is given more concisely and fully than Joseph's forgiveness of his brothers. And, aside from Christ Himself, perhaps no better example is given of one who accomplished this goal successfully and was greatly rewarded in so doing. When evil is dealt to us by the world, we should react in the same way as Joseph, and in so doing, we will reap the eternal rewards given to those who *entrust their souls to a faithful Creator while doing good* (1 Pet 4.19).

Judgment and vengeance belong to God (v 19). The first key to dealing successfully with evil is to distance oneself from desiring revenge. Joseph

---

[10]John J. Davis, *Paradise to Prison*, 304.

understood that the righting of all wrongs belonged in the hands of God, not himself. Paul summed up this point concisely: *Beloved, never avenge yourselves, but leave it to the wrath of God, for it is written, "Vengeance is mine, I will repay, says the Lord"* (Rom 12.19).

Man's evil cannot subvert the providence of God (v 20). Perhaps one of the most comforting points made in all of Scripture is that God is in control. No matter how current events may seem, God is directing them to accomplish His purpose. Regardless of how hard we may strive against Him and His purpose, He will still use our actions to fulfill His wishes. Certainly this is an Old Testament precursor to Paul's declaration that *all things work together for good, for those who are called according to his purpose* (Rom 8.28) and runs closely parallel with Peter's comforting words to *let those who suffer according to God's will entrust their souls to a faithful Creator while doing good* (1 Pet 4.19).

Repay evil with forgiveness and practical affection (v 21). After one has given his desire for vengeance over to God, and has entrusted his soul to God, he must repay evil with good. Peter makes this point clearly in many places in his epistle (*e.g.,* 1 Pet 2.23; 3.19; 4.19). And Paul said, *See that no one repays anyone evil for evil, but always seek to do good to one another and to everyone* (1 Thes 5.15). The good that Joseph repaid his brothers was practical: though they sought to kill him, he sought to preserve their lives in the famine and to continue to provide for them and their children.

Bibliography

Books and Commentaries

Alter, Robert. *Genesis: Translation and Commentary.* New York: Norton and Company, 1996.

_____. *The Art of Biblical Narrative.* New York: Basic Books, Inc. 1981.

Atkinson, David. *The Message of Genesis 1–11: The Dawn of Creation.* The Bible Speaks Today. Downer's Grove: Intervarsity, 1990.

Baldwin, Joyce G. *The Message of Genesis 12–50: From Abraham to Joseph* The Bible Speaks Today. Downer's Grove: Intervarsity, 1986.

Benware, Paul N. *Survey of the Old Testament.* Chicago: Moody Press, 1988.

Blocher, Henri. *In the Beginning: The Opening Chapters of Genesis* Downers Grove: Intervarsity, 1984.

Brown, F. S. Driver & C. Briggs. *The Brown-Driver-Briggs Hebrew and English Lexicon.* Peabody: Hendrickson, 1999.

Bruce, F.F. "The Epistle to the Hebrews." *The New International Commentary on the New Testament.* Grand Rapids: Eerdmans, 1975.

Clarke, Adam. *Adam Clarke's Commentary, One Volume Edition.* Kansas City: Beacon Hill, 1967.

Davis, John J. *Paradise to Prison: Studies in Genesis.* Grand Rapids: Baker Book House, 1975.

De Haan, M.R. *Portraits of Christ in Genesis.* 1966. Grand Rapids: Kregel Publications, 1995.

Dillard, Raymond B. & Tremper Longman III. *An Introduction to the Old Testament.* Grand Rapids: Zondervan, 1994.

Dorsey, David A. *The Literary Structure of the Old Testament: A Commentary on Genesis–Malachi.* Grand Rapids: Baker, 1999.

Driver, S.R. "The Book of Genesis." *Westminster Commentaries.* 1904. 1. London: Methuen & Co. LTD., 1920.

Edersheim, Alfred. *Bible History: Old Testament.* 1876. Peabody Hendrickson, 1995.

Erdman, Charles R. *The Book of Genesis: An Exposition.* 1950. Grand Rapids: Baker Books, 1982.

Finegan, Jack.. *Handbook of Biblical Chronology: Principles of Time Reckoning in the Ancient World and Problems of Chronology in the Bible, Revised Edition.* Peabody: Hendrickson, 1998.

Fox, Everett. *Genesis and Exodus: A New English Rendition with Commentary and Notes.* New York: Schocken, 1990.

Geisler, Norman L. *A Popular Survey of the Old Testament.* Grand Rapids Baker Books, 1977.

————. *Baker Encyclopedia of Christian Apologetics.* Grand Rapids: Baker Books, 1999, 26–28.

Geisler, Norman and Thomas Howe. *When Critics Ask.* Wheaton, Ill Victor Books, 1992.

Glynn, Patrick. *God: The Evidence: The Reconciliation of Faith and Reason in a Postsecular World.* Rocklin: Forum, 1997.

Grant, F.W. *Genesis in the Light of the New Testament.* New York: The Bible Truth Press, n.d.

Guthrie, Donald. "The Letter to the Hebrews: An Introduction and Commentary." *Tyndale New Testament Commentaries.* Grand Rapids Eerdmans. 1983.

Hailey, Homer. *Hailey's Comments: A Compilation of Articles and Writings by Homer Hailey.* 1. Las Vegas: Nevada Publishing, 1985.

Hamilton, Victor P. "The Book of Genesis." 2 vols. *New International Commentary on the Old Testament.* Grand Rapids: Eerdmans, 1990, 1995.

Harris, R. Laird, *et al. Theological Wordbook of the Old Testament.* Chicago Moody Bible Institute, 1980.

Harrison, Roland K. *Introduction to the Old Testament*. 1969. Peabody Prince Press, 1999.

———. *Old Testament Times*. Grand Rapids: Eerdmans Publishing, 1970.

Hasel, Gerhard. *Old Testament Theology: Basic Issues in the Current Debate*. 1972. Grand Rapids: Eerdmans, 1987.

Henry, Matthew. *Commentary on the Whole Bible* (one volume edition) Grand Rapids: Zondervan, 1974.

Jamieson, Robert, A.R. Fausset, David Brown. "Genesis–Esther." *A Commentary on the Old and New Testaments*. 1. Peabody: Hendrickson, 2002.

Jensen, Irving. *Genesis: A Self-Study Guide*. Chicago: The Moody Bible Institute, 1967.

Kaiser, Walter C., Jr. *et al. Hard Sayings of the Bible*. Downers Grove Intervarsity Press, 1996.

———. *Toward Old Testament Ethics*. Grand Rapids: Zondervan, 1983.

———. *Toward an Old Testament Theology*. Grand Rapids: Zondervan, 1978.

Keil, C.F. *Introduction to the Old Testament*. 1869. Peabody: Hendrickson, 1988.

———. "Pentateuch." *Commentary on the Old Testament*. 1. Peabody Hendrickson, 2001.

Kidner, Derek. *Genesis: An Introduction and Commentary*. Downer's Grove: Intervarsity Press, 1967.

Leupold, H.C. *Exposition of Genesis*. 2 Vols. Leupold on the Old Testament. Grand Rapids: Baker Book House, 1942.

Longman, Tremper, III. *How to Read Genesis*. Downer's Grove: Intervarsity Press, 2005.

———. *How to Read the Psalms*. Downer's Grove: Intervarsity Press, 1988.

Mathews, Kenneth A. "Genesis." 2 Vols. *The New American Commentary*. Nashville: Broadman & Holman, 1996, 2005.

McGuiggan, Jim. *Genesis and Us*. Lubbock: International Bible Resources, 1988.

Meek, Theophile J. *Hebrew Origins*. New York: Harper and Row, 1960.

Motyer, Alec. *The Story of the Old Testament*. Grand Rapids: Baker Books, 2001.

Nelson, Ethel R. and Richard E. Broadberry. *Genesis and the Mystery Confucius Couldn't Solve*. St. Louis: Concordia, 1994.

Payne, J. Barton. *Encyclopedia of Biblical Prophecy: The Complete Guide to Scriptural Predictions and Their Fulfillment*. 1973. Grand Rapids: Baker Book House, 1980.

————. *The Theology of the Older Testament*. 1962. Eugene: Wipf and Stock, 1998.

Pickup, Martin. *From the Prophets to the Son: The Use of the Old Testament in the Book of Hebrews*. Currently unpublished.

Roop, Eugene F. *Genesis*. Believer's Bible Church Commentary Scottsdale, Herald, 1987.

Schaeffer, Francis A. *Genesis in Space and Time: The Flow of Biblical History*. Downers Grove: Intervarsity, 1972.

Spence, H.D.M. and Joseph S. Excell. "Genesis, Exodus." *The Pulpit Commentary*. Grand Rapids: Eerdman's, 1950.

Strobel, Lee. *The Case for a Creator: A Journalist Investigates Scientific Evidence that Points Toward God*. Grand Rapids: Zondervan, 2004.

Thompson, Bert. *The Global Flood of Noah*. Montgomery: Apologetics Press, 1986.

Von Rad, Gerhard. *Genesis*. 1956. Philadelphia: The Westminster Press, 1961, Translation.

Vos, Howard, F. *Genesis*. Chicago: Moody Press, 1982.

————. *Genesis and Archaeology*. Chicago: Moody Press, 1963.

Waltke, Bruce K. (with Cathi J. Fredricks). *Genesis: A Commentary*. Grand Rapids: Zondervan, 2001.

Ward, Dene. *Born of a Woman: Woman's Place in the Scheme of Redemption, Teacher's Manual,* revised. Self-published, 2005.

Wenham, Gordon J. "Genesis 1–15" and "Genesis 16–50." *Word Biblical Commentary*. Waco: Word, 1987, 1994.

Westermann, Claus. *Genesis: A Practical Commentary* Grand Rapids Eerdmans Publishing, 1987.

Whitcomb, John C. *The Early Earth: An Introduction to Biblical Creationism, Revised Edition*. Grand Rapids: Baker Book House, 1986.

Whitcomb, John C. and Henry M. Morris. *The Genesis Flood: The Biblical Record and Its Scientific Implications*. Philadelphia: The Presbyterian and Reformed Publishing Company, 1961.

Wood, Leon. *Genesis*. Grand Rapids: Zondervan, 1975.

Young, Edward J. *An Introduction to the Old Testament*. Grand Rapids Eerdmans Publishing, 1949.

————. *Genesis 3: A Devotional and Expository Study*. London: Banner of Truth Trust, 1966.

————. *Studies in Genesis One*. 1964. Phillipsburg: P&R Publishing, n.d.

————. *The Study of Old Testament Theology Today*. Westwood: Fleming H. Revell Co., 1959.

————. *Thy Word is Truth: Some Thoughts on the Biblical Doctrine of Inspiration*. 1957. Grand Rapids: Eerdmans, 1965.

Zuck, Roy B. (ed.). *Vital Old Testament Issues: Examining Textual and Topical Questions*. Grand Rapids: Kregel, 1996.

Journal and Reference

Aaron, David H. "Early Rabbinic Exegesis on Noah's Son Ham and the So-Called 'Hamitic Myth.'" *Journal of the American Academy of Religion*. 63, No.4 (1995): 721–759.

————. "Rejoinder to Steven L. McKenzie and Donald H. Matthews." *Journal of the American Academy of Religion*. 65, No. 1. (1997): 189–192.

Aitken, Kenneth T. "The Wooing of Rebekah: A Study in the Development of the Tradition." *Journal for the Study of the Old Testament*. 30 (1984): 3–23.

Armerding, Carl. "The God of Nahor." *Bibliotheca Sacra*. 106 (1949): 363–366.

Battenfield, James R. "A Consideration of the Identity of the Pharaoh of Genesis 47." *Journal of the Evangelical Theological Society*. 13 (1970): 77–85.

Bechtel, Lyn M. "What if Dinah is not Raped?" *Journal for the Study of the Old Testament*. 62 (1994): 19–36.

Birney, Leroy. "An Exegetical Study of Genesis 6.1–4." *Journal of the Evangelical Theological Society*. 13. (1970): 43–52.

Bledstein, Adrien J. "Was Eve Cursed? (Or Did a Woman Write Genesis?)." *Bible Review*. February (1993): 42–45.

Bromiley, G.W. "Evolution." *The International Standard Bible Encyclopedia*. 2. Grand Rapids: Zondervan, 1979. 212–215.

_____. "God." *The International Standard Bible Encyclopedia*. 2. Grand Rapids: Zondervan, 1979. 493–503.

_____. "Image of God." *The International Standard Bible Encyclopedia*. 2. Grand Rapids: Zondervan, 1979. 803–805.

Burdick, D.W. "Melchizedek." *The International Standard Bible Encyclopedia*. 2. Grand Rapids: Zondervan, 1979. 313.

Busenitz, Irvin A. "Woman's Desire for Man: Gen. 3.16 Reconsidered." *Grace Theological Journal*. 37, No. 2 (1986): 203–212.

Carmichael, Calum. "Some Sayings in Genesis 49." *Journal of Biblical Literature*. 88. (1969): 435–444.

Childs, Brevard S. "A Study of the Formula, 'Until This Day.'" *Journal of Biblical Literature*. 82. (1963): 279–292.

Clifford, Richard J. "Genesis 38: Its Contribution to the Jacob Story." *The Catholic Biblical Quarterly*. 66 (2004): 519–532.

Coats, George W. "Widow's Rights: A Crux in the Structure of Genesis 38." *The Catholic Bible Quarterly*. 34 (1972): 461–466.

Cole, T.J. "Enoch, A Man Who Walked with God." *Bibliotheca Sacra*. 148 (1991): 288–297.

Coppes, Leonard, J. "Yom." *Theological Wordbook of the Old Testament* Chicago: Moody Bible Institute, 1980. 370–371.

Curtis, Edward M. "Structure, Style and Context as a Key to Interpreting Jacob's Encounter at Peniel." *The Journal of the Evangelical Theological Society*. 30, No. 2 (1987): 129–137.

DeWitt, Dale S. "Generations of Genesis." *The Evangelical Quarterly*. 48 (1976): 196–211.

_____. "The Historical Background of Genesis 11.1–9: Babel or Ur? *The Journal of the Evangelical Theological Society*. 22 (1979): 15–26.

Dresner, Samuel. "Rachel and Leah: Sibling Tragedy or the Triumph of Piety and Compassion?" *Bible Review*. April (1990): 22–42.

Duguid, Iain M. "Hagar the Egyptian: A Note on the Allure of Egypt in the Abraham Cycle." *Westminster Theological Journal*. 56 (1994): 419–421.

Ellis, Kent. "Genesis: The Beginnings." *Things Written Aforetime: Florida College Annual Lectures*. Temple Terrace: Florida College Bookstore. 1978. 73–82.

Feldman, Steven. "The Quest for Noah's Flood." *Biblical Archeological Review.* 28 (2002): 56–57.

Foh, Susan T. "What is the Woman's Desire?" *Westminster Theological Journal.* 37 (1975): 376–383.

Futato, Mark "Because It Had Rained: A Study of Gen 2.5-7 with Implications for Gen 2.4-25 and Gen 1.1—2.3." *Westminster Theological Journal* 60 (1998) 1-21.

Gianotti, Charles R. "The Meaning of the Divine Name YHWH." *Vital Old Testament Issues: Examining Textual and Topical Questions.* Grand Rapids: Kregel Resources, 1996.

Gilchrist, Paul R. "Yam." *Theological Wordbook of the Old Testament* Chicago: Moody Bible Institute, 1980. 383–384.

Good, Edwin M. "The 'Blessing' on Judah, Gen. 49.8–12." *Journal of Biblical Literature.* 82 (1963): 427–432.

Goodman, Marvin. "Non-Literal Interpretations of Genesis Creation." *Grace Journal.* 14 (1973): 25–38.

Greenberg, Moshe. "Another Look at Rachel's Theft of the Teraphim." *Journal of Biblical Literature.* 81. (1962): 239–248.

Hamilton, Victor P. "Pana." *Theological Wordbook of the Old Testament* Chicago: Moody Bible Institute, 1980, 727–728.

_____. "Shabat." *Theological Wordbook of the Old Testament.* Chicago Moody Bible Institute, 1980, 902–903.

Hämmerly-Dupuy, Daniel. "Some Observations on the Assyro Babylonian and Sumerian Flood Stories." *Andrews University Seminary Studies.* 6 (1968): 1–18.

Harris, R. Laird. "The Bible and Cosmology." *Bulletin of the Evangelical Theological Society.* 5 (1962): 11–17.

Harris, R. Laird. "Sheol." *Theological Wordbook of the Old Testament* Chicago: Moody Bible Institute, 1980. 892–893.

Harrison, Roland K. "Abraham." *The International Standard Bible Encyclopedia.* Vol. 1. Grand Rapids: Zondervan, 1979. 15–18.

_____. "Cain." *The International Standard Bible Encyclopedia.* 1. Grand Rapids: Zondervan, 1979. 571–572.

_____. "Eden." *The International Standard Bible Encyclopedia.* 2. Grand Rapids: Zondervan, 1979. 16–17.

_____. "Genesis." *The International Standard Bible Encyclopedia*. 2. Grand Rapids: Zondervan, 1979. 431–443.

_____. "Offerings." *Zondervan's Pictorial Bible Dictionary*. Grand Rapids: Zondervan, 1967. 601–602.

Hasel, Gerhard, F. "The Meaning of 'Let Us' in Gn. 1.26." *Andrews University Seminary Studies*. 13, No. 1 (1975): 58–66

_____. "The Significance of the Cosmology in Genesis 1 in Relation to Ancient Near Eastern Parallels. *Andrews University Seminary Studies*. 10, No. 2. (1972): 1–20.

Helyer, Larry R. "The Separation of Abraham and Lot: Its Significance in the Patriarchal Narratives." *Journal for the Study of the Old Testament*. 26 (1983): 77–88.

Hill, Carol A. "The Garden of Eden: A Modern Landscape." *Perspectives on Science and Christian Faith*. 52, No. 1 (2000): 31–46.

Hoehner, Harold. "The Duration of the Egyptian Bondage." *Bibliotheca Sacra*. 129. (1969): 306–316.

Holmgren, Frederick C. "Holding your own against God! Genesis 32.22–32 (In the Context of Genesis 31–33). *Interpretation: A Journal of Bible and Theology*. 44 (1990): 5–17.

Hugenberger, Gordon P. "The Name אדני." *Basics of Biblical Hebrew* Grand Rapids: Zondervan, 2001. 269–270.

Hutchison, John C. "Women, Gentiles, and the Messianic Mission in Matthew's Genealogy." *Bibliotheca Sacra*. 158 (2001): 152–164.

Kaiser, Walter C., Jr. "The Promised Land: A Biblical-Historical View." *Bibliotheca Sacra*. 138 (1981): 302–312.

Kaminski, Carol M. "The Promises to the Fathers." *Basics of Biblical Hebrew*. Grand Rapids: Zondervan, 2001. 343–354.

Kidner, Derek. "Genesis 2.5,6: Wet or Dry?" *Tyndale Bulletin*. 17. (1966): 109–114.

Kilgore, John M. "Abraham: The Friend of God." *Things Written Aforetime: Florida College Annual Lectures*. Temple Terrace: Florida College Bookstore, 1978. 9–20.

Kitchen, K.A. "Joseph." *The International Standard Bible Encyclopedia*. 2. Grand Rapids: Zondervan, 1979.1125–1130.

Kline, Meredith G. "Divine Kingship and Genesis 6.1–4." *Westminster Theological Journal*. 24. (1961): 187–204.

Knight, G.A.F. "Theophany." *The International Standard Bible Encyclopedia.* 4. Grand Rapids: Zondervan, 1979. 827–831.

Lambe, Anthony J. "Judah's Development: The Pattern of Departure–Transition–Return." *Journal for the Study of the Old Testament.* 83 (1999): 53–68.

Landy, Francis. "The Song of Songs and the Garden of Eden." *Journal of Biblical Literature.* 98 (1979): 513–528.

Laniak, Tim. "Believing is Seeing." *Basics of Biblical Hebrew.* Grand Rapids: Zondervan, 2001. 204–205.

Larsson, Gerhard. "The Chronology of the Pentateuch: A Comparison of the MT and LXX." *Journal of Biblical Literature.* (1983): 401–409.

Lewis, Jack P. "The Days of Creation: An Historical Survey of Interpretation." *The Journal of the Evangelical Theological Society.* 32 (1989): 483–455.

————. "The Offering of Abel (Gen. 4.4): A History of Interpretation." *The Journal of the Evangelical Theological Society.* 37 (1994): 481–496.

————. "The Woman's Seed (Gen. 3.15). *The Journal of the Evangelical Theological Society.* (1991): 299–319.

Lindsay, J. "Creation." *The International Standard Bible Encyclopedia.* 1. Grand Rapids: Zondervan, 1979. 800–802.

MacKenzie, R.A.F. "The Divine Soliloquies in Genesis." *The Catholic Bible Quarterly.* 17 (1955): 157–166.

Macrae, Allan A. "Olam." Theological Wordbook of the Old Testament Chicago: Moody Bible Institute, 1980. 672–673.

Matthews, Donald H. "Response: The Cultural Aesthetic of Blackness." *Journal of the American Academy of Religion.* 65, No. 1 (1997): 187–188.

Mathewson, Steven D. "An Exegetical Study of Genesis 38." *Bibliotheca Sacra.* 146 (1989): 373–392.

McGarvey, J.W. "Divine Providence: Joseph." *McGarvey's Sermons Delivered in Louisville, Kentucky, June – September 1893.* Delight: Gospel Light Publishing. 215–231.

McKenzie, Brian A. "Jacob's Blessing on Pharaoh: An Interpretation of Gen. 46.31–47.26." *Westminster Theological Journal.* 45 (1983): 386–399.

McKenzie, Steven L. "Response: The Curse of Ham and David H. Aaron." *Journal of the American Academy of Religion. 65, No. 1 (1997):* 183–186.

Miles, Jack. "Jacob's Wrestling Match: Was It an Angel or Esau?" *Bible Review.* October (1998): 22–23.

Millard, A.R. "Isaac." *The International Standard Bible Encyclopedia.* 2. Grand Rapids: Zondervan, 1979. 883–884.

_____. "Jacob." *The International Standard Bible Encyclopedia.* 2. Grand Rapids: Zondervan, 1979. 948–955.

Miller, Patrick D., Jr. "*Yeled* in the Song of Lamech." *Journal of Biblical Literature.* 85 (1966): 477–478.

Morris, Henry M. and John C. Whitcomb Jr. "The Genesis Flood: Its Nature and Significance." *Bibliotheca Sacra.* 117 (1960): 155–163, 204–213.

Morrison, Martha A. "The Jacob and Laban Narrative in Light of Near Eastern Sources." *Biblical Archaeologist.* Summer, 1983: 155–164.

Morton, Glenn R. "The Mediterranean Flood." *Perspectives on Science and Christian Faith.* 49 (1997): 238–251.

Munday, John C. Jr. "Eden's Geography Erodes Flood's Geology." *Westminster Theological Journal.* 58 (1996): 123–154.

Murray, J. "Adam." *The International Standard Bible Encyclopedia.* 1. Grand Rapids: Zondervan, 1979. 47–50.

Pickup, Martin. "The Seed of Woman." *The Gospel in the Old Testament:Florida College Annual Lectures.* Temple Terrace: Florida College Bookstore, 2003. 49–78.

Parker, Paula. "Between Text and Sermon: Genesis 11.1–9." *Interpretation: A Journal of Bible and Theology.* 54 (2000): 57–59.

Payne, J. Barton. "Satan." *Theological Wordbook of the Old Testament.* Chicago: Moody Bible Institute, 1980. 874–875.

Payne, D.F. "Tower of Babel." *The International Standard Bible Encyclopedia.* 1. Grand Rapids: Zondervan, 1979.382–383.

Pinches, T.G. "Tower of Babel: Archaeological Evidence." *The International Standard Bible Encyclopedia.* 1. Grand Rapids: Zondervan, 1979. 383–384.

Plantinga, Cornelius. "Murder, Envy and the Harvest Princess." *Christianity Today.* 35 (1991): 26–28.

Pratico, Gary D. "What is His Name?" *Basics of Biblical Hebrew.* Grand Rapids: Zondervan, 2001. 304–306.

Riemann, Paul. "Am I My Brother's Keeper?" *Interpretation: A Journal of Bible and Theology.* 24 (1970): 482–491.

Rienstru, M.V. "Eve." *The International Standard Bible Encyclopedia.* 2. Grand Rapids: Zondervan, 1979. 204–205.

Roberts, Phil. "The City of God." *The Gospel in the Old Testament: Florida College Annual Lectures.* Temple Terrace: Florida College Bookstore. 2003. 233–254.

————. "The Role of Satan in the Bible." Unpublished Article. 1981.

Rooker, Mark. F. "Genesis 1.1–3: Creation or Re-Creation?" *Vital Old Testament Issues: Examining Textual and Topical Questions.* Grand Rapids: Kregel Resources, 1996.

Robertson, Thomas G. "Purpose of the Old Testament." *Things Written Aforetime: Florida College Annual Lectures.* Temple Terrace: Florida College Bookstore, 1978. 57–67.

Robinson, R.B. "Literary Functions of the Genealogies of Genesis." *The Catholic Bible Quarterly.* 48 (1986): 595–608.

Ross, Allen P. "Studies in the Life of Jacob, Part 1—Jacob's Vision: The Founding of Bethel." *Bibliotheca Sacra.* 142 (1985): 224–237.

————. "Studies in the Life of Jacob, Part 2—Jacob at the Jabbok, Israel at Peniel." *Bibliotheca Sacra.* 142 (1985): 338–354.

Selman, Martin. "The Kingdom of God in the Old Testament." *Tyndale Bulletin.* 40. (1989): 161–183.

Siemens, David F., Jr. "Some Relatively Non-technical Problems with Flood Geology." *Perspectives on Science and Christian Faith.* 44, No. 3 (1992): 169–174.

————. "More Problems with Flood Geology." *Perspectives on Science and Christian Faith.* 44, No. 4 (1992): 228–235.

Sterchi, David A. "Does Genesis 1 Provide a Chronological Sequence?" *The Journal of the Evangelical Theological Society.* 39, (1996): 529–536.

Stitzinger, Michael F. "Genesis 1–3 and the Male/Female Role Relationship." *Grace Theological Journal.* 2, No. 1 (1981): 23–44.

Stuart, D.K. "Sheol." *The International Standard Bible Encyclopedia.* 4. Grand Rapids: Zondervan, 1979. 472.

————. "Shiloh." *The International Standard Bible Encyclopedia.* 4. Grand Rapids: Zondervan, 1979. 478–479.

Tanner, William F. "Real World Stratigraphy and the Noachian Flood." *Perspectives on Science and Christian Faith.* 48 (1996): 44–47.

Thomas, D.W. "The Baal Myths." *Documents from Old Testament Times* London: Thomas Nelson and Sons, 128–133.

Tucker, Gene. "The Legal Background of Genesis 23." *Journal of Biblical Literature.* 85 (1966): 77–84.

Tucker, Gordon. "Jacob's Terrible Burden in the Shadow of the Text." *Bible Review.* June (1994): 20–28, 54.

Van Broekhoven, H., Jr. "Nephilim." *The International Standard Bible Encyclopedia.* 3. Grand Rapids: Zondervan, 1979. 518–519.

VanGemeren, Willem A. "The Sons of God in Genesis 6.1–4." *Westminster Theological Journal.* 43 (1981): 320–348.

Van Wolde, Ellen. "The Story of Cain and Abel: A Narrative Study." *Journal for the Study of the Old Testament.* 52 (1991): 25–41.

Vos, H.F. "Flood (Genesis)." *The International Standard Bible Encyclopedia* Vol. 2. Grand Rapids: Zondervan, 1979. 316–321.

Waltke, Brice K. "Ark of Noah." *The International Standard Bible Encyclopedia.* Vol. 1. Grand Rapids: Zondervan, 1979. 291.

————. "Cain and His Offering." *The Westminster Theological Journal.* 48 (1986): 363–372.

Walton, John. "The Antediluvian Section of the Sumerian King List and Genesis 5." *Biblical Archaeologist.* Fall, 1981. 207–208.

Whitcomb, John C. "Genesis." *Zondervan's Pictorial Bible Dictionary* Grand Rapids: Zondervan, 1967. 305–307.

Wiesel, Elie. "Esau." *Bible Review.* April (1998): 26–27.

Wilson, J.M. "Angel." *The International Standard Bible Encyclopedia.* Vol. 1. Grand Rapids: Zondervan, 1979. 124–127.

Author Index [1]

Aalders, G.C., 24

Albright, W.F., 171

Alter, R., 256, 271, 388, 395, 397

Banvinck, H., 23

Battenfield, J.R., 174

Bechtel, L., 347, 348, 349

Berg, W. 180

Birney, L., 101, 103, 105, 109

Blocher, H., 25, 33, 35, 39, 47, 49, 51, 57, 60, 61, 62, 63, 64, 70, 71, 72, 74

Boice, J.M., 333

Bromiley, G.W.. 52, 54, 55, 56

Bruce, F.F.. 158, 162, 163, 165

Burdick, D.W.. 162, 163, 164

Calvin, J., 118, 192

Carmichael, C., 484

Chrysostom, J., 487

Coats, G.W., 387

Cole, T.J., 86, 87

Clifford, R.J.. 390, 391

Curtis, E.M., 332, 333, 337

Davis, J.J., 19, 489, 501

Delitzsch, F., 23, 188, 209, 443, 471

DeWitt, D.S., 20, 128

Dods, M., 406

Dorsey, D.A., 24, 93, 94, 123, 177, 368, 373, 398

Duguid, I.M., 141, 181, 243, 244, 245, 246

Edersheim, A., 163

Foh, S.T., 69

Fokkelman, J.P., 301, 316

Fox, E., 30, 263

Geisler, N.L., 89, 90, 105

Gianotti, C.R., 53, 54, 55,

56, 57

Good, E.M.,

Greenberg, M., 315

Guthrie, D., 162, 164, 165

Hammerly-Dupuy, D., 94

Harris, R.L., 383

Harrison, R.K., 18, 20, 21, 42, 43, 48, 76, 106, 127, 132, 140, 180, 248, 250, 282, 315, 419, 450, 478

Hasel, G.F., 26, 31, 42, 43

Helyer, L.R., 138, 149, 153

Hengstenberg, E.W., 227

Henry, M., 50, 51

Hill, C.A., 48

Hoehner, H., 173, 174, 175, 176

Holmgren, F.C., 329

Honeyman, A.M., 396

Houtman, C., 296

Howe, T., 105

---

[1]The eight commentators we cited most frequently (see page 8) have been omitted from this index, except where cited from a work other than their commentary.

Humphreys, W.L. 427

Jacob, B. 230, 499

Kaiser, W.C., Jr., 16, 33, 53, 54, 56, 57, 62, 88, 90, 96, 100, 101, 103, 104, 107, 112, 120, 121, 162, 163, 164, 185, 186, 187, 200, 265, 266, 381, 485, 486

Kilgore, J.M., 135, 136

Kitchen, K.A., 234, 394, 397, 399, 461, 500

Kline, M.G., 103, 167

Lambe, A.J., 391, 424, 466

Landy, F. 238

Laniak, T., 236

Lehmann, M.R., 249, 250

Lewis, J., 77

Longman, T., III, 21, 33, 37, 40, 41, 42, 43, 69, 71, 94, 102, 118, 128, 129, 131, 481

Luther, M., 352

MacKenzie, R.A.F., 68, 73, 202, 203

Macrae, A.A., 150

Mathewson, S.D., 387, 388, 389, 391, 392

McGarvey, J.W., 412, 416

McGuiggan, J., 71, 77, 118, 126, 193, 203, 214, 236, 237, 352, 499

McKenzie, B.A., 455, 458

Meek, T.J., 52

Miles, J., 327

Morris, H.M., 98

Morrison, M.A., 311, 315, 317, 325

Morton, G., 112

Motyer, J.A., 53

Parker, P., 125, 126

Patrick, D. 139

Payne, J.B., 53, 54, 55, 56, 57, 127, 185, 186, 187, 380, 382, 383, 384

Pickup, M., 59, 66, 162, 164, 165, 166

Procksch, O., 427

Riemann, P., 78, 79

Roberts, D.P., 68, 82, 125, 127, 128

Robinson, R.B. 88

Rooker, M.F., 25, 43

Roop, E.F., 30, 83, 158, 193, 204, 248, 298, 404, 438, 493

Ross, A.P., 323, 327, 328, 329, 330, 333

Sarna, N., 147, 235, 343, 350, 395, 403, 429, 443, 449, 452, 500

Schaeffer, F., 21, 34, 63, 72

Speiser, E.A., 41, 42

Sterchi, D.A., 39, 39

Sternberg, M., 255, 427, 475, 498

Stigers, H.G., 387

Stitzinger, M.F., 34, 70

Strobel, L., 41

Stuart, D.K., 381, 382, 383, 486

Thomas, D.W., 41

Thompson, B., 112

Tucker, G., 249, 250, 351

Van Broekhoven, H., Jr., 108

VanGemeren, W.A., 102, 103

Vawter, B., 389

Vilmar, A., 432

Vos, H.F., 426, 438, 491, 495

Vriezen, T.C., 95

Waltke, B.K., 25, 42, 97

Ward, D., 70, 356

Westerman, C., 9, 434

Whitcomb, J.C., 37, 98

Whitelaw, T., 231, 306

Wiesel, E., 271

Wilson, J.M., 185, 187

Wright, C.G.H., 202

Wood, L., 473, 488

Young, E.J., 23, 24, 37, 38, 50, 61, 62, 63, 64, 65, 71, 72, 73, 89, 134

General Index [1]

Abel, 16, 76, 83

Abimelech (chs 20–21), 217, 232
  God speaks to him, 218

Abimelech (ch 26), 274, 278

Abram (Abraham), 131, 133, 152, 243
  Covenant with Abimelech, 233
  First called Abraham, 189
  God speaks to him, 135, 167, 196
  God tests him, 235, 241
  God's covenant with Abraham, 169
  His battle in Canaan, 154, 158, 160
  His children with Keturah, 264
  His death, 265
  His faith, 138, 168, 194, 228
  His hospitality, 197
  His last words, 252
  His son, Ishmael, born, 184
  His son, Isaac, born, 226
  His wealth, 139, 147, 157, 250, 259
  His worship, 140, 148, 151, 189, 233
  Intervenes for Sodom and Lot, 204
  Laughs at promise of a son, 191
  Lies about relationship with Sarah, 141, 217
  Marriage to Keturah, 264
  Nation promise (Israel), 136, 168, 189, 240
  Promise of a great name, 136
  Promise of land, 172, 190
  Promise of a son, 168, 172

Adam, 47, 63, 70

Afterlife, 170, 265, 381

Amalekites, 154, 155, 364

Ammonites, 216

Amorites, 170

Angel of the Lord, 182, 185, 239, 313, 326
  Angels in Jacob's vision, 296, 323

Ark (Noah), 96, 98

Asher, 357, 490

Authorship of Genesis, 18

Babel (tower of), 124, 127
  Location (land of Shinar), 125

Barren(ness), 138, 177, 188, 194, 214, 223, 244, 268, 306

Beersheba, 230, 233, 247, 280, 295, 447, 454

Benjamin, 354, 358, 371, 415, 417, 419, 424, 431, 441, 443, 450, 492

Bethel (see also El-Bethel), 149, 150, 296, 300, 313, 323, 338, 343, 350, 354, 471

Bethuel (Rebekah's father), 257, 260

Bilhah, 354, 357
  Her children with Jacob, 357, 370

Bigamy, 82, 258, 320

---

[1]To conserve space, this index cites the first page of the indexed subject only.

Birthright, 271, 281, 289, 294, 323, 336, 363, 430, 472, 480, 486

Bless(ing), 15, 116, 117, 136, 137, 147, 152, 159, 183, 193, 226, 240, 252, 259, 266, 269, 272, 277, 279, 281, 293, 307, 322, 328, 329, 336, 352, 358, 367, 385, 393, 426, 455, 457, 464, 471, 476, 480, 500

Blood, 42, 68, 76, 80, 117, 285, 377, 379, 416, 419

Cain, 76
  His murder of Abel, 79
  His wife, 81
  His building of the first city, 82
  Land of Nod, 81

Canaan (son of Ham), 120, 124

Canaan/Canaanites (land and its people), 107, 128, 135, 139, 141, 147, 148, 149, 153, 158, 163, 173, 178, 247, 251, 253, 274, 280, 287, 289, 293, 297, 314, 323, 339, 363, 370, 385, 415, 430, 447, 451, 455, 459, 462, 470, 472, 488, 492, 494, 500

Chedorlaomer, 155, 156

Cherubim, 73

Circumcision, 190, 194, 199, 226, 342

Clothing
  Animal skins (God's choice), 72
  Fig leaves (Man's choice), 64
  Jospeh gives brothers clothes, 443
  Joseph's robe
    Receives it, 371
    His brothers take it, 377
  His brothers soak it in animal blood, 379
  Potiphar's wife takes his cloak, 396
  Rebekah deceives Isaac, 285
  Tamar removes widow's garments, 388
  Clothed as prostitute, 388

Covenants between God and man, 36, 57, 98, 118, 169, 189, 194, 475

Covenants between men, 233, 280, 320

Creation, 23, 37
  Animals paraded before Adam, 50
  As evidence for creator/God, 40
  Covenant relationship, 36, 57
  Day-age theory, 28
  Genesis vs. mythology, 23
  Logos, 31, 32

Man's creation, 45
Parallel structure, 24
Plurality of deity (in creation of man), 30
Science and the Bible, 37
Shabbath (Sabbath), 35, 39
Woman's creation, 50

Curse, 65, 68, 71, 80, 114, 120, 137, 180, 284, 287, 483

Dan (city), 18

Dan (son of Israel), 357, 489

Dead Sea, 155, 213

Death, 62, 71, 73, 85, 112, 134, 247, 265, 281, 352, 354, 386, 388, 493, 501

Deborah (Rebekah's nurse), 262, 352

Designations of God
  Almighty, 491
  El-Beth-el, 233, 352
  El-elohe-Israel, 233
  El Elyon (God Most High), 158
  El Olam (Everlasting God), 233
  El Roi (God of Seeing), 183
  El Shaddai, 52, 54, 56, 188, 233, 426
  Elohim, 18, 31, 52, 54, 57, 73, 104, 188, 221, 328, 360, 413, 418
  Fear of Isaac, 320, 322
  God of Abraham, 321
  God of your father, 491
  Mighty one of Jacob, 491
  Shepherd, 475, 491
  Stone of Israel, 491
  Yahweh (YHWH), 18, 35, 43, 52, 55, 57, 83, 127, 159, 162, 167, 170, 186, 196, 203, 212, 240, 257, 279, 283, 296, 312, 321, 356, 360, 389, 393, 418

Dinah, 338, 340, 380
  Humiliated by Shechem, 340, 347
  Avenged by Simeon and Levi, 345

Dothan, 375

Eating of animals, 110, 117

Edomites, 124, 271, 290

Egypt (son of Ham), 124

Egypt (land), 141, 147, 149, 177, 217, 231, 243, 274, 340, 364, 367, 385, 394, 442

Eqyptian bondage (prophecy of), 170, 173

El-Bethel (see also Bethel), 352

Eliezer (Abraham's servant), 140, 152, 167, 252
His worship, 257, 260

Enoch, 85
Walked with God (see also Noah), 86

Ephraim, 284, 412, 450, 471, 477, 491

Er, 386

Esau, 268, 323
Called Edom, 271
His wives, 280, 291, 294, 363
His wealth, 336
Inhabits the land of Seir, 323
Mourns the loss of the blessing, 289
Reunited with Jacob, 335
Sells his birthright, 271

Eve, 61, 68, 72

Faith, 77, 83, 87, 96, 131, 135, 138, 161, 167, 168, 182, 194, 203, 226, 228, 235, 240, 245, 247, 253, 261, 274, 281, 289, 308, 323, 333, 339, 343, 360, 426, 462, 471, 477, 493, 497, 500

Famine, 139, 141, 243, 274, 407, 412, 456, 459

Flood (see also Noah), 93
Ages of Antediluvians, 90
As judgment, 112
Covenant with Noah, 113
Dry vs. dried out *(harev vs. yavesh)*, 114
Eating of animals, 110, 117
Instructions regarding clean animals, 110
Localized vs. universal, 111
Noah's Obedience, 110
Raven and dove, 113
Waters, 110

Gad, 357, 490

Garden of Eden (see also Adam, Eve), 45, 47
Tree of Life, 47
Tree of Knowledge of Good and Evil, 47, 49, 61
Woman's role as helper, 49
Work/labor, 49

Genealogies, 88, 123, 129, 164, 266, 363, 392, 450

Gerar, 217, 275

God of Nahor, 321

God speaks to man, 49, 64, 77, 96, 110, 114, 117, 136, 150, 167, 183, 189, 196, 198, 201, 218, 229, 235, 240, 269, 274, 296, 311, 316, 328, 352, 448

God's omnipresence, 297

Gomorrah (see also Jordan Valley), 155, 202, 206

Goshen, 441, 452, 455, 459

Hagar
Angel speaks to her, 182
As Sarah's property, 177
Egyptian, 177, 243
Given as wife to Abram, 177
Flees from Sarai, 181
Sent away, 228
Wanders in Beersheba, 230

Ham, 119, 123, 163

Hamor, 342

Hammurabi's code, 318

Haran (city), 135, 253, 295

Haran (son of Terah), 133, 152

Headship/subjection, 68, 200

Hebron, 247, 374

Hittites, 247
Ephron the son of Zohar, 248
Esau's wives, 280, 291

Hivites (see Shechemites)

Homosexuality, 208

Hospitality, 197, 207, 255

Idolatry, 135, 253, 258, 297, 307, 315, 322, 350, 489, 491

Isaac, 245, 267
As a sacrifice, 235
Blesses Esau, 289
Blesses Jacob, 287
Finding a wife for him, 253
God's covenant will him, 194
God's promises to him, 275
His birth predicted, 194, 226
His blindness, 281
His death, 354
His plan to bless Esau, 281

His submission and faith, 239, 274, 279
His wealth, 277
His worship, 279
Marries Rebekah, 263
Prays for Rebekah's infertility, 268
Quarrels over wells, 277
Receives blessing, 266
Sends Jacob to find a wife, 293

Ishmael, 193, 227, 244
His name predicted, 183
Nation promise, 183, 229, 231, 266

Ishmaelites (see also Midianites), 378

Israel (see also Jacob), 333, 444, 481

Israelites, 124, 173, 245, 365, 462, 500

Issachar, 358, 488

Jacob, 245, 267, 341, 367
Becomes ill, 471
Becomes Israel, 328, 333, 353
Blesses his sons and Joseph's sons, 473, 480
    Asher, 490
    Benjamin, 492
    Dan, 488
    Ephraim, 475, 500
    Gad, 490
    Issachar, 488
    Joseph, 491
    Judah, 484
    Manasseh, 475
    Naphtali, 490
    Reuben, 482
    Simeon and Levi, 483
    Zebulun, 487
Blesses Pharaoh, 457
Builds a pillar at Bethel, 297, 353
Deceives Isaac, 285
Deceives Laban, 315
Flees from Esau, 290
Fulfills his vow, builds altar at Bethel, 351
God speaks to him in vision, 448
His birth, 270
His death, 493
His diminished faith, 346
His love for Rachel, 302
His reaction to Simeon and Levi's violence, 345, 348
His sons, 356, 464
His sons convince him that Joseph is dead, 379
His sons journey to Egypt for food, 415
His striped, speckled, and spotted flock, 309
His vow, 298
His wealth, 314, 325, 344
His worship, 339, 447, 454
Ladder (his vision), 295
Learns that Joseph is alive, 444
Marries Leah, 304
Marries Rachel, 305
Naming of his children, 356
Prepares to reunite with Esau, 323
Promises repeated to Jacob, 353, 448
Rebukes Joseph (for his dream), 373
Receives blessing from God, 352
Requests to be buried in Machpelah, 462, 471, 492
Returns to Bethel, 350
Returns to Canaan, 311, 370
Seeks peace with Esau, 325
Sends Benjamin to Egypt, 426
Travels to Egypt, 445
Wrestles with the angel/God, 327, 332

Japheth, 120, 123

Jerusalem, 158

Jordan Valley (see also Sodom, Gomorrah), 149, 212, 243

Joseph, 367, 385
As the privileged son, 367, 370
Foreshadows Christ, 440
Forgives his brothers, 501
Given Egyptian name, 411
Hated by his brothers, 371
His birth, 306, 358
His brothers bow before him, 416, 498
His brothers cast him into the pit, 377
His brothers conspire to kill him, 376
His character/righteousness, 395, 397, 398, 459
His cup placed in Benjamin's sack, 431
His death, 501
His dreams, 372, 373
His Egyptian wife, Asenath, 411, 452
His faith, 500
His position of authority in Egypt, 409, 441, 464
His robe of many colors, 371
His sons, 412

Imprisoned, 397
In Potiphar's household, 393
Interprets dreams, 401, 407
Invites brothers to his home, 428
Invites family to live in Goshen, 441, 469
Joseph Cycle: Concentric Pattern, 368
Joseph Cycle: Parallel Pattern, 369
Puts his brothers into custody, 418
Receives birthright, 480
Reconciled with his family, 452, 467
Requests to be buried in Canaan, 500
Reveals his identity to his brothers, 438
Sold to the Midianites (Ishmaelites), 378, 464
Tests his brothers, 467
Vows to bury Jacob in Machpelah, 462, 471, 492

Judah, 15, 367, 398
Decides to sell Joseph, 377
Goes to Timnah, Enaim, 388
His birth, 357
His blessing (Messianic), 484
His leadership, 422, 424, 434, 452, 465
His marriage to Canaanite woman, 385
His repentance, 391
His sons, 386
His wife's death, 388
Learns of Tamar's pregnancy, 390

Judgment, 65, 80, 96, 103, 112, 117, 128, 170, 201, 207, 501

Keeper, 78

Keturah, 189, 264
Her children with Abraham, 264

Laban, 260, 301, 306, 451
Aramean, 316
Brother of Rebekah, 258, 290
Deceives and cheats Jacob, 304, 312
Father of Rachel and Leah, 293
His greed, 258, 301
His idolatry, 307
His polytheism, 258
Proposes a covenant with Jacob, 320

Lamech, 82

Leah, 302, 313
Her burial, 362
Her character, 358, 360
Her children with Jacob, 356
Her marriage to Jacob, 304

Her name, 302
Her son Judah will carry out Messianic line, 361

Levi, 15, 342, 483
And Simeon kill the Shechemite males, 345, 465
And Simeon take back Dinah, 345
Dinah as his full-blood sister, 340
His birth, 356

Lies/lying, 17, 61, 67, 79, 141, 217, 221, 223, 244, 275, 284, 286, 304, 319, 379, 388, 396

Lifespan of the patriarchs, 142, 458, 462

Lot, 134
Accompanies Abram in wilderness, 138
As possible heir to Abraham, 140, 152
Corruption of his family, 215
His capture and rescue, 156, 158
His daughters' sins, 215
His wife's death, 214
His wealth, 148
In Sodom, 204
Journeyed east (Jordan Valley), 149, 243
Journeyed with Abram to Egypt and back, 147
Moabites, as his descendants, 216

Machir (clan of Manasseh), 500

Machpelah, 151, 251, 265, 284, 362, 492, 496

Mahanaim, 323

Mamre, 151

Manasseh, 284, 412, 450, 471, 477

Marriage covenant, 51

Melchizedek, 158, 162

Midianites (see also Ishmaelites), 378

Milcah, 135, 241

Moabites, 216

Moriah, 235, 240

Mosaic authorship, 18

Murder (kill), 79, 82, 117, 143, 290, 342, 376

Nahor, 133, 241

Naked(ness), 63, 119

Naphtali, 357, 490

Negeb, 140, 147

Nephilim, 100, 106

Noah, 93, 123
    "Be fruitful and multiply," 114, 117
    Commanded to build the ark, 96
    Covenant with God (rainbow), 98, 113, 118
    His descendants, 123
    His family, 111
    His obedience, 110
    His sin (drunkenness), 119
    His sons, 87
    Walked with God, 86, 96

Offspring, 59, 66, 110, 138, 150, 168, 172, 183, 215, 228, 240, 254, 275, 293, 325, 386, 449, 474

Onan, 386

One flesh, 51

Pagan creation accounts, 41

Peniel/Penuel, 329, 330

Perez, 392

Perizzites, 148

Pharaoh, 393, 403, 455
    And Sarai, 142
    Blessed by Jacob, 457
    His dream about the cows, 404
    His dream about the grain, 405
    Invites Joseph's family to live in Egypt, 442, 469

Philistines, 277

Phicol (Chapter 21), 232

Phicol (Chapter 26), 279

Plagues, 144

Plain of the Jordan (see Jordan Valley)

Polygamy, 104, 178, 260, 304, 357

Potiphar, 380, 393
    His trust in Joseph, 394, 398
    His wife, 394

Prayer, 193, 203, 219, 222, 231, 254, 268, 298, 324, 331, 358, 360, 426, 454, 489

Promises, 136, 150, 168, 183, 189, 198, 229, 240, 269, 274, 296, 448, 485

Prophecy/Prophet, 219, 283, 480

Rachel, 302, 306, 313, 356
    Her burial, 361
    Her character, 358
    Her children with Jacob, 354, 358
    Her death, 354, 473
    Her materialism, 314
    Her name, 302
    Meets Jacob, 300
    Steals the household idols, 315, 318

Rameses (see Goshen)

Rebekah, 255
    And Abimelech, 144, 276
    Deceives Isaac, 284
    Marries Isaac, 263
    Plans for blessing of Jacob, 283

Redeemed, 476

Repentance, 210, 350, 355, 391, 420, 467

Resurrection (and judgment of Satan), 67

Reuben, 15, 419
    Distraught over Joseph's disappearance, 378
    His birth, 356
    His blessing from Jacob, 482
    His leadership fails, 422, 465
    His sin with Bilhah, 354
    Rescues Joseph from death, 376

Revelation (see also God speaks to man), 14, 170

Righteous(ness), 76, 89, 164, 201, 205, 308, 398

Sabbath, 35, 39

Sacrifice/offering, 26, 76, 114, 140, 151, 236, 240, 276, 322, 339, 350, 447

Salem (see Jerusalem)

Salt Sea (see Dead Sea)

Salvation, 15, 489

Sarai (Sarah), 134
    And Abimelech, 144, 217
    And Pharaoh, 145
    Barren, 138, 177, 223
    First called Sarah, 191

Her death, 247
Laughs at promise of a son (and denies it), 198, 200
Says she's Abram's sister, 141

Seed (see offspring)

Seth, 83

Serpent, 59, 60, 61, 65, 67, 75

Shame, 64, 119, 341, 389

Shechem (land), 140, 338, 374, 478

Shechem (son of Hamor), 340, 342, 344
Humiliates Dinah, 340, 347

Shechemites (or Hivites), 340, 343, 465, 483

Shelah, 386, 388

Shem, 87, 120, 123, 129, 163

Sheol, 381

Shepherd, 76, 299, 308, 370, 449, 453, 456, 475, 491

Shur, 182

Simeon, 15, 342, 483
And Levi kill the Shechemite males, 345, 465
And Levi take back Dinah, 345
Dinah as his full-blood sister, 340
His birth, 356
His Canaanite wife, 451
His son, Shaul, 451
Kept in Egypt by Joseph, 420, 428

Sin, 15, 64, 74, 77, 119, 120, 126, 141, 144, 202, 208, 217, 221, 223, 276, 390, 395, 399, 482

Slavery, 121, 139, 170, 177, 223, 228, 345, 380, 385, 397, 433, 461

Sodom (see also Jordan Valley), 155
Angels travel there, 200, 202
God's judgment on it, 206, 210, 212
Its king, Bera, 155
Lot settles there, 150
Lot sits in its gate, 207
Men of the city, 208, 210

Sons of God and Daughters of Men, 100, 101

Structure and pattern, 22, 24, 93, 115, 128, 133, 177, 267, 368
Toledot structure, 20, 268, 367, 385

Succoth, 338

Tamar, 386
Her children, 391
Poses as prostitute to seduce Judah, 388

Terah, 133, 152

Ur, 135

Worship, 76, 83, 140, 148, 151, 159, 162, 187, 189, 225, 233, 238, 257, 260, 321, 324, 339, 350, 447

Zebulun, 358, 487, 490

Zerah, 391

Zilpah, 357
Her children with Jacob, 357, 370

Zoar, 215

Scripture Index

Genesis

1.1	26		
1.1–2.3	22, 57		
1.2	25, 27, 115		
1.3	25		
1.5	37		
1.6–8	115		
1.9	115		
1.11	98		
1.16	30		
1.17	28		
1.18	30		
1.20	29, 114		
1.20–23	115		
1.22	103, 114		
1.24–25	116		
1.25	98		
1.26	26, 31, 72, 100, 126		
1.26–28	85, 116		
1.27	31, 32, 49, 98		
1.28	103, 116		
1.30	98		
1.31	98		
2.3	39		
2.4–25	57		
2.4–3.24	22		
2.5	45		
2.8–9	45		
2.14	28, 125		
2.16–17	61		
2.15	70, 71		
2.17	28		
2.18	70		
2.19–20	117		
2.24	102		
3.1–5	63		
3.4–5	17		
3.5	72, 137		
3.5–6	125		
3.6	180, 386		
3.7	72		
3.9	182		
3.11	64		
3.12	396		
3.14–19	118		
3.15	290		
3.16	49, 69, 70		
3.17	71		
3.20	83		
3.22	31, 47, 62		
4.1–16	22		
4.3–5	336		
4.7	69, 70, 77		
4.8	290		
4.9	182		
4.10	81		
4.11	78		
4.17–22	22		
4.19	82, 111		
4.19–22	82, 83		
4.19–24	106		
4.23	82, 290		
4.24	82		
4.25–5.32	100		
4.26—16	83, 84		
5.1–32	22		
5.4	81		
5.22–24	82		
5.27	85		
5.32	16, 87, 133		
6.1	101		
6.1–2	101		
6.1–3	104		
6.1–4	22, 101, 103, 104		
6.1–6	83		
6.1–8	100		
6.2	101, 104, 106, 386		
6.3	94, 103, 104		

6.3–5	103	8.16	116	11.18–19	229
6.4	96, 104, 107, 137	8.18	116	11.20–26	124
		8.17	116	11.21	477
6.5	115	8.17–19	116	11.24	90
6.5–6	104	8.20	110	11.26	16, 134
6.5–7	96	8.21–22	115, 118	11.27	268
6.5–8	22	9.1	120	11.27–32	22, 133
6.6	115	9.1–2	116	11.27–25.18	268
6.7	96	9.1–7	93	11.28	18
6.8	98	9.2–3	110	11.30	177
6.9	96	9.5	80	11.32	16, 134
6.9–10	93	9.5–6	118	12.1	297, 311
6.9–9.19	22	9.6	116	12.1–3	447, 448
6.11–12	93, 108	9.8–17	93, 98	12.1–9	133
6.12	119	9.12	121	12.2	229, 252, 447
6.13–22	93	9.13	66	12.2–3	146, 287
6.15	112	9.14–15	113	12.3	157, 180, 204, 307, 394, 398, 455, 463
6.18	98, 99	9.15–16	417		
6.19–21	98	9.18–19	93		
6.22	99, 110	9.19	127	12.4	16, 266, 275, 440
7.1–4	114	9.20–25	224		
7.1–9	93	9.20–27	121	12.5	136
7.4	110	9.20–29	22	12.5–9	140
7.6	16, 87	9.24	16, 133	12.6	351
7.6–10	110	9.29	100	12.6–9	339
7.10–16	93	10.1–5	22	12.7	148, 151
7.11	29, 94, 95	10.6–20	22	12.8	140
7.16	210	10.8	48	12.10	447
7.17–20	93	10.8–12	104	12.10ff	217
7.21–24	93	10.15–18	148	12.10–13	241
7.24–8.1	17	10.19—217		12.10–20	133, 243, 274, 440, 448, 456
8.1	26, 112, 118, 119, 417	10.21–32	22		
		11.1–9	22, 128, 129, 295	12.11	142, 221
8.1–2	115			12.12	143
8.1–5	93	11.4	296	12.13	145
8.2	115	11.5	202	12.14	263
8.3	112	11.7	202	12.14–15	142
8.3–5	115	11.9	127	12.15	340, 386
8.6–12	115	11.10	16, 87	12.16	136, 177, 222, 310
8.6–14	93	11.10–26	163		
8.11	113	11.11	163	12.17	219
8.12	113	11.18	124	12.19	133, 144, 146, 219, 224, 244
8.15–22	93				

13.1–12	324	15.12–13	306	17.12–18	241
13.1–18	133	15.12–16	169	17.13	191, 266
13.5–9	363	15.12–21	448	17.14	191
13.9	149	15.13	173, 251, 456	17.15	195, 329
13.10	243	15.13–14	448	17.15–16	189
13.10ff	216	15.16	162, 173, 500	17.16	168, 198, 472
13.11–12	153, 243	15.17	169, 174, 295	17.16–21	226
13.12	150, 243	15.18	188, 306	17.17	134, 192, 226, 276
13.13	153	15.18–19	172		
13.14–17	151	16.1	243	17.18	193, 237, 245, 265
13.15	135, 266, 275	16.1–2	177		
13.16	168	16.1–4	243, 331	17.18–19	195, 228
14.1–9	157	16.2	177, 178	17.19	193, 195, 198, 226, 266
14.1–24	133	16.3	177, 178, 243		
14.5	155	16.3–4	180	17.20	193, 229, 266
14.7	154, 155	16.4	177	17.21	226
14.8	155	16.5	177, 181	17.23	194
14.9	155	16.5–6	283	17.27	194
14.10	155, 213	16.6	177, 178	18.1	196
14.11	18	16.7–13	375	18.2	203, 256, 375
14.12	156	16.9	179	18.6	156
14.13	151	16.10	186, 229, 266	18.6–7	197
14.14	136, 204	16.11–12	228	18.7	256
14.14–15	316	16.11–13	231	18.10	200, 206, 226
14.17	156	16.12	266	18.10–15	226
14.18	159, 233	16.13	182, 184, 185, 186, 233	18.12	196, 199, 200, 226, 276
14.18–20	160				
14.20	298	16.14	266	18.12–13	192
14.20–24	167	16.15	378	18.15	199, 276
14.22	159	17.1	86, 189, 233, 297, 426	18.16ff	194
14.24	151, 157, 159			18.16–33	133
15.1	169, 297	17.1–18.15	133	18.17	203
15.1–6	169, 400	17.3	192	18.19	201, 202, 207
15.1–16.16	133	17.4–8	189, 195	18.21	167
15.2	138, 140, 252	17.5	136, 195, 329	18.22	203, 206
15.2–3	252	17.6	137, 229, 472	18.22–33	237
15.4–5	229, 448	17.7–8	266	18.25	205
15.4–6	167	17.9–14	189	18.33	194
15.4–7	172	17.10–11	195	19.1	167, 200, 203, 249, 295, 344
15.9–11	233	17.10–12	226		
15.11	402	17.10–14	194	19.1–38	133
15.12	295	17.11	190	19.3	215
		17.12	191	19.8	197, 2102

19.9	210, 211	21.12	227, 228, 245, 265	24.1	252
19.10	211			24.2	462
19.14	276	21.13	229, 266	24.4	257
19.16	211	21.14	220, 227, 237, 280, 322	24.7	260
19.17	214, 215			24.12	252
19.19ff	215	21.16	276	24.14	252
19.21	215	21.17	227	24.16	142, 255, 256
19.22	212	21.18	227, 229, 266	24.17	261
19.24	211	21.20	227, 230	24.18–20	256
19.27	229	21.21	243	24.20	261
19.27–28	217	21.21–32	280	24.23	207
19.29	113, 417	21.22ff	218	24.26f	252
19.30–38	211, 244	21.22–24	320	24.27	252, 257
19.36	124	21.27	232	24.29	261
20.1ff	142	21.31–32	230	24.32	254
20.1–18	133, 274	21.33	447	24.33	252, 261
20.2	232, 274, 340	21.34	247	24.35	394
20.3	219, 223, 448	22.1	297	24.47	257
20.3–4	145	22.2	281	24.50	342
20.3–7	232, 316	22.3	229	24.50–51	258
20.4	217, 219, 223	22.4	236, 242	24.52	252
20.5–6	224	22.8	236	24.54	207, 261, 306
20.6	62	22.9	238	24.56	252, 306
20.7	145, 223	22.11	448	24.57–60	254
20.8	229	22.12	241	24.59	254, 352
20.11	220, 230	22.13	236	24.62	247
20.11–13	223	22.14	236	24.64	156
20.12	141, 223	22.15–18	447	24.66	262
20.13	141, 217, 241	22.18	138	24.67	262
20.14–15	232	22.19	247	25.1	179
20.14–16	144, 219	22.20–24	133	25.1–4	124
20.15	233	22.23	241	25.2	190, 378
20.17	145, 219, 268	23.1	134, 252, 262	25.5–6	228
20.17–18	219	23.1–2	284	25.6	179
21.1–2	268	23.2	247	25.7	263, 264
21.1–22.19	133	23.6	137, 250	25.8	170, 265, 354, 381, 463
21.5	263, 264, 440	23.7	250		
21.8–14	283	23.10	207	25.9	231, 263, 265, 294
21.9	243	23.11	250		
21.9–10	227	23.12	250	25.12	243
21.10–12	241	23.13	250	25.12–18	124
21.11	227, 265, 279	23.15	250	25.17	281
		23.18	207	25.17–18	378

25.19	268	26.31	229	28.13–15	298
25.19–34	267	26.33	447	28.13–16	447
25.19–37.1	268	26.34	256, 280, 293, 363	28.14	297, 351
25.20	256, 262, 263, 268			28.15	298, 313, 449
		26.35–35	455	28.16–19	300
25.21	269	26.35	291, 293	28.17	295, 297, 323, 351
25.21–28	281	27.1–28.9	267, 474		
25.22	269	27.2	281	28.18–19	353
25.22–23	286	27.4	282	28.18–22	350
25.23	273, 281, 481	27.9	282, 379	28.19–22	338
25.26	264, 268	27.12	318	28.20	449
25.28	282	27.14	282	28.20–21	350
25.29–34	273, 281	27.15	287, 379	28.20–22	286, 306, 313
25.30	269	27.17	287	28.21	354
25.31	282, 472	27.21–22	318	29.1–14	257
26.1	275, 297	27.24	286	29.1–30	267
26.1–2	141, 448	27.26–27	285	29.10	255, 257, 316
26.1–35	267	27.27	289, 3031	29.13	322
26.2	275, 279	27.29	138, 282	29.14	316
26.2–3	245	27.31	285	29.15	303
26.3	275, 279	27.34–36	477	29.17	142, 395
26.5	279	27.35–36	310	29.18	281, 301
26.6–11	217, 440, 455	27.37–40	477	29.21	281, 306
26.7	340	27.41	497	29.25	310
26.8	227	27.43	350	29.27	261, 281
26.10	218	27.45	323	29.27–30	356
26.11	62, 279	27.46–28.2	291	29.31–55	356
26.12	275, 394	28.1–22	448	29.31–30.11	451
26.12–13	144	28.2	350	29.31–30.24	267, 356
26.12–14	144	28.3	426	29.32	17
26.13–14	310	28.4	296, 306	30.1	354, 358, 359
26.14	277	28.6–9	280, 293	30.1–8	357
26.16	277, 279	28.8	293	30.3	357, 359
26.18	278	28.9	363	30.3–13	184
26.19	278	28.10–12	267	30.6	178
26.22	275	28.10–16	448	30.9–13	357
26.23–25	447	28.10–17	400	30.11	490
26.24	279, 280	28.10–19	471	30.14–21	358
26.26–31	320	28.11	330	30.15	359
26.27–31	320	28.12	298	30.16	340
26.28–29	218	28.12–17	375	30.17	358
26.29	278	28.13	296, 297, 306	30.20	178

30.22	113, 268, 359, 417	31.35	17, 359	34.15	387
30.22–24	354, 358	31.36–37	351	34.16	343
30.25	281	31.38–42	302	34.25	260, 340, 345
30.25–34	302	31.41	440	34.25–26	379
30.25–43	267	31.42	286, 316, 322, 449	34.25–31	367
30.26	306	31.42–45	300	34.26	345, 348
30.27	394	31.45	321	34.28	483
30.30	394	31.53	320	34.29	450
30.31–34	312	32.1	296	34.30	343, 351
30.36	314	32.1–2	338, 375	34.30–31	372
30.37–39	312	32.1–32	267	34.31	340, 246, 483
30.39	309	32.2	270	35.1	448
31.1	311, 313	32.7	335, 351	35.1–3	343
31.1–2	351	32.9	286	35.1–22	267
31.1–3	311	32.9–12	330	35.4	354, 380
31.1–16	306	32.11	330, 353, 361	35.5	346, 374, 375
31.1–55	267	32.22–32	270	35.6–7	298
31.3	311, 350, 449	32.24–31	312, 448	35.6–13	471
31.3–54	448	32.24–32	375	35.7	233
31.4	313	32.26	206, 327	35.8	262, 284, 492
31.5	286, 312, 449	32.28	326, 331	35.10	355
31.6–7	312	32.29	327	35.11	293, 353, 426, 472
31.7	307	32.30	326, 327	35.11–12	355
31.8	312	32.31	331, 444	35.13	194
31.8–9	312	33.1–20	267	35.14–15	353
31.9–12	309	33.4	335	35.16–18	356
31.10–13	448	33.5	474	35.16–19	358
31.11–13	350	33.6–7	335	35.16–20	318
31.13	306, 338, 350, 448	33.10	327	35.22	120, 355, 367, 377, 465
31.14	315, 259	33.13–17	354	35.23–26	353, 451
31.14–15	302, 312, 317	33.18–20	286	35.27	291
31.19	17, 253, 258, 311, 359, 388	33.19	375, 478	35.28	281
31.20	210, 314	33.20	233, 351	35.28–29	352
31.24	218, 321, 448	34.1–31	267	35.29	266, 338
31.26–27	310	34.1	346, 348	36.2	364
31.29	316	34.2	345, 347, 386	36.3	294
31.31	54, 311, 316, 351, 361	34.3	348, 349	36.4–5	363
		34.4	348	36.6–7	363
31.32	351, 433	34.5	260	36.8	270
31.34–35	359	34.11	260, 348	36.9	124
		34.13	210, 349	36.11	364

36.12	154	38.7	450	41.1–57	369
36.28	362	38.8	391	41.3–4	404
37.2	21, 268, 340, 374, 399, 411, 452, 464	38.9–10	450	40.4	465
		38.10	228	41.9–13	401
		38.11	391	41.10	398
37.2–11	368, 369	38.11ff	466	41.12	157
37.2–50.26	268	38.14	263, 388	41.15	413
37.3	374	38.15	391	41.16	394, 409
37.3–4	270	38.18	485	41.17–18	404
37.4	346, 442	38.20	391	41.21	407
37.4–8	497	38.21–22	388	41.23	407
37.7	372	38.26	391, 465	41.24	405
37.8	372	38.27–30	390	41.27	442
37.9	405, 412	39.1	390, 399	41.28	408
37.10	484	39.1–23	368, 369	41.32	373, 405, 408
37.12–36	368, 369	39.2	464	41.33–36	408
37.14	370, 464	39.2–3	449	41.35	461
37.17	375	39.3	398, 406	41.38	405
37.20	230, 379	39.3–5	455	41.38–29	413
37.21–22	374, 377	39.5	398, 406, 465	41.38–41	406
37.22	230, 345, 420	39.7	396	41.40	410
37.23	376, 396	39.9	218	41.43	404
37.23–24	428	39.10	396	41.45	461
37.24	230, 376	39.12	397	41.46	281, 399
37.26	374	39.12–13	377	41.49	394, 412
37.26–27	421, 464	39.14	157	41.51	417
37.26ff	452	39.19–20	465	41.55	411
37.26–28	424	39.20	393, 465	42.1	415
37.27	484	39.21	449	42.1–38	369
37.28	428	39.22	464, 465	42.1–43.34	368
37.34	334	39.21–23	399	42.4	334
37.28	393, 467	39.23	398, 406, 449, 455	42.6ff	363
37.29	377			42.7	427
37.30	377	40.1–23	389	42.7–8	467
37.32	390, 421	40.1–41.57	368	42.7–9	466
37.34	434	40.3	398	42.9–13	425
37.34–35	466	40.5	218	42.13	346
37.35	382, 449, 452	40.8	392, 405	42.14	467
37.36	393, 399	40.14	403	42.15–20	424
38.1	385, 390	40.15	376, 420	42.21	376, 418, 466
38.1–30	368, 369	40.23	401	42.21–22	466
38.2	386	41.1	218	42.22	379, 424, 465
38.3	386				

42.24	379, 494	45.1–15	438	46.12	450
42.25	431	45.1–28	368	46.15	450
42.36	334, 415	45.2	442, 494	46.17	450
42.37	465, 466	45.3	438	46.18	450, 452
42.37–38	424	45.4	438, 468	46.21	436
42.38	382, 436, 441	45.4–8	391	46.22	450
43.1–44.3	368	45.5	466, 468, 499	46.25	450, 451, 452
43.3–15	466	45.5ff	439	46.26	252, 450
43.6	334	45.5–8	445	46.27	450
43.7	429	45.6	281, 424	46.28–47.12	368
43.8	334	45.7	468	46.29	494
43.8–9	422	45.7–8	439, 498, 499	46.33–34	456
43.9	466	45.8	468	46.34	385, 409, 456, 457
43.11	334	45.9ff	456		
43.15	428	45.10	442, 453	47.3–4	456
43.16	429	45.12	439	47.6	441, 453, 456, 470
43.18	433	45.13	469		
43.20–22	428	45.14–15	469, 494	47.7	455
43.27	468	45.15	438, 469	47.9	281, 334, 474
43.28	428	45.16	411, 438	47.10	455, 493
43.29	467	45.16–28	438	47.11	441, 470
43.30	494	45.16–47.12	369	47.13–15	459
43.32	409	45.17ff	456	47.13–26	369, 441
43.32–34	377	45.17–20	455	47.13–31	368
43.34	467	45.18	442	47.15–26	394
44.1	434	45.19	411, 469	47.20	459
44.1–34	368	45.20	449, 469	47.20–21	406
44.4	428	45.22	377	47.24	461
44.4–45.15	369	45.24	438, 469	47.25–26	406
44.5	434	45.27–28	470	47.26–27	459
44.7	435	45.28	334, 447, 453	47.27	334
44.14	498	46.1	334, 441	47.27–49.32	369
44.15	432	46.1–4	141, 445, 470	47.28	370, 452, 470
44.17	436	46.1–27	368	47.29	253
44.18–34	345, 378, 391	46.2	239	47.29–30	495
44.18–45.3	416	46.2–4	447	47.29–31	463, 470
44.19	425	46.3	462	47.31	272
44.27	436	46.3–4	245, 355, 454	48.1–49.28	368
44.29	441	46.4	450, 494	48.2	334, 471
44.32–34	466	46.5	450	48.4	472
44.33	440, 466	46.8	334	48.5	471, 475
45.1	438, 468	46.8–27	174, 454	48.10	415, 473
				48.12	500

48.13	473	50.24	500	14.23–28	496
48.13–14	471	50.24–25	282, 497, 501	15.6	475
48.13–20	478	50.25	251	17.8–16	364
48.15–16	185	50.26	458	17.14	18
48.17–21	390			20.1	56
48.18–20	475	**Exodus**		20.2	401
48.19–20	471	1.1–4	451	20.6	401
48.20	334	1.5	252, 328	20.8–11	39
48.22	478	1.7	462	20.9–11	35
49.1–28	492	1.8	403, 457	20.11	23
49.3	482	1.8–11	462	21.5–6	452
49.3–4	354, 465, 478	1.8–14	443	21.15	284
49.3–19	451	2.3–6	185	21.16	419
49.4	120	2.15–21	257	21.17	284
49.5–7	3346	2.16	255	22.2–3	428
49.7	346	2.17	257	23.20–21	186
49.9–12	465	2.24	113, 401	23.20–23	185, 186
49.10	472, 473, 486	3.2	186	23.21	186
49.16	489, 490	3.2–6	185	23.24	297
49.17	489	3.4	186, 239, 448	32.6	227
49.18	490	3.5	186	32.13	113
49.19	357	3.7—186		33.20	328
49.25	426	3.13–15	55	34.7	498
49.29	497	3.14	55, 56	34.13	297
49.29–20	362	3.20	186		
49.29–31	251	4.16	54	**Leviticus**	
49.29–33	265, 462, 492	5.1–9	443	1.4	336
49.29–50.14	368	6.2–3	53	2.1	336
49.31	284, 291, 362	6.3	52–54	2.3–7	336
49.33–50.14	369	6.5	113	7.18	336
50.3	494	6.6–8	56	17.11	80, 117
50.5–7	497	7.1	54	18.2	56
50.6	463	7.5	53	18.4	56
50.10	495	9.33–34	46	18.18	305
50.12–13	265	12.20	176	18.21	56, 216
50.14	497	12.35–39	170	18.22	208
50.15	439	12.39	208	18.30	56
50.15–26	368, 369	12.40	88	19.7	336
50.19	501	12.40–41	173–176	19.14	284
50.20	502	13.11–13	236	20.13	208
50.21	500, 502	13.21	171	27.13–33	476
50.23	174, 475	14.9	316, 496	28.29	261
		14.17–18	496	26.3–13	56

Numbers

1.46	174
2.32	174
3.19–38	89
11.5–6	245
11.10	228
11.18–20	245
13.33	107
16.30	382
16.33	382
20.5	245
20.8–12	224
20.14	363, 365
21.5	245
22.6	219
22.22–35	61
26.5–18	451
27.1–11	265
32.39	500
33.2	18
35.12–27	476
36.1–10	500

Deuteronomy

2.12	323
2.23	234
11.1	275
11.10–12	149
12.11	53
13.4	86
15.12–13	306
15.12–17	462
15.18	306
16.21–22	297
17.14–20	365
17.16	246
18.10–22	400
19.6–12	476
21.15–17	265, 482
21.18–19	284
21.19	207
21.22–23	402
22.15	207

22.21	341
22.23–29	347
22.28–29	345
22.29	222, 303
23.3–6	216
23.7	363
23.7–9	364
25.7	207
27.16	284
27.18	284
29.23	214
32.5	102
33.18	487
34.3	213

Joshua

5.14	186
7.14–18	309
8.1–2	324
8.29	402
10.26	402
10.41	441
11.16	441
15.51	441
17.1	500
19.1	484
24.2	135
24.15	170
24.32	339, 478

Judges

3.13	364
3.15–30	492
5.14	492, 500
5.15–16	482
6.3–5	364
6.10	170
6.21	186
6.33	364
6.35	488
7.12	364
8.12	316
8.22–28	378

9.45	214
10.12	364
11.26	88, 174
13.20	186
14.1–2	386
15.1	389
16.25	227
18.2	207
19.4–20	207
20.10	341
20.14–21	492
21.22	260

Ruth

1.11	380
1.12–13	215
1.20–21	54
4.1ff	207
4.5–6	387
4.7–11	476
4.17	168
4.18–22	216

1 Samuel

1.19	113
3.10	239
9.1	364
9.1–2	492
9.11	255
13.3	492
14.47	290
16.12	269
17.34–35	376
17.42	269
18.8	228
25.2	388
25.18	197
26.11–12	295

2 Samuel

4.12	402
5.1–3	484
7.9	137
8.14	290

8.17	163	6.18	210	**Job**	
11.27	228	14.7	290	1.1	240, 364
12.8	354	14.22	290	1.6ff	32, 296
12.11	354	16.6	290	3.13–14	266
12.23	381	25.27	403	3.17	382
13.12	341			3.18–19	382
13.12–14	347	**1 Chronicles**		5.4	207
13.18	371	1.32	264	7.9	382
13.20	342	2.1–2	451	7.12	60
13.22	260	2.2	174	14.11	114
13.23–24	388	3.11–12	88, 90	14.13	113
13.32	342	5.1–2	272, 472	16.18	80
15.24–36	163	5.18	490	17.13–16	382
16.16	458	6.6–14	88	17.16	382
16.20–21	354	7.20–27	174	26.12–13	60
17.15	163	8.40	492	38.4	32
17.27–29	158	12.2–22	492	38.7	32, 102
20.3	354	12.8	490	39.5–8	183
20.8–10	287	12.14	490	42.2	126
21.12	402	12.29	492	42.16	500
24.14	31	21.25	250		
24.24	250			**Psalms**	
		2 Chronicles		8.4	113
1 Kings		3.1	235	9.12	80, 113
1.31	458	25.11ff	290	12.7	79
2.6	382	26.2	290	13.3	382
2.9	382	26.5	236	16.10	381
2.22	354	28.17	290	19.1	14
2.36–46	62			19.1–6	40
6.1	88	**Ezra**		20.1–2	53
8.29	53	1.1–4	249	23.3	53
11.14ff	290	7.3–4	88	25.20	79
14.22–23	297			30.3–4	381
16.24	250	**Nehemiah**		32.1	498
19.6	295	1.11–2.8	399	33.6	25, 26
20.3–7	354	4.9ff	324	49.7	382
22.10	207			49.10	382
22.19–22	32	**Esther**		49.15–16	381
22.19–23	67	2.5	365, 492	54.1	53
		3.1	365	72.17	137
2 Kings		3.10	365	73.15	102
6.13–17	376	4.2	495	74.1–3	113
6.15–17	161, 323	8.3	365	74.12–14	60
		8.5	365		
		9.23–25	365		

74.13	30	27.20	382	**Jeremiah**	
76.1	53	30.16	382	2.2	113
76.2	158, 162	30.20	394	3.17	53
78.35	158	31.23	207	7.12	53
78.67–68	472			4.23–27	26
80.1	476	**Ecclesiastes**		10.2	30
80.17	102	1.14	71	15.15	113
82.1	104	10.2	475	17.6	214
82.6–7	104	12.11–12	2	23.18	32
83.5–6	227	12.13	71	23.22	32
88.10–18	382			25.20	440
89.8–10	60	**Song of Songs**		31.20	113
89.13	475	1.6	342	32.9	250
89.48	382	6.10	258	34.18	171
90.10	95	7.4	257	38.6	376
91.11–13	67	7.10	69	43.13–22	246
94.17	382			48.34	213
98.3	113	**Isaiah**		49.7	364
104.8	112	1.2	185		
104.25	30	3.21	257	**Lamentations**	
104.26	30	5.14	382	4.21	364
105.8	113	6.1–8	32	5.11	347
106.45	113	11.11	125		
107.34	214	14.14–20	381	**Ezekiel**	
110.4	162, 165	15.5	213	1.5ff	73
111.5	113	19.5	114	3.18	80
111.9	53	19.24	137	10.15	73
116.15	80	24.23	258	14.12–20	204
121.4–8	79	27.1	60	16.12	257
127.5	207	30.1–3	246	18.22–23	213
128.6	500	30.26	258	21.26–27	485
141.7	382	30.27	53	21.27	485
148.4	111	31.1–3	246	23.24	293
		36.6–9	246	24.7–8	80
Proverbs		37.4	440	32.3	293
1.12	382	40.11	476	32.20–28	107
3.16	475	42.8	186	33.6	80
9.5	158	43.6	102		
11.12	257	51.2	137	**Daniel**	
12.10	114	51.9–10	60	2.4	458
16.33	309	54.10	255	2.27–30	407
17.6	500	65.25	67	2.28	400
25.1	21			4.1ff	218

5.10   458
6.6   458

Hosea
1.9   55
1.10   102
6.1–3   374
12.4   326
13.14   382

Joel
2.12–13   355

Amos
4.6–12   210
5.10   207
5.12   207
5.15   207
9.2   381
9.12   440

Obadiah
10–12   363

Jonah
1.7   309

Micah
7.17   67
7.18   498

Zechariah
1.10ff   296
1.11   186
1.12   186
3.1–2   186
3.2   67
3.4   186
5.11   125
8.13   137

Malachi
3.1   187
4.5   187

Matthew
1.3   392
1.8   88
1.18   226
1.20   185, 226
2.9   30
4.9   67
5.17–18   13
5.23–24   326
10.37   241
14.11   187
19.4   24
19.4–9   358
23.37–39   213
24.37   112
25.33   475
26.49   287

Mark
2.23–28   35
7.7   62
12.25   102

Luke
1.1–4   21
1.11   185
1.19   185
1.35   226
2.9   185
2.19   374
2.29–30   452
6.27ff   499
15.20   335
17.32   212
19.41–44   214
21.25   30
21.28   30
24.27   13, 18
24.44   13, 18

John
1.1–4   187
1.5–9   27

1.14   187
1.51   296, 298
3.29–30   252
4.5   375, 478
8.41–42   66
8.44   66, 290
10.11   476
11.48   126
12.31   67
12.35–36   27
13.11   287
13.30   295
15.1   487

Acts
1.26   309
2.5–7   126
2.27   383
2.33   475
7.4   16, 134
7.6   173–176
7.22   18
8.1   126
8.4   126
8.30–35   13
9.4   237
13.17–20   173–176
14.7   14
17.24   24

Romans
1.19–20   40
1.20   14
1.26–27   208
4.9–12   136
4.16–17   131
5.12–21   63
5.14   85
8.28   502
9.6–7   264
9.10–13   273
9.11   282
11.1   492

11.17–21	131	2.13–14	70	3.20	111
12.19	502	2.14	63	4.19	499, 501–502
12.29	499				
13.1–5	117	**2 Timothy**		**2 Peter**	
16.18–20	75	2.22	396	2.6–9	207
				2.7	207
1 Corinthians		**Hebrews**		2.8	139, 152
1.18–2.16	404	4.1–11	40	3.4–6	102
6.9	208	6.7	24	3.5	24, 111
7.7–8	49	6.13	240	3.5–7	90, 112
9.27	225	6.16	463	3.8	28
11.7	24	6.16–17	240	3.8–10	170
15.22	63	7.1–3	160		
15.55	383	7.2	164	**1 John**	
		7.3	162, 165	2.15–16	74
2 Corinthians		7.7	457	3.8	66
4.6	24	7.23–24	166	3.12	80
		8.1	35		
Galatians		10.12	35	**Jude**	
3.7–9	136	11.1	236	6	102
3.17	172–176	11.3	24, 26	7	103, 207
3.22–25	13	11.5	87	14	82
3.25–29	136	11.8–19	131		
3.27	73	11.13–16	251, 458	**Revelation**	
4.4	67	11.18–19	229	4.6ff	73
4.29	227	11.19	238	5.5	485
		11.20	269, 289	5.8	73
Ephesians		11.21	273	5.11	73
1.3–14	15	11.22	500	7.5–8	489
4.22–24	355	12.16	273	12.1–5	404
		13.20	476	12.1–13	67
Philippians				12.11	68
2.10	404	**James**		19.10	186
		1.13	235	20.7–10	68
Colossians		4.8	224	22.8–9	186
1.16	25, 41				
2.16–17	36	**1 Peter**			
3.5–6	214	1.5–7	235		
		2.11–17	456		
1 Thessalonians		2.23	502		
5.15	499, 502	2.25	476		
		3.6	200, 247		
1 Timothy		3.19	502		
1.10	208	3.19–20	102		
3.6	61				
2.13	70				

About the Author

Nathan Ward is a professor of Biblical studies at Florida College in Temple Terrace, Fla. He has bachelor's degrees in mass communications and Biblical studies, and a master's degree in religion. He holds memberships in the Evangelical Theological Society and the Society of Biblical Literature.

He, wife Brooke, and son Silas currently reside in Tampa. He can be reached by email at nathan@deward.com.

For a full listing of DeWard Publishing
Company books, visit our website:

www.deward.com

www.ingramcontent.com/pod-product-compliance
Lightning Source LLC
Chambersburg PA
CBHW021207090426
42740CB00006B/158